Frommer's®

Y0-BZK-329

Morocco
1st Edition

by Darren Humphrys

WILEY

Wiley Publishing, Inc.

About the Author

Darren Humphrys is a writer, photographer, and tour guide who left his native Australia in 1997 for an African safari—and stayed. Now residing in his adopted homeland of South Africa and a self-confessed "Africa-phile," Darren has been leading tours to Morocco since 2001. He has also contributed text and images to various African guidebooks and travel magazines.

Published by:

Wiley Publishing, Inc.

111 River St.
Hoboken, NJ 07030-5774

ISBN 978-0-470-18403-5
Editor: Anuja Madar
Production Editor: Suzanna R. Thompson
Cartographer: Andrew Dolan
Photo Editor: Richard Fox
Production by Wiley Indianapolis Composition Services

Front cover photo: Marrakech: Young drummer, Place Jemaa El Fna
Back cover photo: Erg Chebbi, Sahara Desert, Merzouga: Berber Man and Camel Train

For information on our other products and services or to obtain technical support, please contact our Customer Care Department within the U.S. at 800/762-2974, outside the U.S. at 317/572-3993 or fax 317/572-4002.

Wiley also publishes its books in a variety of electronic formats. Some content that appears in print may not be available in electronic formats.

Manufactured in the United States of America

5   4   3   2   1

Contents

List of Maps

Acknowledgments

Two women have traveled the length of this book with me. My partner, Kate Hassall, has shown the understanding of a saint and is my true soul mate. I am infinitely indebted to Anuja Madar and thank her for her confidence, patience, and unwavering belief in this project and in my ability to produce the goods. In Morocco, *shukran bezzef* to the Nassar family (Rachid, Rajaa, Samir), the el Janah family (Hassan, Malika, Meryem, Omar), *sahbis* Bouchaib and Ismaïl, and linguistics expert Assaïd Enmili.

An Invitation to the Reader

In researching this book, we discovered many wonderful places—hotels, restaurants, shops, and more. We're sure you'll find others. Please tell us about them, so we can share the information with your fellow travelers in upcoming editions. If you were disappointed with a recommendation, we'd love to know that, too. Please write to:

Frommer's Morocco, 1st Edition
Wiley Publishing, Inc. • 111 River St. • Hoboken, NJ 07030-5774

An Additional Note

Please be advised that travel information is subject to change at any time—and this is especially true of prices. We therefore suggest that you write or call ahead for confirmation when making your travel plans. The authors, editors, and publisher cannot be held responsible for the experiences of readers while traveling. Your safety is important to us, however, so we encourage you to stay alert and be aware of your surroundings. Keep a close eye on cameras, purses, and wallets, all favorite targets of thieves and pickpockets.

Other Great Guides for Your Trip:

Frommer's Spain
Frommer's Europe

Frommer's Star Ratings, Icons & Abbreviations

Every hotel, restaurant, and attraction listing in this guide has been ranked for quality, value, service, amenities, and special features using a **star-rating system.** In country, state, and regional guides, we also rate towns and regions to help you narrow down your choices and budget your time accordingly. Hotels and restaurants are rated on a scale of zero (recommended) to three stars (exceptional). Attractions, shopping, nightlife, towns, and regions are rated according to the following scale: zero stars (recommended), one star (highly recommended), two stars (very highly recommended), and three stars (must-see).

In addition to the star-rating system, we also use **seven feature icons** that point you to the great deals, in-the-know advice, and unique experiences that separate travelers from tourists. Throughout the book, look for:

Finds	Special finds—those places only insiders know about
Fun Fact	Fun facts—details that make travelers more informed and their trips more fun
Kids	Best bets for kids and advice for the whole family
Moments	Special moments—those experiences that memories are made of
Overrated	Places or experiences not worth your time or money
Tips	Insider tips—great ways to save time and money
Value	Great values—where to get the best deals

The following **abbreviations** are used for credit cards:

AE	American Express	DISC	Discover	V	Visa
DC	Diners Club	MC	MasterCard		

Frommers.com

Now that you have this guidebook to help you plan a great trip, visit our website at **www. frommers.com** for additional travel information on more than 3,600 destinations. We update features regularly to give you instant access to the most current trip-planning information available. At Frommers.com, you'll find scoops on the best airfares, lodging rates, and car rental bargains. You can even book your travel online through our reliable travel booking partners. Other popular features include:

- Online updates of our most popular guidebooks
- Vacation sweepstakes and contest giveaways
- Newsletters highlighting the hottest travel trends
- Online travel message boards with featured travel discussions

The Best of Morocco

Morocco has historically conjured up images of ancient walled cities, desert-crossing camel caravans, Arab sultans, Berber tribesmen, and mud-walled kasbahs shaded by tall date palms. The good news is that the Morocco of today can still deliver this, plus much more. Independent since only 1956, this is a youthful country in more ways than one. The largely under-40 population is being led into a complicated 21st century by a young king, Mohammed VI, intent on retaining Morocco's diversity and traditional customs while encouraging tourism as a major form of economic development. Morocco is filled with unforgettable travel experiences, and somewhere along the journey it will surely test your sense of patience and good nature. This chapter is a personal review of the best of what I feel Morocco has to offer, though I encourage you to discover your own magical Moroccan memories.

1 The Most Unforgettable Travel Experiences in Morocco

- **Meandering Along the Winding Streets of a Medina:** Within Morocco's old walled cities, known as medinas, you can immerse yourself in both the country's past and present. Formerly safe havens from invaders and marauders, today's medinas are intoxicating combinations of traditional and modern, where ancient mosques, crowded souks, and workshops of skilled craftsmen sit side by side with trendy *maisons d'hôte,* candle-lit restaurants, and alfresco cafes. Making the time to wander around a medina's maze of streets, alleys, and lanes—including a few inevitable wrong turns and dead ends—will reward you with a greater insight to these beating hearts of Morocco.

- **Hearing the *Muezzin* Call to Prayer:** Five times a day, the call of *"Al'lah al Akbar"* (God is Great) resonates throughout Morocco, calling the faithful to the mosque to pray. The call comes from the top of the

mosque's tower, called a minaret, and is traditionally the job of the *muezzin,* a sort of town crier. Although nowadays it's mostly a taped version played through loud speakers, the call to prayer is still a beautiful, spiritual sound.

- **Sunrise from the Top of a Saharan Dune:** Whether you've camped in the dunes overnight or slept in a nearby *auberge,* make sure you witness the beginning of a new Moroccan day from the crest of a dune on the edge of the Sahara. Experiencing the desert's utter tranquillity while feeling the cold, soft grains of sand between your toes can be one of the most serene, invigorating, and even spiritual moments you'll ever have. See chapter 7.

- **Celebrating Eid al-Fitr (Feast of Fast Breaking):** Upon the rise of the new moon after the fasting month of Ramadan, Morocco's Muslims—99% of the population—mark the end of the fast with 3 days of celebrations and festivities. Traveling in Morocco during this time showcases the country at its most joyous and friendly, with many travelers being invited into local homes to share in the family feast.

- **Shopping & Haggling in the Souks:** Morocco's craftsmen are some of the most skilled in the world, with generations of families working in ceramics, jewelry, leather, metal, and wood. Many are located within the local markets, called souks, and this is where the shopping bargains are to be found. Bartering is part of the routine for locals, and is an accepted and expected practice within the souks.

- **Cafe Culture:** Do as the Moroccans do, and take some time out during your day to sit down at a pavement cafe, order a *café* or *thé,* and watch the world go by. In a country where bars and pubs are still largely kept out of sight, the cafe—a byproduct of 44 years of French occupation—has become a major social element in Moroccan society. Moroccans come to chat, play endless games of checkers, conduct business meetings, watch football on TV, or simply catch up on the latest local gossip.

- **Seeing Snow-Topped Mountains in Africa:** You don't normally associate Africa with snow-topped mountain peaks, but travel in Morocco anytime between December and March, and you stand a good chance of sighting the powdery stuff on the taller mountains in both the Middle and High Atlas ranges. For the ultimate bragging right of having skied in Africa, head for the village of Oukaïmeden, home to the continent's highest ski lift and 20km (13 miles) of trails. See chapter 6.

2 The Best of Photogenic Morocco

- **Jemaa el Fna (Marrakech):** Marrakech's famed square is the setting for an incredible spectacle that begins in the morning with snake charmers, West African Gnaoua musicians, and veiled *nakkachat* women ready to tattoo any bare piece of flesh with their henna-based designs. Come late afternoon, they are joined by all manner of performers—acrobats, dancers, musicians, and storytellers called *halkas*—and the square's heart converts to the country's largest open-air restaurant. More than 100 food carts offer traditional dishes such as couscous and tagine, along with specialties such as boiled escargot and roasted sheep's head. Surrounding the "show" is a circle of stalls selling freshly squeezed orange juice and dried fruits and nuts. It all adds up to a visual extravaganza, and each "performer" is ready and willing—upon payment of a few dirham—to be photographed. See p. 108.

- **Chouwara Tannery (Fes):** The largest and busiest of Fes el Bali's traditional tanneries, Chouwara is a scene straight out of medieval times. The skins of camels, cows, goats, and sheep are stretched, cured in a concoction that includes cow urine and pigeon droppings, and laid out to dry. Workers in shorts then stomp around in various earthen pits, where the skins are dyed in natural colors taken from indigo (blue), mint (green), poppy (red), and turmeric (yellow). It makes for a stunning picture from the viewpoints above—strategically placed within the various leather shops—though the rancid smell emanating from the cocktail of chemicals certainly makes you earn it. See p. 230.

- **Camel Caravans in the Sand:** Whether in the soft glow of the morning light or silhouetted against the often rapidly setting sun, the image of trekking camels is the stuff of postcards and can be captured in Morocco's sand seas, Erg Chebbi and Erg Chigaga. Here you'll find men (dressed in the flowing blue caftans and robes of the famed Tuareg nomads) walking alongside trains of loping one-humped dromedaries into the seemingly never-ending dunes of Saharan sands. See chapter 7.

- **Majorelle Garden (Marrakech):** Within this popular city sight is the former studio of the original owner, artist Jacques Majorelle, and its brilliant cobalt-blue exterior contrasts strikingly with the surrounding flora of this now botanical garden. Jardin Majorelle's current owner is the very colorful and fashionable Frenchman, Yves Saint Laurent, who ensures the small building regularly receives a fresh lick of color, sometimes simply described as "Majorelle blue" because of its combination of brightness and depth. The garden maintains its standing as a popular visual for Moroccan postcards and coffee table–style books. See p. 143.

- **The Colored Doors of the Medina:** Most architectural beauty within Morocco's medinas is to be found behind the doors of its houses, *maisons d'hôte, medersas,* and mosques. Often overlooked, however, are the doors themselves. The only obvious external feature distinguishing one establishment from the other, the doors of the medina are often a very visual reflection of the status of the family that lives behind it. They can range from simple and practical—often painted in bright blues, greens, reds, or whites— to castlelike creations complete with a brass knocker and mosaic archway.

Those in the medinas of Asilah, Chefchaouen, Essaouira, and Fes and Rabat's kasbah are particularly photogenic.

- **A Rainbow of *Babouches:*** Morocco's traditional slipper is the leather *babouche,* which is worn by men and women of all ages and backgrounds. Styles range from pointed to round-toe in colors covering the whole spectrum of the rainbow. Walk through any market or souk in the country, and you're bound to find the local *babouche* quarter, where literally hundreds of *babouches* are displayed from floor to ceiling. Politely ask the shopkeeper if you can photograph his collection, and you may end up with a pair for yourself. Marrakech's Souk Smata (chapter 5) and Meknes's Souk es Sebbat (chapter 8) are just two market areas devoted to this popular footwear.

- **Spice Cones:** Spices are an everyday ingredient in the cuisine of Morocco and can be purchased from establishments ranging from small medina stalls to large nationwide supermarket chains. At the front of most spice stalls you'll see the various spices displayed in tall, cone-shape mounds within brass or steel vats. The vibrant color of these mounds of henna (green), chile (orange), paprika (red), and turmeric (yellow) are easy subjects for an image that sums up the exotic sights and smells of the country's medinas.

- **Souk des Teinturiers (Marrakech):** Marrakech's dyers' souk is one of the most photogenic—and photographed—areas of the city's medina, and with good reason. While *jellabah*-wearing shopkeepers sit outside their shops, the top of your camera's frame is filled with overhanging fabric and wool, still wet from being recently dyed in bright blues, oranges, reds, and yellows. The colorful subject matter is better some days than others, but give yourself a few consecutive days, and you'll more than likely be able to find your perfect picture. See p. 141.

- **Seffarine Square (Fes):** This busy square, bordering one side of the spiritual Kairouine Mosque, is home to the ancient city's brass and copper workshops. Although the noise generated by the constant banging and clanging can't be captured on film, there's still plenty of scope for great images. Coppersmiths sit cross-legged while shaping everything from small decorative plates to huge cauldrons, and are generally receptive to camera-wielding visitors requesting a photo or two. See chapter 8.

- *Jellabahs* **& Donkeys:** A *jellabah* (a traditional robe with a pointed hood) is still worn throughout the country by both sexes and all ages, and many Moroccans still transport their goods, and themselves, by donkey. An everyday visual, this combination makes for a fascinating picture, especially in the larger towns and cities where the contrast of traditional and modern can be captured as the four-legged subjects plod by a KFC or McDonald's.

3 The Best Kasbahs & Medinas

- **Aït ben Haddou:** One of the country's most picturesque kasbahs is also one of its most easily accessed. Just a 15-minute drive from the country's movie capital, Ouarzazate, Aït ben Haddou has also seen its fair share of Hollywood stars, having been used in movies such as *Gladiator* and *Lawrence of Arabia*. A UNESCO World Heritage site that sees more than 130,000 visitors a year, the kasbah is best visited early in the morning before both the crowds and heat arrive. This is when the first rays of sun light up the kasbah's earthen walls, and imaginative minds can conjure images of a time when this was one of the most important stops on the lucrative West African caravan trade route. See p. 187.

- **Fes el Bali:** Within this ancient medina's walls lies a medieval city as alive today as it was 1,200 years ago. Its 9,500 alleyways, lanes, and streets are largely pedestrian only, and one turn can reveal a heaving mass of people, donkeys, mules, and produce, while another brings a calm, quiet, and cool picture of serenity. Considered Morocco's spiritual heart, it's also one of its most creative, with workshops housing skilled craftsmen found throughout. This is more than a must-see—it's a must-experience. See chapter 8.

- **Essaouira:** This seaside resort's medina is Morocco's most traveler friendly. Large enough to wander around for a couple of days but small enough to never get too lost, it's a delightful mix of modern and traditional. There's a range of stylish yet affordable accommodations to suit all budgets and tastes, as well as a good choice of restaurants and cafes, all combining with traditional sights such as the fish market and jeweler's souk. There's also a large square that's perfect for a coffee break and quality people-watching, which leads onto a quaint port where fishermen still bring in the daily catch and mend their nets. See chapter 10.

- **Kasbah des Oudaïas:** Rabat's elevated and compact kasbah looks out over the mouth of the Oued Bou Regreg, and over the centuries it's seen dynasties come and go and has housed a band of notorious pirates. It's a quiet and airy quarter with a few attractions, a quaint *maison d'hôte,* and both a cafe and viewing *plat-forme* that afford sweeping views of the river mouth and adjoining beaches. A welcoming sea breeze usually sifts its way through the kasbah, making for a very pleasant stroll through its winding alleys, past whitewashed houses and brightly colored doors. See p. 313.

- **Marrakech:** Fes's jet-setting sister is riding a massive tidal wave of popularity at the moment, largely thanks to a sharp rise in international airline routes flying directly from Europe. And who wouldn't want to come here? This city's ancient medina has got it all: shops and souks specializing in most of the country's renowned crafts; a central square, Jemaa el Fna,

where the most fascinating spectacle takes place daily; and a plethora of accommodations and restaurants ranging from traditional and conservative to ultrachic and sexy. See chapter 5.

- **Taroudannt:** Enclosed by an almost unbroken circuit of 16th-century walls and largely ambivalent to the proclaimed marvels of tourism, Taroudannt is as authentic as they come. Lacking any great sights, the attraction of coming here is the staunchly Berber town itself. Travelers can walk the streets without any hassle from touts or faux guides, watching the locals go about their everyday lives without the haste of many other Moroccan towns and cities. See chapter 11.

4 The Best Cultural & Historical Sights

- **American Legation Museum (Tangier):** In 1786, Morocco became the first country to formally recognize the infant United States of America. The Legation building was presented as a gift by Sultan Moulay Slimane to the American people in 1821 and housed the U.S. ambassador for the next 135 years. Conveniently located within Tangier's medina, the now museum houses various exhibitions showcasing the connection between the two countries and the many U.S. citizens who have resided in the city over the years. The Paul Bowles room is dedicated to the late writer, while another room displays a copy of a 1789 letter from George Washington to his "Great and Magnanimous Friend, the Emperor of Morocco," Sultan Moulay Ben Abdallah. See p. 280.

- **Mausoleum of Mohammed V (Rabat):** The burial shrine of the current king's grandfather and father is a place of reverence for Moroccans and visitors alike. A dignified building

watched over by elaborately dressed Royal Guards, the white onyx tombs of Mohammed V and his sons Hassan II and Moulay Abdellah can be viewed from an upper balcony. See p. 313.

- **Ben Youssef Medersa (Marrakech):** Marrakech's 16th-century former Koranic school is one of the country's best examples of Islamic architecture. Try to ignore the steady stream of large tour groups, and marvel at the carved cedar facades and exquisite stucco and *zellij.* Quiet corners can often be found in one of the upper dormitories' cell-like rooms, where up to 800 students were housed. Apart from learning the Koran, students would also immerse themselves in Islamic law and the sciences. See p. 139.

- **Hassan II Mosque (Casablanca):** Built to commemorate the former king's 60th birthday, Casablanca's premier house of prayer is one of the largest in the world, able to house 25,000 worshippers under its retractable roof and another 80,000 in the courtyards and squares outside. Non-Muslims can view the mosque's interior on a guided tour, where the country's master craftsmen pulled out all stops to produce an amazing display of plaster, marble, glass, wood, and *zellij.* See p. 332.

- **Mausoleum of Moulay Ismail (Meknes):** The burial place of Morocco's longest-serving ruler, this is another of the few spiritual monuments open to non-Muslims. A relatively bland exterior and a series of plain yet serene courtyards lead the visitor to a quiet, cool anteroom, resplendent in exquisite *zellij,* carved plaster, and marble columns ransacked from nearby Volubilis. From here, visitors can view the tomb from behind a small barrier and reflect on the life of a man both respected and feared by subjects and opponents alike. See p. 250.

- **Volubilis:** From A.D. 45 to 285, Volubilis was the capital of the Roman province Mauritania Tingitana and the southernmost outpost of the vast empire. Home to at least 20,000 inhabitants during its peak, the city's wealth was built upon exporting vast quantities of olives and wheat back to Rome, as well supplying that city's coliseums with the majority of its gladiator-fighting lions. Virtually deserted by the 11th century and totally flattened by a devastating earthquake in 1755, the ruins of the city were partially excavated and reconstructed during the protectorate era. The site's triumphal arch, forum, and faded but still beautiful mosaics are best discovered during cool early mornings or at sunset. See chapter 8.

5 The Best of Natural Morocco

- **Cascades d'Ouzoud:** The most scenic waterfalls in the country, the Central High Atlas's Cascades d'Ouzoud plunge 100m (328 ft.) into the river below, and the crashing water, surrounding lush woodland, and rural atmosphere have made this a popular tourist stop on the route between Marrakech and Fes. Here you'll also likely encounter the indigenous Barbary macaque monkey. See p. 171.

- **Todra Palmeraie & Gorge:** Following the Oued Todra to its aboveground source provides the traveler with stunning views of the lush, green Todra Palmeraie. Walking within the palmeraie is a wonderful attack on the senses, as fruit and palm trees overlook crops of grains and vegetables. The palmeraie ceases at the entrance to the majestic Todra Gorge, 300m (984 ft.) in length,

50m (164 ft.) across, and with towering 300m-high (984-ft.) walls. Here you'll find the above-ground beginnings of the Oued Todra, and dipping your toes in its icy waters is the best way to relax and take in one of Morocco's most dramatic natural sights. See chapter 7.

- **Erg Chebbi & Erg Chigaga:** Morocco's two most accessible sand seas are fed by the ever-advancing Sahara Desert, and their color can change from golden to rust red, depending on the time of day. They are reached by crossing a flat, rocky desert plain called the *hammada,* and your first glimpse of their mountainous dunes is something to treasure. Comparisons between the two ergs is inevitable (see "Which Desert, Merzouga or M'hamid?" in chapter 7), but whichever one you choose, the effort to get there is definitely worth it. See chapter 7.

- **Western High Atlas:** The western end of the High Atlas mountain range is home to most of Morocco's—and some of North Africa's—highest peaks, and can be conveniently accessed on a day trip from Marrakech or Ouarzazate. The 4,167m-high (13,671-ft.) Jebel Toubkal is often snowcapped for much of the year, while the area's lower grassy slopes and valleys are delightfully pleasant and cool retreats from the hot plains below. See chapter 6.

- **Agadir Bay:** Golden sand stretches around this crescent-shaped bay for 9km (5½ miles), most of which is protected from the often-strong sea breeze. With relatively calm Atlantic waters lapping on the shore, the bay has attracted many international resort chains on the southern edge of Agadir city. Large numbers of tourists lazing on roped-off private beaches is more reminiscent of Europe than Morocco, but the bay is big enough for everyone and is a warm delight for most of the year. See chapter 11.

- **Oualidia Lagoon:** This crescent-shaped lagoon—fringed by golden sands and protected from the crashing Atlantic waves by a naturally formed breakwater—offers perfect conditions for fishing, sailing, surfing, and swimming. It's also home to Morocco's small oyster farming industry. Apart from the summer holiday months of July and August, the otherwise sleepy village on the lagoon's shores offers a select range of comfortable accommodations and fine seafood restaurants, adding up to a great spot for few days of relaxation and recreation. See chapter 10.

- **Middle Atlas Cedar Forests:** Unlike the often-barren High Atlas range, the Middle Atlas often comes as a pleasant surprise with its swathes of forested peaks and valleys. The scent of cedar trees abounds here, and a day's exploration around Ifrane and the nearby Mischiflen crater rewards the traveler with glorious views of these majestic trees. There's also the chance to encounter the indigenous Barbary macaque monkey and breathe in some of the freshest and most aromatic air in Morocco. See chapter 8.

- **Tafraoute & Environs:** Found within the Anti-Atlas range, the boulder-strewn mountains and lush palmeraie around the small village of Tafraoute are an artist's dream. Depending on the time of day, the boulders—some seemingly clinging to the cliff face—can be a palette of gold, gray, or pink. Coupled with valleys of green palmeraie and the white and pink blossoms of almond trees, this is one of Morocco's most scenic yet least visited areas. See chapter 11.

6 The Best Villages

- **Asilah:** This quaint fishing village exudes a Mediterranean-style charm, true to its relatively recent Spanish history, which is amplified by the throngs of Spanish visitors and ex-pats who fill the village during the summer months. Asilah's prestigious International Cultural Festival, celebrating its 30th anniversary in 2008, is worth timing your itinerary around, and has assisted in the general beautification and restoration of the 15th-century medina. See chapter 9.

- **Ifrane:** A French-built mountain resort, Ifrane is a village like no other in Morocco. Thanks to its

Swiss chalet–like architecture, neatly trimmed lawns and gardens, tree-lined lake, and clean, crisp mountain air, a stop in Ifrane is almost like leaving the country. The village is also home to a royal palace and a U.S.-curriculum university. It's a welcome retreat from Fes and Meknes during the hot summer months and enjoys erratic snowfalls during the winter. See chapter 8.

- **Imlil:** The most popular trail head from which to trek Jebel Toubkal, the village of Imlil is witnessing a bit of a boom at the moment, thanks largely to the increasing number of visitors from Marrakech, less than a 2-hour drive away. Sitting in the Aït Mizane valley and 1,740m (5,708 ft.) high, Imlil is a very pleasant place to while away a couple of days. The silence is deafening, the nights are filled with endless stars, and there's a small but quality choice of accommodations. See chapter 6.

- **Chefchaouen:** The Rif mountains' most traveler-friendly village is also one of the country's most picturesque, sitting snugly between the twin peaks from which it takes its name. Chefchaouen's small medina was once off limits to all Westerners, but nowadays it's a decidedly more welcoming place, with plenty of accommodations and restaurants to suit all budgets and a square where breakfast, lunch, and dinner can blend into a day-long affair. See chapter 9.

- **Amezrou:** This small village—across the Oued Dra from its big sister Zagora—meanders through a lush palmeraie and is one of the most authentic desert settlements of the scenic Dra Valley. Although often used only as an overnight stop on the way to/from the Erg Chigaga desert dunes, Amezrou offers the traveler multiple attractions and quality accommodations, and is worth an extended stay if you have the time. See chapter 7.

- **Oukaïmeden:** Morocco's only ski resort is also a beautiful trekking base during the warmer months. At the end of a steep, winding road, Oukaïmeden is little more than a smattering of Swiss-like holiday homes and a few hotels, although this may change in the near future with a proposed Dubai-financed property development. See chapter 6.

7 The Best Shopping

- **Marrakech Medina:** Almost every form of Moroccan arts and crafts can be found within the souks and shops of Marrakech's medina, and it's this gluttony of choice—rather than quality—that makes this the number-one shopping destination for the majority of travelers. From antiques to woodwork, it's all available and ready to be haggled over. See chapter 5.

- **Fes el Bali:** Fes is well known for its high density—and high quality—of carpet emporiums. Although the interested buyer is spoilt for choice, Fes's carpet dealers are like no other, and setting aside enough time for the bargaining and tea-drinking process is essential to a successful purchase. Also within this ancient medina, you'll find a wealth of workshops called *foundouks,* where you can see many of the traditional crafts still practiced. Fassi potters are located just outside the medina's walls and are amongst the best in Morocco. See chapter 8.

- **Souk es Sebbat (Meknes):** This is where you'll find some of the country's finest handmade Moroccan slippers, or *babouches*. Each small stall is jam-packed with rows of colored *babouches,* and the sales pressure is pleasantly minimal. See chapter 8.
- **Tiznit Medina:** Tiznit's Souk des Bijoutiers, or Jeweler's Souk, is a maze of more than 100 small shops selling mostly silver Berber jewelry and accessories. Initially practiced by the town's long-departed Jewish silversmiths, their Berber cousins now continue the tradition within Tiznit's attractive little medina, less than a couple of hours away from modern Agadir. See chapter 11.
- **Essaouira Medina:** Within this seaside resort's increasingly popular medina is an eclectic mix of art galleries, a jeweler's souk, and shops selling everything from local *thuya* woodcrafts and argan oil-based products to surf wear and handmade leather goods. Reflecting the whole medina itself, the hassle from shop owners is relatively mild, and the whole process is much more pleasant than that in nearby Marrakech. See chapter 10.
- **Rabat Medina:** The major bonus of shopping within Rabat's medina is the lack of hard-sell by shopkeepers. Along the main shopping streets of rue Souiqa, Souk Assabbat, and rue des Consuls are shops selling everything from high-quality carpets and handmade *jellabahs* to hand-carved wood furniture and jewelry. See chapter 10.

8 The Most Authentic Culinary Experiences

- **Slurping Down a Dozen Oualidia Oysters:** The seaside village of Oualidia is home to Morocco's oyster farming industry, established back in 1957. Nowadays more than 200 tons of oysters are harvested annually, most of them consumed domestically. Moroccans and visitors can be seen shucking and slurping down oysters' fleshy insides all along the Atlantic coast and often within the fine dining establishments of other inland centers.
- **Eating Your Way Through Tagine Fatigue:** It's the national dish and is the name for both the two-piece clay cooking vessel and the resulting meal. Spend any length of time in Morocco, and you'll become just like everybody else—a discerning tagine connoisseur. Suffering from bouts of tagine fatigue can be countered by discovering delicious variations from the norm, such as lamb tagine with dates and figs, chicken tagine with apricot in saffron sauce, and a vegetable tagine that isn't one big mass of overcooked mush.
- **Trying Couscous by Hand:** The centerpiece of most sit-down meals in Morocco is couscous. Fine, grain-size pieces of semolina lightly steamed in an aromatic broth until light and fluffy, couscous can be served with any meat or vegetable, or a combination of both. When dining with Moroccans, you'll be encouraged to scoop up a handful—use your "clean" right hand—and roll it into a small ball before tossing it into your mouth. This is one of the main reasons why most dinner tables in Morocco are covered with plastic—and easily cleaned—tablecloths.
- **Pouring Your Mint Tea Without Spilling a Drop:** It's the national drink—jokingly described to Westerners as "Moroccan whiskey"—and

is available anywhere, anytime. Traditionally brewed slowly over a charcoal fire and sweetened by large chunks of sugar, the tea is poured from an arm's length height to aerate the brew. This is to be performed two to three times—and tasted after each pour—before the tea is considered ready to drink. See "Chill . . . & Have a Hot Mint Tea" on p. 143.

- **The Freshest Seafood:** In comparison to most Western countries, Morocco's seafood is very reasonably priced with a relatively healthy range of daily catches. Feast on the freshest seafood—handpicked by yourself and chargrilled while you wait—at various fish markets and restaurants throughout the country.

- **A Breakfast *Baghrir* Smothered in *Amlou:*** A *baghrir* is an aerated pancake, similar to a large English crumpet. Moroccans and visitors alike drool over a *baghrir* (still warm from the pan) covered in the argan-based *amlou* paste and topped with crushed cashew nuts.

9 The Most Scenic Drives

- **The Dadès Gorge:** The 35km (22 miles) drive along this gorge's southern edge is one of the most scenic in Morocco. At the northern end of this drive, the gorge narrows considerably, the road rises and then falls in a series of hairpin bends, and one or two strategically placed cafe-restaurants take advantage of the grand views. The Dadès Gorge is often passed over by most visitors, who are intent on reaching the better-known Todra Gorge to its east or the "bright lights" of Ouarzazate to its west. Those self-drivers, however, who take the time to turn off the highway can often have this beautiful gorge to themselves. See chapter 7.

- **Ouarzazate to Zagora:** This 168km (104 miles) stretch of road offers harsh yet beautiful mountain scenery as it winds up and over rocky, barren Jebel Anaouar before descending into the Dra Valley and its string of palmeraie and oases. The two-lane road is in pretty good shape, and there are plenty of opportunities to pull over and take in the views. See chapter 7.

- **Asni to Imlil:** Formerly a potholed gravel track, the road from Asni to the mountain trail head village of Imlil is now tarred the whole way. Along this 17km (11-mile) drive are pretty villages clinging to the cliff sides or nestled on bends of the Oued Mizane, all the while watched over by the looming, often snowcapped peak of Jebel Toubkal. See chapter 6.

- **Tizi n'Test Pass:** The drive from Marrakech to Taroudannt takes in some of the most spectacular mountain scenery in Morocco. Dissecting the Western High Atlas, the road (the R203) has its fair share of hairpin bends and blind corners, and culminates roughly 134km (83 miles) from Marrakech and 87km (54 miles) from Taroudannt at the 2,092m-high (6,864-ft.) Tizi n'Test pass. From here the sweeping views of the Souss plain to the south are simply breathtaking, while the highest peaks of the Western High Atlas loom to the northwest. See chapter 6.

- **Tizi n'Tichka Pass:** An impressive feat of French road building, this pass lies roughly halfway between Marrakech and Ouarzazate on the tarred and relatively wide N9 highway. Higher than the Tizi n'Test to the west, the 2,260m (7,415-ft.) Tizi n'Tichka offers a harsher yet just as spectacular view, with just as many twists and turns in the road to reach it. See chapter 6.

- **The Dadès Valley:** This 70km (43 mile) stretch of highway is also called the Valley of the Kasbahs, thanks to hundreds of desert castles dotted along its route. A section of the valley is also Morocco's premier rose-growing region, and shops selling all manner of rose-based products line the tarred road. There are plenty of opportunities along the way to pull over for pictures of the closer kasbahs. See chapter 7.

- **Tetouan to Chefchaouen:** This drive leaves behind the Mediterranean plain at Tetouan and almost immediately begins the steady incline into the Rif mountains. Along the way are clusters of family compounds and small villages, inhabited by the resilient Riffians, the women often clothed in their distinctive traditional dress and wide-brimmed hats. The drive is only 59km (37 miles), but in the process the hustle and bustle—and extremely busy traffic—of Tangier and Tetouan is replaced by the chilled-out Riffian vibe. See chapter 9.

2

Planning Your Trip to Morocco

At the crossroads of Africa, Arabia, and Europe, 21st-century Morocco is an exotic land of intriguing culture, mesmerizing landscapes, great shopping, and memorable experiences, and is welcoming Western travelers in record numbers. First-time travelers may know little about the country other than the ancient cities of Fes and Marrakech and the quintessential camel treks through the desert, but there's a lot to consider—how to get there; money, health, and safety concerns; where to stay and what to eat; and what to see and where to shop. This chapter, along with chapter 4, will provide you with everything you need to know to make planning your trip to Morocco less daunting.

1 The Regions in Brief

Morocco lies in the far northwestern corner of Africa, across the fabled Straits of Gibraltar from Spain, and was once the western frontier of the known world, called el-Maghreb el-Aksa, or "the Far West." Not including its disputed southern province of the Western Sahara, Morocco is slightly smaller than France or Spain and slightly larger than California, covering an area of 446,500 sq. km (172,395 sq. miles). It's bordered by the Atlantic Ocean to the west, the Mediterranean Sea to the north, and shares borders with Algeria to the east and southeast and Mauritania to the south. A nation of coastline, fertile plains, mountains, and desert, Morocco is a country of distinct geographical regions that have influenced the culture of its inhabitants for hundreds, if not thousands, of years. These geographical and cultural differences, however, are to be found within a relatively compact area, making this country a pleasurable and rewarding place to explore.

MARRAKECH This city is not exactly a region of Morocco, more of a world unto itself. The jet-setting sister of Morocco's four imperial cities, Marrakech is on every traveler's itinerary, and for good reason. Nowhere else is the country's crossroads of cultures more evident than here. This exotic, sexy, pulsating, and confronting city is well and truly on the international scene, and nowadays offers a mesmerizing palate of accommodations, restaurants, festivals, and shopping.

THE HIGH ATLAS Part of the greater Atlas chain that stretches across the country from the Atlantic coast to Algeria and beyond, the High Atlas mountain range is featured on most travelers' itineraries if only because it's the natural barrier between Morocco's coastal, fertile plains and its vast, desert-fringed oases. The "Land of the Berbers," the High Atlas are home to North Africa's highest peaks, including the climber's favorite, the 4,167m-high (13,671-ft.) Jebel Toubkal, along with some of its most beautiful valleys and friendliest people. This is also where many of the country's outdoor activities (trekking, hiking, mountain biking, and even skiing) can be enjoyed.

CENTRAL MOROCCO This region of gorges, valleys, and desert is perhaps the quintessential Morocco that most travelers imagine. Like the High Atlas, also inhabited by the country's Berbers, central Morocco offers vistas of mountain gorges and desert valleys, cut deep with lush, green oases called palmeraie. Both the Todra and Dadès Gorges are easily accessed, and along their winding valleys are some of the most scenic areas of the country. Heading away from the mountains, the land flattens out into the stony, pre-Saharan *hammada* before finally arriving at Morocco's Saharan-fed seas of sand, Erg Chebbi and Erg Chigaga. Out here you can ride a camel into the desert, watch the sun setting over towering sand dunes, and sleep under a starlit African night.

MIDDLE ATLAS, FES & MEKNES The Middle Atlas is perhaps the prettiest of the country's ranges, covered for its greater part with aromatic forests of pine and cedar. These are broken up by carpets of green pasture, where Berber communities—some still nomadic—tend to the herds of cattle and flocks of sheep that feed the country. The Middle Atlas stands watch over the spiritual heart of the country: the former imperial capitals of Fes and Meknes. Fes's ancient walled city, Fes el Bali, is the world's most complete medieval city and is where the first Moroccan dynasty, the Idrissids, built their empire. As with Marrakech, Fes is a popular destination for travelers, many of whom stay in a traditional riad or dar located down one of Fes el Bali's 9,500 alleys and lanes.

Sixty kilometers (37 miles) west of Fes, Meknes was the imperial home of the country's longest reigning and most ruthless ruler, Moulay Ismail. Combined with a visit to the excavated ruins of the Roman city of Volubilis and the pilgrimage village of Moulay Idriss (burial place of the country's "founding father"), Meknes is a hidden gem that delightfully lacks the tourist intensity of Fes.

NORTHWEST MOROCCO The country's northwest sees less travelers than the regions to the south, although history records a long list of other visitors, including invaders and rulers, culminating in the Spanish occupation of the first half of the 20th century. Tangier, a seething, sleazy free-for-all between the 1920s and 1950s, has cleaned its act up recently, and is fast creating itself a niche as a vibrant, affordable Mediterranean resort.

The fishing village of Asilah is home to one of the country's most popular festivals, where artists paint murals on the walls within its quaint medina. Asilah still exudes a village charm, and is a great first stop for those traveling south from Tangier.

The Rif mountain range is the natural border between Europe and Africa. The mountain-side village of Chefchaouen resisted Spanish occupation for 8 years, and before that resisted all Western influence for more than 400 years. Today this picturesque, blue-washed village is a backpacker favorite, thanks largely to its *kif*-induced relaxed vibe.

ATLANTIC COAST Morocco's Atlantic coastline is its most populated region, home to the nation's political and business centers. From the mouth of the Bou Regreg river, Rabat's inhabitants have seen conquerors (which have included pirates) come and go. It's a pleasant city that betrays its title as the country's capital, and its medina and kasbah are remarkably easy to get around.

Most travelers only stop here to connect to other destinations in the country, but Casablanca is the nation's heaving, gritty, working heart, home to more than three million people, all looking for work in a city built by the French due to Tangier's "internationalization." The coastline south of Casablanca is packed with Moroccan holidaymakers every August and delightfully quiet for the rest of the year, other than the large flocks of birds

Morocco

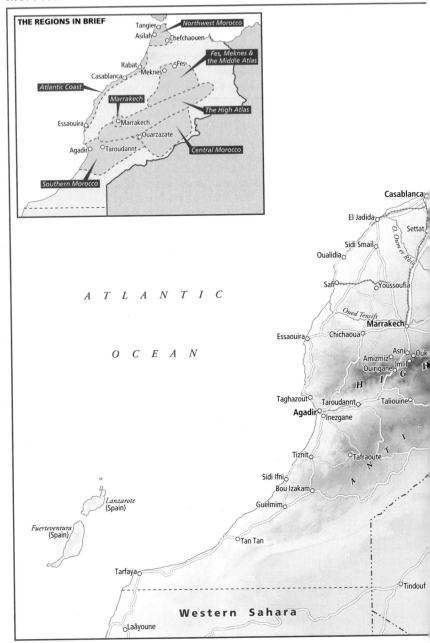

THE REGIONS IN BRIEF

Tangier
Asilah
Chefchaouen
Northwest Morocco

Rabat
Meknes
Fes
Fes, Meknes & the Middle Atlas

Casablanca

Atlantic Coast

Marrakech

The High Atlas

Essaouira
Marrakech
Ouarzazate

Agadir
Taroudannt
Central Morocco

Southern Morocco

ATLANTIC

OCEAN

Casablanca
El Jadida
Settat
O. Oum er Rbia
Sidi Smail
Oualidia
Safi
Youssoufia
Oued Tensift
Marrakech
Essaouira
Chichaoua
Asni
Ouk
Amizmiz
Imlil
Ouirigane
Taghazout
Taroudannt
Taliouine
Agadir
Inezgane
Tiznit
Tafraoute
Sidi Ifni
Bou Izakam
Guelmim

Lanzarote
(Spain)

Fuerteventura
(Spain)

Tan Tan

Tarfaya

Tindouf

Western Sahara

Laâyoune

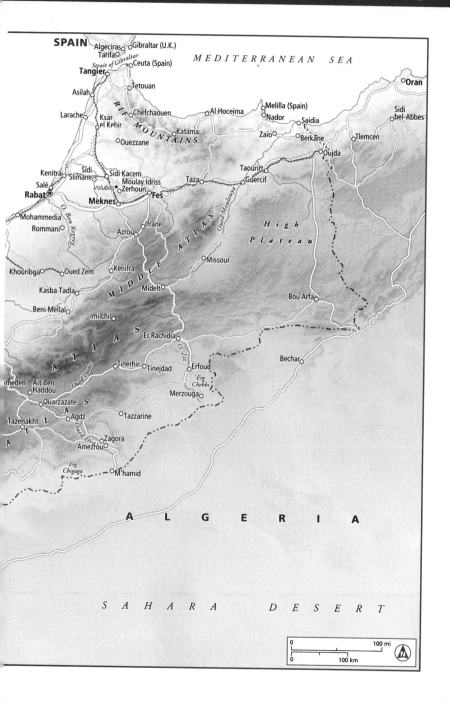

making a stop on their migration between Europe and Africa. Casablanca is also home to one of the world's largest places of worship, the Hassan II Mosque.

The village of Oualidia overlooks a large natural lagoon and is fast becoming a summer destination for in-the-know European holidaymakers. To the south are the country's best surf spots, including the windsurfing town of Essaouira, home to perhaps the country's prettiest medina and one of its major music festivals.

SOUTHERN MOROCCO Besides the beach resort city of Agadir and the popular surfing spots to the city's north, much of this region sees few travelers. It's a pity, because beyond its coastline is the Anti-Atlas mountain range, dotted with villages and palmeraie surrounded by a unique mountain/desert landscape.

The walled town of Taroudannt is dubbed "Little Marrakech," but is much more than just a facsimile of its better-known big sister to the north. Taroudannt is perhaps the one major town in Morocco that's still largely unaware of its attraction to, and therefore its reliance on, tourists. Wandering around its streets and lanes opens up a window on the everyday lives of Moroccans that is hard to come by in the country's better-known spots.

2 Visitor Information & Maps

Morocco's national tourism board, the **Office National Marocain de Tourisme (ONMT),** maintains several offices abroad including: **In the U.S.:** 20 E. 46th St., Suite 1201, New York, NY 10017 (© **212/557-2520**), and P.O. Box 2263, Lake Buena Vista, Orlando, FL 38230 (© **407/827-5335**).

In the U.K: 205 Regent St., London, W1R 7DE (© **020/7437-0073**).

In Australia: 11 West St., North Sydney, NSW, 2060 (© **02/9922-4999**).

In Canada: Place Montréal Trust, 1800 rue McGill College, Suite 2450, Montréal, PQ H3A 2A6 (© **514/842-8111**).

These are really only general information offices and will be able to offer you some glossy pamphlets, perhaps a map of Morocco, and a list of tour operators offering trips to Morocco. You're as likely to get just as much useful information from their sites www.visitmorocco.org and www.tourisme.gov.ma.

Within Morocco, you'll find an ONMT office, or a small Syndicat d'Initiative bureau, in most cities and large towns. Look for their addresses and alternative, destination-specific options in each relevant chapter's "Fast Facts." Unfortunately, their usefulness mirrors that of the international offices. Some useful websites include:

- **www.oncf.ma**: Train timetables and ticket prices.
- **www.marocannonces.com/ morocco_news.php**: English-language Moroccan online newspaper.
- **http://riadzany.blogspot.com**: Moroccan lifestyle e-zine based in Fez.
- **http://theviewfrommorocco.blog spot.com**: Includes reviews on Moroccan restaurants, bars, nightlife, and day tours.
- **http://moroccankitchen.blogspot. com**: The blog of two Moroccan women who operate a riad in Fes; includes recipes.
- **www.amazigh-voice.com**: Berber culture, history, and politics.

For Morocco maps, I've always used the Morocco GeoCenter World Country Map, which includes distances (in kilometers only) between most urban centers and major road junctions on major and secondary roads. It's available at Maps Worldwide (www.mapsworldwide.com) and Stanford's (www.stanfords.co.uk). For destination-specific maps, look in each chapter's "Fast Facts" section.

3 Entry Requirements

PASSPORTS

For information on how to get a passport, go to "Passports" in the "Fast Facts" section of this chapter. The websites listed provide downloadable passport applications as well as the current fees for processing passport applications. For an up-to-date, country-by-country listing of passport requirements around the world, go to the "International Travel" Web page of the U.S. State Department at **http://travel. state.gov**. For entry into Morocco, children traveling on their parents' passports must have a recent photograph affixed to the passport. If this isn't done, the whole family is at risk of being denied entry.

VISAS

Most visitors to Morocco don't need a visa, including citizens from Australia, Canada, New Zealand, the United Kingdom, the United States, and the European Union, including Ireland. Currently, the most notable exceptions are Israeli, South African, and Zimbabwean citizens, who need to apply at a Moroccan embassy or consulate for a 90-day single-entry (around $30/£15) or double-entry (around $50/£25) visa. See the Moroccan Ministry for Foreign Affairs and Cooperation website (**www.maec.gov.ma**) for its current list of visa-exempt countries and a visa application form (in French).

Moroccan embassies abroad include: **In the U.S.:** 1601 21st St. NW, Washington, DC 20009 (© **202/462-7979** or 202/457-0012; www.themoroccan embassy.com). There's also a consulate at 10 E. 40th St., 24th floor, New York, NY 10016 (© **212/758-2625;** www. moroccanconsulate.com).

In Canada: 38 Range Rd., Ottawa, KIN 8J4 (© **613/236-7391;** www.amba maroc.ca). There's also a consulate at 2192 bd. René-Lévesque West, Montréal H3H 1R6 (© **514/288-8750** or 514/288-6951; www.consulatdumaroc.ca).

In the U.K.: 49 Queen's Gate Gardens, London SW75NE (© **020/7581-5001**). The consulate is at Diamond House, 97–99 Praed St., Paddington, W21NT (© **020/7724-0719** or 020/ 7724-0624).

In Ireland: 39 Raglan Rd., Ballsbridge, Dublin 4 (© **31/66-09449** or 31/ 66-09319).

In Australia: 17 Terrigal Crescent, O'Malley, Canberra (© **02/62-900755** or 02/62-900766).

In South Africa: 799 Schoemann St. (corner of Farenden), Arcadia, Pretoria (© **012/343-0230**).

There's no Moroccan embassy or consulate in New Zealand.

Every visitor requires a current passport, valid for at least 6 months from the date of entry and with a minimum of two blank pages. All visitors are given a 90-day entry upon arrival. Extensions are possible, but time-consuming. You must visit the nearest Préfecture de Police (police headquarters) with your passport, four passport-size photos, and a letter from your embassy requesting a visa extension on your behalf. The process can take hours or even days, and usually involves an indefinite amount of bureaucracy depending on the whim of the police involved. It may prove easier to simply cross over to the Spanish enclaves of Ceuta or Melilla in Morocco's north or across the Straits to mainland Spain, and re-enter Morocco after a day or two.

Note: An occupation of "journalist" or "writer" entered on your arrival form can potentially lead to extended questioning as to your intentions while in Morocco. Choosing an occupation less threatening is advised. It's always best to carry around your passport—or at least a copy of the most relevant pages—while in Morocco. Police checks are numerous throughout the country, and usually the only thing they want to do is look at your passport, ask where you're from, and welcome you to Morocco.

MEDICAL REQUIREMENTS

For information on medical requirements and recommendations, see "Health" on p. 33.

CUSTOMS

For information on what you can bring into and take out of Morocco, see "Customs" in the "Fast Facts" section of this chapter.

4 When to Go

Morocco's peak holiday season is from July to September and is as much influenced by Moroccans returning home for their annual holiday as it is by international tourists. This is Morocco's summertime, when the whole country seems to enter holiday mode. The streets are noisier, the beaches are jam-packed, and temperatures—both physically and metaphorically—can soar. Many Moroccans live and work on mainland Europe, and they all seem to take the month of August off to head back to the motherland. Most travel overland in their own vehicles, with seemingly everything bar the kitchen sink strapped to the rooftop, and the congestion at the main ferry ports can be horrendous, especially at the beginning and the end of August. Some *maisons d'hôte* in Fes and Marrakech close their doors for the month of August to escape the heat and the congested streets.

Also keep in mind the Islamic fasting month of Ramadan. During this time, daytime travels and activities may be curtailed or achieved with a noted lack of local enthusiasm. However, to be in the country during this spiritual time, and to witness the happy, festive atmosphere at nighttime, can more than offset any travel inconveniences.

WEATHER

Morocco's summertime heat can have a major influence on the enjoyment of your time in the country and should be taken into consideration when planning your trip. The country's vast coastline is a magnet for locals and visitors alike during summer, with long, sunny days that are cooled by afternoon sea breezes. The higher reaches of the High Atlas, Middle Atlas, and Rif mountains are also pleasant escapes from the heat down on the plains. Traveling inland during this time—especially in central and southern Morocco but also Marrakech, Fes, and Meknes—is extremely uncomfortable.

Spring is considered the best season to experience Morocco. From late March to the end of May, central and southern Morocco are bathed in gloriously warm sunshine, the coast is beginning to warm up, and the mountains, some still hopefully snow-topped, come into their own with crisp, fresh air and none of the haze of the ensuing months.

Central and southern Morocco, as well as Marrakech, offer crisp, sunny days during the colder months (Nov–Mar), but be warned that the nights can be exceptionally cold. Mountain trekkers should also be aware that Morocco's mountainous regions are susceptible to flash flooding during winter (from rainfall) and spring (from melting snow). Roads and villages have been washed away in the past.

Average Monthly High/Low Temperatures & Rainfall

		Jan	Feb	Mar	Apr	May	June	July	Aug	Sept	Oct	Nov	Dec
Agadir	Temp. (°F)	70/45	72/48	73/52	73/55	75/57	77/77	81/64	79/64	79/63	77/59	73/54	70/48
	Temp. (°C)	21/7	22/9	23/11	23/13	24/14	25/16	27/18	26/18	26/17	25/15	23/12	21/9
	Rainfall (in.)	2.0	1.9	1.2	0.7	0.3	0.1	0	0.1	0.3	1.1	2.0	2.2

		Jan	Feb	Mar	Apr	May	June	July	Aug	Sept	Oct	Nov	Dec
Casablanca	Temp. (°F)	63/46	64/50	66/52	68/54	70/57	75/61	77/64	79/66	77/63	73/57	70/54	64/50
	Temp. (°C)	17/8	18/10	19/11	20/12	21/14	24/16	25/18	26/19	25/17	23/14	21/12	18/10
	Rainfall (in.)	2.7	2.3	2.0	1.7	1.0	0.3	0	0.1	0.4	1.8	3.0	3.2

		Jan	Feb	Mar	Apr	May	June	July	Aug	Sept	Oct	Nov	Dec
Erfoud	Temp. (°F)	63/34	66/37	72/43	77/46	86/57	93/61	100/68	100/66	90/63	81/54	70/45	61/36
	Temp. (°C)	17/1	19/3	22/6	25/8	30/14	34/16	38/20	37/19	32/17	27/12	21/7	16/2
	Rainfall (in.)	0.7	0.5	0.2	0.1	0.1	0	0	0.2	0.8	1.0	1.3	0.9

		Jan	Feb	Mar	Apr	May	June	July	Aug	Sept	Oct	Nov	Dec
Fes	Temp. (°F)	61/39	63/41	66/43	72/46	77/52	84/57	95/63	95/63	86/57	77/54	68/46	61/41
	Temp. (°C)	16/4	17/5	19/6	22/8	25/11	29/14	35/17	35/17	30/14	25/12	20/8	16/5
	Rainfall (in.)	3.2	3.8	3.8	3.5	2.0	1.0	0.3	0.2	0.8	2.2	3.5	3.6

		Jan	Feb	Mar	Apr	May	June	July	Aug	Sept	Oct	Nov	Dec
Marrakech	Temp. (°F)	64/39	68/46	72/48	77/52	81/55	90/61	100/66	100/66	90/64	82/57	73/50	66/45
	Temp. (°C)	18/4	20/8	22/9	25/11	27/13	32/16	37/19	36/19	32/18	28/14	23/10	19/7
	Rainfall (in.)	0.9	1.0	1.2	1.1	0.6	0.3	0.1	0.1	0.3	0.8	1.1	1.0

		Jan	Feb	Mar	Apr	May	June	July	Aug	Sept	Oct	Nov	Dec
Tangier	Temp. (°F)	61/48	63/50	64/52	68/54	72/57	77/61	82/66	84/66	81/64	73/59	68/55	64/50
	Temp. (°C)	16/9	17/10	18/11	20/12	22/14	25/16	28/19	29/19	27/18	23/15	20/13	18/10
	Rainfall (in.)	4.3	4.0	3.8	2.5	1.8	0.8	0.3	0.2	1.0	3.7	5.6	5.1

HOLIDAYS

Two types of holidays are celebrated in Morocco. **National public holidays** (*fêtes nationales*) commemorate important dates in the country's more recent history, as well as general Western holidays. All banks, post offices, government departments, and some shops will close on these days, though public transport is only slightly reduced. These holidays are: New Year's Day (Jan 1); commemoration of the Istiqlal Party's Independence Manifesto (Jan 11); Labor Day (May 1); Fête du Throne (July 30); Allegiance Day (Aug 14); Revolution Day (Aug 20);

Youth Day (Aug 21); anniversary of the Green March (Nov 6); Independence Day (Nov 18). The Western public holidays of Good Friday, Easter Monday, Christmas Day, and Boxing Day are sometimes also taken as holidays by some workers, though they are not official public holidays.

Islamic holidays are observed countrywide by all Moroccans, and some can last for 2 days. These holidays are influenced by the lunar-based Islamic, or *hejira,* calendar, which is roughly 11 days shorter than the Western Gregorian calendar and began in the year A.D. 579, when the Prophet

Mohammed was born. Exact dates in the lunar calendar depend upon each new moon, and the holidays listed below are only approximate, having been calculated in advance by Islamic authorities in Fes. The most spiritual time during the Islamic year is the month-long fast of **Ramadan** (see appendix A). The four most important Islamic holidays in Morocco are: **Eid al Fitr,** the Feast of the Breaking of the Fast after Ramadan; **Eid al Adha; Ras as-Sana,** the first day of the Muslim New Year; and **Mouloud,** the Prophet Mohammed's birthday.

The following are a list of major Islamic holidays and their dates for 2008, 2009, and 2010: Ramadan (Sept 1, Aug 22, Aug 11); Eid al Fitr (Oct 2, Sept 21, Sept 10); Eid al Adha (Dec 9, Nov 28, Nov 17); Ras as-Sana (Jan 10, Dec 31, Dec 20); and Mouloud (Mar 20, Mar 9, Feb 26).

MOROCCO CALENDAR OF EVENTS

Morocco hosts many festivals throughout the year, including a fine range of internationally recognized music festivals, feasts, and celebrations linked to the agricultural or Islamic calendar, and regional *moussems*—festivals dedicated to local holy men, called *marabouts,* and displaying a unique blend of Islamic Sufism with traditional Berber beliefs. For an exhaustive list of events beyond those listed here, check http://events. frommers.com, where you'll find a searchable, up-to-the-minute roster of what's happening in cities all over the world.

February

Almond Blossom Festival, Ameln Valley (Tafraoute is the nearest major town). Held in late February to early March when the valley is "snowing" with pink and white blossoms. The festivities move along the valley from one village to the next, with Berber dancing, singing, and, of course, almond tasting. The harvest is heavily dependent on winter rainfall, so contact

Ahmed Ouardarass at Tafraout Aventure (p. 389) for dates.

March & April

International Nomads Festival, M'hamid. Styled along the lines of Mali's Festival in the Desert, this Moroccan version has slowly gained in prestige since its inception in 2003, drawing artists from France, Brazil, and Spain. Performances rotate between two sites: one in a specially constructed nomadic camp in the dunes about 20km (12 miles) from the village and only accessible by 4×4, the other on a stage in the village itself. The event is still small scale, and thus yet to be overrun by tourists, and is held over 4 days in mid- to late March or early April (2008 dates are Mar 20–23). Visit www.nomadsfestival.com (in French) for information.

Moussem of Sidi Abdallah ibn Hassoun, Salé. Held on the eve of Mouloud, the Prophet Mohammed's birthday, this *moussem* is presided over by local brotherhoods. Commencing at around 3pm and continuing for 3 to 4 hours, a procession of candle bearers (a position handed down from father to son) carry large wax candle lanterns to the Grand Mosque, accompanied by music and dancing.

May

Rose Festival, El Kelaâ M'Gouna, Dadès Valley. A colorful (and aromatic) festival held in late May that coincides with the harvest of Damask roses in the valley. Music and dancing are accompanied by the obligatory showers of rose petals, and children line the roads selling fresh garlands.

Festival des Musiques du Desert, Tafilalet region. This weeklong festival of music and dance attracts performers from Arabia and Africa, with styles ranging from blues to traditional folk music. Concerts are held in the central Moroccan towns of Er Rachidia and Rissani, as well as in Meknes. Held in late May. Visit www.festivaldudesert.ma (in French) for information.

TANJAzz, Tangier. This quality jazz festival is held during the latter part of May and attracts some big names from the U.S. and France. Concerts and jazz sessions are held at various hotels throughout the city, including El Minzah Hotel. In 2008, the festival takes place May 28 to June 1. Visit www.tanjazz.org (in French) for information.

June

Gnaoua & World Music Festival, Essaouira. One of the best known of the country's music festivals celebrated its 10th anniversary in 2007, with 25 Gnaoua bands, 250 Moroccan artists, and 150 international musicians. Essaouira is bursting at the seams during the festival, so book your accommodations early. Mid- to late June. Visit www.festival-gnaoua.net.

Moussem of Ben Aïssa, place el Hedim, Meknes. This is one of the country's largest *moussems* and was traditionally the annual gathering of the Aïssoua brotherhood, known for their extraordinary endurance and self flagellation under trance. They still gather here today, but concentrate more on extended sessions of music, as well as worshipping their *marabout,* Ben Aïssa, near the entrance into Meknes from Rabat. Other attractions during the festival include a *fantasia,* where a charge of horses are ridden at full gallop by riders simultaneously firing long-barreled rifles. Takes place over several days on the eve of Mouloud.

July

Festival of World Sacred Music, Fes. This is another of Morocco's most popular music festivals. The 9-day festival has attracted big names such as South Africa's "white Zulu" Johnny Clegg and U2's Bono. Concerts are held throughout the city—some for free—and occasionally at the Roman ruins of Volubilis. Early June. Visit www.fesfestival.com for information.

International Cultural Festival, Asilah. This 30-year-old festival has rejuvenated the Atlantic fishing village of Asilah, and is perhaps the most dedicated cultural event on the calendar. Throughout the village's medina are performances, lectures, exhibitions, and workshops (some for kids) given by an array of international artists, musicians, intellectuals, and lecturers. The festival runs for the entire month.

Marrakech Popular Arts Festival, Marrakech. Traditional performers from all over the country converge on the city for this 10-day carnival that turns Marrakech into one big, open-air theater. Performances are held in former palaces, on Jemaa el Fna, or simply begin impromptu on the street. Usually held in early July. See p. 154.

August

Setti Fatma Moussem, Setti Fatma. This *moussem* is held for 4 days, usually in the middle of August, and celebrates the local *marabout* whose shrine, or *koubba,* is upstream from the village. Non-Muslims aren't allowed into the *koubba,* but the village itself turns out a fantastic carnival, and tourists are welcome. It makes a great day trip from Marrakech.

September

Imilchil Marriage Festival, Imilchil. This 3-day Fête des Fiancés in the Eastern High Atlas has become just as popular with tourists as it has with the locals. Traditionally, it is a time for the region's unmarried men and women to mix and sometimes match. Usually held the first week of September. See p. 173.

Moussem of Moulay Idriss II, Fes. In late September or early October, thousands gather outside this *marabout's* tomb, located close to the ancient city's Kairouine Mosque, to watch processions of brotherhoods coming to pay tribute to their saint, the son of Morocco's founding father and creator of Fes.

October

Date Festival, Erfoud. Once the Tafilalet's delicious dates have been harvested, this otherwise sleepy town at the entrance to Morocco's Sahara comes alive. Performances of Gnaoua and Berber music and dance reflect the region's influences, and there are plenty of free dates to taste. The festival's

dates (no pun intended) vary from year to year, according to the harvest. Contact one of the local hotels or restaurants toward the end of September for a better idea of exact days.

December

Festival International du Film de Marrakech, Marrakech. This is North Africa's version of the popular Cannes festival and screens more than 100 films over 1 week. The festival has attracted big-name Hollywood and Bollywood stars since it began in 2001. The festival dates seem to change every year, so consult their site (www.festivalmarrakech.com) for more details. See p. 154.

5 Getting There

BY PLANE

In 2006, the Moroccan government, in conjunction with Mohammed VI's desire to increase tourism arrivals to 10 million by 2010, invoked an open-skies policy on the country's air transport sector. Several low-cost European airlines leapt at the opportunity, resulting in decidedly more flight arrivals, especially into the tourist hubs of Agadir, Fes, and Marrakech.

Scheduled international flights fly directly into a number of airports in Morocco: Agadir (AGA), Casablanca (CAS), Fes (FEZ), Marrakech (RAK), Ouarzazate (OZZ), Rabat (RBA), and Tangier (TNG). Casablanca is the country's major airport and hub for the national carrier, Royal Air Maroc. If you're flying from anywhere other than Europe, then more than likely your flight will touch down here. Domestic connections are plentiful, and the airport is connected to the national rail network. North American flights, as well as those from Germany, Italy, and the Netherlands, operate from Terminal 3, a short shuttle ride from terminals 1 and 2,

where all domestic flights are operated from and where the main arrivals and departures buildings are located.

If you're departing from Europe, then flying directly into one of the country's other airports is definitely possible, and the decision whether to do so comes down to which destination you wish to begin your journey and the frequency of flights available. All the airports mentioned above are located out of town, but taxis are usually always parked outside to meet incoming flights, or transfers can be prearranged with your hotel.

When departing Morocco, the departure tax is already included in the cost of your ticket, and *most* airport bureaux de change will change your dirham (notes only) back into euros or sometimes U.S. dollars. There are duty-free shops past the immigration counters, but they won't accept dirham, only euros, British pounds, and U.S. dollars.

Region-specific airport information can be found in the "Fast Facts" in each destination chapter.

The national air carrier is **Royal Air Maroc** (© 09000/0800 toll-free in Morocco; www.royalairmaroc.com), which has offices in most major Moroccan cities, as well as in the U.K., Langham House, 32–33 Gosfield St., London, W1W 6ED (© 020/7307-5800), and the U.S., 666 5th Ave., New York, NY 10103 (© 800/446-726 or 974/385-053). Since 2004, Royal Air Maroc has also operated a subsidiary low-cost international airline called **Atlas Blue** (© 0820/09090 within Morocco, or 020/7307-5803 within the U.K.; www.atlas-blue.com). There are flights from a good selection of European destinations including London, and most of them fly directly into Marrakech. Although their prices are reasonably competitive with other budget airlines, they are notorious for experiencing delays and canceling flights.

Regional Airlines (© 082/000082 within Morocco, or 902/180-151 within Spain; www.regionalmaroc.com) is largely a domestic carrier within Morocco, but they have a few flights into Agadir, Casablanca, and Tangier from mainly Spanish destinations.

FROM NORTH AMERICA   Royal Air Maroc flies five times a week from both New York and Montréal direct to Casablanca, with code-share flights out of New York with **Delta Airlines** (© 800/241-4141; www.delta.com); code-share cities include Atlanta, Boston, Chicago, Dallas, Los Angeles, Miami, San Francisco, Seattle, and Washington. *Note:* If you decide to fly via Europe, be sure to check your arrival and departure airports (for example in London: Gatwick, Heathrow, and Luton) and budget enough time for travel between them if need be.

FROM THE U.K.   British Airways, through its franchisee **GB Airways** (© 0870/8509850 in the U.K., or 022/229464 in Morocco; www.gbairways.com), flies daily from London Heathrow to Casablanca and Marrakech, and twice a week to Tangier during summer. From London Gatwick, they fly daily to Marrakech and twice a week to Fes.

Royal Air Maroc flies daily from London Heathrow to Casablanca, twice weekly to Tangier during summer, and daily from London Gatwick to Marrakech. Budget airlines **Atlas Blue** and **EasyJet** (© 0905/821-0905; www.easyjet.com) fly daily from London Gatwick to Marrakech; **Ryanair** (© 0871/246-0000 in the U.K., or 0818/30-3030 in Ireland; www.ryanair.com) flies at least three times a week from London Luton to both Fes and Marrakech; and **Thomsonfly** (© 0870/190-0737; www.thomsonfly.com) flies weekly to Agadir from London Gatwick or Manchester and at least three times a week to Marrakech from either London Gatwick or London Luton. There are also charter flights from London direct to Agadir, organized by all-inclusive tour operators such as **Panorama** (© 0871/664-7984; www.panoramaholidays.co.uk). For just flights to Agadir (that are not part of an all-inclusive package), you'll have to fly to Casablanca and then catch a domestic flight with Royal Air Maroc.

FROM EUROPE   There's a range of airlines flying to Morocco from within Europe, including Air Berlin (www.airberlin.com), Air France (www.airfrance.com), Iberia Air (www.iberia.com), KLM (www.klm.com), and Ryanair, as well as Royal Air Maroc and Atlas Blue.

FLYING FOR LESS: TIPS FOR GETTING THE BEST AIRFARE

- Passengers who can book their ticket either **long in advance or at the last minute,** or who **fly midweek** or **at less trafficked hours,** may pay a fraction of the full fare. If your schedule is flexible, say so, and ask if you can secure a cheaper fare by changing your flight plans.
- Search **the Internet** for cheap fares. The most popular online travel a

gencies are **Travelocity** (www. travelocity.com or www.travelocity. co.uk); **Expedia** (www.expedia.com, www.expedia.co.uk, or www.expedia. ca); and **Orbitz** (www.orbitz.com). In the U.K., go to **Travelsupermarket** (© 0845/345-5708; www.travel supermarket.com), a flight search engine that offers flight comparisons for the budget airlines whose seats often end up in bucket-shop sales. Other websites for booking airline tickets online include **Cheapflights. com, SmarterTravel.com, Priceline. com,** and **Opodo** (www.opodo.co. uk). Metasearch sites (which find and then direct you to airline and hotel websites for booking) include **Side-step.com** and **Kayak.com**—the latter includes fares for budget carriers such as JetBlue and Spirit as well as the major airlines. **Lastminute.com** is a great source for last-minute flights and getaways. In addition,

most **airlines** offer online-only fares that even their phone agents know nothing about.

- Keep an eye on local newspapers for **promotional specials** or **fare wars,** when airlines lower prices on their most popular routes.
- Try to book a ticket **in its country of origin.** If you're planning a one-way flight from Johannesburg to New York, a South Africa–based travel agent will probably have the lowest fares. For foreign travelers on multi-leg trips, book in the country of the first leg; for example, book New York–Chicago–Montréal–New York in the U.S. Refer to some of the Moroccan-based tour operators recommended later in this chapter.
- **Consolidators,** also known as bucket shops, are wholesale brokers in the airline-ticket game. Consolidators buy deeply discounted tickets ("distressed" inventories of unsold seats)

(Tips   Getting Through the Airport

- Arrive at the airport at least 1 hour before a domestic flight and 2 hours before an international flight. You can check the average wait times at your airport by going to the TSA **Security Checkpoint Wait Times** site (http://waittime/tsa.dhs.gov/index.html).
- Know what you can carry on and what you can't. For the latest updates on items you are prohibited to bring in carry-on luggage, go to **www.tsa. gov/travelers/airtravel**.
- Beat the ticket-counter lines by using the self-service electronic ticket kiosks at the airport or even printing out your boarding pass at home from the airline website. Using curbside check-in is also a smart way to avoid lines.
- Help speed up security before you're screened. Remove jackets, shoes, belt buckles, heavy jewelry, and watches, and place them either in your carry-on luggage or the security bins provided. Place keys, coins, cellphones, and pagers in a security bin. If you have metallic body parts, carry a note from your doctor. When possible, pack liquids in checked baggage.
- Use a TSA-approved lock for your checked luggage. Look for Travel Sentry certified locks at luggage or travel shops and Brookstone stores (or online at www.brookstone.com).

Tips Don't Stow It—Ship It

Though pricey, it's sometimes worthwhile to travel luggage free, particularly if you're toting sports equipment, meeting materials, or baby equipment. Specialists in door-to-door luggage delivery include **SkyCap International** (www. skycapinternational.com) and **Sports Express** (in partnership with Virtual Bellhop and Luggage Express; www.sportsexpress.com).

from airlines and sell them to online ticket agencies, travel agents, tour operators, corporations, and, to a lesser degree, the general public. Consolidators advertise in Sunday newspaper travel sections (often in small ads with tiny type), both in the U.S. and the U.K. They can be great sources for cheap international tickets. On the down side, bucket-shop tickets are often rigged with restrictions, such as stiff cancellation penalties (as high as 50%–75% of the ticket price). And keep in mind that most of what you see advertised is of limited availability. Several reliable consolidators are worldwide and available online. **STA Travel** (www. statravel.com) has been the world's leading consolidator for students since purchasing Council Travel, but their fares are competitive for travelers of all ages. **Flights.com** (© 800/ TRAV-800; www.flights.com) has excellent fares worldwide, particularly to Europe. They also have "local" websites in 12 countries. **Lowestfare. com** (© 800/678-0998; www.lowest fare.com) has especially good fares to sunny destinations. **Air Tickets Direct** (© 800/778-3447; www.air ticketsdirect.com) is based in Montréal and leverages the currently weak Canadian dollar for low fares; they also book trips to places that U.S. travel agents won't touch, such as Cuba.

- Join **frequent-flier clubs.** Frequent-flier membership doesn't cost a cent, but it does entitle you to free tickets or upgrades when you amass the airline's required number of frequent-flier points. You don't even have to fly to earn points; **frequent-flier credit cards** can earn you thousands of miles for doing your everyday shopping. But keep in mind that award seats are limited, seats on popular routes are hard to snag, and more and more major airlines are cutting their expiration periods for mileage points—so check your airline's frequent-flier program so you don't lose your miles before you use them. _Inside tip:_ Award seats are offered almost a year in advance, but seats also open up at the last minute, so if your travel plans are flexible, you may strike gold. To play the frequent-flier game to your best advantage, consult the community bulletin boards on **FlyerTalk** (www.flyertalk.com) or go to Randy Petersen's **Inside Flyer** (www.insideflyer.com). Petersen and friends review all the programs in detail and post regular updates on changes in policies and trends.

LONG-HAUL FLIGHTS: HOW TO STAY COMFORTABLE

- Your choice of airline and airplane will definitely affect your legroom. Find more details about U.S. airlines at **www.seatguru.com**. For international airlines, the research firm Skytrax has posted a list of average seat pitches at **www.airlinequality.com**.

- Emergency exit seats and bulkhead seats typically have the most legroom. Emergency exit seats are usually left unassigned until the day of a flight (to ensure that someone able-bodied fills the seats); it's worth getting to the ticket counter early to snag one of these spots for a long flight. Many passengers find that bulkhead seating (the row facing the wall at the front of the cabin) offers more legroom, but keep in mind that bulkhead seats have no storage space on the floor in front of you.

- To have two seats for yourself in a three-seat row, try for an aisle seat in a center section toward the back of coach. If you're traveling with a companion, book an aisle and a window seat. Middle seats are usually booked last, so chances are good you'll end up with three seats to yourselves. And in the event that a third passenger is assigned the middle seat, he or she will probably be more than happy to trade for a window or an aisle.

- Ask about entertainment options. Many airlines offer seatback video systems where you get to choose your movies or play video games—but only on some of their planes. (Boeing 777s are your best bet.)

- To sleep, avoid the last row of any section or the row in front of an emergency exit, as these seats are the least likely to recline. Avoid seats near highly trafficked toilet areas. Avoid seats in the back of many jets—these can be narrower than those in the rest of coach. Or reserve a window seat so you can rest your head and avoid being bumped in the aisle.

- Get up, walk around, and stretch every 60 to 90 minutes to keep your blood flowing. This helps avoid **deep vein thrombosis,** or "economy-class syndrome." See the box "Avoiding 'Economy Class Syndrome,'" p. 34.

- Drink water before, during, and after your flight to combat the lack of humidity in airplane cabins. Avoid alcohol, which will dehydrate you.

⌜Tips⌝ Coping with Jet Lag

Jet lag is a pitfall of traveling across time zones. If you're flying north-south and feel sluggish when you touch down, your symptoms will be the result of dehydration and the general stress of air travel. When you travel east-west or vice versa, however, your body becomes thoroughly confused about what time it is, and everything from your digestive system to your brain is knocked for a loop. Traveling east, say from Chicago to Paris, is more difficult on your internal clock than traveling west, say from London to Atlanta, because most peoples' bodies are more inclined to stay up late than fall asleep early.

Here are some tips for combating jet lag:

- **Reset your watch** to your destination time before you board the plane.
- **Drink lots of water** before, during, and after your flight. Avoid alcohol.
- **Exercise and sleep well** for a few days before your trip.
- If you have trouble sleeping on planes, **fly eastward on morning flights.**
- **Daylight** is the key to resetting your body clock. At the website for **Outside In** (www.bodyclock.com), you can get a customized plan of when to seek and avoid light.

Flying with Film & Video

Never pack film—exposed or unexposed—in checked bags, because the new, more powerful scanners in U.S. airports can fog film. The film you carry with you can be damaged by scanners as well. X-ray damage is cumulative; the faster the film, and the more times you put it through a scanner, the more likely the damage. Film under 800 ASA is usually safe for up to five scans. If you're taking your film through additional scans, U.S. regulations permit you to demand hand inspections. In international airports, you're at the mercy of airport officials. On international flights, store your film in transparent baggies so you can remove it easily before you go through scanners. Keep in mind that airports are not the only places where your camera may be scanned: Highly trafficked attractions are X-raying visitors' bags with increasing frequency.

Most photo supply stores sell protective pouches designed to block damaging X-rays. The pouches fit both film and loaded cameras. They should protect your film in checked baggage, but they also may raise alarms and result in a hand inspection.

You'll have little to worry about if you are traveling with **digital cameras**. Unlike film, which is sensitive to light, the digital camera and storage cards are not affected by airport X-rays, according to Nikon. Carry-on scanners will not damage **videotape** in video cameras, but the magnetic fields emitted by the walk-through security gateways and handheld inspection wands will. Always place your loaded camcorder on the screening conveyor belt or have it hand-inspected. Be sure your batteries are charged, as you may be required to turn the device on to ensure that it's what it appears to be.

- If you're flying with kids, don't forget to carry on toys, books, pacifiers, and snacks and chewing gum to help them relieve ear pressure buildup during ascent and descent.

BY CAR

Self-drivers are best advised to make their way down through Spain to the southern ports of Algeciras or Tarifa, from where there are vehicle ferries making the daily crossing across the Straits of Gibraltar to Tangier (from both), and the Spanish enclave of Ceuta (from Algeciras only). Ceuta is the best port of arrival if you want to head straight into the Rif mountains and across to Fes, while Tangier is a good (and the only) point of arrival for the Atlantic Coast and inland to Marrakech.

Remember that the Spanish-Moroccan border is about 5km (3 miles) inland from Ceuta port. Current costs for your vehicle, depending on the size, are: Algeciras to Tangier 60€ to 105€ ($87–$152); Algeciras to Ceuta 30€ ($44); and Tarifa to Tangier 68€ ($99).

To enter Morocco, you'll need your vehicle's registration papers and a Green Card (*carte verte* in French) insurance document from your insurer. The Green Card proves that your vehicle is at least insured against third-party damage. Some companies won't insure your vehicle for travel in Morocco, so it's best to check beforehand and shop around if you need to buy some. You can also purchase temporary third-party insurance at Spanish and Moroccan ports, but it really is best to arrange this beforehand so you're sure of the coverage you're paying for. A *Carnet de Passage* (issued by motoring organizations worldwide to allow your vehicle to enter most countries without any customs or import fees) is not required for your vehicle to enter Morocco, but you'll need one if you're traveling farther into Africa.

Upon arriving in the Moroccan port, you'll need to complete a Temporary Importation document, which is usually available on the Tangier ferries or otherwise at the Ceuta-Morocco border post. Your vehicle will then be "stamped" into your passport, allowing the vehicle to stay in Morocco for 6 months (but remember that *you* are only given 3 months; see "Entry Requirements" earlier). The vehicle can only leave with you, proving to Moroccan Customs that it hasn't been sold, and therefore no customs or tax on the sale is due.

BY FERRY

Traveling by sea is a wonderful, almost spiritual, way to arrive in Morocco. When sailing from the Spanish port of Algeciras—the most popular point of departure—the Rock of Gibraltar is visible for quite some time before finally fading away into the Mediterranean mist. However, it's not long before the silhouettes of Tangier's minarets appear in the distance.

As mentioned, the most popular route operates between **Algeciras and Tangier,** and during the peak August holiday month, ferries run every hour almost around the clock. Popular alternative routes include **Algeciras to Ceuta** and **Tarifa to Tangier,** though Tarifa is not an "international" port, thus only E.U. passport holders can travel on this route. The crossing from Algeciras to Tangier can take between 80 minutes and 3 hours, depending on the ship, and currently costs range from 35€ to 37€ ($51–$54)

per person. The companies crossing from Algeciras to Ceuta all operate fast catamarans, taking only 35 minutes; the cost is currently 34€ ($49) per person. *Note:* It's worth remembering that Ceuta is still on Spanish soil, which means the port is void of all the border formalities experienced in Tangier. If you're traveling independently, you'll have to catch local bus no. 7 (0.62€–0.67€/90¢–95¢) or a taxi (2.90€/$4.20) from the center of Ceuta to the border. Crossing from Tarifa to Tangier is also by catamaran and takes 35 minutes. The current fare is 29€ ($42) per person.

The ferry companies operating between Morocco and Europe are:

- **Acciona Trasmediterranea** (© **902/ 454645** within Spain; www.tras mediterranea.es): One of the largest companies, sailing between Algeciras and both Ceuta and Tangier; Almeria and Malaga to the Spanish enclave of Melilla; and Almeria to Nador.

- **Buquebus** (© **902/414242** within Spain, or 039/342384 within Morocco; www.buquebus.es): Spanish company sailing between Algeciras and Ceuta.

- **Comanav** (© **022/302412** within Morocco, or 956/570420 within Spain; www.comanav.co.ma): Moroccan-based company sailing between Algeciras and Tangier; Genoa (Italy) and Tangier; Almeria and Tangier, Nador, or Al Hoceima; and Sète (France) and Tangier or Nador.

- **Comarit** (© **956/668462** within Spain, or 039/320032 within Morocco; www.comarit.es): Spanish company sailing between Algeciras and Tangier and Almeria (Spain) and Nador.

- **EuroFerrys** (© **956/652324** within Spain, or 039/948199 within Morocco; www.euroferrys.com): Sails between Algeciras and both Ceuta and Tangier, and Almeria and Nador.

- **FRS** (© **956/681830** within Spain, or 039/942612 within Morocco; www.frs.es): Sails between Tarifa, Gibraltar, and Algeciras (in summer) to Tangier.
- **Limadet** (© **039/933621** within Morocco, or 956/669613 within Spain): A Moroccan-based company that sails between Algeciras and Tangier.
- **Nautas** (© **956/589530** within Spain, or 039/934463 within Morocco; www.nautasferry.com): Sails from Algeciras to both Tangier and Ceuta.

Ferries will always have an on-board restaurant serving meals and drinks, but sometimes not much else. *Note:* Payment, no matter which direction you're heading, is almost always only accepted in euros. Tickets can always be purchased at each company's office or ticket booth located at the ferry terminals. Don't be swayed by any talk of "last ferry leaves now" or "cheapest ticket here" by hustlers. For more information on traveling to Tangier by ferry, including immigration formalities, see p. 266.

6 General Travel Resources

MONEY & COSTS

On the whole, Morocco is inexpensive by Western standards. Moroccans tend to haggle over prices and accept that others will do the same, especially in the country's markets, or souks. The cost of certain services—such as guides, car rental, and mechanical services—can also be negotiated. However, in businesses such as restaurants and grocery, hardware, electrical, and fashion stores, prices are generally fixed. In the bigger cities, prices for virtually everything are higher, especially in the main tourist centers of Marrakech, Agadir, Fes, and Casablanca. In addition to this, prices can rise for public transport and in hotels and restaurants over the post-Ramadan feasts of Eid al Fitr and Eid al Adha, and again in the main tourist centers over the Easter and Christmas/New Year holiday periods.

CURRENCY

Morocco's official currency is the dirham (MAD; abbreviated to dh within Morocco), divided into 100 centimes. Coins are issued in denominations of 1dh, 2dh, 5dh, and 10dh, as well as 10, 20, and 50 centimes. Banknotes are issued in denominations of 20, 50, 100, and 200. At press time, the rate of exchange was 8dh to $1, 16dh to £1, and

11dh to 1€. I often use the website www.oanda.com to check current exchange rates, as well as view the trading history between certain countries to look for recent fluctuations. The dirham is a restricted currency and can't be taken out of the country, is not traded, and is only theoretically available abroad (I have heard of travelers finding the odd bureau de change in London that has a supply). The currency is stable and hasn't fluctuated too much over recent times.

EXCHANGING MONEY

Morocco is still very much a cash society. Throughout the country, it's very difficult to cash traveler's checks or use credit cards. Euros are by far the easiest foreign currency to exchange, and are often accepted as payment if you don't have any dirham on hand. U.S. dollars and British pounds can be exchanged at banks and bureaux de change, but will rarely be accepted as payment. Frustratingly, most banks, as well as bureaux de change, **do not exchange** pre-2000 U.S. notes or the new F-series British pound notes that began circulation in early 2007. Throughout the country you'll also come up against a blanket refusal by any Moroccan to accept any dirham note that is damaged (that includes the slightest

What Things Cost in Morocco	Dirham	US$	UK£
Taxi from the airport	160.00–200.00	20.00–25.00	10.00–13.00
Double room (very expensive)	960.00	120.00	60.00
Double room (expensive)	640.00–960.00	80.00–120.00	40.00–60.00
Double room (moderate)	360.00–640.00	45.00–80.00	23.00–40.00
Double room (inexpensive)	150.00–360.00	19.00–45.00	9.00–23.00
Dinner for one, without wine (very expensive)	240.00	30.00	15.00
Dinner for one, without wine (expensive)	160.00–240.00	20.00–30.00	10.00–15.00
Dinner for one, without wine (moderate)	80.00–160.00	10.00–20.00	5.00–10.00
Dinner for one, without wine (inexpensive)	40.00–80.00	5.00–10.00	2.50–5.00
Local taxi ride	5.00–15.00	.65–1.90	.30–.95
Bottle of water (small)	3.00	.40	.20
Bottle of water (large)	7.00	.90	.45
Cup of tea or coffee	5.00	.65	.30
Bottled beer (Flag Spéciale)	10.00	1.25	.65
Liter (¼ gal.) of petrol	11.00	1.40	.70

tear). The national reserve bank, Bank al Maghrib, will accept all of these, and can be found in each large city. The easiest to locate is the branch in Marrakech (see "Banks & Currency Exchanges" under "Fast Facts" in chapter 5). Scottish pounds and Australian and New Zealand dollars *are not exchangeable* in Morocco.

As the dirham isn't traded international-ly, there's no money-changing black market, and exchange rates vary marginal-ly between banks, bureaux de change, and even most hotels. Changing money at a bureau de change is quicker than at banks, although some banks do have ded-icated booths just for money exchange. A Moroccan bank, the Société Générale du Marocain Banques (SGMB), offers a for-eign exchange ATM—simply labeled EXCHANGE—outside a number of their branches, usually located right next to a regular ATM. This brilliant service exchanges foreign currency while you wait. The exchange rate is the same as what is offered within the branch, but is rounded down to the nearest 10. A few other banks have also installed these ATMs in branches within the larger cities. These ATMS are operational 24 hours a day and have been duly noted where available in each destination's "Fast Facts."

There is always a problem making change in Morocco, and it's often diffi-cult to pay with large banknotes. Always be on the lookout for smaller denomina-tion (10 and 20) bank notes and dirham coins, as this will make your life easier during the daily trials of tipping for serv-ices and paying for inexpensive everyday goods such as bottled water. Good places to break down a large note are the Acima and Marjane supermarkets (noted throughout the "Shopping" sections of each destination) or at the toll booths on the nation's auto routes (if you are self-driving).

You can *usually* exchange dirham back into hard currency—usually only euros—at major airports around the country. They may ask for an exchange receipt, so keep a few handy along your travels. Duty-free shops past the immigration counters do not accept dirham. If traveling by ferry from Tangier, you can try to re-exchange dirham at the bureaux de change at the port entrance or with money changers in Algeciras. Money changers at the Ceuta/Morocco border will do this as well.

ATMs

The easiest and best way to get cash away from home is from an ATM (automated teller machine), sometimes referred to as a "cash machine" or a "cashpoint." The **Cirrus** (© **800/424-7787;** www.master card.com) and **PLUS** (© **800/843-7587;** www.visa.com) networks span the globe. Go to your bank card's website to find ATM locations at your destination. Be sure you know your daily withdrawal limit before you depart.

Some ATMs in Morocco only accept a four-digit personal identification number (PIN); change your five- and six-digit PIN before you're in Morocco. Without the PIN, you can't use the card at an ATM or within a branch, unless it is a credit card, where you can make a cash advance within some banks and bureaux de change. *Note:* Many banks impose a fee every time you use a card at another bank's ATM, and that fee can be higher for international transactions (up to $5 or more) than for domestic ones (where they're rarely more than $2). In addition, the bank from which you withdraw cash may charge its own fee. For international withdrawal fees, ask your bank.

CREDIT CARDS

Credit cards are another safe way to carry money. They also provide a convenient record of all your expenses, and they generally offer relatively good exchange rates. You can withdraw cash advances from your credit cards at banks or ATMs, but high fees make credit card cash advances a pricey way to get cash. Keep in mind that you'll pay interest from the moment of your withdrawal, even if you pay your monthly bills on time. Also, note that many banks now assess a 1% to 3% "transaction fee" on *all* charges you incur abroad (whether you're using the local currency or your native currency).

It's best not to rely on being able to use your credit card when shopping in Morocco. Some large, tourist-friendly shops, especially the carpet emporiums, will have the necessary equipment, but when paying for smaller purchases, cash will be the only form of payment accepted. If you are using your credit card, be aware of the full amount being charged to your card prior to signing off the transaction. The transaction should be in dirham, so be aware of the current exchange rates. Make sure the amount on the transaction slip is clear and concise, and on no occasion agree to signing multiple slips for monthly payments, as there's every chance the slips will be banked all at once, and the door is also left open for those slips to be doctored.

When it's possible to pay for goods and services by credit card, MasterCard and Visa are accepted, but rarely American Express. Diner's Club and Discover cards are not accepted in Morocco.

TRAVELER'S CHECKS

Exchanging traveler's checks can be difficult in Morocco. Most banks and bureaux de change exchange cash only—or will make it plainly obvious that they would prefer not to exchange traveler's checks by asking for all manner of identification and proof of purchase. Personal experience recommends wherever you find an establishment accepting traveler's checks, plan ahead and exchange a bit more than you budgeted. I've found most success with the banks along Tangier's avenue Mohammed V and at branches of the national reserve bank, Bank al Maghrib, throughout the country.

The most common traveler's checks accepted in Morocco—in either euros, U.S. dollars, or British pounds—are those offered by **American Express** (© **800/807-6233,** or 800/221-7282 for card holders—this number accepts collect calls, offers service in several foreign languages, and exempts Amex gold and platinum cardholders from the 1% fee); **Visa** (© **800/732-1322**—AAA members can obtain Visa checks for a $9.95 fee for checks up to $1,500 at most AAA offices or by calling © **866/339-3378**); and **MasterCard** (© **800/223-9920**).

Be sure to keep a record of the traveler's checks serial numbers separate from your checks in the event that they are stolen or lost. You'll get a refund faster if you know the numbers.

TRAVEL INSURANCE

The cost of travel insurance varies widely, depending on the destination, the cost and length of your trip, your age and health, and the type of trip you're taking, but expect to pay between 5 and 8% of the vacation itself. You can get estimates from various providers through **InsureMy Trip.com.** Enter your trip cost and dates, your age, and other information for prices from more than a dozen companies.

U.K. citizens and their families who make more than one trip abroad per year may find an annual travel insurance policy works out cheaper. Check **www.money supermarket.com**, which compares prices across a wide range of providers for single- and multitrip policies.

Most big travel agents offer their own insurance and will probably try to sell you their package when you book a holiday. Think before you sign. **Britain's Consumers' Association** recommends that you insist on seeing the policy and reading the fine print before buying travel insurance. **The Association of British Insurers** (© **020/7600-3333**; www.abi. org.uk) gives advice by phone and publishes *Holiday Insurance*, a free guide to policy provisions and prices. You might also shop around for better deals: Try **Columbus Direct** (© **0870/033-9988**; www.columbusdirect.net).

TRIP-CANCELLATION INSURANCE

Trip-cancellation insurance will help retrieve your money if you have to back out of a trip or depart early, or if your travel supplier goes bankrupt. Trip cancellation traditionally covers such events as sickness, natural disasters, and State Department advisories. The latest news in trip-cancellation insurance is the availability of **expanded hurricane coverage** and the **"any-reason"** cancellation coverage—which costs more but covers cancellations made for any reason. You won't get back 100% of your prepaid trip cost, but you'll be refunded a substantial portion. **TravelSafe** (© **888/885-7233;**

Tips   Hey, Google, Did You Get My Text Message?

If you forget your guidebook at the hotel, send a text message (such as "carnegie deli new york") to © **46645 (GOOGL).** Within 10 seconds, you'll receive a text message with the address and phone number. Look up weather, translations, currency conversions, and more. For more tips, see www.google. com/intl/en_us/mobile/sms/. Regular text message charges apply.

Travel in the Age of Bankruptcy

Airlines go bankrupt, so protect yourself by **buying your tickets with a credit card.** The Fair Credit Billing Act guarantees that you can get your money back from the credit card company if a travel supplier goes under (and if you request the refund within 60 days of the bankruptcy). **Travel insurance** can also help, but make sure it covers against "carrier default" for your specific travel provider. And be aware that if a U.S. airline goes bust midtrip, a 2001 federal law requires other carriers to take you to your destination (albeit on a space-available basis) for a fee of no more than $25, provided you rebook within 60 days of the cancellation.

www.travelsafe.com) offers both types of coverage. Expedia also offers any-reason cancellation coverage for its air-hotel packages.

For details, contact one of the following recommended insurers: **Access America** (© 866/807-3982; www.access america.com); **Travel Guard International** (© 800/826-4919; www.travel guard.com); **Travel Insured International** (© 800/243-3174; www.travel insured.com); and **Travelex Insurance Services** (© 888/457-4602; www.travelex-insurance.com).

MEDICAL INSURANCE

For travel overseas, most U.S. health plans (including Medicare and Medicaid) do not provide coverage, and the ones that do often require you to pay for services upfront and reimburse you only after you return home.

As a safety net, you may want to buy travel medical insurance, particularly if you're traveling to a remote or high-risk area where emergency evacuation might be necessary. If you require additional medical insurance, try **MEDEX Assistance** (© 410/453-6300; www.medex assist.com) or **Travel Assistance International** (© 800/821-2828; www.travel assistance.com; for general information on services, call the company's **Worldwide Assistance Services, Inc.** at © 800/777-8710).

Canadians should check with their provincial health plan offices, or call **Health Canada** (© 866/225-0709; www.hc-sc.gc.ca) to find out the extent of their coverage and what documentation and receipts they must take home in case they are treated overseas.

LOST-LUGGAGE INSURANCE

On international flights (including U.S. portions of international trips), baggage coverage is limited to approximately $9.07 per pound, up to approximately $635 per checked bag. If you plan to check items more valuable than what's covered by the standard liability, see if your homeowner's policy covers your valuables, get baggage insurance as part of your comprehensive travel-insurance package, or buy Travel Guard's "BagTrak" product.

If your luggage is lost, immediately file a lost-luggage claim at the airport, detailing the luggage contents. Most airlines require that you report delayed, damaged, or lost baggage within 4 hours of arrival. The airlines are required to deliver luggage, once found, directly to your house or destination free of charge.

HEALTH
STAYING HEALTHY

Traveling in Morocco generally presents no serious health concerns. If there is one constant health concern, it's that of traveler's diarrhea, sometimes dubbed "Morocco belly" (see "Common Ailments," below).

General Availability of Health Care

No compulsory vaccinations are required to enter Morocco, though travelers arriving from cholera-infected areas may be asked for proof of vaccine, and it's always wise to be up-to-date with your tetanus and typhoid vaccines. Due to the aforementioned stomach distress, it's always good to bring along a course of anti-diarrhea tablets and oral rehydration sachets, although these are usually readily available from the country's pharmacies. Moroccan pharmacists (see "Drugstores" in "Fast Facts") are very well trained, and regularly act as the village doctor. They dispense a far wider range of drugs than their colleagues in the West, and can usually assist with most travelers' ailments. If you need the attention of a doctor, they can usually recommend one for you, some even have a doctor on-site. Moroccan doctors—private and public—are very professional, with most having studied in France.

The level of hospital care in Morocco tends to be dictated by the location. Privately-run *polycliniques* generally offer first-world facilities and can be found in most larger towns and cities. State hospitals are notoriously under-funded and are best visited only for minor injuries;

however, they may be the only option if you are in rural regions. For serious illnesses or injuries, contact your embassy for advice. Throughout the book, I have listed each city's doctors and hospitals where available in the "Fast Facts" section.

Note: Almost without exception, you will have to pay upfront and in cash for any medical treatment and then claim on any travel insurance once you return home. Remember to get receipts for any treatment or medication.

Contact the **International Association for Medical Assistance to Travelers (IAMAT;** © **716/754-4883,** or 416/652-0137 in Canada; www.iamat.org) for tips on travel and health concerns in the countries you're visiting, and for lists of local, English-speaking doctors. The United States **Centers for Disease Control and Prevention** (© **800/311-3435;** www.cdc.gov) provides up-to-date information on health hazards by region or country and offers tips on food safety. **Travel Health Online** (www.tripprep.com), sponsored by a consortium of travel medicine practitioners, may also offer helpful advice on traveling abroad. You can find listings of reliable medical clinics overseas at the **International Society of Travel Medicine** (www.istm.org).

Avoiding "Economy Class Syndrome"

Deep vein thrombosis, or as it's know in the world of flying, "economy-class syndrome," is a blood clot that develops in a deep vein. It's a potentially deadly condition that can be caused by sitting in cramped conditions—such as an airplane cabin—for too long. During a flight (especially a long-haul flight), get up, walk around, and stretch your legs every 60 to 90 minutes to keep your blood flowing. Other preventative measures include frequent flexing of the legs while sitting, drinking lots of water, and avoiding alcohol and sleeping pills. If you have a history of deep vein thrombosis, heart disease, or another condition that puts you at high risk, some experts recommend wearing compression stockings or taking anticoagulants when you fly; always ask your physician about the best course for you. Symptoms of deep vein thrombosis include leg pain or swelling, or even shortness of breath.

Healthy Travels to You

The following government websites offer up-to-date health-related travel advice.

- **Australia:** www.dfat.gov.au/travel
- **Canada:** www.hc-sc.gc.ca/index_e.html
- **U.K.:** www.dh.gov.uk/en/Policyandguidance/Healthadvicefortravellers/index.htm
- **U.S.:** www.cdc.gov/travel

COMMON AILMENTS

MOROCCO BELLY Traveler's diarrhea (locally known as Morocco belly) is the most common ailment suffered by Westerners while traveling in Morocco. As with similar destinations around the world, there's only so much that can be done to try to avoid an upset stomach. Some people religiously stay away from street food, others never order a salad and only drink bottled water, while others only eat peeled or cooked food. All of these are good ideas and recommended—however, I've still seen the most cautious of travelers fall victim. It can happen simply because your body isn't used to the unfamiliar cuisine, or perhaps from a little bout of travel fatigue.

For many, however, traveler's diarrhea is a direct result of dehydration. Morocco's summer months are often oppressively hot—especially for those arriving from more temperate climes—and can sometimes be too much for the body to cope with. Even at other times of the year, Morocco's delightfully warm temperature can disguise the strong effect that the sun can have.

Once you arrive, increasing your daily intake of water is the most effective way to keep Morocco belly at bay. I always recommend two large bottles per day, which takes a bit of effort for those not used to drinking so much water. Most tap water is drinkable, but bottled water is available everywhere, inexpensive, and recommended. If you do suffer from a dose of diarrhea, it's important (especially for children) to replace lost body fluids and salts. Oral rehydration salts, available in any pharmacy, will help. Moroccans swear by a tablespoonful of ground cumin washed down with a swig of water.

It pays to adapt your diet as well. Steer clear from fatty foods, caffeine, alcohol, and dairy products (except yogurt). Eat plain boiled rice or plain steamed couscous, yogurt, and dried biscuits. For a serious dose of diarrhea, start taking an antibiotic and an anti-diarrhea agent.

Note: Mountain and desert trekkers should avoid drinking from rivers and streams, as cases of giardiasis are common. If you must, be sure to boil the water sufficiently or purify it with iodine tablets.

BUGS, BITES & OTHER WILDLIFE CONCERNS The existence of malaria is officially denied by Moroccan authorities, but other sources report very occasional summertime cases in a few of the more northern reaches of the country. Personally, I've never heard of, or seen, anyone suffering from malaria in Morocco. Cover up from dusk until dawn and use good mosquito repellent, and you shouldn't have anything to worry about.

Morocco's Saharan ergs and the surrounding stony *hammada* are home to a number of scorpions and snakes. Although very few of the country's scorpions are venomous—a notable exception being the decidedly nasty *Androctonus australis*—the sting can still be extremely painful, especially if you are allergic. The same goes for the country's snakes, which other than the largely nocturnal and terrestrial Saharan horned viper, are mostly non-venomous. The chances of coming across a snake, however, are slim. All snakes, without exception, are greatly feared by ordinary Moroccans, and no distinction is drawn between venomous and non-venomous species. Snakes are invariably killed whenever and wherever they are found. To be safe, wear closed footwear when outdoors, and shake them out before putting them on. If bitten, try to stay calm and seek medical help as quickly as possible.

Rabies cases are rare but do occur in Morocco. Vaccination against rabies doesn't mean you're immune, and it's worth seeking medical advice if you're bitten.

HIGH-ALTITUDE HAZARDS   More travelers are making day trips from Marrakech to the Jebel Toubkal trail head village of Imlil, which sits 1,740m (5,709 ft.) above sea level. Most people are fine at this altitude, but it's worth knowing your limits and realizing some people may be a little short of breath. For hard-core trekkers who don't wish to spend a day in the village acclimatizing, be aware that the Toubkal-Neltner refuge sits at 3,207m (10,521 ft.) and the Jebel Toubkal peak at 4,167m (13,671 ft.). Altitude sickness, or acute mountain sickness (AMS), can occur as low as 2,500m (8,202 ft.), but serious symptoms don't usually occur until above 3,600m (11,811 ft.). The main cause of altitude sickness is going too high too quickly, and can generally be avoided by planning a sensible trek that allows for gradual altitude acclimatization. Given enough time, your body will adapt to the decrease in oxygen at a specific altitude. Trekking up to 3,000m (9,843 ft.), many people will experience mild AMS. The symptoms—headache, appetite loss, extreme fatigue, and nausea—usually start 12 to 24 hours after arrival at altitude and begin to decrease in severity around the third day. It's important to stay properly hydrated when mountain trekking—experts advise 4 to 6 liters of water per day—and avoid tobacco, alcohol, and depressant drugs such as sleeping pills. Remember the easiest and quickest way to lessen AMS is to descend.

SUN/ELEMENTS/EXTREME WEATHER EXPOSURE   The weather extremes in Morocco can be surprising for some. During the colder months of November to February, the country can experience European-like cold spells bringing cold, wet, and sometimes snowy weather to many regions. Travel through those same regions from June to September, however, and Morocco fulfils its image as a land fringed by Saharan sands and harsh, barren mountains. It's during these hot months that travelers should try to limit their exposure to the sun—especially during the first few days after arrival and at high altitudes—during the heat of the day. Wear a hat and use sunscreen with a high protection factor (SPF 30+), and remember that children are more susceptible to heat exhaustion and dehydration than adults.

WHAT TO DO IF YOU GET SICK AWAY FROM HOME

In Morocco, you will have to pay all medical costs upfront and in cash. See "General Availability of Health Care" under "Health," above. Before leaving home, find out what medical services your health insurance covers. To protect yourself, consider buying medical travel insurance (see "Medical Insurance," under "Travel Insurance," above).

Very few health insurance plans pay for medical evacuation back to the U.S. (which can cost $10,000 and up). A number of companies offer medical evacuation services anywhere in the world. If you're ever hospitalized more than 150 miles from home, **MedjetAssist** (*✆* **800/ 527-7478;** www.medjetassistance.com) will pick you up and fly you to the hospital of your choice virtually anywhere in the world in a medically equipped and staffed aircraft 24 hours day, 7 days a week. Annual memberships are $225 individual, $350 family; you can also purchase short-term memberships.

We list local **hospitals** and **doctors** under "Fast Facts" in each destination chapter.

If you suffer from a chronic illness, consult your doctor before your departure. Pack **prescription medications** in your carry-on luggage, and carry them in their original containers, with pharmacy labels—otherwise they won't make it through airport security. Carry the generic name of prescription medicines in case a local pharmacist is unfamiliar with the brand name.

SAFETY
STAYING SAFE

Morocco is a relatively safe country in which to travel, and the majority of Moroccans are hospitable, friendly, and law-abiding. That said, there are some issues that travelers should be aware of.

In April 2007, two suicide bombings took place outside the U.S. Consulate and the private American Language Center, respectively. There is some conjecture as to whether these were the work of an organized terror group with international links. In 2003, a series of coordinated suicide bombings also occurred in Casablanca, targeting buildings with either Jewish or Western connections. Both of these incidents provoked outrage and disbelief amongst ordinary Moroccans. Although most sympathize with the plight of their Arab neighbors in Palestine and Iraq, there is an accepted distinction between Western travelers and their governments' policies. For more, see "Terrorism in Morocco" in appendix A. Other

than not coming to Morocco at all— which would be an unnecessary overreaction—travelers are best advised to keep up to date with current events during their travels. Before you depart, check for travel advisories for your home country.

Violent crime is generally minimal in Morocco, although there have been incidents of tourists being robbed at knifepoint in various cities and at nighttime on some tourist beaches. Most crimes that occur are acts of sexual harassment (see "Women Travelers" on p. 43) and non-confrontational theft. Pickpocketing, purse snatching, and theft from vehicles are the most common. These are more likely to occur in the country's cities and large towns, crowded medinas, bus and train stations, and beaches, but it pays to be vigilant everywhere. Be particularly alert when withdrawing money from ATMs, and be aware of some of the common tactics used by petty criminals, such as distracting you with questions and small talk while an accomplice is deftly emptying your pockets or backpack. If your hotel offers a safe-keeping area, use it. Otherwise, take away the temptation that might present itself by locking valuables in your bag or suitcase.

Westerners driving rental cars generally stick out and are easily spotted by thieves, so it goes without saying that you shouldn't leave anything of value in an unattended car.

Traveling by train or long-distance bus is generally considered safe, though it pays to keep one eye on your luggage at each stop. Women travelers should look for seats close to those occupied by Moroccan women. The country's taxis— both *petit* and *grand*—are considered generally crime free, but may be poorly maintained and driven recklessly (a request of *"beshwiya"* ["slowly"] may or may not be heeded). Traveling on a crowded city bus can be unsafe.

Tips Guide or No Guide?

Any conversation amongst travelers in Morocco inevitably leads to relating personal experiences about the country's guides. Some people are overflowing in praise, while others are decidedly not. The first question I'm often asked is, "Do I need a guide?" The answer largely depends on what you want to see and how much time you have to see it. If you're an independent traveler with plenty of days to spare and a decent map in your hands, then even the seemingly unnavigable medinas of Fes and Marrakech can be explored without a guide, taking into account the numerous wrong turns and dead ends that you will no doubt experience. Unfortunately, each time you stop to consult a map or your guidebook, you'll likely be interrupted by a steady stream of hustlers and faux guides ever eager to assist you (see "Hustlers & Faux Guides," below).

If you're on more of a time constraint, then hiring a guide for at least half a day is recommended, especially for Fes and Marrakech. At the least, this allows you to get oriented before setting out on your own exploration. Personally, I don't think a guide is necessary for any of Morocco's other medinas or cities. Keep in mind that hustlers and faux guides tend to leave you alone when you are in the company of an official guide.

If you do hire a guide, I strongly recommend hiring an official guide. Official guides have been properly trained, vetted by the Moroccan National Tourism Board (ONMT), and (in the case of English-speaking guides) are understood easily. All of these benefits are not guaranteed in the case of a faux guide. Official guides will also be more relaxed and will walk alongside you while dispensing their knowledge. Faux guides, fearful of incurring the wrath of the Brigade Touristique (see below), usually walk two or three steps in front of their clients so as to not appear as if they are guiding. It's true that many faux guides are simply looking for work in a country with

HUSTLERS & FAUX GUIDES

Morocco's infamous hustlers and unofficial guides come in many different guises, from baby-face students to well-dressed gentlemen. Hustlers or touts tend to pounce on travelers who are looking lost or newly arrived, and will proceed to tell all sorts of horror stories such as the buses aren't operating, the hotel is closed, your desired destination isn't safe, or that you are walking in the wrong direction. These men are tricksters, conmen, thieves, even drug dealers. Their sole mission is to glean you of your money, and they are a very unfortunate part of many travelers' tales. Leading you to particular hotels, shops, and sometimes even restaurants usually means some commission coming their way. Unofficial guides—called faux guides—are generally less intimidating, if not slightly more annoying. For most, guiding is the only profession they know, and the only reason they aren't officially qualified is for socioeconomic reasons. Some can be very entertaining and knowledgeable, but most are very persistent to get any business from you, sometimes resorting to a hustler's tactics. Although a stronger police presence in recent years (thanks largely to the establishment of the Brigade Touristique) has removed a lot of hustlers and faux guides high unemployment and low social welfare and are unfairly treated. However, the Moroccan tourism authorities have recently recruited and licensed more guides, and I feel it is only fair to employ the services of those who have made the effort to become official. Official guides can be hired from tourist offices and most good hotels, and are mentioned throughout this guide. They can identify themselves by a brass badge or laminated card. Decide beforehand what you want to see and do, and then discuss this with your guide before agreeing on an itinerary and cost.

It's true that guides—official or otherwise—receive up to 40% commission from shopkeepers in return for bringing them clients. This commission is invariably added on to the cost of your purchase. If you don't want to visit any shops, then be clear and firm about this before setting out with your guide. If you do want to visit some shops, however, perhaps concentrate less on how much commission your guide will receive and more on what a great opportunity it is to find out more about the item.

The current rate for an official guide is 180dh ($23/£12) for half a day and 350dh ($44/£22) for a full day. This is not a per-person cost, though if you are a large group then it's expected you will add on a bit more, say 100dh ($13/£6.25). If you are being guided for a whole day, then you are expected to pay for the guide's lunch. If you are eating at one of the guide's preferred restaurants, however, lunch will most probably be given to the guide for free. For a guided tour devoid of any shops—and hence the chance for the guide to earn any extra money—I advise offering to pay more for his services before you depart. This will hopefully negate any sly attempts to direct you into a shop while on tour. Should you be pleased with the service provided by your guide, feel free to tip as a form of encouragement for the guide to continue with their high standards and low hassle.

from the streets, it can appear at times that they have found other ways and means to continue their profession. Travelers that I've spoken to recently related incidences where they encountered hustlers and faux guides on the trains, especially those traveling to Fes and Marrakech, and on the ferries coming from mainland Spain. Bus and train stations, largely unpatrolled by the Brigade Touristique, continue to be a hangout for many.

Getting rid of hustlers and faux guides can become a difficult and frustrating task. Some confrontations can become ugly, with the hustler becoming verbally abusive and accusing the traveler of racism toward Muslims. The best approach is to keep your sense of humor and initially ignore the unwanted attention entirely, followed by continuous, polite, and direct rebukes if necessary.

DRUGS Morocco has strict penalties for those caught purchasing, using, or dealing drugs. This includes *kif,* as the local marijuana is called. However, *kif* is smoked by many Moroccan men, especially in the northwest part of the country. Historically, the Moroccan police took a fairly lenient attitude toward its consumption, but in recent years there have been sporadic but concerted efforts to curb its use, including the arrest of foreigners caught indulging. Spanish border police are also known to prosecute travelers (suspected as traffickers) caught in possession of *kif* as they enter the country from Morocco. See the box "The Rif & Her *Kif*" on p. 286 in chapter 9.

POLICE   The Moroccan police force is still styled on the French system, comprising the Sureté National, who wear navy blue uniforms and are responsible for enforcing the law in urban areas, and the Gendarmerie, who wear gray uniforms and are to be found in the rural areas and at major road junctions and town entrances. In some of the major cities, such as Fes, Marrakech, and Tangier, there is a Brigade Touristique, which has been specifically formed to curtail the actions of touts and faux guides. Generally, law enforcement officers in Morocco are polite to travelers, although they often ask to see your identification, preferably a passport, and, if driving, obviously a driver's license. Their overall helpfulness, however, can be limited, especially concerning action over theft. Usually, they are quite happy to complete a police report for travel insurance purposes, but actual efforts to retrieve the stolen goods may be laborious at best.

7 Specialized Travel Resources

TRAVELERS WITH DISABILITIES

Unfortunately, Morocco offers very little assistance to people with disabilities, and traveling in the country requires a certain amount of adventurous spirit, good humor, and determination. There are no disabled services or adapted transport, and there's a distinct lack of adapted infrastructure, such as wheelchair-friendly ramps, signs in Braille, or beeping and flashing pedestrian crossings. Moroccans are usually very supportive of those with disabilities and generally willing to assist without looking for something in return.

The most difficulty faced by wheelchair-bound travelers will be daily challenges such as crowded pavements, busy streets, drivers with no regard for pedestrians, and rutted medina alleys. If choosing between the major cultural cities of Fes and Marrakech as your prime destination, I recommend the relatively flat Marrakech as opposed to Fes, with its hillside medina, steep lanes, and multitude of steps. Traveling by private car or as part of an organized tour will be the best way to get around Morocco. Bus and train travel will be difficult due to the steps that will have to be negotiated and the lack of wheelchair-friendly areas once you're on. If you do travel by public transport, I recommend *grands* taxis.

All disabled travelers should be aware that very few hotels offer adapted accommodations. Not all hotels have elevators, but there are usually ground-floor rooms. *Maisons d'hôte* by their very nature are usually old houses with steep, narrow staircases and are located in difficult corners of the medina. Some will be accessible for wheelchairs and may have adequate-size ground-floor rooms, but on the whole the more feasible accommodations options will be found in the new hotels, especially in Agadir and Marrakech.

Organizations that offer a vast range of resources and assistance to disabled travelers include **MossRehab** (© 800/CALL-MOSS; www.mossresourcenet.org); the **American Foundation for the Blind** (AFB; © 800/232-5463; www.afb.org); and **SATH (Society for Accessible Travel & Hospitality;** © 212/447-7284; www.sath.org). **AirAmbulanceCard.com** is now partnered with SATH and allows you to preselect top-notch hospitals in case of an emergency.

Access-Able Travel Source (℃ 303/232-2979; www.access-able.com) offers a comprehensive database of travel agents from around the world with experience in accessible travel; destination-specific access information; and links to such resources as service animals, equipment rentals, and access guides.

Many travel agencies offer customized tours and itineraries for travelers with disabilities. Among them are **Flying Wheels Travel** (℃ 507/451-5005; www.flying wheelstravel.com) and **Accessible Journeys** (℃ 800/846-4537 or 610/521-0339; www.disabilitytravel.com).

Flying with Disability (www.flying-with-disability.org) is a comprehensive information source on airplane travel. **Avis Rent a Car** (℃ 888/879-4273) has an "Avis Access" program that offers services for customers with special travel needs. These include specially outfitted vehicles with swivel seats, spinner knobs, and hand controls; mobility scooter rentals; and accessible bus service. Be sure to reserve well in advance.

Also check out the quarterly magazine *Emerging Horizons* (www.emerging horizons.com), available by subscription ($16.95 year U.S.; $21.95 outside U.S).

The "Accessible Travel" link at **Mobility-Advisor.com** (www.mobility-advisor.com) offers a variety of travel resources to disabled persons.

British travelers should contact **Holiday Care** (℃ 0845-124-9971 in U.K. only; www.holidaycare.org.uk) to access a wide range of travel information and resources for disabled and elderly people.

GAY & LESBIAN TRAVELERS

Homosexuality is considered relatively common, though rarely acknowledged, amongst Moroccan men. Even though illegal and punishable with imprisonment, the lack of everyday integration between the sexes has lent itself to a general and subtle tolerance toward male effeminate behavior. Platonic affection between Moroccan males—such as holding hands, which is a sign of friendship and respect—is freely shown, and some of the Berber tribes (the Atlas Chleuh, for example) are known as particularly tolerant toward homosexual behavior. Lesbianism is relatively uncommon and definitely not acknowledged, as it portrays a weakness on both the woman—she's expected to get married and bear children—and her family.

For both gays and lesbians, discretion is advised. Avoid public displays of affection, as this is something that is even frowned upon when shown by a heterosexual couple. Tangier—the world's first gay resort—is still considered somewhat gay friendly. Marrakech certainly has a mini gay scene, thanks largely to the number of gay French couples now residing there.

The International Gay and Lesbian Travel Association (**IGLTA;** ℃ 800/448-8550 or 954/776-2626; www.iglta.org) is the trade association for the gay and lesbian travel industry, and offers an online directory of gay- and lesbian-friendly travel businesses and tour operators. **Gay 1st Travel** (℃ 407/850-9770; www.gay1sttravel.com) is a U.S.-based tour operator catering to both business and leisure clients interested in traveling to destinations that cater to the gay lifestyle. They offer an 11-day "Discover Morocco" tour, traveling from Casablanca to Marrakech via the Imperial cities, central Morocco, and Essaouira.

Beyond the Mask (www.mask.org.za) has gay-based information and news articles on each African country, including Morocco. **Gay Morocco** (http://gay morocco.tripod.com) offers chat rooms for homosexuals traveling to or living in Morocco.

Gay.com Travel (℃ 800/929-2268 or 415/644-8044; www.gay.com/travel or www.outandabout.com) is an excellent online successor to the popular *Out &*

About print magazine. It provides regularly updated information about gay-owned, gay-oriented, and gay-friendly lodging, dining, sightseeing, nightlife, and shopping establishments in every important destination worldwide. British travelers should click on the "Travel" link at www.uk.gay.com for advice and gay-friendly trip ideas.

The Canadian website **GayTraveler** (www.gaytraveler.ca) offers ideas and advice for gay travel all over the world.

The following travel guides are available at many bookstores, or you can order them from any online bookseller: *Spartacus International Gay Guide* (Bruno Gmünder Verlag; www.spartacusworld.com/gayguide); *Odysseus: The International Gay Travel Planner* (www.odyusa.com); and the *Damron* guides (www.damron.com), with separate annual books for gay men and lesbians.

SENIOR TRAVEL

Moroccans as a whole greatly respect the contributions and wisdom of society's elders, but unfortunately that consideration doesn't necessarily translate into automatic deferential treatment of senior tourists. While senior travelers on an organized tour will be treated with respect and patience, traveling by public transport produces very little of either when it comes to finding a seat. There are no special discounts offered to senior travelers in Morocco, apart from fare reductions offered by some ferry companies plying the route to/from Spain.

Seniors should also pay particular attention to the daytime temperatures during summertime (see "When to Go," earlier in this chapter).

Members of **AARP**, 601 E St. NW, Washington, DC 20049 (© **888/687-2277**; www.aarp.org), get discounts on hotels, airfares, and car rentals. AARP offers members a wide range of benefits, including *AARP: The Magazine* and a monthly newsletter. Anyone over 50 can join.

Many reliable agencies and organizations target the 50-plus market. **Elderhostel** (© **800/454-5768**; www.elderhostel.org) arranges worldwide study programs for those aged 55 and over, including an escorted tour to Morocco. **ElderTreks** (© **800/741-7956** or 416/558-5000 outside North America; www.eldertreks.com) offers small-group tours to off-the-beaten-path or adventure-travel locations, including Morocco, restricted to travelers 50 and older.

Recommended publications offering travel resources and discounts for seniors include the quarterly magazine *Travel 50 & Beyond* (www.travel50andbeyond.com) and the best-selling paperback *Unbelievably Good Deals and Great Adventures That You Absolutely Can't Get Unless You're Over 50 2005–2006* (McGraw-Hill), by Joann Rattner Heilman.

FAMILY TRAVEL

Moroccans are extremely family oriented, and children are an important and very visible part of Moroccan society. Traveling with your small children will undoubtedly attract more attention (in a good way) and may very well turn your holiday into something memorable, as shopkeepers wave you into their stores, waiters offer you free cups of tea, and local guides invite you home to meet their family. As with most Arabic cultures, children generally stay up later then those in the West, playing unsupervised and being sent on errands.

On a practical level, there are a few challenges that will be faced in Morocco when traveling with babies or small children. Baby-changing facilities are nonexistent, and while disposable diapers are available in the supermarket chains and some pharmacies, you'll be lucky to find them outside of the cities and larger towns. Other specific items such as special foods and sunscreen are also best brought from home. Heating up formula should never be a problem, as cafes—and boiling water—are found everywhere, as is long-life milk. My suggestion is to look for the national supermarket chains **Acima** and **Marjane**. These French-owned supermarkets are like any in the Western world and will be good places to stock up on supplies for your children. I've mentioned them in the relevant "Shopping" sections throughout the book.

Most hotels allow children under 12 to sleep in their parent's room. Children under 2 (and sometimes up to 6) are usually free. Children under 12 are usually charged half price. However, you should definitely inquire as to the size of the room before handing over any money. Quite often the hotel will be leaving you to your own devices when it comes to sleeping configurations; what's in the room is all that you'll get. Sometimes it's worth considering the expense of a larger suite or asking for two cheaper interconnecting rooms. Some *maisons d'hôte* don't accept children, as the thin, echoing walls and thin, narrow staircases aren't exactly child friendly. Many mid- to top-range hotels and *maisons d'hôte* will gladly organize a babysitter for you, although specific English-speaking babysitters may need to be organized well in advance.

Traveling by public transport with children can be both challenging and rewarding. On buses and in *grands* taxis, children small enough to share your seat or sit on your lap can usually travel for free. If not, you will probably be charged full fare. Train travel is a great way to get around and obviously allows little ones to move around a lot more. Children under 4 travel free, while those under 12 are charged half fare. While most international car-rental firms proclaim to offer baby or child seats, you'll be best to make sure of this in advance.

Take note of my words regarding the summertime heat, remembering that children are more susceptible to dehydration and heat stroke, as well as the most common ailment befalling most tourists in Morocco—traveler's diarrhea.

U.K. travel company **Panorama** (*©* **0871/664-7984;** www.panorama holidays.co.uk) has packages for families to Agadir, Essaouira, Marrakech, and Ouarzazate. **Families Worldwide** (*©* **0845/051-4567;** www.familiesworldwide.co.uk) is also based in the U.K. and offers specialist family tours to Morocco with itineraries that include hiking and camel trekking, as well as a general sightseeing tour.

To locate accommodations, restaurants, and attractions that are particularly kid friendly, refer to the "Kids" icon and the "Especially for Kids" sections throughout this guide.

Tip: If your child is big enough to play football (soccer in the U.S.), bring along a ball. It's the national game of Morocco and is played on any bare patch of ground (including medina alleyways) at any time of the day and half the night. Your child will be "king for a day" once the local kids see the ball.

Recommended family travel websites include **Family Travel Forum** (www.familytravelforum.com), a comprehensive site that offers customized trip planning; **Family Travel Network** (www.familytravelnetwork.com), an online magazine providing travel tips; and **TravelWithYourKids.com** (www.travelwithyourkids.com), a comprehensive site written by parents for parents offering sound advice for long-distance and international travel with children.

WOMEN TRAVELERS

Encountering unwanted attention from Moroccan men is unfortunately a possibility for female travelers. The relative lack of social interaction between the sexes in Morocco results in men having little exposure to women other than their immediate family. They often see Western women as not being bound by Morocco's social restrictions, and perhaps have a not-so-respectful assumption of them via easily accessible Internet pornography. This assumption of availability emboldens the Moroccan male to make advances on female travelers that they would never attempt with Moroccan women. This generally takes the form of catcalls and straight-up come-ons. Blonde women may be singled out, and women traveling alone generally receive more attention than most. Women on the receiving end of nonphysical sexual harassment should do what Moroccan women do: Ignore it. Showing confidence and self assurance also seems to deter a lot of would-be Romeos. I've often explained the situation to female travelers by comparing the male harasser to your 13-year-old brother—full of bravado and not much else, especially when isolated from his friends. What you are basically trying to project is that you wish to be treated with the same respect and standards as Moroccan women, who regularly put up with catcalls but will never stand for anything more, especially unwanted physical attention such as groping. Should this happen, make a scene, and Moroccans around you will come to your assistance and often strongly admonish your attacker. If you're in one of the major medinas, ask for the Brigade Touristique.

Dressing modestly—a long skirt and loose, long-sleeve shirt—can help. Having said that, I've seen Western women wearing *jellabahs* (the traditional robe worn by local women) on the receiving end of lewd comments. Traveling with a male can help you avoid verbal harassment; however, be prepared to call him your "husband" on occasions.

All of this sounds terribly negative, but most women never receive any harassment and are nothing but glowing in their praise for the respect shown to them. Try not to be paranoid or aggressive toward all Moroccan men. It's extremely rare for harassment to go any further than the odd catcall or lewd remark. If you do need to escape at any time, head for the nearest *salon de thé* (upmarket teahouse) or cafe-restaurant (but not the local all-male cafe) to gather yourself.

Check out the award-winning website **Journeywoman** (www.journeywoman.com), a "real-life" women's travel-information network where you can sign up for a free e-mail newsletter and get advice on everything from etiquette to safety. The travel guide *Safety and Security for Women Who Travel* by Sheila Swan and Peter Laufer (Travelers' Tales Guides), offering common-sense tips on safe travel, was updated in 2004.

JEWISH TRAVELERS

Jews first set foot in Morocco in pre-Christian times, accompanying the Phoenicians on their trade excursions along the country's coastline. Jews also joined waves of Muslims escaping persecution during the Christian conquests of southern Spain. Since the Arab Islamic invasions from the 8th century onward, the two faiths have coexisted mostly in peace, although at times the Jews were used as scapegoats or favored purely for their business acumen. The silversmiths of today are also a product of the craft practiced by many Moroccan Jews up until as late as the 20th century. Prior to World War II, the Jewish population was around 225,000, and although no Jews were sent to concentration camps, they did suffer acts of humiliation under the French Vichy government. After the war, a steady stream of immigration to Israel turned into a flood after independence in 1956, and today's population of Moroccan Jews is considered to number around 10,000 at the most.

Since independence, the ruling Alaouite dynasty has continued a tradition of tolerance and support toward the country's Jewish minority. Hassan II was particularly active in the 1980s in trying to bring peace to the Israeli/Palestine conflict. King Mohammed VI has inherited his father's tolerance, with the appointment of prominent Jewish citizen André Azoulay as one of his royal advisors. In 2000, after two youths vandalized a Tangier synagogue, Mohammed VI appeared on television, decrying the act of interfaith disrespect; the two youths were subsequently sentenced to a year in prison. In 2003, a coordinated series of suicide bombs targeted both Western and Jewish businesses in Casablanca. It's debatable whether the attacks were an act of anti-Semitism or were more of an assault on the country's social and political order, the king himself, and the West in general.

In times past, Jews traditionally lived in a part of the medina called the Mellah (see "Salt & the Jews" on p. 232). Most have now moved out into the ville nouvelle, although some old synagogues still remain. The majority live in Casablanca, where a visit to the only Jewish museum in the Arabic world (p. 333) is well worth the time. Morocco's Jews are an aging population, as most Jewish youths travel to Israel, the U.S., and France to study.

Jewish travelers in Morocco needn't take any special precautions other than those concerning all travelers. The **Conseil des Communautes Israelites du Maroc** (**CCIM;** ℂ **022/222861;** comjuive@ mail.cbi.net.ma) is based in Casablanca and represents the Jewish community in most matters within Morocco. **Morocco Custom Travel** ⍟⍟⍟ (ℂ **866/966-7622** toll-free or 209/466-3105; www.morocco customtravel.com) is a specialist in tailor-made itineraries and tours to Morocco, with suggested itineraries that include "Spiritual Morocco," which focuses specifically on the country's long Jewish history.

STUDENT TRAVEL

Youth or student cards can sometimes get you a discount on entry to various sights, including museums, in Morocco. They can be used when booking domestic flights with the national air carrier, Royal Air Maroc, which offers up to 60% discounts. Discounted travel on the country's trains is also available, but this involves paying and applying for a separate card at the train station (see "By Train" in "Getting Around Morocco," later in this chapter).

The **International Student Travel Confederation** (**ISTC;** www.istc.org) was formed in 1949 to make global travel more affordable for students. Check out its website for comprehensive travel services information and details on how to get an **International Student Identity Card (ISIC),** which qualifies students for substantial savings on rail passes, plane tickets, entrance fees, and more. It also provides students with basic health and life insurance and a 24-hour helpline. The card is valid for a maximum of 18 months. You can apply for the card online or in person at **STA Travel** (ℂ **800/781-4040** in North America; www.statravel.com), the biggest student travel agency in the world; check out the website to locate STA Travel offices worldwide. If you're no longer a student but are still under 26, you can get an **International Youth Travel Card (IYTC)** from STA, which entitles you to some discounts. **Travel CUTS** (ℂ **800/ 592-2887;** www.travelcuts.com) offers similar services for both Canadians and U.S. residents. Irish students may prefer to turn to **USIT** (ℂ **01/602-1904;** www. usit.ie), an Ireland-based specialist in student, youth, and independent travel.

SINGLE TRAVELERS

Morocco is a popular destination for solo travelers, especially backpackers. Moroccans are very friendly, and traveling alone amongst them on public transport has brought about many memorable conversations and experiences. If at any time you would prefer some company or a traveling companion, there are always plenty of fellow travelers around, especially in Essaouira, Fes, and Marrakech. Single female travelers may encounter some harassment, however. See "Women Travelers," above.

On package vacations, single travelers are often hit with a "single supplement" to the base price. To avoid it, you can agree to room with other single travelers or find a compatible roommate before you go from one of the many roommate-locator agencies.

TravelChums (© 212/787-2621; www.travelchums.com) is an Internet-only travel-companion matching service with elements of an online personals-type site, hosted by the respected New York–based Shaw Guides travel service.

Many reputable tour companies offer singles-only trips. **Backroads** (© 800/462-2848; www.backroads.com) offers "Singles + Solos" active-travel trips to destinations worldwide.

For more information, check out Eleanor Berman's classic *Traveling Solo: Advice and Ideas for More Than 250 Great Vacations* (Globe Pequot), updated in 2005.

8 Sustainable Tourism/Eco-Tourism

Each time you take a flight or drive a car, carbon dioxide is released into the atmosphere. You can help neutralize this danger to our planet through "carbon offsetting"—paying someone to reduce your carbon dioxide emissions by the same amount you've added. Carbon offsets can be purchased in the U.S. from companies such as **Carbonfund.org** (www.carbonfund.org) and **TerraPass** (www.terrapass.org), and from **Climate Care** (www.climatecare.org) in the U.K.

Although one could argue that any vacation that includes an airplane flight can't be truly "green," you can go on holiday and still contribute positively to the environment. You can offset carbon emissions from your flight in other ways. Choose forward-looking companies that embrace responsible development practices, helping preserve destinations for the future by working alongside local people. An increasing number of sustainable tourism initiatives can help you plan a family trip and leave as small a "footprint" as possible on the places you visit.

Responsible Travel (www.responsibletravel.com) contains a great source of sustainable travel ideas run by a spokesperson for responsible tourism in the travel industry. **Sustainable Travel International** (www.sustainabletravelinternational.org) promotes responsible tourism practices and issues an annual *Green Gear & Gift Guide.*

You can find eco-friendly travel tips, statistics, and touring companies and associations—listed by destination under "Travel Choice"—at the TIES website, www.ecotourism.org. Also check out **Conservation International** (www.conservation.org)—which, with *National Geographic Traveler,* annually presents **World Legacy Awards** (www.wlaward.org) to those travel tour operators, businesses, organizations, and places that have made a significant contribution to sustainable tourism. **Ecotravel.com** is part online magazine and part eco-directory that lets you search for tour companies in several categories (water-based, land-based, spiritually oriented, and so on).

In the U.K., **Tourism Concern** (www.tourismconcern.org.uk) works to reduce social and environmental problems connected to tourism and find ways of improving tourism so that local benefits are increased.

The **Association of British Travel Agents** (ABTA; www.abta.com) acts as a

Frommers.com: The Complete Travel Resource

It should go without saying, but we highly recommend **Frommers.com,** voted Best Travel Site by *PC Magazine*. We think you'll find our expert advice and tips; independent reviews of hotels, restaurants, attractions, and preferred shopping and nightlife venues; vacation giveaways; and an online booking tool indispensable before, during, and after your travels. We publish the complete contents of more than 128 travel guides in our **"Destinations"** section covering nearly 3,600 places worldwide to help you plan your trip. Each weekday, we publish original articles reporting on **"Deals and News"** via our free **Frommers.com Newsletter** to help you save time and money and travel smarter. We're betting you'll find our new **Events** listings (http://events.frommers.com) an invaluable resource; it's an up-to-the-minute roster of what's happening in cities everywhere—including concerts, festivals, lectures, and more. We've also added weekly **podcasts, interactive maps,** and hundreds of new images across the site. Check out our **"Travel Talk"** area featuring **message boards** where you can join in conversations with thousands of fellow Frommer's travelers and post your trip report once you return.

focal point for the U.K. travel industry and is one of the leading groups spearheading responsible tourism.

The **Association of Independent Tour Operators** (**AITO;** www.aito.co.uk) is a group of interesting specialist operators leading the field in making holidays sustainable.

Note: See chapter 4 for detailed information about eco-friendly tour guides and itineraries throughout the country.

9 Staying Connected

TELEPHONES

Coin-operated phones can be found in private *téléboutiques* within every village, town, and city. You can make local and international calls from here, though you will need a stack of coins—thankfully there is always an attendant on hand to dispense change. Card-operated public phones are scattered everywhere, including outside post offices. Cards can be bought from the post office, newspaper stalls, and *tabacs* (news agency–cum–tobacconist). Per-minute costs to landline numbers are currently 1dh (13¢/5p) for local calls, 1.50dh (20¢/10p) for national calls, 2.60dh to 3.75dh (35¢–45¢/15p–25p) for calls to Europe, and up to 7dh (90¢/45p) to elsewhere.

To call Morocco from another country:

1. Dial the international access code: 011 from the U.S.; 00 from the U.K., Ireland, or New Zealand; or 0011 from Australia
2. Dial the country code 212
3. Dial the Moroccan number minus the first 0.

To make domestic calls within Morocco: For all calls within Morocco, drop the country code; the full area code (including the first 0) must be dialed along with the number. All numbers in Morocco begin with a three-digit area code. Codes beginning with 02 or 03 are landline numbers; all other numbers are mobile numbers.

To make international calls from Morocco: To make international calls from Morocco, first dial 00 and then the country code (U.S. or Canada 1, U.K. 44, Ireland 353, Australia 61, New Zealand 64). Next, dial the area code (drop the first 0 if there is one) and number. For example, if you wanted to call the British Embassy in Washington, D.C., you would dial 00-1-202-588-7800.

For directory assistance & operator-assisted calls: Dial 160 for a number within Morocco, and dial 126 for numbers to all other countries.

Toll-free numbers: There are no toll-free numbers within Morocco, and calling a toll-free number in the U.S., U.K., or anywhere else from Morocco is not toll-free. In fact, it costs the same as an overseas call.

CELLPHONES

The three letters that define much of the world's wireless capabilities are **GSM** (Global System for Mobile Communications), a big, seamless network that makes for easy cross-border cellphone use throughout Europe and dozens of other countries worldwide. In the U.S., T-Mobile, AT&T Wireless, and Cingular use this quasi-universal system; in Canada, Microcell and some Rogers customers are GSM, and all Europeans and most Australians use GSM. GSM phones function with a removable plastic SIM card, encoded with your phone number and account information. If your cellphone is on a GSM system and you have a world-capable multiband phone such as many Sony Ericsson, Motorola, or Samsung models, you can make and receive calls across civilized areas around much of the globe. Just call your wireless operator and ask for "international roaming" to be activated on your account. Unfortunately, per-minute charges can be high—usually $1 to

$1.50 in western Europe and up to $5 in places such as Russia and Indonesia. GSM coverage in Morocco is generally excellent, bar the more inaccessible regions in the mountains and within the country's desert ergs.

For many, **renting** a phone is a good idea. While you can rent a phone from any number of overseas sites, including kiosks at airports and at car-rental agencies, I suggest renting the phone before you leave home. North Americans can rent one from **InTouch USA** (✆ 800/872-7626; www.intouchglobal.com) or **RoadPost** (✆ 888/290-1606 or 905/272-5665; www.roadpost.com). InTouch will also, for free, advise you on whether your existing phone will work overseas; simply call ✆ 703/222-7161 between 9am and 4pm EST, or go to **http://intouchglobal.com/travel.htm**.

There are no phone rental companies within Morocco. However, **buying a phone**—or using your own if it is compatible—is often economically attractive, as Morocco has a cheap prepaid phone system. You can buy phones in Morocco for as little as $100 (£50). The major local GSM provider is Méditel. Shops selling Méditel SIM cards and prepaid top-ups are located in all urban centers, large or small. A SIM card currently costs 200dh ($25/£13), and top-ups can be purchased from any Méditel shop or from *tabacs* and general stores countrywide. The SIM card is valid for 6 months upon the first call. Each top-up extends the SIM for another 6 months, but the SIM must be used within a 6-month period or else it expires and cannot be used again. Domestic calls cost 1dh (13¢/6p) per minute to other Méditel numbers and 3.50dh (44¢/22p) per minute to other GSM numbers and local landlines. International calls cost up to 20dh ($2.50/£1.25) per minute, depending on the destination and the time of day. All incoming calls are free.

VOICE OVER INTERNET PROTOCOL (VOIP)

If you have Web access while traveling, you might consider a broadband-based telephone service (in technical terms, **Voice over Internet Protocol,** or **VoIP**) such as Skype (www.skype.com) or Vonage (www.vonage.com), which allows you to make free international calls if you use their services from your laptop or in a cybercafe. The people you're calling must also use the service for it to work; check the sites for details. Most cybercafes (see below) throughout the country will be using these programs already, complete with headset, microphone, and Web cam.

INTERNET/E-MAIL

Morocco has truly joined the Internet era. While there is a growing number of home users, socioeconomic reasons (most people can't afford a home computer) dictate that the majority of Moroccan users frequent Internet cafes—called "cyber"—found in virtually every city, town, and even village that has electricity and telephones. The users are generally teenage Moroccans, who sit for hours during the evening participating in international chat rooms. Most cybercafes don't censor what their users are watching—there's no government censorship—and Western travelers may be shocked to find themselves sitting next to a young Moroccan lad who is surfing some pretty hard-core porn sites. Moroccans have also fully taken to speaking to loved ones via VoIP calls (see above) from their local cybercafe.

Tip: You'll find most keyboards in Morocco are designed with Arabic-language users in mind, so some letters will be in a different place from what you're used to. To bring up the @ symbol, simultaneously press Alt Gr and either the number 0 or à keys.

Online Traveler's Toolbox

Veteran travelers usually carry some essential items to make their trips easier. Following is a selection of handy online tools to bookmark and use.

- **Airplane Food** (www.airlinemeals.net)
- **Airplane Seating** (www.seatguru.com and www.airlinequality.com)
- **Foreign Languages for Travelers** (www.travlang.com)
- **Moroccan Government Website** (www.maroc.ma/PortailInst/An/home)
- **English-Language Moroccan Newspaper** (www.marocannonces.com/morocco_news.php)
- **Lifestyle in Morocco** (http://theviewfrommorocco.blogspot.com) includes reviews on restaurants, bars, nightlife, and day tours.
- **Time and Date** (www.timeanddate.com)
- **Travel Warnings** (http://travel.state.gov, www.fco.gov.uk/travel, www.voyage.gc.ca, or www.dfat.gov.au/consular/advice)
- **Oanda, the Currency Site** (www.oanda.com)
- **U.S.-Moroccan sites** (www.washingtonmoroccanclub.org and www.wafin.com)
- **Visa ATM Locator** (www.visa.com), **MasterCard ATM Locator** (www.mastercard.com)
- **Weather** (www.intellicast.com and www.weather.com)

WITHOUT YOUR OWN COMPUTER

In Morocco, by far the easiest way to check your e-mail and surf the Web is in one of the country's Internet cafes. Connection speed varies but is usually pretty fast. The cost for 30 minutes is around 5dh (65¢/30p). Cybercafes usually open between 9 and 10am, not closing until 10 to 11pm most days, although some will close for a few hours at midday Friday. To find cybercafes in your destination, check **www.cybercaptive.com** and **www.cyber cafe.com**. I've also included specific recommendations in the "Fast Facts" section of each destination.

WITH YOUR OWN COMPUTER

Within Morocco there is a growing number of hotels, *maisons d'hôte,* and cafes that offer free high-speed Wi-Fi access or charge a small fee for usage. Most laptops sold today have built-in wireless capability. To find public Wi-Fi hotspots at your destination, go to **www.jiwire.com**; its Hotspot Finder holds the world's largest directory of public wireless hotspots.

For dial-up access, most business-class hotels throughout the world offer dataports for laptop modems.

Wherever you go, bring a **connection kit** of the right power and phone adapters, a spare phone cord, and a spare Ethernet network cable—or find out whether your hotel supplies them to guests. See "Electricity" in the "Fast Facts" section, later in this chapter.

---

10 Packages for the Independent Traveler

Package tours are simply a way to buy the airfare, accommodations, and other elements of your trip (such as car rentals, airport transfers, and sometimes even activities) at the same time and often at discounted prices.

One good source of package deals is the airlines themselves. Most major airlines offer air/land packages, including **American Airlines Vacations** (© 800/321-2121; www.aavacations.com), **Delta Vacations** (© 800/654-6559; www.deltavacations. com), **Continental Airlines Vacations** (© 800/301-3800; www.covacations. com), and **United Vacations** (© 888/ 854-3899; www.unitedvacations.com).

Tips Ask Before You Go

Before you invest in a package deal or an escorted tour:

- Always ask about the **cancellation policy.** Can you get your money back? Is there a deposit required?
- Ask about the **accommodations choices and prices** for each. Then look up the hotels' reviews in a Frommer's guide and check their rates online for your specific dates of travel. Also find out what types of rooms are offered.
- Request a complete **schedule** (escorted tours only).
- Ask about the **size** and demographics of the group (escorted tours only).
- Discuss what is included in the **price** (transportation, meals, tips, airport transfers, and such; escorted tours only).
- Finally, look for **hidden expenses.** Ask whether airport departure fees and taxes, for example, are included in the total cost—they rarely are.

Several big **online travel agencies**—Expedia, Travelocity, Orbitz, Site59, and Lastminute.com—also do a brisk business in packages.

U.K. travel company **Panorama** (© 0871/664-7984; www.panorama holidays.co.uk) has good airfares to Morocco from various U.K. destinations, as well as air/hotel packages to Agadir, Essaouira, Marrakech, and Ouarzazate. Another U.K. company, **Sovereign** (© 0871/200-6677; www.sovereign. com) has a good choice of air/land packages to Marrakech from select U.K. airports. **Sunway** (© 01/231-1888; www. sunway.ie) has a range of air/land packages throughout the year to Agadir with return flights from Dublin included.

Travel packages are also listed in the travel section of your local Sunday newspaper. Or check ads in national travel magazines such as *Arthur Frommer's Budget Travel Magazine, Travel + Leisure, National Geographic Traveler,* and *Condé Nast Traveler.*

11 Escorted General-Interest Tours

Escorted tours are structured group tours with a group leader. The price usually includes airfare, hotels, meals, tours, admission costs, and local transportation.

RECOMMENDED TOUR OPERATORS
U.S. & U.K. COMPANIES

- **Abercrombie & Kent** (© 800/323-7308; www.abercrombiekent.com) is one of the world's leading luxury tour operators, and has been organizing quality travel itineraries and group tours since 1962. Their Morocco tours include a 14-day "Morocco Revealed," which takes in the major sights from Casablanca to Marrakech and includes cocktails with the former U.S. ambassador to Morocco. There's also a 9-day private tour taking in Morocco's four imperial cities.
- **Adventures Abroad** (© 800/665-3998 in the U.S. and Canada, or 0114/247-3400 in the U.K.; www. adventures-abroad.com) prides itself on operating quality, small-group holidays worldwide in three categories: active, cultural, and family. They offer 8-day and 15-day tours of Morocco, as well a visit to the country within tours of Spain and Portugal, Tunisia, or Libya.

- **Audley Travel** (© 01993/838400; www.audleytravel.com) arranges personalized tours for the discerning traveler based on each client's particular interests. Their North Africa and Arabia department can tailor-make itineraries to specific regions of Morocco such as Fes and the north, Marrakech and the mountains, central Morocco, or a combination of all three.
- **Authentic Morocco** (© 0845/0944725; www.authentic-morocco. com) is Liz Williams' U.K.-based company specializing in personalized custom itineraries to Morocco with well-respected English-speaking guides. Liz specializes in working with Western travelers—especially females. There are numerous sample itineraries, including New Year's Eve in the desert and specialist photographic tours, but it's the custommade tours that make this company stand out.
- **The Best of Morocco** ⚲ (© 1249/467-165; www.morocco-travel.com) is a Moroccan specialist based in the U.K. with an office in Marrakech. They've been organizing tailor-made holidays to Morocco for more than 40 years, and now offer an extensive

selection of accommodations, itineraries (both general and specialist), and general information.

- **GAP Adventures** (© **800/708-7761** in the U.S., 0870/999-0144 in the U.K., or 1300/796618 in Australia; www.gapadventures.com) operates group tours for independent-minded travelers and currently offers three itineraries in Morocco: an 8-day "Morocco Sojourn" from Marrakech to Essaouira via the Western High Atlas; an 8-day "Morocco Hike & Bike" through parts of the Western High Atlas and central Morocco; and a 14-day "Highlights of Morocco" tour from Casablanca to Marrakech, visiting most of the country's major sights.

- **Gateway2Morocco** (© **800/997-6612;** www.gateway2morocco.com) is a young company offering personalized tours of Morocco. Based in the U.S. with Moroccan connections, their itineraries are many and varied, catering to general interest along with specialist tours such as arts and culture, golfing, Jewish heritage, outdoor adventures, and honeymooners.

- **Marrakech Voyage** (© **888/990-2999;** www.morocco-travel-agency. com) is a U.S.-Moroccan agency specializing in custom-made, fully escorted tours for individuals and groups. They have an extensive selection of suggested itineraries, including tours coinciding with some of the country's many festivals.

- **Martin Randall Travel** ☆☆ (© **020/8742-3355;** www.martinrandall. com) is considered the U.K.'s leading cultural travel specialist, with more than 180 art, music, archaeology, history, and architecture tours to Europe, the Middle East, and beyond. Groups are around 17 people and are accompanied by expert lecturers. Their itineraries change

each year; the 2007 Moroccan tour traced the Saharan gold trade that opened Morocco to the world.

- **Morocco Custom Travel** ☆☆☆ (© **866/966-7622** or 209/466-3105; www.moroccocustomtravel.com) is a professional and dependable firm run by Peggy Ward Engh, who divides her time between the U.S. and Marrakech. A wide range of services is provided, with custom-made tours for individuals, conventions, and incentives. Their suggested itineraries include "Spiritual Morocco," which looks at the country's long Jewish history, and "The Ancient Route of the Moors," which showcases the history and gold age of Andalusia.

- **Overseas Adventure Travel** (© **800/493-6824;** www.oattravel.com) is a specialist in natural history and "soft-adventure" tours, with optional add-on excursions. The group size is never more than 16, and tours are led by naturalists. Their 15-day "Morocco Sahara Odyssey" travels from New York to Casablanca through central Morocco, Meknes, Fes, and Marrakech, and includes 3 nights in private desert tented camps.

- **Trafalgar Tours** (© 020/7574-7444 in the U.K., or 866/544-4434 in the U.S.; www.trafalgartours.com) has been operating since 1947 and offers holiday packages worldwide, including quality escorted coach tours to Morocco. The coaches are luxury 49-seaters, with air-conditioning and an on-board washroom. Their 10-day "Best of Morocco" is a return tour from Casablanca and includes the imperial cities and some of central Morocco. Some of their tours of Spain and Portugal also travel across the Straits of Gibraltar to visit parts of Morocco.

- **Tribes Travel** (© **01728/685971;** www.tribes.co.uk) is a U.K.-based fair trade travel company operating tailor-made holidays to destinations in Africa, Asia, and South America. They offer itineraries throughout the majority of Morocco, ranging from 9- to 14-day tours, as well as shorter holidays in Essaouira and Marrakech.

MOROCCO-BASED COMPANIES

- **Blue Men of Morocco** (℃/fax **952/467562;** www.bluemenofmorocco.com) is owned and operated by American Elena Hall, who divides her time between her two bases in Spain and Merzouga, on the edge of the Erg Chebbi desert dunes. She offers a range of itineraries, including combinations of Morocco with southern Moorish Spain.

- **Compass Odyssey** (℃ **061/250746** or ℃/fax 021/439-2225; www.compassodyssey.net) is my own responsible-tourism company, specializing in small-group escorted tours of Morocco and South Africa. I lead two trips around Morocco every spring, with an emphasis on sightseeing and one-of-a-kind cultural experiences that benefit both locals and travelers.

- **Craft Treasures of Morocco** ★★★ (℃ **024/783543;** www.styles-morocco.com) is an escorted tour of Morocco's famous craft workshops, led by British-based Arabic-historian Jennifer Scarce and Essaouira-based craft specialist Alison MacDonald. The tour goes beyond the tourist shops, taking clients to the artisans themselves.

- **Fes Art et Culture Travel** (℃ **061/250249;** fact@menara.ma) utilizes the services of one of Morocco's best guides, Hassan el Janah, and operates tours of Fes and the rest of Morocco. While the company's emphasis is on the country's renowned art and culture, they also offer general interest itineraries and special-interest themes such as festivals and history.

- **Menara Tours** (℃ **024/446654;** tours@menara-tours.ma) is one of the country's leading inbound tour operators, with offices in Marrakech, Agadir, Casablanca, and the U.S. They offer the full range of travel services, including tailor-made, fully escorted tours for individuals and groups, as well as internal flights and airport meet and greets.

- **Moroccan Club Travel** ★ (℃ **024/331594;** www.mct.ma) is based in Marrakech, with partners in Japan and the U.S. Their very friendly English-speaking staff operates tours Morocco-wide, including 4WD tours to Morocco's Saharan dunes, a "Just for Women" tour that includes numerous encounters with local Moroccan women, and an 11-day "Grand Morocco Tour" from Casablanca.

- **Mountain Voyage Morocco** (℃ **024/421996;** www.mountain-voyage.com) is the Moroccan branch of U.K.-owned Discover Ltd., owner of the Kasbah du Toubkal in Imlil. They offer a range of services, including tailor-made escorted itineraries by land or air, private villa rentals, and corporate or private event coordination.

- **Naturally Morocco** ★★★ (℃ **028/551628** or 01239/654466 U.K.; www.naturallymorocco.co.uk) is a very professional U.K.-based responsible and sustainable tourism operator offering personalized tours, activities, and accommodations within Morocco. Their Moroccan office, based in Taroudannt, is a combined guest-house–cum–cultural and environmental center. From here they operate a fantastic and diverse selection of cultural and environmental experiences.

Despite the fact that escorted tours require big deposits and predetermine hotels, restaurants, and itineraries, many people derive security and peace of mind from the structure they offer. Escorted tours—whether they're navigated by bus, motorcoach, train, or boat—let travelers sit back and enjoy the trip without having to drive or worry about details. They take you to the maximum number of sights in the minimum amount of time with the least amount of hassle. They're particularly convenient for people with limited mobility and can be a great way to make new friends.

On the downside, you'll have little opportunity for serendipitous interactions with locals. The tours can be jam-packed with activities, leaving little room for individual sightseeing, whim, or adventure—plus they often focus on the heavily touristed sites, so you miss out on many a lesser known gem.

12 Getting Around Morocco

Getting around this compact country is pretty straightforward, thanks to a far-reaching network of public transport. Rail, bus, and collective—or *grands*—taxis pretty much cover most of the country, with larger transit-vans and Berber trucks covering the more inaccessible areas.

However, although the coverage may be good, it always pays to have a bit of "Moroccan time" up your sleeve, as delays can sometimes occur on public transport.

BY PLANE

Most international travelers only fly within Morocco when connecting directly from an international flight, such as New York to Marrakech, where you will more than likely change planes onto a local carrier in Casablanca. Domestic flights are relatively expensive when compared to road and rail, and are subject to frequent delays that often negate the quicker flying time. As there are only two domestic air carriers, competition is low and fares are relatively high. Both carriers have an extensive network of flights servicing the country, mostly emanating from Casablanca.

The two carriers are the national airline **Royal Air Maroc** (✆ **09000/0800;** www.royalairmaroc.com), which has offices in most major Moroccan cities, as well as in the U.K., Langham House,

32–33 Gosfield St., London, W1W 6ED (✆ 020/7307-5800), and in the U.S., 666 5th Ave., New York NY 10103 (✆ 800/446-726 or 974/385-053); and **Regional Airlines** (✆ **082/000-082** within Morocco, 902/180-151 within Spain, or 121/842-5559 within Portugal; www.regionalmaroc.com).

BY TRAIN

The state-run **Office National des Chemins de Fer** (ONCF; ✆ **090/ 203040** within Morocco; www.oncf.ma) operates a safe and comfortable rail network connecting most cities west of the Atlas Mountains, including Fes, Meknes, Tangier, Rabat, Casablanca, and Marrakech. ONCF's subsidiary, **Supratours** (see below), runs buses linking some other destinations to the rail network, such as Essaouira. Rail travel in Morocco is quite cheap when compared to that in Europe and North America. A first-class ticket on the network's longest journey—the 15-hour, 825km (510 miles) trip from Oujda to Marrakech—costs 420dh ($53/ £26).

Timetables rarely change, although special schedules are arranged during Ramadan and the two subsequent festival times of Eid al Fitr and Eid al Adha. Timetables are usually posted within the station, or can be viewed on the ONCF website (*horaires* for schedules, *tarifs* for the fare). Station counter staff can also print the schedule between two particular stations. Punctuality and reliability can be hit or miss on the network, with trains operating with Swiss-like precision at times, and other times running frustratingly late. There are two types of trains, Train Navette Rapide (TNR), also called *ordinaire,* and Train Rapide Climatisé (TRC), also called *train à supplement* or *train noble.* Almost all intercity services are TRC trains, which are air-conditioned and offer both first- and second-class travel. Drinks and snacks are available on the train, and smoking is (theoretically) not allowed in compartments, just the carriageway.

First-class compartments have six seats, second class have eight. All overnight trains have couchettes, and some also offer sleeper cars. Couchettes consist of four or six bunk beds in each compartment, while sleeper cars offer one or two beds, a toilet, and washbasin. Each couchette and sleeper car has its own attendant for security, who'll also wake you in time for your stop. Couchettes and sleepers must be booked in advance, with a couchette costing an additional 90dh ($11/£6) on top of your ticket, and sleeper cars costing no more than 350dh ($44/£22), depending on the length of the journey. Reservations can be made from within Morocco only, and can be made 2 months in advance for couchettes, while first-class tickets for other journeys can be reserved 1 month in advance. Tickets prebooked over the phone must be collected from the departure station at least 4 hours before departure. Second-class seats can't be prebooked. Other than that, you can simply purchase your ticket at the station before departure, or even on the train, although this incurs a supplement. Prebooking is especially recommended for overnight couchettes and for travel during Eid al Fitr and Eid al Adha. Also, first-class fares on many routes can get sold out, so it's worth getting to the station early, as second class on some routes is often overbooked and commuters can be left standing in the aisle. All tickets are sold at train stations—payable in cash only—and authorized travel agents. The flipside of being so organized is that many Moroccans are unaware of, or don't understand, the concept of prereserved seating, and you may well find someone in your seat. If you have any difficulty in procuring your allotted seat, there are conductors moving through the trains regularly.

Tickets are valid for 5 days and are worth hanging onto during the journey, as conductors check them on the train and often collect them at the arrival station. A return *(retour)* ticket is exactly double the price of a one way *(aller simple),* and any journey that includes a Supratours service (called a Road & Rail ticket) can only be booked one way.

There are a few reductions and discounts available. The Billet Week-end offers a 25% reduction on return journeys of a minimum of 360km (223 miles) made over the same weekend. The Carte Fidelité, which costs 149dh ($19/£9) and is valid for 1 year, is for those over 26 years old and gives a 50% discount on 16 one-way, second-class journeys. The Carte Jeune costs 99dh ($12/£6) and offers the same discount for those under 26. There are also reductions available for small children, seniors, and families. You can inquire at any train station; you'll need a photocopy of your passport and a passport-size photograph.

Most luggage, including surfboards and bicycles, can be taken on as carry-on. Moroccan train conductors are friendly, well informed, and helpful. They usually announce—in Arabic and French—each station well in advance, but many stations are poorly signposted, so it pays to stay alert as to when your station should be coming up; don't be afraid to ask your fellow passengers. Platforms on some stations are only accessed by walking across the tracks. The stations themselves usually offer luggage storage for up to 24 hours for 10dh ($1.25/65p) per item.

BY BUS

Buses are the cheapest and most popular way to get around Morocco, and they have by far the greatest reach. A complex network of private bus companies crisscrosses the country, with many competing lines covering the most popular routes. The "big four" are Compagnie de Transports Marocains (CTM), SATAS, Trans Ghazala, and Supratours. **CTM** (© **022/438282** or 022/753677; www.ctm.co.ma) is the privatized national carrier and the most reliable. Their network covers the entire country, and buses depart on fixed schedules with numbered seating. **SATAS** and **Trans Ghazala** are the best of the private lines, operating largely in the country's south and north, respectively. **Supratours** (© **022/298163** central reservations; www.supratours.ma) operates in conjunction with the national rail carrier, ONCF. Their routes supplement ONCF's schedule to destinations south of Marrakech (including Agadir and Essaouira) and to the northern cities of Tetouan and Nador, and are direct point-to-point services. All of these companies offer well-maintained, air-conditioned buses, and due to seat numbering, don't oversell. They also, theoretically, only pick up and drop off from designated stops.

All the other private companies operate with smaller fleets, often running on a definitive timetable and departing only when the driver and his attendants think the bus is sufficiently full. These operators are very competitive for business, often paying commission to hustlers and touts. Their fleets can be poorly maintained, with vehicles driven recklessly in order to arrive at particular destinations before their competitor. Their advantage over the bigger companies is their access to the country's smaller villages and more inaccessible towns.

Some companies, CTM included, operate overnight services on long distance routes, such as between Fes and Marrakech; Casablanca and Tangier; and Casablanca and Er Rachidia. From June to September, these services are a popular—and cooler—alternative to traveling during the day.

Fares can be as little as 20dh ($2.50/£1.25) for the 1-hour journey between Fes and Meknes, and even the 12- to 15-hour long-haul routes cost no more than 230dh to 250dh ($29–$31/£14–£16).

Most towns in Morocco have a main bus station, called a *gare routière*. This can sometimes be similar to the Western perception of a bus station, but can also be a simple patch of ground. More often than not, it will be located some distance from the center, but there are usually *petits* taxis parked nearby. Some cities have more than one *gare routière*. This is in addition to CTM, who largely operate from their own terminals, which are located outside their offices. Supratours buses operate either from the train station or from their own office. In the larger towns and cities, the *gare routière* can feel intimidating upon arrival. Each bus company will have a ticket counter, usually displaying their departures in the window. Normally upon arrival, Western travelers are approached by ticket touts called *courtiers*. Although overwhelming initially, *courtiers* do usually know their stuff and can be handy in some of the busier stations. Advise your destination, and you will be directed to the appropriate ticket counter. A *courtier* earns a small commission for every passenger he brings to the company, but he will also expect a small tip from you for his service. To get the most value out of this service, and some peace of mind, I always ask to be shown to the particular bus that I will be traveling on before I purchase my ticket.

It's worth trying to buy your ticket in advance, especially if you're traveling to a popular destination or wish to travel with one of the companies mentioned above. At the very least, try to arrive early in the day to give yourself the most options.

This is particularly wise in the smaller towns, where buses traveling through are already full and therefore don't stop.

When traveling with the companies mentioned above, luggage is usually charged by weight. You should be given a receipt, and your luggage will be stowed for you. With the private companies, you are normally charged a per-item fee, paid to an independent porter. Either way, it's never normally any more than 10dh ($1.90/95p) per piece. Most *gare routière*

and CTM stations have a luggage storage where you can leave your bags for up to 24 hours for around 10dh ($1.90/95p) per piece.

In rural areas, such as the High Atlas villages, there may be no bus or *grand* taxi services. In their place you will normally find trucks or lorries *(camions)* and transit vans *(transits)*. They operate pretty much the same as *grands* taxis and can be a fun and memorable way to travel around the far reaches of the country.

Driving Distances (Km/Miles) in Morocco

	Agadir	Casablanca	Erfoud	Essaouira	Fes	Marrakech	Meknes	Ouarzazate	Rabat	Tangier
Agadir	X	511/ 318	853/ 530	173/ 107	756/ 470	273/ 170	740/ 460	375/ 233	602/ 374	880/ 547
Casablanca	511/ 318	X	637/ 396	351/ 218	289/ 180	238/ 148	229/ 142	442/ 275	91/ 57	341/ 212
Erfoud	853/ 530	637/ 396	X	756/ 470	430/ 267	580/ 360	408/ 254	376/ 234	546/ 339	675/ 419
Essaouira	173/ 107	351/ 218	756/ 470	X	640/ 398	176/ 109	580/ 360	380/ 236	442/ 275	692/ 430
Fes	756/ 470	289/ 180	430/ 267	640/ 398	X	483/ 300	646/ 401	198/ 123	303/ 188	
Marrakech	273/ 170	238/ 148	580/ 360	176/ 109	483/ 300	X	467/ 290	204/ 127	321/ 199	579/ 360
Meknes	740/ 460	229/ 142	408/ 254	580/ 360	60/ 37	467/ 290	X	652/ 405	138/ 86	267/ 166
Ouarzazate	375/ 233	442/ 275	376/ 234	380/ 236	646/ 401	204/ 127	652/ 405	X	528/ 328	783/ 487
Rabat	602/ 374	91/ 57	546/ 339	442/ 275	198/ 123	321/ 199	138/ 86	528/ 328	X	250/ 155
Tangier	880/ 547	341/ 212	675/ 419	692/ 430	303/ 188	579/ 360	267/ 166	783/ 487	250/ 155	X

BY *GRAND* TAXI

Morocco's collective taxis, called *grands* taxis, are the work horses of the country's public transport system, operating in every corner throughout the day and night, linking villages with towns and towns with cities. They are usually old Mercedes sedans and are located at organized ranks next to bus stations, train stations, and even street corners. Most routes are short and regular, with longer or less popular

routes normally leaving early in the morning. *Grands* taxis always travel with six passengers—two in the front next to the driver and four in the back. If it sounds cramped, you're right. Travelers with just a slightly bigger budget than stone broke often choose to pay for two seats and claim the front seat for themselves. This is an especially good idea for single female travelers. Many taxi drivers will try to push this onto Western travelers, however. If you only want to pay for one seat, you can use the words *"wa-hed"* (one) and *"collectif"* (collective taxi). The fares are fixed, and drivers rarely attempt to overcharge Westerners, though they often try to add on extra for luggage, which is fair if you're accompanied by a surfboard or three suitcases, but not for any reasonable piece of luggage.

Within each chapter of this guide, I've given many examples of routes and their corresponding fares. *Grands* taxis leave when full, and there's no system of pre-booking a seat. A good option for small groups or families is to charter a whole taxi. This allows for much more freedom within the journey (rest and toilet stops, for example), and can often be organized by your hotel. Although it seems obvious that the cost of chartering a whole *grand* taxi should be six times the single fare, this isn't always the case. Bargain hard.

There are some pertinent safety concerns attached to traveling in *grands* taxis. Many drivers are under pressure to work long hours, and falling asleep at the wheel is a definite possibility on night drives, so it's best to travel by day. Within that busy day, a driver is trying to fit in as many journeys as possible, and will often drive as if there is no one else on the road. Overtaking on blind corners is common on many *grand* taxi journeys. Added to this is the lack of available seat belts, because it's either too cramped within the vehicle or there quite simply aren't any. Needless to say, when chartering a *grand* taxi, stress on the driver your expectations toward his driving.

BY CAR

Given enough time, driving yourself around Morocco is a great way to enjoy the country—if it wasn't for Moroccan drivers. Accident rates are very high, and aggressive driving practices and lack of road safety awareness by pedestrians, cyclists, and moped riders can make for a stressful experience. However, if you can handle what sometimes feels like a driving free-for-all and desire maximum flexibility and independence, then self-driving in Morocco is definitely plausible. The road network linking the country is generally very good, with some European-standard motorways (called auto-routes), many other well-surfaced (though sometimes narrow) secondary and minor roads, and a network of dirt roads, called *pistes,* through the Atlas ranges.

The minimum driving age in Morocco is 18, though most rental companies will only rent to those 21 and older. You must have both your driving license and passport available for inspection by police at any time. An international driver's license isn't required, so long as your domestic license bears your photograph. Driving in Morocco is on the right-hand side, the same as in continental Europe and North America, and most roundabouts apply the French rule, where priority is given to those entering, rather than those already on, the roundabout. On the motorways the speed limit is 120km per hour (75 mph), while on other open roads the limit is 100km per hour (62 mph). In built-up areas the limit is usually 40km per hour (25 mph). Road signs advising the speed limit are relatively common, but so are police checks and speed traps. Oncoming motorists usually flash their lights to warn of an approaching road block or speed radar. On-the-spot fines for speeding start at 400dh ($50/£25). If you're caught speeding, pay the official fine rather than *baksheesh* (a bribe); this will perhaps lessen the seemingly inherent corruption within Morocco's police force.

Motorways are superb for getting quickly between the major cities and regions, as they connect Tangier, Rabat, Casablanca, Fes, Meknes, Marrakech, and El Jadida. An extension connecting Ceuta to Tangier will be completed by the end of 2008, and work is underway on a Marrakech to Agadir extension. Toll stations are located regularly along the routes, and the cost (calculated on the distance traveled and the size of vehicle) is very reasonable given the quality of the roads. For example, the current cost for a sedan is 107dh ($13/£6.70) from Tangier to Casablanca; 20dh ($2.50/£1.25) from Casablanca to Rabat; and 145dh ($18/£9.05) from Casablanca to Marrakech. The toll stations are about the only services in Morocco that always have change, so pay with your notes and keep the change for everyday use. Modern roadside petrol stations–cum–restaurants are also dotted along the routes, as are emergency assistance patrols.

Fuel is referred to as "petrol" or "essence," with leaded petrol called *super,* unleaded *sans plomb,* and diesel *gasoil.* Leaded and unleaded currently cost around 11dh ($1.38/69p) per liter, and diesel is around 8dh ($1/50p) per liter. Four liters is approximately 1 gallon. Leaded and diesel fuel are both usually available at all petrol stations, located throughout the country, but sparsely between towns in rural areas. Unleaded can be difficult to procure sometimes, and it's therefore best to fill up whenever you can; the Afriquia stations are your best bet. If you break down, Moroccan mechanics are experts at getting your car back on the road. Parts for most cars, especially French makes, are usually readily available.

Driving in Morocco's cities can be extremely daunting. One particularly crazy time is nearing sunset during Ramadan. The mad rush to finish work and get home (it's traditional to break each day's fast with family or close friends) brings about even crazier driving tactics than normal. Conversely, the hour or so after sunset sees the streets practically void of any traffic, motorized or pedestrian. If you can time your entry or exit with this time of the Ramadan day, you'll have a free run.

Parking in Morocco's urban centers can be difficult. Most top-end hotels will offer private parking, while street-side parking is attended to by *gardiens. Gardiens* are often licensed by the local authorities to keep a watch over vehicles in a given area. *Gardiens* only earn money from the tips they receive from drivers. He may ask for a fee, or tip, upfront if you are staying for more than a day, as sometimes arguments break out between a day-shift and night-shift *gardien* as to who has earned the money. Budget on 10dh ($1.25/65p) per shift, and you'll keep everybody happy. If you're lucky, you might even find your car has been washed before you depart. ***Note:*** Red- and white-stripe curbing means no parking.

The major international car-rental firms are all represented in Morocco, with agencies in most of the major cities and airports. These include Avis (© **022/312424;** www.avis.com), Budget (© **022/313124;** www.budget.com), Europcar (© **022/313737;** www.europcar.com), Hertz (© **022/484710;** www.hertz.com); and National/Alamo (© **022/472540;** www.nationalcar.com). There are also countless local car-rental firms, the most reliable of which are mentioned in the "Fast Facts" within each chapter. To rent a car in Morocco you'll need to be 21 years or older and theoretically have a year's driving experience. Group A vehicles, usually a small, four-door hatch or sedan, are the smallest available and perfectly adequate for most road touring in Morocco. The next size up is Group B, usually a small to medium four-door sedan, which will have a bit more power and may offer air-conditioning and a music system. Generally, it can be difficult, but not impossible, to acquire an automatic-gear rental car.

Car rental is a very competitive industry in Morocco, and daily rates ebb and flow according to season, demand, and supply. Costs for a Group A can range from 350dh to 500dh ($44–$63/£22–£31) per day with unlimited mileage. These rates will usually include basic third-party insurance, but I recommend paying an extra 50dh to 100dh ($6.25–$13/£3.15–£6.25) per day for Collision Damage Waiver (CDW) insurance. This usually still has an excess of between 3,000dh and 5,000dh ($375–$625/£188–£313), which can be waived by paying a Super Collision Damage Waiver of around 50dh ($6.25/£3.15) per day. There's usually no additional fee for an additional driver, but each driver's name must be recorded on the rental agreement. Most companies request an imprint of your credit card as a deposit.

All of the above costs are usually non-negotiable with the international firms, especially if you prebook, but can often be negotiated with the local firms, especially outside of high tourist season (June–Sept). Although this can be advantageous for your wallet, first compare the logistical and mechanical assistance offered between companies. Also, not many local companies offer one-way rentals.

BY *PETIT* TAXI

Operating in all cities and large towns are local taxis called *petits* taxis. These small four-door vehicles are the most convenient and inexpensive way to get around town. They are usually a four-door hatch, and those operating in each city or town are all colored the same; beige in Marrakech and turquoise in Tangier, for example. Government-regulated drivers are only allowed to carry up to three passengers, though these can all be traveling on separate fares, and are only allowed to travel within the city/town limits. At all times, request (sometimes this becomes a demand) the driver to charge by his electronic meter, as he is legally bound to no matter the time of day or night. After 8pm, a 50% surcharge kicks in. Fares are usually no more than 15dh to 20dh ($1.90–$2.50/95p–£1.25) per trip—not per person—and are quite often less.

13 Tips on Accommodations

Morocco offers the traveler an extremely appealing range of year-round accommodations, including trendy medina houses, world-class luxury hotels and beach resorts, desert and mountain kasbahs, and grand sultan palaces. Luxury options have increased considerably over recent years, but there are still plenty of mid- to lower-range accommodations as well. Advance reservations are recommended during the holiday season from June to September, as well as over the Easter and Christmas/New Year periods. This applies year-round in Marrakech. You'll also need to prebook if you want to stay in a medina *maison d'hôte,* where it's almost geographically impossible to simply arrive and ask for a room.

Hotels in Morocco are distinguished between those that are classified by the Moroccan tourist board and those that aren't. As in most countries, the government's hotel-rating system means that establishments are awarded stars for the presence of certain facilities—pool, restaurant, elevator, and so on—more than for standards of service and luxury. Thus, it is not always true that the accommodations with the most stars are necessarily the most comfortable or atmospheric. In Morocco, it's best not to rely too much on the star system, as inspections of classified hotels are erratic, and regardless of their star rating, hotels can charge whatever they wish. Unclassified hotels tend to be inexpensive places, usually with communal showers and toilets, few facilities, and in the cities are often located within the medina. Other unclassified hotels, such as those in central and southern Morocco, often offer mattresses on their roof terraces or under large Berber tents, and can be a bargain for budget travelers. Classified hotels in the cities are usually found in the **ville nouvelle,** and although most lack any

Riads, Dars & *Maisons d'Hôte*

Morocco's medinas are the ancient walled cities constructed through the ages by the country's various dynasties, protected from invaders by the imposing walls that now separate the medina from the rest of the city. The traditional dwellings within the medina are called riads or dars. The Arabic word *"riad"* translates to "garden," while *"dar"* simply means "house," and this is the main distinction between the two dwellings. Both typically have no windows onto the street outside, instead having all windows opening inward to an open-air central courtyard that is the heart of the house. The service areas—kitchen, hammam, and laundry—are normally on the entrance side near the street.

The courtyard in a true riad has both a fountain and garden, or at least some fruit trees. Riads tend to have many salons on multiple levels, often on all four sides but sometimes on only three sides, with the garden up against the fourth wall. A dar mirrors a riad in much of its design, but is generally smaller. While it might have a fountain, it lacks the central garden in the courtyard. The principal elevating characteristics of both dwellings are their sanctuary from the busy streets outside and their interior courtyards that are open toward the sky.

During the protectorate years, the French created new cities (ville nouvelle) outside the medinas, condemning the medinas to becoming the poor neighborhoods of contemporary Moroccan cities. Moroccan families abandoned their medina dwellings in favor of apartments or villas in the new neighborhoods outside. Rural families, sometimes up to a dozen, moved into the medina houses, paying rent to unscrupulous landlords who kept maintenance of the buildings to a minimum. Toward the end of the 1990s, however, and coinciding with a general surge of tourism interest toward Morocco, some Europeans and prosperous Moroccans began buying and restoring the medina's riads and dars, initially as holiday homes. While abroad, many of these foreign-based owners were faced with security and maintenance concerns of their medina dwellings, and some began to open them as guesthouses, called *maisons d'hôte,* as a way of paying for these additional year-round expenses.

great character with mainly Western-style rooms, they do offer value for money. During the cold winter and hot summer, these hotels—usually in the moderate price bracket and upward—come into their own, offering rooms with reverse-cycle air-conditioning and showers with a good supply of hot and cold water. Some hotels offer half board (*demi-pension,* meaning breakfast and dinner are included), which can be a good deal, especially in the more isolated areas where there aren't too many alternative dining options.

Morocco's other major style of accommodation is the guesthouse, or **maison d'hôte** (see box below). Generally, *maisons d'hôte* are in the expensive and very expensive price range, offering services similar to what you would expect from a four-star hotel. Initially concentrated within Marrakech, but now found in great number throughout the country, Morocco's medina *maisons d'hôte*—simply called riads in much travel literature—have become one of the world's most chic accommodations styles. They are generally owner-managed, and each has its own distinct soul that is a personal reflection of the owners themselves. Inside you're more than likely to find romantic bedrooms, personal service, fantastic rooftop terrace views, and delicious breakfasts (if not dinners as well), all in a relaxed, intimate setting amidst the hustle and commotion of the medina. On the flip side, however, your room may lack air-conditioning or heating; offer little privacy due to thin, echoing walls and curtained entrances with no locks; and only be accessible by climbing numerous flights of steep, narrow stairs.

Most medina *maisons d'hôte* can only be accessed by foot. Staying within the medina offers the benefit of being within walking distance of the majority of sights and attractions, and presents an authentic experience of medina life. If you are considering staying within the medina but are traveling with small children, take note that *maisons d'hôte* usually consist of two to three levels of rooms in close quarters, and noise carries easily from within. Many *maisons d'hôte* also have plunge or small swimming pools that aren't supervised or cordoned off, as well as stairways or roof terraces that aren't the safest places for crawling or investigative little ones. It is because of both these noise and safety concerns—let alone any practical problems concerning bed space within the rooms—that some *maisons d'hôte* simply refuse to accept children.

The popularity of this accommodations style has skyrocketed in recent years, bringing with it a few unscrupulous property developers who are merely looking to make some easy money through minimum investment. Although the website may look stunning, it's always worth checking out any recent online reviews on a *maison d'hôte* (such as www.tripadvisor.com) or, if possible, viewing the establishment before handing any money over.

Note: In your hotel or *maison d'hôte* bathroom, taps labeled C and F stand for *chaude* (hot) and *froid* (cold).

Throughout this guidebook, I've separated hotel listings into several broad categories: **Very Expensive,** 960dh ($120/£60)

and up; **Expensive,** 640dh to 960dh ($80–$120/£40–£80); **Moderate,** 360dh to 640dh ($45–$80/£23–£40); and **Inexpensive,** under 360dh ($45/£23). These are rack rates for a double room in high season, and include all government taxes including a recently introduced Tourist Promotion Tax (TPT) of 5dh to 15dh (65¢–$1.90/30p–95p) per person per night, depending on the grade of accommodations. Some accommodations, however, are yet to implement the tax, and I've noted this where applicable.

Tip: During the quieter months, many hotels (but not *maisons d'hôte*) will give room discounts or offer *petit déjeuner* (breakfast) if it's not already included. Most of the time you'll have to inquire first, though, as nothing will be automatically given to you. Also, don't be fooled by the lure of a "minibar." In Morocco, this generally means that there is a small—and empty—fridge in your room. However, I've made this distinction in the amenities where applicable (so minibar does indeed mean minibar).

Making advance reservations with many unclassified and inexpensive hotels is usually only achieved over phone, often with reception staff who speak only French, or at best a little English. Most other levels of accommodations will accept reservations by fax or email, requiring a credit card number to confirm the room for you. Many *maisons d'hôte* and high-end hotels quote in euros but will accept cash payment in either euro or dirham. Most hotels and *maisons d'hôte,* except the inexpensive establishments within the medina, will accept payment by credit card, but some will add a 5% bank administration fee to your bill, and others will frustratingly advise you when checking out that their machine is broken and request you to draw large sums of cash from a bank ATM.

A few international chains operate in Morocco, most notably the Hilton in

Rabat; the Hyatt and Sheraton in Casablanca; Le Meridien in Casablanca and Marrakech; and Sofitel, which among its seven Moroccan properties includes those in Agadir, Essaouira, Fes, Marrakech, and Rabat. The **Atlas Hospitality Group** (www.hotelsatlas.com) is a Moroccan company with a number of resorts and hotels throughout Morocco. Most of their properties were existing hotels that have been bought by the group and refurbished. Like all chains, they have a certain similarity between them, but the rooms are fitted with quality finishings and are on the whole a very good value. **Kenzi Hôtels** (www.kenzi-hotels.com) operates 10 hotels in Morocco. The hotels are all four- or five-star, but are generally tired and overpriced, most not having been refurbished since they opened in the late 1980s or early '90s. A lot of their business comes from large tour groups and Moroccan businessmen. The **Ibis hotel chain** (www.ibishotel.com) operates a string of midrange hotels throughout Morocco. Their hotels are usually found near transport centers, mainly train stations, and are all styled along similar lines, with compact, functional rooms.

Some websites worth checking out for accommodations in Morocco include: www.hipmorocco.com, www.marrakech-medina.com, and www.riadomaroc.com.

SURFING FOR HOTELS

In addition to the online travel booking sites **Travelocity, Expedia, Orbitz, Priceline,** and **Hotwire,** you can book hotels through **Hotels.com, Quikbook** (www.quikbook.com), and **Travelaxe** (www.travelaxe.net).

HotelChatter.com is a daily webzine offering smart coverage and critiques of hotels worldwide. Go to **TripAdvisor** or **HotelShark.com** for helpful independent consumer reviews of hotels and resort properties.

It's definitely a good idea to **get a confirmation number** and **make a printout** of any online booking transaction. Communication problems between English-speaking accommodations booking services and the mostly French- or Arabic-speaking staff at each particular hotel or *maison d'hôte* has been known to cause incorrect or even totally absent bookings.

SAVING ON YOUR HOTEL ROOM

The **rack rate** is the maximum rate that a hotel charges for a room. Hardly anybody pays this price, however, except in high season or on holidays. To lower the cost of your room:

- **Ask about special rates or other discounts.** You may qualify for corporate, student, military, senior, frequent flier, trade union, or other discounts.
- **Dial direct.** When booking a room in a chain hotel, you'll often get a better deal by calling the individual hotel's reservation desk rather than the chain's main number.
- **Book online.** Many hotels offer Internet-only discounts, or supply rooms to Priceline, Hotwire, or Expedia at rates much lower than the ones you can get through the hotel itself.
- **Remember the law of supply and demand.** You can save big on hotel rooms by traveling in a destination's off season or shoulder seasons, when rates typically drop, even at luxury properties.
- **Look into group or long-stay discounts.** If you come as part of a large group, you should be able to negotiate a bargain rate. Likewise, if you're planning a long stay (at least 5 days), you might qualify for a discount. As a general rule, expect 1 night free after a 7-night stay.
- **Sidestep excess surcharges and hidden costs.** Many hotels have adopted the unpleasant practice of nickel-and-diming guests with opaque surcharges.

When you book a room, ask what is included in the room rate and what is extra. Avoid dialing direct from hotel phones, which can have exorbitant rates. And don't be tempted by the room's minibar offerings: Most hotels charge through the nose for water, soda, and snacks. Finally, ask about local taxes and service charges, which can increase the cost of a room by 15% or more.

- Consider the pros and cons of **all-inclusive** resorts and hotels, such as those offered in Agadir. The term "all-inclusive" means different things at different hotels. Many all-inclusive hotels include three meals daily, sports equipment, spa entry, and other amenities; others may include most alcoholic drinks. In general, you'll save money going the "all-inclusive" way—as long as you use the facilities provided. The downside is that your choices are limited and you're stuck eating and playing in one place for the duration of your vacation.

- **Book an efficiency.** A room with a kitchenette allows you to shop for groceries and cook your own meals. This is a big money saver, especially for families on long stays.

- **Consider enrolling in hotel chains' frequent-stay programs,** which are upping the ante lately to win the loyalty of repeat customers. Frequent guests can now accumulate points or credits to earn free hotel nights, airline miles, in-room amenities, merchandise, tickets to concerts and events, discounts on sporting facilities—and

even credit toward stock in the participating hotel, in the case of the Jameson Inn hotel group. Perks are awarded not only by many chain hotels and motels (Hilton Honors, Marriott Rewards, Wyndham ByRequest, to name a few), but individual inns and B&Bs. Many chain hotels partner with other hotel chains, car-rental firms, airlines, and credit card companies to give consumers additional incentive to do repeat business.

LANDING THE BEST ROOM

Somebody has to get the best room in the house. It might as well be you. You can start by joining the hotel's frequent-guest program, which may make you eligible for upgrades. A hotel-branded credit card usually gives its owner silver or gold status in frequent-guest programs for free. Always ask about a corner room. They're often larger and quieter, with more windows and light, and they often cost the same as standard rooms. When you make your reservation, ask if the hotel is renovating; if it is, request a room away from the construction. Ask about nonsmoking rooms and rooms with views. Be sure to request your choice of twin, queen-, or king-size beds. If you're a light sleeper, ask for a quiet room away from vending or ice machines, elevators, restaurants, bars, and discos. Ask for a room that has been recently renovated or refurbished.

If you aren't happy with your room when you arrive, ask for another one. Most lodgings will be willing to accommodate you.

14 Tips on Dining

Moroccan cuisine reflects the country's history, with elements of Africa, Arabia, and the Mediterranean adding spice and color to a rich array of fresh produce available throughout the country. Combined with the culinary traditions of both

the Berbers and Arabs, dining in Morocco truly becomes an experience rather than just a meal.

Moroccans tend to eat three meals a day, in similar fashion to the Western world, but usually taken after prayer.

Tips for Digital Travel Photography

- **Take along a spare camera—or two.** Even if you've been anointed the "official" photographer of your travel group, encourage others in your party to carry their own cameras and provide fresh perspectives—and backup. Your photographic "second unit" may include you in a few shots so you're not the invisible person of the trip.
- **Stock up on digital film cards.** At home, it's easy to copy pictures from your memory cards to your computer as they fill up. During your travels, cards seem to fill up more quickly. Take along enough digital film for your entire trip or, at a minimum, enough for at least a few days' of shooting. At intervals, you can copy images to CDs. Many camera stores and souvenir shops offer this service, and a growing number of mass merchandisers have walk-up kiosks you can use to make prints or create CDs while you travel.
- **Share and share alike.** No need to wait until you get home to share your photos. You can upload a gallery's worth to an online photo-sharing service. Just find an Internet cafe where the computers have card readers, or connect your camera to the computer with a cable. You can find online photo-sharing services that cost little or nothing at Kodak's EasyShare gallery (**www.kodak.com**), Snapfish (**www.snapfish.com**), or Shutterfly (**www.shutterfly.com**).
- **Add voice annotations to your photos.** Many digital cameras allow you to add voice annotations to your shots after they're taken. These serve as excellent reminders and documentation. One castle or cathedral may look like another after a long tour; your voice notes will help you distinguish them.
- **Experiment!** Travel is a great time to try out new techniques. Take photos at night, resting your camera on a handy wall or other support as your self-timer trips the shutter for a long exposure. Try close-ups of flowers, crafts, wildlife, or maybe the exotic cuisine you're about to consume. Discover action photography—shoot the countryside from trains, buses, or cars. With a digital camera, you can experiment and then erase your mistakes.

—*From* Travel Photography Digital Field Guide *(Wiley Publishing, Inc.; 2006)*

Breakfast is usually served from 7am onward, with most cafes opening at this time and serving a small selection of pastries and fresh bread to accompany a mint tea or coffee. Western travelers often despair at the lack of diversity when it comes to hotel breakfasts; expect baguettes, croissants, orange juice, tea and coffee, and not much else in most lower- to midrange accommodations. Staying in a higher-end accommodations should reward you with additions to the norm, such as fresh Moroccan breads, yogurt, cereals, fresh fruit, and perhaps eggs.

Lunch is considered the most important meal of the day, hence the midday closure of most businesses, shops, and offices from noon to 2pm, sometimes 2:30pm. It's therefore also the longest meal, and can include any number of courses. The traditional lunch—often offered by top-end and palace-style restaurants—begins with a meze selection of olives and cold and cooked salads, and can fill you up on its own. This is usually followed by a tagine, couscous, or both. Rarely will Moroccans use cutlery; rather they will eat with their freshly washed right hand (the left mainly used for passing food around), using *khübz* (bread) to mop up the juices and sauce. Mint tea, and perhaps sweet pastries, may then be offered for dessert, followed by an early afternoon nap.

Dinner tends to be served after the sunset prayer, and is more along Mediterranean and Latin times, from 7 or 7:30pm to 10:30 or 11pm. A popular pastime in Morocco—and one I am particularly fond of—is an after-dinner stroll, followed by an ice cream or cake and coffee. Families are usually in the streets, squares, and parks after dinner to socialize, play, chat, and generally watch and mingle.

I have separated restaurant listings throughout this book into four price categories based on the average cost per person of a meal, not including tip. The categories are **Very Expensive,** more than 240dh ($30/£15); **Expensive,** 160dh to 240dh ($20–$30/£10–£15); **Moderate,** 80dh to 160dh ($10–$20/£5–£10); and **Inexpensive,** less than 80dh ($10/£5). A compulsory 10% government tax (called TTC) is usually included in the cost of each item on your menu. If it isn't, it's normally stated somewhere at the bottom. Very rarely, however, will a service charge be included in your bill, so a tip of at least 10% is expected, no matter if you've had a meal or just a drink. Expensive restaurants are usually the only ones that accept credit cards, and even those that claim to can sometimes bring your card back asking for payment in cash, usually due to telecommunication problems or, I kid you not, because they've run out of paper in the credit card machine. Also watch out for a 5% bank administration fee that is sometimes added to your bill.

Because Morocco is a predominantly Muslim country, alcohol is not served at all restaurants; I have noted where it's available in the review's listing information.

For more on Moroccan cuisine, see appendix A.

FAST FACTS: Morocco

American Express **American Express** is represented in Morocco by the travel agency Voyages Schwarz, with branches in Casablanca, 2 av. Hassan Souktani, Fourth Floor, Apt 10 (② **022/203552**), and 2 av. Prince Moulay Abdellah (② **022/ 278054**); Marrakech, Residence Nadia, 22 rue Moulay Ali Cherif (② **024/ 437469**); and Tangier, 54 bd. Pasteur (② **039/936028**). These are only agents, however, and the services offered may be limited. They can usually issue traveler's checks—but often won't cash them—and hold mail for clients, but they don't cash personal checks or accept wired money.

Area Codes Much of Morocco changed fixed-line area codes in 2006. South of (but not including) Casablanca, all numbers changed their prefix from 04 to 02. For example, Marrakech changed from 044 to 024. Many published telephone numbers still contain the old area codes.

ATM Networks See "Money & Costs" on p. 29.

Business Hours The Moroccan working day is a combination of both Western and Eastern cultures. For example, most Moroccans eat three meals a day at the usual meal times of breakfast, lunch, and dinner. However, most will also work from 9am to 7pm, with short breaks during the day to pray and an extended lunch break. Shops in the medina will usually open at 8 or 9am and stay open until 8 or 9pm. Business hours for the country's banks are Monday to Friday 8:15am to 3:45pm, though during Ramadan these are shortened from 9am to 2:30pm, depending on the bank. Government departments work from Monday to Thursday 8:30am to noon and 2 to 6:30pm, and Fridays 8:30 to 11:30am and 3 to 6:30pm.

Car Rentals See "Getting Around Morocco" on p. 54.

Currency See "Money & Costs" on p. 29.

Customs **What You Can Bring Into Morocco:** Tobacco (200 cigarettes/100 cigarillos/25 cigars), alcohol (1 liter), perfume (150ml), eau de toilette (250ml), electrical and photographic goods, and a bicycle.

What You Can Take Home from Morocco: All locally made crafts and souvenirs, including a reasonable amount (not in the dozens) of fossilized, ornamental, and semi-precious stones. Objets d'art and antiques theoretically require signed authorization from the Ministry of Culture, though this is only required for expensive or large items, and will be taken care of if purchased from any reputable shop owner. *Note:* It is forbidden to import/export the national currency, the Moroccan dirham.

U.S. Citizens: For specifics on what you can bring back and the corresponding fees, download the invaluable free pamphlet *Know Before You Go* online at **www.cbp.gov.** (Click on "Travel," and then click on "Know Before You Go! Online Brochure".) Or, contact the **U.S. Customs & Border Protection (CBP)**, 1300 Pennsylvania Ave., NW, Washington, DC 20229 (© **877/287-8667**), and request the pamphlet.

Canadian Citizens: For a clear summary of Canadian rules, write for the booklet *I Declare,* issued by the **Canada Border Services Agency** (© **800/461-9999** in Canada, or 204/983-3500; www.cbsa-asfc.gc.ca).

U.K. Citizens: For information, contact **HM Customs & Excise** at © **0845/010-9000** (from outside the U.K., 020/8929-0152), or consult their website at www.hmce.gov.uk.

Australian Citizens: A helpful brochure available from Australian consulates or Customs offices is *Know Before You Go.* For more information, call the **Australian Customs Service** at © **1300/363-263,** or log on to www.customs.gov.au.

New Zealand Citizens: Most questions are answered in a free pamphlet available at New Zealand consulates and Customs offices: *New Zealand Customs Guide for Travellers, Notice no. 4.* For more information, contact **New Zealand Customs,** The Customhouse, 17–21 Whitmore St., Box 2218, Wellington (© **04/473-6099** or 0800/428-786; www.customs.govt.nz).

Driving Rules See "Getting Around Morocco" on p. 54.

Drugstores Drugstores, or chemists, are called *pharmacie* in Morocco. Pharmacies are found everywhere in Morocco, from the smallest hamlet to the largest city. Most pharmacists obtain their qualifications in France, and the standard of health care—including in some emergency situations—is exceptional. Operating hours differ from place to place, but pharmacies generally open around 9am and close late at night, having closed for one or two breaks during the day. After hours, pharmacies open on a roster basis, each week's late-night facilities being displayed on the front door. Most larger towns and cities will also have a *pharmacie du nuit,* which is open all night.

Electricity Electricity is generally reliable and available throughout Morocco, barring obvious places such as the top of Jebel Toubkal or in the dunes of central Morocco. Moroccan power points accept the European two-pin plug only, and run on a 220V/55Hz current. International adaptors are very hard to find within the country, so bring your own.

Embassies & Consulates The following embassies are in Rabat: **Canada,** 13 bis rue Jaâfar as Sadiq, Agdal (© 037/687400; www.dfait-maeci.gc.ca/morocco); **South Africa,** 34 rue des Saadiens, Hassan (© 037/706760; www.dfa.gov.za); **U.K.,** 28 av. SAR Sidi Mohammed, Souissi (© 037/633333; www.britishembassy.gov.uk/morocco); and **U.S.,** 2 av. Marrakech (aka av. Mohammed el Fassi), Ministères (© 037/762265; www.usembassy.ma).

The **U.S.** also maintains a consulate in Casablanca, 8 bd. Moulay Youssef (© 022/264550; http://casablanca.usconsulate.gov), as does the **U.K.,** 36 rue de la Loire, Polo (© 022/857400). The **U.K.** operates another consulate in Tangier at 9 rue Amerique du Sud (© 039/936939). **Australians** are provided consular assistance by the Canadian embassy, or must otherwise contact the Australian embassy in France, 4 rue Jean Rey, Paris (© 1405/93300; www.dfat.gov.au). **Irish** citizens are represented by their embassy in Portugal at Rua da Imprensa a Estrela 1–4, Lisbon (© 121/3929440; www.dfa.ie). There are also two Honorary Consuls of Ireland in the COPRAGRI Building, Boulevard Moulay Ismail, Km 6.3 Route de Rabat, Aïn Sebaa, Casablanca (© 022/660306), and in the Hotel Kenzi Europa, boulevard du 20 Août, Agadir (© 028/821212). **New Zealanders** are represented by their embassy in Spain at Calle del Pinar 7, Madrid (© 915/230226; www.nzembassy.com), but in an emergency can call on the U.K. Moroccan embassy or consulates.

Emergencies In any **emergency,** dial © 19 from anywhere in Morocco, which will connect you with the local police. For a **public ambulance,** dial © 15. On the other end of the line, however, may be someone who speaks only Moroccan Arabic or French at best. In the medinas of the major cities, ask a local shopkeeper to find you the Brigade Touristique. I've mentioned these and listed the various numbers for fire departments, ambulances, and hospitals—where available—in the "Fast Facts" sections throughout the book.

Etiquette & Customs **Appropriate Attire:** Although wholeheartedly Muslim and conservative by nature, Moroccans are also understanding of, and have been exposed to, Western culture. Unfortunately, many Westerners take this tolerance to the extreme, and dress as if they were back home. Travelers will be treated with undoubtedly higher respect by all Moroccans if dressed conservatively. For men it's worth looking around and seeing the type of dress generally worn by all Moroccan men: collared shirt or T-shirt covering the shoulders, long pants or jeans, and sandals or shoes. Running shorts, sleeveless shirts, and beachwear are only worn when playing sports or at the beach, and if worn at other times are almost tantamount to wearing only your underwear. For women, dressing conservatively can range from loose, long pants, shoulder-covering short-sleeve shirts, and shoes or sandals to a full-length Moroccan robe, called a *jellabah*.

Greetings: Moroccans are more formal in social situations than most Westerners. Queries about one's marital status and children are considered polite, and greetings should always include queries as to the health and well-being of one's family. Always greet with your right hand, as your left is traditionally considered unclean. Kissing cheeks is practiced between members of the same sex—especially if they are friends—but should not be performed between opposite sexes unless each is well known to the other. When entering someone's home, it's considered polite to remove your shoes, especially before entering the living/dining area. If your host doesn't require such politeness, they will quickly inform you.

Gestures: Using your index finger to motion a person to approach you is considered impolite. Moroccans—as with most non-Western cultures—beckon someone by placing the palm downward and sweeping the hand towards themselves.

Avoiding Offense: In Morocco, taboo conversation subjects include the royal family, the political situation in the Western Sahara and Algeria, and drugs. It's also wise to be prudent when talking about Islam and Al'lah (God). Although non-Muslims are not expected to fast during Ramadan, it's considered polite to eat, drink, and smoke indoors, or at least away from the public eye. At any time of the year, but especially during Ramadan, show respect in both dress and demeanor if you are near a mosque. Photographing a mosque is usually acceptable, so long as you're not too close or appear to be photographing the interior. You may be invited to come closer, but it's best to wait for this. Photographing border checkpoints, military, police, or airport installations is strictly forbidden.

Eating & Drinking: In Islamic (and Arabic) cultures, the left hand is considered unclean, as this is the hand with which a person performs sanitary tasks. Moroccans, therefore, rarely eat with their left hand, perhaps only using it to drink from or maybe to pass bread. If you are eating from a communal tagine, eat with your right hand only. The respectful procedure when offered food is to politely decline and, if offered again, to accept a small portion. Reciprocating the offer is also considered polite, and will afford respect. To decline an offer of food, simply pat your stomach and shake your head, followed by *"La, shukrran"* (No, thank you).

Punctuality: Punctuality is not one of the trademarks of Moroccans. Tasks are often achieved in "Moroccan time," which can be anything from a half-hour late for personal appointments to even arriving the next day. The exception to this rule is the country's guides—especially the faux guides and hustlers—who will be waiting long before any agreed time.

Hammams: Traditionally, Moroccan women used to bathe nude, but nowadays this isn't always the case, with many younger women (and most travelers) electing to go topless but wear underwear or bikini bottoms. This will not cause offense; those who choose to also wear a bra or bikini top may do so, but local women will wonder why the visitor doesn't, like them, bare all. Men, both Moroccan and Western, bathe in shorts. It's not necessary to shower beforehand.

The Global Etiquette Guide To Africa and the Middle East (Wiley Publishing, Inc.; 2002), written by cross-cultural expert Dean Foster, has some handy information for both business and leisure travelers on general cultural issues between Arabs and Westerners, and includes some specific advice regarding Morocco.

Holidays See "Holidays," earlier in this chapter.

Hospitals See "Health" on p. 33.

Internet Access See "Staying Connected," earlier in this chapter.

Language Moroccan Arabic (sometimes called *Darija*) is the country's official language. A distinctive dialect of the worldwide Modern Standard Arabic (MSA), it is largely a spoken, rather than written, language. Newspapers and official documentation will therefore usually be written in MSA. Moroccan Arabic is constantly evolving, and includes words adapted from Spanish, English, and French. French is widely spoken throughout the country, and is the language of business, commerce, and, to a large degree, tourism. English is becoming a popular language to learn in universities, and is spoken frequently in heavily touristed areas. The regional languages of the country's Berbers are widely spoken in the Atlas mountains and central Morocco, although French and some English will be spoken in the more touristed areas. For a Moroccan Arabic/French/English glossary, see appendix B.

Laundromats Very few laundromats are found within Morocco, and even fewer are self-service. Most Moroccans wash their everyday clothes at home, and use dry cleaners (*m'sbana* in Arabic, *pressing* in French) for their suits, *jellabahs*, and other fine dresswear. Where applicable, I've mentioned the laundry options available to travelers within each chapter's "Fast Facts" section.

Legal Aid If you need legal assistance, your first (and only) option is to contact your embassy or consulate. Remember that it is illegal to bribe a police officer or public official in Morocco—even though the practice is commonplace. If you have been dealing with a local guide, sometimes they can help with translation, though they will be very wary of treading on the police's toes.

Liquor Laws Contrary to preconceived notions, liquor is available throughout much of Morocco. Many Moroccans—mainly men—drink, but do so privately. The legal drinking age for Moroccans is 18, but for visitors this is a gray area, as most establishments will serve you no matter what the age (within reason, of course). Moroccan bars, called brasseries, are usually smoky, dingy drinking dens frequented by Moroccan men and prostitutes. Most top-end restaurants and many *maisons d'hôte* will also offer alcohol, as will nightclubs in the resorts of Agadir and Marrakech. The business hours of these establishments vary from town to town, but you'll find most restaurants are closed by 11pm and local brasseries by midnight, while nightclubs and hotel bars may stay open until 4 or 5am, especially in tourist areas. To find a shop selling alcohol, it's best to ask at your hotel reception, or locate a branch of the national supermarket chains Acima and Marjane, mentioned where applicable in the "Shopping" sections throughout this book. Drinking alcohol in public is frowned upon and downright ignorant if practiced near a mosque.

Lost & Found Be sure to tell all of your credit card companies the minute you discover your wallet has been lost or stolen, and file a report at the nearest police precinct. Your credit card company or insurer may require a police report number or record of the loss. Most credit card companies have an emergency toll-free number to call if your card is lost or stolen; they may be able to wire you a cash advance immediately or deliver an emergency credit card in a day or two.

There's no Moroccan emergency number for American Express, Visa, or MasterCard cardholders, so all companies offer a reverse-charge phone number to the U.S.: **American Express** (© **336/393-1111**); **Visa** (© **410/581-9994** or -3836); and **MasterCard** (© **636/722-7111**). If you need emergency cash over the weekend when all banks and American Express offices are closed, you can have money wired to you via **Western Union** (© **800/325-6000**; www.westernunion.com).

Mail The Moroccan postal service **(Maroc Post)** is fairly reliable, with postcards and letters taking between 1 to 3 weeks to international destinations, depending on where you post from. A postcard or small letter costs 7dh to 8dh (90¢–$1/45p–50p) to Europe, 9dh to 12dh ($1.15–$1.50/55p–75p) to the U.S., and 10dh to 15dh ($1.25–$1.90/65p–95p) to Australia. A package weighing 1kg (2.2 lbs.) costs around 110dh ($14/£6.90) to Europe, 150dh ($19/£9.40) to the U.S., and 195dh ($24/£12) to Australia and New Zealand. Post offices are open Monday to Friday 8am to 4:15pm, and Saturday 8 to 11:45am. Stamps *(timbres)* can be purchased from post offices and sometimes from souvenir shops and *tabacs,* which also sell cigarettes and sometimes newspapers. Separate parcel counters are found in all post offices, and all packages need to be inspected beforehand. **DHL** and **FedEx** offices are located at various cities within the country, and are listed in each applicable city's "Fast Facts."

Newspapers & Magazines All major newspapers and magazines in Morocco are in either Arabic (MSA) or French. Weekly international editions of *The Guardian, Herald Tribune,* and *Time* magazine can sometimes be found at newspaper vendors in the major cities, and are listed where applicable in each city's "Fast Facts" section.

Passports Allow plenty of time before your trip to apply for a passport. Processing normally takes 3 weeks, but can take much longer during busy periods (especially spring). If you need a passport in a hurry, you'll pay a higher processing fee.

For Residents of Australia: You can pick up an application from your local post office or any branch of Passports Australia, but you must schedule an interview at the passport office to present your application materials. Call the **Australian Passport Information Service** at © **131-232,** or visit the government website at www.passports.gov.au.

For Residents of Canada: Passport applications are available at travel agencies throughout Canada or from the central **Passport Office,** Department of

Foreign Affairs and International Trade, Ottawa, ON K1A 0G3 (℗ **800/567-6868**; www.ppt.gc.ca).

For Residents of Ireland: You can apply for a 10-year passport at the **Passport Office**, Setanta Centre, Molesworth Street, Dublin 2 (℗ **01/671-1633**; www.irl gov.ie/iveagh). Those under 18 and over 65 must apply for a 3-year passport. You can also apply at 1A South Mall, Cork (℗ **021/272-525**), or at most main post offices.

For Residents of New Zealand: You can pick up a passport application at any New Zealand Passports Office or download it from their website. Contact the **Passports Office** at ℗ **0800/225-050** in New Zealand or 04/474-8100, or log on to www.passports.govt.nz.

For Residents of the United Kingdom: To pick up an application for a standard 10-year passport (5-year passport for children under 16), visit your nearest passport office, major post office, or travel agency. Or, contact the **United Kingdom Passport Service** at ℗ **0870/521-0410,** or search its website at www. ukpa.gov.uk.

For Residents of the United States: Whether you're applying in person or by mail, you can download passport applications from the U.S. State Department website at **http://travel.state.gov**. To find your regional passport office, either check the U.S. State Department website, or call the **National Passport Information Center** toll-free number (℗ **877/487-2778**) for automated information.

Photographic Needs Photo stores can be found all over Morocco. Although the number of these shops offering digital services—such as copying images to CD and selling digital accessories—are increasing, for the moment most shops' services usually revolve around film-processing services and the supply of film (usually only Fuji and/or Kodak, and only 100 ASA) and sometimes camera batteries.

Police See "Safety" for information on Morocco's police forces. For **police** assistance, dial ℗ **19** anywhere in the country.

Restrooms There are very few public restrooms in Morocco, and those that are anywhere near hygienic I have mentioned in each destination's "Fast Facts." Most restaurants will allow you to use their *toilette* if you ask politely. Sometimes there might be a small fee, or if there is an attendant keeping them clean, 2 to 3 dirham (25¢–40¢/15p–20p) is expected.

Safety See "Safety," earlier in this chapter.

Smoking Smoking is common and an accepted part of the Moroccan lifestyle, thus there aren't many designated nonsmoking areas to be found. This isn't so much of an inconvenience at the outdoor cafes and restaurants, but if you are sensitive to smoke, then it's worth checking out the haze in an indoor cafe or restaurant before you sit down. Thankfully, it's considered impolite to smoke inside public transport.

Taxes The main indirect tax in Morocco is a value-added tax (VAT), with rates of between 7% and 14% included in the cost of basic goods and services, including those offered in all restaurants and hotels. A recently introduced Tourist Promotion Tax (TPT) is supposed to be added onto the cost of your accommodations. During the research of this book, I found some accommodations already doing this, some are adding it on to your bill at the end of your stay, and some are not even aware of it. The amount is between 5dh and 15dh (65¢–$1.90/30p–95p) per person per night, depending on the grade of accommodations.

Time Zone Morocco is on Greenwich Mean Time year-round. The Spanish enclaves of Ceuta and Melilla keep Spanish time, which is GMT plus 1 hour in winter, and GMT plus 2 hours in summer. Remember to keep this in mind when traveling by ferry from/to the Spanish mainland.

Tipping Tipping is expected by Moroccans for every service provided to you, whether you requested the service or not. Sometimes those asking for a tip are bordering on begging considering the assistance or service—if any—that was given. However, it's best not to fight this national habit and rather enjoy your time with no hassle. The expected minimum tip for any meal or drink is 10%. For informal services such as parking attendants and luggage porters, I usually give 5dh to 10dh (65¢–$1.25/30p–65p). If asked to tip when taking a photo, I usually pay 10dh to 20dh ($1.25–$2.50/65p–£1.25). For guiding services it depends on how much guidance was given and whether it was any good or not. For official guides, budget on a 10% tip per person. For faux guides who have perhaps assisted with a small navigational problem, 5dh to 10dh (65¢–$1.25/30p–65p) is enough. For other services such as petrol attendants and taxi drivers, I usually round up to the nearest 5 dirham. These are relatively small amounts and are worth shelling out to both create harmony between Moroccans and tourists and save you from continuous hassle and agitation.

Useful Phone Numbers

- U.S. Dept. of State Travel Advisory: ✆ 202/647-5225 (manned 24 hr.)
- U.S. Passport Agency: ✆ 202/647-0518
- U.S. Centers for Disease Control International Traveler's Hot Line: ✆ 404/332-4559
- U.S. Embassy in Rabat: ✆ 037/762265
- U.K. Embassy in Rabat: ✆ 037/633333
- Canadian Embassy in Rabat: ✆ 037/687400

Water Much of Morocco's water is potable but may upset Westerners' stomachs (see "Common Ailments" on p. 35). Bottled drinking water is available everywhere and is inexpensive, although some restaurants charge an exorbitant markup. From any street-side shop, a 1.5-liter bottle of water will cost no more than 8dh ($1/50p).

3

Suggested Morocco Itineraries

Where else in the world can you spend your morning swimming in the ocean, eat lunch amongst snowcapped mountains, and end the day by watching the sun set over Saharan sands? Granted, you'd be pushing it to achieve this—though it is possible—but it illustrates the range of diverse landscapes and experiences that Morocco offers. The relatively compact area, good roads, and reliable public transportation allow travelers to squeeze a lot into each day. In just 2 weeks, most of Morocco's must-see destinations can be visited, while those with less time may have to prioritize between the coast and the desert. All of the itineraries listed here are scheduled pretty tightly, and those traveling by public transport may need to factor in an extra day here and there.

1 Marrakech & Essaouira in 1 Week

This popular itinerary combines the mysterious allure of Marrakech with the relaxed coastal vibe of Essaouira. Throw in a day visit to the valleys below the often snowcapped Western High Atlas, and you'll get more than enough out of your weeklong holiday.

Day ❶: Arrive in Marrakech

Marrakech's weather can be energy-sapping hot or surprisingly cold, depending on the time of year. Either way, give yourself time today to get used to the temperature as well as the city's general hustle and bustle. An afternoon ride on the double-decker **City Sightseeing bus** (p. 144) is a perfect, hassle-free way to get your bearings and absorb the atmosphere, passing the city's iconic sights such as the **Koutoubia Mosque** (p. 138) and **Jemaa el Fna** (p. 108). Later this afternoon, make your way to the incomparable cuisine and entertainment spectacle taking place on Jemaa el Fna.

Day ❷: Discover the Medina

Today's the day to "enter the fray" and discover this city's heart and soul. Hire a guide for a morning walking tour, taking in one or two historical sights, a visit to a

herboriste and some of the souks, and a stop along the way for a mint tea. You'll no doubt be led to a few shops along the way, so make the most of the situation by taking mental notes of each item's general price and quality, preparing yourself for a return visit should you be seriously interested in something. If you haven't already done so, be sure to head to Jemaa el Fna for the late afternoon and evening show. Perhaps treat yourself tonight with dinner at one of the city's many romantic and ambience-filled restaurants in the medina such as **Café Arabe** (p. 132) or **Narwama** (p. 132), or **Le Grand Café de la Poste** (p. 134) in Guéliz.

Day ❸: Visit the Mountains

Head to the nearby Western High Atlas, only a 1- to 2-hour drive away from the sprawling metropolis of Marrakech (but up to 10°F cooler and with far less

hassle and noise). Around the villages of **Imlil** (p. 161), **Ouirgane** (p. 162), and **Oukaïmeden** (p. 162), you'll find some of the country's tallest mountain peaks, inhabited by overwhelmingly friendly Atlas Berbers, and places to have lunch or a mint tea that range from rustic local teahouses to five-star international restaurants.

Day ④: Essaouira

Three to 4 hours away from Marrakech is Essaouira, easily Morocco's most likeable seaside resort. After checking into one of the medina's many *maisons d'hôte*, soak up the atmosphere with a wander along the city's pedestrian-only streets, including visits to the numerous **souks** (p. 140) such as Souk el Ghezel, known as the

Spice Souk; La Joutia, the town's flea market; and place Marché de Grains (the old corn market). Catch the sunset atop the ocean-facing ramparts, **Le Skala de Kasbah,** followed by a dinner of fresh seafood at one of the port's relaxed fish grills.

Day ⑤: Sand, Shops & Seafood

Quality beach time—usually best in the morning before the sea breeze cranks up—and visits to a few of the medina's shops and galleries is best combined with a long, lazy lunch and a romantic dinner in any number of medina and beachside restaurants. Call in to see the El Asri family in the **Souk des Bijoutiers** (Jeweler's Souk; p. 353), find a bargain in Abdellatif al Koujdaih's **carpet shop** (p. 356), and discover the many benefits of argan oil in **Arga d'Or** (p. 356). Take an extended lunch break at the **Océan Vagabond** beach shack (p. 351), and finish the day with a sunset dinner at the legendary beachfront institution **Le Chalet de la Plage** (p. 350).

Day ❻: Back to Marrakech
Arrive back in Marrakech with enough time to complete any outstanding shopping, followed by a last visit to Jemaa el Fna. Perhaps spoil yourself with an overnight stay in one of the palmeraie's all-inclusive, luxurious villas such as the regal **Dar Ayniwen** (p. 128) or chic **Dar Zemora** (p. 128).

Day ❼: Going Home
Most direct flights to the U.K., as well as those to Casablanca for connecting flights to elsewhere, depart from Marrakech in the morning.

2 Marrakech & the Sahara in 1 Week

This week affords a taste of the more popular vision of Morocco—the exotic city of Marrakech along with some of the country's most scenic pre-Saharan oases and sand dunes. Some travelers will substitute the Erg Chigaga dunes for those at Erg Chebbi, though they may find themselves spending more time traveling than they would like.

Days ❶ & ❷
See days 1 and 2 in "Marrakech & Essaouira in 1 Week," above.

Day ❸: Amezrou Palmeraie
Today's journey up and over the Western High Atlas to Zagora is a long one, but the spectacular drive includes both mountainous and desert scenery. Overnight in the quiet palmeraie of **Amezrou** (p. 191) and enjoy the clear, starlit night.

Day ❹: Erg Chigaga Desert Dunes
Make time for a fascinating morning's walk through the village of Amezrou, organized through the **Bienvenue Amezrou** project (p. 191). In the afternoon, head to the end of the tarred road at **M'hamid** (p. 192) and continue on to the imposing sand sea of **Erg Chigaga** (p. 192). Be there in time to watch the hazy sunset atop one of its 300m-high (984-ft.) dunes. You can sleep outside under the stars or inside a traditional goat-hair Berber tent.

Day ❺: Ouarzazate
A predawn rise will afford you a magical, serene sunrise before setting out on the long drive back past M'hamid and Zagora to the French-built city of **Ouarzazate** (p. 178), Morocco's film capital. Ouarzazate has a good range of hotels and restaurants, and if there's a movie shoot in town, you might even spot a Hollywood star or two.

Days ❻ & ❼: Back to Marrakech
From Ouarzazate to Marrakech, detour to the mud-walled kasbahs of **Aït Ben Haddou** (p. 187) and **Telouet** (p. 168). Upon arrival in Marrakech, finish off your shopping list or take a stroll through the lesser visited areas within the medina, such as the kasbah and **Mellah,** or Jewish quarter (p. 141). If you've had your fill of medina madness, consider splurging on a night out in the **palmeraie** (p. 128). Prepare to head home the next morning.

3 Fes, Meknes & the Sahara in 1 Week

This busy week is a great mix of history, culture, and landscape. Unless you desperately wish to visit Marrakech, I consider this a better 1-week option, combining both medina and desert.

Day ❶: Arrive in Fes

Staying within Fes el Bali's (Old Fes) walls is the only way to experience this ancient city. Navigating your way around can initially be overwhelming, so prearrange with your accommodations for an escort to guide you to their doors. If you have time, stop off at one of the **medina viewpoints** (p. 223).

Day ❷: Discover the Medina

Spend the day wandering some of the 9,500 lanes and alleys accompanied by an official guide or the excellent *Bab to Bab* book and map. Tonight may be a good night to don your tourist hat and enjoy the dinner spectacular at **Restaurant al Fassia** (p. 224).

Day ❸: Meknes, Volubilis & Moulay Idriss Zerhoun

Two of the country's most sacred sites, along with its best preserved Roman ruins, can all be visited as a day tour from Fes. The **Mausoleum of Moulay Ismail** (p. 250) is a tranquil, serene place in Meknes and is one of the few shrines in the country that is open to non-Muslims. The village of **Moulay Idriss Zerhoun** (p. 253) is a place of pilgrimage for Moroccans, who come here to pay homage to the founder of the country's first Islamic dynasty. Non-Muslims aren't allowed to enter his shrine but are welcome to wander the village's steep, winding streets and to absorb the almost festive atmosphere that emanates from here.

Best visited at the start or end of the day, the ruins of the Roman city of **Volubilis** (p. 254) are well worth a visit. Partially restored during colonial times and currently undergoing renovation to its visitor center, the 40-hectare (99-acre) site contains a triumphal arch, forum, and basilica, along with some slowly fading mosaics.

Day ❹: Atlas Mountains to the Desert

Travel through both the Middle and High Atlas ranges on your way to the country's northern sand dunes. The landscape changes from fertile farming plains to mountains dotted with cedar trees or sliced by deep gorges and palmeraies before flattening out to the pre-Saharan *hammada*. The sleepy town of **Erfoud** (p. 203) awaits at the end of this long day's travel.

Day ❺: Step onto Saharan Sands

A short drive from Erfoud brings you to the various accommodations at the foot of the Erg Chebbi, a "mountain range" of sometimes rust, sometimes gold sand dunes fed by the shifting sands of the Sahara desert. Do as the locals do and follow lunch with an afternoon siesta. Later in the day, hop on board your one-humped steed for a 1- to 2-hour camel trek to your overnight camp amongst the dunes. Enjoy sunset atop one of this sand sea's 150m-high (492-ft.) dunes before spending the night under the stars.

Day ❻: Back to Fes

After a magical sunrise, your camel will return you to your hotel where breakfast and a welcome shower are followed by a long day's drive back through the High and Middle Atlas ranges to Fes. Alternatively, stay the night in the university mountain village of **Ifrane** (p. 257) and continue to Fes the next morning.

Day ❼: Going Home

Some direct flights to the U.K. depart later in the day, so you may have time to visit the **Mellah,** or Jewish quarter (p. 232), of Fes el Jdid (New Fes) or take one last wander up Fes el Bali's main thoroughfares, Tala'a Kbira or Tala'a Sghira, finishing the walk with a mint tea at one of the cafe-restaurants near **Bab Bou Jeloud** (p. 226).

4 The Imperial Cities in 10 Days

This itinerary is big on culture, bypassing the Saharan side of the Atlas mountain ranges to visit Morocco's present and past imperial capitals. Although Casablanca was never the country's capital, it has become the economic heartbeat of the country and is worth a stop if only to visit Rick's Café and say, "Play it again, Sam."

Days ❶ & ❷

See days 1 and 2 in "Marrakech & Essaouira in 1 Week," above.

Day ❸: Marrakech to Fes

It's a long day's travel, but self-drivers should have time to break the journey with a visit to the **Cascades d'Ouzoud** (p. 171). Arriving into Fes after dark can be a little challenging, so ask your accommodations for clear directions.

Days ❹ & ❺: Fes

Spend the next 2 days wandering around the ancient city of Fes el Bali. Giving yourself this much time allows for both a guided morning walk—visiting sights such as the **Bou Inania Medersa** (p. 229), **Nejjarine Museum of Wooden Arts & Crafts** (p. 231), and **Chouwara Tannery** (p. 230)—as well as a look (from the outside) of the spiritual **Kairouine Mosque** (p. 230). You'll also have plenty of time to explore on your own. Be sure to dine one night at the **Restaurant al Fassia** (p. 224); it's touristy but great fun.

Day ❻: Volubilis, Moulay Idriss Zerhoun & Meknes

Visit the ruins in the Roman city of **Volubilis** (p. 254) early in the morning to beat both the crowds and the heat. Have lunch in the nearby spiritual village of **Moulay Idriss Zerhoun** (p. 253), watching the pilgrims as they come to visit the shrine of the founding father of Morocco. Arrive in **Meknes** (p. 238) in the early afternoon and visit another important shrine, that of the country's longest-serving ruler, Moulay Ismail. Stay the night in one of Meknes's few medina riads.

Day ❼: Rabat

Rabat (p. 299) has been the capital since the beginning of the French protectorate in 1912. It's a pleasant city cooled by the afternoon Atlantic sea breeze and lacks the general noise and bustle of Morocco's other major cities. This afternoon, visit the **Mausoleum of Mohammed V** (p. 313), the burial place of the current king's father and grandfather. On the same site is the imposing 12th-century **Hassan Tower** (p. 313), looking out over the mouth of the Oued Bou Regreg. Stroll through the medina and up along rue des Consuls to the charming **Kasbah des Oudaïas** (p. 313).

Day ❽: Casablanca

South of Rabat is the nation's economic capital, Casablanca (p. 317). Stroll downtown (largely a French creation) to admire the many Art Deco buildings still standing. An early evening aperitif at **Rick's Café** (p. 329) is highly recommended. If you don't wish to stay for dinner, head to the restaurant and bar strip opposite the central market.

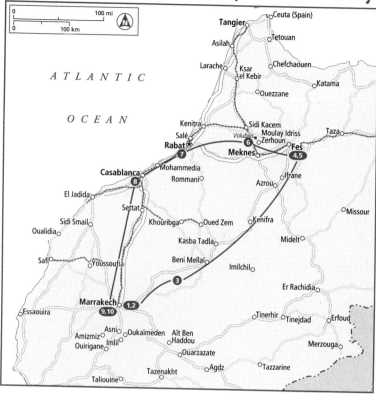

Days ❾ & ❿: Back to Marrakech

A new highway has made today's travel faster and more bearable. Arrive back in Marrakech for any last-minute shopping or for another fix of people-watching on Jemaa el Fna. Prepare to leave early to late morning the next day.

5 Morocco in 2 Weeks

Days ❶ & ❷

See "Marrakech & Essaouira in 1 Week," above.

Day ❸: Over the High Atlas & toward the Saharan Sands

Leave the plains behind and travel up and over the mighty Western High Atlas via the Tizi n'Tichka pass. Stop off at the very picturesque, mud-walled kasbah at **Aït ben Haddou** (p. 187) before spending the night in Morocco's very pleasant movie capital, **Ouarzazate** (p. 178).

Day ❹: Valleys & Gorges

Enjoy the beautifully scenic drive along the **Dadès Valley** (p. 196), also called The Valley of a Thousand Kasbahs. Reach Tinerhir by afternoon and make your way up the Todra Valley, following the path of the Oued Todra to where it bubbles up from the earth below at the foot of the 300m-high (984-ft.) **Todra Gorge** (p. 198). If the weather's warm, sleeping on a hotel rooftop within the gorge allows for some excellent star gazing.

Morocco in 2 Weeks

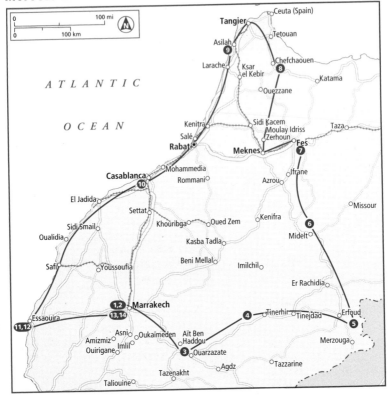

Day ❺: The Saharan Sands
Reach your accommodations at the foot of the Erg Chebbi dunes—near the small villages of Merzouga and Hassi Labied—by mid-afternoon. If you're up for it, board your trusty camel for a 1- to 2-hour trek into the sand dunes of **Erg Chebbi** (p. 202). Sunset and sunrise on top of your own dune is an almost spiritual experience for some.

Day ❻: Over the Atlas Mountains to Fes
This is a long day's journey traveling up and over both the High and Middle Atlas mountain ranges, and will take some perseverance and planning if traveling by

public transport. If you're staying within the Fes el Bali medina, prearrange your accommodations and ask for clear directions to their front door, or arrange an escort to guide you.

Day ❼: Ancient Fes
With more than 9,500 lanes and alleys within Fes el Bali's walls, it may be best to arrange a guide to show you the major sights for half a day, followed by some of your own exploration and shopping.

Day ❽: The Rif to Chefchaouen
If you have your own transport, depart Fes early and visit the nearby sights of **Meknes** (p. 238), **Moulay Idriss Zerhoun**

(p. 253), and **Volubilis** (p. 254). Today's final destination is the Rif mountain village of **Chefchaouen** (p. 285). Enjoy an evening of excellent people-watching on **place Outa el Hammam** (p. 291), the village's heart.

Day ❾: From Mountains to Ocean

Rise early for a short hike up to the **Spanish Mosque** (p. 291) or take a morning stroll through the luminous blue streets of Chefchaouen. Travel down the Rif mountains by afternoon, arriving in Tangier with enough time to continue on to the popular seaside village of **Asilah** (p. 292). If you've traveled in good time, you'll be sitting on the medina's ramparts by sunset, gazing out into the Atlantic Ocean.

Day ❿: Heading South along the Coast

A morning arrival in **Rabat** (p. 299) will give you enough time to visit the Mausoleum of Mohammed V, the burial shrine of the current king's father and grandfather, and the adjoining Hassan Tower before continuing on to nation's "other" capital, **Casablanca** (p. 317). Wander through the city's small medina, arriving at **Rick's Café** (p. 329) in time

for early-evening aperitifs or late evening for a cocktail and some tunes from resident piano man Issam Chaaba.

Day ⓫: Essaouira

Visit the monumental **Hassan II Mosque** (p. 332)—one of the world's largest and open to non-Muslims—before setting out for the seaside town of **Essaouira** (p. 338), a long-standing traveler's favorite. Enjoy dinner at the fresh seafood grills between the medina's main square and the port.

Day ⓬: Beach & Shopping

Take your time today to enjoy Essaouira's beach and medina. In between sessions of sunbathing and shopping, enjoy more fresh seafood at the basic restaurants located within the medina's fish market, or find a cozy, warm restaurant for an intimate, candle-lit meal.

Days ⓭ & ⓮: Back to Marrakech

Arrive back in Marrakech by afternoon to seek out some last-minute shopping in the medina's souks or at one of the specialist boutiques in the ville nouvelle. Splurge tonight on a romantic dinner at one of the city's fine restaurants, or be in the thick of the action on Jemaa el Fna before flying out tomorrow morning.

4

The Active Vacation Planner

Morocco is a prime destination for the active and adventurous traveler. Throughout the country, you'll find ways to experience Morocco's diverse culture and natural landscapes and, at the same time, enjoy a wide range of sports and activities. Morocco's compact size affords travelers the luxury of catching a wave before breakfast, heading up to the mountains for a prelunch hike, and finishing the day astride a camel on the edge of the Sahara.

Within Morocco is a well-established adventure travel industry that is run by both international and local operators, and offers a range of both "soft" and "hard" options. Whether you want adventure travel to be the focus of your trip or you want to treat it as an extra to a more conventional holiday, there are a number of ways to approach it.

This chapter outlines everything from tour operators offering combination or special-interest packages to the best locations in Morocco to enjoy specific activities. Some activities—such as birdwatching and mountain trekking—are

located within Morocco's underfunded national parks and nature reserves. Although the government has recently created four new national parks, the total protected area within Morocco is less than 1%. Of that miniscule amount, much of the land is still used by bordering communities for grazing and firewood, and information centers or other visitor facilities are practically nonexistent. By far the country's most-visited park is the **Toubkal National Park** in the Western High Atlas, and there's talk that the government may begin charging an admission levy (there are no entrance fees to any of the country's protected areas) on visitors, a move already agreed to in principle by many trekking operators, so long as the funds are used toward the park itself. At the end of this chapter, I've highlighted the small group of eco-tourism operators who are truly dedicated to responsible and sustainable tourism within Morocco, as well as educational and volunteer options for those who are interested in a more in-depth, extended stay in the country.

1 Organized Adventure Trips

Because many travelers have limited time and resources, organized adventure-travel packages, arranged by tour operators abroad or in Morocco, are a popular and time-efficient way to enjoy activity- and time-specific trips such as climbing Jebel Toubkal or weeklong biking and hiking tours. It's also a good way to experience an activity within a broader sightseeing itinerary.

Group travel can produce several advantages over independent travel. The most obvious is having all your accommodations and transport prearranged, and some (if not all) of your meals included in the cost of a package. Reasonably experienced and professional tour operators should also be able to transport you to each destination or activity without the snags and long delays that those traveling on their own can encounter in Morocco. As an added bonus, you'll have the opportunity to meet like-minded travelers. Joining an organized mountain-trekking tour will usually include prearranged porters or muleteers to carry extra equipment—sometimes even your own backpack. Dedicated independent travelers will no doubt point out that it always costs extra for the convenience of having all your arrangements handled, and paid for, in advance.

In the best scenario for organized active vacations, group size is kept small (10–16 people) in comparison to the large, escorted bus tours, and tours are conducted by qualified guides knowledgeable about a particular activity. Within this chapter, I've mentioned when specific tours or activities are led by specialists, such as naturalists, professors, and the like. Be sure to ask about difficulty levels when you're choosing an active tour. While most companies offer "soft adventure" packages suitable for those in decent (but not necessarily phenomenal) shape, others focus on more strenuous activities geared toward athletic and seasoned adventure travelers.

Moroccan-based operators dedicated to adventure travel are still very thin on the ground, and those that are involved are usually either owned by non-Moroccans and also have a base outside the country, or are activity specific and are therefore mentioned in this chapter under each specialist activity. Other local companies that pertain to adventure-travel specialists are really just general-interest tour operators that have caught on to this particular market and offer a few activities only when specifically requested, and usually within a much broader base of general sightseeing tours. I have listed such companies in chapter 2. However, it's worth noting that many tour operators contract their ground operations to a locally based outfit that then deals with even smaller operations (such as guides and muleteers for mountain trekking), resulting in some of your tour cost trickling down to the Moroccans themselves.

TOUR OPERATORS

- **Andante Travels** (© 01722/713800; www.andantetravels.co.uk) has been organizing archaeology and ancient-history tours from their U.K. base since 1985. Their group sizes are small, and groups are accompanied by both a tour manager and a specialist lecturer guide. Their current Morocco offering is the annual 9-day tour to Marrakech, Fes, and Volubilis, plus they have an additional tour penciled in for 2008 that visits prehistoric engravings and paintings in the Souss Valley and Anti-Atlas.

- **Biotrek Adventure Travels** (© **866/246-8735** toll-free or 540/349-0040; www.biotrektours.com) was created by Sunny Reynolds, a professional photographer, in 1991. The company organizes tours to countries including Morocco, India, Tanzania, Costa Rica, and Guatemala. Trips depart from Washington, D.C., and groups are never more than 10 people.

- **Dragoman Overland** (© 01728/861133; www.dragoman.com) is based in the U.K. and operates grassroots tours in their own overland-style trucks through Africa, the Americas, and Asia. The tours are usually camping-oriented with group participation, and the trucks are self-sufficient with cooking equipment, water tanks, and tents. They have a 2-week round-trip from Marrakech that is specially geared toward families, with a combination of camping and hotels. The tour visits central Morocco attractions such as the Aït ben Haddou kasbah, the Dadès Valley, and the Erg Chebbi desert dunes, along with the Western High Atlas village of Imlil and the Atlantic port city of Essaouira. Morocco is also included in their 5-week overland from Malaga, Spain, to Dakar, Senegal.

- **Epic Morocco** ★★ (© 020/8150-6131; www.epicmorocco.co.uk) is a small U.K.-owned, Marrakech-based tour operator. Owned and managed by Anglo-French couple Charlie Shepherd and Melodie Selvon, they specialize in high-quality, small-group mountain biking, walking, and horse-riding tours in Morocco. They offer a fascinating "Walking with Nomads" experience, which accompanies a family from the Aït Atta tribe as they make their annual migration with their flocks to greener pastures in either the High Atlas or Jebel Sarhro mountain regions. Other tours offer hiking and biking combinations, or they can tailor-make tours to suit.

- **Explore! Worldwide** (© 0870/333-4001; www.explore.co.uk) is a U.K.-based operator specializing in small-group adventure holidays worldwide (currently more than 300 tours to more than 130 countries). Their tours cover a wide range of styles, accommodations, and themes such as cycling, trekking, astronomy, and history, as well as dedicated family adventures. They currently offer 18 trips in Morocco, ranging from 5-day mountain treks to a 10-day itinerary that takes in Andalusian Spain.

- **Imaginative Traveller** (© 0800/316-2717 toll-free or 01473/667337; www.imaginative-traveller.com) is a U.K.-based outfit specializing in small-group adventure travel worldwide. Their tours come in a range of styles catering to everyone from the independent-minded to the connoisseur traveler. They offer 13 itineraries in Morocco, some of them led by their own leaders and some by local guides. The 15-day "Morocco Caravan" is a good mix of trekking and sightseeing, with plenty of free time for exploring.

- **Intrepid Travel** ★ (© 1300/364-512 toll-free or 03/8602-0500; www.intrepid travel.com) is an Australian-based adventure-travel specialist that has been taking travelers "off the beaten track" since 1989. They offer small-group tours for individuals, couples, and families, with varying levels of comfort and activities. Their current selection includes a dozen tours within Morocco, which includes trekking, cycling, and photographic and general-interest itineraries, along with a few other tours combining a visit to Morocco within a larger tour of southern Europe or North Africa.

- **Journeys International** ★★ (© 800/255-8735 toll-free or 734/665-4407; www.journeys-intl.com), based in the U.S., offers small group (4–12 people) natural-history tours guided by naturalists. Trips include an 8-day "Morocco Imperial Cities" tour, which gives you an in-depth look at the country's cultural and historical centers, and a more general 12-day "Discover Morocco."

- **KE Adventure Travel** (© 800/497-9675 toll-free in the U.S., or 0176/877366 and 1303/321-0085 in the U.K.; www.keadventure.com) is a leading independent-adventure-travel specialist offering a range of tour styles to more than 140 destinations worldwide. Their Moroccan itineraries are unique and diverse, ranging from an 8-day camel trek for families to a 15-day trekking/white-water rafting combo.

- **Nomadic Expeditions** (© 0870/2201718; www.nomadic.co.uk) is a U.K.-based company offering overland-style, group-participation tours in Morocco. Clients travel in self-sufficient overland safari trucks, complete with all cooking and camping gear and a driver and tour leader. Eight- and 15-day round-trip itineraries depart Tangier regularly from May to October, and there's also an 8-day round-trip from Marrakech that visits central Morocco and is hotel-based rather than camping.

- **Wilderness Travel** (© 800/368-2794 toll-free or 510/558-2488; www.wilderness travel.com) is a U.S.-based tour company specializing in cultural, hiking, and wildlife tours worldwide. Their 15-day "High Atlas Trek" travels from Casablanca to Marrakech via the Central High Atlas, and includes a 6-day trek around the Aït Bou Guemez Valley, with an optional 4-day extension to climb Jebel Toubkal. There's also a 15-day "Camels to Casbahs" tour from Casablanca to Marrakech via central Morocco and Essaouira. These two tours are arranged with tiered pricing (the cost varies according to group size). They also offer a 10-day private tour from Casablanca to Marrakech via central Morocco, with an Essaouira extension.

- **World Expeditions** (© 888/464-8735 toll-free in the U.S., 866/606-1721 toll-free in Canada, or 020/8545-9030 toll-free in the U.K.; www.worldexpeditions. com) is one of the world's original adventure-travel companies, organizing Himalayan treks since 1975. Their tours typically offer general-adventure tours as well as activity-specific trips such as sea kayaking, cycling, trekking, and mountaineering. They are highly regarded for their responsible tourism and environmental philosophies, and offer three tours in Morocco consisting of a 13-day trekking/sightseeing combo, a 14-day general sightseeing itinerary, and a combination of the two.

2 Activities A to Z

With so many outdoor options in Morocco, how do you choose? Here's a list of the various activities available, where to participate in them, and tour operators that specialize in related trips (though many of them will also offer the activity as part of a wider cultural sightseeing tour).

BALLOONING

In the late 1990s, Virgin founder Sir Richard Branson chose Morocco as his departure point for an ultimately unsuccessful attempt to circumnavigate the globe by balloon. The country is tailor-made for ballooning, one would think, with its scenic mountains, largely unspoiled coastline, and sweeping seas of Saharan sand dunes. It's taken a while, but there is now one sole outfitter operating balloon flights in Morocco. **Ciel d'Afrique** (© 024/432843; www.cieldafrique.info) is the passion of exuberant Frenchman Maurice Otin. His Marrakech-based operation offers scenic flights of the wide plains around (but not over) Marrakech and Ouarzazate, with the Western High Atlas as a backdrop. Hour-long flights start from 2,050dh ($256/£128) per person (half-price for kids under 10), with additional extras offered such as a champagne breakfast and video footage. It's best to contact Maurice as early as possible so that weather conditions can be taken into consideration.

BIRD-WATCHING

Morocco is one of North Africa's best birding locations. There's a wide range of easily accessed sites in a rich diversity of habitats that are often very different to those found in neighboring Europe. More than 480 species have been recorded in Morocco, and birders can usually find something of interest throughout the year. Having said that, the period from March to May is considered the optimum bird-watching season, as a wide variety of species—both resident and migrant—are present, and the weather is generally mild and sunny. Morocco is an important stop for millions of migrants on their way to and from western Europe, and more than 100 species are considered regular winter visitors. Morocco offers good opportunities to see a range of birds such as larks, raptors, warblers, water birds, and wheatears, along with a few specific species that are difficult to find elsewhere.

Merja Zerga 🐦🐦 (80km/50 miles south of Tangier) was declared a Ramsar Wetland of International Importance back in 1980, and is one of the largest lagoons in Morocco. During the winter months, it's possible to see more than 1,000 greater flamingoes, 30,000 ducks, 40,000 Eurasian coots, and 50,000 waders here. The small fishing village of Moulay Bousselham looks out over the lagoon, as well as the near-deserted Atlantic shoreline. Nearby is another Ramsar lagoon, the small but attractive **Lac de Sidi Boughaba** 🐦 (30km/19 miles north of Rabat), which is also known for its large winter flocks. Present at various times of the year here are various raptors such as the marsh harrier, montagu harrier, black-shouldered kite, and occasionally Eleonora's falcon. Occasionally spotted at both lagoons are the rare slender-billed curlew and marsh owl.

The **Souss-Massa National Park** stretches for 70km (43 miles) south of Agadir and is bordered by the Oued Souss and Oued Massa. Best visited between September and April, the mouths of both rivers are amongst the best bird sites in the country, offering excellent viewing of waders such as avocet, black-winged stilt, and oystercatcher, as well as numerous species of gulls and terns roosting on the sand bars. Also present are many large water birds such as great cormorant, little egret, greater flamingo, grey heron, spoonbill, white stork, and the less common purple heron and glossy ibis. The area leading up to the mouth of the Oued Massa is considered the best spot in Morocco to sight the critically endangered waldrapp, better known as the northern bald ibis, which breeds on the nearby coastal cliffs. The large concentration of water birds consequently attracts numerous species of raptors such as Bonelli's eagle, marsh harrier, and Barbary, lanner, and peregrine falcons.

The islands offshore from the attractive seaside port of **Essaouira** are one of the world's largest—and Morocco's only—breeding sites for the endangered Eleonora's falcon. This migrant breeder resides here from late April to the end of October, and while the protected islands offer very limited access, the falcon can often be seen hunting at the mouth of the Oued Ksob, to the south of Essaouira's wide bay, during the prebreeding months of May and June.

In the **Western High Atlas** mountains, both the highly sought-after white-rumped swift and Levaillant's woodpecker can often be seen in the valleys around Asni and Imlil, along with large flocks of both red-billed and alpine chough. The pleasant drive from **Marrakech to Oukaïmeden** passes through several habitats and offers diverse sightings such as rufous bush robin, alpine swifts, and black wheatear. The little-known crimson-winged finch is a rare resident that can be spotted around Ouakaïmeden, as well in the higher reaches of the **Middle Atlas.**

Possible sightings in the fertile lower valleys of both the **Oued Todra** and **Oued Dadès** include common bulbul, gold finch, hoopoe, scops owl, white stork, and blue tit, along with blackbird, nightingale, and various warblers. Breeding specifically in the Dadès Valley is the great spotted woodpecker. Both valleys are also good spots to sight spring migrants, including the pretty European bee-eater, while their gorges offer possible sightings of long-legged buzzard and golden and Bonelli's eagles.

Following the course of the often-dry Oued Dra, the **Dra Valley,** at various times through the year, is home to many varied species, including little owl and Egyptian vulture. From April to September, the sought-after blue-cheeked bee-eater can also be spotted here, as well as in the palm groves of the **Tafilalt** region around Erfoud and Merzouga.

Another prized Moroccan sighting is the tristram's warbler, which breeds solely in the scrub of the High Atlas mountains (but is a winter visitor to both the Dadès and Dra valleys) and the tamarisk trees found along the fringe of the **Erg Chebbi** desert dunes near Merzouga. It also winters in the **Souss Valley,** which is well known for regular sightings of tawny eagle and dark chanting goshawk.

Special mention must also be made of the impressive migration across the **Straits of Gibraltar,** which can be observed onshore within the vicinity of Tangier. More than 250 mainly European species have been recorded making the 15km (9-mile) crossing—mainly between March and May and August and October—including bee-eaters, finches, flamingoes, gulls, larks, shearwaters, swallows, and wagtails, along with high concentrations of raptors and storks.

As yet, there are no Moroccan-based English-speaking tour operators offering specialized birding tours, and local English-speaking specialists are also sparse. In the village of Moulay Bousselham, local ornithologist Hassan Dalil (© **068/434110**) comes highly recommended from fellow travelers, as witnessed in the Birder's Log housed in Restaurant Milano, on the one main street. Mohammed Zaki (© **066/659392;** zaki tours@yahoo.fr) specializes in the general wildlife (birdlife in particular) of Morocco's mountains and desert regions, and is often contracted by various U.K.-based operators. Saïd Ahmoume is Naturally Morocco's resident wildlife guide, with a particular passion for botany and ornithology. He can be contacted through Naturally Morocco (see "Responsible Tourism," later).

Some of the better English-language websites for birding in Morocco are **Go-South** (www.go-south.org), which also has an extensive archive of field reports; **African Bird Club** (www.africanbirdclub.org), a general information website; and **Bird Links to the World** (www.bsc-eoc.org/links), which, as the name suggests, is a dedicated site of links to other birding websites. An Internet chat forum—in English and French—dedicated to Moroccan birding can be found at http://fr.groups.yahoo.com/group/moroccobirding.

Considered the most comprehensive Moroccan ornithological field guide is the *Collins Bird Guide* (Collins, 1999) by Lars Svensson, Killian Mullarney, Dan Zetterstrom, and Peter J. Grant. Although it's subtitled "The Most Complete Guide to the Birds of Britain and Europe," the book's 392 pages cover Morocco as well. For something that's easier to pack, I recommend *A Birdwatchers' Guide to Morocco* (Prion Ltd., 2003) by Patrick and Fédora Bergier. The easy-to-read layout includes directions and a map to access each location, though its one downfall is the lack of any pictures for identification. *Birding in Morocco* (Gostours), by Dave Gosney, is a DVD covering a birding expedition by the author and is full of great footage of many of Morocco's birds.

TOUR OPERATORS

- **Field Guides** ✦ (© **800/728-4953** toll-free or 512/263-7295; www.fieldguides. com) is a specialist bird-watching tour operator with trips worldwide. They operate an irregular trip to Morocco—the next is in September 2009—that takes in the country's Atlantic coastline, Atlas mountain ranges, and central desert landscapes. Group size is usually limited to 14 participants.

- **Heatherlea** ⭐⭐ (☏ **01479/821248;** www.heatherlea.co.uk) is one of the U.K.'s leading wildlife holiday operators, specializing in birding tours worldwide. Their annual 11-day Morocco tour, usually departing at the end of March, is a round-trip from Marrakech, taking in the best birding sites of the Western High Atlas and central and southern Morocco. Group size is limited to 14 participants.
- **Naturetrek** (☏ **01962/733051;** www.naturetrek.co.uk) has more than 20 years' experience in operating natural history and wildlife holidays, including specialist bird-watching tours. This U.K.-based company currently offers four trips to Morocco, including a 5-day "Bald Ibis Break" and a 15-day itinerary that includes 10 days trekking through the Western High Atlas in search of birds and wildflowers.
- **Spanish Nature** ⭐⭐ (☏ **616/891359;** www.spanishbirds.com/spanishnature) is a small Spanish-based tour operator leading bird-watching trips throughout the year to Costa Rica, Spain, and Morocco. They are renowned for their leisurely paced itineraries and quality guides. Most Moroccan tours run for 11 days, and group size is kept to a maximum of 12.
- **Wings** (☏ **888/293-6443** toll-free; www.wingsbirds.com) has been offering bird-watching tours worldwide for the past 30 years. Their current brochure includes "Morocco in Fall," an 8-day ramble of the Souss Valley and Agadir coastline, which also includes an off-shore pelagic day trip. This trip is limited to 16 participants and includes two specialist leaders.

COOKING

An increasing number of travelers are combining their loves of cuisine and culture. Moroccans take great pride in their culinary skills, as well as their reputation as exemplary dinner hosts, and are always eager to share their kitchen knowledge. In the past, however, the language barrier proved a difficult hurdle for English-speaking travelers, but recently a few select options have begun operating in Fes and Marrakech. Clients are exposed to the other side of the kitchen, joining the cook as he or she visits the local produce souk, butcher, spice seller, and others. This is followed by hands-on instruction in the kitchen, after which you can sample your labor of love in a sit-down meal. Besides the operators listed below, some *maisons d'hôte* in Fes and Marrakech offer 1-day cooking lessons exclusively to their guests, such as **Dar Roumana** (p. 218) in Fes and **Dar les Cigognes** (p. 118) in Marrakech.

TOUR OPERATORS

- **Fes Cooking** ⭐⭐⭐ (☏ **015/866144;** www.fescooking.com) is operated by Lachen Beqqi, a young Fes-based chef who has quietly built up a reputation as a superb culinary guide. His English is as good as his humor, and clients rave about his culinary knowledge and his love for his country. Courses offered range from a single day lesson to a weeklong "Culinary Adventure," which includes visits to a Meknes winery and the Middle Atlas Berber village of Azrou.
- **The International Kitchen** (☏ **800/945-8606** toll-free or 312/467-0560; www.theinternationalkitchen.com) is based in the U.S. and has been providing cooking school vacations since 1994. It offers a range of itineraries to France, Italy, Spain, and Morocco, where its 7-day tour is based in Fes. Cooking lessons are intermingled with tours of the city as well as visits to nearby Meknes and Volubilis.

- **Rhode School of Cuisine** (© 888/254-1070 toll-free or 252/790222; www. rhodeschoolofcuisine.com) is a well-respected specialist gourmet holiday operator offering tours in Italy, France, and Morocco, where its Moroccan cooking school is based in a top-end *maison d'hôte* in Marrakech's palmeraie. It offers weeklong tours that cater to both culinary and gourmet guests, the former for those who wish to be in the kitchen, the latter for those who don't.
- **Souk Cuisine** (© 073/804955; www.soukcuisine.com) is a cooking school based in a riad within Marrakech's medina. Operated by English-speaking Dutchwoman Gemma Van de Burgt, the 1-day cooking classes are a great way to get to know Marrakech a little better and are very reasonably priced. There are also multiple-day options in conjunction with staying at a nearby *maison d'hôte.*

DESERT TREKKING

Morocco's Saharan sand dunes are the stuff of legend, and sitting astride a camel as the sun sets over the golden sands is surely the best way to experience them. The dunes are called ergs, or islands of sand fed by the Sahara Desert to the south, isolated from the main ocean of sand by a hard, stony barrier called *hammada.* Their ageless scenic beauty and sense of tranquillity, combined with their close proximity to the rest of the country, make desert trekking one of the country's most popular and rewarding experiences. The most easily accessible sand dunes are Erg Chebbi, at Merzouga, and Erg Chigaga, 55km (34 miles) south of M'hamid. There are other smaller dunes closer to M'hamid (Lehoudi and Messouira) and Zagora (Nakhla and Tinfou), as well as along the road between Tinejdad and Erfoud, but they will disappoint if you have come looking for waves of dunes rolling into the horizon.

Exploring the desert can last as little as a couple of hours to a multiple-week caravan trek. Most travelers opt for an overnight excursion, with the mode of travel—camel, 4WD, or a combination of both—dependent on your choice of sand dunes (p. 177). It's possible to organize this independently, but if you wish to head straight out to overnight in the dunes, you'll need to arrive very early at your *auberge* or pre-book. Camel treks should include all of your meals; some will also include bottled water, but it's worth taking an extra personal supply as well. I normally budget on two large bottles per night, plus a bottle of red wine for sunset on the dune. Blankets and rugs are provided, but they are usually communal, so you may want to take your own sleeping bag or inner sheet. Very rarely will any medical supplies be carried.

Desert camps are usually a collection of semi-permanent Berber tents, made from goat's hair. They keep the sand out if the wind is blowing, and are also naturally heated by the sun, which is good for the colder months when nighttime temperatures are decidedly chilly. Some camps, however, might not be as solitary as you'd imagined. The camp may be used by more than one company, or your individual booking may have been combined with others. If you're looking for solitude rather than company, remember that you can simply pick up your blankets and rugs and move out of the camp onto your own secluded dune. Even sleeping 30m (100 ft.) away will give you your own little piece of starlit Sahara.

Visiting the dunes is possible year-round, but from June to August the heat can be distressingly overwhelming. If you must visit at this time, I recommend Erg Chebbi due to the choice of *auberges* at the dunes' edge—especially if you're traveling with children—rather then the long, hot drive out to Erg Chigaga.

Camel treks organized locally start from 200dh ($25/£13) per person for a 2-hour excursion and 350dh ($44/£22) for an overnight stay in the dunes, including dinner and breakfast. Some companies offer 2 days/1 night return excursions from Fes or Marrakech, but they may only visit the smaller dunes near Zagora or will be traveling exceedingly long days to fit everything in within the 2 days.

TOUR OPERATORS

There are numerous operations—local and international—that organize desert experiences, but most of these companies include a desert trek as part of a wider tour of Morocco. These operators are either mentioned earlier in this chapter (see "Organized Adventure Trips") or in chapter 2 (see "Escorted General-Interest Tours"). Most of the hotels and *maisons d'hôte* mentioned in chapter 7 also organize desert excursions for their guests. Apart from the operators already recommended in chapter 7, other desert specialists include:

- **Blue Men of Morocco** (©/fax **952/467562;** www.bluemenofmorocco.com) is run by American Elena Hall, who divides her time between her two bases in Spain and Merzouga. Married to a local Berber, she is a desert expert and personally organizes each traveler's itinerary.
- **Desert Dream** (©/fax **024/885343;** www.sahara-desert-dream.com) is a Ouarzazate-based outfit specializing in desert excursions by both camel and 4WD, and recommended by fellow travelers.
- **Equatorial Travel** ✸✸✸ (© **01335/348770;** www.equatorialtravel.co.uk) is a small U.K.-based outfit operating on fair-trade principles and specializing in central and southern Morocco desert excursions, especially the area encompassing the Dra Valley down to Erg Chigaga.
- **Mountain Travel-Sobek** (© **888/687-6235** toll-free or 510/594-600; www.mt sobek.com) was one of the pioneers of adventure travel, offering trips since 1969. Their 2-week "Morocco Camel Trek" travels from Marrakech to Fes via the Dra Valley, Erg Chebbi, and Meknes, and includes a 4-day vehicle-supported camel trek.

GOLF

Introduced to Morocco by the British back in 1917, the sport of golf gained the royal seal of approval during the late 1960s, when King Hassan II became hooked. Pictures in the press showed Hassan II decked out in the latest golf wear—cigarette in one hand, putter in the other—playing the game with like-minded heads of state. A spate of course building followed, and today there are around 20 golf courses in Morocco ranging from 9 to 36 holes, some of which were designed by well-known masters Jack Nicklaus, Robert Trent Jones, and Jones's protégé, Cabell B. Robinson. Crown Prince Moulay Rachid shares his late father's passion for the game and has established a Royal Golf Academy, as well as taken on the presidency of the Royal Moroccan Golfing Federation.

The best known of the country's courses is at the **Royal Dar es Salaam Golf Club** (© **037/755864**) in Rabat. Set in a forest of cork, eucalyptus, and oak trees, the club offers two 18-hole courses (called red and blue), and one 9-hole (green) course. The red course—rated in the world's top 100 golf courses by *GOLF* magazine—plays host to Morocco's annual **Hassan II Golf Trophy** (www.hassan2golftrophy.com). Founded in 1971, the invitation-only tournament has previously hosted names such as Billy Caspar, Lee Trevino, Payne Stewart, Nick Price, Vijay Singh, Colin Montgomerie, and 2006 winner Sam Torrance. There's also a corresponding ladies tournament—the Lalla Meryem Cup—as well as a very popular 3-day pro-am, where amateurs get to play with a different professional each day.

The beachside resort city of Agadir is home to three clubs: the 9-hole **Agadir Royal Golf Club** (✆ 028/248551), the 45-hole **Dunes Golf Club** (✆ 028/834690), and the 36-hole **Golf du Soleil** (✆ 028/337330; www.golfdusoleil.com). Within the environs of Marrakech are three 18-hole courses: the **Marrakech Royal Golf Club** (✆ 024/409828 or 024/404705), **La Palmeraie Golf Club** (✆ 024/368766; www.pgpmarrakech.com), and the **Amelkis Golf Club** (✆ 024/404414). Other 18-hole courses can be found along the Atlantic coast in **El Jadida** (El Jadida Golf Club; ✆ 023/352251), where America's Favorite Golf Schools (www.afgs.com) has recently opened their first non–North American golf school; **Mohammedia** (near Casablanca; ✆ 023/324656); and the recently lengthened **Royal Country Golf Club** (✆ 039/938925) in Tangier. Nine-hole courses include those at **Casablanca** (within the Anfa Hippodrome; ✆ 022/365355 or 022/361026); **Fes** (✆ 035/665210); **Meknes** (✆ 035/530753; www.royalgolfmeknes.com), where the course is floodlit at night and is perhaps the only course in the world located within royal grounds; and **Ouarzazate** (✆ 024/882218 or 024/882486).

Morocco's golf courses are usually open every day to players of any handicap, other than Rabat's red course, which is only open to players of a handicap of 18 or less. Greens fees are around 400dh ($50/£25) for 9 holes and 550dh ($69/£34) for 18. Most clubs will rent full golf bags (200dh–300dh/$25–$38/£13–£19) and golf carts (200dh–400dh/$25–$50/£13–£25), and caddies are usually compulsory, costing between 60dh and 100dh ($7.50–$13/£3.75–£6.25).

Agadir's **Golf du Soleil** and Marrakech's **La Palmeraie Golf Club** both offer packages that include greens fees and other extras, along with prereservation of preferred tee times.

Online golf magazine **Golf Today** (www.golftoday.co.uk) includes a course directory for Morocco. For a recent appraisal of some of the country's golf courses, read Chaka Travel (see below) Managing Director Mark Marias's reviews on the company site.

TOUR OPERATORS

- **Exclusive Golf** (✆ **0870/8704700;** www.exclusivegolf.co.uk) has been organizing specialist golf holidays since 1988 and offers packages to both Marrakech and Rabat, usually with special deals that include free greens fees.
- **International Golf Adventures** (✆ **800/4581792** toll-free or 07092/010677 in the U.K.; www.golfcom.net) offers a number of top-end packaged golf holidays to Morocco playing at some of the Atlantic coast courses, as well as in Marrakech. Tours generally include quality accommodations, most meals, transport, and greens fees.
- **Pure Vacations** (www.purevacations.com) is a U.K.-based travel specialist offering golf packages from London for 7 or 14 nights in Marrakech and five rounds at the La Palmeraie course.

Other tour operators that can create golf-centric itineraries are: **Chaka Travel** (✆ **028/9023-2112;** www.chakatravel.com); **The Golf Holiday Company** (✆ **08701/121-315;** www.golfholidaycompany.com); and **The Best of Morocco** (✆ **08450/264-585;** www.morocco-travel.com).

KITESURFING & WINDSURFING

Essaouira's wide bay offers a variety of conditions for both kite surfers and windsurfers, and annually hosts a leg of the Kiteboard Pro World Cup. The "Windy City" experiences almost daily winds ranging from 20 to 35 knots, and with no reef or strong current, the shallow 3km-wide (1¾-mile) bay is perfect for all skill levels. June through August, morning conditions can range from flat to a slight wind chop—and is usually when beginner's classes are taken—while wind speeds in the afternoon can reach up to 35 knots. For the rest of the year, particularly in spring and autumn, the North Atlantic swell, assisted by wind speeds of between 20 to 30 knots, makes for particularly good wave-sailing conditions, especially on the southern side of the bay. This end of the bay is generally considered the kitesurfing zone, though wave sailors also congregate here, while beginners of both sports may feel more comfortable in the relatively calmer waters closer to the port.

The small beach of **Moulay Berzouktoune,** 20km (12 miles) north of Essaouira, offers one of the best wave-sailing locations outside Europe. Known simply as Moulay, both the current and cross-shore wind here is stronger than that at Essaouira and is only for experienced wave sailors. Similar in wind strength and wave size is **Sidi Kaouki,** about 10km (6 miles) south of Essaouira. Conditions here, however, can vary, and stretched along the beach are a few different entry points for both intermediate and experienced wave sailors.

Kitesurfing and windsurfing schools in Essaouira include the beachside **Club Mistral-Skyriders** (② 024/783934; www.club-mistral.com) and nearby **Magic Fun Afrika** (② 061/103777 or 061/170410; www.magicfunafrika.com), both of which also rent equipment. Note that most schools will only rent kitesurfing equipment if you are experienced enough to ride upwind and can perform self-rescue, generally considered IKO level 3. Less experienced kitesurfers can sometimes still rent equipment, but there may be a 30% surcharge for supervised rental.

Essaouira surf shops **Gipsy Surfer** (② 061/947092) and U.K.-owned **No Work Team** (② 024/475272) both sell kitesurfing and windsurfing equipment.

TOUR OPERATORS

Most international tour operators offering kitesurfing holidays to Morocco contract their ground operations to **Skyriders,** the Moroccan branch of Club Mistral (see above), including **Planet Kitesurf** (② 0870/749-1959; www.planetkitesurf.com), a U.K.-based travel operator specializing in kitesurfing holiday packages.

MOUNTAIN BIKING

With terrain ranging from coastal plains to mountain passes, Morocco's diverse landscape has been consistently attracting mountain bikers for more than 20 years. The country's well-maintained roads, vast network of dirt tracks *(pistes),* and mountainside footpaths offer very rewarding biking. However, at times this can be tempered, especially on the main roads, with the kamikaze-like nature of most Moroccan drivers. Most bikers, therefore, prefer riding in the biker-friendly Atlas mountain ranges and central Morocco. Popular routes include the roads and *pistes* that pass through the pink granite boulders around the Anti-Atlas village of Tafraoute; the Central High Atlas *pistes* and footpaths along the Aït Bou Guemez Valley; Marrakech to Taroudannt via the spectacular Tizi n'Test pass; and the "desert run" down the Dra or Ziz valleys.

Mountain biking in Morocco can be enjoyed year-round, although the summer heat—from June to September—can be overwhelming and severely dehydrating for most riders. Riding at this time of the year may be best kept to the cooler-but-busier Atlantic coastline. Conversely, the warm days and cool nights experienced throughout most of inland Morocco during the northern hemisphere winter can be simply delightful. Besides the aforementioned danger from Morocco's erratic drivers, mountain bikers may also experience some problems with local children, who have at times been known to harass and even throw stones at riders for no apparent reason, other than to get a reaction. The best reaction, therefore, is to grin and bear it, and try to quickly ride your way out of the situation. On the other side of the coin, mountain bikers are also likely to experience friendliness and hospitality from local villagers, ranging from advice and lifts to food and water.

Pedal-power transportation is very common amongst Moroccans, and in most cities, towns, and villages you'll find a local repair shop where patch-up jobs can be performed and where spare tires and tubes can usually be sourced. It's still worth bringing along specific spares, such as brake blocks, cable, and spokes, as well as a puncture repair kit. Remember that not all *pistes* appear on the map, and navigation without a guide generally requires planning and caution.

When you're tired of sitting in the saddle, Morocco's expansive public transport network makes traveling with your bike relatively easy. Most bus companies will gladly carry your bike for around 20dh ($2.50/£1.25), as will *grands* taxis (if they have space).

Tip: Villages and roadside stops can be few and far between when you're traveling on your own steam, so be sure to stock up on plenty of water and snacks at the beginning of each day. Bringing along a portable water filter is a good idea, as any public water that you find during the day may not be drinkable.

Renting good-quality mountain bikes once in Morocco isn't recommended, and if you want to travel independently, you'll need to bring your own. An exception is **Tafraout Aventure** (© **028/801368**; www.tafraout-aventure.com), which hires out reasonable bikes—some with shock absorbers—from their office in Tafraoute in the Anti-Atlas.

General information on biking can be found on the site of the U.K.'s national cycling association, the Cycle Touring Club, or **CTC** (© **0870/873-0060**; www.ctc. org.uk), and members can access Morocco trip reports from fellow members. The **Trento Bike Pages** (www.trentobike.org) collects worldwide biking tour reports, and always has a good selection of fairly recent reports from rider experiences in Morocco.

TOUR OPERATORS

- **BikeHike Adventures** (© **888/805-0061** toll-free; www.bikehike.com) is a U.S.-based tour operator specializing in multisport adventures around the world. Their 10-day Morocco tour is a round-trip from Marrakech to the Erg Chigaga desert dunes, passing over the Western High Atlas and along the Dra Valley. This tour typically combines biking with a few days of traveling by 4WD and an overnight camel trek.

- **Cycling Holidays** (© **0870/235-1356**; www.cyclingholidays.org) is affiliated with the British CTC (see above). They usually offer a tour to Morocco each year, which is a round-trip from Marrakech taking in the Tizi n'Test pass and parts of southern Morocco.

- **Unique Trails** (www.uniquetrails.com) is a Web-based outfit specializing in guided biking tours worldwide. They offer two 10-day Moroccan itineraries, one traversing the High Atlas and riding through the Dadés Gorge and the other over the High Atlas and down through the Dra Valley.

- U.K.-based **Wildcat Adventures** ★★ (© **1786/816-160**; www.wildcat-bike-tours.co.uk) is considered the leading mountain bike and road cycling specialist operating tours to Morocco. They offer numerous all-inclusive guided tours, both mountain and road biking, throughout the year, which usually include bike hire, qualified guides, and back-up transport. Their popular 14-day "Morocco Adventure" visits the coastline and mountains of southern Morocco, while an 11-day "Morocco Multi Sport Tour" combines biking with hiking and an overnight camel trek.

MOUNTAIN TREKKING

With its four distinct mountain ranges—**High Atlas, Middle Atlas, Anti-Atlas,** and the **Rif**—Morocco offers the walker, hiker, and mountaineer an incredible and rewarding variety of scenery, climate, and terrain. Besides Jebel Toubkal and its northern approaches, Morocco's mountains see relatively few travelers and can feel practically deserted when compared to those of Europe and North America. Just as rewarding as exploring the mountains themselves is encountering the Berbers who live in the valleys and on the lower slopes. These resilient mountain folk are renowned for their hospitality, and along with their picturesque kasbah villages—often surrounded by steep terraces of crop and fruit and nut trees—never fail to leave an impression.

If you have the time, trekking through the mountains is one of the must-dos in Morocco. The variety of terrain and differing degrees of access offer something for everyone, from walking through aromatic forests to scrambling over granite boulders.

One of the most popular mountain treks is the ascent of **Jebel Toubkal** ✸✸✸ (4,167m/13,671 ft.), North Africa's highest peak and part of the Western High Atlas. The mountain is the centerpiece of the Toubkal National Park, created in 1942 and Morocco's oldest. The usual starting point for this trek is the trail head village of Imlil, and to a lesser degree the ski-resort village of Oukaïmeden. Soft trekking is also popular here, with many trails passing through the region's valleys and villages, providing pleasant day and multiday walks, especially during summer when the heat in Marrakech can become unbearable. Other trekking spots include the **Aït Bou Guemez Valley** ✸✸ in the Central High Atlas, a beautiful part of the High Atlas range and trail head valley for ascents of Morocco's third-highest peak, **Ighil Mgoun** (4,071m/13,356 ft); **Jebel Sarhro** and **Jebel Siroua,** two ranges on the south side of the High Atlas requiring a degree of trekking self-sufficiency; the cedar forests, lakes, and craters around **Ifrane** in the Middle Atlas and only 2 hours' drive from Fes or Meknes; the boulder-strewn Anti-Atlas cliffs and fertile palmeraies around **Tafraoute** ✸; and the peaks and valleys of the Rif mountains, to the south of the relaxed village of **Chefchaouen** ✸.

It's possible to walk, hike, and climb in Morocco year-round. Some regions, however, are better explored during certain seasons. Generally speaking, Morocco's mountain ranges are at their most pleasant during late spring, when winter snows are almost entirely melted away, visibility is good, and the days are warm, while nights are still fresh enough to require warm bedding and a cup of hot mint tea. Trekking in snow-topped regions during early spring (Mar–Apr) requires some caution, as this is a time for flash floods caused by melting snow. November to February can be bitterly cold in Morocco's mountains, and some of the higher passes and peaks—including Jebel Toubkal—may be impassable, although others such as Jebel Sarhro, Jebel Siroua, and parts of the Anti-Atlas can still provide sunny days and pleasant trekking. Heading to the mountains during summer (June–Sept) is a great way to escape the heat from the plains (coastal or desert) below, although trekking in the exposed Rif mountains and in some of the Atlas's lower valleys may not be so pleasant.

The Islamic fasting month of Ramadan can also be a time to avoid trekking. Although Morocco's mountain Berbers are generally relaxed about most things, most will be reluctant to work during this time. Most trekking companies will have made prior arrangements for this, but independent trekkers may have to modify their plans to fit in with the locals.

An increase in visitors exploring Morocco's mountains over the past 10 or so years has coincided with a general upsurge in Morocco's economy, and today some regions have become decidedly more developed, boasting recently acquired services such as electricity and telecommunications, a more organized trekking infrastructure providing qualified guides, and a wider choice of accommodations. In a far-sighted attempt to balance the needs of the environment with those of the people, the High Atlas Tourist Code (p. 163) has been developed by the villagers living in the Aït Mizane Valley, below Jebel Toubkal, which has led to a waste-disposal service and a 4WD ambulance service. Development is less evident in other mountainous regions, and trekkers will have to be more resourceful when it comes to accommodations and guiding services, and be aware of their environmental impact, such as using gas heating rather than firewood and waste disposal.

Besides the comparative luxury available in the Western High Atlas, most other trekking regions offer limited, and sometimes very basic, accommodations options. The Club Alpin Français (CAF) operates five refuges in the Toubkal National Park, including the Neltner-Toubkal refuge, from where most ascents to the Toubkal peak depart from. Right next to this refuge, a new and decidedly better appointed private refuge opened in June 2007. Some trekking regions are equipped with *gites d'étape,* basic village houses licensed to serve hot meals and provide lodging for tourists. *Gites d'étape* have proven to be an important boost to the local economy, with the revenue generated from lodging a relatively low number of trekkers equivalent to a year's farming.

All of the trekking regions listed above have at least one principle village where independent trekkers can engage the services of mountain guides, mules to carry bags, and cooks if required. Hiring a qualified *guide de montagne* (mountain guide) is recommended, even for experienced trekkers, for their all-purpose benefits of translator, navigator, negotiator, and first-aid officer, and also for the purely economical benefit it brings to their family and village. Officially accredited mountain guides have been trained at the Centre de Formation aux Métiers de Montagne at Tabant in the Aït Bou Guemez Valley, and should carry a photo identity card to prove it. **Note:** Also trained at the center, but for only 1 week, are *accompagnateurs.* These "escorts" are not qualified to a lead a trip on their own, and should only be hired as trek assistants. More than 400 accredited mountain guides operate throughout Morocco, many of which can be hired from bureaux des guides (guide offices) located in Imlil, Setti Fatma, Azilal, Tabant, and El Kelaâ M'Gouna, near Boulmane du Dadès. To locate a guide in other regions, asking around normally yields quick results; just be sure to check his credentials. When negotiating an independent trek with a guide, make sure to discuss in detail your desired itinerary, objectives, and expectations, and assess the need for a cook and mules. Also ensure that everyone is agreed on the accommodations and catering situation while on trek. Before setting off, also agree on a price for all services provided. The daily rate for a guide currently starts at 300dh ($38/£19) per group, but this can vary according to the season and location. A mule (including its handler, called a muleteer) currently costs an extra 150dh ($19/£9.40) per day. Your guide will usually receive free accommodations, but you may have to cover his food costs. Budget on also giving the guide (and muleteer) at least a 10% tip on top of all of these costs. El Aouad Ali (known simply as Ali; © **066/637972;** http://trekmorocco.squarespace.com/working-with-ali) comes highly recommended by renowned Atlas guru Hamish Brown (see below).

Maps—topographical or otherwise—of Morocco's trekking regions are notoriously hard to come by, especially within the country. The only maps to be consistently found are the Moroccan *Division de la Cartographie* topographical map of the Jebel Toubkal Massif, including the lower valleys around Amizmiz, Oukaïmeden, Taliouine, and the Tizi n'Test; and a more basic map of the Ighil Mgoun Massif, published by West Col, which also has some useful information on possible routes and circuits. These are available online at Map Shop (www.themapshop.co.uk), Maps Worldwide (www.mapsworldwide.com), and Stanfords (www.stanfords.co.uk).

Michael Peyron's two-volume *Great Atlas Traverse* (West Col, 1990) remains the definitive guidebook on trekking in the Atlas mountains. It covers the author's linear traverse from the western Anti-Atlas across to Midelt, and gives a fair bit of background information. *Trekking in the Moroccan Atlas* (Trailblazer, 2000), by Richard Knight, is well researched and offers lots of useful "before you go" information, though is slightly unambitious and only covers the most popular trekking routes, with only sketched maps. The revised edition of Karl Smith's *Trekking in the Atlas Mountains* (Cicerone, 2004) is a compact, waterproof guide with route descriptions of some Toubkal, Mgoun, and Sahro treks, unfortunately with hardly any maps. *Climbing in the Moroccan Anti-Atlas* (Cicerone, 2004), by Claude Davies, is an excellent, compact guide for experienced climbers heading to the crags near Tafraoute.

If your French is up to scratch, then the website for the Moroccan branch of **Club Alpin Français** (www.cafmaroc.co.ma) contains a wealth of trekking information. **Nomadic Morocco** ★★★ operates a very handy and informative blog (http://nomadicmorocco.blogspot.com) with regular updates on trekking conditions, mainly in the Western High Atlas.

TOUR OPERATORS

By far the easiest way to trek in Morocco is through a specialist operator. Nowadays, travelers are spoiled for choice, as the number of operators, both local and international, offering mountain treks is considerable. In addition to those listed below, see "Organized Adventure Trips," earlier in this chapter.

LOCAL

- **Bureau des Guides d'Imlil** (©/fax **024/485626;** bureau.guides@yahoo.fr) is located in the trail head village of Imlil (p. 161). They coordinate the availability of the region's accredited mountain guides, and can arrange everything from overnight ascents of Jebel Toubkal to multiday hikes that include a guide, mules, accommodations, and meals.

- **Kasbah du Toubkal** (© **024/485611;** www.kasbahdutoubkal.com) has its own mountain guide office in Imlil and offers a range of trekking options for guests as well as for nonresidents at an additional cost. Along with all-inclusive ascents of Jebel Toubkal, among other trekking options offered is a full-day "deluxe" trek into the surrounding countryside, complete with lunchtime picnic. The kasbah itself is also a nice lunch stop for day-trippers and has a million-dollar rooftop view.

- **Nomadic Morocco** (© **078/875057;** www.nomadicmorocco.com) is run by Irish-French couple Des and Nathalie Clark, who are based in Taroudannt. They specialize in high-quality, personalized mountain treks throughout Morocco, and are also involved in numerous health projects in some of the villages they trek through. Sister company **Toubkal Mountain Guides** (www.toubkalmountain guides.com) specializes in climbing Jebel Toubkal, including 3- to 5-day winter ascents.

INTERNATIONAL

- **Hamish Brown** (℗/fax **01592/873-546**) is an Atlas expert, having visited Morocco's mountains for more than 40 years. He occasionally leads specialist tours, and it's worth getting in touch with him. His Atlas Mountains Information Services (same number as above) is a good source of information, and often has copies of maps that are hard to come by.

- **Journey Beyond Travel** (℗ **765/387-4404** in the U.S., or 072/882529 in Morocco; www.journeybeyondtravel.com) is a small tour operator offering a range of itineraries to the Toubkal, Mgoun, and Rif trekking regions.

- **Sherpa Expeditions** (℗ **020/857-7217;** www.sherpaexpeditions.com) has been specializing in guided walks since 1973, and offers two tours to Jebel Toubkal and one to Jebel Sarhro. For the past 10 years, it has also offered unique self-guided walking holidays, and the 8-day "Inn-to-Inn" walk, although accompanied by a local guide/muleteer, is a great combination of organized and independent.

- **Walks Worldwide** (℗ **01524/242-000;** www.walksworldwide.com) has a great range of Morocco trekking itineraries for all levels of interest and fitness. Besides Jebel Toubkal, they also have guided tours to Jebel Sarhro, the Rif mountains, and a deluxe, easy-going 7-day "Morocco In Style" itinerary.

SKIING

Anytime from November to April, the peaks of the Western and Central High Atlas offer the opportunity for African skiing. Although obviously incomparable to the slopes of Europe and North America, skiing in Morocco offers the more intrepid skier an intoxicating mix of sport, culture, and adventure. The country's two better-known ski fields are only a 1- to 2-hour drive from Marrakech and Fes, respectively, and returning to these ancient, bustling, and much warmer cities after a day out in the snowy wilderness is a typically Moroccan attack on the senses.

Morocco's only true ski resort is at **Oukaïmeden** (p. 162), 70km (43 miles) south of Marrakech. When conditions are good, 3,263m-high (10,705-ft.) Jebel Oukaïmeden's north-facing slope has up to 20km (13 miles) of trails on eight marked *pistes,* with access provided by one chair lift and five surface lifts. The headline black run would fit right in at a European resort, but the lack of slope maintenance—and the prevalence of submerged rocks—can make the downhill challenging. The quality and length of Oukaïmeden's snow season has varied greatly over recent years, but your best bet is between mid-January and mid-February, when unfortunately it can also get horrendously busy on the weekends. Ski equipment can be hired in the village, which is only 200m (655 ft.) from the chair lift station, but can be of an amazingly varied quality, and you may also have to bargain for the cost. Gear can also be rented in Marrakech, but it's really worth bringing your own if you're a serious skier. When there's enough snow cover, the volcanic crater of **Mischliffen,** near the Middle Atlas village of Ifrane (p. 257), also offers a fun day's skiing, with a few trails that are great for beginners, accessed by a couple of surface lifts or by simply hiking up the slopes. There's usually some equipment for hire in Ifrane.

Also possible on the Atlas's peaks and slopes is ski mountaineering, or *ski randonné.* Popular with the French and Swiss, the sport is becoming more common nowadays in the Western High Atlas and on the slopes above **Aït Bou Guemez Valley** in the Central High Atlas. This off-*piste* skiing requires regular carving skis with special mountaineering bindings that allow the heel to release when climbing, and can be fixed when skiing down. Removable skins for the bottom of the skis will also better enable you to go uphill. You'll have to bring all this equipment with you.

Irish-Moroccan trekking company **Nomadic Morocco** operates a very handy and informative blog (http://nomadicmorocco.blogspot.com) with regular snow and weather updates.

TOUR OPERATORS

There are no specialist tour operators offering Morocco skiing itineraries. Hotels in Ifrane and Oukaïmeden will usually be able to assist prospective skiers with equipment and transport to their respective ski fields. Getting to any other snow-covered areas usually requires high levels of perseverance and adaptability, but this can prove to be part of the adventure. Ski mountaineering in Morocco requires the assistance of a guide, who will organize accommodations, mules, porters, and even cooks. If you wish to pre-organize this, try contacting the **Bureau des Guides d'Imlil** (©/fax **024/485626;** bureau.guides@yahoo.fr), the official mountain guide center for the entire Western High Atlas region, or **Kasbah du Toubkal,** also in Imlil (© **024/ 485611;** fax 024/485636; www.kasbahdutoubkal.com).

SURFING

Morocco's Atlantic coastline has a good selection of mostly uncrowded surf breaks, and when combined with the country's culture, cuisine, and other attractions, they make for a fascinating "surfari." Although surfing in Morocco was initially introduced by Americans and Australians in the '70s, Europeans and Moroccans are now the most common of those out in the water. In the past decade, the sport has gained in popularity, assisted by King Mohammed VI, who is patron of the Oudayas Surf Club in Rabat. There are now surf schools, shops, and camps dotted along the coastline, as well as a number of domestic competitions and surf riders' associations.

Although September through April is when you'll find the most consistent swells, decent surf occurs throughout the year, thanks to swells generated by the North Atlantic depressions combined with light offshore trade winds. Localism is yet to rear its ugly head in any great fashion, at least by Moroccans anyway, who are still rapt to share their waves with "cool" foreign surfers.

Point, reef, and beach breaks are to be found all the way from north of Rabat (Mehdiya Plage) to south of Agadir (Sidi Ifni). Between El Jadida and Safi are some excellent right-handers, as well as the beginner-friendly lagoon at Oualidia. Farther south there are quite a few breaks between Essaouira and Agadir, including **Imessouane** (another long right-hand break and a personal favorite) and the world-class wave at **Anchor Point,** just north of the surfer's village of Taghazout (p. 378). As with most exotic surfing destinations, the most convenient way to access Morocco's surf breaks is by renting a car.

Recommended surf schools include **Surfland** (© 023/366110), overlooking the Oualidia lagoon; **Kahina** (© 028/826032; www.kahinasurfschool.com) at Imessouane; and **Rapture** (© 062/879389; www.rapturecamps.com) in Tamraght, near

Taghazout. In Essaouira are **Club Mistral** (© 024/783934; www.club-mistral.com) and **Magic Fun Afrika** (© 061/103777 or 061/170410; www.magicfunafrika.com), which offer lessons and rent, sell, and repair equipment.

The Stormrider Guide Europe—The Continent (Low Pressure, 2006), by Bruce Sutherland, includes the best available write-up on Morocco's surf spots, while the site for **Global Surfers** (www.globalsurfers.com) offers plenty of specific information on most of Morocco's breaks and has a handy forum where current localized information can be sourced.

TOUR OPERATORS

- **Nomad Surfers** (© **971/306992;** www.nomadsurfers.com) is a Spanish-based company offering surfaris worldwide, including Morocco, where they have an operation in Tamraght, near Taghazout.
- **Pure Vacations** (www.purevacations.com) is a U.K.-based travel specialist offering holidays worldwide, and has recently commenced an Ultimate Moroccan Surf Tour. The 7-night tour begins and finishes in Agadir, and includes return flights from London, all accommodations, meals, transport, and an accompanying surf guide and life guard.
- **Surf Maroc** (© 01794/322-709; www.surfmaroc.co.uk) is a U.K.-based operation offering surf holidays, lessons, and yoga retreats from their Taghazout operation.
- **Zoco Boardriding Adventures** (© **0871/218-0360** in the U.K., or 020/ 8144-1035 from elsewhere; www.zocotravel.com) offers surfing holiday packages, including a 7-night Morocco tour specifically for groups (school, surf clubs, university), which includes accommodations, surf tuition, meals, and transport.

3 Ecological & Cultural Travel

Today's traveler is increasingly looking for more than just superficial sights and experiences. Many visitors come to Morocco hoping to scratch beneath the surface and really get to know the country and, more importantly, its people. Travelers will be confronted daily with random opportunities to interact with Moroccans; many times you'll be invited to share a glass of mint tea, often at the home of the person offering. There are also other, more organized avenues, which take away the initial concerns of safety and communication difficulties. These include volunteering on regional development projects, studying Moroccan Arabic at a local language school, or joining a specific community-based tour.

RESPONSIBLE TOURISM

Eco-tourism has become the fastest-growing sector within global tourism and is promoted by the now well-known saying, "Take nothing but memories, leave nothing but footprints." The International Ecotourism Society (TIES) defines eco-tourism as "responsible travel to natural areas that conserves the environment and improves the well-being of local people." True eco-tourism is still in its infancy within Morocco, contrary to the marketing of many local and international companies. Moroccans are largely ambivalent toward their environmental footprint, mostly through lack of education but also because it is a luxury that most don't have the time or money to afford. The government is also partly to blame, as basic infrastructure such as waste disposal and sewage are criminally lacking in some parts of the country. The amount of waste that litters many of the country's waterways, beaches, roadsides, and mountains is a sight that Western travelers consistently mention as disappointing and worrying.

However, it is only through increasing demand from international visitors that some tour operators, travel agencies, and accommodations are beginning to operate with truly dedicated ecologically sound principles and practices.

The Web-based travel directory **responsibletravel.com** (© **01273/600-030** in the U.K.) lists thousands of "eco holidays" available worldwide, including a vast selection in Morocco. Jane Bayley's **Naturally Morocco** ✸✸✸ (© **01239/654-466** in the U.K.; www.naturallymorocco.co.uk) is considered the leader in eco-travel in Morocco. This U.K.-based responsible and sustainable tourism operator also has a cultural and environmental center in Taroudannt, from where it offers a range of hands-on cultural and environmental experiences. Clients can choose between diverse themes such as anthropology, language, cooking lessons, architecture, music, art, and wildlife. It also operates as a travel agency, recommending similar-principled accommodations and tours throughout the rest of Morocco. **Equatorial Travel** ✸✸✸ (© **01335/348-770** in the U.K.; www.equatorialtravel.co.uk) is a small U.K.-based travel company owned by friendly journeyman John-Paul Rodgers. It offers small-group, personalized tours to central and southern Morocco, with a heavy emphasis on the local culture. Besides desert excursions, it also offers an itinerary that culminates in the Essaouira Gnaoua & World Music Festival, a photographic tour escorted by a professional photographer, and itineraries structured toward families. Operating on fair-trade principles and practices, up to 20% of the company's profit is redirected back to the communities with which it works. **Tribes Travel** (© **01728/685-971** in the U.K.; www.tribes.co.uk) is an independent specialist-travel company based in the U.K. operating tailor-made holidays to a number of exotic destinations, including Morocco. It practices fair-trade principles, combining discerning travel with the needs of local communities, intended to protect both biodiversity and cultural diversity. The Tribes Foundation concentrates on poverty alleviation, education, cultural preservation, and conservation projects within the destinations that Tribes Travel operates. The company offers a range of itineraries throughout the majority of Morocco, as well as organizing weekend breaks in Marrakech.

VOLUNTEERING

Volunteer programs abroad used to be the exclusive domain of students and youth travelers, but with the increasingly high profile of eco-tourism, a desire from the average traveler to become more involved in the country he or she is visiting has increased. Collectively being dubbed "voluntourism," more and more short-term volunteer projects are now being offered by tour operators to complement the choice of volunteer and exchange programs already offered by an established network of volunteer organizations. No matter how short or long, volunteering in Morocco is a great way to see the country in more depth and to greater appreciate the harsh realities faced daily by many locals. Most volunteer organizations are not-for-profit entities that charge participants to go abroad, combining home stays with voluntary service in a variety of community service projects. Voluntourism operators are private tour operators that typically offer 1- to 3-week accommodated holidays, combining sightseeing with the opportunity to assist locals on short-term development projects.

Cross-Cultural Solutions ✸✸ (© **800/380-4777** toll-free or 914/632-0022; www.crossculturalsolutions.org) has offices in the U.S., U.K., Canada, and Australia, and has recently begun placing volunteers in a variety of locally run organizations dedicated to improving the life of residents in and around Rabat. Programs run from 3 to 12 weeks and are typically geared toward those that assist children and empower women. **Different Travel** (© 02380/669-903; www.different-travel.com) is a U.K.-based voluntourism specialist offering worldwide volunteering holidays. Their annual 9-day Moroccan Sahara Challenge is specifically geared toward sponsored travelers raising funds for their selected charity and includes 2 days working alongside Berber villagers to refurbish a community center. The **Peace Corps** (© 800/424-8580 toll-free; www.peacecorps.gov) has been placing American volunteers of all ages and backgrounds in local communities worldwide since 1961. In 1963, Morocco was one of the first countries (73 so far) to invite the Peace Corps to assist in its development. Since then, more than 3,500 Peace Corps volunteers have served in the country in a dazzling array of fields ranging from bee-keeping to urban development. Currently, the sectors of environment, health, small business, and youth development are open to volunteers. **Projects Abroad** ✦✦ (© 888/839-3535 toll-free; www.projects-abroad.org) is based in the U.S. with a local office in Rabat, and places Care & Community volunteers in orphanages and centers for children with special needs in and around Rabat.

Operation Smile ✦✦✦ (© 888/677-6453 toll-free or 757/321-7645; www.operationsmile.org) coordinates more than 30 Medical Mission sites in 25 countries, providing free surgeries for thousands of children to repair facial deformities such as cleft lips and cleft palates. They have been well established in Morocco for the past 10 years, with mission partnerships in Casablanca, Fes, Tangier, and others. They welcome medical specialists—plastic surgeons, pediatricians, speech pathologists, dentists—as well as fourth- or final-year medical students to volunteer on annual 2-week missions to Morocco, which besides treating up to 150 children also provides an educational opportunity for local health-care professionals.

SPANA ✦✦✦ (© 020/783-13999; www.spana.org) is a U.K.-based animal welfare organization that operates veterinary centers, mobile clinics, and educational programs throughout North and West Africa and the Middle East. Their Morocco branch (p. 111) has been operating since 1925, and provides a volunteer vet scheme whereby graduate vets are offered the opportunity to work for up to 3 months in one of the country's refuges.

LANGUAGE PROGRAMS

One of the best ways to learn more about both Islamic and Moroccan culture is to enroll in an Arabic language program. Although Moroccans speak their own unique dialect, courses are also conducted in Modern Standard Arabic (MSA), which is used throughout the Arabic world. Additionally, Morocco is also a good place to learn French, as it is still used widely in the country, especially in business and tourism.

For learning Arabic, the best-known language school is the **Arabic Language Institute in Fes (ALIF)** ✦✦✦ on the eastern edge of the ville nouvelle at 2 rue Ahmed Hiba (© 035/624850; fax 035/931608; www.alif-fes.com). It offers small-group courses in all levels of MSA and colloquial Moroccan Arabic throughout the year. Most courses consist of 6-week (120 hr.) sessions, though there are special content-based courses (3 weeks) and private or specialized lessons can also be arranged. The current costs (excluding materials, accommodations, and living expenses) are 5,200dh ($650/£325) for 3 weeks, 9,400dh ($1,175/£588) for 6 weeks, and 200dh ($25/£13) per hour for private instruction (discounted rate for two or more students). Located in a large Moorish-style villa, ALIF also shares its classrooms and grounds with the American Language Center, providing a good place for meeting young Moroccans. In addition to their courses, they also offer a range of cultural and social activities to students.

In Rabat, the highly regarded **Center for Cross-Cultural Learning (CCCL),** avenue Laalou, Derb Eljirari, 11 Zankat Elhassani (© 037/202365; fax 037/202367; www.cccl-ma.com), is located in a 19th-century riad within Rabat's medina. It organizes a variety of cultural and educational activities, including courses in both MSA and colloquial Moroccan Arabic. Its "semi-intensive" (4 weeks/60 hr.) and "intensive" (6 weeks/90 hr.) programs are great for visitors. As part of its partnerships with various U.S. educational institutions, it also offers study-abroad programs, as well as adult programs that combine language lessons with field trips, excursions, and cultural performances.

DMG Arabophon (© 035/603475 or 035/749893; www.arabophon.com) specializes in Moroccan Arabic, but also offers lessons in MSA, Berber Amazight, French, and German. Along with standard Moroccan Arabic courses of 4 weeks or longer, they also offer a series of traveler-friendly introductory courses including a half-day Curious Explorer. The main office is in Fes, and they have branches in Casablanca, Rabat, and Meknes. **Institut Français** (www.ambafrance-ma.org/institut) has cultural centers located in most of Morocco's major cities, and offers French-language courses along with various cultural activities. **Projects Abroad** ✸✸ (© 888/839-3535; www.projects-abroad.org) is headquartered in New York and has a local office in Rabat. It offers Arabic- and French-language courses, and places you with a local family who converses in the corresponding language. Sixty hours of private, one-on-one tuition is included each month, and participants choose the length of stay.

5

Marrakech

A true crossroads of Africa, Arabia, and Europe, Marrakech (sometimes spelled Marrakesh) is, for many travelers, the experience to which all others in the country are compared. The city thrives as Morocco's imaginative center and attracts visitors throughout the year with its arts and crafts and various festivals.

An imperial capital on more than one occasion, this ochre-colored city has a surprisingly limited number of attractions, but it offers a complete sensory experience that is immediately captivating. Its dynamic mix of traditional folklore and exotic imagery is drawing record numbers of travelers (and settlers) from l'Occident (the West) into its ancient, bustling medina. However, amidst this surge in popularity, Marrakech has been able to preserve its individual mystique and timeless allure.

Berber in origin, Marrakech looks and feels like the very definition of a Moroccan desert capital. The Almoravids, the first great Berber dynasty, established themselves here in the 1060s before going on to conquer northern Morocco and southern Spain. The original settlement—nothing more than a camp and market surrounded by a thorn-tree perimeter—eventually became the capital of the dynasty's empire and underwent a major expansion during their 80-odd years of rule. Unfortunately there is very little evidence today of Almoravid construction, as the orthodox and reforming Almohads—the dynasty that made their way down the High Atlas mountains to overthrow the Almoravids—destroyed most of the city's "impure" architecture and commenced a building spree of their own. This was one of Marrakech's greatest periods, as the city benefited from being the capital of an Almohad empire that reached as far as modern-day Libya. It was during the reign of the third Almohad sultan, Yacoub el Mansour, that the great Koutoubia Mosque and minaret was constructed, and a succession of Arabic creative types—philosophers, poets, scholars—took up residence in el Mansour's court, establishing Marrakech's reputation as a place of creativity and expression.

Upon the demise of the Almohads, the city was largely neglected by the proceeding dynasties until the Saâdians took control of the then famine-struck city in the 1520s. The Saâdians restored imperial glamour upon Marrakech as they regained control of the Atlantic coast from the Portuguese and conquered the powerful West African kingdom of Timbuktu, taking control of the extremely lucrative caravan routes. During this time, the city emerged as a cultural and commercial hub, and the eclectic mix of Atlas Berbers (with their produce, livestock, and crafts), southern caravans (laden with slaves, gold, and ivory), Arabic scholars, Jewish traders, and European consuls shaped the city.

Marrakech fell into disrepair upon the demise of the Saâdians, but regained some of its status with the arrival of the French. For the majority of the French colonial occupation (1912–56), Marrakech and its surrounds were run as a virtual mini-kingdom by the pasha T'hami el Glaoui. The French preferred to govern Morocco's isolated territories through sympathetic local rulers and assisted el Glaoui in extending his, and their, control over all areas of the south. In the 1930s, the French constructed their ville nouvelle, which attracted Western travelers who took advantage of the newly built railway line that still deposits large amounts of visitors here every year. El Glaoui was a legendary party thrower, and at his elaborate banquets, Americans and Europeans—Winston Churchill was considered a personal friend and invited the pasha to the coronation of Queen Elizabeth II—were showered with gifts of gold and diamonds and encouraged to indulge in whatever vice took their fancy. At the time, Marrakech was recognized as the true capital of the south, and today it is the second largest trading center in the country after Casablanca.

The result of this somewhat boisterous history is a city that is at a vibrant crossroads of cultures. The daily life in the medina is, for the most part, absolutely authentic, though you'll find many restaurants and souvenir shops surrounding the main square of Jemaa el Fna.

Marrakech is surrounded by extensive palm groves, yet there are also sandy, arid areas that, when combined, give the city a semi-Saharan feel. Marrakchis are renowned for their humor and gregariousness—something that, for the traveler, may not be fully on display at first glance. Immigration from the surrounding rural areas is high, and the constant competition for work has led to the city gaining a bad reputation for hassling travelers. A special Brigade Touristique (tourist police) was established about 10 years ago to clamp down on the problem, and though it's been generally successful, haggling tourists (and unemployment) still exists.

This Venice of Morocco, as coined by part-time resident and fashion icon Yves Saint Laurent, is eccentric, enchanting, exhausting, enticing, and exasperating all within a moment's difference and deserves its current status as a popular and easily accessible example of the mysterious l'Orient.

1 Orientation

ARRIVING

BY PLANE In 2006, the Moroccan government deregulated the country's airline industry and invoked an open-skies policy to increase the number of tourists coming to the country. Marrakech has been the greatest beneficiary of the policy as evidenced by an explosion (24 at last count) of international airline routes flying directly into the city from Europe. All domestic and international flights land at **Marrakech-Menara Airport** (© **024/447910**), located 4 km (2½ miles) southwest of the city center. All flights arrive at Terminal 1, and at press time a huge new arrivals building was underway and expected to be completed during the course of 2008. The current arrivals hall houses rental-car services, an ATM, and two currency exchange booths that are usually open from 8am to 7pm—but can sometimes be closed during these times and open during others for no apparent reason. Though you'll generally find a bank or bureau de change near your hotel or be able to exchange cash (they may not accept traveler's checks) at your hotel, it's best to pick up some Moroccan dirham at the airport just in case.

Many hotels and *maisons d'hôte* are happy to arrange an airport pickup for you. A taxi from the airport to the medina or ville nouvelle takes about 15 minutes and should cost between 100dh and 150dh ($13–$19/£6.25–£9.40). Expect to pay more if you have a lot of luggage, and keep in mind that *petits* taxis (and sometimes *grands* taxis) increase their fare by 50 percent after 8pm. Taxis from the airport (but not those operating around town) generally accept euros and sometimes U.S. dollars or British pounds, but you'll receive change only in dirham. Around town, *grands* taxis operate on a set-fare basis that depends on the route, while *petits* taxis operate by a meter that charges by distance. However, for those taxis operating from the airport, this is rarely the case, so it's best to agree on a fare before you and your luggage are deposited inside the vehicle.

Taxi drivers are found in the parking lot directly outside the arrivals hall. Be prepared for a chorus of, "Hello, taxi?" as you approach them, and don't be surprised if arguments break out between drivers over who claimed you first, as there is no order to the system. *Note:* Whether you're traveling by private hotel car or taxi, be sure that the driver fully understands the name and location of your hotel. There are incidences of bogus private transfer operators posing as your hotel's representative and taking you to a completely different hotel in the hope that you won't realize the "mistake" so that he will earn commission from the hotel. Taxi drivers are also known to try this scam.

ALSA, the city's public bus company, operates a very convenient shuttle (bus no. L19) between the airport and the city, making numerous stops in Hivernage, Guéliz, and the medina, along with both the bus and train stations. Catch the bus from the airport in the public parking lot outside the arrivals building. One-way tickets are 20dh ($2.50/£1.25); round-trip tickets, valid for 2 weeks, are 30dh ($3.75/£1.90). Daily service begins at 6:15am from Jemaa el Fna and terminates at 12:30am at the ONMT (Office National Marocain de Tourisme) on place Abdelmoumen Ben Ali in Guéliz.

BY TRAIN   All trains arrive and depart from Marrakech's recently refurbished train station (© **024/447703**), southwest of place du 16 Novembre on avenue Hassan II, a short taxi ride (around 10dh/$1.25/65p) to Guéliz, Hivernage, or the medina. Storage lockers are available at the station for 10dh ($1.25/65p) per day. Trains depart daily for Marrakech from most of the western half of Morocco (there are no trains in either the Atlas or Rif mountains or central Morocco). Some of the more popular routes are from Casablanca (3½ hr.; 84dh–125dh/$11–$16/£5.25–£8); Fes (7½ hr.; 180dh–276dh/$23–$35/£11–£17); Meknes (7 hr.; 162dh–247dh/$20–$31/£10–£15); Rabat (4½ hr.; 112dh–170dh/$14–$21/£7–£11); and Tangier (9½ hr.; 190dh/$24/£12). There is also a popular overnight service from Tangier that currently departs at 9:30pm and arrives in Marrakech at 8:40am. If you want to sleep in a couchette, there's an additional 100dh ($13/£6.25) supplement to the above rate. From destinations such as Agadir, Essaouira, and Tetouan, you'll be traveling all or part of your journey on the ONCF bus service called Supratours. Reservations are only accepted up to 1 month prior to departure and can be made either over the phone (© **090/203040** from within Morocco), at ticket booths in each station, or through authorized agents. Payment at the station is by cash only; some agents accept credit cards.

BY BUS   Buses to Marrakech arrive daily from almost everywhere in Morocco south of the Rif mountains, including Agadir (4 hr.; 70dh–90dh/$8.75–$11/£4–£5.65); Casablanca (4 hr.; 50dh–80dh/$6.25–$10/£3.15–£5); Erfoud (10 hr.; 160dh–195dh/ $20–$24/£10–£12); Essaouira (3½ hr.; 35dh–60dh/$4.40–$7.50/£2.20–£3.75); Fes (10 hr.; 150dh–170dh/$19–$21/£9.40–£11); Meknes (9 hr.; 140dh–160dh/$18– $20/£8.75–£10[0]); Ouarzazate (5 hr.; 65dh–70dh/$8.15–$8.75/£4.05–£4.40);

Rabat (5½ hr.; 80dh–105dh/$10–$13/£5–£6.55); Taroudannt (7½ hr.; 60dh/$7.50/ £3.75); Tangier (11 hr.; 150dh/$19/£9.40); and Zagora (9½ hr; 100dh/$13/£6.25). Besides the train station–based Supratours and CTM's international services, which operate from their office in Guéliz (see below), all long-distance bus companies arrive at the *gare routière*, or bus station (© 024/433933), just outside the medina's walls at Bab Doukkala. It's a busy, bustling, and not-too-pretty building with up to 30 24-hour ticket booths covering a large number of destinations and companies. It's open around the clock and offers a convenient luggage storage service (8dh/$1/50p per bag).

From the *gare routière* you can venture straight into the medina or walk south for about 15 minutes to reach avenue Mohammed V, from where you can head to the center of Guéliz or through the medina's Bab Nkob to Jemaa el Fna. Alternatively, there are usually plenty of *petits* taxis around the *gare routière* that will take you this short distance for around 10dh to 15dh ($1.25–$1.90/65p–95p). For onward travel from Marrakech, all companies, except Supratours and CTM's international services, depart from the bus station, where they each have their own ticket booths (you must pay in cash). For an early-morning departure, it's advisable to purchase your ticket the day prior to both ensure your seat and allow you time to ignore the touts and purchase your ticket in peace. CTM (© 022/438282 central reservations; www.ctm.ma) and Supratours (© 022/298163 central reservations; www.supratours.ma) buses to and from Marrakech are regularly full, so again it's best to prebook your seat no matter where you're departing from—sometimes this is best done by booking at their office or agency rather than by phone. You can also purchase tickets (cash only) for any CTM bus from their office at 12 bd. Zerktouni, Guéliz (© 024/448328), open 24 hours a day.

BY *GRAND* TAXI Most long-distance *grands* taxis to and from Marrakech arrive just north of the *gare routière* at Bab Doukkala. Those plying the route to High Atlas destinations around Jebel Toubkal, such as Asni, Ijoukak, and the Ourika Valley, depart from a terminal 3km (1¾ miles) outside the medina's Bab er Rob, which is best reached by *petit* taxi. *Grands* taxis to Marrakech depart throughout the day from Agadir (3½ hr.; 100dh/$13/£6.25); Casablanca (3 hr.; 105dh/$13/£6.55); Essaouira (3 hr.; 100dh/$13/£6.25); Ouarzazate (3½ hr.; 80dh/$10/£5); Setti Fatma (2 hr.; 25dh/$3.15/£1.55); and Taroudannt (4 hr.; 100dh/$13/£6.25).

BY CAR Driving into Marrakech from other parts of the country can range from surprisingly easy to downright suicidal, depending on the time of day, your navigational skills, adjustment to the aggressive driving nature, and experience with the French rule, where priority is given to those entering, rather than those already on, a roundabout. The amount of traffic on the roads, which includes trucks, buses, cars, horse-driven carts, and any number of mopeds, attests to this being the largest city in southern Morocco. The main arrival destinations of Jemaa el Fna, Guéliz, and the airport are generally well signposted no matter which direction you are coming from. Once you're on avenue Mohammed V, which is the main thoroughfare between Jemaa el Fna and Guéliz, it's reasonably easy to find most Guéliz and Hivernage hotels. However, be aware that many of the smaller side streets are one-way—if you are starting to get frustrated, a good option is to park in the general vicinity and locate your hotel on foot. If your destination is the pedestrian-only Jemaa el Fna, your best bet is to head down avenue Mohammed V as far as the Koutoubia Mosque and pull into a nearby 24-hour parking lot (25dh/$3.15/£1.55 per 24 hr.)—you will see their blue-and-white signs—and continue on foot.

There never seems to be enough parking in Marrakech, so if your hotel offers this premium service, use it. No matter where you find parking, remember to locate the parking attendant, or *gardien,* if he hasn't already introduced himself, and advise how many hours or days your vehicle will be parked. He may ask for a fee, or tip, upfront if you are staying for more than a day, as sometimes arguments break out between a day-shift and night-shift *gardien* as to who has earned the money. Budget on 10dh ($1.25/65p) per shift, and you'll keep everybody happy. If you're lucky, you might even find your car has been washed before you depart. *Note:* Red-and-white-stripe curbing means no parking.

Unless you're driving out of Marrakech directly from the airport, car rental pickup is best organized from your hotel. You don't need a car while in Marrakech, and navigating your way from the airport into the city is an unnecessary strain. Conversely, if you are driving into Marrakech from elsewhere and flying straight out, then dropping off your rental car at the airport is a good idea, as it is well signposted from most highways entering Marrakech and is therefore relatively easy to manage.

VISITOR INFORMATION

The **ONMT (Office National Marocain de Tourisme),** on avenue Mohammed V at place Abdelmoumen Ben Ali (© **024/436131**), is open Monday to Friday 8:30am to noon and 2:30 to 6:30pm, Saturday 9am to noon, and 3 to 6pm on Sunday. Although this is the region's main tourist office, the offerings are limited to a free map, a list of recommended accommodations and restaurants, and some pretty useless glossy brochures. There is also a local Syndicat d'Initiative, or tourist information bureau, 170 av. Mohammed V (© **024/230886**), which is open the same days and hours but is even less useful.

The **Institut Français,** Route de la Targa, on the outskirts of Guéliz (© **024/ 446930;** www.ifm.ma), is open 9am to 7pm Tuesday to Saturday and regularly shows films and hosts exhibitions, plays, and other cultural events. Set amongst pleasant gardens, there is an open-air theater, cafe, and a library housing a small collection of Moroccan-related French literature.

Last Exit Marrakech is a free English-language magazine that's published monthly and includes some handy write-ups on the city's restaurants. It's available at many hotels and restaurants, as well as Café du Livre (p. 137).

CITY LAYOUT

Despite its size, Marrakech is reasonably easy to navigate thanks to the two clearly defined areas: the ancient walled **medina** and the French-designed **ville nouvelle.** The medina's walls enclose a surprisingly open, busy area with the fascinating Jemaa el Fna—a broad square lined with food and juice stalls that hosts all manners of entertainment daily—at its heart. It is only once you reach here that you encounter, to the north and south, the seemingly never-ending maze of alleyways that are what most people expect from this city. Heading west from Jemaa el Fna, past the city's most prominent landmark, the minaret of the Koutoubia Mosque, along avenue Mohammed V, and through Bab Nkob will bring you to the ville nouvelle. The two main areas of the ville nouvelle that are of interest to travelers are Hivernage and Guéliz. Hivernage is home to a selection of mainly expensive hotels and offers little of interest other than the photogenic Menara Gardens and a number of nightlife options. Guéliz is the working center of the ville nouvelle, and it is here that you'll find the bulk of Marrakech's offices, shops, and cafes along with a high concentration

Jemaa el Fna

The pulsating heart of Marrakech is no doubt Jemaa el Fna, where medieval and modern mix comfortably on a huge, open square that daily plays host to one of the most fascinating spectacles in the world. The activity on the square never slackens, though different times of the day and night have their own distinctive character.

For such a historical place, it is not entirely known when or how Jemaa el Fna came into being. The popular explanation comes from its literal translation as "assembly of the dead," and refers to when the square was a place of execution, complete with severed heads on display, well into the 19th century. Whatever the square's original meaning, it is agreed that it has probably played the joint role as the medina's open market area and social focal point since the earliest days of settlement. Immediately upon independence in 1956, the new "modern-thinking" government converted the square into a corn market and parking lot. This unpopular move lasted less than a year before the square's tourism and social value became obvious, and it reverted back to its traditional role. In 1994, the entire square was tarred for a GATT, or General Agreement on Tariffs and Trade (now WTO, or World Trade Organization) meeting, and in 2002 it was deemed pedestrian-only, a popular move appreciated by Marrakchis and visitors alike. In 2001, UNESCO proclaimed the "cultural space" on Jemaa el Fna as one of only 90 "outstanding examples of the world's intangible cultural heritage."

First and foremost, Jemaa el Fna is a social meeting place for Marrakchis and visiting Moroccans, with much of the entertainment, particularly in the evening, aimed at Maghrebi-speaking locals rather than visitors, which only makes the experience even more authentic for the traveler. During the day, the western part of the square can be relatively quiet, with just a few troupes of snake charmers, monkey handlers, and metal castanet-clanging Gnaoua musicians jostling for your attention along with veiled women, termed *nakkachat,* armed with henna ready to tattoo your hands and feet in the traditional style. These acts are circled by a string of stalls selling freshly squeezed orange juice for just a few dirhams a glass. To the east of this action, you'll find hawkers with all manner of unusual goods spread out on the ground for perusal. The city's West African history can often be seen here in the potion salesmen, or *herboristes,* purveyors of various animal body parts and unusual dried herbs and spices still used today in traditional medicine. Here you may find local dentists displaying their most recent extractions in neat piles as some sort of assurance, along with public scribes and fortune tellers, although unless you can speak Arabic, you might be better spending your money on a photo rather than a reading. Toward late afternoon, don't miss the square's acrobats. There may also be jugglers, magicians, and child boxers (girls included) along with what seems to be the most traditional and popular, at least for the locals, entertainment—the *halkas*. These tellers of myths and fables derive their name from the circle in which the crowd gathers around to hear the storyteller. Sometimes accompanied by a musician, he will recite his tale well into the evening, with appropriately dramatic pauses for passing the collection hat around.

In addition to entertainment, you'll find row upon row of open-air food stalls. Here the hawkers, some with an amazing array of one-liners spoken fluently in a variety of languages, can be painfully persistent for your dining business until you choose a stall and are sitting down—come armed with a sense of humor, and your experience will remain pleasant. Joining the juice stalls on the perimeter of the square are others selling dates, figs, apricots, and nuts, all of which you can try before you buy.

Music is a constant throughout the day but rises to a crescendo come early evening and continues unabated well into the night. Within 20 paces you may encounter full-blast renditions of traditional Atlas Berber, hypnotic *gnaoua*, and popular Moroccan folk. These simultaneous performances combine to create a powerful din that draws you in the closer you get to the square.

The most popular time of the day to visit Jemaa el Fna is late afternoon, and the presunset rush to find a seat at one of the rooftop cafes overlooking the square can become ugly. See the box, "Dining with a View," later in this chapter for the lowdown on the best spots.

Late afternoon is also the best time to take photos on the square, when both the daytime "workers"—regal-looking turbaned herbal doctors, cross-legged snake charmers, and veiled henna ladies—and nighttime performers—leather-faced Atlas Berber musicians, veiled she-boy dancers, and circus-dressed acrobats—are out. And don't forget the water sellers, with their brightly colored wide-brim hats and goatskin water vessels. Bring along plenty of Moroccan dirham (foreign currency is generally scowled at) in small change if you are planning on taking photos, as all of these people rely on gratuities. I usually make a standard, upfront payment of 10 dirham ($1.25/65p), which allows me to shoot a number of images with a relaxed subject who isn't worried about whether payment will be forthcoming or not after the event.

Remember to watch your wallet and other valuables once you enter the square, as it is an obvious draw for pickpockets. The prevalence of street children during the evening is also on the rise. Female travelers should be careful when crowding around an act, as this unfortunately affords an opportunity for the odd bit of groping. The ever-present Brigade Touristique is on hand to stop much of the hustling by guides and shopkeepers, but can be conspicuous sometimes by their lack of action when some other unfortunate act takes place.

of the city's moderately priced hotels. Most sights and areas of interest, however, are in the medina. North of Jemaa el Fna are the souks and some of the city's more important religious monuments, while to the south is the old Jewish quarter (the Mellah) and the kasbah, home to many of the medina's past and present palaces.

To the northeast of the city is the area known as the palmeraie, home to more than 100,000 date palms whose origins, legend has it, come from the Almoravid leader Youssef ben Tachfine's extensive army, who left behind thousands of discarded seeds during their initial siege of the city in the 11th century. Today this is where many of the city's chic luxury villas are housed.

Tip: Although the medina is relatively easy to navigate on your own, a guide can be handy to both give you insight into the area and protect you from the plethora of fellow guides who surreptitiously attach themselves to you as "your friend." See "Guide or No Guide?" (p. 38) for further information.

2 Getting Around

Getting around Marrakech is relatively straightforward thanks to the two distinct areas of the medina and ville nouvelle, which are joined by avenue Mohammed V. The only real geographically challenging area is the maze of nonsignposted alleys and souks to the north of Jemaa el Fna. You might consider taking a guide here (you'll certainly have enough offers), though you should still give yourself some time to explore on your own.

BY BUS   You aren't likely to need a bus within the city, although bus no. 1, which runs right up avenue Mohammed V from the Koutoubia Mosque to Guéliz, can be a fun way of traveling this busy route and only costs 3dh (40¢/20p); it helps to have exact change. For information on the **Marrakech City Sightseeing** open-top buses, see p. 144.

BY *CALECHE*   These green, horse-drawn carriages are part of Marrakech's scenery and are a great way to see the city. An added incentive during peak hours is the relative ease with which you can catch a *calèche* rather than a *petit* taxi (plus these carriages can carry twice the amount of cargo—six people at a squeeze). You'll find *calèches* lined up between Jemaa el Fna and the Koutoubia Mosque, as well as outside some of the more expensive hotels. Most routes have a fixed price; 30dh ($3.75/£1.90) from Jemaa el Fna to Guéliz; 90dh ($11/£5.65) for a complete circuit of the medina's wall; or an hourly charge of 100dh ($13/£6.25), though reconfirm this with the driver before you set off.

BY FOOT   As the majority of Marrakech's attractions are in the pedestrian-only section of the medina, be prepared for a lot of walking. From Guéliz or Hivernage, Jemaa

---

Tips **"When in Rome . . ."**

As with any travel, be aware of what the locals do and when they do it. In Marrakech, take note of the lack of activity from midday to about 3pm, which is the hottest part of the day. Try to give yourself a break during this time; perhaps even head back to your hotel for a midday siesta. During the oppressively hot months of July and August, dehydration is a real risk, so carry some bottled water, which is cheap and available everywhere.

Looking After Morocco's Beasts of Burden

SPANA (Society for the Protection of Animals Abroad) was founded in the 1920s by two British women, Kate Hosali and her daughter Nina, who were visiting North Africa and appalled at the maltreatment of the region's animals. Today, the British-registered charity operates 19 veterinary centers and 21 mobile clinics throughout North and West Africa and the Middle East, and treats more than 300,000 animals annually.

SPANA has been working in Morocco since 1925, and today this work entails providing free veterinary care to working animals and a mobile veterinary unit that regularly travels to the High Atlas village of Imlil to care for tourist-trekking mules.

In Marrakech, SPANA operates an educational center with an animal refuge and veterinary hospital, which is open to the public. The center, SPANA's largest in the country, has information about their work; interactive displays showing the link between the environment, animals, and humans; and a steady stream of patients in its busy clinic.

The center issues licenses to *calèche* drivers and implants a microchip into each horse's neck to effectively track its medical history. Unhealthy horses are issued a ticket, and a second consecutive ticket results in the horse being admitted as a patient—ensuring only the fit are working on the street. An annual ceremony each May applauds those who care for their horses. This is a great day to visit the center, but visitors can drop in at any time. The center is located in the suburbs at Cité Mohammadi, Daoudiat. All *calèche* drivers should know where it is. Most staff members are non-English speaking, so to ensure that Mohammed Faifaite, the highly likeable English-speaking technician, is available, call © **024/303110,** or contact the center via e-mail by visiting www.spana.org.

el Fna is a 15- to 30-minute walk depending on the location of your hotel, which can be a pleasant stroll early in the morning or late afternoon, but is not recommended during the heat of the day, when it is better to catch a taxi or *calèche.* Majorelle Garden is close to some hotels in Guéliz, as are the Menara Gardens to Hivernage, though I would still recommend taking public transport and saving your legs for the medina.

BY TAXI *Petits* taxis are the most convenient and inexpensive way to get around the city. You'll find the small, beige-color, government-regulated vehicles everywhere. At your hotel, you can usually ask the reception staff to organize one for you, or otherwise you can simply stand on the side of the street and hail one. Drivers are only allowed to carry up to three passengers at a time, but be aware that if there is a vacant seat, you may pick up an additional passenger. At all times, request (sometimes this becomes a demand) the driver to put on the meter, which he is supposed to do no matter the time of day or night. Most trips within the main tourist areas of Guéliz, Hivernage, and the medina should cost no more than 15dh ($1.90/95p) during the day and a bit more after 8pm, when a 50% evening surcharge kicks in. For transport to the airport, the metered fare can rise up to between 60dh and 100dh

($7.50–$13/£3.75–£6.25), though it's best to agree on a price with the driver before-hand, as Marrakchi taxi drivers are notorious for refusing to use the meter for fares to/from the airport and for adding on luggage surcharges at the end of the ride. *Petits* taxis operate solely within the city environs, but remember that some parts of the medina are only accessible on foot. If you're traveling in a group and your exploration plans for the day include the more scattered city sights, then chartering a *grand* taxi for the day may be worthwhile. These beige-color Mercedes sedans take a maximum of six passengers—four is comfortable—and cost around 250dh ($31/£16) for the day. You can find them at Bab Doukkla bus station and by the post office in Guéliz, or ask at your hotel.

FAST FACTS: Marrakech

Airport See "Arriving," in "Orientation," earlier in this chapter.

Banks & Currency Exchanges Banks and ATMs are quite prominent throughout the city. In Guéliz, there's a concentration around place Abdelmoumen Ben Ali, including the **BMCI** branch at 35 bd. Zerktouni (© **024/448109**), which offers both a bureau de change (Mon–Fri 9am–5:30pm, Sat–Sun 9:30–11:30am and 4–7pm) and a 24-hour exchange ATM. **WAFA**'s bureau de change and ATM, on the corner of avenue Mohammed V and rue de la Liberté, is open Monday to Friday 8:15am to 6:45pm, Saturday 9:15am to 12:30pm and 3 to 6:45pm, and Sunday 9:15am to 3:45pm.

In the medina, the main banking area is off the south side of Jemaa el Fna, where the state-run **Bank al Maghrib** (Mon–Fri 8am–3pm) will cash traveler's checks, damaged notes, pre-1999 U.S. notes, and the new British pound notes, all of which may be rejected at other banks. Just around the corner on rue Moulay Ismail is a **WAFA** bureau de change (Mon–Fri 8am–7pm, Sat 9am–1pm and 2–6pm, Sun 9am–4pm), and on rue Bab Agnaou is an **SGMB** 24-hour exchange ATM. If all else fails, try any of the more expensive hotels.

Car Rentals The major international firms can be found on or near avenue Mohammed V, including **Avis,** 137 av. Mohammed V (© 024/433727); **Budget,** 68 bd. Zerktouni (© 024/431180); **Europcar,** 63 bd. Zerktouni (© 024/431228); **Hertz,** 154 av. Mohammed V (© 024/449984); and **National/Alamo,** 1 rue de la Liberté (© 024/430683). All of these have desks in the arrivals hall at the air-port as well, which are usually open from 8am to 10pm. Reputable local com-panies include **Medloc,** 75 rue ibn Aïcha, first floor (© 024/435757 or 061/1 81389), and **Loc Auto,** Galerie Commercial Liberté, corner of avenue Mohammed V and rue de la Liberté (© 024/436051 or 061/242394).

Consulates See "Consulates" in "Fast Facts: Morocco" on p. 66.

Dentists & Doctors **Dr. Gailleres,** 112 av. Mohammed V (© **024/449136**), and **Dr. Hamid Laraqui,** 203 av. Mohammed V (© **024/433216**), are both recommended dentists who speak good English. **Dr. Taarj Bel Abbass,** in the Polyclinique de Sud, 2 rue de Yougoslavie, Guéliz (© **024/447999** or 024/448372), speaks rea-sonably good English and also comes recommended. Other recommended doc-tors are **Dr. Samir Bellmezouar** (© **061/243227**) and **Dr. Frédéric Reitzer** (© **024/ 439562** or 061/173803).

Drugstores Pharmacies are very prevalent in the city. There are several along avenue Mohammed V between place Abdelmoumen Ben Ali and place de la Liberté. On Jemaa el Fna, at the beginning of rue Bab Agnaou, is **Pharmacie de la Place.** Most pharmacies are open 8:30am to 12:30pm, 4 to 8pm, and 8:30pm to 1am Monday to Saturday. Most will post a list of after hours pharmacies on their front door. An all-night pharmacy operates on the western edge of Jemaa el Fna, beside the Commissariat de Police, but there is usually a line. Instead, try **Pharmacie de Nuit,** outside the medina on rue Khalid ben Oualid, just off place de la Liberté (✆ 024/430415), where a doctor is usually available.

Emergency For **general emergencies** and the **police,** call ✆ **19.** For the **Brigade Touristique,** call ✆ **024/384601.** To report a **fire,** call ✆ **16.** In a **medical emergency,** call ✆ **024/404040** for a doctor on call (and public ambulance service); the voice on the other end may only speak Arabic or French. See "Dentists & Doctors," above, and "Hospitals," below, for more options. Call ✆ **024/443724** for a **private ambulance** service.

Hospitals **Polyclinique du Sud,** 2 rue de Yougoslavie, Guéliz (✆ **024/446399** or 024/447999), and **Clinique al Koutoubia,** rue de Paris, Hivernage (✆ **024/438585**), are both private clinics with high standards and usually have staff on hand that can speak some English.

Internet Access In the medina there's a fair smattering of cybercafes located on or near the pedestrian-only rue Bab Agnaou. In Guéliz, try **Cyberland,** 61 rue de Yougoslavie, and **Téléboutique,** 36 bd. Zerktouni, opposite the BMCI bank. Many riads and high-end hotels offer Wi-Fi, as do **Café des Epices** (p. 134) and **Café du Livre** (p. 137).

Laundry & Dry Cleaning There are no self-service laundries in Marrakech, but *pressings* (dry cleaners) are widespread in the ville nouvelle. A shirt or pair of pants costs around 15dh ($1.90/95p). **Pressing Imilchil,** 17 rue Tarik ben Ziad, is open daily from 8am to 9pm. Otherwise you can ask at your hotel reception, though this can prove expensive as they usually charge per item. Often your hotel's cleaning staff will do your laundry privately to earn some money on the side, a practice usually accepted by the management. A plastic shopping bag of laundry shouldn't cost you more than 30dh ($3.75/£1.90), but I wouldn't trust them with your favorite dress or white shirt.

Maps Tourist maps of Marrakech are fairly easy to obtain once you arrive. Different versions of essentially the same map plan are readily available for free from most hotels, tourist shops, or the ONMT office in Guéliz. The easiest to read, though it usually costs around 10dh ($1.25/65p), is the *Marrakech Evasions* version. This particular map marks all of the city's sights as well as a fair number of its accommodations and eating establishments. The most detailed city map, including the medina, is the *Plan Guide de Marrakech,* one of a series printed by the **Librairie DSM** (✆ **022/310281**) in Casablanca. This small booklet costs 85dh ($11/£5.30) and even has a street directory, but can be hard to find. I found it at the airport in the small shop in the Terminal 2 departures hall, but also try the bookshops listed on p. 147.

Newspapers Some shops down rue Bab Agnaou, off Jemaa el Fna, sometimes stock international weekly editions of the *Guardian* and *International Herald*

Tribune. There are also newsstands outside the ONMT office and along avenue Mohammed V in Guéliz, which sell various U.S. and British dailies and magazines.

Photographic Needs **Labo Photo Mondial,** on rue Bab Agnaou, is open daily from 9am to 8pm and sells a range of film, memory cards and USB sticks, and battery chargers and batteries for both cameras and camcorders. **Labo Photo Felix,** 133 av. Mohammed V, in Guéliz is open daily from 9am to 12:30pm and 3 to 6pm. In addition to stocking most digital accessories, they can burn your images onto a CD the same day.

Police The **Brigade Touristique** has a station at the north end of rue Sidi Mimoun. They generally have English-speaking staff and are specifically trained to deal with instances of hassle or theft involving tourists. There's also a regular Commissariat de Police on the west side of Jemaa el Fna.

Post Office & Mail Marrakech's **main post office,** which receives all *poste restante* mail, is on place du 16 Novembre, avenue Mohammed V, Guéliz, and is open Monday to Friday 8am to 4:15pm, Saturday 8 to 11:45am. There is a separate office on the side for sending parcels (which must be inspected first) and Western Union services. The medina post office is on Jemaa el Fna, next to the Bank al Maghrib. You'll also find many shops within the medina, as well as most expensive hotels, that sell postcard stamps. A **DHL** office is located at 113 av. Abdelkarim el Khattabi, Guéliz (✆ 024/437647). It's open Monday to Friday 8:30am to 6pm and on Saturdays 8:30am to noon. **FedEx** (✆ **024/448257**) is in the same building and has the same hours.

Restrooms There is a public toilet, or WC, amongst the plant nurseries in the western corner of Jemaa el Fna. Alternatively, your best bet is to politely ask for the *toilette* in any reasonable-looking restaurant. Sometimes there might be a small fee or, if there is an attendant keeping them clean, 2 to 3 dirham (25¢–38¢/13p–19p) are expected. If you're close to place du 16 Novembre in Guéliz, try the **McDonald's.**

Safety Generally, your personal safety never feels threatened other than being hassled for business by unofficial guides and shopkeepers in the medina. Female travelers may also encounter unwanted attention while wandering around Jemaa el Fna at night. In both cases, the best approach is to keep your sense of humor and initially ignore the unwanted attention entirely, followed by a polite, but direct, rebuke if necessary. If the irritant persists, walk into the closest shop or restaurant and ask them to contact the tourist police. If you are in the company of a male friend, it will be presumed that you are a couple, which can sometimes work in the female's favor with regards to any sexual harassment. However, be prepared for a barrage of questions as to why you don't have any children yet.

Taxis See "Getting Around," earlier.

Telephone Marrakech's **city code** has recently changed from 044 to **024.**

3 Where to Stay

Marrakech is Morocco's most popular tourist destination and is also emerging as one of the northern hemisphere's hottest property markets. This is most noticeable in the medina by the number (current estimates reach 500) of recently renovated foreign-owned houses, called riads (open-top central courtyard with a garden) or dars (central courtyard without the garden or no central courtyard at all). The great majority of these are operated as *maisons d'hôte*—Moroccan versions of the traditional B&B. Also within the medina are a number of inexpensive, backpacker-style hotels located around the pedestrian-only rue Bab Agnaou. Outside the medina's walls, the main concentration of hotels is in Guéliz, the bustling center of the ville nouvelle, or in the quiet, leafy, and well-to-do suburb of Hivernage. Out in the vast palmeraie, on the northeastern out-reaches of the city, are some truly luxurious villas. *Maisons d'hôte* are generally in the expensive to very expensive bracket, although there are a few select places that are cheaper. Moderately priced hotels in Guéliz, by comparison, are numerous, while most, if not all, accommodations in Hivernage are at least expensive if not very expensive. Villas in the palmeraie are, by their very definition, very expensive.

Choosing your accommodations in a city like Marrakech is hugely important. At times the frenetic pace of life here can be overwhelming, and the place that you retreat to each day needs to be a source of comfort. The riads, dars, and *maisons d'hôte* within the medina offer the full "local" experience, usually at a price that comes with welcome concessions to modern living. Outside Marrakech's walls, the hotels in Guéliz and Hivernage generally offer facilities such as a swimming pool, one or more restaurants, 24-hour reception, and an elevator, along with rooms that are air-conditioned and have TVs. Both suburbs have a good choice of restaurants and nightlife, and your hotel will generally only be a long walk or short taxi ride from the medina. The palmeraie is a wide expanse that can be both exotic and dusty, depending on whether you are inside or outside your walled villa, and is too far out to be reached from the city by foot. Personalized yet discreet service, five-star trimmings, and days lounging by the pool are the order of the day out here. My suggestion? Although the nice hotels in Guéliz and Hivernage offer more facilities and are sometimes better value for money, it's only by staying in the medina that you can truly experience this ancient and exotic city. For a perfect combination of culture and relaxation, consider splurging on a couple nights out in the palmeraie after your time in the medina.

No matter where you stay in Marrakech, late-night street noise generally isn't a problem except for some of the backpacker hotels, which look out onto rue Bab Agnaou, where the evening promenade can continue well into the night. However, if you stay in a *maison d'hôte,* remember that you are in a residential neighborhood and that children play, dogs bark, and donkeys bray. Winter nights in Marrakech can be surprisingly cold, and the availability of hot water can be an issue at many hotels during this time (even those that claim to offer it 24 hr. a day can sometimes only produce what is best described as a lukewarm trickle). At this time of year, take into consideration that central heating, or any heating for that matter, can be painfully absent from many places. I'm not kidding when I say that it's not unusual to see guests dressed in overcoats and woolly hats at the breakfast table. ***Note:*** Read my "Tips on Accommodations" in chapter 2.

Marrakech

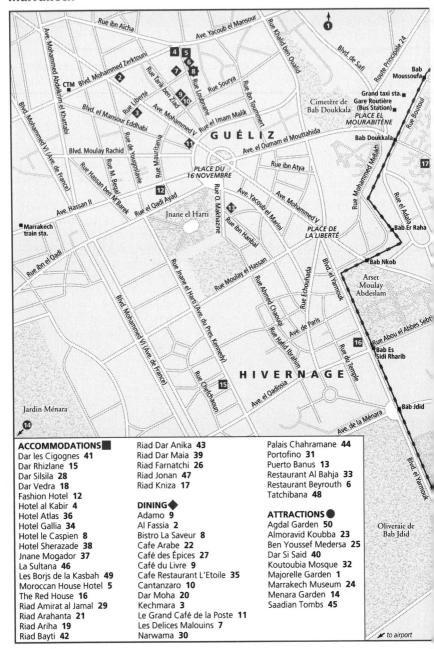

ACCOMMODATIONS ■
Dar les Cigognes **41**
Dar Rhizlane **15**
Dar Silsila **28**
Dar Vedra **18**
Fashion Hotel **12**
Hotel al Kabir **4**
Hotel Atlas **36**
Hotel Gallia **34**
Hotel le Caspien **8**
Hotel Sherazade **38**
Jnane Mogador **37**
La Sultana **46**
Les Borjs de la Kasbah **49**
Moroccan House Hotel **5**
The Red House **16**
Riad Amirat al Jamal **29**
Riad Arahanta **21**
Riad Ariha **19**
Riad Bayti **42**

Riad Dar Anika **43**
Riad Dar Maia **39**
Riad Farnatchi **26**
Riad Jonan **47**
Riad Kniza **17**

DINING ◆
Adamo **9**
Al Fassia **2**
Bistro La Saveur **8**
Cafe Arabe **22**
Café des Épices **27**
Café du Livre **9**
Cafe Restaurant L'Etoile **35**
Cantanzaro **10**
Dar Moha **20**
Kechmara **3**
Le Grand Café de la Poste **11**
Les Delices Malouins **7**
Narwama **30**

Palais Chahramane **44**
Portofino **31**
Puerto Banus **13**
Restaurant Al Bahja **33**
Restaurant Beyrouth **6**
Tatchibana **48**

ATTRACTIONS ●
Agdal Garden **50**
Almoravid Koubba **23**
Ben Youssef Medersa **25**
Dar Si Said **40**
Koutoubia Mosque **32**
Majorelle Garden **1**
Marrakech Museum **24**
Menara Garden **14**
Saadian Tombs **45**

↙ to airport

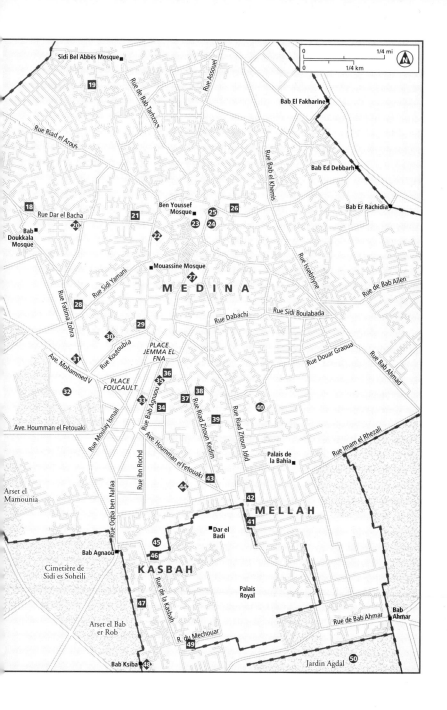

MEDINA
VERY EXPENSIVE
Dar les Cigognes ⚐ Located in the medina's kasbah and within walking distance to Jemaa el Fna, the "House of Storks" is actually two houses joined by an enclosed upper-level bridge, which spans a laneway marking the historical boundary between the old Islamic and Jewish quarters. Swiss-American owned and lovingly restored by respected local architect Charles Boccara, Dar les Cigognes offers a bit of luxury and an exotic ambience without being pretentious. The fresh air and natural light in the twin courtyards are best appreciated from one of the numerous lounges that are strategically placed in various niches and salons coming off the ground floors. Surrounding the courtyards are 11 themed, well-appointed rooms including the decadently ruby-red Harem, with its own fireplace; the sparkling Silver room, resplendent in wall-to-wall silver *tadelakt* and a lace-draped four-poster bed; and my personal favorite, the Safari, decked out in earth tones with various sub-Saharan objets d'art, a large painting depicting a colonial-era hunting party, and a king-size bed (which can be converted into twins).

Neatly tucked into the enclosed bridge are the guest-only hammam and spa, where scrubs, massages, and beauty treatments, including traditional henna tattooing, are available; there's also a Jacuzzi. The roof terraces, which look straight out onto the flock of storks who permanently roost on the ramparts of the Royal & El Badi palaces across the road, have great views of the Western High Atlas and are bedecked with tables and chairs for a sunny breakfast (served until 10:30am) or a romantic glass of wine at sunset. The house kitchen serves traditional Moroccan cuisine for lunch and dinner by reservation, and the cooks are only too happy to pass on their culinary skills to interested guests via a pre-arranged cooking lesson. The morning Stork News, which highlights the day's major world news stories and is served with a cup of coffee (in your room should you request), is a nice touch. *Note:* The outside noise here can at times last well into the night, as one of the main thoroughfares through the kasbah passes right by the doorway of the first house, so request one of the rooms in the second house.

108 rue de Berima, Medina, Marrakech. ⓒ 024/382740. Fax 024/384767. www.lescigognes.com. 11 units. 1,800dh–2,300dh ($225–$288/£113–£144) double; 2,800dh ($350/£175) suite. Children under 2 stay free in parent's room, 2–12 300dh ($38/£19), 13–18 380dh ($48/£24). Rates include breakfast and afternoon mint tea. Peak-season supplement Mar 23–May 14 and Dec 19–Jan 6. AE, MC, V. Public parking lot nearby. **Amenities:** Restaurant; hammam and spa; concierge; boutique; laundry service; Wi-Fi; library. *In room:* A/C, hair dryer, safe.

Riad Amirat al Jamal ⚐⚐ *(Finds)* This American-owned riad was once part of an Alaouite palace—the battlement niches are still in place—and is in a prime location just off Jemaa el Fna and in the shadow of the Koutoubia Mosque. Peggy Ward Engh bought this ochre-colored riad in 2007, and through her personal touches and determination, she has transformed the "Princess of Beauty" into a very special place. The large pool in the center courtyard is surrounded by tall, bird-attracting palms and sets the tone for luxury. A small salon/library—a former prayer room—is furnished with sacred objets d'art from manager Rachid Izemreten's Middle Atlas Aït Ourayne tribe, satellite TV, and a large fireplace. The rooms have all been individually decorated by Peggy and include touches such as a welcome pack of complimentary toiletries and snacks, bedside nightlights, and bathrooms with a portable vanity mirror and twin shower heads. The riad is also going green by changing bath towels only on request and recycling as much as possible—note the dried orange-peel potpourri. Rachid, whose staff are extremely friendly and hard-working, speaks English fluently, and is a highly regarded tour guide to boot. Breakfast is served poolside under a small columned terrace. Pass by the riad's private hammam—guests are also welcome to book the services of housekeeper–cum–beauty therapist Fatima—on the way up to twin rooftop terraces furnished with woven-raffia lounge chairs.

33 rue Fhal Zefritti, Laksour, Medina, Marrakech. © 024/444070 or 066/491706. www.amirataljamal.com. 5 units. 1,785dh–2,840dh ($223–$355/£112–£178) double. Rates include breakfast. Children under 12 stay free with parent in Terrace Duplex only. Peak-season supplement Dec 15–31. MC, V. The riad is only accessible on foot but parking is close by. **Amenities:** Pool; hammam; roof terrace. *In room:* A/C, fridge, safe.

Riad Dar Anika   *Anika* is Arabic for "elegant" and is an accurate description for this British-owned riad, which opened in 2005. Built on the site of an old parking lot, the building's odd shape makes full use of the available space and has a private entrance off one of the busiest pedestrian-only streets in the medina. Its location can't be beat, as it is only meters away from a taxi drop-off point and within short walking distance of many of the medina's sights and restaurants. Although you would assume there would be increased street noise, once you pass through the heavy wood door, the out-side hustle and bustle quickly dissipates. Traditional design is nicely combined with modern trimmings throughout the riad (blessedly during winter this equates to con-sistently hot water). A large, open-top marble courtyard offers a large, bright salon—air-conditioned in summer and fireplace heated during winter—a small hammam with massage room, and a small pool that allows some level of privacy by being built into a covered niche in the wall.

The rooms all face inward and are of various sizes. All are well appointed, especially the sole suite, which has a sofa and its own fireplace. The emphasis on mood lighting in each room, especially the Riad room, can bother some guests who prefer more nat-ural light, but at night you'll find it sets a romantic ambience throughout the riad. Breakfast is served on a narrow terrace on the first floor (grab a table early if the riad is full), and there's a large terrace on the roof with funky woven-grass chairs, big umbrellas, and a Moroccan-style tent with brightly colored low-lying lounges. Dinner is served on request, but since you are in the heart of the medina, there are plenty of choices nearby.

112 rue Riad Zitoun Kedim, Medina, Marrakech. © 024/391740 or 061/109340. Fax 024/391751. www.daranika. com. 9 units. 1,150dh–1,800dh ($144–$225/£72–£113) double; 2,500dh ($313/£156) suite. Rate includes breakfast, bottled water, and 1 free use of hammam. TPT not included. Peak-season supplement Mar 8–Apr 8 and Dec 15–Jan 6. Minimum 5-night stay Dec 22–Jan 1. AE, MC, V with 5% fee. Street parking available nearby. **Amenities:** Restau-rant; pool; hammam; Internet. *In room:* A/C, fridge, hair dryer, safe.

Riad Farnatchi   Located at the northern edge of the souks and around the corner from the oldest *farnatchi*—the below-ground fire pit used to heat the hammams—is this chic, intimate, and luxurious riad. Retired, award-winning British hotelier Jonathon Wix spent 2 years converting three small riads into a personal holiday home before, in 2004, deciding to open the doors to paying guests who have included the likes of Angelina Jolie and Russell Crowe. This celebrity status has by no means affected the attention to service afforded upon nonsuperstar guests, thanks to British manager Lynn Perez and her staff, who are present 24 hours a day to attend to any request. This is one boutique riad where you feel like you're getting what you paid for.

The original trio of riads were as much as 400 years old, but there's nothing ancient about the amenities here, which include a brand-new white-marble hammam and 7m (23-ft.) heated swimming pool (bashful bathers should note it is right near the riad entrance). Rooms are stocked with personally designed and crafted furniture, Egyptian-cotton linens, Hungarian goose-down pillows, and a computerized music/movie system and flatscreen TV. Every room is a suite and also has a private terrace. A nice touch is the set of complimentary *jellabah* and *babouches* that are laid out on the bed awaiting your arrival, as well as predinner canapés.

Even when full, the riad feels intimate and private with numerous salons located around the twin courtyards and a large rooftop terrace with plenty of lounge chairs. Romantic candle-lit dinners are available to guests. The kitchen bakes its own Berber bread and offers a different *menu d'jour* every night. The riad also provides take-out service from an international restaurant nearby.

2 Derb el Farnatchi, Medina, Marrakech. (C) **024/384910.** Fax 024/384913. www.riadfarnatchi.com. 9 units. 3,400dh–4,750dh ($425–$594/£213–£297) double. Children under 2 stay free in parent's room. Rate includes breakfast, airport transfers, *babouches* and *jellabah* (to take home), free use of hammam 4–7pm, and unlimited tea, coffee, and bottled water. TPT not included. Peak-season supplement and minimum 5-night stay Dec 20–Jan 7. Closed Aug. AE, MC, V. Accessible by foot only. **Amenities:** Pool; hammam; concierge; free Internet and laptop use. *In room:* A/C, central heating, satellite TV, iPod dock, on-demand movies, Wi-Fi, modem point.

Riad Kniza ★★★ This 18th-century riad has been in the family for almost 200 years and offers the complete package of traditional architecture, authentic furnishings, and, above all, overwhelmingly hospitable service. Mohammed Bouskri has "seen it all" as a guide for the past 35 years with clients that have included former U.S. President Richard Nixon and A-list Hollywood stars, and wife Najat is one of Marrakech's most renowned antiques dealers. Their passion since 2003 is Riad Kniza, named after their daughter and now managed by son Kamal. The seven rooms and suites are located on two floors around two open-air courtyards, the smaller of which will house a heated swimming pool and hammam by early 2008. Two salons come off the main courtyard and are furnished in Oriental antiques and furniture, and each have a fireplace. There are also fireplaces in all but one of the rooms and suites, which are charming combinations of traditional style and modern conveniences, furnished with lush fabrics of ruby satins and creamy silver velvets. The large roof terrace has two shaded areas with lounges and floor cushions and is a popular spot for both breakfast and a candle-lit dinner, served by the very professional yet personable English-speaking staff. Riad Kniza is located very close to Bab Doukkala, one of the better-known entrances to the medina, and is an easy 10-minute walk from Jemaa el Fna.

34 Derb Hotel, off rue Bab Doukkala, Medina, Marrakech. (C) **024/376942.** Fax 024/378365. www.riadkniza.com. 7 units. 2,420dh–3,850dh ($303–$481/£151–£241) double. Rates include breakfast, airport transfers, all nonalcoholic drinks; half-day city tour with stay of 3 nights. TPT not included. Low-season rates Jun 16–Sept 14. AE, MC, V. 10% discount for cash payments ($, £, €, dirham). Accessible by foot only; parking close by. **Amenities:** Restaurant; pool; concierge; free Internet, Wi-Fi, and laptop use. *In room:* A/C, satellite TV, Wi-Fi, safe.

EXPENSIVE

Riad Arahanta *(Value)* *(Kids)* Scottish owners David and Ross were staying in this 300-year old family home while house hunting and ended up liking the place so much, they bought it. Their Riad Arahanta (Burmese for "the enlightened ones") maintains much of the original atmosphere, which is evident upon arrival when guests are handed a key to the front door. All of the rooms are on the ground floor (David and Ross live on the first floor) and consist of two doubles with their own bathrooms and two singles that share a modern bathroom—a great combination for a family or group of friends. As Arahanta is an old, traditionally built house with rooms insulated by overly thick walls and cooled by a shady courtyard, air-conditioning isn't needed and

— I don't speak sign language.

A hotel can close for all kinds of reasons.

Our Guarantee ensures that if your hotel's undergoing construction, we'll
let you know in advance. In fact, we cover your entire travel experience.
See www.travelocity.com/guarantee for details.

You'll never roam alone.

simply adds to the authenticity. The rooftop terrace is large and nicely overgrown with potted plants. The riad staff includes a housekeeper who is the excellent kitchen cook and a manager who will bring items to the house should guests become despondent with the haggling in the souks. Located extremely close to the old Glaoui Dar el Bacha palace, which is guarded 24 hours a day and therefore extends an atmosphere of security around the area, this isn't a fancy riad by any stretch of the imagination, but it's certainly a welcoming, relaxed, and very affordable place to stay.

14 Derb Tizougarine, Dar el Bacha, Medina, Marrakech. ©/fax 024/426390 or 072/844364. http://perso.wanadoo. net.ma/arahanta. 4 units. 350dh ($44/£22) single; 800dh ($100/£50) double; 10,000dh ($1,250/£625) weekly for whole riad. Children stay free in parent's room. Rates include breakfast. No credit cards. Accessible by foot only; parking nearby. **Amenities:** Kitchen for guest use; lounge. *In room:* Fan and heater (on request), no phone.

Riad Ariha *Value*

Riad Ariha is at least a couple of hundred years old and was restored with owner Barbara's deep fascination and respect for Moroccan interiors. "Zen meets Morocco" is Barbara's theme for the space, and entering the riad's simple, white-dominated interior is a pleasant and instantly calming surprise. Both a small plunge pool and a linen-draped salon lead off from the small inner courtyard, where *bejmat* flooring adds to the earthy and peaceful ambience. Also on the ground floor is a small hammam for two; in-room aromatherapy massages can be arranged.

The five reasonably sized bedrooms are named after various aromatic plants or trees and have white and natural *tadelakt* walls, white-linen drapes, and bright bedspreads. Jasmine is located on the more private first floor and is a perfect example of restrained luxury with its fireplace and small sitting area. On the rooftop is a small terrace with Barbara's version of a Bedouin tent, with its natural linen roof and walls. For those wishing to partake in some serious tanning, the two sun lounges are complimented by an outdoor shower. There are also fantastic views looking toward the Ben Youssef Mosque, which reminds one that although located within the medina, Riad Ariha is still a good 15-minute walk from the bustle of Jemaa el Fna.

90 Derb Ahmed el Borj, Kaa Sour, Sidi bin Slimane, Medina, Marrakech. © 024/375850, 073/784678 in Morocco, or 866/689-9901 toll-free from North America. www.riadariha.com. 5 units. 770dh–990dh ($96–$124/£48–£62) double. Children under 12 165dh ($21/£10) with parent (2 rooms only). Rates include breakfast. TPT not included. Peak-season supplement Dec 17–Jan 2 and Apr–May; low-season rates July–Aug. MC, V. Accessible by foot only; organize pickup with riad. **Amenities:** Plunge pool; meals by request; free Internet and Wi-Fi; satellite TV. *In room:* A/C, central heating, safe.

Riad Bayti ✦✦

This funky and relaxed riad opened in 2002 and is fast becoming the house (*bayti* means "our house" in Arabic) of choice for young 20- and 30-somethings looking for a cultural experience at a reasonable cost. Located on the edge of the Mellah (Jewish quarter) just past a covered market of spices and jewelry, young owners Diego and Marylen are proud of both the Moroccan and Jewish history of their riad, which dates back to 1836. Inside the nondescript entrance is a playful combination of traditional architecture and modern styling. There's a large courtyard with *bejmat* and plenty of greenery, as well as a first-floor terrace with carved-wood railings and an L-shape salon of low lounges and brightly colored cushions that looks over the swimming pool. A separate, cozy dining room for home-cooked meals and a small library are also located on the ground floor.

Unusual for most riads, all the guest rooms are on the first floor, ensuring some quiet and privacy, although inside the good-size rooms (some will comfortably accommodate a third bed), the lack of a door between bedroom and bathroom requires guests to at least be close friends. On the rooftop is a covered lounge that is popular at any time of the day for reading and relaxing, as well as affording great views of the nearby Royal and Badi palaces. Diego and Marylen are both attentive hosts and good company, and you'd be hard-pressed to find a more easygoing, affordable riad.

35 Derb SKCA, Bab Mellah, Medina, Marrakech. ℭ/fax 024/380180 or ℭ 066/254654. www.riad-bayti.com. 6 units. 880dh ($110/£55) double; 1,045dh ($131/£65) suite. Rates include breakfast, afternoon tea, airport transfers for 6-night stay. TPT not included. Peak-season supplement Feb 10–Mar 12, Mar 31–Apr 30, and Dec 18–Jan 5. MC, V with 5% fee. Accessible by foot only; parking nearby. **Amenities:** Pool; laundry service; library w/satellite TV; reception safe; Wi-Fi. *In room:* A/C, no phone.

MODERATE

Jnane Mogador *(Value)*   Down a quiet lane off one of the main thoroughfares leading to Jemaa el Fna is proof that "budget" and *"maison d'hôte"* can be happy bedfellows within the medina. Built in 2000 by Mohammed Araban, one of Marrakech's most experienced hoteliers, Jnane Mogador's heavy 19th-century-style front door opens up to a traditionally designed open-top courtyard complete with *zellij* flooring, a fountain, and overhanging greenery. Rooms of varying size look out over the courtyard, and *moucharabieh* (veiled windows opening outward) let in fresh air. Earthy, pastel-color walls contrast with the bright, natural-fiber bedspreads. Small, bright, *tadelakt*-rendered bathrooms, unusual for Moroccan accommodations in this price range, are in every room. The sole Mogador suite is in the same style as the other rooms but is larger with a king-size bed, lounge, private terrace, and air-conditioning.

On the first floor is a small salon with low-lying lounges and a fireplace, and the rooftop terrace looks straight out to the Western High Atlas mountains. Here you can have breakfast (30dh/$3.75/£1.90) under the sun or beneath the covered Moroccan tent. A below-ground hammam and massage room are recent additions (see "Hot & Steamy: Hammams" on p. 148). At times the reception area can get quite busy and the staff consequently a trifle gruff, but overall it's a cheery place with a distinct "international traveler" atmosphere. It's often full, so book ahead.

116 rue Zitoun Kedim, Derb Sidi Bouloukat, Medina, Marrakech. ℭ 024/426324 or 024/426323. www.jnane mogador.com. 18 units. 290dh ($36/£18) single; 380dh ($48/£24) double; 460dh ($58/£29) triple; 520dh ($65/£33) quad; 700dh ($88/£44) Mogador suite. MC, V. Accessible only by foot. **Amenities:** Cafe; hammam; Internet. *In room:* Satellite TV.

Riad Dar Maia *(Value)*   This is one of the best value riads of this standard within the medina. Maria, an English-speaking Spaniard who also converses effortlessly in French, opened this place in 2006. This is a traditional dar rather than riad, and the small courtyard is only open on three sides, as it is bordered by a brilliant white wall on one side. A small fountain at its base is a pleasant concession to the dar's name, which translates to "Riad of Water," and leads to a small, brightly colored salon where guests can watch a movie or listen to music. The comfortable rooms are named after the colors that grace their walls—green, orange, pink, turquoise, or white. Strips of colored glass beads are all that separate the bedroom from the bathroom, so make sure you're comfortable with your roommate. The rooftop is literally the crowning glory of Maia, with funky woven-grass chairs, umbrellas, and a small covered salon with a flop-down lounge. It can be a bit difficult to find the correct lane that leads to the riad, but its location is very convenient to both Jemaa el Fna and the sights and restaurants within the southern section of the medina.

31 Derb Zouina, off rue Riad Zitoun Jdid, Medina, Marrakech. ℭ 024/376231 or 063/067805. www.riad-dar-maia.com. 5 units. 605dh–770dh ($76–$96/£38–£48) double. Children under 12 stay free in parent's room. Rates

include breakfast. Peak-season supplement Apr, Oct, and Dec. No credit cards. Accessible by foot only; parking off rue Riad Zitoun Jdid. **Amenities:** Internet. *In room:* A/C, no phone.

INEXPENSIVE

Hotel Atlas *(Finds)* This friendly gem is one of the newest and cleanest of all the budget hotels on or near rue Bab Agnaou. Opened in 2002, it has three levels of rooms facing a traditional open-top central courtyard with potted palms and Moroccan lanterns. The rooms are of various configurations and offer good value options for single or group travelers. The rooms are all clean and bright, if at times a little stuffy, with carved-wood doors, modern tiling, wrought-iron furniture, and hand basins. Separate showers and toilets are located on each floor, though there are only three of each to service everybody, so either wake up early or sleep in. Five rooms are located on the roof terrace and come with individual air-conditioning, as they would otherwise be oppressively hot during the summer. Also on the terrace are some woven chairs, umbrellas, and mosaic tables for writing those postcards.

50 rue Sidi Bouloukate, Medina, Marrakech. ℂ 024/391051. 21 units. 90dh ($11/£5.65) single; 170dh ($21/£11) double; 250dh ($31/£16) triple; 280dh ($35/£16) quad; 320dh ($40/£20) quinary. No credit cards. Accessible by foot only. *In room:* Basin, no phone.

VILLE NOUVELLE
VERY EXPENSIVE

Dar Rhizlane ✹✹✹ *(Kids)* Owner Ahmed Sadke and renowned local architect Charles Boccara have transformed this former villa into one of the most charming accommodations in the city. Surrounded by multistory hotel complexes in well-to-do Hivernage, Dar Rhizlane (Ahmed's daughter's name) is as good as anywhere in the medina or the palmeraie, plus it's conveniently located.

A lush garden of bamboo, bougainvillea, citrus trees, palms, roses, and succulents hosts the afternoon's complimentary high tea and surrounds two separate houses, which are bisected by a central salon furnished with leather armchairs and heavy Berber carpets. Menzeh, the main building, houses 10 different-size rooms and suites that enjoy either private garden terraces or balconies, along with a ground-floor reception room complete with antiques and a wrought-iron chandelier. At the rear of the property is Garden Villa Rayyane, where the recently renovated restaurant stands along with two more suites and a room. Aside the pavilion is an open-air bar, and between the two buildings is a large swimming pool, heated in winter and surrounded by sun lounges.

All rooms and suites are elegantly furnished with Moroccan antiques and furniture, lots of cushions and carpets, as well as traditional beehive-shape fireplaces. The bathrooms are nice and big with gilded-copper washbasins. Although it's more of a romantic retreat, families are most welcome. Both the medina and Guéliz are within walking distance (though you wouldn't want to in the heat of the day), and both *calèches* and *petits* taxis are just outside the front gate.

Av. Jnane el Harti (formerly av. du Président Kennedy), Hivernage, Marrakech. ℂ 024/421303. Fax 024/447900. www.dar-rhizlane.com. 19 units. 3,150dh ($394/£197) double; 5,800dh–8,000dh ($625–$1,000/£363–£500) suite. Rates include breakfast and afternoon tea. Children 2–12 half price in parent's room; under 2 free. AE, MC, V. Off-street parking. **Amenities:** Restaurant; bar; pool; babysitting; Wi-Fi. *In room:* A/C, satellite TV, fridge, hair dryer, safe.

The Red House ✹ This Moroccan-owned and -managed *palais d'hôte* is in a great location just outside the medina walls in Hivernage. Opened in 2001, the former mansion is set behind high walls on a large corner block of neatly trimmed grass and extensive gardens; it's a total feast for the eyes once you set foot inside. Guests have a private entrance that leads past the large, heated outdoor pool into a grand salon and reception area. Another entrance, which is open for nonguest diners, leads to a grand restaurant. The combined space of these areas is the size of a small medina neighborhood, and you'll see traditional Moorish *zellij*, gold-edge stucco, *tazouakt*, white-and-green marble-tile flooring, antique furniture, and heavy Arabic carpets.

Some of the rooms are indeed red, while others are in shocking blue or light pastels. The emphasis on luxury extends past the king-size beds and big-screen TVs to the bathrooms, some with both a regular stand-up shower and a separate massage-spray shower. The Imperial is a two-bedroom, two-bath suite with its own large, private balcony, and is perfect for families. The young and attentive staff makes The Red House something special; 44 are on hand to serve a maximum of 18 guests. Breakfast is served until a leisurely 2pm.

Bd. el Yarmouk, Hivernage, Marrakech. ℂ **024/437040** or 024/437041. Fax 024/447409. www.theredhouse-marrakech.com. 8 units. 2,600dh ($325/£163) double; 3,100dh ($388/£194) suite; 6,500dh ($813/£407) Imperial suite. Rates include airport transfers and breakfast. Peak-season supplement Apr 1–May 10 and Dec 21–Jan 5. MC, V. Off-street parking and private garage available. **Amenities:** Restaurant; snack bar; pool w/attendant; 24-hr. room service; 24-hr. reception. *In room:* A/C, cable and satellite TV, DVD player, Wi-Fi, fridge, hair dryer, safe.

EXPENSIVE
Fashion Hotel This newcomer to the Guéliz hotel scene is located on a very busy street, but once guests enter the modern and stylish reception—with just as stylish a reception staff—the noise quickly subsides. The rooms and suites occupy the first five floors, with an indoor swimming pool and hammam occupying the sixth. The rooms are large and well designed, decorated in reds, oranges, and yellows with low-lying beds, thick Berber rugs upon clay-tile flooring, and good-size bathrooms with large shower/tub combos. A modern ground-floor cafe serves an especially biting espresso and is open late.

45 av. Hassan II (corner of rue Mauritania), Guéliz, Marrakech. ℂ **024/423707**. Fax 024/423727. 40 units. 684dh ($86/£43) double; 970dh ($121/£61) suite. Children under 2 stay free in parent's room. MC, V. **Amenities:** Cafe; pool; hammam. *In room:* A/C, satellite TV.

MODERATE
Hotel al Kabir This modern, airy hotel is one of a group of similar standard hotels in this area of Guéliz. Mainly used by tour groups and reservation agencies, the Hotel al Kabir's rooms, accessible from three elevators, are all clean, modern, and well appointed, if a tad sterile, and the bathrooms are a reasonable size with shower/tub combos. The five suites are slightly larger than the rooms—the extra space filled with a small lounge—and aren't a particularly good value in comparison. The L-shape building curls around a very pleasant, clean, and underused pool that is relatively private though only a shuffle away from the bar. You can bypass the hotel's restaurant for the excellent dining options nearby.

Corner of bd. Zerktouni and rue Loubnane, Guéliz, Marrakech. ℂ **024/439540** or 024/434150. Fax 024/448020. 95 units. 291dh ($36/£18) single; 382dh ($48/£24) double; 800dh ($100/£50) suite. MC, V. Reserved st. parking available. **Amenities:** Restaurant; bar; pool. *In room:* A/C, satellite TV.

Hotel Le Caspien ⊛ Opened in 2004 and located on a quiet street minutes away from Guéliz's many restaurants and shops, this pleasant hotel has a modern feel even though the design is essentially traditional. The brick/cement exterior hides a central courtyard–cum–lobby, where *zellij* and clay tiling are complemented by marble floors

Kids Family-Friendly Hotels

Dar Ayniwen (p. 128): Although it's marketed as a romantic getaway, many families enjoy the dar's large, walled grounds. Little ones can splash around in the large pool, run around the lawn, and visit the tortoise colony (22 at last count). The complimentary transport to and from town is greatly appreciated at the end of a long day, as is the in-house chef's adaptability come meal time.

Dar Rhizlane (p. 123): Within no time, kids survey the backyard of this house and immediately set to work exploring the nooks and crannies of the various gardens and structures. Breakfast picnics laid out on the lawn will surely herald a perfect start to the day for little ones on holiday.

Moroccan House Hotel (see below): What makes this city-center hotel attractive to families is the choice of three- and four-bed rooms. The enclosed swimming pool is a rarity for this standard of hotel, as is the availability of cereal at the roof-top breakfast buffet.

Riad Arahanta (p. 120): David and Ross welcome kids into their home-cum-riad. Reasonably priced rooms and a very reasonable weekly rate for the whole riad make this an attractive option for large families, and access to the kitchen will be appreciated by those who need to heat up or prepare meals for babies and fussy eaters.

and lots of natural light. The rooms are entered through dark, heavy medieval-like wood doors, but inside you'll find pastels, wood beams, clay tiling and *zellij,* and Moroccan art, carpets, and lamps. The bathrooms are modern, if small, and have shower/tub combos. The suites are similar to the rooms, only larger. One of the two in-house restaurants, Bistro La Saveur (p. 135), has seating both at the front and rear of the lobby, the latter leading out to a moderate-size pool with a bizarre, fake-rock mini-waterfall. This is the hotel's one failing in design, as the location of the pool affords absolute minimal privacy. The first-floor Moroccan restaurant has traditional music and dancing every Friday night. The staff are numerous and friendly.

12 rue Loubnane, Guéliz, Marrakech. ⓒ 024/422282. Fax 024/420079. www.lecaspien-hotel.com. 38 units. 550dh ($69/£34) double; 800dh ($100/£50) suite. Excludes TPT. Children 2–12 pay half price in parent's room; under 2 free. MC, V. Limited street parking. **Amenities:** 2 restaurants; pool; boutique. *In room:* A/C, satellite TV, safe.

Moroccan House Hotel *(Finds (Kids*   From the outside you wouldn't know it, but this is one of the most colorful and personable hotels in Marrakech. As the name suggests, the design here is more like a house than a standard block hotel, and after the initial surprise at the extravagantly painted and decorated interior, the place starts to grow on you. The lobby, also the central courtyard, is saturated with *zellij, tazouakt* ceiling and furniture, and different-colored Iraqi glass panels. Various standards of rooms are entered through heavy wood and studded doors of bright blue, which are opened with massive keys worthy of something grander. The visual feast continues with a choice of various brightly colored interiors furnished with faux-antiques and lace-draped four-poster beds. Each bathroom has its own water heater and bath/shower combo, and comes supplied with a range of complimentary toiletries (a nail scrubber, for instance). The two styles of suites are larger than the rooms and offer more luxuries such as a fridge, hair dryer, and in-bathroom phone. Although the hotel offers to accommodate up to four people in all its star-based room categories, only the five-star Prince suites can do this comfortably.

Many guests choose to eat dinner in-house at one of the three Moroccan salons. True to the house theme, dinner guests are encouraged to sit together with fellow guests. Although the hotel operates a dry bar, guests are welcome to bring their own alcohol. A breakfast buffet is served in a Moroccan tent on the rooftop terrace. The pool is located at the rear of the building and is only accessed by a stairway below the lobby/courtyard, thus affording a certain level of privacy usually lacking in this standard of hotel. Many guests comment fondly about the hotel's ambience and the genuine friendliness of the staff. The hotel is conveniently close to many of Guéliz's better restaurants and shops.

3 rue Loubnane, Guéliz, Marrakech. ⓒ 024/420305 or 024/420306. Fax 024/420297 or 024/420298. www.moroccan househotels.com. 50 units. 3-star rooms: 405dh ($51/£25) single, 484dh ($61/£30) double; 4-star Pacha suites: 455dh ($57/£28) single, 624dh ($78/£39) double; 5-star Prince suites: 527dh ($66/£33) single, 764dh ($96/£48) double, 917dh ($115/£57) triple, 1,128dh ($141/£71) quad. TPT not included. Breakfast buffet 55dh ($6.90/£3.45). Children under 10 stay free in parent's room. MC, V. Limited street parking available. **Amenities:** Restaurant; pool; free Wi-Fi. *In room:* A/C, satellite TV, modem point, safe.

MORE ACCOMMODATIONS IN MARRAKECH

Marrakech has become a popular, year-round destination, and despite the amazing number of accommodations within the city, finding a place to sleep can sometimes be difficult. Most of the ever-increasing number of riads and dars within the medina have less than 10 rooms and are regularly prebooked. Here are a few places to try when the above are already full.

Dar Silsila 🏠🏠   This popular choice is located near Jemaa el Fna. *Silsila* means "chain," and English-speaking owner Jean Patrick translates this into taking care of his guest's needs from arrival to departure. The entire dar has a chic Asian/African ambience, while the four bedrooms are individually themed and elegantly decorated.

11 derb Jdid Laksour, Medina, Marrakech. ⓒ 067/352005. Fax 024/449215. www.darsilsila.com. 4 units. 1,100dh–1,540dh ($130–$182/£67–£94) double. Children under 12 330dh ($41/£21). Low- and peak-season costs also apply. No credit cards. Accessible on foot only. **Amenities:** Restaurant; lounge w/fireplace. *In room:* A/C, hair dryer, safe.

Dar Vedra 🏠🏠   Owners Didier and Sebastian manage this restored 18th-century riad, whose dark heavy-wood beams are off-set by a brilliant white exterior and soft, muted interiors. Vivian and Pancho Man—the two resident tortoises—wander in the twin open-top courtyards, one of which houses a small heated pool; room no. 1 is just steps away. A single room offers a bit of luxury for solo travelers. The large rooftop terrace is almost in the shadow of the Bab Doukkala mosque.

3 Derb Sidi Ahmed ou Moussa, Bab Doukkala, Medina, Marrakech. ⓒ 024/389370 or 072/387973. Fax 024/380082. www.darvedra.com. 6 units. 759dh ($90/£46) single; 1,199dh–1,419dh ($142–$168/£74–£86) double. Children under 2 stay free in parent's room. Breakfast included. Low- and peak-season costs apply. Closed Jan. MC, V. 3% discount for on-site cash payments. Accessible on foot only. **Amenities:** Restaurant; pool; lounge w/fireplace, satellite TV, and stereo; Internet. *In room:* A/C, no phone.

Hotel Gallia   Since 1929, this French-run hotel has been a favorite for budget travelers. Located a 15-minute walk from Jemaa el Fna, the restored mansion has spotlessly clean rooms of different sizes and decor, some with air-conditioning and a private bathroom. All rooms either look onto one of the two tiled courtyards, which are shaded by a huge palm tree that attracts riotous flocks of finches, or are located on the rooftop terrace. Book ahead by fax if possible.

30 rue de la Recette. ℭ 024/445913. Fax 024/444853. 20 units. 270dh ($34/£17) single; 420dh ($53/£26) double. Breakfast included. No credit cards. Limited street parking available. *In room:* A/C (in most).

Hotel Sherazade ✿   Another very popular budget traveler haunt, this hotel is down a quiet lane within a few minutes' stroll from Jemaa el Fna. Rooms of different sizes and configurations—some with a private bathroom and air-conditioning—are spread throughout two former mansions that are connected by a rooftop terrace. The German-Moroccan owners preside over their staff, who are renowned amongst former guests for their genuine friendliness. The breakfast (50dh/$6.25/£3.15) in the rooftop tent is just as warmly received, while the Sherazade's close proximity to the nearby mosque—and its early morning *muezzin*—sometimes isn't.

3 Derb Jemaa, rue Riad Zitoun Kedim, Medina, Marrakech. ℭ 024/429305. www.hotelsherazade.com. 23 units. 170dh–430dh ($21–$54/£11–£27) single; 260dh–650dh ($33–$81/£16–£41) double; 600dh–650dh ($75–$81/£38–£41) small apt. Peak-season costs apply. No credit cards. Accessible on foot only. **Amenities:** Restaurant. *In room:* A/C (in some).

La Sultana   This is one of the largest and most luxurious riads in the medina. Located right next door to the Saâdian Tombs, La Sultana combines four riads and offers everything you would expect from a member of the "Great Hotels of the World," including a large heated pool, hammam and spa, library, gym, and a variety of bars and restaurants.

403 rue de la Kasbah, Medina, Marrakech. ℭ 024/388008. Fax 024/387777. www.lasultanamarrakech.com. 20 units. 2,561dh–4,741dh ($320–$593/£160–£296) double; 3,597dh–8,175dh ($450–$1,022/£225–£511) suite; 6,540dh–9,537dh ($818–$1,192/£409–£596) apt. Breakfast included. Children under 2 stay free in parent's room. MC, V. Limited street parking close by. **Amenities:** 2 restaurants; 3 bars; pool; gym; hammam and spa; laundry service; Internet; library. *In room:* A/C, fireplace, satellite TV, DVD/CD stereo, minibar w/complimentary nonalcoholic drinks, hair dryer, safe.

Les Borjs de la Kasbah   This boutique hotel, located behind the defensive *borjs* (walls) of the medina's kasbah, was created out of six small townhouses and one riad. Rooms are finished in warm earthy shades and combine traditional with modern touches such as free Wi-Fi and towel warmers. Five rooms are available to solo travelers. The hotel has a village-like atmosphere and includes two salons, a lounge bar, and a restaurant known for its international cuisine. At press time, a pool and spa complex were under way. The Franco-British owners have made a conscious effort to run an environmentally friendly hotel with the use of solar power, energy-efficient lighting, and waste management policies.

Rue du Mechouar, Kasbah, Medina, Marrakech. ℭ 024/381101. Fax 024/381125. www.lesborjsdelakasbah.com. 18 units. 1,100dh ($138/£69) single; 1,600dh–1,900dh ($200–$238/£100–£119) double; 2,400dh ($300/£150) suite. Breakfast and airport transfers included. Low- and peak-season costs apply. Children 5–12 250dh ($31/£16) in parent's room; under 5 free. MC, V. Limited street parking available. **Amenities:** Restaurant; 2 bars; pool; hammam and spa. *In room:* A/C, satellite TV, Wi-Fi, fridge, hair dryer, safe.

Riad Jonan *(Finds*   In a quiet neighborhood in the kasbah of the medina, rooms at this riad overlook twin, open-top courtyards, one with a plunge pool. The rooms are all en-suite and decorated in traditional Moroccan style. This is a friendly, homely place that's efficiently run by live-in English owners Howard and Martyn, who doubles as the excellent in-house chef.

35 Derb Bzou, off rue de la Kasbah, Medina, Marrakech. © 024/386448 or 071/234628. www.riadjonan.com. 11 units. 880dh–1,360dh ($110–$170/£55–£85) double. Breakfast included. Peak-season costs apply Easter, Christmas, and New Year. MC, V (both via PayPal). Limited street parking 50m (165 ft.) away. **Amenities:** Restaurant; lounge w/satellite TV; pool. *In room:* A/C (in some), fridge (in some), hair dryer (in some), safe (in some).

PALMERAIE

Dar Ayniwen ★★★ *(Kids)*   Jacques Abtan built this family villa out in the oasislike palmeraie in 1983, but once the kids moved out, he opened up his "House of Palm Trees" to the public and now presides with son Stéphane over one of the best accommodations in Marrakech. The villa is set amongst 2 hectares (5 acres) of beautiful gardens, where guests will likely come across tortoises, guinea fowl, and Jacques (tending to his beloved plants) on their morning stroll—you may even be treated to an impromptu botany lesson. The grand Moorish villa is spacious and generously decorated with Jacques's other passion—early-20th-century Moroccan antiques and protectorate-era paraphernalia. The rooms (all suites) are lavishly decorated and have large bathrooms, even larger bedrooms, and a separate lounge area with a home-entertainment system. Some also come with a fireplace. The larger Pavilion Romane, out in the garden, is ideal for small families.

Guests can spend time in the marble hammam and book massages and beauty treatments, or else lounge by the heated pool, which is surrounded by a lush green lawn. Dar Ayniwen's best-kept secret is its cuisine, which you can enjoy anywhere on the property, including your room, keeping with the Abtans' philosophy of attentive service in an unobtrusive style. Dar Ayniwen is a 10- to 15-minute drive from Jemaa el Fna, and a free shuttle service is available at any time of day or night (just be sure to give them advance warning).

Tafrata, Palmeraie, Marrakech. © 024/329684 or 024/329685. Fax 024/329686. www.dar-ayniwen.com. 7 units. 2,500dh–4,200dh ($313–$525/£156–£263) double. Children under 12 stay free in parent's room. Rates include airport and urban transfers and breakfast. Peak-season supplement Dec 17–Jan 2 and Feb 5–May 26. Minimum 7-night stay over Christmas and New Year. AE, MC, V. Parking on grounds. **Amenities:** Restaurant; pool; hammam; concierge; room service; babysitting; library. *In room:* A/C, satellite TV, DVD/stereo, Wi-Fi, safe.

Dar Zemora ★★   Paul and Lindsay Kentish's discreet boutique villa is a perfect retreat from the dust and hustle. Opened in 2003, Dar Zemora sits amongst 1.2 hectares (3 acres) of palms, roses, citrus trees, jasmine, and bougainvillea, and consists of a main five-bedroom house, a separate pavilion, and a 25m-long (82-ft.) heated outdoor pool. The bedrooms (two suites and three rooms) are finished in smooth earth-color *tadelakt* walls, hand-painted ceilings, *bejmat* flooring covered with large rugs, and traditional and modern furnishings. The two suites also come with a fireplace, four-poster bed, and private terrace. The pavilion—a mini-house with two bedrooms, two outside terraces, and a small kitchenette—is perfect for families, although they're not keen on accommodating tots due to the unsupervised pool.

What makes Dar Zemora special, I feel, are the reception areas. Two large, indoor salons, where aperitifs are taken each night, have comfortable sofas, big armchairs, plenty of coffee-table books, and smooth background music. Both lead outside to the open-side Fan Room, with tall white-linen drapes, colorful floor cushions, and Moroccan lanterns. There's also a cozy library with leather armchairs, a fireplace, and free Internet and Wi-Fi. A separate hammam and massage room, available to guests only, are located within the gardens. Concierge Youssef and Jamal are always on hand should you need something, and in-house cooks Jamila and Rachida work from a home-style kitchen serving up decadent breakfasts and gourmet six-course international or Moroccan dinners. For those looking to book an entire riad for a special occasion, Dar Zemora is the perfect place.

72 rue el Andalib, Palmeraie, Marrakech. © 024/328200. Fax 024/328201. www.darzemora.com. 2,800dh ($350/£175) double; 4,160dh ($520/£260) suite and 1-room pavilion; 1,600dh ($200/£100) additional pavilion room. Children under 2 stay free in parent's room. Rates include breakfast and bottled water. Peak-season supplement over Easter and Christmas/New Year. Minimum 3-night stay over Easter; 5 nights Christmas/New Year. Closed for 3 weeks in Aug. MC, V. Parking on grounds. **Amenities:** Restaurant; pool, hammam; free Internet and Wi-Fi; library. *In room:* A/C, central heating, portable DVD players available upon request, iPod dock and preloaded iPod, hair dryer, safe.

4 Where to Dine

Visitors to Marrakech have plenty of dining options to choose from. Up until a few years ago, choices were limited to Moroccan, European, or a fusion of the two, but the recent rise in both visitors and foreign residents has diversified the city's gastronomic scene, which is fast becoming a major attraction in its own right.

Setting and ambience play an important part in Marrakech's dining scene. Those looking for romantic candle-lit dinners—complete with world lounge music, rose petal–strewn fountains, and incense-filled air—will be spoiled for choice. However, if your preference or budget makes you hanker for something a bit livelier or cheaper, there are still enough options.

I strongly recommend joining the evening spectacular on Jemaa el Fna for at least one meal. Some travelers refuse to eat here, regarding the hygiene standards below par, but compared to many of the cheap to mid-range restaurants in town, the kitchens here, visible for all to see, may actually be cleaner. My advice is to try it, even if you only indulge in a bowl of traditional *harira* soup. However, should the smell of up to 100 food stalls simultaneously cooking everything from couscous to sheep's brains be too much for you, there are numerous terrace cafe-restaurants overlooking the square offering reasonably priced Moroccan and European dishes (see "Dining with a View," below). Marrakech's restaurants are located both inside and outside the medina walls. Some, especially those in the more residential corners of the medina, can be a bit difficult to find, so it's best to ask the restaurant to send an escort to accompany you from your accommodations. Outside the medina, many of the better restaurants are located on or near avenue Mohammed V and boulevard Mohammed Zerktouni. All of those recommended here are relatively easy to locate on your own and are not too far off the main streets.

MEDINA
VERY EXPENSIVE

Dar Moha ☆☆ MOROCCAN   This restored riad has been offering one of the city's most distinguished dining experiences for almost 10 years. The riad—whose past residents include the secretary to the Pacha el Glaoui of Marrakech and French designer Pierre Balmain—is the perfect spot for a romantic dinner.

The interior rooms are elegantly furnished with antique Asian art and furniture, but for the majority of the year the back garden is where you'll want to be. Ten-meter-high (33-ft.) walls, painted in Majorelle Garden blue, surround a central swimming pool. Candle-lit tables, covered with rose petals, are spread around the pool, shaded by a garden of giant umbrella trees, banana palms, and bougainvillea. Uniformed, friendly, English-speaking waiters and live yet unobtrusive Gnaoua and Andalusian music complete the ambience.

Dining with a View

At some stage of your meanderings in the medina, you'll probably want to stop and rest at one of the cafe-restaurants overlooking the constant activity on Jemaa el Fna. All of them are open every day, usually from 9am to 11pm. Here's a rundown of the most prominent (a map of these listings can be found on the inside front cover of this book):

Café-Restaurant Argana   As much a landmark as an eating establishment, the Argana is just steps from the action. The upstairs terrace restaurant affords a fantastic view of the square from the tables closest to the railing, while the cafe downstairs offers sidewalk seating. The food, everything from a mint tea and pastry to a three-course dining experience, is not half bad, either. Located in the northern souk on the side of the square. ℂ 024/445350.

Les Terrasses de L'Alhambra   This slick operation is one of the newer places on the square. The ground floor is set aside for drinks and ice cream, with comfy tables both on the pavement and in the air-conditioned interior. The open-air terrace upstairs is a good spot if you're looking for a quick meal of pizza, pasta, or salad. In the far northeast corner, next to the Qessabin Mosque. ℂ 024/427550.

Le Marrakchi   Another relative newcomer to the square, the two-story Le Marrakchi is dominated by traditional *zellij* on the first floor and panoramic windows on the second. The young owner, Noureddine Fakir, originally from Casablanca, seems to have gotten both the ambience and the menu just right, as witnessed by the usual line of waiting diners. The decor includes low, comfortable chairs, wooden shutters, and lots of candles, while two set menus feature local specialties. This air-conditioned restaurant serves alcohol and opens at noon. In the northeast corner. ℂ 024/443377.

Café de France   Thanks to three levels of seating, an unpretentious atmosphere, and later hours (10 or 11pm in winter, midnight or 1am in summer), the "old dame" of the square is still as popular as ever with both locals and visitors alike. The ground floor has plenty of seating both inside and out, with separate areas for dining (the food is nothing special, however) and (nonalcoholic) drinking. Located on the east side of the square and close to both the Qessabin Mosque and the turbaned herbs and potions vendors, this is my favorite people-watching spot. The two upper levels are usually fairly quiet and offer a relatively secluded setting. No phone.

La Place   Inconspicuous at ground level, this restaurant's covered second-floor terrace is a hidden gem for those searching for the perfect spot to take in the sunset. Although relatively small, with room for only about six tables,

Then there's the food. Chef Mohammed (Moha) Fedal worked in Switzerland for 14 years and offers a delicious set menu of what can only be described as *nouvelle Marocain*. Familiar dishes have been given a distinctive twist such as the beef tagine with figs and walnuts cooked with cinnamon and argan oil, and a vegetable couscous topped with caramelized pumpkin and raisins. The portions are an agreeable, rather the terrace offers a great view looking westward across Jemaa el Fna to the Koutoubia Mosque. The restaurant serves three set menus of standard Moroccan fare, but you're welcome to have just a drink. Located next door to Café de France. No phone.

Restaurants N'Zahia & Toubkal These two outdoor pavement-level restaurants sit side-by-side in the far southeast corner of the square and are especially popular for their no-frills breakfasts consisting of croissants, *pain au chocolat,* and fresh *khübz, msemmen,* and *baghrir.* Be warned that it can get hot here under the midday sun. No phone.

Les Premices This is the newest cafe-restaurant on the square and is a definite step up in class. Les Premices offers indoor and outdoor seating at its ground-floor cafe and its terrace restaurant, and is a good choice for everything from a short mint tea break to a romantic dinner. The reasonably priced menu (in French and English) offers Moroccan standards such as couscous and tagine, as well as a range of seafood, meat dishes, pastas, and pizzas. Located in the southeast corner. No phone.

Hotel CTM & Le Grand Balcon du Café Glacier These two old stalwarts provide arguably the best views of Jemaa el Fna, and don't they know it—aside from the occasional splash of paint, everything has stayed the same for the last 10 years. Their balconies provide prime views of the extravaganza unfolding below; the CTM also offers the most uninterrupted view of the Koutoubia Mosque. It can get a little crowded up here at the end of the day as people jostle for that perfect sunset picture. Both places serve only drinks (nonalcoholic) on their balconies, and patrons must place an order to gain access. The Le Grand Balcon du Café Glacier also has a pavement-level cafe where it serves a basic breakfast. Located side-by-side on the southern edge of the square. No phone.

Boulangerie Patisserie Mic Mac It's hard to compete with the Mic Mac for the freshest, cheapest breakfast on the square. More of a bakery than a cafe, the pastries and breads are baked on the premises and purchased, along with your coffee or tea, at the counter. There's a small seating area just outside that's nicely shaded in the morning and offers a pleasant view of place de Foucauld; depending on the wind direction, you could pick up the unpleasant scent of horses and *calèches* awaiting passengers. The Mic Mac closes early, at around 7pm. Located behind the post office and technically on rue Moulay Ismail. No phone.

than overwhelming, size, and an entree of meze is a meal in itself. Dessert is also a delight; I recommend the *chakchouka* saffron-stewed apple. Vegetarians won't have a problem here; just be sure to let your waiter know at the start of the meal. Lunch time can get quite busy with groups, so I suggest coming in the evening to make the most of both the setting and cuisine.

81 rue Dar el Bacha (taxis can drop you right at the door). © **024/386400** or 024/386264. Fax 024/386998. www.
darmoha.ma. Reservations recommended. Alcohol served. 240dh ($30/£15) lunch; 460dh ($58/£29) dinner. MC, V.
Tues–Sun noon–3pm and 7:30–11pm.

Narwama ✦✦✦ THAI/MOROCCAN/MEDITERRANEAN   Owner Ali Bous-
fiha's Narwama has all the markings of a trendy restaurant. The former DJ pumps his
own mix of world lounge music into the former UNESCO World Heritage building,
which has a huge central courtyard and two adjoining salons swathed in hues of deep
ochre and charcoal. Low-lying, candlelit tables with dark cushioned chairs surround a
fountain of flames and water (the restaurant's name translates to "fire and water" in
Arabic), and an attentive and attractive staff usher Thai, Moroccan, and Mediterranean dishes to locals and tourists alike. All three cuisines have equal importance in
the kitchen, with specialty chefs for each (including two from Thailand). The menu
is lengthy and includes almost 100 dishes. It's not cheap, but there's something for
everyone, and the servings are filling without being oversize.

30 rue Koutoubia. © **024/440844** or 072/508700. www.narwama.bousfiha.com. Reservations recommended. Alcohol served. Main courses 150dh–225dh ($19–$28/£9.40–£14). Taxes not included. MC, V. Daily 7–11pm. Restaurant
accessible by foot only. Follow the sign down the well-lit passageway 50m (164 ft.) from the beginning of rue
Koutoubia. Make sure to walk to the end of the passage and not into the poolside restaurant of Les Jardins de la
Koutoubia hotel.

EXPENSIVE

Cafe Arabe ✦ ITALIAN/MOROCCAN/CAFE   For almost 4 years, this stylish
cafe/lounge bar/restaurant has been carving its own niche within the medina. The Italian owners have come up with a menu (in English) of both Italian and Moroccan classics that includes ricotta and spinach cannelloni and couscous *aux sept légumes* (I can
report that it does indeed come with seven different vegetables). Those looking for
coffee and cake can choose from a delectable selection of homemade tarts and cakes;
on my last visit the choices included a meringue and cream *pavlova* with strawberries,
and a pear and chocolate cake. The staff is young and friendly, and the background
lounge music fits the bill perfectly. An open courtyard with citrus trees provides shade
for the lunch crowd; in the evening fairy lights create romance. To one side of the
courtyard is a small fire-engine-red lounge—one of the few stand-alone bars in the
medina—with thick cushions and mirrored flowers that wind up the high ceiling.
Passing through the courtyard brings you to a couple of colorful, intimate salons that
are perfect for a predinner aperitif, and upstairs you'll find more lounge areas and
tables. Topping it off, literally, is a canvas-shaded, cushion-strewn terrace with fantastic medina views that is perfect for a midafternoon mint tea.

184 rue el Mouassine. © **024/429728.** Fax 024/429725. www.cafearabe.com. Alcohol served. Main courses 80dh–
130dh ($10–$16/£5–£8.15); cakes and desserts 80dh ($10/£5). MC, V. Daily 10:30am–11:30pm.

Tatchibana *(Finds* ✦✦ JAPANESE   If proof was needed that change has swept over
Marrakech in the last few years, then surely the recent opening of a Japanese restaurant is it. After a busy career dealing in fine wine exports to Japan, Albrecht Jerren-
trup, along with partner Jean-Claude Demaria, decided to semi-retire in Marrakech.
Albrecht, however, couldn't live without his sushi, so they built this slice of Japan in a
quiet corner of the medina's kasbah. Tatchibana (citrus flower) is no tacky imitation,
however. Stepping down from street level through the curtained entrance brings you
to two floors of (air-conditioned) peace and tranquillity. The space fuses the Far East
with Morocco and features an abundance of wood complemented by a palette of

black, white, and red. There's also a small, sunken, open-top courtyard with a low-lying table and cushioned chairs on a bed of white pebbles. The cuisine is authentic with a hint of *nouvelle,* mirroring the influences of the Japanese head chef. Separate set menus for lunch and dinner offer a choice of four courses that, although not cheap (some main dishes incur an additional supplement), are generous in size and delectable in taste. All the standards are available including sushi nigiri, sashimi, tempura, maki, and teriyaki, but there are also a few different offerings such as slivers of duck in green-tea ravioli. The menu changes every 3 months in symbiosis with the seasons, and vegetarians are catered to on request.

38 Derb Bab Ksiba (about 20m/65 ft. from the medina's Bab Ksiba). ©/fax 024/387171. www.tatchibana.com. Reservations recommended. Alcohol served. Main courses 150dh–180dh ($19–$23/£9.40–£11) lunch, 200dh–250dh ($25–$31/£13–£16) dinner. No credit cards. Tues 7:45–10:30pm, Wed–Sun 12:30–2:30pm and 7:45–10:30pm. Closed mid-Sept to mid-Oct.

MODERATE

Palais Chahramane (Kids) MOROCCAN   Of all the *spectacle Marocain* (dinner/dance) restaurants in Marrakech, this is my favorite, despite the masses of tour groups that binge their way through here every day. This is a Moroccan feast for all the senses, so expect to be overloaded with food and bombarded with music and dance, all in a setting that is, indeed, palatial. The stairs and entrance hallway—themselves a tribute to Moroccan artisanship—lead to a gigantic dining room of traditional, low-lying circular tables, cushioned lounges and chairs, room-size Berber and Arabic carpets, and intricate *zellij* and stucco walls and ceilings. If your arrival hasn't been announced by the wailing and drumming of the resident Atlas Berber musical troupe, expect them, or the in-house Andalusian or Gnaoua quartet, to give you a tableside performance at some point in the evening.

The food, like the entertainment and surroundings, is grand. Diners choose from set six-course menus that revolve around similar starters and desserts—Moroccan salads, fresh fruit, Moroccan pastries, mint tea—with a choice of individual main courses such as *kefta* (meatball) tagine with egg, vegetable couscous, or grilled lamb. And so you won't forget the experience, waiters (in traditional dress) have become experts at taking pictures of you and the in-house belly dancer.

6 rue Sidi Bouchouka. © 024/389918. www.palaischahramane.com. Reservations recommended. Alcohol served. Set menus 150dh ($19/£9.40). No credit cards. Daily noon–3pm and 7:30–11pm.

Portofino (Kids) ITALIAN   Almost in the shadow of the Koutoubia Mosque, this Italian-owned-and-operated restaurant is a great choice within the medina for those who are suffering from tagine fatigue. Although only steps away from the busy pavement, the setting is quiet and intimate with simple and modern decor. A traditional wood oven (all the way from Modena, Italy) fills the restaurant with the aroma of sizzling pizzas. The staff is young and friendly, and the meals are usually served in pretty good time. The menu includes the usual suspects: a large range of pizzas and handmade pastas such as spaghetti, penne, lasagna, cannelloni, and gnocchi. There are also meat and seafood dishes. The house specialty is the *pesce al salé,* an oven-baked sea bass encrusted in salt, which is peeled off by your waiter to expose succulent slabs of white meat, served with steaming rice and vegetables. There are also a couple of *menu enfants* for kids that include hamburgers and fries. Sitting by the front window allows for a great view of the Koutoubia and the passing throngs, while a table closer to the open kitchen at the back offers a little more privacy.

279 av. Mohammed V. ✆ **024/391665**. Main courses 60dh–130dh ($7.50–$16/£3.75–£8.15). MC, V. Daily noon–3pm and 7–11pm.

INEXPENSIVE

Café des Epices 🍴🍴 CAFE   This is my favorite place for people-watching in the medina. For 2 years, Youness el Ghoul and his extended family have been dispensing information and a menu that includes tasty sandwiches, salads, pastries, and spiced teas and coffees to flush-faced tourists looking for a rest stop. The rooftop terrace is a great place to enjoy the sunset, while the first-floor chill-out lounge has become a meeting place for young, arty Marrakchis. The interior walls are traditional ochre *tadelakt* and the atmosphere is new world, with a soundtrack to match. The cafe is Wi-Fi connected.

Place Rahba Qedima. ✆ **024/391770**. Main courses 25dh–40dh ($3.15–$5/£1.60–£2.50). No credit cards. Daily 8am–8pm.

Cafe Restaurant L'Etoile MOROCCAN/CAFE   Located on the busy rue Bab Agnaou just off Jemaa el Fna, this is a good option for lunch or a cheap sit-down dinner. The outside tables—if you can grab one—are a great spot for a coffee-and-pastry breakfast, but you may want to sit inside the air-conditioned cafe once the sun is out in full force. A small mezzanine level at the rear offers privacy, and upstairs you'll find an open courtyard with an enclosed balcony and a few mosaic tables and wrought-iron chairs. While there is no view from this level, the top terrace offers a glorious view of Jemaa el Fna. The menu spans the usual range of salads, soups (a bowl of *harira* Marrakchia for only 10dh/$1.25/65p), panini and sandwiches, tagines, couscous, and grilled meats, plus they'll rustle up a Moroccan-style hamburger or chicken burger for the little ones. Their fresh juices aren't bad either. A daily three-course *menu Marocain* offers a choice of dishes and mint tea. The toilets, by the way, are some of the cleanest this close to the square.

49 rue Bab Agnaou, place Jemaa el Fna. ✆ **024/391942**. Main courses 25dh–60dh ($3.15–$7.50/£1.60–£3.75), menu *Marocain* 100dh ($13/£6.25). No credit cards. Daily 8am–10pm.

Restaurant Al Bahja 🍴 MOROCCAN   I can sum up my favorite local restaurant in four words: cheap, busy, quick, and tasty. Chez Bahja has been overseeing his immensely popular eatery for more than 20 years, and it's my guess that the menu hasn't changed much during that time. After you make it past the in-house butcher's display case at the entrance, you have a choice: natural ventilation or air-conditioning, which can be found downstairs. The place is usually packed with locals, but you'll see the occasional tourist partaking in Moroccan standards such as couscous or tagine with meat or vegetables. The menu also offers a house salad, omelets with a variety of fillings, and set meals that include an entree, olives, yogurt, and mint tea. The decor—yellow and white plastic tablecloths that make it easy to wipe away breadcrumbs and olive pits—is nothing to write home about, but this is an exceptionally good value for lunch if you're in the area and looking to mix with the locals.

Rue Bani Marine (between the Bank al Maghrib and the post office on the south side of Jemaa el Fna). No phone. Main courses 20dh–36dh ($2.50–$4.50/£1.25–£2.25); set menus 55dh–65dh ($6.90–$8.15/£3.45–£4.05). No credit cards. Daily 11am–10pm.

VILLE NOUVELLE
VERY EXPENSIVE

Le Grand Café de la Poste INTERNATIONAL/CAFE   This one-story mansion built in the 1920s was originally a post office and then enjoyed the role of Café Pacha during the days of the Pasha El Glaoui's rule. After years of neglect, it's been restored to its former glory with a colonial ambience complete with white linen cushions upon rattan chairs and wicker-cane lounges; lazy wood ceiling fans attached to thick, dark beams on high ceilings; and a climbing, wrought-iron staircase that could have been in *Gone With the Wind*. Diners—Moroccan yuppies, well-to-do expats, and tourists—prefer the outdoor tables under the covered front balcony, but those seeking an intimate meal or respite from a cold winter night should head inside, where tall palms anchor terracotta pots, the sounds of smooth jazz fill the air, and candles provide a soft glow. Menus differ for breakfast, lunch, and dinner and include a fry-up of eggs, bacon, and potatoes; goat cheese salad; roast chicken with thyme and olives; Oualidia oysters; and lamb shank with potato gratin. The menu is expensive by most tastes, but despite the restaurant's high-brow appearance, it's generally relaxed and friendly.

Corner of bd. El Mansour Eddahbi and av. Imam Malik (behind the main Guéliz post office). © 024/433038. Fax 024/422714. www.grandcafedelaposte.com. Reservations recommended. Alcohol served. Main courses 90dh–190dh ($11–$24/£5.65–£12). MC, V. Daily 8am–1am.

EXPENSIVE

Al Fassia ☪☪ MOROCCAN   Once you pass the traditionally dressed doormen, this place is all-female and is run like a family kitchen. Set up by the well-known Chab family 20 years ago, this oft-cramped but always popular restaurant is now successfully managed by Myra Chab as a cooperative where many of the staff are also financially involved. A variety of Moroccan dishes are available, including specialties that require a day's notice such as the *dalaa mbakhra* (steamed lamb shoulder) and *chaâra medfouna* (steamed vermicelli garnished with pigeon). The tagines and couscous here go against the grain in both ingredients and size. Chicken with caramelized pumpkin and lamb with eggplant are just two of the 13 tagine choices, and you're served a portion that you might actually be able to finish. The desserts are delicious, so leave space for some *seffa* couscous in butter, sugar, milk, and cinnamon. The place is always busy and can sometimes feel a bit stuffy and smoky. The occasional family argument has been known to occur between the women, but this only serves to make Al Fassia all the more authentic.

55 bd. Mohammed Zerktouni (about 50m/165 ft. from av. Mohammed V). © 024/434060 or 024/437973. Reservations recommended. Main courses 90dh–110dh ($11–$14/£5.65–£6.90); set menu (lunch only) 145dh ($18/£9.05). Taxes not included. AE, MC, V. Daily noon–2:30pm and 7:30–11pm.

Bistro La Saveur INTERNATIONAL/THAI   I'm usually not keen on eating in hotel restaurants while in Morocco, but this one, attached to the Le Caspien Hotel, is definitely a cut above the norm. The menu is a mix of French, Italian, and Thai, and the service is of a profoundly higher standard than the usual in-house restaurant. The French and Italian dishes are your classical meat, seafood, and pasta dishes, in addition to pizzas made in the restaurant's wood oven. For something different, try the duck terrine with pistachios in mustard sauce, or the prawn and ricotta ravioli. The Thai menu includes soups, salads, curries (yellow, red, and green), and noodle or rice stir-fries. Diners are given a choice of three dining areas: an enclosed, street-side canopy, the restaurant proper at the rear of the small lobby, and beside the swimming pool. All three areas are decked out with modern furniture and white linen and offer a surprising amount of intimacy.

12 rue Loubnane, Guéliz. © 024/422282 or 024/422283. www.lecaspien-hotel.com. Alcohol served. Main courses 100dh–130dh ($13–$16/£6.25–£8.15). AE, MC, V. Daily noon–2:30pm and 7–10:30pm.

Puerto Banus *(Finds* SEAFOOD Marrakech is only 160km (99 miles) away from the major fishing port of Safi, so when owner Nouredine and his manager/uncle Youssef say they offer the freshest seafood, they're not lying. This delightful little *hacienda* is largely off the tourist trail and has been consistently popular with both Marrakchis and foreign residents since it opened in 1991. The friendly and professional staff presides over a menu that includes seafood tapas, seafood *pastilla*, Oualidia oysters, fried *fruits de la mer*, and various fish dishes. There are also a few beef and chicken dishes available as well as a very reasonably priced lunch *menu du jour* consisting of a salad buffet, entree, and dessert. However, there's not much for vegetarians other than a few salads and a vegetable tagine. The dining areas are divided between a tiled patio with wrought-iron chairs and an indoor space with whitewashed walls, dark-wood furniture, and a fireplace.

Rue Ibn Hanbal (opposite the Surète Nationale and tennis club). © 024/446534. www.restaurant-puerto banus.com. Alcohol served. Main courses 120dh–150dh ($15–$19/£7.50–£9.40). Taxes not included. DC, MC, V. Daily noon–3pm and 7:30–11pm.

MODERATE

Cantanzaro *(★★★* ITALIAN A bland exterior has not kept this from becoming one of Marrakech's most popular restaurants. Charming hosts Jawad and Geneviève Amrani, recently joined by their dapper son Mehdi, have been welcoming locals and visitors alike into their simply furnished Italian restaurant and pizzeria for more than 20 years now, and they're only getting busier. This place *smells* like an Italian restaurant should, due in large part to the wood-burning oven in the open kitchen. Waiters in red waistcoats and bow ties usher a wide range of pizzas, including a Royal topped with mince, prawns, mushrooms, and ham (yes, ham), and pastas such as penne in creamy tomato and vodka sauce. The baked eggplant topped with grilled parmesan makes for a particularly pleasant starter, while the obligatory tiramisu almost meets its match with the home-style apple crumble.

42 rue Tarik Ibn Ziyad. © 024/433731. Reservations recommended. Alcohol served. Main courses 60dh–100dh ($7.50–$13/£3.75–£6.25). MC, V. Mon–Sat noon–2:30pm and 7:15–11pm.

Kechmara MOROCCAN/INTERNATIONAL/CAFE Brothers Pascal and Arnaud Foltran have taken a piece of old Morocco and updated it for new Marrakech. This former mechanic's garage now houses a light and airy, white-on-white retro bistro/cafe. The air-conditioned ground-floor cafe is minimalist-European in style, with Finnish-designed furniture, Murano-glass lighting, shiny chrome accents, wood floors, and high ceilings. The white walls are usually adorned with work from local and international contemporary painters and photographers. You'll find both Moroccans and Westerners, though not so many tourists, here at any time of the day, but it is especially popular around lunchtime when the young and stylish staff have to concentrate on serving rather than looking beautiful. The menu is very reasonably priced and offers breakfast up to 11am—a personal favorite is the *Equilibre* of tea/coffee, orange juice, white cheese, and fresh fruit salad, but you can also have good ol' eggs on toast if you wish. This is followed by a selection of light meals, including salads, sandwiches, or toasted panini, up to 7pm. Lunch and dinner are from an a la carte menu of Moroccan and Mediterranean classics, along with some French-influenced *menus du jour*. Available throughout the day and night are a range of fresh juices, milkshakes, teas, coffees, and cakes. The upstairs roof terrace is shaded by woven-grass umbrellas, and although it lacks a view, it's a pleasant spot for an early evening drink during the warmer months.

3 rue De La Liberté, Guéliz. ℂ **024/422532** or 024/434060. www.kechmara.com. Alcohol served on terrace. Main courses 50dh–90dh ($6.25–$11/£3.15–£5.65); set menus 115dh–150dh ($14–$19/£7.20–£9.40). MC, V. Mon–Sat 7am–midnight.

Restaurant Beyrouth ⚑ LEBANESE   Vegetarians tired of the mundane choice between vegetable couscous, tagine, or pizza will rejoice in this cozy restaurant recently opened by larger-than-life chef Richard Chebli. An enclosed alfresco section at the entrance is decorated in traditional Moroccan style, complete with a mosaic fountain, while a larger upstairs room is more simply furnished and serves alcohol. The menu is surprisingly large; there are more than 30 dishes that include standards such as hummus, tabbouleh, moussaka, *moutabbal,* falafel, and *chawarma.* The meze platters, for two to five people, include a vegetarian option, and are a good choice if you feel like a bit of everything. For dessert try the traditional *mouhallabieh,* a melt-in-your-mouth mousse perfumed with orange and rose water.

9 rue Loubnane, Guéliz. ℂ **024/423525.** www.restaurant-beyrouth.com. Alcohol served. Main courses 50dh–80dh ($6.25–$10/£3.15–£5). MC, V. Daily 11am–11pm.

INEXPENSIVE

Adamo *Finds* ⚑⚑⚑ PATISSERIE   It's a tough call, but this is *the* best patisserie in town. Bruno Maulion's little slice of heaven has been forging its way to the top of the pile since 2003, and although it's only one street back from avenue Mohammed V, only locals in the know seem to make their way here. Freshly baked cookies in glass jars sit atop a display full of delicious croissants and tarts—both sweet and savory—and a number of bright, colorful, and especially creamy gâteaux. There are a few tables and chairs both inside and out, so you can savor the taste of your chosen delight right there and then, washed down by a choice of coffees, teas, fresh juices, and milkshakes. There's a fair selection of ice cream flavors as well.

44 rue Tarik ben Ziad. ℂ **024/439419** or 061/439419. www.traiteur-adamo.com. Croissants and cakes 20dh–30dh ($2.50–$3.75/£1.25–£1.90). No credit cards. Daily 7:30am–1pm and 4–9pm. Closed for 3 weeks mid-July to early Aug.

Café du Livre ⚑⚑⚑ INTERNATIONAL   This bookstore-cum-restaurant isn't easy to find, but once you're inside and slouched into one of the chocolate velvet chairs or lounges, you may not want to leave. Converted from an upstairs apartment and a downstairs garage, the space is simple and uncluttered with lots of windows and a fireplace in the restaurant. The bookstore is stocked from floor to ceiling with more than 2,000 new and second-hand fiction and nonfiction titles in both English and European languages. There is also a well-stocked collection of books on Morocco, as well as recently published English-language newspapers and magazines. A few strategically placed armchairs beckon the reader to sit down with coffee and cake; bring your laptop because free Wi-Fi is also available. The dining and reading areas are separated by an open kitchen from where salads, soups (try the pumpkin and ginger), sandwiches and burgers, a mushroom risotto, and freshly baked cakes are available. Brunch-style breakfasts and an afternoon high tea—served between 4 and 6pm with a complimentary brownie—are also part of the daily routine. Try the tapas plate of hummus, tapenade, *aubergine de caviar,* and pâté for an early dinner, when a selection of beers, wines, and spirits is also available.

44 rue Tarik ben Ziad (off to one side of the entrance to Hotel Toulousain). ℂ **024/432149.** www.cafedulivre.com. Alcohol served. High tea 25dh ($3.15/£1.60); main courses 70dh–95dh ($8.75–$12/£4.40–£5.95). MC, V. Mon–Sat 9:30am–9pm.

Les Delices Malouins ⚲ CREPERIE/CAFE   Young French lads Pierre and Steve recently opened this bright cafe, which is a breath of fresh air in the ville nouvelle. Simply furnished with wood tables and director's chairs, this air-conditioned space is already becoming a favorite for guests of nearby hotels who are tired of the standard Moroccan offering of bread, bread, and more bread. The house specialties are crêpes, which come in a standard or buckwheat mixture and are topped with sweet or savory toppings that include honey, chocolate, preserves, cheese, and eggs. Homemade cakes are also regularly available.

68 rue de la Liberté, Guéliz. ⓒ 024/431200 or 073/811472. Crêpes 15dh–40dh ($1.90–$5/95p–£2.50). No credit cards. Daily 9am–10pm.

5 What to See & Do

The majority of Marrakech's attractions lie within its ancient city walls and are best located from the focal point of Jemaa el Fna. As you walk past the snake charmers and orange juice stalls and tentatively enter the maze of alleys and lanes leading off in seemingly haphazard directions, you come to realize that you are well and truly in the medina. Some of the sights south of Jemaa el Fna are scheduled stops on the City Sightseeing Bus tour (see below), but for the very worthwhile places of interest north of Jemaa el Fna, such as the souks, Ben Youssef Medersa, and Marrakech Museum, you'll have to rely on foot power. Outside of the medina are the gardens Agdal, Menara, and Majorelle, the latter known for its photogenic cobalt-blue building as well as its gardens.

IN THE MEDINA

Koutoubia Mosque ⚲⚲⚲   About 100m (300 ft.) west of Jemaa el Fna is Marrakech's most prominent landmark, the Koutoubia Mosque. Its towering minaret is visible for miles in any direction and is the focal point from which the French laid out the road network in their ville nouvelle. The name, meaning the Bookseller's Mosque, reflects the honorable trade that used to be practiced in a nearby souk.

The mosque was constructed, and reconstructed, in the 12th century by the Andalusian-conquering Almohad dynasty and lies on the site of a former Almoravid mosque. It was this prior occupation by the Almoravids, whom they considered heretics, which likely spurred the Almohads to build a new, "pure" mosque rather than renovate the existing structure. Unfortunately, someone got the measurements wrong, and the mosque was not correctly oriented toward Mecca—indicated inside the prayer hall by the *mihrab,* or prayer niche. Even though worshippers can correct this directional problem when commencing prayer, the Almohads decided to build a second, correctly aligned mosque alongside the original. Both buildings were constructed during the reign of Abdullah el-Mumin (1130–63) and existed side-by-side until the older structure eventually fell into disrepair.

Standing on the mosque's esplanade with your back to Jemaa el Fna, the ruins of the original are visible to your right. The existing mosque's principal feature is its 13m-wide (41-ft.) and 68m-high (221-ft.) minaret, completed by el-Mumin's grandson, Sultan Yacoub el Mansour (1184–99). This is the oldest and most complete of the Almohad's three great towers—the others are the Tour Hassan in Rabat and the Giralda in Seville, Spain—and was considered the blueprint for all future Moroccan-Andalusian architecture. Given a clean-up for the beginning of the new millennium, the tower is especially stunning when floodlit each night. ***Note:*** As with most Islamic places of worship in Morocco, the interior of the mosque is off limits to non-Muslims. If you happen to be traveling on the Tizi n'Test road in the Western High Atlas between Marrakech and Taroudannt, stop off at the visitor-friendly Tin Mal Mosque (p. 164) from which the Koutoubia was modeled.

Av. Mohammed V, opposite place de Foucauld and Jemaa el Fna.

NORTH OF JEMAA EL FNA

Musée de Marrakech   On place Ben Youssef is the Musée de Marrakech, housed in Dar Mnebbi, a palace built in the late 19th century for Mehdi Mnebbi, a former Moroccan defense minister and ambassador to Britain. Post-independence, the palace was taken over by the state and gradually fell into disrepair before being privately restored and reopening in 1997 as the museum. The former palace now houses temporary contemporary art exhibitions (some pieces are for sale) in what were the palace kitchens, as well as permanent displays of traditional arts and crafts in what were the main hall and the now-restored hammam. Most of the information panels are in French only. The building's centerpiece is a peaceful covered inner courtyard with a towering brass chandelier hung above a central fountain. This is a good place to rest your legs, although sometimes the tranquillity can be shattered by large tour groups. There is a small cafe and a bookshop in the entrance courtyard.

Place Ben Youssef. © 024/441893. www.museedemarrakech.ma. Admission is in conjunction with Ben Youssef Medersa and the Almoravid Koubba. Cash only; must be paid at museum. Three monuments 60dh ($7.50/£3.75) adults, 30dh ($3.75/£1.90) child under 18; 2 monuments 40dh ($5/£2.50) adults, 20dh ($2.50/£1.25) child under 18. Daily Apr–Sept 9am–7pm; Oct–Mar 9am–6pm.

Almoravid Koubba   Although perhaps uninspiring at first glance, this is in fact the only Almoravid building to have survived the fervent renovation spree undertaken by the Almohads who succeeded them. The Almoravid Koubba, or Koubba Ba'adiyn, is a small, domed building that may have been an ablutions annex to the original Ben Youssef Mosque. The dome's design was the model for the classic shapes and motifs used in future Moroccan design. The Koubba was built well below today's ground level, and until an excavation project in the 1950s had been covered as a result of the numerous rebuildings of the mosque. You now have to walk down two flights of stairs to reach the interior where, besides the fascinating dome and ceiling design, you can also see a water cistern set into the floor and remains of the fountains used by the faithful for performing ablutions before prayer. Photographs of the excavation project are on display inside the ticket room.

About 20m (66 ft.) from the Marrakech Museum.

Ben Youssef Medersa 🌟🌟🌟   Down a lane to the north of place Ben Youssef is the entrance to the 16th-century Ben Youssef Medersa, a former Koranic boarding school attached to its namesake mosque, where students used to learn Islamic law, science, and the Koran. A stunning example of the Saâdian dynasty's attention to detail and craftsmanship, this is one of Marrakech's most important Islamic monuments. A peaceful and meditative place when not invaded by large tour groups (come around lunchtime or at the end of the day), the Medersa is centered around an unusually large square courtyard containing a rectangular pool and wide, columned arcades on two sides. Above them are the dormitory quarters where the up to 800 students were crammed into cell-like rooms. Note the well-weathered cedar-wood carving on the upper facades of the main courtyard as well as the exquisite *zellij* and stucco on the arcades' floors, walls, and pillars. At the far end of the courtyard you'll see the wood dome of the prayer hall, where the interior is best preserved, especially the *zellij*. Set in the wall and, as always, in the direction of Mecca is a five-sided *mihrab*, or prayer niche, decorated with pine cone and palm motifs and Arabic inscriptions.

About 30m (100 ft.) to the right as you depart the Marrakech Museum.

SOUKS

Between Jemaa el Fna and the Ben Youssef Mosque is a seemingly never-ending maze of shops selling a wide variety of high-quality crafts along with a fair amount of tacky souvenirs. These are Marrakech's souks—among the best in Morocco—and shopping aside, a morning's exploration amongst these craftsmen and traders is an experience not to be missed. The main entrance to the souks is to the left of the Qessabin Mosque, via either a small potter's souk or the olive stalls on Souk Ableuh. The following is a general description of each souk, though nowadays the borders have become a bit blurry.

Note: The first time you venture into the medina's souks can be both geographically and emotionally challenging. While you can rest assured that once you are on a main thoroughfare you'll eventually emerge at a landmark or one of the medina gates, there's no way to avoid the offers you will get from "friends" to take you through the souks for a small fee or a visit to an uncle's shop. Keeping calm in this situation is key. For those who think this might be too much too handle, I suggest hiring an official guide (see "Guide or no Guide?" on p. 38) for at least your first morning of exploration. The benefit is twofold in that you will become accustomed to life in the souks and get your bearings, all the while avoiding the hagglers due to the presence of your guide. Once you're ready to set out on your own, you can consult the map on the inside front cover of this book.

Souk Semmarine   An archway marks the beginning of the souk area proper, and rue Souk Semmarine, which is flanked mainly by shops selling textiles and numerous souvenir stalls, is covered by a vast iron trellis.

Souk Larzal, Souk Btana & Place Rahba Kedima ✦✦✦   Just before the fork at the end of rue Souk Semmarine, a narrow lane to the right leads to a small square, place Rahba Kedima. To the right of the square is Souk Larzal, an early-morning wool market and afternoon secondhand-clothing bazaar, and the aromatic Souk Btana, which deals in fresh sheepskins. Place Rahba Kedima is home to a number of apothecary stalls (sometimes called Berber chemists) selling traditional cosmetics and herbal potions of both plant and animal origin, and old women sit selling wool hats and woven baskets.

Souk Zrabia   Still on place Rahba Kedima, a passageway in the far left leads to yet another, smaller covered square and the carpet souk known as Souk Zrabia, or *Le Criée Berbère* (the Berber auction). Prior to the French occupation in 1912, this was the site of Marrakech's slave auctions, held just before sunset every Wednesday, Thursday, and Friday. The slaves were mostly kidnapped West Africans who had been brought in with the caravans plying the route between West and North Africa and farther east into the Levant. Nowadays you'll find carpets—and lots of them.

The *Kissarias*   Back out on rue Souk Semmarine, the road continues on as rue Souk el Kebir and forks to the left into rue Souk el Attarin. To the left of rue Souk el Kebir is a covered area known as the *kissarias*—markets selling mainly everyday clothing and footwear but also a fair smattering of textiles and souvenirs. To the right of Souk el

Kebir is a small lane of jewelers called the Souk des Bijoutiers (look up for the sign saying BIJOUTERIE TEGMOUTIENE).

Souk Cherratin   Beyond the *kissarias* at the northern end of rue Souk el Kebir is a maze of alleys called Souk Cherratin. Here you'll find the leatherworker's souk, with dozens of sandal cobblers and bag, belt, and purse makers spread amongst other smaller souks of carpenters and tourist shops.

Souk el Attarin & Souk Smata   Taking the left fork off rue Souk Semmarine brings you onto rue Souk el Attarin—the spice and perfume souk—and the other side of the *kissarias,* where you will find Souk Smata, also known as Souk des Babouches in reference to the slipper makers found here.

Souk Chouari & Souk Haddadine   To the west of Souk Smata is the carpenter's souk, Souk Chouari, with its beautiful aroma of cedar. Beyond here is the noisy Souk Haddadine, home to the city's blacksmiths.

Souk des Teinturiers ✹✹✹   South of Souk Chouari is Souk des Teinturers, Marrakech's colorful and photogenic dyers' souk, where wool and fabric are dyed and left hanging across the alleyways to dry. There are souvenir shops here but nothing specific to the dying process.

Souk des Chaudronniers   Farther west of Souk Chouari is an ornate 16th-century fountain and the Mouassin Mosque. South of here is Souk des Chaudronniers, where you'll find the city's coppersmiths.

SOUTH OF JEMAA EL FNA

Dar Si Said   This small palace was built by Si Said, *vizier* (minister) under Moulay Hassan, the last effective sultan of precolonial Morocco. An attractive building with shady, pooled courtyards, it is now home to the Museum of Moroccan Arts. Exhibits include a fascinating display of Berber daggers and jewelry made of amber, ivory, and silver; beautiful carpets from the High Atlas; Taroudannt oil lamps; Marrakchi leatherwork; and distinctive blue pottery from Safi and green pottery from Tamegroute, near Zagora. At the end of the main entrance corridor is the museum's oldest and most treasured artifact—an 11th-century rectangular marble basin originally transported from Islamic Spain by the Almoravids and left undamaged for centuries. Prominent throughout the building is the collection of finely carved, mainly Berber woodwork. The exhibit explanations are in Arabic and French only, but it's still worth a look.

Rue Riad Zitoun Jdid. ✆ 024/389564. Admission 20dh ($2.50/£1.25) adults; 10dh ($1.25/65p) children 5–12. Wed–Mon 9am–noon and 3–6pm.

The Mellah ✹   The old Jewish Quarter was created in the kasbah area of Marrakech's medina by the Saâdians in 1558. At the time, the Jewish community controlled most of the Saâdian's important sugar trade and comprised the majority of Marrakech's bankers, jewelers, metalworkers, and tailors. During its heyday in the 16th century, the Mellah enjoyed substantial autonomy with its own fountains, gardens, synagogues, and even souks. Although the present Mellah, renamed Hay Essalam, is much smaller and almost entirely Muslim, the area still has an individual character when compared to the rest of the medina. The streets are narrower, the houses are higher, and the shops are smaller (until the French arrived in 1912, Jews were not allowed to own property outside the Mellah, so all expansion took place within the defined walls of the quarter). Post-Saâdian, conditions here have historically been worse than elsewhere in the medina, but that is rapidly dissipating as

Marrakech's property boom begins to reach the area. There are very few (estimates reach only as high as 250) Jews left in Marrakech, and most now live outside the medina's walls. However, one or two synagogues are still in use for Friday and Saturday services. The blue-and-white Alzama synagogue has an upstairs gallery *(ezrat nashim)* for women, peculiar in Morocco where women traditionally remained at the entrance to the synagogue or in a separate room. On the floor above are a Talmud Torah school, soup kitchen, and community center. Finding the synagogue is difficult, so it's best to ask once in the Mellah for directions—usually a child will guide you for a small fee. This is a largely residential area and as such the attraction is being able to view Marrakchi life away from the touristed areas.

East of place des Ferblantiers; best entered through the adjoining covered market, or *kissaria*.

Saâdian Tombs This high-walled compound, shaded with palms and dotted with bright *zellij*-topped tombs, is the final resting place of the Saâdian dynasty's sultans, princes, and other members of the royal household. The principal structures were built in the late 1500s by Sultan Ahmed el Mansour, who lies in the larger of the two main mausoleums within the compound in a central room called the Hall of the Twelve Columns. This central hall is spectacular, with soft light from an ornate lantern filtering down onto the Sultan's tomb and those of his son and grandson. The other smaller, older mausoleum houses the tombs of el-Mansour's mother and the founder of the Saâdian dynasty, Mohammed ech Sheikh. Between them, the two mausoleums house 66 tombs, while out in the courtyard and garden you'll find more than 100 others.

The whole compound was sealed off during the reign of Sultan Moulay Ismail, the first of the Alaouites to take control of Morocco from the Saâdians, who destroyed virtually everything else the Saâdians had constructed (the el Badi palace next door, for example). The tombs were rediscovered in 1917 when a French resident general noticed the tomb formations on an aerial survey map and constructed a passageway from the side of the adjoining mosque. The sealed-off tombs were in a fairly good state and have since also been restored.

The tombs are popular on guided tours and thus can get crowded, so try and visit very early in the morning or late in the afternoon. The passageway to the tombs is well signposted and lies directly to the right of the Kasbah Mosque, whose tall minaret is easy to locate. There are English-speaking guides (20dh/$2.50/£1.25) at the entrance, and a couple of relaxing cafes across from there.

Rue de la Kasbah. Admission 10dh ($1.25/65p) adults; 3dh (40¢/20p) children 5–12. Daily 8:30–11:45am and 2:30–5:45pm.

OUTSIDE THE MEDINA
THE GARDENS

Jardin Agdal These gardens were first established in the 12th century and over time have expanded to cover more than 400 hectares (988 acres). Surrounded by walls, with gates at each corner, the gardens house large groves of fruit and olive trees along with a series of pools, all of which are fed by a system of underground channels that amazingly come all the way from the Ourika valley at the base of the Atlas mountains, more than 30 km (18 miles) away. The largest of the pools, Sahraj el Hana (Tank of Health), is flanked by an old *minzah* (pavilion) where the last precolonial sultans would have enjoyed extravagant picnics and parties. The pathways around the pool's edge are paved, shaded, and a delight for a picnic.

The garden constitutes the southern edge of the medina. The entrance is on the northwestern edge and is called Bab el Arhdar. Free admission. Daily 8:30am–5:30pm.

Majorelle Garden   This small botanical garden was created in the 1920s by French artist Jacques Majorelle and reflects his affection for contrast and strong color. The scent and color of bamboo thickets, huge cacti, multicolored bougainvillea, and towering palms is offset by the brilliant cobalt-blue of Majorelle's former studio, now a small Museum of Islamic Arts. Inside are some of the artist's engravings and paintings of the Atlas range as well as a personal collection of North African artifacts belonging to the garden's current owner, Algerian-born designer Yves Saint Laurent, who has a villa nearby. The garden is one of the city's more popular sights and, at only 4.8 hectares (12 acres), can become a little crowded at times. Nevertheless, the layout of the garden lends itself to a feeling of tranquillity and is a welcome break from the busy streets outside. A nice way to reach the garden from the medina is by horse-drawn *caléche*. The gardens are also a stop on the Marrakech City Sightseeing bus's Romantique circuit (p. 144).

Av. Yacoub el Mansour, Ville Nouvelle. Entrance is on a small street on the east side of the garden. www.jardin majorelle.com. Garden admission 30dh ($3.75/£1.90) adults, 15dh ($1.90/95p) children 5–12; museum 15dh ($1.90/95p) adults, 10dh ($1.25/65p) children 5–12. Daily Oct–May 8am–5pm; June–Sept 8am–6pm. No picnics allowed.

(Tips   **Chill . . . & Have a Hot Mint Tea**

Morocco's medinas are amazing, though sometimes daunting, places to explore. Particularly in Marrakech, however, visitors try to pack too much into the day and furiously rush around ticking off the sights, bartering for souvenirs, and clicking away on their camera without realizing they are missing the one must-have experience—the medina atmosphere. If you can, take some time to unwind in a nearby cafe and sip on a sweet, piping hot *atei benna'na'* (mint tea). The drink is an institution all over Morocco, and even at the most local of cafes a ritual is often followed.

A small pot (be careful of the hot handle) shouldn't cost more than 10dh ($1.25/65p), and the first glass should be poured from an arm's-length height, repotted, and poured again to both aerate the liquid and properly mix the flavors of tea (first introduced in Tangier by the English during the Crimean War), fresh mint, and sugar. This ritual can vary in length of time and height of pour, depending on your location and the inclination of your waiter or host. The flavor and sweetness can also vary greatly, but you can be almost certain that your tea will come presweetened unless you order it *"la sukka"* (pronounced "la *soo*-ka").

In Marrakech's medina, try **Café des Epices** on place Rahba Qedima (p. 134); the terrace of **Café-Restaurant Argana** on place Jemaa el Fna (p. 130); the literary cafe–cum–art gallery **Dar Cherifa** on Derb Cherifa Lakbir, off rue Mouassine (© **024/426463**); or the air-conditioned *salon de thé* at the back of **Patisserie des Princes** halfway down rue Bab Agnaou. For a spicy cinnamon *chai*, look for the *hunja* stalls, with their big copper urns, that roll onto the southern edge of Jemaa el Fna around 5pm daily.

Get on the Bus

The arrival of the international sightseeing bus franchise **City Sightseeing** (© 024/339637; www.city-ss.com) in Marrakech is proof that the city is positioning itself as a major player amongst the world's tourist destinations. The bright red, open-top, double-decker bus offers two continuous hop-on, hop-off circuits—Marrakech Monumental (18 stops) and Marrakech Romantique (7 stops)—on a first-come, first-served basis. The buses are equipped with a multilingual—English, French, Italian, Japanese, Portuguese, Russian, and Spanish—audio system that provides a brief commentary of the major points of interest. Of the two circuits, the Monumental is by far the more popular, as it includes stops in both Guéliz and Hivernage (including the Menara Gardens) as well as within the medina. The Romantique heads out to the palmeraie and golf courses via the Majorelle Garden, and is more of a scenic drive.

Tickets for each circuit, valid for 24 hours, can be purchased at the pickup/drop-off points (see below) and cost 130dh ($16/£8.15) adults, 65dh ($8.15/£4.05) kids 6 to 16, and free for 5 and under. The Monumental circuit runs every 30 minutes from 9am to 7pm and lasts about 30 minutes. The Romantique circuit takes 1 hour and 10 minutes and runs from 1 to 5:30pm. Both circuits pick up at the ONMT tourist office in Guéliz, while the most accessible pickup points for Monumental include Jemaa el Fna; the Saâdian Tombs and Palais Bahia in the medina; Hotel Le Marrakech and McDonald's on avenue Mohammed V; and the hotels Royal Mirage, Le Meridien, and Andalous in Hivernage.

Menara Gardens ★★ (Kids More an olive grove than a park, this is the most popular of Marrakech's gardens for both picnicking locals and camera-wielding tourists who visit for the picture-postcard pool with green-tiled pavilion, or *minzah,* dwarfed by the High Atlas mountains in the background. It's stunning during the clear, snow-capped winter months. Aside from its photogenic qualities, however, the Menara is a peaceful place to escape the summer heat and the city's hustle and bustle. This is a stop on the Monumental circuit on the Marrakech City Sightseeing bus (see above).

Av. de la Ménara, on the western edge of the city past Hivernage. Free admission. Daily 8:30am–5:30pm.

6 Especially for Kids

Moroccans love children, which can be both a godsend and an irritant, as every shopkeeper in the souks will wave you into his store to both acquire your business and interact with your young one. There is plenty to keep your children's attention while you wander around the **souks**—music shops with lots of drums; Berber pharmacies (called *herboristes*) with brightly colored concoctions; butcheries with the odd sheep or camel's head prominently displayed. The souks are very busy areas with lots of pedestrian traffic, so be sure to keep an eye on your kids. After you're done shopping, check out the entertainment on Jemaa el Fna, where you'll also find a number of **cafes and patisseries.** If the enclosed spaces are making the kids antsy, the **Menara Gardens** (see above) is a good place to let little legs run free for a while. A ride around the medina's walls on a *calèche* or aboard the open-top double-decker City Sightseeing bus can be a quick fix for tired kids, and those who miss their familiar burgers and fries can stop at the **McDonald's** on place de la Liberté.

Kasbah Le Mirage, Sidi Brahim Quarter in the palmeraie (© 024/314444), offers 1- to 2-hour camel rides, while **Atlas Karting,** on the road to Safi (© 024/331717 or 061/237687), has a mini-kart racing circuit along with 45km (28 miles) of quad biking trails. For a day at the "beach," take the kids to the newly opened **Oasiria,** 5km (3 miles) from the city on the Asni road (© 024/380438; www.oasiria.com). They'll love the wave pool, water slides, pools, and lagoons, plus there are grassed areas and a couple of restaurants. It's open 10am to 6pm daily from April to August, and Friday to Sunday during the rest of the year. A free shuttle bus runs from June 15 to August 31, picking up from both the parking lot opposite the Koutoubia Mosque and place du Harti in Guéliz at 9:30, 10:15, 11, and 11:45am, and 1:30, 2:25, and 3pm. The bus drops you right at the entrance to Oasiria. At the end of the day, the shuttle bus departs for the return journey into town at 5, 5:45, 6:30, and 7:15pm.

In the evening the entertainment continues on Jemaa el Fna or at **Chez Ali** (© 024/307730), on the outskirts of the city in Jaafary palmeraie, where Disneyland meets Morocco in a nightly dinner extravaganza complete with Berber musicians, belly-dancing, fireworks, a mock wedding, and a show from charging, gun-wielding horsemen. The kids (and maybe the grownups, too) will love it, and be sure to bring plenty of change for tipping the steady stream of performers who visit your table during the course of the night.

7 Shopping

Nobody leaves Marrakech without buying *something*. Although some particular crafts are better procured elsewhere—ceramics from Fes and silver jewelry from Tiznit—most travelers come here to make their purchases. Almost every form of Moroccan arts and crafts can be found amongst Marrakech's labyrinth of shops. Leatherwork, brassware, and copperware are traditionally of high quality and reasonable cost in Marrakech, but there's so much of everything here that it's easy to suffer from souk overload. An initial visit to the **Ensemble Artisanal,** on avenue Mohammed V between Jemaa el Fna and Bab Nkob (© 024/443503), can help to overcome this. Here, you can see skilled craftsmen and women at work and browse amongst the many items for sale without the pressure that you may encounter in the souks. Unlike the medina's shops and souks, the prices here are more or less fixed, although slightly higher. If anything, coming here before you begin your serious souk shopping gives you an idea of the maximum you should pay and, just as importantly, what to look for in terms of quality and workmanship.

Outside the medina's walls in Guéliz, along avenue Mohammed V and boulevard Zerktouni, you'll find some chic boutiques offering the latest in European fashion, leatherware, and beauty products. For fresh produce, groceries, toiletries, and alcohol, **Acima** supermarket, on the corner of avenues Mohammed V and Abdelkarim el Khattabi (© 024/430453), is open daily from 9am to 10pm. Farther along avenue Abdelkarim el Khattabi is the Western-style, air-conditioned **Marjane Hypermarket** (© 024/313724). Open daily from 9am to 9pm, it sells everything from groceries and general foodstuffs (including bacon) to cookware and computers. There's also a well-stocked liquor store here that stays open for non-Muslims during Ramadan, as well as a bank with an ATM, a McDonald's, and a photo store. They also have a second store on the outskirts of the city on the Marrakech-Essaouira road with the same hours.

If you are intimidated by shopping in the medina, think about hiring an official guide (p. 38) for half a day. All of my recommended Marrakech accommodations will be able to organize an English-speaking guide for you. Although he (I am, unfortunately, yet to meet a female guide in Morocco) may direct you into shops where he will earn commission from your purchases, remember that if you don't buy, he won't earn, so he is playing for both sides, so to speak, which can ultimately be to your benefit. Although bartering is considered compulsory practice, don't get too hung up on it. Before you begin, ask yourself how much you'd like to pay for the item. Keep that figure in mind if you start feeling pressured to pay far more than you had planned, although check yourself if you find you're haggling over a difference in price that, when converted back to your native currency, is relatively small and not worth the stress. Remember, you can always walk away. Take no notice of the shopkeeper's bleeding heart story or over-the-top displays of frustration and temper. Make your purchase a happy memory.

Caution: As in other parts of Morocco, it's best not to rely on being able to use your credit card when shopping. Some shopkeepers, especially the carpet emporiums, will have the necessary equipment, but when paying for smaller purchases, cash—usually dirham but sometimes euros or dollars—will be the only form of payment accepted. If you are using your credit card, be aware of the full amount being charged to your card prior to signing off the transaction. Some shopkeepers will record the purchase amount in dirham, so be aware of the current exchange rates. I recently heard from one traveler who was assured by the shopkeeper that she could pay with her credit card over six monthly installments and signed six separate transaction slips only to find out a few days, and many miles, later that the shopkeeper had processed all six payments simultaneously; there was no credit left on her account.

SHOPPING A TO Z
ANTIQUES
Bazaar Marzouk   Now into its fourth generation of buying and selling antiques, this store's warehouse is full to the brim with artifacts, ceramics, jewelry, carpets, and furniture from all over North Africa. Open daily 9am to 7pm. 100 rue Mohammed el Beqal, Guéliz. ℂ **024/447444.**

Bouchaib Complexe D'Artisanat   Rue Bab Doukkala and rue Dar el Bacha carry a number of antiques dealers, and this, down in the kasbah, is the most conveniently located. This place brings in the tour groups, but the sheer range of products (not all antique), all at fixed prices, makes it a hassle-free one-stop "department" store. Rue de la Kasbah, about 30m (100 ft.) south of the Saâdian Tombs. ℂ **024/381853.** www.bouchaib.net.

Trésor des Nomades   Mustapha Blaoui's shop is probably the best known and most highly respected antiques warehouse in town. Inside you'll find a mind-boggling array of ornamentation and furnishings from ceremonial daggers, Berber jewelry, and candlesticks to lanterns, tables, and chairs. 142–144 rue Bab Doukkala, in the medina. ℂ **024/385240.**

ART
Gallery 21   This gallery hosts temporary exhibitions of both Moroccan and international artists at two locations in Guéliz. The first is open Monday to Saturday 12:20 to 2:30pm and 5 to 10pm, the latter Monday to Saturday 10am to 1pm and 4 to 8pm. 55 bd. Zerktouni. ℂ **024/434996.** 36 rue de la Liberté. ℂ **024/431268.**

Karim Kabadi Karim sells fascinating framed copies of original black-and-white photographs portraying Marrakech in the early 1900s in his small shop. 142 rue Riad Zitoun Kedim. ℂ 073/015331.

La Qoubba Gallery This gallery in the medina displays an interesting collection of originals and prints—for sale and generally quite affordable—from local artists. Open daily from 9am to 1pm and 2:30 to 6:30pm. At the beginning of rue Souk Talaa, just off place Ben Youssef. ℂ 024/380515. www.art-gallery-marrakech.com.

BEAUTY

The benefits of argan oil (produced from trees exclusive to southwest Morocco) are only beginning to be known in the Western world (p. 354), but you can get a jump on everyone at two new shops in the medina. *Tip:* If you are anywhere near the Acima or Marjane supermarkets (p. 43), have a look at their argan oil and spice collection. Although obviously lacking the medina shopping atmosphere, you are very likely to find the same products at a fraction of the price.

Assouss Argane Here you'll find a nicely presented range of creams and soaps (50dh–250dh/$6.25–$31/£3.15–£16) and cooking and essential oils (130dh–250dh/$16–$31/£8.15–£16). The delicious *amlou* spread sells for 100dh ($13/£6.25), and the sales girls are usually willing to let you try before you buy. Open daily 9am to 8pm. 94 rue Mouassine. ℂ 061/729678.

Dar Argane 🌟 *Finds* Marrakech's first organic health shop has a well-laid-out show-room with every argan product currently available, including shower gel (50dh/$6.25/£3.15), shampoo (100dh/$13/£6.25), soaps, creams, and oils. They also sell olive and rose oil products, dried herbs, jams, and herbal teas that can be instantly brewed for you in the attached cafe. Av. Houmman el Fetouaki, about 50m (164 ft.) from rue Riad Zitoun Kedim. ℂ 060/544992. www.arganicaoil.com.

L'Artisan Parfumerie Duty-free's not cheap anymore, so pick from 100 of your favorite (imitation) designer perfumes here for 49dh ($6.15/£3.05) per 50ml (1.7 oz.). Open daily from 9am to 9pm. On rue des Banques, off Jemaa el Fna. No phone.

LB Cosmetics 🌟🌟🌟 The chic jet-set comes here for locally and naturally produced organic beauty products. The small shop smells fantastic, and they have a huge range of products for sale at reasonable prices for both body and bath, all labeled with LB Cosmetics' distinctive calligraphy design. Open Monday to Saturday 10am to 1pm and 4 to 8pm. 13 rue Moulay Ali (behind the Hotel Diwane). ℂ 061/284467. www.lineaire-b.com.

Les Parfums du Soleil 🌟🌟🌟 Marrakchi botanist-turned-*parfumier* Abderrazak Benchaâbane has become a bit of a star nowadays (his original business partner was Yves Saint Laurent), and his current *eaux de toilette* includes Soir de Marrakech, an evocative blend of amber, musk, vanilla, patchouli, and citrus oils. It sells for 500dh ($63/£31). Open Monday to Saturday 9am to 1pm and 3 to 7:30pm. Rue Tarik ben Ziad, between bd. Zerktouni and rue ibn Aïcha (around the corner from LB Cosmetics). ℂ 024/422627. www.lesparfumsdusoleil.com.

BOOKSHOPS

ACR Librairie Like Librairie Dar el Bacha (below), this shop in Guéliz carries a good selection of glossy coffee table–style books on various Moroccan themes such as architecture and the country's Berbers, as well as a few English-language guidebooks to Morocco. Open Monday to Friday 9am to 1pm and 3 to 7:30pm. 55 bd. Zerktouni. ℂ 024/446792.

Hot & Steamy: Hammams

The traditional Turkish steam bath plays an important role in the community as a gathering place for both men and women. Within Morocco, there are public hammams in almost every city, town, and village, and this is often the only place to get clean for those households that still lack running water. There's also a strong religious connotation attached to the hammam, with many Muslims cleansing themselves here before prayer. Morocco's public hammams are largely welcoming to visitors, bar those located close to mosques and other Islamic monuments. Public hammams are strictly segregated—some may be men- or women-only, or have separate entrances, while others are open to a particular sex at specific hours or on separate days. Entrance is usually 5dh (65¢/30p) per person per session, paid to an attendant at the hammam entrance, where bathers belongings are stored for safekeeping.

Once changed into hammam attire, bathers head into the steam rooms, locate an empty bucket and scoop, find a spot to sit down, and begin the process of opening the pores through sweating, interspersed with an alternate dousing of hot and cold water from the bucket, filled from a communal tap located within the room. Moroccans also like to indulge in some *grommage* (a rigorous exfoliation performed with a harsh, flannel glove), a body wrap or hair wash using a fine clay mixed with herbs and lavender called *ghassoul*, or a simple body wash with *sabon bildi*, a black, oily, olive oil–based, gel-like soap. There are usually attendants on hand who offer these traditional services, as well as an on-the-floor massage, for a small gratuity of around 20dh ($2.50/£1.25).

Reception staff at any good hotel or *maison d'hôte* will be able to direct travelers to the nearest public hammam. Take your own towel, a change of underwear/shorts, soap (though this can usually also be purchased at the

Café du Livre ★★★ This peaceful haven in Guéliz has Morocco's best selection of English-language books for both loan and sale that includes a good number of Moroccan fiction and nonfiction. Recent English-language newspapers are also available to read while you relax in one of the supercomfy lounge chairs. The cafe hosts an afternoon high tea and serves food (salads, sandwiches, tapas) and alcohol (available at dinner time; p. 137). Open Monday to Saturday 9:30am to 9pm. 44 rue Tarik ben Ziad, off to one side of the entrance to Hotel Toulousain. ✆ 024/432149. www.cafedulivre.com.

Librairie Dar el Bacha This is the only true bookshop in the medina, and its floor-to-ceiling shelves are packed with books on Moroccan art, literature, and cuisine. Although the majority of them are in French, there are a few English-language guidebooks and coffee table–style books available. They also host regular book launches and other events. Rue Dar el Bacha. ✆ 024/391973. www.darelbacha.com.

CARPETS
Berber Shop *Finds* For an intimate, relaxed experience, visit Mohammed Aggani, a genuinely nice gentlemen who speaks perfect English. He only sells carpets made from

hammam), shampoo (if required), and a plastic mat to sit on. Tourist-friendly and in-house hammams (such as those listed below and throughout this book) will usually provide the towel and soap, and won't require the plastic mat. For information on hammam etiquette, refer to the "Fast Facts" section in chapter 2.

In the medina is **Hammam Ziani**, 14 rue Riad Zitoun Jdid (© **062/715571**), where you can get a massage, scrub, seaweed bath, mud wrap, bathrobe, and toiletries bag for 300dh ($38/£19). A simple massage and scrub is 155dh ($19/£9) Monday to Thursday and 165dh ($21/£10) Friday to Sunday and public holidays. Open daily for men and women (separate entrances) from 8am to 10pm.

Les Secrets de Marrakech, 62 rue de la Liberté, Guéliz (© **024/434848**), is a very classy hammam and spa that offers a variety of massages, aromatherapy treatments, body wraps, and pedicures. They also sell an exquisite range of natural soaps, scrubs, bath salts, and oils. A full 1½-hour package costs 580dh to 680dh ($73–$85/£36–£43), and includes entrance into the hammam followed by a *grommage*, body wrap in *ghassoul* or argan and cinnamon oil, and a massage. Open Monday to Saturday for both genders from 10am to 8pm.

Many *maisons d'hôte* and high-end hotels have in-house hammams, but most of these are for guests only. The small hammam and massage room at the **Jnane Mogador** (p. 122), however, is open to the public by appointment between 9am and 11pm daily. It offers a Berbère Hammam exfoliation scrub, natural soap wash, and mud body wrap for 125dh ($16/£8); a range of 45-minute massages including sports, Californian, Thai, and shiatsu runs from 180dh to 400dh ($23–$50/11–£25).

the women of his own Aït ben Haddou tribe near the desert outpost of M'hamid. Open daily 9am to 7pm. 214 rue Riad Zitoun Jdid. © **061/210283** or 069/973760.

Souk Zrabia   You can't beat this place for pure selection. Inside this covered souk are up to a dozen shops selling every shape, size, and color carpet, rug, and *kélim* available. The pressure to buy can be quite intense, but if you truly wish to purchase, this is the place. Prices vary greatly due to the quality of both craftsmanship and negotiation, but small *kélims* can go for as little as 1,000dh ($125/£63); medium Berber rugs (2×2m/6½×6½ ft.) for 5,000dh ($625/£313); and a 4×4m (13×13 ft.) reversible carpet can sell for 32,000dh ($4,000/£2,000).

FASHION

Kif Kif 𝔊𝔊   This is a gem of a shop, decked out in lime green and burgundy and selling original designs by Marrakech resident designer Stéphanie Bénetère. There's a great range of clothing (for babies and kids as well) along with jewelry, napkins, very original *babouches*, belts, stationery, and home accessories including cushions and oil burners. Open daily 9am to 1pm and 4 to 7:30pm. 6 rue el Ksour, off rue Sidi el Yamani, in the medina. ℂ 061/082041. www.kifkifbystef.com.

Kulchi ⭐ Close to Kif Kif (above), this shop sells owner Florence Taranne's popular label of light, colorful clothing along with raffia shoes, leather handbags, and screen-printed T-shirts. If you're looking to take home some world lounge music, pick up resident Buddha Bar DJ and producer Claude Challe's *Le Grand Orchestre du Comptoir de Marrakech* for 200dh ($25/£13). Open Monday to Saturday 9am to 1pm and 4 to 7:30pm. There's a second boutique inside Comptoir Darna restaurant (p. 153) open Monday to Saturday from 4pm to midnight. 1 rue el Ksour. ℂ 024/429177.

La Maison du Kaftan ⭐ Come here if you want to dress like the locals do. Since 1980, this two-level store has been selling kaftans and *jellabahs* to both Marrakchis and visitors, including film stars such as Samuel L. Jackson. There are literally thousands in here to choose from, in all the colors of the rainbow. Prices start at 200dh ($25/£13) for a lightweight cotton kaftan to as high as 5,000dh ($625/£313) for a special occasion *jellabah*. 65 rue Sidi el Yamani, in the Mouassine neighborhood of the medina. ℂ 024/441051.

La Perle Fassi *Babouches,* the traditional Moroccan slippers, are for sale seemingly everywhere, but for minimal hassle, high quality, and fixed prices, turn into Sidi Berrada's shop in the medina. You'll find a huge choice for both women and men, most of which aren't any more than 120dh ($15/£7.50). Open daily 9am to 9pm. 5 rue Souk Semmarine. ℂ 024/442333.

HOUSEWARES

Abdelkarim Elazri *Finds* Ouarzazate-born Abdelkarim Elazri designs, creates, and sells the most original mint tea glasses in the medina. If you can't find what you want from his large selection, let him know what you're after, and he'll make it for you. He also has a fair range of teapots for sale. The glasses sell for 10dh ($1.25/65p) each. Open daily from around 9am to noon and 2 to 9pm. If Abdelkarim isn't around, ask one of the neighboring shopkeepers to contact him. 38 rue Riad Zitoun Jdid. ℂ 071/842628.

Zen Bougie ⭐⭐⭐ Owner Naouri's passion for candles led him to open his little "cave" in the medina in 2004. His nonmelting designs are to be found in many of Marrakech's riads and restaurants and come in all colors and sizes, sometimes decorated in copper, glass, henna, and even *thuya* wood. Prices start from 50dh ($6.25/£3.15). Open daily 9am to 1pm and 3 to 8pm. 10 rue el Ksour. (ℂ 024/391989.

JEWELRY

El Abidi Nasser Eddine ⭐⭐⭐ Whether you buy something or not (he's not cheap), this should be your first stop for jewelry. For 30 years, Sidi Nasser has been selling both antique and original jewelry. The shop now has a carved-wood frontage and is air-conditioned, but the service and craftsmanship are steeped in tradition. His English-speaking staff are happy to explain the history behind each design and the materials used. Examples include necklaces made from trade beads of Tibetan turquoise and Afghani lapis, and black coral encrusted in silver. Open daily from 9am to 8pm. At the south end of rue Souk Semmarine in the medina, shop no. 9. ℂ 024/441066.

Souk Fondouk Louarzazi Here you'll find two cramped levels of treasure troves selling reasonably priced Berber jewelry. On place Bab Ftouh.

LEATHERWARE

Hassan Zemouuri's 🏺 Inside you'll find a large selection of all things leather, including jackets, caps, *babouches*, belts, *poufes* (foot cushions), and bags of all shapes and sizes, including attractive handbags inlaid with old coins for 200dh ($25/£13). Open daily 9am to 8pm. Next door to Jamal Hadzoui's *thuya* wood shop (see below) in the medina's Mouassine neighborhood.

Latif Art & Deco This small shop specializes in leather bags, belts, and sandals— with the odd leather cowboy hat—at very reasonable prices. Open daily 9am to 6pm. 116 rue Dar el Bacha. 🕾 062/085594.

MUSIC

Tamouziqua 🏺🏺 Mustapha Mimani's shop in the medina sells all manner of traditional Moroccan and Arabic musical instruments including drums, string, and percussion, some of which he makes himself in his workshop around the corner. Open daily 9am to 9pm. 86 rue Riad Zitoun Jdid. 🕾 071/518724.

SPICES & *HERBORISTES*

Stalls and small shops within the medina selling spices can be instantly recognized by the tall, cone-shape mounds of red (paprika), yellow (turmeric), and green (henna) on display at their entrances. Spices are an essential item in everyday Moroccan cooking, so their availability is widespread and therefore not as exhilarating of a shopping experience. Prices should be fixed (around 20dh/$2.50/£1.25 per 100g/¼ lb. for any standard spice) and the transaction swift, though in the more touristy areas of the medina, the shopkeeper may attempt to fleece you.

Providing far more entertainment are the medina's Berber chemists, or *herboristes,* who display animal skins, dried herbs, and caged tortoises at their entrances. Generally open every day from 9am to 7pm, they also sell spices, including a mixture of 35 different varieties known as *ras el hanout.* However, they specialize in herbal medicines and oils. Constipation, diabetes, weight loss, depression, bladder, liver or skin problems, and impotence are just some of the ailments that can be miraculously "cured" with the concoctions that are paraded in front of you. A good *herboriste* is a pharmacist, salesman, and entertainer all in one.

Herboriste du Paradis 🏺🏺🏺 *Kids* This is one of the largest chemists, overseen by one of the best English-speaking *herboristes,* Saïd Telecom. In the medina, next to the Almoravid Koubba. 🕾 024/427279.

Sloubi For a more laid-back experience, try this English-speaking family's narrow shop. In the lane joining rue Souk Semmarine and the southwest corner of place Rahba Kedima, shop no. 6, third on the right. No phone.

WOODWORK

Aux Merveilles du Bois Jamal Hadzoui specializes in products made from the *thuya* tree found farther south. The pieces are smooth and shiny, and you can choose from backgammon and chess boards, chests and jewelry boxes inlaid with mother of pearl, candlesticks, photo frames, and even life-size footballs. A regular-size backgammon board should sell for around 200dh ($25/£13). Open daily; closed for lunch on Fridays. 1 rue Mouassine, in the Medina. 🕾 024/441786.

8 Marrakech after Dark

Today's Marrakech seems to be living two lives, both as a playground for international jet-setters and a place where tradition still runs deep. This dichotomy is most visible when surveying the available options for a night on the town.

Those seeking a taste of old Morocco should spend at least 1 night at Jemaa el Fna. Arrive before evening to watch the sunset, followed by an array of musicians, storytellers, and dancers. After you've sampled the square, stroll along the adjoining rue Bab Agnaou, or take a seat on Abd el Moumen Square (in front of the Koutoubia Mosque) and end the night with some prime people-watching.

Culture seekers should coincide their visit to the city with one of Marrakech's festivals (see "Festivals," below), while those who prefer a night of dancing and drinks will find everything from lounges to what claims to be the biggest club in Africa.

BARS

There was a time when most watering holes in the city were either of the all-male, sawdust-floor variety or the exclusive domain of the more expensive hotels, but nowadays there's a fair smattering of sophisticated, chic establishments where both genders can enjoy a drink without hassle.

Within the medina, choices are limited if you don't wish to have a meal with your drink. There are stand-alone bars at **Cafe Arabe** (p. 132) and **Narwama** (p. 132), while next to the Mellah is the Asian-chic **Kosybar** ✦✦, place des Ferblantiers (© 024/380324; http://kozibar.tripod.com), which has been hugely popular since it opened in 2005. This former riad offers something different on each of its three floors. The small ground-floor bar, decorated with a zebra-skin hide, is a great spot for an evening of drinking and dancing. The second level combines shades of ochre and olive with heavy, dark-wood furniture and the original *zellij* flooring. On the terrace you'll be rewarded with a superb view of the medina, the top of the El Badi Palace, and the resident flock of storks who regularly cruise by at eye level. The terrace has heaps of comfy lounges and is a great place to chill out with a cold beer or a bottle of wine (the selection must be one of the largest in the country, no doubt thanks to the owner's family connection to the award-winning Les Celliers de Meknès winery). Kosybar is open daily from noon to midnight.

For surroundings a little more distinguished, there are a couple of piano bars worth a visit. **La Maison Arabe,** 1 Derb Assehbe, off rue Bab Doukkala (© 024/387010), is one of the larger riads within the medina. Its sub-Sahara-theme lounge has a stylish cocktail list. The lighting is low and the atmosphere reserved, making this the perfect spot for an aperitif or nightcap. The aptly named **Piano Bar,** within the mammoth Hotel les Jardins de la Koutoubia, 26 rue Koutoubia (© 024/488800), is very low key and rarely busy in the evening. The bow-tied staff members are pretty much at your disposal, while the resident piano player tries out his best Frank Sinatra impersonation. Come here if you want somewhere to drink and talk without the fuss and noise of the outside world.

In Guéliz, the restaurants **Le Grand Café de la Poste** (p. 134), **Kechmara** (p. 136), and **Café du Livre** (p. 137) are great places to enjoy a drink. If you're simply looking for a refreshing ale during the heat of the day, inside the **Grand Café de L'Atlas,** avenue Mohammed V at place Abdelmoumen Ben Ali, is a bar where Moroccan men and the odd tourist can sink one down away from the public eye. The compact **Le Lounge,** next to the Diwane Hotel, 24 rue Yougoslavie (© 024/433703), is Daniel

Guillard and Christian Hofer's affordable, unpretentious lounge bar that nightly attracts a loyal set of locals as well as a few stray tourists. The staff members are young, pretty, and friendly; drinks are served either in the downstairs lounge or the smoky upstairs mezzanine. The interior is sleek and modern, with black and red colors throughout. The music is largely dance, house, or funk, and wide-screen TVs show the latest music videos. There's a reasonable menu, including tapas, available, and most diners prefer to take their meals under the covered alfresco terrace.

Out in well-to-do Hivernage is the icon of Marrakech nightlife, **Comptoir Darna** ✸✸✸, rue Echouhada (② **024/437702;** www.comptoirdarna.com). The two-level former villa is renowned for its sexy Franco-Asian groove and is one of *the* places to see and be seen. Low lighting, scented candles, and Moroccan lamps are strategically placed in the ground-floor restaurants. Diners can choose from low-lying tables under the Berber tent, or inside the charcoal and ochre restaurant proper. Head out to the small garden where you can lounge on the lime, orange, and red cushions and heavy Berber carpets. A wide, central staircase leads up to the real reason to come here: the haremlike bar decked out in charcoal, orange, and burgundy veils where resident and guest DJs spin the latest in Euro-Arabian dance music. Oh, and did I mention the exotic dancers? Dress hot and arrive thirsty (and bring plenty of money).

DANCE CLUBS

Up until a few years ago, Marrakech's nightclub scene had become quite seedy, but recently some very classy (and very expensive) clubs have opened up in tune with the general trend that is sweeping the city. Most are located in Hivernage or farther out in a new *zone hôtelière* on boulevard Mohammed VI. They usually don't get busy until after midnight and may charge admission ranging from 150dh to 300dh ($19–$38/ £9.40–£19), which includes your first drink. Alcohol is generally available at exorbitant prices, and although the city is inundated with tourists for the greater part of the year, the dance clubs are mainly the domain of European residents, seasonal visitors, and young well-to-do Marrakchis. Come dressed to impress.

Consistently one of the hottest places in town since it opened in 2004 is **Theatro** ✸, at the Hotel es Saadi on avenue Quadissia, Hivernage (② **024/448811;** www.theatro-marrakech.com). Converted from an old theater and with the original stage still intact, this place, at times, rivals Europe with its unabashed on-stage hedonism (visualize semi-naked people lounging around on four-poster beds surrounded by flame throwers). At other times, it's simply a high-end techno dance club and a good place to show off your best moves.

Out past Hivernage is **Pacha Marrakech,** Complexe Pacha, boulevard Mohammed VI (② **024/388400;** www.pachamarrakech.com), which bills itself as the biggest club in Africa (and possibly the loudest). This kasbah-style club, an outpost of the clubbing giant Pacha in Ibiza, pumps out 50,000 watts of DJ-mixed music that pulses through your body (it even makes your nose vibrate). It boasts two restaurants and a huge swimming pool (more for trying to look good next to rather than to actually swim in) in addition to its neon cavelike nightclub and lounge. It can be a bit quiet during the week, so try to go on Saturday night when international guest DJs are flown in.

Farther out, on the Ourika road, is **Bô & Zin** ✸✸ (② **024/388012;** www.bo-zin. com), which can be a bit hit-and-miss with its cuisine (mainly French and Thai), served within the various rooms inside. However, it definitely hosts a pretty good late-night party, with both a resident DJ and guest musicians out in the garden. During

Festivals

Marrakech is widely regarded as the creative soul of Morocco (with respect to Fes, which is definitely the spiritual heart of the country), and a number of annual festivals hosted by the city help to confirm the view. Specific dates can vary from year to year, but it's worth preplanning your trip to coincide with one of the following:

Dakka music—polyrhythmic percussion beats accompanied by extended chanting—has been performed for centuries by the craftsmen of Marrakech's souks in tribute to Sabaatou Rijal, the city's seven spiritual guards. For 10 days each February, the **Dakka Marrakchia Festival** brings together the craftsmen/performers from seven of Marrakech's districts for nightly performances in Jemaa el Fna as well as the city's Théâtre Royal.

The **Festival International du Film de Marrakech** (www.festival-marrakech. com) aims to be North Africa's version of the Cannes Film Festival, and over its 6-year history, its has attracted the likes of Martin Scorsese, Francis Ford Coppola, Susan Sarandon, Jeremy Irons, and Roman Polanski, along with a host of Arabic, European, and Indian film stars. More than 100 films are shown during the weeklong festival, and select films are shown nightly on a huge screen in the northwest corner of Jemaa el Fna. Although the exact dates vary, it's always hosted toward the end of the year.

Friendship Fest (www.friendshipfest.com) is a musical event promoting peace and friendship between the cultures of North America and Morocco. The most recent concert, held in 2006 over 3 nights outside Bab Ighli and next to the Agdal Garden, drew more than 200,000 people who had come to see some of North America's most popular Christian rock acts (Joy Williams and The Crabb Family, for example) perform alongside popular Moroccan contemporary and traditional music stars. The event is free.

The **Marrakech Popular Arts Festival** is held over 10 days each June or July. During the festival, Marrakech becomes a big open-air theater packed with traditional performers from all over Morocco—High Atlas Berbers, Riffian-Andalusians, southern Gnaoua-ians, and Arabic belly dancers. The majority of performances take place in the El Badi Palace or on Jemaa el Fna, which becomes even more frenzied than usual. Each day is topped off by an evening performance by gun-wielding horsemen just outside Bab el Jdid.

summer it's usually packed with beautiful people being served by beautiful staff—it's that kind of place.

LIVE MUSIC

For the ultimate in live music, look no further than the nightly concert on Jemaa el Fna. Besides this obvious choice, live music in Marrakech seems to revolve around troupes of Andalusian or Gnaoua musicians performing as part of a dinner show, like that at **Palais Chahramane** (p. 133), or one-man synthesizer shows in the smoky (and usually depressingly empty) bars of some expensive hotels. However, if you don't mind a dose of live Latino cover music, then a trio of clubs recently opened in Guéliz may do the trick.

For Afro-Brazilian inspiration, try the pulsating **Afric'n Chic** 𝒜𝒜★, 6 rue Oum Errebia, behind Hotel Le Marrakech (© **024/431424;** www.africnchic.com). The bar is at the front of this so-called "tribal lounge," where objets d'art from all over the African, Asian, and Latino world blend in with Moroccan specialties such as mosaic tables, brightly colored cushions, and ceramic pottery. There's a restaurant/lounge farther inside, but the live Latino, jazz, and blues music, which usually cranks up just after the 7 to 9pm happy hour, can be enjoyed from either spot.

Offering something totally different is **Trio Latino,** on the corner of boulevard Zerktouni and rue Tarik ben Ziad (© **024/433070**). Multitalented Rémi Leviconte is the current one-man show performing in this bar/restaurant. Every night, except Monday, he smoothly moves from Robbie Williams to Barry White to Frank Sinatra, depending on the preference of the audience, in between servings of Tex-Mex cuisine. This "music hall" seats about 70, and on a busy night, the atmosphere is pure fun.

There's also **Montecristo,** 20 rue ibn Aïcha (© **024/439031;** www.montecristo-marrakech.com). Although it takes itself far too seriously and the food is nothing special, the saving graces for this two-story, floodlit mansion are the shedlike Bar Latino and the even smaller Bar Africaine, where live music generally pumps out from late evening until the early hours. The number of high-class prostitutes in residence can be a concern, but if this doesn't trouble you, drink and salsa the night away.

Live classical music (both Andalusian and European) sometimes makes its way to Marrakech, generally courtesy of the **Institit Français,** Route de la Targa on the outskirts of Guéliz (© **024/446930;** www.ifm.ma). Keep an eye out around town for posters promoting upcoming performers.

9 Side Trips from Marrakech

OURIKA VALLEY
30–70 km (19–43 miles) S of Marrakech

The High Atlas mountains hover tantalizingly close to Marrakech, and if you don't have the time to explore them in great detail, some areas are easily accessible for either a day or overnight excursion. During the oppressively hot summer months, a drive up to the Ourika Valley is a pleasant and popular escape for both locals and visitors alike. The main places of interest, for a day's excursion at least, are the winter ski resort of Oukaïmeden (also a great spring/summer hiking spot) and the riverside village of Setti Fatma, site of one of Morocco's biggest *moussems,* which takes place in mid-August. Both villages are only about 70km (43 miles) south of Marrakech, and most travel agencies in the city offer guided day tours, or you can charter a *grand* taxi for the day. Adventure travelers should consider setting aside a few days to explore the area further, as there are opportunities for mountain biking, rock climbing, hiking, trekking, and, in winter, skiing. Bird-watching around **Oukaïmeden** 𝒜𝒜 can be quite rewarding at the end of spring and during summer and autumn. These and other High Atlas destinations are discussed in more depth in chapter 6.

GETTING THERE   Buses and *grands* taxis for Setti Fatma depart daily from a terminal 3km (1¾ miles) outside the Bab er Rob medina gate, best reached by *petit* taxi. During winter, a separate, direct route to Oukaïmeden operates daily from the same terminal. For the rest of the year, take Setti Fatma transport as far as the turn-off, from where you should be able to catch a stray *grand* taxi or hitch a ride heading up to the resort. Chartering a *grand* taxi from Marrakech for the day is a very good option if there are even just two of you, purely for the convenience factor. They can usually be chartered either from the Bab er Rob terminal or directly from your hotel. Rates average around 500dh to 600dh ($63–$75/£31–£38) for the day. *Note:* Remember to pay at the end of the day, not the beginning, and make sure upfront that all costs and itinerary are agreed upon. If you're driving yourself, the road is well signposted heading out of Marrakech. After around 35km (22 miles), the road starts to wind upward and stays very scenic, whether you continue on to Setti Fatma or turn right up to Oukaïmeden

BARRAGE LALLA TAKERKOUST
35km (22 miles) SW of Marrakech

A short drive from Marrakech on the road to Amizmiz is the Barrage Lalla Takerkoust dam. Constructed by the French in the 1930s to irrigate the surrounding Haouz plains and generate additional electricity for Marrakech, the dam's lake is the closest thing to a beach the city has to offer—and it's not half bad. Along the lake's 7km-long (4⅓-mile) shoreline are opportunities to jet- and water-ski as well as kayak—a paddle across to the more secluded, far side of the lake can even involve a bit of turtle spotting. For the more refined, perhaps, you can take things a bit slower in a pedal boat, stroll along the water's edge, or simply find a nice spot for a picnic and enjoy the view over to the peaks of the Western High Atlas. All year round, the lake is a heavenlike escape from Marrakech's medina, perfect for a day's outing or even longer. Numerous well-established hotels are located around the lake, most of which also accept day visitors for lunch and have their own private beaches offering the aforementioned watersports. The motorized activities usually cost 200dh ($25/£13) for 10 to 15 minutes.

The small hotel **Le Relais du Lac** (© **061/187472**; www.hotel-relaisdulac-marrakech.com) is renowned for both its service and Moroccan-French cuisine and has a great little bar and swimming pool overlooking the lake. Should you wish to stay the night, they have nine rooms, all en-suite and air-conditioned, and also offer a night's sleep in a Bedouin tent overlooking the lake. Rates are 650dh ($81/£41) for a double room, 350dh ($44/£22) for a double tent; breakfast is included.

GETTING THERE The village of Lalla Takerkoust is located on the road to Amizmiz. Buses and *grands* taxis for Amizmiz operate daily from a terminal 3km (1¾ miles) outside the Bab er Rob medina gate, best reached by *petit* taxi. Once in Lalla Takerkoust, the best route to the lake *(barrage)* is a left turnoff on the Amizmiz side of the bridge—from here it's about 3km (1¾ miles) to the lake's shores. Chartering a taxi from Marrakech will cost about 400dh ($50/£25) round-trip, and make sure payment is deferred until your driver has transported you back to the city. If you're driving yourself, take the Asni/Taroudannt (not the Ourika) road southwest for 5km (3 miles) and then stay straight (for Amizmiz), as this road forks left for Asni and Taroudannt. It's a lovely drive through mostly barren plains, and the road around the lake affords lots of sightseeing and picnic spots as well as a few rural villages.

The High Atlas

When Sir Winston Churchill and President Franklin D. Roosevelt headed for Marrakech after the Allies' Casablanca Conference in 1943, Churchill told his travel companion, "I must be with you when you see the sunset on the snows of the Atlas Mountains."

Beautiful, rugged, and sometimes harsh, the High Atlas mountains save Morocco from being another Saharan-battered country of Africa's north. Rising abruptly from the Atlantic coast near Agadir and stretching northeasterly across Morocco toward the Algerian border, the High Atlas encompass some of the most scenic and intriguing regions of the country. Visitors have the chance to stand on the summit of a peak and look down in awe and self-contemplation, seemingly upon the rest of the world, invigorated by the sense of nature and culture that pervades the range. Yes, there are some well-trodden, almost over-hyped areas, but there are also places that, with a little planning and flexibility, will have you wondering if you've entered the land that time forgot.

An obvious physical barrier between Morocco's encroaching southern desert sands and fertile northern farmlands, the High Atlas are also home to a Berber population that has historically acted as a cultural buffer between their nomadic cousins of the Saharan south and the Arab-dominated northern plains. Living amongst a landscape characterized by jagged peaks and steep-sided valleys, High Atlas Berbers are tough and resilient rural folk who, particularly away from the few touristed areas, still live in their traditional manner in flat-top villages constructed from a mix of stone and packed earth, called *tabout*. Part of their culture is the well-known warmth and hospitality they extend to travelers.

The High Atlas is separated into roughly three regions—western, central, and eastern. The **Western High Atlas** is home to North Africa's highest peak and has long been the most popular trekking destination in Morocco. Here you will also find the country's only ski resort, along with a number of pretty villages scattered amongst the region's valleys. This is the most popular region of the High Atlas, and consequently offers the widest range of accommodations and adventure pursuits. Its close proximity to Marrakech supplies the region with a steady stream of visitors and, more recently, improved infrastructure, but the impact of tourism and development on both the villagers and the land appears to be reaching a critical point. The increased accessibility to its higher reaches is putting a strain on an area that has traditionally lacked environmental services. Aware of this impact, some villages banded together to instigate a trekkers code (see "The High Atlas Tourist Code" on p. 163), informing visitors of their environmental and cultural responsibilities. Some international tour companies have reacted positively to the challenge by conducting Clean up Toubkal days, and there is also talk of an entrance fee being charged to all those entering the Toubkal National Park as a way to raise funds for better management of its environment.

Morocco's south is accessed by routes running through the Western High Atlas, and the views afforded by the numerous *tizis*, or passes, are alone worth the drive.

The **Central High Atlas** also offers excellent trekking, as well as providing four-wheel drivers with a seemingly never-ending network of dirt tracks, or *pistes*, that eventually wind over and down the range to arrive in the fertile valleys of the Middle Atlas or the dramatic gorges of the south. The northern flank of the region is beginning to be discovered, having been in the past the relatively exclusive domain of intrepid travelers and small groups. The eco-friendly architecture in the higher reaches here is both fascinating and inspirational, and it's mostly in these local structures that travelers can choose to stay in and experience the extremely friendly nature that the Berbers of this region, in particular, are renowned for.

The **Eastern High Atlas** rises north from the lower Middle Atlas, while the southern flank is dissected by dramatic gorges, which carve a passage southward toward the Sahara. This section of the High Atlas was one of the last in Morocco to accede to colonial rule, and is more closely linked to the southern oases area than the other High Atlas regions to its west. Its barren landscape is dotted with traditional *ksour* (castles) and broken only by the odd village or pasture. Like the Central High Atlas, the region's *tizis* and *pistes* are popular with four-wheel drivers. The *pistes* are everyday thoroughfares for the local Berber trucks and link the more remote Atlas villages with one another. For the traveler, Berber trucks provide a leisurely, cheap, and fascinating way to travel around. On the western fringe of the Eastern High Atlas is the formerly remote village of Imilchil and its annual marriage market, a traditional fair that's heavily marketed as a tourist attraction but still manages to retain most of its cultural and social significance.

1 Western High Atlas

When talking about the High Atlas, most literature and marketing focuses on the western section of the range—and with good reason. This area is one of the most scenic regions in all of Morocco, a land of majestic, sometimes snowcapped, mountains; verdant valleys; terraced fields; and remote Berber villages. The main focus for trekkers is the Toubkal National Park, centered around the 4,167m-high (13,671-ft.) Jebel Toubkal. The park is usually approached via Asni, a ramshackle village worth a stop only for its Saturday souk, which attracts its fair share of day-tripping busloads. Upward from Asni is the attractive village of Imlil, from where most ascents of Jebel Toubkal depart and where there's an established infrastructure of accommodations, guides, and mule transport. The more energetic and experienced may wish to trek from the scenic Ourika Valley or the nearby ski resort of Oukaïmeden, both villages worthy of a visit in every season. It's also possible to get an authentic feel for the mountains and the people who live amongst them by spending a couple of days exploring the range's lower passes, valleys, and villages. Amizmiz, for example, is a pleasant base for day walks and mountain biking. Every Tuesday, the village also hosts a Berber souk that is one of the largest in the Atlas. On the Tizi n'Test road to Taroudannt are Ijoukak and Ouirgane, pleasant alternatives for trekking the surrounding peaks and valleys and close to the spiritual Tin Mal Mosque. For those with less time, the Western High Atlas can simply present a scenic day's drive from Marrakech.

If possible, try to include a drive over one of the region's dramatic passes—the Tizi n'Test, Tizi n'Tichka, or Tizi Maachou.

It's possible to trek in the Western High Atlas year-round, though winter conditions can sometimes border on dangerous above the snow line. Lower down, the region is a pleasant escape at any time of the year, although nights can always be a bit brisk. I personally enjoy traipsing around lower Toubkal in late spring, between April and May, when the flowers are in bloom. The days are warm and still relatively clear, and there is usually still some snow on the higher peaks.

ESSENTIALS
GETTING THERE

BY BUS & *GRAND* TAXI Buses and *grands* taxis depart from a terminal 3km (1¾ miles) outside the Bab er Rob medina gate, best reached by *petit* taxi, to Amizmiz (1–1½ hr.; 15dh–20dh/$1.90–$2.50/95p–£1.25); Asni (1½–2 hr.; 15dh–20dh/ $1.90–$2.50/95p–£1.25); and Setti Fatma (1½–2 hr.; 15dh–25dh/$1.90–$3.15/ 95p–£1.55). During winter, a separate, direct route to Oukaïmeden operates daily from the same terminal (2½–3 hr.; 25dh–30dh/$3.15–$3.75/£1.55–£1.90), or otherwise take Setti Fatma transport as far as the Oukaïmeden turnoff, from where you should be able to find a stray *grand* taxi or hitchhike heading up to the resort. For Imlil, catch a *grand* taxi or public transit van from Asni at the main rank at the entrance to the walled souk for around 20dh ($2.50/£1.25) one way. Ouirgane can be reached by any bus or *grand* taxi traveling the Tizi n'Test road from Marrakech's Bab Doukkala station (1½–2½ hr.; 30dh/$3.75/£1.90) or Taroudannt (4–5 hr.; 80dh/ $10/£5); sometimes you can pick up a ride in Asni for either direction.

Grands taxis can also usually be chartered from Marrakech for the day, either from the Bab er Rob terminal or directly from your hotel. For Imlil or Oukaïmeden, rates average around 300dh ($38/£19) one way. For a full day's outing to Oukaïmeden and Setti Fatma, or Imlil and Ouirgane, expect to pay between 500dh to 600dh ($63–$75/£31–£38). *Note:* Remember to pay at the end of the day, not the beginning, and agree on all costs and the itinerary upfront.

BY CAR The main road heading south from Marrakech is well signposted in both Guéliz and the medina (look for the signs to Oukaïmeden). For Amizmiz, Asni, Imlil, and Ouirgane, take the Asni/Taroudannt turnoff opposite Bab er Rob in the southwest corner of the medina. After 5km (3 miles), the road forks left for Asni and Taroudannt; stay straight for Amizmiz. The road from Asni to Imlil has been tarred for some years now and is in reasonably good condition. For Oukaïmeden and Setti Fatma, stay on the Oukaïmeden road past the medina walls. After around 35km (22 miles), the road starts to wind upward and stays very scenic whether you continue on to Setti Fatma or turn right up to Oukaïmeden. *Note:* Petrol stations are few and far between once out of Marrakech, so fuel up before you depart.

Driving in this region is only for confident drivers, as the traffic can become very busy during the warmer months, especially on weekends, when Marrakchis head for the hills. From winter to early spring, the roads are prone to flooding, and visibility can be poor. From Asni to Ouirgane and farther up and over the Tizi n'Test pass there are many hairpin bends.

VISITOR INFORMATION The **Centre d'Informations Touristique Ourika** (© 068/465545), 33km (20 miles) from Marrakech on the road to Oukaïmeden/ Setti Fatma, provides brochures, information, and a map of the various attractions in the Ourika Valley. It's open daily 9am to 5pm. For those planning a trek independently, the **Bureau des Guides d'Imlil** (©/fax **024/485626;** bureau.guides@yahoo.fr) in the center of Imlil is the official mountain guide center for the entire region. The center is a wealth of information on every aspect of trekking the High Atlas and is staffed by registered guides, most of them English speaking. The office is on the central square and is open daily from 8am to 7pm during summer and 9am to 5pm during the colder months.

FAST FACTS   There are no banks in the Western High Atlas. The accommodations listed here will, however, usually accept payment in—and sometimes exchange—major foreign currencies (cash only and preferably euros).

    Pharmacie Asni, on the main Marrakech-Taroudannt road in Asni (© **024/462006**), is open daily from 8am to 9pm.

    A four-wheel-drive **ambulance** services the villages of the Aït Mizane valley, including Imlil and Asni, and is easiest contacted via the hotels **Kasbah du Toubkal** (p. 166) or **Dar Imlil** (p. 166).

    There are private coin-operated *téléboutiques* in Asni, Imlil, and Oukaïmeden. Internet access is available at **Cyber Asni** on the main Marrakech-Taroudannt road in Asni. It's open daily 9am to 11pm.

    A set of four **maps** covering the regions around Amizmiz, Oukaïmeden, Taliouine (the southern approach to Jebel Toubkal), and the Tizi n'Test is rarely found within Morocco (try the grocery shops adjoining the square in Imlil) but is readily available from major bookstores in the U.K. and online.

GETTING AROUND

BY FOOT   It goes without saying that the easiest way to explore the mountains is by foot. For those not wishing to wander off alone, hiring a guide can be easily arranged. In Imlil, visit the **Bureau des Guides d'Imlil** (above). Elsewhere, simply inquire at your hotel or a local restaurant or cafe, and a guide will miraculously appear. Try to hire only those guides who are officially registered with the Association des Guides et Accompagnateurs en Montagne and who will have this status noted on their Moroccan ID card. Expect to pay around 250dh ($31/£16) per day for these mountain specialists.

BY MULE   For those wishing to explore more than the general environs surrounding your hotel/village of choice but not wishing or able to do this by foot, hiring a mule for the day is the only option. The Atlas mountains are crisscrossed with an established network of mule trails, and no matter where you are staying, a mule—and accompanying muleteer—will be available for hire. In the Toubkal area, each mule generally has its own muleteer; in other areas, one muleteer may look after two to three mules at a time. Rates start from around 150dh ($19/£9.40) per half-day for the mule, with an additional tip of up to 50dh ($6.25/£3.15) for the muleteer. For general information regarding the condition of Morocco's mules, donkeys, and horses, see "Looking After Morocco's Beasts of Burden" in chapter 5.

BY ORGANIZED TOUR   In Marrakech, every hotel and *maison d'hôte* will be able to organize day and multiday tours to the Western High Atlas. One very reputable company that is experienced with English-speaking travelers is **Imagine le Voyage,** corner of rue Mouahidine and rue Bani Marine in the medina (© **024/427977;** fax 024/427972; www.saharaexpe.ma). A full-day excursion to either the Ourika Valley or

Ouirgane starts at 250dh ($31/£16) per person, and to Imlil from 400dh ($50/£25) per person. See p. 83 for more operators.

WHAT TO SEE & DO

Amizmiz More a town than a village, Amizmiz (pronounced "amz-*meez*") itself doesn't offer much scenic beauty, but its surrounding countryside makes it worth the trip. A track winding above the town leads to a forest of eucalyptus trees and a *maison forestière* (ranger's station), from where there are great walking and mountain-biking trails. You can also rent bikes in nearby Ouirgane (p. 162). The landscape is dotted with terraced groves of olive and lemon trees, and in spring the scent of lavender and thyme abounds. The town's Tuesday souk is billed as one of the largest Berber markets of the Atlas region and comes across as a type of mini-Marrakech, with stalls of spices and fresh produce interspersed with the occasional barber, blacksmith, and the odd, sometimes very odd, entertainer. The area around Amizmiz lacks the hardcore trekking vibe or oft-pretentious skiing scene of the neighboring Ourika Valley, but, particularly when combined with a visit to the Lalla Takerkoust lake (see "Side Trips from Marrakech" on p. 155), it's a very pleasant place to visit. Plus it's less than an hour away from the hustle and bustle of Marrakech.

58km (36 miles) SW of Marrakech.

Asni The hassling from touts can be quite intense here, but the weekly Saturday souk is worth a stop. Local produce (this is a big fruit-growing region) and livestock sit side by side with dentists and barbers, and sometimes you'll come across a 500-strong mule "parking lot," each beast adorned with a thick, brightly colored saddle. Should you be headed for some serious trekking, this is also the best, and cheapest, time to stock up on supplies. Arrive early to avoid the busloads of day-tripping tourists.

Above the village are the lower, forested slopes of the limestone Kik Plateau, which is a great place for a walk, particularly in spring when nature lays down carpets of alpine flowers.

48km (30 miles) S of Marrakech, 173km (107 miles) NE of Taroudannt.

Ijoukak Ijoukak is situated on the high ground above the meeting points of the Agoundis and Nfis valleys, and offers an alternative, less trodden trekking route up to Jebel Toubkal. The village is a busy tea and tagine stop between Marrakech and Taroudannt. The Tin Mal Mosque (see "Fortress of an Empire," below) is about 8km (5 miles) southwest from Ijoukak, and is clearly visible beside present-day Tin Mal, to the west of Oued Nfis and the main road. Don't confuse it with the Talat-n-Yacoub kasbah, on the southern edge of Ijoukak to the east of the main road, which was home to the Goundafi clan, one of three tribal families who controlled the three traditional trade routes between Marrakech and the Saharan interior until colonial times. You can easily dedicate a day or two to exploring this area.

94km (58 miles) S of Marrakech, 127km (79 miles) NE of Taroudannt.

Imlil ✶✶✶ Most trekkers who arrive here are on a mission to climb Jebel Toubkal, while less energetic travelers are choosing to simply visit the village as a day or overnight trip from Marrakech. The village, 1,740m (5,708 ft.) high and a steep road climb up the Aït Mizane Valley from Asni, is a pleasant and deafeningly quiet place (once you make it past the initial clamor of area guides). The surrounds offer beautiful walks amongst the almond, apple, cherry, and walnut trees, affording opportunities for quiet contemplation. Imlil clings to the banks of the Mizane River, and therefore is susceptible to flooding during winter and early spring, when the road from Asni is often damaged.

In 1996, Oscar-winning director Martin Scorsese transformed the village and surrounding peaks into Tibet for his film biography of the Dalai Lama, *Kundun*. A waste disposal system, now self-funded, was welcome compensation for the village's inconvenience. In 2004, a hammam (for villagers only) was constructed as a result of another fund-raising initiative, and is now an important communal focal point for residents of Imlil and the surrounding villages.

17km (11 miles) S of Asni.

Ourika Valley (Vallée de l'Ourika) & Oukaïmeden

This is a picturesque area of gorges, which gets its name from the terraced fields running alongside the river. Its scenic beauty, cool and clean air, and close proximity to Marrakech make it a popular day-trip destination, as evidenced by the number of restaurants and souvenir stalls dotted along the route, as well as a proposed Dubai-financed property development.

The valley proper begins at the small roadside village of Souk Tnine de l'Ourika, which, as its name translates to, hosts a Monday market. Similar to the Saturday market in nearby Asni, it receives its fair share of tourists. Farther along is a turnoff to **Oukaïmeden** ★★, a ski base during the winter and a beautiful starting point for trekking during the warmer months. If the aforementioned property development is approved, the village will evolve into a golf course–cum–ski resort, with a water park, exclusive shops, and faux beachfront. Jebel Oukaïmeden's chair lift—once the highest in the world at 3,273m (10,739 ft.) above sea level—will likely also receive a makeover. For more on skiing here, see p. 97.

During the warmer months, the peak of Jebel Oukaïmeden (3,263m/10,705 ft.) is within easy hiking reach of the village. It's a moderate 650m (2,133 ft.) ascent and offers stunning views, especially at sunset. For a truly peaceful and refreshing break—during summer it's about 10 degrees cooler up here than in Marrakech—I recommend a day or two here. Birders may wish to note the crimson-winged finch is an elusive resident here. At the end of the Ourika Valley's tarred road is Setti Fatma, rebuilt after devastating floods in 1995 and hence a mishmash of faceless concrete housing blocks and more traditional homes. Nestled amongst grassy terraces, walnut groves, and mountain peaks, the village's setting is still stunning and an alternative starting point for treks of Jebel Toubkal and its environs. About a 30-minute scramble up into the rocky foothills just above Setti Fatma is a series of waterfalls (called cascades by the locals) flanked by the occasional cafe. The lower falls are relatively easy to access, but the higher ones can sometimes be a bit tricky—there are always plenty of guides willing to take you up. The *moussem* of Setti Fatma is one of the most important festivals in Morocco and takes place over 4 days every August. See "Morocco Calendar of Events" on p. 20.

30–70km (19–43 miles) S of Marrakech.

Ouirgane ★★ *Finds*

Set in a green valley of the Oued Nfis, this peaceful village is a great spot to stop between Marrakech and Taroudannt or as an alternative day-trip destination from Imlil or the Ourika Valley. There are plenty of easy walks around the village, some with great views looking down onto the wide river. Mountain biking (100dh/$13/£6.25 per day), horseback riding (500dh/$63/£31 for half-day), and trekking with a local guide (250dh/$31/£16 per day) with mules (50dh/$6.25/£3.15

The High Atlas Tourist Code

As Marrakech continues to witness an increase in tourist arrivals, more travelers are venturing out of the city and into the Western High Atlas to absorb its stunning natural beauty, quiet rural life, and opportunities for trekking and other outdoor adventure sports. This increase in human traffic is placing unprecedented pressure on the very people and landscape that attracts the visitor in the first place. Waste, both human and artificial and deposited by locals and visitors alike, is becoming increasingly visible. Added to this are numerous social development issues, such as access to health and education facilities, and sustainable, year-round employment opportunities—all of this in an area where electricity and telecommunications were unheard of a decade ago. An impending multimillion-dollar golf and ski resort in Oukaïmeden will also create its fair share of environmental and social challenges.

On a positive note, the past decade has witnessed the successful implementation of some joint initiatives between the region's residents, local government, and various private businesses, including a 4WD ambulance service in the Aït Mizane Valley and Clean Up Toubkal days implemented by numerous foreign-based trekking companies.

In 1998, Discover Ltd, a U.K.-Moroccan responsible-tourism operator, which also owns and operates the Kasbah du Toubkal near the village of Imlil, instigated the High Atlas Tourist Code, a code of conduct for all those traveling in the High Atlas, particularly the Western High Atlas. The code was jointly developed and endorsed by various regional players, including the villagers themselves, and highlights an activity's potential to impact, positively and negatively, the region. Signs in Arabic, English, and French have been erected at strategic points around the popular Jebel Toubkal area, stating the code and asking visitors to respect the mountains and keep them waste free. The code also requests visitors to consider the cultural implications of their actions—such as refraining from drinking alcohol and eating pork (in align with Islamic principles)—while the trekking code follows guidelines set by most national parks and reserves around the world, including removing litter, not making open fires, and not removing plants or other wildlife. Importantly, the code also asks that visitors encourage their local guide to adhere to this same conduct.

Travelers should examine where, when, and how they can utilize services, purchase products, and contribute to projects that directly benefit the locals (or ask your tour company to what extent they follow this guideline), and when possible, always take your trash with you.

per hour) can be organized from the village's two hotels (I review one of these on p. 164), where you can also indulge in some fine cuisine.

15km (9⅓ miles) SW of Asni, 63km (39 miles) S of Marrakech, 158km (98 miles) NE of Taroudannt.

Fortress of an Empire

The founding father of the Almohad empire was Ibn Toumert, and it was from Tin Mal (sometimes spelled Tinmel) that his extremely orthodox and reformist Islamic movement took seed, eventually to reign over the entire Maghreb and Andalusian Spain. Born around 1080 in the Atlas mountains, a young Ibn Toumert left on a quest of spiritual learning and exploration that delivered him first to the Moorish capital of Cordoba and then farther on to the great Islamic centers of learning in the East, where he became an accomplished theologian. During this time, Ibn Toumert formed a defined set of principles for what he believed Islam stood for and how its followers should live.

In 1117, he arrived back in his homeland with a small group of followers and found much to disapprove of in Almoravid-ruled Morocco. Like all good Atlas Berbers of the time, Ibn Toumert held a traditional contempt for the desert-originating Almoravids, and he began preaching about the impure nature, as he saw it, of a ruling dynasty that indulged in blasphemous pleasures such as wine and one that allowed women prominent roles in society. He and his followers traveled to Marrakech and lambasted the Almoravid court for their un-Godly ways. The emir at the time, Ali Ben Youssef, was a particularly pious man, and tolerated Ibn Toumert's ranting. He even organized a theological debate between his court's most learned elders and Ibn Toumert. Ibn Toumert held his own, and the debate failed to disprove his theories. Ben Youssef's aides advised him to execute the fanatical upstart, but it was only after Ibn Toumert knocked the emir's sister from her horse because she wasn't wearing a veil (as was her desert tradition) that he banished Ibn Toumert and his followers, known as the Almohads. The Almohads headed for the remote mountains above Marrakech, and finally settled in Tin Mal, building a simple mosque and settlement from where they proceeded to convert the scattered Atlas Berber communities to the strict doctrine of simple living and acquiescence to one God, as practiced and preached by Ibn Toumert, or Mehdi (the chosen one), as he was known.

To subdue and convert the tribal villages must have been quite an achievement considering their fiercely self-reliant, independent nature. It is widely accepted that much of the conversion took place with barbaric force—"convert or die," so to speak—and the Mehdi, aided by his trusted

WHERE TO STAY & DINE
ASNI
Kasbah Tamadot 𝄐𝄐   In 1998, Sir Richard Branson was in Morocco looking for a launch site to commence his circumnavigation around the world by hot-air balloon. His mother Eve found him the early 1900 Kasbah Tamadot. Opened in 2005 after being renovated for 7 years to match the standard of Virgin's other hideaway retreats, this is pure luxury—with a price to match. Set on the road from Asni to Imlil, with a view of the Mizane River running down from Jebel Toubkal more than

deputy, the Algerian Abd el-Mumin, was known to enforce his strict, puritan teachings in a very disciplined manner, regularly handing out punishment in public to those whose faith was deemed to be floundering.

Ibn Toumert died in 1130, and it was Abd el-Mumin who really expanded the Almohad's control in the neighboring mountain ranges, eventually establishing a disciplined military force that swept down onto the fertile plains to conquer the Almoravids first in Fes and then, in 1147, Marrakech—barely 25 years after their banishment from the city.

The mosque of Tin Mal that is visible today formed part of a larger, more fortified town (the settlement served as state treasury during the empire's early years) that was constructed over the original in 1154. Although the mosque is roofless today, its classical Almohad design—subsequently used in the construction of the Koutoubia Mosque in Marrakech—can still be appreciated. Central to this design is the T-shape interior with a central aisle leading to the *mihrab*, or prayer niche, decorated in the characteristically Almohadic palmettos, rosettes, and scallops. Strangely, however, the minaret was placed over the *mihrab*, ultimately restricting how high it could be built. This design fault is apparent today, as the minaret and its sweeping vista of the Nfis valley is off-limits due to severe structural damage.

Although the Almohad seat of power eventually moved to Marrakech, Tin Mal remained their spiritual home. The Mehdi's tomb took on the aura of a holy shrine, and the man himself was elevated to saint status, something which he surely wouldn't have liked given his life's directive of worshipping one God.

The mosque was restored in the 1990s after a donation by one of the country's largest private corporations. The original *mihrab*, minaret, and the majority of internal arches remain intact.

The mosque is still used for midday Friday prayers, but visitors are free to enter any other day (aside from the Hassan II Mosque in Casablanca, this is the only other mosque in Morocco where non-Muslims are allowed to enter). The mosque's *gardien*, French-speaking Mohammed Fillali (© 062/725612), lives directly below and is usually on hand to escort you around at any time of the day. Admission is free, but a 20dh ($2.50/£1.25) tip to Mohammed is appreciated.

of the mountain itself, the sprawling kasbah is a mix of Moroccan and Indian, full of antique and contemporary artwork. All the spacious rooms have balconies and are simply furnished but with luxury touches such as towel warmers (it gets cold up here) and dinner-plate-size shower heads. The library–cum–cigar room—decked in blood-red *tadelakt* walls, charcoal tiling, a large fireplace, and telescopes—is delightfully opulent. There are heated indoor and outdoor pools and a hammam. The Kanoun restaurant serves exquisite, fresh North African fusion cuisine, open to nonguests for lunch (noon–3pm) and dinner (7:30–10:30pm). You'll come here to relax and indulge, but if you feel like being active, horseback riding, tennis, and hiking can be organized.

Asni-Imlil road, 3.5km (2 miles) from Asni. © 024/368200. Fax 024/368211. www.virgin.com/kasbah. 18 units. 3,685dh–7,370dh ($461–$921/£230–£461) single; 4,015dh–7,700dh ($502–$963/£251–£481) double. Low-season discounts apply Jan 6–Feb 28 and July 1–Aug 31. Minimum stays may apply at certain times. Rates include breakfast. AE, MC, V. **Amenities:** Restaurant; 2 pools; tennis; gym; hammam; salon; boutique; massage; library w/Internet. *In room:* A/C, heater or fireplace, CD/DVD player, fridge, towel warmer, *babouches.*

IMLIL

Café Soleil   Located steps away from the village parking lot–cum–trekking assembly point, this large hotel/restaurant overlooks the river and is always busy with trekkers. Run by the friendly and easy-going Omar, the hotel has older, spartan rooms with either beds or mattresses on the floor, or newer rooms—opened in July 2007—with heated flooring and fireplaces. An in-house hammam is also a recent addition. All rooms have individual gas hot-water systems. The reception/restaurant opening out to a large garden overlooking the river is heaven on a warm sunny day. The restaurant serves food all day (they do a nice breakfast with eggs for 30dh/$3.75/£1.90) and is a popular hangout where trekkers converge to outdo each other with hard-core trekking stories.

Central village parking area, Imlil. © 024/485622. Fax 024/485622. cafesoleil44@yahoo.fr. 24 units. 180dh ($23/£11) double (half board); 260dh ($33/£16) double (full board). No credit cards. **Amenities:** Restaurant; hammam. *In room:* No phone.

Dar Imlil ★★ (Value   Often used as an overflow if Kasbah du Toubkal (below) is full, this is the best value accommodations in the village. Dar Imlil is at the top of the village (but only a few paces from an accessible road) beside the Mizane River, which adds an even greater sense of tranquillity than there already is.

Rooms are spread out over two floors and are nicely furnished in local fabrics. In the winter, you'll appreciate the heating and thick, warm *jellabahs.* The deluxe rooms also have private balconies; ask for the Amtarfor room, which has views of the river. A large courtyard of clay and *bejmat* leads onto a lounge that converts to a dormitory when needed. The rooftop terrace is Dar Imlil's best feature, where guests can laze on lounges of white linen while taking in views of Jebel Toubkal and the Aït Mizane Valley; in the colder months, tall gas heaters are a thoughtful touch. The small kitchen serves delicious Moroccan food, and nonguests are welcome for lunch (180dh/$23/ £11; noon–3pm) and dinner (220dh/$27/£14; 7:30–10pm).

Top end of village, across the river and directly on the right, Imlil. © 061/692765 or 068/253451. darimlil@yahoo.fr. 7 units plus dormitory salon. 1,320dh ($154/£83) double on ground floor; 1,200dh ($150/£75) double on terrace; 300dh ($38/£19) dorm bed. Children under 5 stay free in parent's room. Rates include breakfast. MC, V. **Amenities:** Restaurant; 2 lounges. *In room:* A/C, heating, CD/DVD player, tea/coffeemaker, *babouches, jellabah.*

Kasbah du Toubkal ★★★   Formerly a local feudal chief's summer palace, brothers Chris and Mike McHugo bought this once-ruined kasbah and renovated it—by hand and only with traditional materials transported by mule—with the help of local guide and friend Haj Maurice, who now manages this responsible-tourism role model with his lovely wife Arkia. Opened in 1995, this is more of an experience than a hotel. Its location, clinging to a rock face above a mountain stream and under the shadow of snowcapped Jebel Toubkal, is surely one of the most dramatic and beautiful in the world. More than just a pretty face, however, the kasbah houses a hammam, rustic rooms of different sizes, and a self-contained private house. In the main building are three Berber salons that sleep 7 to 12 people dorm-style. This main building is the social center of the property with a large lounge/communal room with fireplace. Most guests and day-trippers take their meals on the rooftop; the kitchen whips up an amazing number of fine, home-cooked meals supplied from the kasbah's own vegetable garden. There is no on-site liquor license, but you're welcome to bring your own alcohol.

Kasbah du Toubkal's philosophy is focused on uplifting the Imlil village and the Aït Mizane Valley, and many of the locally made crafts found throughout the property—wool bed covers, lanterns, honey-drizzlers, *harira* soup spoons made from the local walnut tree, and watercolor postcards—are for sale.

Office and collection point across from village parking lot; 10-min. walk or mule ride to the kasbah, Imlil. ℗ 024/485611 or 061/343337. Fax 024/485636. www.kasbahdutoubkal.com. 12 units. 1,760dh–4730dh ($220–$591/ £110–£296) double; 440dh ($55/£28) dorm bed; 8,470dh ($1,059/£529) house (sleeps 6). Children under 5 stay free in parent's room. Rates include breakfast and use of the hammam. Community fee (5%) added to all rates. Minimum 2-night stay unless single night is available. MC, V if prepaid online; no credit cards on property. **Amenities:** Restaurant; 2 lounges; hammam; trekking. *In room:* Heater, CD player, fridge, tea/coffee, *babouches, jellabah.*

OUIRGANE

Au Sanglier qui Fume ⭐ This friendly mountain inn was originally built in the early 20th century to accommodate French Foreign Legion soldiers as they built the nearby bridge. Family-run since it opened in 1945, "The Smoked Wild Boar" is a ramshackle assortment of rooms that range from large, colorful standard rooms with private courtyards to two-room suites (can accommodate four) with a fireplace, lounge, and terrace. The hot water can take a while to reach your shower, but it will come. The property centers around a large swimming pool with lots of private, shaded areas for reading and resting. The restaurant is a popular stopover for travelers and is very much of the bed-and-breakfast style. Don't be surprised if the family dog comes to pay a visit. The staff, Amine and Rachis, are very welcoming. Breakfast is served on a glorious terrace; lunch and dinner are three-course Franco-Moroccan *menus du jour* that change daily.

Next to the bridge, Ouirgane. ℗ 024/485707. Fax 024/485709. www.ausanglierquifume.com. 25 units. 325dh– 585dh ($41–$73/£20–£37) single; 415dh–625dh ($52–$78/£26–£39) double. Children 11–15 200dh ($25/£13) in parent's room; under 11 130dh ($16/£8). Rates include breakfast. No credit cards. **Amenities:** Restaurant; lounge; pool; quad and mountain bike hire. *In room:* Fireplace (in most), fridge, no phone.

OUKAÏMEDEN

Hôtel de L'Angour Better known as Chez Juju, after its French-Canadian owner, this local legend's rooms have seen better days, but the downstairs restaurant and bar— oozing protectorate-era nostalgia—are worth a visit. The rooms have 1970s-era furnishings with old bathrooms; the toilets are out in the hallway. Good value three-course meals are the order of the day (125dh–139dh/$16–$17/£7.80–£8.70), accompanied by the coldest beer in Morocco and, if you sit outside, sweeping views of Jebel Oukaïmeden. They also do a kids meal of chicken, fries, and dessert (95dh/$12/£5.95).

At the southern end of the village, Oukaïmeden. ℗ 024/319005. Fax 024/319006. 18 units. 780dh–860dh ($98– $108/£49–£54) double. Rates include breakfast and dinner. No credit cards. **Amenities:** Restaurant; bar; lounge. *In room:* No phone.

Le Courchevel This large, faux–Swiss chalet is the newest accommodations in Oukaïmeden. At the end of the village, the hotel's orange-stained exterior will thankfully begin to pale after a few summers, and inside has everything you could ask for. Spread out over two floors are two restaurants—one with a mainly French menu and the other Italian—and a bar with large stone fireplaces throughout. In true alpine style, there's a heated indoor pool and hammam to soothe those sore muscles after a hard day on the *pistes*. The rooms are simply furnished in a modern design, all with private bathrooms and some with their own balcony and million-dollar view. Some can accommodate up to two additional beds. During ski season, a ground-floor night-club is open 11pm to 3am.

At the southern end of the village, behind Hôtel de L'Angour (Chez Juju), Oukaïmeden. ℂ **024/3159092** or 068/048034. www.lecourchevelouka.com. 46 units. 585dh ($73/£37) double with garden view; 675dh ($84/£42) double with mountain view. Children 3–8 pay 30% in parent's room; 2 and under free. Discounts available for 2- to 7-night stays. No credit cards. **Amenities:** 2 restaurants; bar; nightclub (in season); pool; hammam; lounge room w/satellite TV/DVD; babysitting (in season). *In room:* No phone.

MOUNTAIN PASSES

Tizi n'Test   The 2,092m-high (6,863-ft.) Tizi n'Test pass lies on a 170km (106-mile) stretch of road (the R203) that is one of the most spectacular and breathtaking routes in Morocco. Winding its way up and down through the heart of the Western High Atlas, the road passes beautiful valleys and isolated villages before eventually reaching the Tizi n'Test pass, with its sweeping views of both the High and Anti-Atlas mountains. This former trade route between the deep south and Marrakech was controlled by the Goundafi clan until as recently as the 1920s. **Gite Tizi n'Test** (ℂ **071/157124**) is at the top of the pass, usually with a very welcome fireplace during winter and a steaming pot of mint tea. About .5km (⅓ mile) farther south is **La Belle Vue Hotel,** which makes a great stop for lunch and has sweeping views of the Souss plain below. An abandoned red van, which ran out of steam on its way to the top, now houses a pottery stall. Be aware that heavy clouds and mist can sometimes cut vision to dangerously low levels. Signs on the exit from Marrakech or Taroudannt will indicate if the pass is closed due to snowfall.

40km (25 miles) SW of Ijoukak, 87km (54 miles) NE of Taroudannt.

Tizi n'Tichka   Roughly halfway along the main highway between Marrakech and Ouarzazate, this pass is a spectacular piece of French engineering built to replace the main caravan route connecting south and north. Along its route is a fascinating contrast of environments ranging from the rich, red-soil farming plains and fertile valleys above Marrakech to barren peaks and oaseslike palmeraies facing the pre-Sahara. Scattered along the route are small villages and welcome roadside cafes. At 2,260m (7,413 ft.), the pass is higher than the Tizi n'Test to its west and affords a similarly exhilarating, if somewhat bleaker, vista from its peak. There are souvenir stalls precariously perched all along the higher reaches of the pass, and look out for salesmen waving brightly colored—sometimes by artificial means—fossils and minerals at your vehicle as you round the hairpin bends.

If you have time, I recommend a side visit to Telouet and the Dar Glaoui kasbah that dominates the village. This former "castle of the sand," fast rejoining the very earth from which it was built, was the base for the el-Glaoui clan, who controlled much of southern Morocco from the late 1800s until Moroccan independence in 1956, as well as the caravan route of which the main highway has now replaced. The kasbah is an absurdly huge, dramatic building, and although the maze of locked rooms and connecting passageways are mostly off limits—for safety reasons—it's still worth a visit if only to marvel at the extravagance of this modern-day dynasty. The turnoff to Telouet is about 6km (3¾ miles) south of the pass and 21km (13 miles) along a narrow, scenic, pot-holed road.

The turnoff to the kasbah is about .5km (⅓ mile) past the village; don't be fooled by faux guides claiming that you have to park in the village and walk. *Gardien* Abdul Karim is around every day from 8am to 6pm to let visitors into the kasbah—with a front door key whose size defies description—and will give you a short tour of those areas safe to visit, including the former reception rooms and main hall. A tip of 10dh ($1.25/65p) is appreciated.

At the turnoff to the kasbah, past Telouet village, is Ahmed Boukhsas' **Auberge Telouet** (C 062/134455; www.telouet.com), which has comfortable rooms available (150dh–300dh/$19–$38/£9.40–£19) and both a large indoor restaurant and an outside Berber tent serving Moroccan standards daily from 7am to midnight.

A direct bus to Telouet from Marrakech (4 hr.; 45dh/$5.65/£2.80) departs daily at 3pm from Bab Gehmat (the southeastern medina gate), returning for Marrakech at 7am the next day. A bus from Ouarzazate (3 hr.; 35dh/$4.40/£2.20) departs daily at noon, returning for Ouarzazate at 7am the next day.

103km (64 miles) SE of Marrakech, 98km (61 miles) NW of Ouarzazate.

Tizi Maachou   A less dramatic pass (1,700m/5,577 ft.) than those to the east, this makes for a pleasant drive (rather than somewhere to stop) on the 4-hour journey between Marrakech and Agadir. Intrepid trekkers with their own transport may wish to diverge from the main highway at Imi n'Tanoute to explore the remote Tichka Plateau, a beautiful area of isolated Berber villages and trekking paths far from the more established routes around Jebel Toubkal. **Cafe-Restaurant Des Voyageurs,** on the main road passing through Imi n'Tanoute, is a pleasant place to stop for lunch or a mint tea; it's open daily 8:30am to 11pm.

123km (76 miles) SW of Marrakech, 126km (78 miles) NE of Agadir.

2 Central High Atlas

The Central High Atlas is beginning to witness a rise in the number of foreign visitors, but it's still the quintessential remote, rugged mountain range. On its north side, as the range melds into the Middle Atlas, are the highest mountains outside the Toubkal area and some of the most isolated villages you'll ever come across—electricity and telecommunications only recently became available. The valleys and gorges rising up to the 4,068m-high (13,346-ft.) Ighil M'goun offer excellent trekking, and recently the peak has started to see some skiers crossing its slopes in the winter. The Aït Bou Guemez (sometimes spelled Aït Bougamez) Valley, 70km (43 miles) of winding road and *piste* heading south and upward from the robust town of Azilal, is the most popular route to the peak, but is also a beautiful and unspoiled trekking area in its own right. Heading southwest from here, in the direction of Marrakech, are the natural wonders of the Cascades d'Ouzoud and Imi n'Ifri. Over and beyond Ighil M'goun are some breathtaking gorges and *pistes* leading down the southern flank of the Central High Atlas to the Dadès Valley and the country's oases region (see chapter 7).

Even though modernization is making its way here—a tarred road, for example, now affords access to some villages in the Aït Bou Guemez Valley that in the recent past would be cut off after a heavy snowfall—this is a vastly untouristed region in comparison to the popular environs of Jebel Toubkal, which means only the most basic of services and accommodations, or *gîtes,* are available. Most of the villagers speak only their local Berber or Tamazigh dialect with perhaps a few words of Maghrebi Arabic.

The Central High Atlas can be visited and trekked year-round, although you should be fairly experienced and accompanied by a local guide if you're tackling the higher peaks in winter. While the winter days enjoy their fair share of sun, the nighttime temperature can drop dramatically. In summer the valley's mild temperatures are a welcome break from the sometimes oppressive heat of the plains below.

ESSENTIALS
GETTING THERE
BY BUS   Traveling from the south, the regional centers of Demnate and Azilal can be reached by buses departing daily from Marrakech's Bab Doukkala bus station (2 hr. to Demnate, 30dh/$3.75/£1.90; 3½ hr. to Azilal, 70dh/$8.75/£4.40). Coming from the north, buses depart daily from the main bus station in the strategic transport hub of Beni Mellal (2 hr. to Azilal, 40dh/$5/£2.50; 3½ hr. to Demnate, 43dh/$5.40/£2.70).

BY *GRAND* TAXI   *Grands* taxis operate from terminals adjacent to the bus stations mentioned above in both Marrakech (1 hr. to Demnate, 55dh/$6.90/£3.45; 2½ hr. to Azilal, 65dh/$8.15/£4.05) and Beni Mellal (1 hr. to Azilal; 40dh/$5/£2.50). Separate *grands* taxis also ply the route all day between Demnate and Azilal (35dh/$4.40/ £2.20), with the Aït Bou Guemez Valley accessed by *grands* taxis operating from the latter.

BY CAR   Marrakech and Beni Mellal lie almost 200km (124 miles) apart on the major N8 highway, which originates in Fes. From Marrakech, take this highway for 18km (11 miles) to the R210 turnoff for Demnate, which is 80km (50 miles) farther on, via Tazzerte—this is a more scenic and less trafficked road than the R208 road to Demnate, whose turnoff is just past Tamlet farther along the N8. If you're coming from Beni Mellal, take the N8 for 20km (12 miles), and turn left onto the R508 for a stunning scenic drive via Afourer to Azilal, 68km (42 miles) away.

BY ORGANIZED TOUR   Many companies in Marrakech offer day tours to the Cascades d'Ouzoud with a short visit to Imi n'Ifri. See p. 83 for a list of tour operators.

VISITOR INFORMATION   The regional **Délégation du Tourisme** (© 023/ 458722) is in Azilal on avenue Hassan II, near the Hotel Assounfou, and is friendly but largely ineffectual. They do have a handy list on their window of late-night pharmacies and a notice board inside with brochures from local hotels.

FAST FACTS   **WafaCash** (© 023/478942) and **Banque Populaire** (© 023/894571) both have branches with bureaux de change in the center of Demnate, just past the entrance arches, open Monday to Friday 8:15am to 3:45pm. In Azilal, at the turnoff to the valley, there are also branches of WafaCash (© **023/368462**) and Banque Populaire (© **023/617854**), open Monday to Friday 8:15am to 3:45pm.

Post offices in both Demnate and Azilal are located on the main Demnate–Beni Mellal road, and are open Monday to Friday 8am to 4:15pm and Saturday 8 to 11:45am.

In Demnate, **Pharmacie Nouvelle** (© **023/896784**), opposite the post office, is open 8:30am to 9pm Monday to Friday. In Azilal, at the junction with the road up to the valley, is **La Grande Pharmacie de l'Atlas** (© **023/458408**), open 9am to midnight.

WHAT TO SEE & DO
Aït Bou Guemez Valley   This valley is quite simply one of Morocco's most beautiful areas, a scenic expanse of green pastures, barley fields, meadows of wildflowers, and the occasional fruit orchard. The area, 14km (8¾ miles) long and at times 1km

(⅔ mile) across, is crisscrossed by year-round streams, which make their way down from the M'goun massif. The area was nicknamed by early French trekkers as La Vallée Heureux (the Happy Valley) on account of the relaxed and friendly nature of the local Berbers. Unlike the High Atlas of Jebel Toubkal, the Aït Bou Guemez has more vegetation, including conifer forests. Tabant, the main village in the valley, hosts a great Sunday souk and is also the location of the Centre de Formation aux Métiers de la Montagne (CFAMM), the only official mountain guide training school in the country. Pleasant day and multiday hikes—as well as longer treks to the 4,068m-high (13,346-ft.) Ighil M'goun—commence from Tabant or from numerous smaller villages such as Imelghas, Agouti, and Aït Mohammed, where *gîte* accommodations, meals, guides, and mule transport can be organized. The road from Azilal is tarred all the way to Tabant via a recent diversion through Agouti. The original *piste* via Aït Mohammed can still be traveled on—it's pretty rough in stages—but is often impassable during the snow season. Either road offers stunning views of steep ascents and subsequent descents.

79km (49 miles) SE of Azilal, 270km (168 miles) E of Marrakech, 167km (104 miles) SW of Beni Mellal.

Cascades d'Ouzoud

Set in a lush valley and falling about 100m (328 ft.) into the river below, the Cascades d'Ouzoud are the most beautiful waterfalls in the country. The combination of crashing water, dense wood areas, laid-back rural atmosphere, and daily rainbow displays are making the waterfalls an increasingly popular destination for day-tripping visitors from Marrakech or overnight stays for those traveling between the city and Fes. The small village of Ouzoud—whose name is Berber for "delicious," likely chosen because of the surrounding olive groves—spreads up the hills around the waterfalls. Visitors can walk amongst the olive and almond trees, or head to the nearby village of Tanagh-Melt, about 1.5km (1 mile) away from the waterfalls' lower pools. This fascinating medieval hamlet, set on the steep slopes of the wooded hills, is connected by a series of semi-underground passages. Back at the falls, there are numerous lookout points and terraced cafe-restaurants (the local Barbary ape population is quite cheeky around here, so watch your food), and the best photographs can be taken in the mid- to late-afternoon when the sun works its way over the falls and the rainbows are at their widest.

Traveling between Demnate, Ouzoud, and Azilal is pretty straightforward, with buses and *grands* taxis plying the route throughout the day. Once in Ouzoud, follow the trail of hotel signs and souvenir stalls to find the waterfalls. If you'd like to stop over, there are a few hotels within spray-range, the best by far being the **Riad Cascades d'Ouzoud** (© **023/459658;** www.ouzoud.com), an ochre-colored former residence restored in an eco-friendly manner and exuding a welcoming warmth, both from the Algerian-born owner and the often-roaring salon fireplace. There are six en-suite rooms, each with an individual character and some with their own fireplace. The interior courtyard is centered around an orange tree, and there are numerous spots to lounge; you can also head to the rooftop terrace to enjoy the view. The riad offers a wide range of day trips including guided hikes into the surrounding hills, donkey treks to a local village market, or a day on the lake of the nearby Bin el Ouidane dam. Rooms are 650dh ($81/£41) for a double, half price for kids between 5 and 10. Meals are also available.

170km (106 miles) NE of Marrakech, 130km (81 miles) SW of Beni Mellal.

Imi n'Ifri   Six kilometers (3¾ miles) south of Demnate is the "door to the cave," known in the local Berber dialect as Imi n'Ifri, a natural rock bridge formed by the collapse of an underground cave system. Views are spectacular from both above and down below, where the Wadi Méhasseur flows between the sheer, vertical rock walls while swifts and choughs flit about overhead. At the bottom of the ensuing gorge is an opening whose shape is similar to the outline of the African continent. There are guides in the parking lot but they aren't necessary, as the steps down the gorge and into the cave are clearly visible. Take your swimsuit, as the river is usually flowing and makes for a refreshing dip.

If you don't have your own transportation, you can charter a *grand* taxi from the bus and taxi terminal in Demnate, or alternatively set out on foot for the 1½-hour hike. A half kilometer (⅓ mile) beyond Imi n'Ifri is **Riad Aghbalou** (© **061/768359;** www.iminifri-riad.com), which has comfortable rooms with and without private bathrooms (275dh–440dh/$34–$55/£17–£28 double, including breakfast). They also have a restaurant serving lunch and dinner with a pleasant view over the surrounding fields.

104km (65 miles) NE of Marrakech, 146km (91 miles) SW of Beni Mellal.

3 Eastern High Atlas

The eastern reach of the High Atlas is definitely the lesser known—and visited—of the range, although it holds just as much scenic, and decidedly more historic, drama than the central and western regions. The Eastern High Atlas is nature's buffer zone between the relatively lush, cedar-topped Middle Atlas and the harsh, palmeraie-dotted Saharan south, and visitors will notice the change from the traditional, low-level, earthen homes of the Middle Atlas Berbers to the famous *ksour* and kasbahs of the southerners.

The highest peaks in this section of the range are on its northern flank, centered around the 3,747m-high (12,293-ft.) Jebel Ayachi, which rises to the south of Midelt, a Berber frontier-type town on the plains between the Middle and High Atlas. Connecting Midelt to the region's southern side is the only major road, from which a number of other minor roads, mainly *pistes,* branch off into the High Atlas and eventually emerge at the Todra or Dadès Gorges (see chapter 7) or the western reach of the Middle Atlas. It's a fascinating route and is as dramatic as the passes of the Western High Atlas.

The northern ascent from Midelt via the curiously named Tizi n'Talrhmeht (Pass of the She-Camel) is short and steep before flattening out to desertlike plains, which mark the beginning of the southern *ksour.* These castlelike fortresses are often shadowed by old French Foreign Legion posts, as this whole area was historically notorious for attacks on caravans and travelers by the Berber Aït Haddidou tribe. Only in the 1930s, 20 years after the beginning of colonial rule, did the French finally subdue these nomadic tribesmen. Rich, the major town of these plains, is watered by the Oued Ziz. Following the water course west will eventually bring you to the village of Imilchil, its nearby annual festival steeped in romance and tragedy (see "The Moroccan Romeo & Juliet" on p. 175). Going south from Rich, the route passes through the dramatic Ziz Gorges before finally arriving at the administrative and military center of Er Rachidia and the beginning of the vast pre-Sahara.

This is a sparsely populated region of mainly harsh, rugged terrain. Accommodations are available, mostly in Imilchil, though the standards are basic, which means no central heating or electric sockets in the bathrooms for your appliances. However, I find that the cuisine and hospitality make up for this. Winter in the Eastern High Atlas can produce some gloriously mild, sunny days, followed by freezing nights and an irregular fall of snow in the higher areas around Imilchil. On the other hand, summer can be stifling, especially on the southern flanks, where you can be confronted by the hot Saharan winds.

ESSENTIALS
GETTING THERE

BY BUS   Midelt and Er Rachidia are major transport hubs with daily bus connections to other centers on both the northern and southern flanks of the Eastern High Atlas. Rich (1½ hr. from Midelt, 40dh/$5/£2.50; 2 hr. from Er Rachidia, 50dh/$6.25/£3.15) is a major stop on the main R13 road, with more than a dozen buses plying the route between Midelt and Er Rachidia daily.

BY *GRAND* TAXI   There are plenty of *grands* taxis running between Midelt and Er Rachidia, taking about an hour less than the bus and costing 50dh to 60dh ($6.25–$7.50/£3.15–£3.75). Between Rich and Imilchil, minibus and transit van taxis run throughout the day along the 130km (81-mile) tarred road. The scenic drive can take up to 3 hours including pickup/drop-offs and costs 65dh ($8.15/£4.05).

BY BERBER TRUCK   Also known as *camionettes,* these regional buses often run between villages in a particular area, coinciding the day's travel with each village's weekly souk. It's possible to travel a large portion of the Eastern High Atlas this way, particularly between Midelt and the Todra and Dadès gorges (see chapter 7) via Imilchil, from where you can also try your chances north toward the Middle Atlas.

BY CAR   The R13 runs between Midelt and Er Rachidia, and is a pleasant drive; make sure the brakes are working properly. The road west from Rich is paved all the way to Imilchil, and passes stunning gorges, *tizis,* and valleys. Some of the *pistes* branching off both of these roads are navigable in a standard 2WD vehicle, but you may encounter the odd sandy bog or sharp-edge tire-puncturing section. There is a petrol station on the R13 at the turnoff to Rich/Imilchil, although it only sells diesel and leaded fuel.

FAST FACTS   All main services in Rich are located on the town square as you come from the Midelt–Er Rachidia highway: **Banque Populaire,** with an ATM, open Monday to Friday 8:15am to 3:45pm; **Pharmacie Agdoude** and **Pharmacie Rich,** open daily from 9am to 8pm; **post office,** open Monday to Friday 8am to 4:15pm, Saturday 8 to 11:45am; and **Cyber Karamanet** Internet cafe, open daily 9am to 11pm. In Imilchil's small village center is a post office, open Monday to Friday 8am to 4:15pm, Saturday 8 to 11:45am; and a few small shops selling basic groceries.

WHAT TO SEE & DO

Imilchil   This usually peaceful village surrounded by mountains is turned on its head every September for the 3-day Fête des Fiancés, or marriage market. The festival is an important community event for the Aït Hadiddou, Aït Izdeg, Aït Morghad, and Aït Yahia clans (usually with only one or two families in residence), who use the opportunity to socialize, trade livestock, and purchase clothing and hardware before the snow isolates their villages until spring. Here it's the girls—adorned in a ceremonial *serdal* (a wool headband decorated with coins and coral) and eyes rimmed with *kohl* (a heavy dark charcoal)—who are the star attraction. Singing, mingling, and dancing take place, and if both families agree on a match, a formal engagement, or even a marriage, takes place. The festival is more of a formality, as most of the match-making has taken place before the event, and traces back to the story of Isli and Tislit (see "The Moroccan Romeo & Juliet," below) and the days of French occupation, when the Bureau des Affaires Indigènes would arrive during the annual local fair for the compulsory registering of all births, deaths, and marriages.

The tourism board is guilty of perpetuating the legend surrounding the festival, and today thousands of foreign visitors arrive armed with cameras. Regardless, the main purpose of the festival still holds true, and I encourage you to head to the perimeter and walk amongst the more than 30,000 Berbers in attendance, some of whom are sure to invite you into their tent for a cup of mint tea. The exact dates of the festival change each year, though it's usually held the last weekend of September. ONMT offices around the country post the dates around February. Otherwise, contact the ONMT (© **037/673918**; www.onmt.org.ma or www.tourisme.gov.ma) for more details.

During the festival the area is literally covered with tents. Outside of this time, accommodations are limited to a few hotels in the middle of the village. The best is Bessou Chabou's **Chez Bassou** (©/fax **023/442402** or 068/564475; www.chezbassou. com), which has 15 simply furnished rooms, 10 with private bathrooms, for 100dh to 250dh ($13–$31/£6.25–£16). His restaurant also cooks up a very tasty chicken tagine for 40dh ($5/£2.50). Two kilometers (1¼ miles) north of town on the road to lakes Isli and Tislit is **Auberge Kasbah Adrar** (© **023/442184**), with comfortable rooms and shared bathrooms for 150dh to 250dh ($19–$31/£9.40–£16) double.

209km (130 miles) SW of Midelt, 194km (121 miles) NE of Er Rachidia, 130km (81 miles) W of Rich.

Ziz Gorges The Ziz Gorges were formed by the river of the same name, which begins west of Rich before it veers south to carve a passage through the rocky Eastern High Atlas down to the pre-Saharan Tafilalt, sprouting palmeraies along its course. About 25km (16 miles) from Rich, the river-shadowing Midelt–Er Rachidia road descends through the Zaalal Tunnel, also known as Tunnel du Legionnaire—a 200m (656-ft.) passage blasted through the mountains by the French in 1930 to open the route to the Saharan south—and enters the stunning Ziz Gorges. Around 2km (1¼ miles) long and at times almost as high, the gorges are both dramatic and photogenic, subtly changing color as the day wears on. The surrounding barren mountain landscape, interrupted by the odd watered oasis or cliffside *ksour,* only serves to accentuate the sense of isolation and awe.

(Tips **A Picture is Worth 1,000 Words . . . & Some Change**

As with the rest of Morocco, the locals here generally expect payment when being photographed. I always budget on around 10dh ($1.25/65p), and if requested, gladly hand this over. Make this payment directly to the person involved and not via one of the faux guides or hustlers who wander around the festival preying on tourists.

The Moroccan Romeo & Juliet

Isli and Tislit were in love. Their families, from the Aït Hadiddou clan, were sworn enemies, and after the couple confessed their love to their parents, they were forbidden to marry. Heartbroken, they knew it would be impossible to live apart. Their flow of tears was said to form two lakes under the shadow of the mountains, and it was here that the young lovers exchanged vows and drowned themselves to be spared from a life of heartache. Their warring families were guilt-ridden, and the clan's elders, determined that it never happen again, granted their youth the right to choose their own life partner. The twin lakes, which bear the names of Isli and Tislit, are just north of Imilchil.

Imilchil's popular Fête des Fiancés is held near the burial site of Sidi Mohammed el Maghani, the patron saint of the Aït Hadiddou. Marriages that were blessed by this holy man were said to be long and happy, and the tradition continues today with betrothal ceremonies taking place at his tomb over the 3-day festival.

There are a couple of viewpoints and picnic spots along the route, and I encourage you to hop out and take in the view. Heading south, the gorges emerge near the wide Barrage Hassan Addakhil, a Moroccan-built dam providing irrigation and electricity to the region and lessening the threat of flash flooding farther downstream. The route, and consequently the Eastern High Atlas, bottoms out at the nearby administrative and military center of Er Rachidia, from where most travelers continue on to the desert oases and sands.

83km (52 miles) S of Midelt, 43km (27 miles) N of Er Rachidia.

7

Central Morocco: Gorges, Valleys & Desert

Over the other side of the mountains lies the Morocco that most travelers imagine. A land of palm-fringed oases; a turbaned nomad astride his one-humped steed; a fortresslike mud-walled kasbah; and Saharan dunes rising above a harsh, unforgiving plain. This image wasn't merely dreamt up by some movie director—it's real. The French-made cities of Ouarzazate, Er Rachidia, and Erfoud are merely stepping stones to a land that still largely operates on "desert time," working with the sun rather than the clock.

History flows out here, and Morocco's sands of time have seen it all. Here were the days when the earliest camel caravans passed through on their way to and from the valuable salt lands of West Africa, and armies of zealots built their desert empires before setting out to conquer as far away as Libya and Spain. Today you'll find rally drivers saying goodbye to the last vestiges of civilization before they continue their race through the desert to the westernmost point of Africa in Dakar.

The rich history hasn't stopped modernity from reaching the region. Looked at through the eyes of a virgin visitor, the advent of good roads, electricity, Internet, and satellite TV might shatter the untouched desert image. But look a bit deeper, and you'll see people, a mixture of the original ancient tribes and Bedouin and Berber immigrants, who've got the blend right. Modernization and tradition are given equal status, and over time, the best of both worlds have been accepted into daily life—and today's travelers now reap the benefits. Where once travel was only by slow bus or even slower camel, it's now possible to reach the edge of Morocco within a day or so (some tours from Fes or Marrakech manage to have their clients sleeping under Saharan stars that same night). Upon returning from a desert adventure, an air-conditioned room and swimming pool await, and e-mails to family and friends can now be done that very same day. All of this is now readily available in what is still essentially a land on the edge of the desert.

This is the desert Morocco of tourism folklore and is best absorbed rather than merely viewed. A stay of even just 2 nights (try for 3) in the region will reward the traveler with the stories, pictures, and memories that are secretly hoped for when Moroccan travel plans are originally made.

There's a lot to see in central Morocco, but at the same time some travelers believe that it all provides essentially the same experience. Perusing the region harshly, one could say that there are three valleys, two gorges, and two "deserts." Everywhere, bar the last 50km (31 miles) to one of the desert dunes, is easily reached by most means of transport. Renting a car (p. 180) out here is a popular option amongst independent travelers. The roads are pretty good, traffic is nowhere near as hectic as the cities in the country's north, and traveling by public transport affords only fleeting glimpses of

Which Desert, Merzouga or M'hamid?

Although I am loathe to compare, the choice between Morocco's two most accessible desert experiences is one often faced by travelers.

First, let it be known that neither of the dunes most visited—Erg Chebbi at Merzouga and Erg Chigaga at M'hamid—are the Sahara desert per se. These ergs are massive sand seas separated from the main Saharan ocean by barren, rocky, predesert plains called *hammada*. That said, when you're climbing up one of their dunes (Erg Chebbi's are up to 150m/492 ft. high, and Erg Chigaga's double this) and look across to nothing but more sand, the definition becomes a moot point.

A very good tarred road meets up with the southern half of the Erg Chebbi dunes about 30km (19 miles) south of Erfoud. Around the village of Merzouga the dunes are no less than .5km (⅓ mile) from this road, and you can drive right up to them. This easy access allows the traveler to safely wander into the immediate dunes without needing a guide. Erg Chigaga, on the other hand, can only be reached from M'hamid, more than 50km (31 miles) away, and requires a 2-hour 4WD journey or a 5-day camel trek.

Accommodations at the dunes vary greatly between the two. A string of *auberges* ranging from basic to luxury have sprung up alongside Erg Chebbi due to its direct access, and travelers can now view the dunes from the cool waters of a swimming pool or while sipping a cold drink atop a roof terrace. No such luxuries have been allowed at Erg Chigaga, however, and after the long journey, travelers are housed in temporary Berber tents and will be lucky if they can have a shower in the one concession to civilization, a small communal ablutions block.

At times both dunes witness their fair share of crowds, while at other times you can have the sand to yourself. The guides and villagers that you encounter in both Merzouga and M'hamid are generally of the same desert ilk, with most guides dressed in flowing blue robes in imitation of the famed indigo-swathed nomadic warriors of the Saharan Tuareg tribe.

For some, the choices available at Erg Chebbi are what tip the scales. Trekking by camel farther into the dunes—it takes about 1 to 1½ hours—and overnight in Berber tents is still possible. Most travelers take up this option, with a return the next morning to shower and breakfast at an *auberge* before heading back to Erfoud and beyond. For those heading to Erg Chigaga, there is no choice but to trek into the dunes. The return trip involves the long journey to M'hamid and, for most, continuing all the way back to the relative luxury in Zagora or Ouarzazate. However, for some it's the entire journey to Erg Chigaga that attracts. Travelers truly feel they are heading to the edge by traveling off the tar and past herds of camels, along dry river beds and via deep wells to eventually arrive at the secluded dunes.

Companies operating specifically to one erg or the other are listed in this chapter. For general companies operating from Marrakech and elsewhere, see p. 83.

scenery as your vehicle speeds past. If you do travel by public transport, make sure to grab a window seat to take full advantage of the fantastic views.

Tip: Petrol stations are few and far between in central Morocco. If you're driving on your own, top up your tank whenever and wherever you can, especially if your car runs on *sans plomb*, unleaded fuel, which isn't available at every petrol station.

1 Ouarzazate

Ouarzazate (pronounced "war-za-zat") is a French creation—a once isolated military outpost that still exudes a frontier-type atmosphere despite its position as the major administrative center of the region. Discovered by Hollywood in the 1960s and 1970s, hotel developers flocked to the town during the 1980s and embarked on a hotel-building spree in anticipation of a tourism boom that has never really risen to the expected heights. There are, however, a number of film studios based in the town that attract their fair share of big budget productions, and when combined with a steady stream of overnighting tour buses, the town's hotels seem to tick over nicely.

Ouarzazate for most travelers is simply a transit point en-route to the desert or the High Atlas, but no matter how long your stay, you'll be struck by the town's pleasant lack of noise and hustle and the laid-back nature of its almost 50,000 inhabitants. Befitting its status as a regional center, Ouarzazate offers most modern facilities and services. Combine this with the city's few sights, consistently sunny days, and proximity to the region's attractions, and Ouarzazate can be a very pleasant base for a few days of exploring.

ESSENTIALS
GETTING THERE
Ouarzazate is one of the major transport hubs of central Morocco and is well connected to the rest of the country by air or land. Most travelers arrive as part of an organized tour or on a self-drive holiday. Those traveling by public transport can easily reach the city by bus or *grand* taxi from the major cities of Agadir, Casablanca, and Marrakech, as well as the closer regional centers of Tinihir (from Er Rachidia or Erfoud) and Taroudannt.

BY PLANE Ouarzazate's small Taourirt Airport (© 024/882383) is only 2km (1¼ miles) northeast of the town. Inside the arrivals/departure building is a Banque Populaire bureau de change, but it operates with very sporadic hours and isn't to be counted upon. There is also a small cafe and souvenir shop. There is no bus service from the airport, but *petits* taxis are always around to meet incoming flights and will charge around 30dh ($3.75/£1.90) to take you to your hotel or into town. They will only accept dirham, but will stop at a bank in town or you can usually exchange money at your hotel. Most hotels will organize an airport pickup if you arrange this with them before your arrival. Remember that *petits* taxis are only authorized to travel within the town's environs, so if you intend to move on without staying in Ouarzazate, they can only take you as far as the bus or *grand* taxi station.

BY BUS Ouarzazate is well served by the country's bus network, and buses arrive at least once a day from Agadir (8 hr.; 90dh–110dh/$11–$14/£5.65–£6.90); Casablanca (9 hr.; 130dh–140dh/$16–$18/£8.15–£8.75); Erfoud (7 hr.; 90dh/$11/£5.65); Er Rachidia (6 hr.; 65dh/$8.15/£4.05); Marrakech (5 hr.; 65dh–70dh/$8.15–$8.75/£4.05–£4.40); Fes (14 hr.; 150dh/$19/£9.40); M'hamid (7½ hr.; 60dh/$7.50/£3.75);

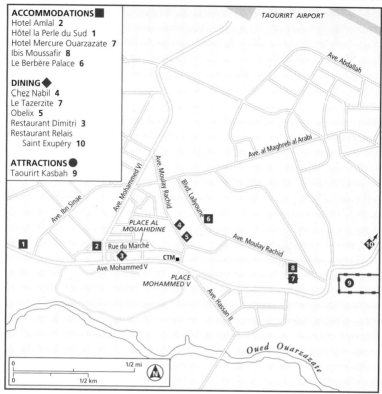

ACCOMMODATIONS ■
Hotel Amlal **2**
Hôtel la Perle du Sud **1**
Hotel Mercure Ouarzazate **7**
Ibis Moussafir **8**
Le Berbère Palace **6**

DINING ◆
Chez Nabil **4**
Le Tazerzite **7**
Obelix **5**
Restaurant Dimitri **3**
Restaurant Relais
 Saint Exupéry **10**

ATTRACTIONS ●
Taourirt Kasbah **9**

Taroudannt (5 hr.; 65dh–75dh/$8.15–$9.40/£4.10–£4.70); Tinerhir (5½ hr.; 60dh/$7.50/£3.75); and Zagora (4½ hr.; 40dh/$5/£2.50). CTM (© **024/882427**) buses operate from their own station in the center of town on avenue Mohammed V.

All other bus companies operate from Mahta *gare routière,* 2km (1¼ miles) north-west of town off the N9 road to Marrakech, from where it's an easy (though often hot) 20-minute walk into the town center, or you can catch a *petit* taxi for around 10dh ($1.25/65p).

BY *GRAND* TAXI *Grands* taxis for Marrakech (4 hr.; 80dh/$10/£5) and Zagora (3 hr.; 65dh/$8.15/£4.05) operate from the *gare routière,* while those heading for Zagora depart from both the *gare routière* and the satellite suburb of Tabounte, across the river and south of the city center.

BY CAR Ouarzazate is fairly easy to navigate thanks to the one main road, avenue Mohammed V, which runs the length of the town coming from either Marrakech or Tinerhir and from which the majority of hotels and restaurants can be accessed. About halfway along avenue Mohammed V, opposite the post office, is the well-signposted turnoff south to Zagora and the Dra Valley.

VISITOR INFORMATION

The **Delegation du Tourisme,** at the turnoff to Zagora on avenue Mohammed V (© **024/882485;** fax 024/885290), is open Monday to Friday from 8:30am to 4:30pm, but doesn't offer much more than a list of the hotels and restaurants in Ouarzazate.

Ouarzazate is a relatively small city, and its center is very easy to navigate. Some travelers don't even venture out of their hotel while in Ouarzazate, but if you do, most services and sights are along avenue Mohammed V, the main road running west-east from Marrakech to Tinerhir, and the small rue du Marché running parallel 1 block north. *Petits* taxis operate within the city and can be useful if you are wishing to travel during the heat of the day between the Taourirt Kasbah and your hotel.

FAST FACTS: Ouarzazate

Banks & Currency Exchange There is a string of banks along avenue Mohammed V with ATMs and bureaux de change (though they rarely exchange traveler's checks) open Monday to Friday 8:15am to 3:45pm. The **SGMB** branch, near place du 3 Mars at the west end of avenue Mohammed V (© **024/886308**), has a 24-hour exchange ATM, and the **Banque Populaire** branch between the police station and the post office (© **024/868573**) has a separate bureau de change open Monday to Thursday 8am to noon and 2 to 6pm, Friday 8am to noon and 3 to 7pm, and Saturdays and public holidays 9am to noon and 3 to 6pm.

Car Rentals There are quite a few car-rental firms based in Ouarzazate. The local companies can often have the best deals, but make sure they offer a 24-hour assistance service and that your car is equipped with a good spare tire and the tools with which to change it. Also, be sure to read the fine print with regard to driving off the tarred road. If you want to drop the car off in Marrakech or elsewhere, you may have to shop around.

Most companies are found on avenue Mohammed V or coming off its west end at place du 3 Mars. **Avis** is just east of place du 3 Mars on avenue Mohammed V (© 024/888000 or 061/491459); **Budget** is at 28 av. Mohammed V (© 024/884202); **Europcar** (© 024/882035) and **National/Alamo** (© 024/885244 or 066/782786) are both at place du 3 Mars; and **Hertz** (© 024/882084) is at 33 av. Mohammed V.

Galaxy Car, 8 av. Moulay Rachid (opposite Obelix restaurant, p. 185; © 024/885598 or 067/595854), and **Desert Evasion,** 2 av. Mohammed V (© 024/888682 or 061/243106), are very reputable local firms with both sedans and 4×4s. Plan on paying up to 600dh ($75/£38) per day for a small, four-door sedan, less for rentals of 7 days or longer. Some companies offer 4WDs for around 1,350dh to 1,500dh ($169–$188/£84–£94) per day, and about an extra 400dh ($50/£25) per day for a driver/guide.

Consulates See "Fast Facts: Morocco" in chapter 2.

Doctors Dr. **Kabir Lahcen** is located in the Clinique Chifa, avenue Moulay Rachid (© **024/883588**), above Pharmacie Chifa.

Drugstores Pharmacies are dotted throughout the city center and open Monday to Friday 8:30am to 12:30pm, 2:30 to 7:30pm, and 8 to 10:30pm, and Saturday 8:30am to 12:30pm. **Pharmacie Centrale** is located at 31 av. Mohammed V (next to Hertz; © **024/882601**), and **Pharmacie Chifa** is on avenue Moulay

Rachid, next to the Supermarché Dadès (© **024/883588**). The all-night **Pharmacie du Nuit** (© **024/882490**) is located at the beginning of avenue Mohammed V, opposite the post office, open nightly 10:30pm to 8:30am.

Hospitals The public hospital, **Hôpital Bougafer** (© **024/882444**), is located at the far east end of avenue Mohammed V between the city center and Taourirt Kasbah.

Internet Access **Ouarnet** is at 19 av. Mohammed V; Cyber Marché is at the west end of the pedestrian-only section of rue du Marché; and **Cyber Vallée des Kasbahs** is on avenue Moulay Rachid, next to the Supermarché Dadès.

Laundry The small **Point d'Eau Lavanderie** (© **062/836864**) is next to Hotel Amlal (p. 183) on rue du Marché, open Saturday to Thursday 8:30am to 8pm. There are only a couple of washers and one dryer; an attendant will wash, dry, and fold a 5-kilogram (11-lb.) bag for 50dh ($6.25/£3.15).

Maps & Newspapers **Supermarché**, 13 av. Mohammed V, sells a selection of country maps and guidebooks, as well as 1- to 5-day-old U.K. and U.S. newspapers.

Photographic Needs **Labo Ennakhil**, 16 av. Mohammed V, and **Agfa Image Centre**, 2 av. Moulay Rachid (opposite Obelix restaurant, p. 185), are open daily 9am to noon and 3 to 8pm and sell a range of film and a few memory cards.

Police The **Commissariat de Police** (© **19**) is on avenue Mohammed V, 100m (330 ft.) west of the post office.

Post Office The main **post office** is on the corner of avenue Mohammed V and rue de la Poste, opposite the turnoff south to Zagora. It's open Monday to Friday 8am to 4:15pm and Saturday 8 to 11:45am. There's a small postal agency next to the Taourirt Kasbah (p. 186) with the same hours.

Restrooms There are no public toilets in the city center. Your best bet is to ask at **Restaurant Dimitri** (p. 184) or the cafe-restaurant next to **Hotel Amlal** (p. 183).

Safety The city center of Ouarzazate is a very safe place to walk around day or night. If you are self-driving, be sure to lock your car as there has been an increase in petty theft and car break-ins.

Telephone Ouarzazate's **city code** has recently changed from 044 to **024**.

Tour Operators There are many tour operators located in the center of Ouarzazate, all offering the same excursions down the Dra Valley to the Saharan sands south of M'hamid. Since 1998, Abdelouahid Aabi's **Desert Evasion,** 2 av. Mohammed V, opposite the police station (© **024/888682** or 061/243106; www. desert-evasion.net), has been one of the most reputable. For a private tour of the region, contact **Nawfal Kabbaj** (© **024/882809** or 062/836864). A very amiable and relaxed guide, Nawfal speaks excellent English and specializes in themed tours of the region such as archaeology, birding, and botanical tours, along with the other mainstream destinations.

WHERE TO STAY

Thanks to a burgeoning film industry and a handy location that's an easy day's drive from Erfoud, Marrakech, and Taroudannt, Ouarzazate has a good selection of accommodations to suit all budgets. In the past, supply heavily outweighed demand, but

Ouarzazate is greatly benefiting from Morocco's determined push for increased tourism. Most travelers still only stay for 1 night, but there are more and more travelers arriving each year. Accommodations are spread out and, as previously mentioned, some travelers don't even venture off their hotel grounds. For those who do, *petits* taxis are easy to hail on avenue Mohammed V to return to your hotel.

The temperature in Ouarzazate can be stifling in the summer months of July and August and bitterly cold from December to February, so it's definitely worth considering a room with air-conditioning or heating, respectively.

VERY EXPENSIVE

Le Berbère Palace   This is the hotel of choice for movie stars, luxury tour groups, and dusty, grizzled travelers returning from a desert excursion who don't care about the expense. This sprawling kasbah-village lives up to its hefty price tag on most accounts. Rooms and townhouselike suites are spread throughout the grounds in one- and two-story villas, each with their own balcony and tiled throughout, with large bedrooms, a lounge area, and a modern bathroom with tub/shower combo. The grand lobby leads onto a public area dotted with movie memorabilia—Caesar's throne is a popular photo prop. From here you can access three restaurants—international, Moroccan, and a pizzeria—as well as a separate large lounge bar with free Wi-Fi and an oversize plasma TV, and the hotel's 25m (82-ft.) pool. Beside the pool is a white-linen Bedouin tent with a shaded lounge. It's all very professional, if at times impersonal, with piped smooth jazz music and plenty of staff on hand. The restaurants, however, are overpriced, and you'd be better off walking the 15 minutes into town and enjoying both the restaurants and the livelier local atmosphere.

Tip: Ask for a discount upon arrival. Although they loathe to reduce the room price, they are usually very quick to upgrade you if the hotel is quiet.

Bd. Laâyoune, Quartier Mansour Eddahbi, Ouarzazate. (C) **024/883105** or 024/882139. Fax 024/883071. www. ouarzazate.com/leberberepalace. 232 units. 2,000dh–2,600dh ($250–$325/£125–£163) double; 3,200dh–4,200dh ($400–$525/£200–£263) suite. Children under 2 stay free in parent's room. TPT not included. Buffet breakfast 130dh ($16/£8.15). AE, MC, V. **Amenities:** 3 restaurants; 2 bars; pool; tennis; hammam; Jacuzzi; sauna; salon; massage; dry cleaning; boutique. *In room:* A/C, satellite TV, fridge.

EXPENSIVE

Hotel Mercure Ouarzazate   The combinations in this chain hotel work very well. Throughout the two-level building is a mix of traditional *tabout* (rammed earth) and stone architecture with funky, contemporary colors and design. The comfortable, tile rooms are a bit on the small side but have a few Moroccan touches—Berber carpets, mosaic-tile headboards—to accompany the modern furnishings and bathroom with a separate toilet. All rooms have a balcony, though it's shared between two and lacks any outdoor seating. The public areas are outstanding. Three lounges accompany the large and modern bar—one with a stone fireplace; another with burgundy walls and low tables; and another with pillows and cushions strewn on the floor and a wide window affording fantastic views of the nearby kasbah—all of which surround a good-size swimming pool. A ground-floor restaurant (Le Tazerzite, p. 184) leads to a balcony with stunning views of the kasbah and the usually dry Oued Ouarzazate; I recommend the buffet breakfast. Along with the Ibis Moussafir hotel (see below), its sister property next door, the Mercure is close to the kasbah but a good 25-minute walk from the city center; a solitary computer providing free Internet access in the lobby can save a trip into town.

Av. Moulay Rachid, Ouarzazate. ℂ 024/899100. Fax 024/899101. www.mercure.com. 68 units. 858dh ($107/£54) double. Children under 2 stay free in parent's room. Online discounts available. Rates include breakfast. TPT not included. MC, V. On-site parking. **Amenities:** Restaurant; bar; pool; tennis court; sauna; 24-hr. room service; dry cleaning; 24-hr. reception; free Internet; Wi-Fi. *In room:* A/C, satellite TV, fridge, hair dryer, safe.

MODERATE

Hôtel la Perle du Sud *Value*   Located on the main street on the western edge of the city center, this is a good value hotel. A range of different-size rooms are available, all of them well appointed and with heavy wood furnishings, Moroccan carpets, and *tadelakt*-finished bathrooms. The suites come with a small salon; some also with a balcony. Although the road-facing rooms aren't that noisy, you can also request an inward-facing room. The licensed restaurant—with both a buffet and an a la carte menu—looks out to a sunny outdoor area with a poolside bar, woven-grass sun lounges, and a large, clean pool with faux-rock waterfall. The English-speaking staff are very friendly, and you may want to book ahead, as this place is popular with film crews.

40 av. Mohammed V, Ouarzazate. ℂ 024/888640. Fax 024/888646. www.hotelperledusud.com. 68 units. 500dh–550dh ($63–$69/£31–£34) double; 750dh–1,100dh ($94–$138/£47–£69) suite. Children 2–12 half price in parent's room; under 2 free. TPT not included. Buffet breakfast 60dh ($7.50/£3.75). MC, V. **Amenities:** Restaurant; bar; pool; Internet; Wi-Fi. *In room:* A/C, satellite TV, fridge, hair dryer.

Ibis Moussafir *Value* *Kids*   As with other hotels in Morocco under this chain, this is a great value for your money. The large three-story, *tabout*-rendered building may attempt to look like a kasbah on the outside, but inside you'll find no surprises. The compact rooms are carpeted with modern finishings and are still relatively fresh. A ground-floor restaurant leads off to one side of the reception and serves a menu of international standards with a nice salad buffet and comfort food for the kids. However, I recommend eating at Le Tazerzite (p. 184) in the Mercure next door. To the other side of reception is a cozy lounge bar. Children will love the large pool, surrounded by a good supply of sun lounges and no less than three Berber tents for shade. It's within short walking distance to the Taourirt Kasbah and about a 25-minute walk from the city center.

Av. Moulay Rachid, Ouarzazate. ℂ 024/899110. Fax 024/899111. www.ibishotel.com. 104 units. 591dh ($74/£37) double. Children under 12 stay free in parent's room. Low-season rates apply. Breakfast buffet 47dh ($5.90/£2.95). MC, V. On-site parking. **Amenities:** Restaurant; bar; pool; 24-hr. room service; babysitting; dry cleaning; 24-hr. reception; Internet. *In room:* A/C, satellite TV, hair dryer (upon request).

INEXPENSIVE

Hotel Amlal   This is a good, clean, cheap hotel located on a quiet street in the city center. Owner Youssef Mimoun refurbished the Amlal in 2007, and now all rooms, although simply furnished, are clean and come with reverse-cycle air-conditioning. The rooms are on the upper floors (only accessible by stairs) with a small lounge on the first landing. Some rooms will take up to four adults (one double and two singles). On the ground floor is a cafe-restaurant, and there's an unguarded parking lot at the entrance.

24–25 Lot du Centre, rue du Marché, Ouarzazate. ℂ 024/884030. Fax 024/884600. 28 units. 200dh ($25/£13) single; each additional person (including children) 50dh ($6.25/£3.15). No credit cards. **Amenities:** Restaurant. *In room:* A/C, satellite TV.

WHERE TO DINE

For those who don't wish to dine in-house, there's a small but vibrant restaurant scene in Ouarzazate offering a good selection of international and Moroccan cuisine. Most are located close together at the east end of avenue Moulay Rachid, although there's more atmosphere on nearby rue de la Poste and avenue Mohammed V. No matter where you dine, however, make your way to the pedestrian-only rue du Marché after dinner for the evening promenade, where you'll see Ouarzazate families out and about, many of them sampling the best ice cream in town at **Patisserie-Glacier des Habouss** on place al Mouahidine. It's open daily from 6am to 10pm and is also a bakery, offering a good spot for a pastry and coffee/tea breakfast. **Paradis Jus de Fruits,** at the west end of the pedestrian section on rue du Marché, serves delicious freshly squeezed juices daily from 9am to 9pm.

EXPENSIVE

Restaurant Relais Saint Exupéry ⟨ INTERNATIONAL   Owner Jean-Pierre pays tribute to French pilot, explorer, and writer Antoine Saint Exupéry in this little piece of colonial France on the edge of Ouarzazate. Smooth jazz and blues music plays in the background as you choose from a mind-boggling choice of seven-course meals. The courses range from a seasonal soup to Berber cheese perfumed with saffron, while the entrees tread through every style of cooked meat imaginable, including *cheval* (horse) and *dromedaire* (camel). Vegetarians are left with three choices from the 50-odd on the menu. The courses aren't large, and it makes for a fine dining experience that is quite unexpected given its location. A separate lunch menu that includes a starter, roast chicken with fries or spaghetti, and chocolate crêpes caters to the passing tour bus brigade, while a kids' menu offers a starter, steak with mashed potatoes or fries, and homemade ice cream. You'll need a taxi to get here.

13 av. Moulay Abdellah, corner of Ouarzazate-Tinerhir rd. on the far east end of Ouarzazate. ℂ 024/887779. Fax 024/888444. www.relaissaintexupery.com. Set menus 98dh–275dh ($12–$34/£6.15–£17) dinner, 140dh ($18/£8.75) lunch; 70dh ($8.75/£4.40) kids' menu. Alcohol served. AE, MC, V with 5% administration fee. Daily noon–2:30pm and 6:30–10:30pm. Closed July.

MODERATE

Le Tazerzite INTERNATIONAL/MOROCCAN   For a hotel-restaurant, located within the Mercure Ouarzazate, that could afford to coast along with a steady stream of in-house clients, this is a very impressive setup that is open to nonguests for both lunch and dinner. Diners choose from a daily buffet or a la carte menu. The buffet consists of a small selection of salads and desserts, and both vegetarian and meat main courses usually cooked *à la tagine* style. I recommend choosing from the menu, however, where there is a bit more variety such as an exquisite starter of *zaalouk* (eggplant purée mixed with thyme, tomato, and *épices* [spices] *aux Dra*), followed by a chicken tagine in honey and rose water and a dessert of frangipani tart with seasonal fruits and ice cream. There's also a seasonal kids' menu. The restaurant offers indoor and outdoor seating. Inside the stylish, deep-red interior are comfortable, thickly woven grass chairs set around nicely spaced tables; a glass wall that constitutes one side of the pool creates a funky aquarium effect. The outside veranda continues the stone and wood theme of the hotel and is very pleasant on warmer evenings. True to the contemporary theme throughout the hotel, the waitstaff is young, attractive, and efficient.

Hotel Mercure Ouarzazate, av. Moulay Rachid, Ouarzazate. ℂ 024/899100. Fax 024/899101. www.mercure.com. Starters 30dh–40dh ($3.75–$5/£1.90–£2.50); main courses 95dh–125dh ($12–$16/£5.95–£7.80); buffet 160dh ($20/£10); kids' menu 55dh ($6.90/£3.45). Alcohol served. MC, V. Daily noon–3pm and 7:30–10:30pm.

Restaurant Dimitri INTERNATIONAL/MOROCCAN   In 1928, Chez Dimitri opened for business in Ouarzazate—the first restaurant in the then frontier outpost. The owner's son is now in charge of one of the most consistently popular restaurants in town. Located in the heart of the city center—it's often used as a geographical locater for travelers—the interior has a touch of the Mediterranean but the walls are all Hollywood, with autographed pictures of stars and wannabe stars who have come for dinner. A wood-fire stove keeps things warm in winter, but the outside veranda is the obvious dining spot in the warmer months. The menu has a wide variety of dishes ranging from a delicious chicken tagine with dates and figs and tagliatelle with salmon to Thai-style stir-fried beef and, of course, a house *moussaka*. Make sure to leave room for a chocolate mousse or bananas flambéed in dark rum. Befitting the Mediterranean connection, there's a good wine and aperitif/digestive menu. Although Dimitri's food is wholesome rather than outstanding, the location and atmosphere are unrivalled.

22 av. Mohammed V, Ouarzazate. ✆ 024/887346. Appetizers 50dh–60dh ($6.25–$7.50/£3.15–£3.75); main courses 70dh–130dh ($8.75–$16/£4.40–£8.15). Alcohol served. MC, V. Daily noon–2:30pm and 7–10:30pm.

INEXPENSIVE

Chez Nabil 🐾 MOROCCAN   This busy, sociable place is popular with both locals and travelers for its inexpensive, tasty food and fast service. Most diners eat alfresco on high-back wrought-iron chairs under umbrellas of woven grass. There is also a small air-conditioned section inside that looks onto the open kitchen. The menu is mainly Moroccan and the servings are plentiful. *Pastilla*, grilled meats, and tagines are available, or there is a good variety of salads, omelets (vegetarians will enjoy the veggie-filled Berber omelet), and hamburgers, though you may wish to pass on the *burger à cheval* (horse). If you're around on Friday, try the couscous. Alcohol is not available for purchase, but you can bring your own.

Av. Moulay Rachid, next to Supermarché Dadès, Ouarzazate. ✆/fax 024/884545. Sandwiches/burgers 20dh–40dh ($2.50–$5/£1.25–£2.50); main courses 40dh–60dh ($5–$7.50/£2.50–£3.75); *pastilla* 110dh ($14/£6.90). No credit cards. Daily 7:30am–11pm.

Obelix INTERNATIONAL/MOROCCAN   One of a string of restaurants along this road, the Obelix offers a fine dining experience at a very reasonable price. Autographed pictures of movie stars adorn the walls of the Egyptian-theme interior, complete with temple columns and hieroglyphics. There are a few tables outside looking onto the street that are preferable on balmy evenings, as it can get stuffy inside. The menu includes Moroccan classics such as tagine, couscous, and brochettes along with a choice of pizzas, pastas, grilled meats, soups, and salads; try the *zaalouk* (pulped eggplant) to start. The service is always efficient and friendly, and a reasonable wine list is available.

11 av. Moulay Rachid, Ouarzazate. ✆ 024/887117. Entrees 30dh–40dh ($3.75–$5/£1.90–£2.50); main courses 40dh–80dh ($5–$10/£2.50–£5). Alcohol served. MC, V. Daily noon–3pm and 6–10:30pm.

WHAT TO SEE & DO

Atlas Film Studios   In the early 1960s, *Lawrence of Arabia* film director David Lean was the first to take advantage of Ouarzazate's potential as a movie location, the town's exotic scenery, clear skies, and availability of "authentic-looking" locals providing an attractive location for all movies involving ancient, desert-based storylines. In 1983, Moroccan entrepreneur Mohamed Belghmi, recognizing the need for a permanent filmmaking studio in the area, constructed the Atlas Film Corporation Studios on the outskirts of town. Other studios have since followed, and a string of Hollywood productions have spent time filming here including *Jewel of the Nile, Kundun, Gladiator, Black Hawk Down, Alexander the Great, Kingdom of Heaven,* and *Babel.* Atlas remains the biggest and busiest of the town's film studios and is generally open to visitors for a tour of some of the old construction sets. It's really only for movie buffs, but it's a fun way to spend 30 minutes and borders on a surreal experience as you walk past a Tibetan monastery and an Egyptian temple.

5km (3 miles) from Ouarzazate on the western (Marrakech) approach to town. (© 024/882166. Admission 50dh ($6.25/£3.15) adults, 25dh ($3.15/£1.55) children. 30-min. tours daily 9am–6pm, except when filming is in progress. If you don't have your own transport, take a taxi—petit or grand—here, but negotiate a return fare (around 40dh/$5/£2.50) and collection time, as there are no taxis at the studios. Pay the driver on the return journey.

Taourirt Kasbah   Ouarzazate's only real sight of historical interest is the former el Glaoui palace, the Taourirt Kasbah. The el Glaoui clan controlled one of the major southern caravan routes to West Africa and were given extensive power by the French during colonial rule in exchange for keeping the southern tribes subdued. The Taourirt Kasbah was built in the 19th century and reached the height of importance during the 1930s, when the el Glaoui powers were at their peak. Although located at a strategic junction of the caravan routes, the kasbah was never actually resided in by the el Glaoui chiefs. Housed here would have been the second tier of command, such as the dynasty's sons and cousins and their extended—numbering in the hundreds— entourages of servants, builders, and craftsmen. The palace has close to 300 rooms and within the kasbah were more than 20 riads.

The kasbah today is partly ruined, but it's still inhabited on its rear side by a small group of villagers who are always willing to show you around for 15dh to 20dh ($1.90–$2.50/95p–£1.25). You can only enter the former palace from the main entrance, however. The palace has been restored, with assistance from UNESCO, and it is this section of the kasbah that visitors are shown. Rambling off in all directions from a main courtyard—originally the souk area—visitors can see the former reception rooms, harem room, and palace kitchens. Some of the upstairs area affords fabulous views of the remainder of the kasbah as well as the Oued Ouarzazate in one direction and the High Atlas in the other. If you're not part of a large group, guides, waiting for business at the entrance, will often show you a few more rooms if you're interested. Ask for the very pleasant, English-speaking guide Mohammed Amrani.

East end (Tinihir direction) of av. Mohammed V. Admission 10dh ($1.25/65p) adults; 3dh (40¢/20p) children 12 and under. Guides available for 70dh ($8.75/£4.40) for a 2-hr. tour. Daily 8am–6pm. The kasbah is about a 30-min. walk from the post office or a 10dh ($1.25/65p) petit taxi ride.

SHOPPING

Most travelers are on their way to/from the major shopping experiences in Marrakech or Fes, and as a consequence the pressure to buy when browsing the shops in Ouarzazate can be quite intense. Opposite the kasbah is the **Kissariat Artisinal,** where a maze of stores sell a good range of curios such as pottery, carpets, lanterns, scarves, and spices. Next door, on the corner of Mohammed V, is another string of shops; the pressure here is slightly less than that at the Kissariat. Agnaou el Houssaine's **Antiquities de Sud** (© 024/883730) is filled with antiques and Saharan/West African objets d'art, as well as a bric-a-brac selection that is beginning to suspiciously look like junk. All of the shops here are open daily from 9am to sunset.

For everyday items, **Super Marché,** on avenue Mohammed V (next to the BMCE bank), is well stocked with groceries, cold meats, dairy products, toiletries, and even alcohol. It's open every day from 8am to 10pm. **Supermarché Dâdes,** on avenue Moulay Rachid, has a wider range of groceries and a large cold-storage section, and is open every day from 8am to 1pm and 4 to 10pm

Azedine Bendra Originally a potter in Safi, Azedine Bendra's watercolors were discovered in Ouarzazate by a UNESCO worker in 2001 and are now exhibited in France and Marrakech. A biography has recently been written about him and the journey he took both geographically and spiritually to arrive in Ouarzazate and begin his life as a painter. His paintings depict the rural life of central and southern Morocco in soft, wide brushstrokes of pale blues, browns, and grays. Those from his collection that aren't snatched up by exhibitors and galleries are sold from a small shop on avenue Mohammed V between Hertz and the mosque. Open daily with flexible hours between 8am and 8pm. No phone. www.kasbahdupeintre.com.

Ensemble Artisinal Opposite the entrance to Taourirt Kasbah, this is an interesting mix of museum, gallery, and retail where you'll find some good-quality—though not necessarily cheap—crafts at more or less fixed prices. Especially interesting is the Centre du Tapis at the rear where you can see—and buy—carpets being handmade by women from the local Ouzgita tribe. The women are welcoming, and it's a great experience to sit with them at their large looms and see their swift, nimble work. Open daily 9am to 12:30pm and 3 to 6pm. Centre du Tapis closed weekends. Av. Mohammed V, opposite Taorirt Kasbah. No phone.

Le Paon de l'Arganier Right across from Le Berbère Palace (p. 182) is this delightful little shop run by Chahira Yakoubi for the Minatou Association. The association coordinates the marketing, distribution, and retailing of handmade products produced by various women's cooperatives in central and southern Morocco. Inside the shop you'll find great gift ideas such as argan oil (p. 354) soap, lamps with Berber motifs in henna, slippers, photo albums, notebooks, handbags, and a range of linen decorated in traditional yet modern Berber and Saharan motifs. The shop is usually open Wednesday to Monday 8am to 12:30pm and 3 to 9pm, but this can be seasonal. 5 bd. Laâyoune, Ouarzazate. ✆ 024/884197.

SIDE TRIPS FROM OUARZAZATE
AÏT BEN HADDOU
29km (18 miles) NW of Ouarzazate, 209km (130 miles) SE of Marrakech

The village of **Aït Ben Haddou** ✶✶✶ receives up to 130,000 visitors each year, and every one of them is coming to view the same thing. Perched upon a low hillside overlooking an often-dry riverbed, the Aït Ben Haddou *ksour*, or kasbahs, are one of the most scenic sights in the country. Towering defensive walls and elaborately decorated corner towers surround the collection of houses, stables, lofts, and even a mosque—all constructed from a mix of red earth and stone called *tabout*—connected by a maze of narrow, winding lanes. Probably established as early as the 11th century, the site was an important stronghold of the clans that controlled the lucrative southern caravan trade that passed through here and Telouet (p. 168). This strategic geographical importance was severely diminished in 1936 by the French construction of the Tizi n'Tichka road to the west. The *ksour* has since remained virtually abandoned, bar a few families that still reside here eking out a rural existence that is now somewhat subsidized by travelers who climb past their kasbahs on the way to the hilltop. A ruined fortified granary, or *agadir*, sits atop the hill and lays testament to the historical reasoning behind the kasbah's strongly defensive position—their highly prized supply of grain. Since the late 1970s, the kasbahs have been used for numerous movie shoots with the odd bit of Hollywood restoration work undertaken, even though a

---

Moments A Trip Down Memory Lane

As mentioned, the kasbahs receive their fair share of visitors, most of whom stop only for a picture before moving on. If you can, stay the night. Rise early— before the tourists *and* the touts—and find a spot next to the pebble-strewn riverbed. As the sunlight begins to cross the *ksour* walls, visualize the site during its prime—before the west coast of Africa was discovered by the seafaring nations of Europe; before the French built a faster, safer route through the Atlas; before the border with Algeria was closed. Caravans of more than a hundred camels—laden with cloth, glass, and other wonders from the modern world—would pass by here en route from Marrakech to the kingdoms of Timbuktu and the old Sudan, returning months later with their booty of gold, ivory, salt, and slaves.

UNESCO heritage listing of the site in 1983 has assisted the Moroccan government in retaining some control over its exploitation.

The best time of day to visit is very early in the morning when the red-earth *tabout* contrasts strikingly against the bright blue sky—and while the tour groups are still eating breakfast in Marrakech or Ouarzazate.

To reach the hilltop and the ruined *agadir,* simply enter the *ksour* through one of the entrances—reached by walking across the usually dry Oued Mellah from one of the hotel parking lots in the new village—and follow the maze of lanes uphill until you eventually come out at the top.

Note: The kasbahs are still inhabited and some of the residents don't take kindly to being photographed or intruded upon. This is fair enough considering how many people pass by each day. Quite often you'll be accosted as you proceed through one of the *ksour's* entrances by a "doorman" demanding entry. This is a quandary on which I have had conflicting local advice. On the one hand, it could be considered fair payment to hand over 10 dirham ($1.25/65p) to a member of the kasbah's families in exchange for tromping through their backyard. On the other hand, this can lead to squabbles between the families as to who receives the money, if indeed the "doorman" is an actual family member and not just an enterprising nobody. My advice is to abstain from any payment if you are simply traipsing up to the hilltop and especially if you are being accosted by an unlikely sort. However, if you stop to take photographs along the way or are invited, as can often happen, inside one of the houses, then I recommend paying for the privilege.

GETTING THERE

Twenty kilometers (12 miles) from Ouarzazate, on the main road to Marrakech, is a small roadside settlement with a signposted turnoff for the narrow tarred road to Aït Ben Haddou, 9km (5½ miles) away. Buses traveling to Aït Ben Haddou are few and far between, with the majority only stopping at the turnoff from where you can usually catch a *grand* taxi (10dh/$1.25/65p) to the village. A better idea, if traveling from Ouarzazate, is to charter a *grand* taxi for the return trip (350dh/$44/£22 per taxi).

WHERE TO STAY & DINE

Dar Mouna 🌟🌟 Abdellah Mouna's family-run guesthouse was the first in the village and is the one of the friendliest, with a terrace that looks directly over the riverbed to their old house in Aït Ben Haddou. Constructed in *tabout* throughout, the main building surrounds a cozy interior courtyard with comfortable lounges and a clay-brick fireplace that is perfect on cold winter nights. The rustic inward-facing rooms are on two levels opening on to the courtyard. Low-lying beds with natural-fiber spreads and floors covered with Berber rugs, grass mats, and lamb's wool hides complement the rustic, earthen walls. Most rooms have good-size bathrooms with ceramic basins atop stone pedestals and large walk-in showers; the sole suite has a small, separate lounge room and a private terrace.

Note: The kasbah view that is offered with the more expensive rooms is only through a small window and partly obscured by decorative ironwork.

An earth and stone restaurant adjoining the main building is furnished with wrought-iron furniture and has two fireplaces and a small lounge area. The 30-seat restaurant offers a *menu du jour,* for lunch and dinner, of fine, home-cooked Moroccan fare. Nonguests are welcome with prior notice. Note that the restaurant isn't air-conditioned and doesn't serve alcohol, though you can bring your own.

The large *terrasse panoramique* stretches the length of Dar Mouna and is where you will want to spend most of your time. Woven grass umbrellas afford some shade from the sun as you while away the hours simply looking across to the famous *ksour.* Request your meals to be taken out here. A garden at the rear of the small, walled property has a vegetable patch to supply the restaurant, as well as a swimming pool and some woven-grass sun lounges, though at press time, this area was in need of some attention.

Aït Ben Haddou village; follow signs from the road for 200m (655 ft.). © 028/890840 or 061/385720. Fax 028/823080. www.darmouna.com. 12 units. 550dh–620dh ($69–$78/£34–£39) double; 650dh ($81/£41) suite. Children under 2 stay free in parent's room. Rates include breakfast. TPT not included. Restaurant: *Menu du jour* 100dh ($13/£6.25). MC, V. Covered parking. **Amenities:** Restaurant; lounge; pool. *In room:* A/C.

2 The Dra Valley & Desert Dunes

In Neolithic times, the Oued Dra—Morocco's longest river—flowed all the way to the Atlantic, heading southeast from what is now Ouarzazate before turning directly to the west, around M'hamid. Until this elbow, the Dra watered a string of seven palm groves including Ternata (Zagora), Fezawata (Amezrou), and M'hamid. The valley of the Dra was warm and humid before it started to drain. Rock carvings in the area depict a tropical land inhabited by elephants, rhinoceros, lions, ostrich, gazelles, and crocodiles. Until modern times, the Dra produced the much-sought-after tainting agents of indigo and a red-color *lac* (a pigment secreted by a particular family of insects onto the branches of a host tree). The M'hamid palm grove was especially strategic over the centuries as one of the main trading posts for the trans-Saharan caravans. Amber, ivory, musk, salt, and slaves from the south, and fabric, silk, spices, and sugar from the north would be exchanged here along with the local dates, indigo, and *lac.* Control of the valley was paramount for Morocco's dynasties, and many a sultan came to grief trying to subdue the region's indigenous—and ferociously independent—Drawa tribes.

It was from the Dra Valley in the 11th century that Morocco's first great Berber dynasty, the Almoravids, launched their eventual conquest of the country and beyond into Spain. The Saâdians, in the late 16th century, also accumulated vast power and wealth by controlling the Dra from where their empire extended south to the great

Songhai kingdoms of Gao and Timbuktu. Also recognizing the importance of the valley was the Alaouite sultan Moulay Ismail (p. 238), who sent his son to govern the Dra for a quarter of a century, building many kasbahs, or *ksour,* and developing the valley. Peace, however, was a foreigner here for most of Morocco's history until the French eventually pacified the area in 1931.

Since the 1990s, the region has experienced a new invasion—4WDs speeding through the villages on their way to a Saharan experience. This has attracted a generation of blue-turban touts and guides who pounce on independent travelers in desperation for much-needed work. Those who are driving, especially, should be aware of the touts' age-old scam of hitching a ride "to see my brother in the next village," or "my car is broken and I need to get to the village for repairs," or of tales that small vehicles can't make the journey all the way to M'hamid. The heat here, however, breeds a patient and unhurried person, and for the most part the touting for business is low key and not too obtrusive.

The road from Ouarzazate to Zagora is simply spectacular, as it first winds up and across the Jebel Anaouar before joining the Dra Valley and its fertile strip of palmeraie and settlements. From Zagora, the landscape is that of the harsh *hammada* (barren plains of hardened dirt and stone); this prepares travelers for the end of the road at M'hamid and the bumpy journey—or slow camel ride—to the edge of the Sahara.

GETTING THERE

The road all the way to M'hamid is good, although it's always worth budgeting extra travel time for any mishaps and carrying more water than normal. There are daily buses and *grands* taxis connecting Ouarzazate, Zagora, and M'hamid, but, if possible, driving yourself from Ouarzazate is easily the best option, allowing for visits to as many oases and villages as takes your fancy.

BY BUS   Buses service Zagora reasonably well, with daily departures from Casablanca (5 hr.; 170dh/$22/£11); Erfoud (9 hr.; 80dh/$10/£5); Er Rachidia (10 hr.; 110dh/$14/£6.90); Marrakech (10 hr.; 90dh/$11/£5.65); and Ouarzazate (4½ hr.; 40dh/$5/£2.50). CTM is located at the south end of the main road, boulevard Mohammed V. They only have one departure per day, at 7pm to Marrakech and beyond to Casablanca. All other services operate from a new *gare routière* at the north entrance to town. There is a daily bus from Zagora to M'hamid (2 hr.; 20dh/$2.50/£1.25). All buses operate from the dusty junction in M'hamid where the tarred road ends.

BY *GRAND* TAXI   *Grands* taxis operate throughout the day (when full) to Zagora from Ouarzazate (3 hr.; 65dh/$8.15/£4.05) and M'hamid (1½ hr.; 25dh/$3.15/£1.55). In Zagora they still operate from the old *gare routière* in the middle of town, a frustrating 15-minute walk from the new bus station. In M'hamid they stop at the same junction as the buses (see above).

BY ORGANIZED TOUR   Ali Yassine's very professional, family-run **Caravane du Sud** (© **024/847569;** fax 024/847497; caravane.sud@gmail.com) is located at the main junction as you enter Amezrou after crossing the Oued Dra. His English-speaking staff can arrange 2-hour camel treks to the small dunes at nearby Nakhla and various other excursions of up to 3 weeks. Ahmed Hajja's **Zbar Travel** (© **068/517280;** fax 024/848184; www.zbartravel.com) can be found next door to the Hotel Elghizlane in M'hamid. Ahmed's ancestry goes all the way back to the first Bedouin Arabs who migrated here from Yemen, and he intimately knows the dunes around M'hamid. A 2-hour camel trek to the Erg Lehoudi and Erg Messouira dunes, with an overnight stay in Berber tents, costs 370dh ($46/£23) per person including dinner and break-fast. An overnight stay at Erg Chigaga costs 200dh ($25/£13) per person with meals, 1,320dh ($165/£83) for a six-seater 4WD, or 370dh ($46/£23) per day per camel.

FAST FACTS   All services offered in **Zagora** are located on the main road from Ouarzazate, boulevard Mohammed V, along a 1km (⅔-mile) stretch between the north entrance arches and the south junction to Foum Zguid or Amezrou.

Banque Populaire (© 024/859372) is located in the middle of boulevard Mohammed V and has a 24-hour exchange ATM, while **BMCE** (© 024/879649), at the northern end, and **Credit Agricolé** (© 024/860042), next to Banque Populaire, both have ATMs and bureaux de change open Monday to Friday 8:15am to 3:45pm.

The **post office** is located at the south end of boulevard Mohammed V and is open Monday to Friday 8am to 4:15pm and Saturday 8 to 11:45am.

Pharmacie Zagora, opposite Cyber Draa (© 024/847195), and **Pharmacie Assa-fare,** near the BMCE bank (© 024/895390), are open Monday to Saturday 7:30am to 1pm, 3 to 8pm, and 9:30pm to 1am. The all-night Pharmacie du Nuit is opposite Banque Populaire.

Cyber Cafe Albahas is just off the north end of boulevard Mohammed V. Cyber Draa is close to Banque Populaire, and **Cyber Agharas** is next door to CTM. All of them are open daily from 9am to noon and 3 to 10pm.

Labo Photo Zagora, opposite the *grand* taxi station, sells and processes film and has a very limited stock of memory cards and other digital accessories.

At the entrance to M'hamid is a very small cluster of hotel-restaurants, a couple of shops, an Internet cafe, and a disproportionate number of tour operators. Stopping here can be quite intense upon arrival as hordes of "blue men" gather around to offer you trips into the desert.

WHAT TO SEE & DO

Amezrou   Most travelers, at best, stop in Zagora or Amezrou for only 1 night on a speeding visit to the Erg Chigaga dunes past M'hamid. Although the physical experi-ence of walking in the Saharan sands is not to be missed, staying a few days in Amezrou can ultimately offer a far more rewarding and interesting desert experience. Here you slow down and start to see past the hot, harsh landscape and get to meet the resilient, independent Drawa and Berber locals and see the hidden lushness of the oases they live in.

Antoine Bouillon from Dar Raha (below) has initiated the **Bienvenue Amezrou** project. Six young villagers have been trained as **guides** and walk visitors through various parts of the Amezrou palmeraie, conveying their knowledge primarily on the village's his-tory, culture, and geology, as well as other diverse themes such as an introduction to Islam. The guides are currently booked via Dar Raha, but at the time of writing they were about to become self-sufficient and work out of a small office opposite the dar. This office will eventually become a center for youth development programs and further education. Day walks cost around 300dh to 400dh ($38–$50/£19–£25) depending on the tour and group size.

On the southern edge of Amezrou in the former Jewish kasbah, or Mellah, are the village's **silversmiths.** The craft was historically the domain of Berber and Arab Jews (they controlled the silver trade along this former caravan route) until as recently as the early 20th century, when they then began to migrate to Casablanca, France, and Israel. The skill was passed on to Amezrou's Berber Muslims and continues today in its traditional form. Abdullah Chjai has been designing, molding, melting, and making silver jewelry by flame, wind bellows, hand, and hammer for the past 25 years. The designs come from traditional Berber, Drawi, and Saharwi symbols. His sons have followed in his footsteps and are happy to show visitors the process on their rooftop workshop above **Maison la Kasbah** (© **024/846598**) on the southern edge of Amezrou village.

Squeezed between the imposing Jebel Zagora and the Oued Dra and its peaceful, fertile palmeraie is where the best accommodations can to be found and cultural tours of the town's *ksour,* palmeraie, and silversmiths can be organized.

170 (105 miles) S of Ouarzazate.

The Dunes   The 40km-long (25-mile) **Erg Chigaga** ★★★ dunes—some climbing to 300m (985 ft.) high—are about 55km (34 miles) south of M'hamid and can only be reached by 4WD or camel. For more on Erg Chigaga, see p. 177. Closer and smaller dunes can be found at Erg Lehoudi and Erg Messouira, 8km (5 miles) north and south of M'hamid, respectively. Erg Lehoudi, especially, gets its fair share of day-trippers from Ouarzazate and Zagora.

Jebel Zagora   This small mountain rises up behind Amezrou to keep watch over the valley, and is worth climbing for the sweeping views of the Dra Valley to both the north and south. Seeing the valley from up high, the historical importance of controlling this route throughout the ages becomes obvious. At the moment, a ghastly half-built concrete shell of a hotel has been stubbornly left standing while the owner continues to look for ways to acquire the planning permission he was initially denied. A road from the north side of the Jebel leads up to this point. If you're driving, the road continues from there but is dangerously narrow.

M'hamid   At the end of the tar road is the scruffy village of M'hamid. Technically M'hamid Jdid (new M'hamid), there's not a lot here to attract travelers except to stock up on water or organize a trip into the dunes. M'hamid Kedima is the attractive old village set in the palm grove on the other side of the dry Oued Dra. Picturesque kasbahs—some still inhabited by the Aït Haratin, descendants of West African slaves who settled here—are dotted amongst the palms and shifting sands, and it was here that the great camel caravans would stop. For a time gold was even melted and stamped here, a craft practiced by the region's long-gone Jewish population.

98km (61 miles) S of Zagora, 266km (165 miles) S of Ouarzazate.

Zagora   The Zagora of today is very much a French creation, with few architectural traces left of the ancient *ksour* that in centuries past would deal with the passing caravan trade. It's the major administrative center of the Dra Valley, but for travelers it's pretty much a one-road town, and if you don't need to take advantage of the town's services, then you're very likely to drive straight through. The hassle from touts and guides here used to be intolerable, and although you will still receive many enquiries about your desert plans if you hang around for any length of time, the serious hassling seems to now be the domain of the desperate touts farther south in M'hamid. Some maps still indicate the tar road ending in Zagora—the reason why the French set up headquarters here rather than the then-bigger village of Amezrou—but it now continues over a low concrete runway across the Oued Dra to link up with Amezrou and continue for another 98km (61 miles) south to M'hamid where it abruptly ends. The arches at the southern end of Zagora were demolished in the process, and along with them the famous sign depicting *Tombouctou à 52 jours* (Timbuktu in 52 days)—by camel—although a replica has been painted at the new junction with the road west to Foum Zguid.

If you're around on Wednesday or Sunday, the marketplace in the center of town comes alive with the largest souk south of Ouarzazate. This is a true village market with local produce (dates especially), livestock, everyday hardware, and some handicrafts.

168km (104 miles) S of Ouarzazate.

WHERE TO STAY & DINE
AMEZROU

Dar Raha 🌙🌙 This is the real deal: three family houses only minimally restored to provide access between them, no air-conditioning or electronic gadgets, shared bathrooms (the originals of the building), and a central courtyard and kitchen that is the heart of the house. Antoine Bouillon and Josiane Morillon have made their "House of Rest" a vehicle for a much greater passion involving the conservation of Amezrou's kasbah, its architecture, history, environment, and its people. To this end, they have converted one of the rooms into a gallery displaying the artwork of some now-famous local artists. Guests are welcome to visit the artists in their homes, or the artists are happy to come to Dar Raha to talk about their work. Staying at Dar Raha truly feels like being in someone's home, and the smells of earth, food, plants, and livestock that emanate from its various parts only add to this sense. Toward the end of each day, guests often converge on the rooftop terrace to enjoy the view over the kasbah and palmeraie before moving down to the salon to enjoy some home-cooked Moroccan cuisine. The rustic rooms are very simply, though tastefully, furnished. The lack of luxuries and private bathrooms won't be to everybody's taste, but you'd be hard-pressed to find a more genuine, authentic experience. *Note:* There is one single room, but it is very small.

Amezrou kasbah, Amezrou. ℂ 024/846993 or 070/023696. Fax 024/846180. http://darraha.free.fr. 9 units. 220dh ($28/£14) single; 410dh ($51/£26) double. No credit cards. Closed Jun 15–Aug 31. **Amenities:** Restaurant; art gallery. *In room:* Fan (upon request), no phone.

Riad Lamane Set within the palmeraie is this lush, shady, rambling property with an amazing choice of rooms and restaurants. *Lamane* is Berber for "confidence," and there's been a healthy dose of it involved in this riad's construction. At the entrance is a two-level building with very large, modern rooms built in a *tabout* and *tadelakt* combination; ask for the Waha room with its private balcony. At the rear of the property are seven individual bungalows with more combinations of *tabout* and *tadelakt,* along with colorful Iraqi glass, heavy wood furniture, and local textiles. With toilets designed like royal thrones and ornate metal and bone dressers, these rooms border precariously between chic and tacky, but there's no doubting the five-star intent. To one side of the property are five furnished Berber tents with lockable doors and a communal ablutions block. These tents, however, are without air-conditioning and are oppressively hot for most of the year. In between the two sets of accommodations are two restaurants—one under a large Berber tent and the other in a more solid structure—both of them with a lounge and low-lying tables. Here you'll also find a glorious, keyhole-shape pool, though it's not the most private of locations, and the sub-Sahara theme Bar Amdicar with camel-leather chairs and palm trees rising through the ceiling. There's also a third restaurant at the entrance of the property. Nonguests are welcome for meals; three-course set menus of very good Moroccan cuisine cost 150dh ($19/£9.40).

Amezrou palmeraie, Amezrou. Cross the Oued Dra, and turn right before the irrigation channel. ☎ **024/848388.** Fax 024/848389. www.riadlamane.com. 19 units. 1,000dh ($125/£63) double room; 1,200dh ($150/£75) double bungalow; 250dh ($31/£16) per person Berber tent. Children under 5 stay free in parent's room. Rates include half board. MC, V. Parking. **Amenities:** 3 restaurants; bar (unlicensed); pool. *In room:* A/C, fridge.

Villa Zagora ⭐⭐⭐   From the moment you enter the walled garden of Villa Zagora, the heat and dust you've endured to get here rapidly begin to recede. Michèle Arnaud's little kasbah is a true retreat, set below the road level in the Amezrou palmeraie. A wide veranda looks out over a large, multilevel garden that affords plenty of private, shaded areas. Here you'll also find a heavenly pool that is kept crystal clear by jack-of-all-trades Ahmed. Inside the two-story villa is a small inner courtyard, dining room with fireplace, plus a large suite with a private terrace and small lounge. The other rooms are located on the first floor; room no. 5 has its own balcony looking out over the irrigation channel into the palmeraie. Personal touches include mosquito netting over the large windows and heaps of wardrobe space. On the rooftop terrace is a Berber tent with separate bathroom, which is offered to small groups or families. Michèle and manager Mohammed Haoua, who speaks perfect English, keep everything simple, quiet, and running smoothly.

Amezrou Palmeraie, Amezrou. Turn left at Amezrou T-junction after crossing Oued Dra. ☎ **024/846093.** www.mavilla ausahara.com. 6 units. 572dh ($72/£36) double; 726dh–990dh ($91–$124/£45–£62) double with private bathroom; 220dh ($28/£14) per person in Berber tent. Children 4–12 100dh ($13/£6.25) discount in parent's room; under 4 free. Rates include breakfast. AE, MC, V. **Amenities:** Restaurant; pool. *In room:* A/C, fan.

M'HAMID

If you need to stay the night in M'hamid, the hotels Sahara and Elghzlane offer very basic rooms for around 120dh ($15/£7.50) double. Five hundred meters (⅓ mile) to the west, across the Oued Dra, is Hassan Naamani's **Relais Hamada du Dra** (☎/fax **024/848086** or 062/132154; www.relaishamadadudraa.com). Set amongst pleasant grounds of palm, olive, and oleander trees are two en-suite rooms and six Berber tents with communal bathrooms for around 80dh ($10/£5) per person. There's a pool and an on-site restaurant with a large central fireplace.

An alternative to staying in M'hamid is the **tented camp,** or *bivouac,* of Zbar Travel (p. 190), about 2km (1¼ miles) south of the village. Nine Berber tents and one restaurant tent encircle the small campsite, with an ablutions block with toilets and hot showers set to one side. Cost is 200dh ($25/£13) per person including all meals.

Dar Azawad ⭐⭐⭐   On the road into M'hamid, in a palm grove called Ouled Driss, is Vincent Jaquet and Christian Jeannerot's stunning Dar Azawad. At one with its surroundings, each of the 15 individually decorated mini-kasbahs—built by local artisans with only local materials—are both rustic and luxurious, thanks to Vincent's natural eye for flair and detail. *Tabout* walls hold up palm tree beams and bamboo ceilings, and shiny, earthy *tadelakt*-rendered bathrooms house large walk-in showers. There are also eight Berber tents with private bathrooms. All rooms and tents are furnished with local cloth and artifacts that Vincent has picked up around Morocco. At the entrance to the property is a large reception-cum-bar that leads out to the heavenly, crystal-clear swimming pool. Set to one side is the restaurant that bears the stamp of Vincent's 12 years under legendary French chef Joël Robuchon. Nonguests are welcome for lunch and dinner. Dar Azawad is heavily involved with the development of Ouled Driss, ranging from employing and training villagers to providing transport for local schoolchildren.

Ouled Driss, M'hamid. © **024/848730.** www.darazawad.com. 23 units. 1,400dh–1,800dh ($175–$225/£88–£113) double; 1,000dh ($125/£63) double tent. Children 2–12 50% discount in parent's room; under 2 free. Discounts for stays of 2 nights or longer. Rates include half board. Lunch or dinner *menu du jour* 150dh ($19/£9.40). MC, V with 5% fee. On-site parking. **Amenities:** Restaurant; bar; pool. *In room:* A/C, no phone.

ZAGORA

Hôtel la Palmeraie   Zagora's first hotel was built in 1950 and has been under the management of the Zouzi family since 1969. The old dame has definitely seen grander times, but her large rooms are still the budget traveler's best option in Zagora. Travelers have a choice of rooms with shared bathrooms, private bathrooms, or private bathrooms and air-conditioning. The hotel's public areas are very popular, with a separate bar and restaurant serving an outdoor area that includes shaded tables and a swimming pool. A three-course set menu for 90dh ($11/£5.65) is a pretty good value, offering eggplant salad, beef tagine or vegetable couscous, fresh fruit, and more. The beer here is cold and cheap.

Bd. Mohammed V, at the Amezrou/Foum Zguid junction. © **024/847008.** Fax 024/847878. 57 units. 90dh–120dh ($11–$15/£5.65–£7.50) single; 130dh–210dh ($16–$26/£8.15–£13) double. Breakfast 24dh ($3/£1.50). No credit cards. On-site parking. **Amenities:** Restaurant; bar; pool. *In room:* A/C (some), no phone.

3 Dadès Gorge & Dadès Valley

From humble beginnings, the Oued Dadès carved a trail south through the High Atlas mountains before veering west to form the Dadès Valley. With the semi-desert to one side and often snowcapped peaks on the other, the journey alongside the Oued Dadès from the top of its gorge to its spring-fed palm groves is one of the most tranquil and scenic in Morocco.

GETTING THERE

The highway between Ouarzazate and Er Rachidia/Erfoud passes through Boumalne du Dadès, the main transport hub of the Dadès Valley, as well as the town of El Kelaa M'gouna and the village of Skoura.

BY BUS   Buses depart daily for the region from Casablanca (12–13 hr.; 160dh–180dh/ $20–$23/£10–£11); Er Rachidia (4–5 hr.; 35dh–50dh/$4.40–$6.25/£2.20–£3.15); Erfoud (5–6 hr.; 50dh–70dh/$6.25–$8.75/£3.15–£4.40); Tinerhir (2–3 hr.; 15dh– 25dh/$1.90–$3.15/95p–£1.55); and Zagora (5–6 hr.; 50dh–70dh/$6.25–$8.75/£3.15– £4.40).

BY *GRAND* TAXI   There are always *grands* taxis running the short distances between Ouarzazate and Skoura, Skoura and El Kelaa M'gouna, El Kelaa M'gouna and Boumalne du Dadès, and Boumalne du Dadès and Tinerhir. Fares range from 10dh to 25dh ($1.25–$3.15/65p–£1.55). *Grands* taxis and minibuses run fairly frequently throughout the day from Boumalne du Dadès up the Dadès Gorge to Msemrir, the village at the top of the gorge.

VISITOR INFORMATION

In Boumalne du Dadès is the **Bureau des Guides,** next to Cafe des Fleurs at the west end of the town center (© **067/593292;** hamou57@viola.fr). Born and bred in Boumalne du Dadès and an official guide since 1995, Hamou Aït Lhou is a fountain of knowledge on the geology and culture of the Dadès. He can arrange all manner of outings and treks (for example, a full-day trek at the Dadès Gorge, including lunch with a Berber family, for 250dh/$31/£16 per person), or can simply impart some knowledge for those going their own way. The small bureau is open daily when he's not out in the field.

FAST FACTS The main Tinerhir-Ouarzazate highway runs through the small town center of Boumalne du Dadès as avenue Mohammed V. Here you'll find a branch of **Banque Populaire** (✆ 024/808623) with a bureau de change and ATM, open Monday to Friday 8:15am to 3:45pm.

Pharmacie du Dadès (✆ 024/807683) is opposite the mosque, open Monday to Saturday 7:30am to 1pm, 3 to 8pm, and 9:30pm to 1am. Next door is **Taziri Net** cybercafe, open daily 9am to 11pm.

WHAT TO SEE & DO

Dadès Gorge ✫✫✫ This is a narrow, winding, and simply spectacular gorge, and the 35km (22-mile) drive along its southern section is one of the best in Morocco. At times the gorge can be wide and low, but at other times the cliff face is up to .5km (⅓ mile) deep. The gorge narrows considerably near the village of Aït Oudinar (25km/16 miles from the Boulmalne du Dadès), and the road ascends rapidly in a series of hairpin bends before rejoining the river. After passing through a very narrow and picturesque section, the gorge opens up to continue into the High Atlas. There are plenty of viewpoints along the way, and the villages dotted along its path are just as scenic as the gorge itself.

Boumalne du Dadès, 124km (77 miles) NE from Ouarzazate, 108km (67 miles) SW from Tinerhir. Scenic drive for 35km (22 miles) from turnoff at south entrance to Boumalne du Dadès.

Dadès Valley This valley stretches more than 70km (43 miles) from Boulmane du Dadès to the Skoura palm grove and is coined the Valley of the Kasbahs with good reason. In centuries past this was a lawless, dangerous land, and to protect themselves from marauding invaders and continuous battles between rival clans, families erected hundreds of castles along the fertile valley floor. These kasbahs were made of *tabout* and palm-tree beams, but since the 1930s, times have not been so dangerous, and many kasbahs have begun to rejoin the earth from whence they came as families move into more modern housing, sometimes located right next to the original kasbah. A section of the valley has taken to rose farming, and there are numerous shops along the highway selling rose water, oil, soap, and other products.

43–113km (27–70 miles) NE from Ouarzazate, 53km–123km (33–76 miles) SW from Tinerhir.

WHERE TO STAY
DADES GORGE

Auberge Le Vieux Château du Dadès This long, narrow hotel, squeezed between the road and Oued Dadès, offers very good value rooms with a million-dollar-view. Various standards of reasonable size, simply furnished rooms are available. All come with a private bathroom and some have river views. There are also some larger rooms with their own riverside balcony; try to ignore the ghastly pink bathrooms. Although air-conditioning is rarely needed, at press time four new rooms were being constructed and will include this amenity. A large restaurant services both guests and day-trippers. Furnished with Moroccan-style low-lying tables, the setting is enhanced by the constant background sound of the flowing river and birdsong. At times this hotel can be dead quiet and lacks a lively atmosphere, but that's not what you're here for anyway. The river can be accessed directly from the hotel.

Rte. des Gorges du Dadès, Km 27. © 024/831261. Fax 024/830221. 30 units. 360dh ($45/£23) double. Children 6–13 50% discount in parent's room; under 6 free. Rates include half board. No credit cards. Off-road parking. **Amenities:** Restaurant. *In room:* No phone.

Hotel Berbere de la Montagne ♠

This small riverside inn is in a beautiful, shady location at the end of the dramatic section of the gorge, just as it begins to widen and head farther into the mountains. The tall poplar trees add a European feel to Mohamed Asmoun's establishment, set in large pleasant grounds with plenty of open space to find a sunny or shady spot to watch the river or read a book. Inside you'll find small, simply furnished rooms with white walls and bamboo ceilings, some with a narrow bathroom and others sharing facilities. The rooms open inward to a central sitting room. On the ground floor is a cozy restaurant/salon, with a well-used fireplace, that serves delicious home-style Moroccan fare. Meals can also be taken on a shady outdoor terrace, and nonguests are welcome.

Rte. des Gorges du Dadès, Km 34. ©/fax 024/830228. www.berbere-montagne.ift.fr. 10 units. 300dh ($38/£19) double (shared bathroom); 560dh ($70/£35) double (private bathroom). Children 5–15 100dh ($13/£6.25) in parent's room; under 5 free. Rates include half board. MC, V. On-site parking. **Amenities:** Restaurant. *In room:* A/C or fan.

Hotel Timzzillite *Finds*

Mohamd Arif, from the nearby village of Aït Oufi, has built his restaurant-hotel atop a sheer cliff face .5km (⅓ mile) up from the Oued Dadès below. The rooms are blessed with stunning, unobstructed views looking southward down the gorge, and are simply but tastefully furnished with large beds, a small table, and a narrow bathroom. Each room has a walk-in shower fed by an individual gas hot-water system. On the levels closer to the road are a large restaurant-salon (with a gas heater for the colder months) and the roadside cafe and terrace complete with Berber tent, swings for the kids, wrought-iron tables, and a small shop selling basic necessities. Nonguests are welcome. The hotel is in an isolated section of the gorge, and the silence and solitude offered by staying here are undoubtedly the attraction.

Rte. des Gorges du Dadès, Km 28. © 077/264347. 4 units. 500dh ($63/£31) double. Rates include half board. No credit cards. On-site parking. **Amenities:** Restaurant. *In room:* No phone.

DADES VALLEY
Skoura

The Skoura palm grove was created in the 12th century by the Almohad sultan Yacoub el Mansour and today is still where some of the best dates in the country are grown alongside orchards of almonds and figs.

Dar Ahlam ♠♠♠ *Kids*

Down a winding track and across the dry Oued Dadès sits the inconspicuous front door to one of Morocco's premier accommodations. Set amidst 2 hectares (5 acres) of gardens, the "House of Dreams" is the work of Frenchman Thierry Teyssier. Within a renovated 1920s kasbah, every tiny detail—and I mean every tiny detail—has been considered, designed, and immaculately styled by Thierry and a team of professionals that include a landscaper, *parfumeur,* chef and *pâtissier,* and an interior-lighting specialist. The result is a five-star experience from the moment you are greeted at the door by English-speaking managers Jean Luc and Anna. Earthy colors and lots of natural cloth abound, be it in the grand salon, where aperitifs and digestifs are taken each night, or the different theme suites and villas. No two rooms are alike: The Riad suite has a claw-foot tub for two, and the Ethnique suite has a decidedly sub-Saharan feel.

The villas are perfect for families, with individual pools and multiple bedrooms. The cuisine is *nouvelle Marocain,* and most of the ingredients are sourced from the on-site vegetable garden. Meals are taken wherever and whenever you wish. There's a large out-door heated swimming pool, hammam, and massage room. You are also assigned your own personal guide—one of more than 25 staff from villages within the Skoura palmeraie—who meets you upon arrival to discuss what you want to see or do, which can include biking through the palmeraie, hiking in the nearby Atlas, hot-air ballooning, or a candle-lit dinner at dusk beside a secluded oasis. Dar Ahlam is very expensive and out of the way, but this is one place that delivers on its promises.

Kasbah Madini, Douar Oulad Sheik Ali, Skoura palmeraie. Directions given upon reservation; pickup from Marrakech or Ouarzazate available. (024/852239. Fax 024/852090. www.darahlam.com or www.maisonsdesreves.com for reservations. 12 units. 8,250dh–15,400dh ($1,031–$1,925/£516–£963). Rates all-inclusive, including meals, drinks, laundry, and activities. AE, MC, V. Closed mid-July to mid-August. **Amenities:** Restaurant; pool; hammam; fragrance salon and shop; massage room. *In room:* A/C, fireplace, safe, no phone.

4 Todra Palmeraie & Gorge

This is one of Morocco's most visited natural sights. From the former oasis (now major town) of Tinerhir, the lush **Todra Palmeraie** ✶✶✶ that feeds off the Oued Todra winds upstream for 15km (9⅓ miles) before reaching the entrance to **Todra Gorge** ✶✶✶. The palmeraie is a stunning sight, a river of green slicing through the otherwise endless, rocky, brown landscape. Down here is a thriving agricultural industry—palm and fruit trees, crops of grains and vegetables—that supplies the region year-round. This is possible thanks to the Oued Todra that rises above the ground opposite the Hotel Yasmina (p. 200) to casually flow down to Tinerhir before again descending below the earth to feed the numerous palm groves farther down its course. There are a couple of handy viewpoints alongside the road.

Understandably popular with tour groups, independent travelers, and Moroccans, Todra Gorge can be quite busy some days, but it's worth it for the first view from its narrow mouth. Only 50m (165 ft.) across and with 300m-high (985-ft.) walls, this is the gorge at its most dramatic. During certain times of the year, the height of the cliffs and the axis of the sun prevent any direct sunlight from reaching the gorge's floor. Mid- to late afternoon is generally the best time to visit, as the sun is absorbed by the gorge's walls and produces beautiful shades of orange and red. The largely hidden Oued Todra emerges as a spring here, and the cool stream is a nice spot to dip your toes and watch the comings and goings of visitors and locals. The gorge, 300m (985 ft.) in length, opens up into a valley on the northern end, which is popular with hikers. The road is tarred from here to the village of Tamatoucht, 17km (11 miles) farther up, and there are usually roadside Berber tents selling water along the way.

GETTING THERE

BY BUS Buses depart daily for Tinerhir from Casablanca (11 hr.; 150dh/$19/ £9.40); Er Rachidia (3 hr.; 35dh–50dh/$4.40–$6.25/£2.20–£3.15); Erfoud (4 hr.; 50dh/$6.25/£3.15); Marrakech (10 hr.; 100dh/$13/£6.25); and Ouarzazate (5 hr.; 45dh/$5.65/£2.80). They operate on, or across the road from, place Principale, on the west side of the gardens in the center of town.

BY *GRAND* TAXI *Grands* taxis operate throughout the day to Tinerhir from Ouarzazate (4 hr.; 55dh/$6.90/£3.45) via Boumalne du Dadès (1 hr.; 15dh/$1.90/ 95p); Erfoud (3 hr.; 50dh/$6.25/£3.15); and Er Rachidia (3 hr.; 50dh/$6.25/£3.15). *Grands* taxis park on the east side of the gardens. From here you can also catch a *grand* taxi heading up the Todra Palmerie to the gorge (30 min.; 10dh/$1.25/65p). Chartering one for the return journey to Todra Gorge will cost around 200dh ($25/£13) for a couple of hours.

FAST FACTS In the bustling town center of Tinerhir, you'll find most services within a .5km (⅓ mile) along avenue Mohammed V, the main Ouarzazate–Er Rachidia road.

At the west end of this stretch are branches of the banks **BMCE** (© 024/870694), **Credit du Maroc** (© 024/803562), and **Banque Populaire** (© 024/894138), all with ATMs and bureaus de change, open Monday to Friday 8:15am to 3:45pm.

Tinerhir's post office is in the *grand* taxi parking lot on the east side of the gardens. It's open Monday to Friday 8am to 4:15pm and Saturday 8 to 11:45am.

Pharmacie Todgha (© 024/834166) is at the east end of avenue Mohammed V, open Monday to Friday 8:30am to 12:30pm and 3:30 to 7:30pm, and Saturday 8:30am to 12:30pm.

Internet can be accessed at **Fecom,** in the small square off avenue Mohammed V, opposite the gardens. The store also sells computer accessories and blank CDs, and is open daily 8:30am to noon and 3 to 8pm.

Labo Photo al Fath, next to Pharmacie Todgha, sells and processes film and has a small stock of memory cards, batteries, and battery chargers. It's open daily 9am to noon and 2:30 to 8pm.

WHAT TO SEE & DO

Both the Todra Palmeraie and Todra Gorge are equally scenic and fascinating, and I recommend you explore both by foot. Access paths down into the palmeraie are dotted along the course of the 15km (9⅓ miles) road that runs from Tinerhir. The gorge is also very popular with rock climbers.

English-speaking El Houssaïne ("call me Hassan") Abdel Fadel (© 070/223076, or ask at Hotel Yasmina) is from the Aït Ousal clan that have lived in the palmeraie for centuries. Joining him for even half a day will leave you with a greater knowledge of the botany and geology of the Todra and deeper affection for the people who live here. Full-day walks along the palmeraie floor or up the gorge, including lunch with his family (palmeraie) or local shepherds in a cave (gorge), cost 100dh ($13/£6.25) per person. Full-day mule treks, mountain biking, and rock climbing (with equipment) can also be organized.

WHERE TO STAY

Hotel Amazir *Finds* Though it opened in 2001, the small and cheerful Amazir still feels fresh and new. The hotel's location on a bend in the palmeraie makes it ideal for exploring the crops, palms, and fruit trees and absorbing the way of life here. The reasonable-size rooms are simply furnished, have private bathrooms, and are finished with Berber carpets and natural fiber curtains and bed covers. Some rooms have a balcony with either river or palmeraie views. The one suite, which can accommodate up to four people, has a balcony literally atop the river with comfortable cane lounges to enjoy the view. It's the sound of rushing water and bird song and the absence of traffic noise that I love about this place. The large ground-floor restaurant is Moroccan in style with *zellij* and an ornate stucco ceiling; a well-located fireplace is welcoming during the colder months. During summer the pool is very popular, along with the sun lounges sitting on its terrace, which overlooks the river. Campers can pitch their tents on the palmeraie floor for 20dh ($2.50/£1.25).

10km Route des Gorge, Tinerhir. ℂ **024/895109.** Fax 024/895050. www.lamazir.com. 20 units. 600dh ($75/£38) double; 800dh ($100/£50) suite. Children 6–16 50% discount in parent's room; under 6 free. Christmas/New Year supplement applies. Rates include half board. MC, V with 5% fee. Covered parking. **Amenities:** Restaurant; pool. *In room:* A/C.

Hotel Yasmina   This is the better of two hotels located in the narrow gorge, set against the sheer cliff face and directly next to the Todra spring. Owned and managed by two local brothers, the Yasmina is a large hotel that's popular with all types of travelers, from adventure tour groups to 4WD convoys. There's a choice of standard or newer rooms; all of them are pretty basic but clean and comfortable. They also cater to day-trippers who visit the gorge, hence the four restaurants. A large Berber tent with a Moroccan lounge looks out over the spring and is the recommended place to take meals and relax with a book or chat with one of the many fellow travelers. The restaurant pumps out a lot of meals during the day, yet the soups, tagines (*kefta* with egg is a specialty), and fresh fruit have hit the spot for me every time. The twin rooftop terraces afford the best view of the gorge—a favorite pastime is sitting back and counting rock-climbing goats—and budget travelers can sleep under the stars here on the mattresses provided. There are also a few rooftop rooms, but they can become oppressively hot during the summer. The hotel is powered by a diesel generator that is switched off around midnight, but it's located about 50m (164 ft.) from the hotel and rarely upsets with its noise.

Todra Gorge, Tinerhir. ℂ **024/895118.** Fax 024/895075. www.todragorge.com. 48 units. 400dh ($50/£25) double; 50dh ($6.25/£3.15) roof-terrace mattress. Rates include half board. No credit cards. On-site parking. **Amenities:** Restaurant. *In room:* No phone.

5 Ziz Valley & Desert Dunes

The Ziz River leaves its craggy gorges behind (p. 174) at the city of Er Rachidia and continues its southward journey for another 100km (62 miles) along the Ziz Valley to the Moroccan pre-Sahara (*hammada*). Along the way, the largely hidden river feeds a string of oases and brings life to what would otherwise be dirt and stone. Dotted along its green belt are groups of kasbahs, or *ksour,* built to protect families in what was, until the 1930s, a largely lawless land. Some of the Ziz *ksour* have been abandoned for modern housing (the need for walled security no longer exists), but many are still standing and can be viewed from various roadside viewpoints alongside the valley.

At the valley's southern extreme is an area known as the Tafilalt, sometimes spelled Tafilalet or Tafilet. From the 8th to the 10th centuries, this was an independent kingdom, wealthy from its trading role on the ancient Saharan caravan routes traveling through here between west and northeast Africa. *Filalis,* the people of the Tafilalt, have kept this independent streak through the centuries. The Alaouites, still sitting on the throne today through King Mohammed VI, originated here with the desert sultan Moulay Rachid, and the French met with fierce resistance in the Tafilalt for almost 20 years before finally succeeding in their "pacification program" of the area.

The Oued Ziz completes its journey under the Erg Chebbi, a sweeping sea of sand 30km (19 miles) long and 7km (4⅓ miles) wide, isolated from the Sahara ocean by the Moroccan *hammada*. Ultimately, this is the destination that makes the hot journey worthwhile. The combination of 150m-high (490-ft.) dunes, sometimes gold, sometimes rust red, with indigo-robed nomads, oases of date palms, and trains of camels is the quintessential desert landscape.

One-Humped Wonder

If the Sahara is thought of as an ocean—an analogy that makes the history of the desert a little less strange—then the oases are its islands; the nomadic tribes its mariners, pilots, and pirates; and camels its ships.

The camel would seem to have been introduced into the Western Sahara in the first 500 years A.D. It has proven almost impossible to trace the stages of its immigration, but there is no doubt that its arrival represented a development as revolutionary in its way as the replacement of the stagecoach by the railroad. Prior to the coming of the camel, men used both horses and pack oxen in the Sahara. Neither of these animals fell completely out of use, but the camel, with its extraordinary capacity for traveling long distances with little or no water, was far better adapted for the strenuous conditions of the desert. The camel made possible the establishment of regular trading caravans across the Sahara. They also increased the insecurity of desert life by enabling the strong to prey more effectively on the weak, gradually transforming the political patterns of the Sahara.

GETTING THERE

Er Rachidia and Erfoud are the transport hubs of the Ziz. Er Rachidia holds no interest for travelers, and most bypass the city or catch connecting transport straight away. Heading for the dunes from the west, it's better to catch transport direct to Erfoud. If you're heading north after the dunes, you'll have to travel through Er Rachidia anyway.

BY BUS Er Rachidia is well served by the country's bus network, and buses arrive at least once a day from Casablanca (11 hr.; 170dh/$21/£11); Erfoud (1½ hr.; 15dh/$1.90/ 95p); Fes (9 hr.; 110dh/$14/£6.90); Marrakech (11 hr.; 135dh/$17/£8.45); Meknes (8½ hr.; 105dh/$13/£6.55); Midelt (3 hr.; 40dh–60dh/$5–$7.50/£2.50–£3.75); Ouarzazate (6 hr.; 65dh/$8.15/£4.05); Tinerhir (3 hr.; 35dh–50dh/$4.40–$6.25/£2.20–£3.15); and Zagora (10 hr.; 110dh/$14/£6.90). All buses, including CTM (© 035/572024), operate out of the central *gare routière* at the southwest entrance to the city.

Buses to Erfoud operate daily from Er Rachidia (1½ hr.; 15dh/$1.90/95p); Fes (9½ hr.; 100dh–110dh/$13–$14/£6.25–£6.90); Marrakech (10 hr.; 160dh–195dh/$20–$24/ £10–£12); Meknes (10 hr.; 100dh–110dh/$13–$14/£6.25–£6.90); Midelt (4½ hr.; 55dh–75dh/$6.90–$9.40/£3.45–£4.70); Ouarzazate (7 hr.; 90dh/$11/£5.65); and Tinerhir (4 hr.; 50dh/$6.25/£3.15). **CTM** (© 035/576886) operates from their office on boulevard Mohammed V, between place des F.A.R. and the main Er Rachidia–Merzouga road, avenue Moulay Ismail. All other bus companies come and go from place des F.A.R., about 300m (984 ft.) from avenue Moulay Ismail.

BY *GRAND* TAXI *Grands* taxis operate between Er Rachidia and Erfoud (1 hr.; 20dh/ $2.50/£1.25); Midelt (2 hr.; 35dh/$4.40/£2.20); and Tinerhir (3 hr.; 50dh/$6.25/ £3.15). *Grands* taxis in Erfoud operate from the bus station at place des F.A.R and run throughout the day to Tinerhir (3 hr.; 50dh/$6.25/£3.15).

To reach the village of Merzouga and the *auberges* nearby, *grands* taxis depart irregularly throughout the day from place des F.A.R. (20dh/$2.50/£1.25). Be firm and clear with regards to your chosen *auberge,* as some accommodations pay a commission to taxi drivers for clients.

BY CAR Thanks to the tar road from Erfoud to Merzouga and beyond, self-drivers no longer need a guide to reach the dunes. About 10km (6¼ miles) west of Rissani toward Merzouga, the various *auberges* have installed road signs to advise when to turn off the tar onto the sand and stone of the *hammada*. Follow the signs and stay on the worn tracks, and you'll be fine. An alternative route heads east from the center of Erfoud and arrives at the northern end of Erg Chebbi, but this should only be attempted with a guide and preferably in a 4WD vehicle.

FAST FACTS Most services in Erfoud are found on avenue Moulay Ismail (the main Er Rachidia–Merzouga road) or boulevard Mohammed V, which connects place des F.A.R. with avenue Moulay Ismail.

Branches of **BMCE** (© 035/530284) and **Banque Populaire** (© 035/561907), both with ATMs and bureaux de change, are on avenue Moulay Ismail, open Monday to Friday 8:15am to 3:45pm.

Erfoud's **post office** is on the corner of avenue Moulay Ismail and boulevard Mohammed V, open Monday to Friday 8am to 4:15pm and Saturday 8 to 11:45am.

The town's **police station** is on the south side of place des F.A.R.

Dr. Fatiha Lemjimer (© 035/576520 or 061/355684) has a clinic on rue al Moukawama at the southwestern edge of place des F.A.R.

Air-conditioned **First Net** cybercafe is opposite Superette Chez Adil, on avenue Moulay Ismail, and is open Saturday to Thursday 10am to midnight and Friday 2pm to midnight. It also has Wi-Fi access.

Superette Chez Adil is at the northeast end of avenue Moulay Ismail and sells a wide range of groceries, cold meats, dairy products, toiletries, and photographic supplies including memory cards. It's open daily 8am to 10pm.

Merzouga village (50km/31 miles south of Erfoud) is a dusty conglomeration of houses and shops servicing the local smattering of Erg Chebbi *auberges*. At the turnoff to the village from the highway is a new post office and bureau de change, open Monday to Friday 8am to 4:15pm and Saturday 8 to 11:45am. Just .8km (½ mile) farther is the village square, where you'll find some cafes, grocery stores, and a few shops selling souvenirs and film. There's also **Merzouga@Net** cybercafe and **Trans Sahara Pharmacie** (© 035/590689).

WHAT TO SEE & DO

An isolated wave of sand dunes some 30km (19 miles) long and 7km (4⅓ miles) wide, **Erg Chebbi** ✪✪✪ is definitely worth the journey to get there. Emotions of wonder and excitement usually accompany a traveler's first sight of this surreal mountain range–like mass of gold, pink, and red. The hot, hard, black *hammada* leading up to edge of Erg Chebbi only adds to the dramatic vista. A string of *auberges* run parallel to the dunes from west of Erfoud all the way south just beyond the village of Merzouga. Every one of them can organize camel treks into the dunes lasting 1 hour to overnight. An overnight excursion typically includes a dinner of mint tea, tagine, and fruit; bedding of blankets or rugs; and breakfast the next morning back at the *auberge*. For more information and recommendations, see p. 177 and p. 204.

Hassi Labied is a small hamlet north of Merzouga and about .5km (⅓ mile) from the highway; it's within walking distance from Dar el Janoub (p. 204) and Kasbah Mohayut (p. 205). Here you'll find Centre Shop selling groceries, spices, and photographic accessories, and Kem Kem, which has an irregular Internet service and rents out mountain bikes for 100dh ($13/£6.25) per day.

The Amraoui family, former nomads–turned–entrepreneurs, settled in Hassi Labied more than 40 years ago and has been welcoming visitors for 17 of those years into their **Dépôt Nomade** (ⓒ/fax **035/577303** or **061/259687**). Inside this air-conditioned treasure trove is a wealth of crafts and souvenirs. "We specialize in beauty," say Chez Amraoui, and the selection of carpets (some hard-to-find Bedouin Arabic carpets) in all colors and sizes confirms his sales pitch. In other rooms you'll find such diverse items as leather *poufes,* wind bellows, walking sticks, drums, cotton throws, lanterns, scarves, jewelry, and chess sets. There are flowing blue *gandoras* (for men) and caftans (for women) if you wish to dress like a local, as well as locally handmade shawls. It's open daily from 9am to 6pm, but they'll open up after hours on request. The village of Hassi Labied and Dépôt Nomade are 4km (2½ miles) north of Merzouga and 46km (29 miles) south of Erfoud.

WHERE TO STAY & DINE IN ERFOUD

Kasbah Tizimi 𝒻 These are the best accommodations in Erfoud and it's worth staying 2 nights if you've come out of the desert but want to lap up some more sun. A sprawling kasbah-style complex on the outskirts of town, Kasbah Tizimi has a range of rooms, suites, and apartments spread out over three buildings. The kasbah complex was built in 1997, and here you'll find very good value rooms with clay-tile floors, walk-in showers, and high bamboo ceilings simply furnished and with local Berber-design bed covers. The riad complex opened in 2003, and the rooms are more modern in style and larger than those in the kasbah. The separate suites overlook the pool and are much larger, with four-poster beds, an L-shape lounge, and tub/shower combos. Also overlooking the pool are a couple of two-room apartments that can accommodate a family of five.

The large swimming pool is very clean but could do with a few more sun lounges and umbrellas. An underused poolside snack bar is handy for those staying in for the day. Small gardens of oleander and bougainvillea are set throughout the property, attracting chirpy finches and adding a tranquil touch to an already peaceful ambience. A large restaurant, decorated in an unfortunate sky- and navy-blue combination, serves the tour bus masses at lunchtime, but the very decent breakfasts and dinners are thankfully a more private affair. A large *salon de thé,* with wide-screen TV and lots of comfortable lounges, leads to a well-stocked bar.

The service throughout the Tizimi is professional and relaxed, and any place in Morocco that has an Employee of the Month award must be doing something right. It's about a 30-minute walk to the center of Erfoud, but Kasbah Tizimi's location isn't as much of a negative as one might first assume.

Rte. de Jorf (.5km/⅓ mile along Erfoud-Tinejdad rd.), Erfoud. ⓒ 035/576179 or 035/577374. Fax 035/577375. www. kasbahtizimi.com. 73 units. Kasbah room 487dh ($61/£30) double; riad room 600dh ($75/£38) double; 900dh ($113/£56) suite; 1,500dh ($188/£94) apt. Low-season prices available. Children 2–12 25% discount in parent's room; under 2 free. TPT not included. MC, V. Covered parking. **Amenities:** Restaurant; lounge; bar; pool; Internet. *In room:* A/C, satellite TV (apt and suite).

Restaurant al Andalous MOROCCAN/INTERNATIONAL Abdelkarim M'Sid's clean white restaurant serves up a no-nonsense menu of good value dishes. Choices include salads, omelets, and soups (try the *harira*), along with tagines, spaghetti bolognese, *pastilla,* and grilled meats. He can also cook up a lamb *mechoui* (roast) with a few hours' notice. The local specialty of *tagine de kalia* (minced mutton with a spicy mix of tomatoes, onion, egg, and peppers) is recommended. There's an adjoining cafe that serves a pastry and coffee/tea breakfast. Alcohol is not available for purchase, but you can bring your own.

North end of av. Moulay Ismail. ☎ 035/578188 or 066/040179. Main courses 65dh–95dh ($8.15–$12/£4.05–£5.95); *tagine de kalia* 65dh ($8.15/£4.05). No credit cards. Daily 7am–11pm.

Restaurant Dakar MOROCCAN   This new restaurant has a very pleasant garden setting (despite a large, tacky fountain) and an air-conditioned dining area decorated in natural tones. The Moroccan menu has the usual choice of tagines, omelets, grilled meats, and couscous. They also offer *medfouna filalia,* but I recommend the Restaurant des Dunes' wood-fire oven for this (see below). Three-course set menus offering a choice of salads and tagines with a fruit dessert are a good value. Alcohol is not available for purchase, but you can bring your own.

North end of av. Moulay Ismail, opposite Ziz petrol station, Erfoud. ☎ 035/578554 or 061/351652. Main courses 40dh–80dh ($5–$10/£2.50–£5); set menus 70dh ($8.75/£4.40). No credit cards. Daily 7am–11pm.

Restaurant des Dunes MOROCCAN/ITALIAN   This restaurant, located at the north end of avenue Moulay Ismail, is popular with independent travelers. The Moroccan menu includes the usual standards of tagine, couscous, and brochettes, but also offers two local specialties: *tagine de kalia* and a traditional Moroccan flat loaf, *medfouna filalia,* stuffed with your choice of meat or vegetable and baked in a wood-fire oven. There's also a wide choice of Moroccan three-course set menus. The oven pumps out a good selection of pizzas as well. The stone-wall interior with wood beams and bamboo ceiling is furnished with wrought-iron tables and high-back chairs. Across the road is the original restaurant, now a popular cafe.

North end of av. Moulay Ismail, opposite Ziz petrol station, Erfoud. ☎ 035/576793. Fax 035/577765. Pizzas and *medfouna filalia* 40dh–50dh ($5–$6.25/£2.50–£3.15); *tagine de kalia* 40dh ($5/£2.50); main courses 40dh–55dh ($5–$6.90/£2.50–£3.45); set menus 75dh–100dh ($9.40–$13/£4.70–£6.25). No credit cards. Daily noon–3pm and 6–10pm.

WHERE TO STAY & DINE IN ERG CHEBBI

Dar el Janoub ★★   Opened in 2005, the "House of the South" is one of the most pleasant *auberges* on the dunes. The lobby wall is adorned with symbols of the Berber alphabet, and from there on managers Omar and Driss are at your service. The rooms and suites are all constructed from *tabout,* and throughout the walled property this earthy theme continues. Inside the small rooms is an accent wall of pastel-color *tadelakt,* bamboo ceilings, and neutral bedcovers made from local textiles. The bathrooms have walk-in showers and large shower heads. Room nos. 5, 7, 8, 10, and 11 all have dune frontage and can be requested with your reservation. As consolation, rooms that don't enjoy dune frontage have a small, individual rooftop terrace with dune views. The suites are larger and all open onto the dunes. All the rooms and suites are deliberately void of TVs and phones to sustain the peaceful atmosphere. A large pool—one of the first at Erg Chebbi—is well designed, allowing for some privacy while sunbathing. A very large restaurant is both air-conditioned and has a fireplace. The restaurant opens out to a ground-floor terrace with cane lounges, wrought-iron tables, and direct access to the dunes. An upstairs terrace affords even clearer dune views. Nonguests are welcome to use both the pool and restaurant.

Hassi Labied; turn off 3km (1¾ miles) before Merzouga. ☎/fax 035/577852 or 068/471516. www.dareljanoub.com. 21 units. 1,000dh ($125/£63) double; 1,200dh–1,400dh ($150–$175/£75–£88) suite. Children 3–12 50% discount in parent's room; under 3 free. Rates include half board. TPT not included. Nonguests pay 50dh ($6.25/£3.15) for swimming pool; 120dh ($15/£7.50) lunch or dinner. MC, V. **Amenities:** Restaurant; pool. *In room:* A/C.

Hotel Yasmina   Located at the less busy, north end of Erg Chebbi, the Yasmina has long been a favorite for the budget conscious. A recent addition of a swimming pool has perhaps lifted the prestige of the Yasmina, but the same laid-back, international-traveler vibe remains. The large rooms are in somewhat garish shades but are light, clean, and cool with private bathrooms. Mattresses on the rooftop terrace are also available. The dunes begin right outside the large salon, where the staff—all local lads—usually start up a jamming drum session after dinner, which is served in a separate, refined restaurant (bring your own alcohol). Many adventure-tour groups pass through here, but rather than a distraction, this only adds to the atmosphere. A seasonal lake often forms beside the hotel after spring rains, attracting flamingoes.

Erg Chebbi; look for sign about 10km (6¼ miles) west of Rissani. ⓒ 061/351667. Fax 035/774071. www.hotel yasminamerzouga.com. 20 units. 500dh ($63/£31) double. Children under 5 stay free in parent's room. Rates include half board. TPT not included. No credit cards. **Amenities:** Restaurant; pool. *In room:* No phone.

Kasbah Mohayut ✿✿✿   Mohmmed Oubadi and his family are the friendly, welcoming hosts in this rambling kasbah that used to be their home. Built in *tabout* throughout with ceilings supported by palm-tree beams, there are various room styles available, all of them simply furnished with low-lying beds covered with handmade textiles, a small lounge, and good-size bathrooms. The rooms aren't well lit with natural or artificial light, which keeps them cool, but nighttime readers will need to bring a light. Room nos. 11 and 12 are more recent additions, are poolside, and have their own fireplace. Tranquil inner courtyards connect the series of buildings within the walled kasbah, the largest courtyard housing the keyhole-shape pool surrounded by plenty of sun lounges and chairs. To accentuate the silence on the dunes, which come right up to the kasbah walls, the public areas, which include an air-conditioned restaurant (bring your own alcohol) and rooftop terrace, are concentrated at the front of the property away from the dunes. Four covered parking bays will be appreciated by self-drivers.

Hassi Labied; turn off 4km (2½ miles) before Merzouga. ⓒ **066/039185.** Fax 035/578428. www.mohayut.com. 22 units. 400dh (50/£25) double; 500dh ($63/£31) double (new rooms). Children 4–10 120dh ($15/£7.50) in parent's room; under 4 free. Rates include half board. TPT not included. No credit cards. **Amenities:** Restaurant; pool. *In room:* A/C.

8

Fes, Meknes & the Middle Atlas

Within this chapter lies the soul of Morocco. With its jet-setting cousins Casablanca and Marrakech attracting the glitter, and the desert palmeraies to the south attracting the gold, this region has, throughout the centuries, been the rock of the country.

The beginnings of the country started here, when Moulay Idriss I set foot in el-Maghreb el-Aksa, "the Far West," and found shelter amongst the Berber tribes living within the remnants of the Roman city of Volubilis. A great-grandson of the Prophet Mohammed, Moulay Idriss I and his son, Idriss II, created the first semblance of a unified, independent Morocco on the banks of the Wadi Fes. From here dynasties would come and go, but no matter where their power was based, Fes would always feature strongly in their plans.

The *zaouia* of Idriss I is in the holy city named in his honor, Moulay Idriss Zerhoun. Non-Muslims are now allowed to enter this town—though not the holy tomb—and it makes for a fantastic day trip when combined with a visit to Volubilis. Although direct Roman rule was relatively brief, this southernmost outpost of their empire comes to life with a walk along the city's excavated streets, houses, forum, and triumphal arch.

Most visitors travel here via Meknes, an imperial city built during the reign of Morocco's longest serving—and most notorious—ruler, the Sultan Moulay Ismail. His mausoleum, a peaceful, contemplative, and truly spiritual sanctuary, is one of only a few Moroccan monuments of this stature open to non-Muslims.

Throughout this relatively short time span, the quiet, welcoming range of the Middle Atlas has watched over the theatrics occurring down on the fertile plains. With its cool, temperate climate and forests of towering cedar, the Middle Atlas is a surprise to most visitors who take the time to venture up here from the twin imperial cities down below. In the past, time-strapped travelers would bypass this whole region, or at best visit Fes for a day or two on the way to coastal or desert destinations. But Fes is entering a renaissance period. Word is getting out that within a few hours airtime from the frantic, modern, Western world, there's a medieval city that still lives and breathes within its ancient walls.

1 Fes ★★★

Fes is the spiritual heart of Morocco and is the most ancient, and indeed the greatest, of the country's imperial cities. It's one of the undisputed highlights of any visit to Morocco. Within the walls of its medina, Fes el Bali (Old Fes), lies the world's largest intact medieval city. More than 9,500 narrow streets and dim alleyways wind endlessly up and down, around and around, crammed with people, music, noise, and smells.

Whether arriving from within Morocco or elsewhere, nothing can prepare you for this assault on the senses.

Fes means different things to different people. To some, it is a center of the decorative arts, world famous for its leather and metalwork and the skill of its master craftsmen, or *maâlem*. Others may see it as the home of the Kairouine Mosque, the second largest in North Africa and neighbor of the oldest university in the world. For others still, Fes conjures up an image of the quintessential fabled Arab city from a time when traveling merchants from the Middle East traded with nomads from the Sahara and Berbers from the mountains.

It was in the year 786, 150 years after the death of the Prophet Muhammad, that one of his descendants set foot in Morocco. Idriss Ben Abdallah Ben Hassan Ben Ali was destined to become Moulay Idriss, patron saint of Morocco and founder of Fes. Blamed for a failed rebellion against the Arabian Abbaysids, he had fled Baghdad and come to el-Maghreb el-Aksa of the Muslim world.

Idriss settled in the Roman city of Volubilis and was quickly accepted among the local Berbers as their spiritual leader, or *imam*. Before long, he established Morocco's first independent Islamic kingdom, the Idrissid dynasty. He began his empire (which was later named in his honor) near Volubilis, but during his short reign (he was poisoned in 791 by an Abbaysid assassin) he also laid the foundation for a new capital in a shallow basin of the Wadi Fes, strategically situated at the junction of Morocco's major trading routes. Idriss fathered a son, Idriss II, with a Berber woman, and by 809 the young Idriss set about continuing his father's work and began expanding the town of Fes in earnest.

The town's growth was rapid, boosted early in the 9th century by two waves of migrations that formed the religious and artistic base from which the city still emanates today. The first were Muslim refugees fleeing civil war in Cordoba, who settled on the east bank of the river in an area that became known as Adwat al Andalus, "the Andalusian Quarter." These Andalusians included craftsmen, merchants, and learned citizens who brought along their experience of urban life and their ancestral techniques in masonry and the craft industry. The second influx came from Jewish and Muslim immigrants from the holy Tunisian city of Kairouan, who brought with them their business acumen and spiritual knowledge. It was the Kairouanese who founded Fes's famed Kairouine Mosque and theological college. Together, these two migrations ensured that for centuries to come, Fes was to be a center of intellect and creativity.

The city continued to grow in the 11th century, with the coming of the Berber Almoravids who constructed Fes's ancient water and sewage system, an incredible feat of hydro-engineering that to this day is in full working order. The city's golden age, literally, came with the rise to power of the Merenids and their predecessors, the Wattasids. For 300 years, these dynasties ruled from Fes, which greatly benefited from the pious nature of their sultans (a building spree of mosques and *medersas* included the Bou Inania on Tala'a Kebira) as well as the expansion of the West African caravan routes and the gold, ivory, and slaves that came with them. They also constructed an entirely new city—Fes Jdid, or New Fes. In the 16th century, amid the chaos of the fall of Granada, the last Muslim kingdom in Spain, hundreds of thousands of Jewish and Muslim refugees fled to North Africa, many settling in Fes Jdid. From then on, Fes was to figure little in Moroccan history, as political power shifted to Meknes and Marrakech. That is, until 1912, when it became the unwilling stage for the signing of the infamous Treaty of Fes that handed Morocco to France and Spain. Open rebellion broke out just 2 weeks later, and 80 Europeans were lynched. The next day, the French bombarded the city and promptly moved the seat of power to Rabat. Although this may have initially appeared as a humiliating episode for the city, in a sense it actually reasserted its status as the center of national pride.

The city, it must be remembered, is not one but three. Constructed at different times in history and for different reasons, the combination of Fes el Bali, Fes Jdid, and the French-designed ville nouvelle was described to me by a local Fassi as *une ville authentique*—a real city. One finds things here that exist nowhere else." This uniqueness led, in 1980, to Fes becoming the first Islamic and Arab city to be designated a World Heritage site, joining Venice and Havana, among others. At the time, more than 300,000 people lived within the city's ancient walls, which were close to bursting at the seams. UNESCO recognition brought about a plan to rescue the city via the Agence pour la Dédensification et la Réhabilitation de la Médina de Fès, or ADER-FES. Since then, through various inducements, the population of Fes el Bali has been reduced to somewhere near 200,000 while the city's total urban area has grown to 800,000. In a project that could last as long as 20 years, ADER-FES has identified 11 *medersas,* 320 mosques, 270 *foundouks,* and more than 200 hammams, houses, or public ovens worthy of preservation. Some structures are famous and have undergone or are undergoing restoration already—for example, the Kairouine Mosque, the Bou Anania Medersa, the Nejjarine Fountain, and the Foundouk Nejjarine (see the Nejjarine Museum of Wooden Arts & Crafts on p. 231). Others are only known to locals, who feel they represent key aspects of the city's cultural heritage.

This resurgence of pride in the architectural beauty of Fes is also being helped along by increased flight arrivals into the city courtesy of the government's 2006 open-skies policy, and the seemingly weekly immigration of Westerners—including a marked increase of Brits—restoring and moving into the medina's old dars and riads. Whether this will turn Fes into the "new Marrakech" is a question being asked by some. Certainly, Fes has become one of the world's "in" exotic destinations in recent years, attracting a traveler that historically would have journeyed to places less confronting. The recent introduction into the medina of a Brigade Touristique to curtail the hassle from unregistered guides only adds to the city's marketable stature. For a city that desperately requires employment for its impatient youth, tourism can bring fast and direct economic benefits. But whether this comes at the expense of the very culture and tradition that attracts the traveler in the first place is yet to be seen. For the moment, Fes deserves all the attention she is receiving. To walk within its old walls is to witness a city that is heaving and claustrophobic, fascinating and frustrating, decrepit and majestic, inspirational and wondrous, and waiting to be discovered every day.

ORIENTATION
ARRIVING
BY PLANE   Despite more flight arrivals from the U.K. and Europe, thanks to the government's 2006 open-skies policy, Fes's airport appears able to handle the increase without the sort of expansion that is taking place in Marrakech. All domestic and international flights land at Fes-Saïss airport (*©* **035/624800**), 15km (9⅓ miles) south of the city. In the small arrivals and departures hall are rental-car services, an ATM, and two currency exchange booths open 8am to 8pm, although these hours seem flexible. Though you'll generally find a bank or bureau de change near your

accommodations, it's best to pick up some Moroccan dirham at the airport just in case. On the mezzanine level is a cafeteria, while on the ground floor is a small shop/*téléboutique* selling postcards. On the return leg of your trip, there's a duty-free shop after immigration; note that only major currencies and credit cards are accepted—dirham are not.

Many hotels and *maisons d'hôte* are happy to arrange an airport pickup for you, usually with one of their preferred taxi drivers for around 150dh ($19/£9.40). This is especially recommended if you are staying in the medina, as not all taxi drivers will know the location—and best drop-off point—of your accommodations. The drive from the airport to the ville nouvelle takes 15 to 20 minutes, 5 to 10 minutes more to the medina. Taxis are located directly outside of the airport, and the fare to anywhere in Fes is currently fixed at 160dh ($20/£10) up to 8pm and 200dh ($25/£13) after. Taxis from the airport (but not those operating around town) generally accept euros and sometimes U.S. dollars or British pounds, but you'll receive change only in dirham.

A local bus (no. 16) operates a fairly reliable service between the airport and train station. It runs every half-hour from 6am to 11pm, costs 3dh (40¢/20p), and takes about 30 minutes. The bus stop is directly outside the airport.

BY TRAIN   All trains arrive and depart from the city's sole station (© 035/930333), located in the ville nouvelle at place du Roi Faycal, about a 10-minute walk or very short taxi drive from avenue Hassan II. At press time, a new station was being built adjacent to the current building. Inside the original station are an ATM and a couple of ticket counters. There is luggage storage accessible from the building's exterior, where locked bags can be left for 10dh ($1.25/65p) per item per day; it's open daily from 6am to 8pm. There are usually red *petits* taxis waiting outside the station; a fare to avenue Hassan II or boulevard Mohammed V should cost no more than 5dh (65¢/30p), and to the medina, which is too far away to walk, should cost 10dh to 15dh ($1.25–$1.90/65p–95p). *Note:* Insist that any taxi driver use his meter.

Trains depart daily for Fes from most of the western half of Morocco (there are no trains in either the Atlas or Rif mountains or central Morocco and the oases). Some of the more popular routes are from Casablanca (4 hr.; 103dh–155dh/$13–$19/£6.45–£9.70); Marrakech (7½ hr.; 180dh–276dh/$23–$35/£11–£17); Meknes (45 min.; 18dh–26dh/$2.25–$3.25/£1.15–£1.65); Rabat (3 hr.; 76dh–115dh/$9.50–$14/£4.75–£7.20); and Tangier (5–6 hr.; 97dh–145dh/$12–$18/£6.05–£9.05). From destinations such as Agadir, Essaouira, and Tetouan, you'll be traveling all or part of your journey on the ONCF bus service Supratours. Reservations are only accepted up to 1 month prior to departure and can be made either over the phone (© 090/203040 from within Morocco only), at ticket booths at each station, or through authorized agents. Payment at the station is by cash only, but some agents will accept credit cards.

BY BUS   Buses to Fes arrive daily from almost everywhere in Morocco, including Agadir (12 hr.; 230dh–250dh/$29–$31/£14–£16); Casablanca (5 hr.; 80dh–90dh/$10–$11/£5–£5.65); Chefchaouen (5 hr.; 50dh–60dh/$6.25–$7.50/£3.15–£3.75); Erfoud (9½ hr.; 100dh–110dh/$13–$14/£6.25–£6.90); Marrakech (10 hr.; 150dh–170dh/$19–$21/£9.40–£11); Meknes (1 hr.; 20dh/$2.50/£1.25); Ouarzazate (14 hr.; 150dh/$19/£9.40); Rabat (4½ hr.; 50dh–60dh/$6.25–$7.50/£3.15–£3.75); and Tangier (6 hr.; 70dh–80dh/$8.75–$10/£4.40–£5).

Besides CTM services, which operate from their office in the ville nouvelle (see below), all long-distance bus companies arrive at the *gare routière* (© 035/732992), just outside the medina's walls, diagonally north of Bab Mahrouk. Open around the clock, it's a busy building consisting of ground-floor restaurants, cafes, and ticket counters, and offers a handy luggage storage service (5dh/65¢/30p per bag) open 6am to midnight.

Bab Mahrouk and nearby Bab Bou Jeloud are an easy walk across the double-lane road, as is Bab Aïn Zleten in the other direction—so long as you're not weighed down or battling the heat of the day. For other medina entrances (Bab Jdid, place Rcif, Bab Guissa, and Access Oued Zhoun) and the ville nouvelle, there are always plenty of *petits* taxis directly outside the *gare routière*. It shouldn't cost more than 10dh to 15dh ($1.25–$1.90/65p–95p) to reach your destination. For onward travel from Fes, all companies except CTM depart from the bus station, where they each have their own ticket booths (you must pay in cash). For an early-morning departure or during high season to Chefchaouen, Marrakech, and Tangier, it's advisable to purchase your ticket the day before. CTM (© 022/438282 central reservations; www.ctm.ma) operates from their own station on the corner of rue Tetouan and rue Kandar (© 035/732992) in the ville nouvelle. CTM's international services to Spain and France also operate from here. It's a 15-minute walk along rue Kandar and boulevard Mohammed V to place Mohammed V, or a short taxi ride.

BY *GRAND* TAXI   Most long-distance *grands* taxis operate throughout the day from the *gare routière,* including those for Meknes (20dh/$1.75/90p) and Rabat (55dh/$6.90/£3.45). Those plying the route to Ifrane (23dh/$2.90/£1.45) operate from a parking lot opposite the CTM station in the ville nouvelle.

BY CAR   Driving into Fes can be a bit daunting due to the various entries into the city, depending on where you're coming from. Arriving from Meknes or the airport, the main thoroughfare in the ville nouvelle, avenue Hassan II, is reasonably easy to locate by following the signs to Centre Ville. To head toward the medina from here is then relatively straightforward; simply head for the McDonald's and then continue straight. For Bab Jdid and place Rcif, continue straight until signposted to turn left. If your destination is Ahmed Mekouar Square, then make sure you turn left at the traffic lights at the bottom of the alley between the ville nouvelle and the medina, onto avenue Allal el Fassi. From here you continue straight to Ahmed Mekouar Square. For Bab Bou Jeloud, the *gare routière,* Bab Aïn Zleten, Bab Guissa, and Access Oued Zhoun, turn left off avenue Allal el Fassi onto avenue de l'Unesco to drive through the medina to the other side, through Bab Chems, where a right turn puts you on the main road alongside the western wall, from where you can access all of the above. The road from Chefchaouen/Ouezzane arrives at the northern edge of the medina, from where you can choose to follow the western or eastern side of the medina walls.

Parking on avenue Hassan II is relatively easy. For boulevard Mohammed V, which is one-way only, heading south from avenue Hassan II to place Mohammed V, there's a secure parking lot opposite the Central Marché and Jardin Lalla Amina. In the medina, there's a small parking lot on an open patch of land between Bab Mahrouk and Bab Bou Jeloud. Secure parking is found at Ahmed Mekouar Square (formerly place d'Istiqlal), Access Oued Zhoun, and Aïn Zleten; figure on paying 20dh ($2.50/£1.25) per day for secure parking. ***Note:*** Red-and-white-stripe curbing means no parking.

Unless you're driving out of Fes directly from the airport, car rental is best organized from your hotel. You don't need a car while in Fes, and navigating your way from the airport into the city is an unnecessary strain. Conversely, if you are driving into Fes from elsewhere and flying straight out, then dropping off your rental car at the airport is a good idea, as it is well signposted from most highways entering Fes.

VISITOR INFORMATION

There's a **Syndicat d'Initiative,** or tourist information bureau, on place Mohammed V (© 035/623460; fax 035/654370), open Monday to Friday 8:30am to noon and 2:30 to 6:30pm. It has friendly staff but is largely ineffectual.

The **Arabic Language Institute (ALIF)** and the **American Language Center** are located on the eastern edge of the ville nouvelle at 2 rue Ahmed Hiba (© 035/ 624850; fax 035/931608; www.alif-fes.com). They organize social and cultural events—usually for students only—and can be a good source of local information regarding home-stays and English-language teaching positions.

The best map/book of the medina is Hammad Berrada's *Fez from Bab to Bab, Walks in the Medina* (160dh/$20/£10; in English and French). The glossy spiral book is easy to carry, and includes good directions, interesting information, and hand-drawn maps to accompany 11 gate-to-gate walks. Included with the book is the most detailed map of the medina available. Most of the smaller *derbs* (lanes) are marked, and the color combination makes it easy to read. Another handy medina map is found in the Fes-Boulemane Regional Tourism Council's *The Fes Medina Tourist Circuits* (100dh/$13/ £6.25; in English and French). Thin and easy to carry, the book takes readers along six themed circuits with interesting info on the main sights along the way. These books are usually for sale at **Librairie Nouvelle** (© 035/685493), 46 av. Hassan II, next door to the Hotel de la Paix in the ville nouvelle. It's open Monday to Saturday 9am to 6:30pm (Fri closed noon–2:30pm). Some *maisons d'hôte* also sell them; ask your reception.

CITY LAYOUT

Fes's medina and ville nouvelle are clearly defined thanks to the Sebou Valley that separates the two. The medina consists of Fes el Bali, the original city where you'll spend most of your time, and Fes el Jdid, a 13th-century addition containing the former Jewish quarter and the Royal Palace.

Fes el Bali contains more than 9,500 alleys and lanes—almost all of them navigable only by foot—and for the traveler is the most geographically daunting of anywhere in Morocco. Bab Bou Jeloud receives the most pedestrian traffic due to its easy access to the busy thoroughfares of Tala'a Kbira (great slope) and Tala'a Sghira (little slope). These two lanes are relatively easy to navigate and give access to the medina's heart around the *medersa's* Attarine and Seffarine and the Kairouine Mosque. Some of the sights are concentrated around this very busy quarter of narrow and twisting lanes, however accommodations, restaurants, and shops are scattered fairly liberally throughout the medina. The two squares accessible by car—Ahmed Mekouar and Rcif—are handy geographical landmarks.

The French-designed ville nouvelle is easy to navigate thanks to the double-lane avenue Hassan II, which runs through its center, and its offshoot boulevard Mohammed V. Most hotels, restaurants, and banks are centered around these two streets.

GETTING AROUND

The distance between Fes's medina and ville nouvelle is usually too great to walk, and with the easy access to cheap buses and *petits* taxis, there's no real reason to bother. If you like to walk, there's plenty available within the medina. Once you're in the

---

Fun Fact **Fes or Fez?**

The Western name for the city is drawn from its Arabic name *"fas,"* which itself refers to a pickaxe of silver and gold presented to Moulay Idriss I to use in tracing the outlines of his new city. There is no one correct way to translate Arabic words into Western characters. The French have always referred to the city as "Fes," while Americans tend to use "Fez." Fassis themselves use Fes, most likely due to the long history of colonial French presence in Morocco.

---

medina, however, you'll be faced with the choice of navigating its thoroughfares on your own or with a guide. If you're only visiting for a day or two, then I strongly suggest hiring a guide for at least half a day, followed by some personal exploration. For more on the pros and cons of hiring a guide, see "Guide or No Guide?" on p. 38. Those who wish to explore the medina on their own should consider purchasing either or both of the books mentioned in "Visitor Information," above, which are loaded with easy-to-read information on the sights and attractions within the medina.

BY BUS The city has a very reliable local bus service but can at times be hopelessly overcrowded. Try to avoid the early-morning and late-afternoon rush hours, along with the midday rush on Friday.

Bus no. 9 operates a handy round circuit beginning in the ville nouvelle at place Allal al Fassi (formerly place Atlas)—across from the CTM bus station—via avenue Abdellah Chefchaouni and place de la Résistance (McDonald's) to Ahmed Mekouar Square, returning via avenue Hassan II and avenue des F.A.R. Bus no. 10 runs from the train station via the *gare routière,* Bab Guissa, and Access Oued Zhoun to Bab Fettouh. Bus no. 12 operates between Bab Bou Jeloud and Bab Fettouh via Bab Guissa and Access Oued Zhoun. Bus no. 19 runs between the train station and Bab Rcif. Bus no. 47 connects the train station with Bab Bou Jeloud.

Note: These route numbers are posted on the side of the bus. There are numbers on the back of the bus, but these are insignificant to its route.

BY FOOT Whether in the ville nouvelle or medina, it's often easiest to simply walk around Fes. It takes about 10 minutes to walk from one end of avenue Hassan II to the other, and about the same to negotiate the busy section of boulevard Mohammed V from the corner of avenue Hassan II to place Mohammed V. Within the medina you obviously have little choice but to walk. Even at a good pace it can still take at least 15 minutes to walk from Bab Bou Jeloud along Tala'a Kbira to the Attarine Medersa and up to another 10 minutes to negotiate the heavy pedestrian traffic before arriving at place Rcif.

Tip: The months of July and August can be oppressively hot in Fes, and this heat is amplified within the confines of the medina. Be aware of your body heat, stop for a mint tea here and there, and drink plenty of bottled water, which can be bought everywhere.

BY TAXI *Petits* taxis are the most convenient way to travel between the medina and ville nouvelle. You'll find the small, red, government-regulated vehicles everywhere. You can usually ask your hotel reception staff to organize one for you, or otherwise you can simply stand on the side of the street and hail one. Drivers are only allowed to carry up to three passengers at a time, but be aware that if there is a vacant seat, you may pick up an additional passenger. At all times, request the driver to put on the meter, which he is supposed to do no matter the time of day or night. Most trips between the ville nouvelle and medina should cost no more than 15dh ($1.90/95p) during the day and a bit more after 8pm, when a 50% evening surcharge kicks in. *Petits* taxis operate solely within the city environs; for transport to the airport you can charter a *grands* taxi through your hotel or at the *gare routière*. These Mercedes sedans take a maximum of six passengers and cost around 160dh ($20/£10) for the one-way trip.

FAST FACTS: Fes

Banks & Currency Exchange Within the medina, there's a branch of **SGMB** with an ATM at Bab Bou Jeloud. The branch is open Monday to Thursday 8:15am to 4pm and Friday and Saturday 8:30am to noon. The 24-hour ATM accepts all cards and also changes foreign currency. **Banque Populaire** has a branch with an ATM halfway along Tala'a Sghira at Souïqt Bensafi, open Monday to Friday 8:15am to 3:45pm. Out in the **ville nouvelle**, banks can be found from place Yacoub el Mansour (formerly place Florence) to place Mohammed V via boulevard Mohammed V. Halfway along this stretch of boulevard Mohammed V, **Wafa** has a bureau de change open Monday to Friday 8am to 6pm and Saturday 9am to 1pm. The **BMCE** branches at place Yacoub el Mansour and place Mohammed V, open Monday to Friday 8:15am to 3:45pm, will usually exchange traveler's checks and process cash advances on credit cards. One block west of place Yacoub el Mansour, on avenue Lalla Meriem, is an **SGMB 24-hour exchange ATM.** The state-run **Bank al-Maghrib**, on place Yacoub el Mansour (Mon–Fri 8am–3pm), will usually cash traveler's checks, damaged notes, pre-1999 U.S. notes, and the new British pound notes, all of which may be rejected at other banks.

Car Rentals The major international firms can be found in the ville nouvelle including **Avis,** 50 bd. Chefchaouani (© 035/626969); **Budget,** 6 bd. Lalla Asmaa (© 035/940092); **Europcar,** 45 av. Hassan II (© 035/626545); and **Hertz,** Kissariat de la Foire on boulevard Lalla Meryem (© 035/622812). Those with desks at the airport include **Avis** (© 035/626969), **Europcar** (© 061/171325), **Hertz** (© 063/614212), and **National/Alamo** (© 063/111960); all are usually open from 8am to 10pm. A reputable local company, **Tijania Car,** 7 av. des F.A.R. (© 035/653737 or 061/194028), also has a prominent desk at the airport (© 074/774730). Rates are around 350dh to 500dh ($44–$63/£22–£31) per day for a small, four-door sedan with unlimited mileage and insurance.

Consulates See "Fast Facts: Morocco" in chapter 2.

Doctors **Dr. Jamal Wakkach,** 2 rue Benzakkour, on place Hussein de Jordainie (© **035/656565**), speaks relatively good English and comes recommended.

Drugstores Pharmacies can be found easily throughout the city. In the medina, at Bab Bou Jeloud, is **Pharmacie Bab Bou Jeloud** (© 035/643385); farther down along Tala'a Kbira, at Qantrat Bourous, is **Pharmacie La Medina** (© 035/634458); and on Ahmed Mekouar Square is **Pharmacie du Maroc** (© 035/633574). In the ville nouvelle, **Pharmacie Bahja** (© 035/623867) is on the corner of boulevard Mohammed V and avenue Abdelkarim Khattabi; **Pharmacie de**

France (© 035/614398) is at 48 av. Hassan II. All general pharmacies in Fes operate Monday to Friday 8:30am to 12:30pm and 3:30 to 8pm, and Saturday 8:30am to 1pm. After-hours pharmacies are listed on the front door. The **Pharmacie du Nuit** (© 035/623380), on avenue Moulay Youssef between the ville nouvelle and Fes el Jdid, is open nightly from 9pm to 6am and usually has a doctor in residence.

Hospitals **Clinique Ryad,** on place Hussein de Jordainie (© **035/960000** or 035/656565), is a private clinic with high standards and usually has staff on hand that can speak some English.

Internet Access Cybercafes can be found in both the medina and ville nouvelle. In the medina, at the bottom end of Tala'a Kbira on Qantrat Boutros, is **Internet; BathaNet** is on Derb Douh, between Bab Bou Jeloud and Ahmed Mekouar Square; while opposite the parking lot on Ahmed Mekouar Square, on avenue Allal Fassi, are **London Cyber** and **Cyber Didi. Cyber Hatim** is next door to Cinema el Amal on boulevard Ahmed ben Mohammed Alaoui, about 300m (985 ft.) south of Bab Rcif. In the ville nouvelle, **Cyber Club** is above the *téléboutique* 1 block south of place Mohammed V on boulevard Mohammed V. **Cyber@ Téléboutique** is at 52 av. Hassan II. Some medina *maisons d'hôte* now offer Wi-Fi, as does **Cafe Clock** (p. 226).

Laundry & Dry Cleaning There are no self-service laundries in Fes. There is an unnamed *pressing* (dry cleaner) on Ahmed Mekouar Square, next to the post office. In the ville nouvelle is **Pressing Dallas,** 44 rue Asilah (between Hotel Mounia and av. Mohammed es Slaoui). Both are open Monday to Friday 8am to 7pm and Saturday 9am to 1pm. A shirt or pair of pants costs around 15dh ($1.90/95p). Otherwise you can ask at your hotel reception, though this can prove expensive as they usually charge per item. Often your hotel's cleaning staff will do your laundry privately to earn some money on the side, a practice usually accepted by the management. A plastic shopping bag of laundry shouldn't cost you more than 30dh ($3.75/£1.90), though perhaps don't trust them with your favorite white shirt or dress.

Maps & Books The books *Fez from Bab to Bab, Walks in the Medina* and *The Fes Medina Tourist Circuits* (see "Visitor Information," above) are good sources for information on the sights and attractions within the Fes medina. They are usually for sale at **Librairie Nouvelle** (© 035/685493), 46 av. Hassan II, next door to the Hotel de la Paix in the ville nouvelle; it also sells some beautiful coffee table–style books on Morocco. It's also worth asking at your accommodations if they sell either. The tourism council also produces a free *Carte Touristique* map with pretty good maps of both the medina and ville nouvelle. On my last visit, I managed to pick one up at the Hotel Olympic (p. 223) in the ville nouvelle, not far from the Syndicat d'Initiative. **Librairie el Fikr el Moaser,** 15 av. Abdallah Benchakroun (formerly rue du 16 Novembre), opposite the Centrale Marché, sells guide books and coffee-table books of Morocco, some in English. It's open Monday to Saturday 9am to 6:30pm (closed Fri noon–2:30pm).

Newspapers **Librairie el Fikr el Moaser** (see above) sells the international weekly newspaper *Guardian Weekly* and the odd English-language copy of

Time, Newsweek, and *The Economist.* Also try the newsstands along boulevard Mohammed V, between avenue Hassan II and place Mohammed V, in the ville nouvelle.

Photographic Needs **Labo Tazi,** on the pedestrian-only section of avenue Abdelkarim Khattabi in the ville nouvelle, sells a range of film, as well as a few memory cards. At press time, they were installing hardware and software to burn your digital images onto CD. Labo Tazi is open Monday to Friday 9am to 7pm and Saturday 9am to 1pm.

Police For **general emergencies** and the **police,** call © **19.** There's a **Commissariat de Police** beside the post office on the corner of avenue Hassan II and boulevard Mohammed V in the ville nouvelle, while in the medina there's one located on Derb Douh, to the right of the post office on Ahmed Mekouar Square. This is where the medina's **Brigade Touristique** is located. Another police station can be found on boulevard Ahmed ben Mohammed Alaoui, about 200m (655 ft.) south of Bab Rcif.

Post Office & Mail Fes's **main post office,** which receives all *poste restante* mail, is in the ville nouvelle on the corner of avenue Hassan II and boulevard Mohammed V and is open Monday to Friday 8am to 4:15pm and Saturday 8 to 11:45am. There's a section inside for sending parcels (that must be inspected first) and Western Union services. The **medina post office** is on Ahmed Mekouar Square and is open Monday to Friday 8am to 4:15pm and Saturday 8:30am to noon. You'll also find many shops within the medina, as well as most expensive hotels, that sell postcard stamps. A **DHL** office is located in the ville nouvelle within the Royal Mirage Hotel (formerly the Sheraton) on the corner of avenue Hassan II and avenue des F.A.R. (© **035/930909**). It's open Monday to Friday 8:30am to 6:30pm and on Saturdays 8:30am to noon.

Restrooms Although some traditional ablutions rooms are being restored as part of the Fes medina rehabilitation project, they are generally difficult to locate. Should you need a toilet during your exploration of the medina, try any of the dining places recommended below or time your toilet break with a visit to the **Nejjarine Museum** (p. 231), which has modern and clean toilets on each of its two floors. In the ville nouvelle, again try any of the recommended dining options or the **McDonald's** at the north end of avenue Hassan II heading toward the medina.

Safety Although Fes el Bali is still largely pedestrian-only, there's recently been an increase in the number of mopeds, scooters, and motorcycles breaching the city's walls. The riders of these bikes are invariably in a hurry to get somewhere and can be quite blasé about the speed with which they pass you. It appears that they are in the medina to stay, so be on the lookout as you're also trying to dodge the donkeys, mules, and motorized carts. Your personal safety, however, generally never feels threatened other than being hassled for business by unofficial guides and some shopkeepers in the medina. Female travelers may also encounter unwanted attention while wandering around the medina, even when dressed conservatively. If the irritant persists, walk into the closest shop or restaurant and ask them to contact the tourist police. If you are in the company of a male friend, it will be presumed that you are a couple, which can sometimes work in the female's favor with regards to any sexual harassment, though be prepared for a barrage of questions as to why you don't have any children yet.

Telephone Fes's **city code** has recently changed from 055 to **035**.

WHERE TO STAY

Ten years ago, the majority of quality accommodations in Fes were located in the ville nouvelle. Things have changed, however. The recent resurgence of interest in Fes, from both would-be residents and everyday travelers, has been the catalyst for an explosion of guesthouses, or *maisons d'hôte,* opening within the city's ancient walls. Although yet to reach the proportions seen in Marrakech, there is now a fantastic choice of places to stay here. What *can* be compared with Marrakech, however, is a dearth of decent budget accommodations within the medina, and the majority of better value hotels in this price bracket are still to be found in the ville nouvelle.

Choosing where you stay in Fes is important. The distance between the medina and the ville nouvelle is, for most, too great to walk. For some this can be a blessing, with daily visits into the oppressively busy medina tempered by retreats back to the openness and greenery of the ville nouvelle. Some travelers, however, never set foot in the ville nouvelle, preferring the all-enveloping life within the medina. If you are visiting during the very hot months of July and August or the wintry and very cold months from November to January, these factors become even more important in your decision. Hotels in the ville nouvelle tend to include reverse-cycle air-conditioning in their rooms and can supply a welcome stream of hot water in your bathroom—not-so-small factors that can be the difference between a good night's sleep and a bad one. *Maisons d'hôte* in the medina rarely offer any artificial climate control other than the odd fan or electric heater, and at times the hot water supply can be erratic, although you can be certain that if this is the case, your host and staff will make more of an effort to assist you than those in the ville nouvelle hotels. Read my "Tips on Accommodations" (p. 60) for more information.

Having stayed over the years in both Fes's medina and ville nouvelle, I lean more toward recommending the medina. I've enjoyed staying in the ville nouvelle—especially when my wallet hasn't been as full as I would like—and watching the evening promenade on the recently landscaped avenue Hassan II is one of my favorite pastimes. However, nothing escapes the fact that you are missing out on the chance to experience daily life in one of the world's greatest living medieval cities—without any real sacrifices to modern living.

MEDINA
Very Expensive

Dar Anebar *(Finds* In the "uptown" section of the medina, a 5-minute walk from the landmark Sofitel Palais Jamaï, is Ahmed Azami's former family home–turned–elegant *maison d'hôte.* His cousins, Abdelhamid and Nadia, undertook an 18-month restoration before the dar opened in 2006, and the result is captivating. A dark entrance opens onto a very spacious courtyard of *zellij* tiling and Marrakchi-ochre *tadelakt* walls. This earthy color scheme continues throughout the riad and makes for a pleasant change

Fes

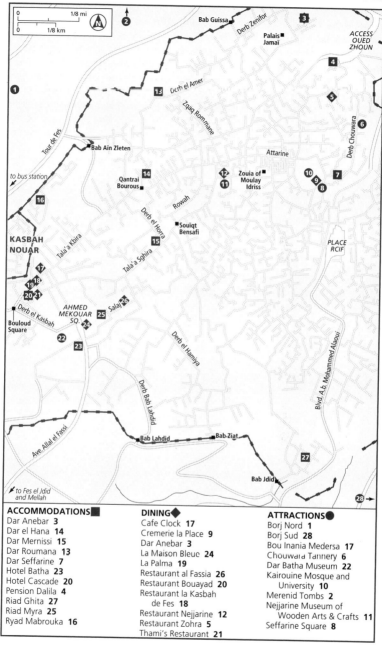

ACCOMMODATIONS ■
Dar Anebar 3
Dar el Hana 14
Dar Mernissi 15
Dar Roumana 13
Dar Seffarine 7
Hotel Batha 23
Hotel Cascade 20
Pension Dalila 4
Riad Ghita 27
Riad Myra 25
Ryad Mabrouka 16

DINING ◆
Cafe Clock 17
Cremerie la Place 9
Dar Anebar 3
La Maison Bleue 24
La Palma 19
Restaurant al Fassia 26
Restaurant Bouayad 20
Restaurant la Kasbah
de Fes 18
Restaurant Nejjarine 12
Restaurant Zohra 5
Thami's Restaurant 21

ATTRACTIONS ●
Borj Nord 1
Borj Sud 28
Bou Inania Medersa 17
Chouwara Tannery 6
Dar Batha Museum 22
Kairouine Mosque and
University 10
Merenid Tombs 2
Nejjarine Museum of
Wooden Arts & Crafts 11
Seffarine Square 8

from other, garish interiors. A variety of room sizes and configurations are offered, including the two-room Oumkeltoum suite, which was the former apartment of the family's matriarch, Lalla Anebar. The Amina suite has interconnecting rooms that can accommodate two people in each. All of the rooms are stylishly furnished without being over the top, and include refurbished bathrooms with all the modern conveniences and large bathtubs. Nice welcoming touches in the rooms include flowers, a fruit basket, and chocolates on the pillows. Dar Anebar's rooftop takes full advantage of its elevated position and is a perfect spot for an extended brunch or a sunset drink. Ahmed is the consummate professional and is always around to help guests negotiate the medina, find a guide, or head out on day trips. See p. 224 for more on Dar Anebar's cuisine.

Note: "Uptown" does mean "up" in Dar Anebar's case. It's a good 15- to 20-minute uphill walk from the Kairouine Mosque, but downhill all the way from Sofitel Palais Jamaï.

15 Derb el Mitter, Zenjfor, Medina, Fes. ℂ 035/635785 or 066/202614. Fax 035/637473. www.daranebar.com. 5 units. 990dh ($124/£62) single; 1,540dh–1,760dh ($193–$220/£96–£110) double; 2,310dh ($289/£144) Amina quad; 3,025dh ($378/£189) Oumkeltoum suite. Children under 12 stay free in parent's room. TPT not included. MC, V. Accessible by foot only; pickup available from Sofitel Palais Jamaï. **Amenities:** Restaurant. *In room:* A/C, satellite TV, fridge, hair dryer (on request), safe (on request).

Dar Roumana ☾☾☾   This could be the best all-around package in the medina: an authentically restored, early-20th-century riad; exceptional medina views from the rooftop terrace; and owned and managed by an American cordon-bleu chef and her flamenco guitarist husband. Jennifer Lapostol endured 3 years of renovation work, much of it conducted personally, before her "House of Pomegranate" was ready for business. During this time, the *zellij*, stucco, and cedar wood of this once grand dar were brought back to life. Additions were made in the form of a small salon with fireplace, a courtyard fountain, a second rooftop with *the* view, and completely refitted bathrooms. The result is stunning, with rustic, earthy colors somehow blending perfectly with the more traditional aspects. The romantic Roumana suite includes a clawfoot bathtub for two, while the Quormosa suite is handy for three-person families with a single bed located on a separate mezzanine level.

To extend the already peaceful atmosphere within, there are no TVs or phones in the rooms, but a satellite TV/DVD is set up in the salon. Jennifer's fusion Moroccan-Mediterranean cuisine is surely destined for larger audiences, but for now it's her guests who are the lucky ones, especially when she conducts her twice weekly day-long cooking classes that begin with a recipe book, visit to the market, and time in the Dar Roumana kitchen, and end with an after-dinner guitar serenade by her husband, Sebastian.

30 Derb el Amer, Zqaq Rommane, Medina, Fes. ℂ 035/741637 or 060/290404. Fax 035/635524. www.dar roumana.com. 5 units. 1,210dh–1,430dh ($151–$179/£76–£89) double; 1,265dh ($158/£79) Quormosa suite triple. Children under 6 stay free in parent's room. Rates include breakfast. MC, V with minimum 4,000dh ($500/£250) payment. Accessible by foot only. **Amenities:** Restaurant; salon/library; rooftop terrace; cooking lessons. *In room:* A/C (in some), safe.

Riad Myra ☾☾   This is the *palais d'hôte* of the Chab family, well respected in both Fes and Marrakech, where Myra now runs the popular Restaurant al Fassia (p. 224). Sister Meryem and her husband Mustapha now manage Riad Myra for the family, keeping the standard of service at an exceptionally high level. The bedrooms are sumptuously furnished and decorated in a mix of traditional Moroccan and antique English, with heavy drapes and bed covers of gold and burgundy. A large courtyard of deep-cushioned lounges surrounds an eight-pointed star fountain and is both a meeting area and restaurant for riad guests. A roof terrace offers private corners for sunbathing and reading. What sets Riad Myra apart from a lot of its competition is Meryem and Mustapha—both have lived in either the U.S. or U.K. and can easily relate to Western travelers' questions and concerns. Their well-trained, professional staff delivers friendly service in a peaceful and relaxed atmosphere.

13 rue Salaj, Batha, Medina, Fes. ℂ 035/740000 or 035/638080. Fax 035/638282. www.riadmyra.com. 12 units. 1,500dh ($188/£94) double; 2,000dh–2,400dh ($250–$300/£125–£150) suite. Children under 5 stay free in parent's room. Rates include breakfast. Secure parking at Ahmed Mekouar Sq. (200m/655 ft.). Accessible by foot only. MC, V. **Amenities:** Restaurant; library; Internet. *In room:* A/C, satellite TV, fridge, hair dryer.

Ryad Mabrouka   It's a bit of a walk up the alleyway to Ryad Mabrouka ("luck"), but once you've arrived, you'll find one of the medina's most popular *maisons d'hôte.* Michel Trezzy and his partners Pierre and Caroline have got the combination just right: an authentically restored 14th-century mansion in one of the quieter corners of the medina staffed by trilingual (Moroccan Arabic, English, and French) Moroccans who have been trained in all aspects of good hospitality by Michel himself. The tall mansion has a feeling of seclusion thanks to high walls surrounding the almost-overgrown back garden and pool, but this doesn't equate to feeling hemmed in. A large, open-top courtyard opens out to the garden, while a first-floor enclosed veranda affords a magical view above the high wall and into the medina beyond. The spacious bedrooms, also with high ceilings, are carved cedar wood, *zellij,* and stucco with large, modern *tadelakt* bathrooms. The entire house is decorated in a refined mix of Moroccan antiques and French artwork that reflects Michel's taste. Ryad Mabrouka's cuisine is well known, and most guests choose to dine in most nights, having returned by late afternoon to enjoy aperitifs and the sunset on the veranda or the large roof terrace.

25 Derb el Mitter, Aïn Zleten, Medina, Fes. ℂ 035/636345. Fax 035/636310. www.ryadmabrouka.com. 8 units. 1,150dh–2,000dh ($144–$250/£72–£125) double. Children 4–12 350dh ($44/£22) in parent's room; under 4 free. Discount Jan 7–Feb 14, Jun 16–Aug 31, and Nov 16–Dec 19. TPT not included. Rates include breakfast. Secure parking within 100m (330 ft.). Accessible by foot only. MC, V. **Amenities:** Restaurant; pool. *In room:* A/C, hair dryer, safe, no phone.

Expensive

Dar Seffarine 🏅🏅🏅   Highly rated since it opened in 2006, this palatial dar is as authentic as they come and sits comfortably within the medina's historic quarter. Alaâ, an Iraqi-born architect, and Kate, a Norwegian graphic designer, undertook 2½ years of extensive restoration on Dar Seffarine, and the result is simply magnificent. A grand courtyard of 10m-high (33-ft.) columns; large, original hand-painted cedar wood doors; and a vast floor of original *zellij* lead onto two floors of large, airy, sparsely furnished suites with discreet bathrooms and low-lying beds. Stairs lead past a small guest kitchen up to a large rooftop terrace, where you can take in a grand view over the Sebou Valley with a glass of wine. The main kitchen is on the ground floor and opens out to a quaint courtyard where guests join Kate and Alaâ for delicious breakfasts—the best I've had in Morocco—and dinners that are equal to anything available outside.

14 Derb Sbaâ Louyati, Seffarine, Medina, Fes. ℂ 071/113528 or ℂ/fax 035/635205. www.darseffarine.com. 6 units. 550dh ($68/£34) single; 770dh–880dh ($96–$110/£48–£55) double; 1,100dh–1,320dh ($138–$165/£69–£83) suite. No children under 12. Rates include breakfast. Accessible by foot only; directions upon booking or phone from place Bab Rcif for escort. MC, V with 4% fee. **Amenities:** Restaurant; guest kitchenette. *In room:* A/C in 2nd-floor suites and rooms.

Riad Ghita This restored 16th-century riad is in a quiet residential corner of the medina and is one of the most peaceful you'll come across. Riad Ghita is Moroccan owned and managed, and this local influence is visibly apparent in its furnishings—lots of traditional antique-style furniture and plush gold and burgundy lounges—and its interior architecture of *zellij* and stucco walls and carved-cedar wood doors and ceilings. There's also plenty of blue and pink, which can seem garish at first, but only adds to the local flavor. Rooms and suites of varying sizes come with lounges or separate seating areas with coffee tables, and the bathrooms are a mix of traditional and modern. Guests divide their time between a spacious and light courtyard with a retractable sun roof and comfortable lounges that are perfect for an afternoon mint tea, and the split-level rooftop terrace that catches the breeze and affords a great view across the medina. An in-house restaurant serves up fine Moroccan cuisine (also popular with nonguests), and the friendly and discreet staff are always on hand.

52 Bou'ajjara, Bab Jdid Rcif, Medina, Fes. (C) 035/740901 or 061/202235. Fax 035/740921. www.riadghita.com. 7 units. 935dh ($117/£58) double; 1,045dh–1,265dh ($131–$158/£65–£79) suite; 1,430dh ($179/£89) royal suite. Children 5–15 330dh ($41/£21) in parent's room; under 5 free. Peak- and low-season prices apply. Rates include breakfast. Secure parking close by. Accessible by foot only. MC, V. **Amenities:** Restaurant; salon/TV room; laundry service; complimentary tea and pastries upon arrival. *In room:* A/C, satellite TV, bottled water.

Moderate

Dar el Hana 🏵🏵🏵 *Finds*   This little "house of tranquillity," off busy Tala'a Kbira, is a real home away from home. Aussie Josephine came to Fes for a 12-month adventure and liked it so much, she decided to stay. The almost-300-year-old house was once owned by the *imam* of the nearby mosque and has been left largely untouched bar a few concessions to modern living. Each room is different: The Jacaranda suite can accommodate a third person in a separate sitting room; the Hibiscus room has welcoming external windows; and the Acacia room is excellent for two single travelers. The building's heart is a small patio on the first floor with a narrow kitchen to one side. Here everyone gathers for a communal breakfast—and dinner if requested—and can also spend the day enjoying an on-site cooking lesson. The combination of rooms and the kitchen make Dar el Hana a perfect choice for groups of friends or families to rent out. Everything is little here, but in a nice way. The rooftop terrace is small but has enough space for everyone; an outdoor shower helps to cool down while sunbathing, while a round mosaic table is a popular spot for sunset drinks. *Maisons d'hôte* are a reflection of their owners, and friendly, welcoming, diminutive, and lively Dar el Hana is definitely that.

22 Farran Couïcha, off Tala'a Kbira, Aïn Zleten, Medina, Fes. (C) 035/635854 or 076/286584. www.darelhana.com. 3 units. 605dh–825dh ($76–$103/£38–£52) double; 1,045dh ($131/£65) triple; 2,090dh ($261/£131) entire house per night, minimum 2 nights. Children 2–12 220dh ($28/£14) in parent's room; under 2 110dh ($14/£7). Peak-season supplement Dec 23–Jan 6 and during the Festival of World Sacred Music (p. 21). Secure parking at Bab Aïn Zleten. Accessible by foot only. No credit cards. **Amenities:** Restaurant (on request); salon/library; portable phone for incoming/outgoing calls (user pays); Wi-Fi. *In room:* A/C (2 rooms), fan/heater (1 room).

Dar Mernissi 🏵🏵🏵 *Finds*   U.K.-born ex-DJ Louis McIntosh's Dar Mernissi, named after the building's original owners, only opened in 2007 but has already become the house of choice for those looking to be in the thick of the medina. The relaxed and fun atmosphere attracts artists, musicians, and other creative types, who always seem to be popping in for a visit. The design of Dar Mernissi is different to most of those in the medina. The basementlike ground floor is a comfortable, chill-out room, and the first floor is like a self-contained apartment, complete with a marble-top kitchen counter where Louis has been known to show off his culinary skills. Black-and-white tile flooring is also a step away from the norm. It's only on the second floor that you'll find tradition in the form of a spacious salon with high ceilings and brightly colored Iraqi glass—although even here you'll find a larger-than-life picture of Rolling Stones guitarist Keith Richards, Louis' friend and long-time Morocco fan. Rooms—three with private bathrooms—are spread out over three levels, one with a small private garden. A refurbished split-level rooftop terrace of beige-and-green *zellij*, complete with its own shallow, *zellij* lounging pool, affords a great view of the busy life down below on Tala'a Sghira.

Corner of Tala'a Sghira and Derb el Horra Medina, Fes. © 035/637779 or 010/167405. www.louis-fes.blogspot.com. 4 units. 440dh ($55/£28) single; 505dh–770dh ($63–$96/£32–£48) double. Children 8–15 165dh ($21/£10) in parent's room; under 8 free. Rates include breakfast. Parking at Aïn Zleten (70m/230 ft.). Accessible by foot only. No credit cards. **Amenities:** Basement lounge; Wi-Fi. *In room:* No phone.

Hotel Batha

This is a popular choice for travelers wanting good-value rooms in an excellent location. The Hotel Batha has been around for years and was at one time the only accommodations of choice this far into the medina. It's a little frayed around the edges now but still manages to cling to some past grandeur. Rooms are a mix of bland '80s furnishings with a splash of traditional *zellij*, and are a reasonable size with decent bathrooms. They all surround a large central courtyard and fountain that leads to a large, welcoming pool that affords some privacy when compared to other hotels. Also at this end of the property, in a building that was the British Consulate until 1989, is the Churchill lounge bar, which is a great spot during winter to sit in large leather armchairs in front of the fire with a glass of wine. Also located here is a restaurant serving Moroccan and international cuisine, but I recommend heading outside and eating elsewhere. At the rear, also accessible from Museum Street, is Le Consul bar, a lively place most nights and one of very few public places in the medina that serves alcohol. There's a steady stream of tour groups coming through here—there's parking right outside the front door and always a few Fes guides waiting for business—but in a hotel this big, it adds some atmosphere.

Ahmed Mekouar Sq., Batha, Medina, Fes. © 035/741077. Fax 035/741078. 62 units. 327dh ($41/£20) single; 452dh ($57/£28) double; 558dh ($70/£35) triple. MC, V. **Amenities:** Restaurant; 2 bars; pool; elevator. *In room:* A/C, satellite TV.

Inexpensive

Hotel Cascade

This old dame has been one of the most popular medina cheapies for years now, and its location certainly can't be beat. Located just inside Bab Bou Jeloud and within walking distance from the *gare routière,* the Cascade has seen better days but still offers simple, clean rooms at basement prices in a very friendly atmosphere. Some rooms conveniently take up to three people, while others have nice big windows. Shared showers and toilets are located out in the hallways and can get busy at times, though there are also separate wash basins scattered around. During summer they offer mattresses on the twin rooftop terraces, the higher of the two with a fantastic view over the comings and goings at Bab Bou Jeloud.

26 rue Serrajine, Bab Bou Jeloud (about 30m/100 ft. on the right-hand side), Medina, Fes. © 035/638442. 18 units. 60dh–70dh ($7.50–$8.75/£3.75–£4.40) per person. Secure parking available 200m (655 ft.) west of Bab Bou Jeloud. Accessible by foot only. No credit cards. *In room:* No phone.

Pension Dalila

This budget hotel, opened in 2003, is a real bargain and popular with young, international travelers. Rooms have brightly colored floors and are tiled, simply furnished, and spotlessly clean. All rooms come with a private bathroom, though the bathrooms for room nos. 9 and 10 are out in the hall, which is somewhat compensated for by having a balcony. The rooftop terrace is a quiet spot for reading or writing, while the busy ground-floor cafe is a good place to meet fellow travelers and enjoy the simple breakfast menu (25dh–35dh/$3.15–$4.40/£1.55–£2.20). Because the hotel is located on the edge of the medina in a busy residential area, the front-facing rooms can be a bit noisy late at night. Taxi access and parking is right outside the front door, while the Kairouine Mosque and place Seffarine are only 10 to 15 minutes away. It can get full, so try to book ahead or arrive early.

26 Bab Oued Zhoun, Medina, Fes. ℂ 035/740657. 12 units. 120dh ($15/£7.50) single; 200dh ($25/£13) double; 300dh ($38/£19) triple. Children under 8 stay free in parent's room. Parking at front door. No credit cards. **Amenities:** Cafe. *In room:* No phone.

VILLE NOUVELLE
Very Expensive

Dar Ziryab ✷✷ *Kids*   Since 2001, Jalil el Hayar's Dar Ziryab has been the accommodations of choice for those wanting the culture and authenticity of a medina *maison d'hôte* with the openness and easy access of the ville nouvelle. Located in a residential area just behind the Royal Mirage (formerly Sheraton) and Crown Palace hotels, this house is a living museum—cum–art gallery, decorated in expertly crafted *zellij*, stucco, carved cedar, and colored Iraqi glass. The restaurant/salon is simply stunning. Tiled throughout but warmed by Moroccan carpets and *kélims*, there's a homeliness to Dar Ziryab that you wouldn't expect from such a grand mansion. The rooms are all very private, some with a terrace and fireplace, but open onto a central lounge room often used for communal aperitifs before dinner. Jalil's wife is an excellent cook and serves traditional Moroccan cuisine that is equal to anything available in Fes. For families, there's a split-level corner suite with two beds and a private yard.

Corner of rue Lalla Amina and rue Lalla Malika, Ville Nouvelle, Fes. ℂ 035/621561 or 061/173997. Fax 035/623167. www.darziryab.com. 8 units. 800dh ($100/£50) single; 1,200dh–1,600dh ($150–$200/£75–£100) double; 2,400dh ($300/£150) suite. Children 3–12 25% discount in parent's room; under 3 free. Rates include breakfast. Private parking available. AE, MC, V. **Amenities:** Restaurant; hammam; babysitting; laundry service; library; Wi-Fi. *In room:* A/C, satellite TV, CD player.

Hotel Menzeh Fes   Often beset by tour groups, this large, aging hotel still exudes more character than its modern, bland competitors, helped along by a fantastic view—best taken from the rooftop bar—across the Sebou Valley to the Fes medina. An enormous, grand reception area greets guests who can then travel up to their room in a glass-side elevator that takes advantage of the view. A range of traditionally decorated rooms are available; the standard double is very spacious with a king-size bed, two-seater lounge, and large, modern bathroom with a tub/shower combo. Some suites come with a private terrace and separate lounge area, or with a small Jacuzzi and bigger bathroom. Request a top-floor room with a medina view—not all rooms face the medina, and of those that do, the view from the lower floors is partially obscured by a McDonald's. The main restaurant is a beautifully grand structure with four massive columns holding up an intricately painted ceiling and chandelier. This is the sister hotel to Hotel Menzeh Zalagh, located 1 block away with similar rooms and a pool open to guests from both hotels.

28 rue Abdessalam Serghini, Ville Nouvelle, Fes. ℂ 035/943849. Fax 035/943834. menzeh.zalagh@fesnet.net.ma. 130 units. 950dh ($119/£59) single; 1,300dh ($163/£81) double; 2,000dh–2,800dh ($250–$350/£125–£175) suite.

Children under 5 stay free in parent's room. Breakfast 120dh ($15/£7.50). TPT not included. Secure parking available across the road. AE, MC, V. **Amenities:** 2 restaurants; rooftop bar; boutique. *In room:* A/C, satellite TV, fridge, hair dryer.

Moderate

Hotel de la Paix
Just outside the inexpensive bracket, this hotel is located right on avenue Hassan II. Hotel de la Paix has been around for a while and is popular with Moroccans, tour groups, and independent travelers. The English-speaking reception is always efficient and friendly. There are some recently renovated rooms that although still small now have nice contemporary furnishings and tile throughout, with large, modern bathrooms. The older rooms are still very adequate and are carpeted. Enjoy breakfast a few doors down at Le Paris (p. 228).

44 av. Hassan II, Ville Nouvelle, Fes. ℂ **035/622148.** 42 units. 285dh ($36/£18) single; 365dh ($46/£23) double. Street parking available. MC, V. **Amenities:** Restaurant; bar; elevator. *In room:* A/C, satellite TV.

Hotel Mounia
This is one of the better hotels within this price range in Fes's ville nouvelle. A grand reception area of *zellij* and marble leads to the in-house restaurant and a separate lounge and bar area, which gets quite busy with local clientele as the evening progresses. Rooms are comfortable, clean, tiled, and functional, with built-in wardrobes and a modern bathroom with 24-hour hot water in the bath/shower combo. The hotel is located on a quiet side street close to place Mohammed V and the area's restaurants, and is a 10-minute walk from avenue Hassan II. It's popular with tour groups, but absorbs the noise quite well when busy.

Tip: Inward-facing rooms would appear quieter but often catch the noise and live Moroccan music emanating from the popular bar below, whereas street-facing rooms normally aren't that noisy. Also, while breakfast is decent (and included), I wouldn't recommend the restaurant.

60 bd. Zerktouni, Ville Nouvelle, Fes. ℂ **035/624838** or 035/650771. Fax 035/650773. www.hotelmouniafes.ma. 83 units. 424dh ($53/£27) single; 536dh ($67/£34) double. TPT not included. Breakfast 39dh ($4.90/£2.45). Limited street parking available. MC, V. **Amenities:** Restaurant; bar; elevator. *In room:* A/C, central heating, satellite TV.

Inexpensive

Hotel Olympic (Value)
This is the best cheapie in the ville nouvelle considering its central location and good-value rooms. Admittedly it lacks any great atmosphere other than early morning, when adventure tour groups scoff down their breakfast before moving on. Nonetheless, this small hotel continues to keep its independent clients happy thanks to clean and comfortable tiled rooms, some looking out over the ville nouvelle's central market, with small but functional bathrooms. There's also usually a guide or two hanging around if you're interested.

Rue Houman el Fatouaki, off bd. Mohammed V, Ville Nouvelle, Fes. ℂ **035/932682** or 035/944683. Fax 035/932665. www.hotel-olympic-fes.com. 31 units. 242dh ($30/£15) single; 292dh ($37/£18) double; 377dh ($47/£24) triple. Children under 5 stay free in parent's room. Breakfast 31dh ($3.90/£1.95). Secure parking available 50m (164 ft.) east of hotel. MC, V. **Amenities:** Restaurant. *In room:* A/C, central heating, satellite TV.

Hotel Splendid
Renovated in 2007, the Splendid now offers impressive amenities and rooms for a hotel in this price bracket. A bright, tiled reception area leads to a pleasant restaurant on one side and an air-conditioned bar on the other. At the rear of the property is a large, clean pool, although it's not as private as one would like, and you need to move away from it to do any sunbathing. There's also a first-floor terrace. The modern rooms, housed in two separate blocks, are plainly furnished but nice and light, with reasonably sized bathrooms and walk-in showers. The hotel is located on a quiet side street close to place Mohammed V and some of the ville nouvelle's restaurants.

9 rue Abdelkarim el Khattabi, Ville Nouvelle, Fes. © **035/622148** or 035/650283. Fax 035/654892. 70 units. 284dh ($36/£18) single; 348dh ($44/£22) double; 449dh ($56/£28) triple. Breakfast 31dh ($3.90/£1.95). Children under 5 stay free in parent's room. Limited secure parking available. MC, V. **Amenities:** Restaurant; bar; lounge w/TV; pool. *In room:* A/C, satellite TV.

WHERE TO DINE

The choice of dining options in Fes reflects the culture of the city's two distinct areas. Within the ancient walled city, authentic Moroccan food is the cuisine of choice, with only the setting, ambience, and price being the difference. This apparent lack of choice sits easily; to eat anything else while surrounded by such history and tradition would seem out of place. Out in the ville nouvelle is a surprisingly small selection of restaurants with a range of cuisines and settings.

The restaurants recommended below are all relatively easy to find, though for those in the medina it always helps to reset your bearings when you're departing for the walk back to your accommodations.

MEDINA
Very Expensive

Dar Anebar 🎭🎭🎭 MOROCCAN   This classy *maison d'hôte* is also a very fine restaurant. Open for dinner only, candles, soft lighting, and low background music set the scene for an intimate meal, enhanced by discreet table placement. After a large selection of Moroccan "tasters" (be careful not to fill up), diners can choose to indulge in chicken tagine with preserved lemons, a fluffy vegetable couscous, lamb tagine with figs and almonds, or a pigeon *pastilla*. Dessert is a traditional sweet *pastilla* with nuts and milk custard followed by mint tea or freshly brewed coffee. This is top-end Moroccan cuisine with a homely touch, served at a suitable pace and overseen by owner/manager Ahmed, who ensures quality service without being intrusive.

15 Derb el Mitter, Zenjfor. © **035/635785** or 066/202614. Fax 035/637473. www.daranebar.com. Reservations recommended. 3-course set menu 300dh ($38/£19); 4-course set menu 400dh ($50/£25). Alcohol served. MC, V. Daily 7:30–11pm. Accessible by foot only; pickup available from Sofitel Palais Jamaï.

La Maison Bleue 🎭🎭🎭 MOROCCAN   Housed in one of "The Most Romantic Hotels of the World," La Maison Bleue serves exceptional traditional cuisine in a setting that is indeed romantic and worth the splurge. Mehdi el Abbadi converted his family's early-20th-century home into Fes's first *maison d'hôte*, and sister Kenza turned the kitchen and ground floor into one of the city's premier gourmet experiences. Aperitifs and olives are served in the marble-floor courtyard, while Andalusian or Gnaoua musicians play softly in the background; a *zellij* fountain provides a sound of tranquillity. Candle-lit tables are spread throughout three intimate salons. The four-course set menu changes with the seasons, but can include a meze of Moroccan salads, chicken or pigeon *pastilla*, and a delightful dessert of sliced orange in cinnamon. The ambience is matched by the service, which is attentive and discreet. Vegetarians should let their preferences be known at the start of the meal.

2 Ahmed Mekouar Sq., Batha. © **035/741843**. Fax 035/740686. www.maisonbleue.com. Reservations recommended. Set menu 500dh ($63/£31) guests; 550dh ($69/£34) nonguests. Includes wine and beverages. MC, V. Daily 7:30–11pm.

Restaurant al Fassia MOROCCAN 🧒 *Kids*   This is the most popular dinner show in Fes. Located just off Ahmed Mekouar Square, this palace/restaurant provides a show, complete with flashing lights, on a large carpeted courtyard surrounded by exquisite *zellij;* hand-carved stucco; intricate, hand-painted *tazouakt* ceilings; and brightly colored Iraqi glass. Ten acts perform throughout the evening, including a

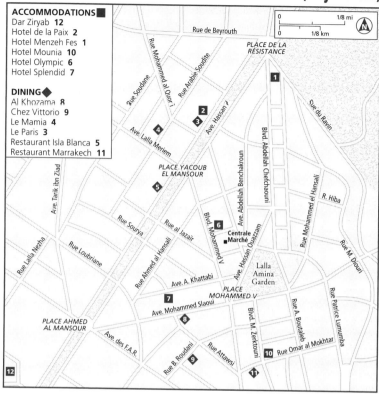

Fes Ville Nouvelle (City Center)

ACCOMMODATIONS ■
Dar Ziryab **12**
Hotel de la Paix **2**
Hotel Menzeh Fes **1**
Hotel Mounia **10**
Hotel Olympic **6**
Hotel Splendid **7**

DINING ◆
Al Khozama **8**
Chez Vittorio **9**
Le Mamia **4**
Le Paris **3**
Restaurant Isla Blanca **5**
Restaurant Marrakech **11**

four-piece Andalusian house band, a belly dancer, and a mock traditional wedding between two lucky diners. This scene is not for everyone, but can be fun if you're into it. Six menus offer five courses of various Moroccan classics, all delightfully presented, delicious, and large—you'll be doing well to eat everything that's put in front of you. The service can at times be a little gruff, but with so many meals and courses to serve, it's perhaps understandable.

21 rue Salaj (laneway opposite Hotel Batha). ✆ 035/637314. Set menus 250dh–600dh ($31–$75/£16–£38); 50dh ($6.25/£3.15) surcharge for floor show. 10% service tax not included. Alcohol served. MC, V. Daily 7–11:30pm.

Restaurant Nejjarine MOROCCAN Opened in 2006, Jalil Laghmri's restaurant is the perfect spot for an authentic Moroccan feast in the medina. As the name suggests, this 100-year-old building is located just steps from the Nejjarine Museum of Wooden Arts & Crafts (p. 231). Guests can dine in either a covered courtyard of Fassi *zellij* and intricately carved and painted cedar, or in any of the three large salons surrounding the courtyard, furnished with Moroccan-style lounges and silk cushions. The four-course meals include a delicious meze of Moroccan salads, tagines, or chicken or pigeon *pastilla,* accompanied with couscous and followed by fresh fruits and mint tea. For a breath of fresh air, head up to the rooftop terrace for a fantastic medina view. Jalil gets a few tour groups (for the most part his diners are individual travelers and their guides), and both the setting and service befit the classy ambience he has established.

9 rue Dermami, Nejjarine. © 061/259052. Set menus 120dh–220dh ($15–$28/£8–£14). MC, V. Daily noon–4pm.

Moderate

Restaurant Zohra MOROCCAN   Since 1993, this friendly, family-run restaurant has been serving simple, tasty Moroccan food to travelers looking for authentic cuisine at very reasonable prices. Diners can sit in any of the four salons, all furnished in the typical Moroccan style with low lounges (tired-looking but still comfortable) and tables with quirky wall hangings such as antique clocks, drums, and animal skins. Set menus offer all standard Moroccan staples such as *harira* soup, couscous, brochettes, *pastilla,* and tagine—try the chicken with almonds—with *salade Marocain* and pastries. The restaurant can be difficult to find but is very well known by the locals, who should be able to steer you in the right direction if you're struggling.

3 Derb Aïn Nass Blida, off Zenqat Blida. © 035/637699. Set menus 80dh–90dh ($10–$11/£5–£5.50). No credit cards. Sat–Thurs noon–10pm; Friday noon–3pm and 7–10pm.

Inexpensive

A string of eateries can be found within 50m (165 ft.) of the Bab Bou Jeloud medina entrance heading down rue Sarrajine. Hugely popular for the unbeatable people-watching location and cheap food—rather than the quality of the cuisine prepared in kitchens of questionable hygiene—some of these eateries are only distinguishable from each other by the color of their faux-satin covered chairs. The menus cover the Moroccan standards of brochettes, tagine, and couscous along with omelets, fries, and sandwiches. Unsuspecting travelers who stop to ponder where they will eat are soon beset upon by fast-talking touts competing for their business.

Restaurant Guenoune sums up the cheeky attitude that prevails here by stating on their English-language menu, "Our beef and chicken are mad cow- and bird flu-free." Locals—both Fassi and ex-pats—swear by **Thami's Restaurant** ✷✷, at the beginning of Tala'a Sghira, in the corner. Thami's *kefta* tagine with egg, fish dishes, and *pastilla* are all highly recommended; Thami also speaks English. Standing over the crowd is **Restaurant la Kasbah de Fes,** which climbs more than two stories with two separate roof terraces. **Restaurant Bouayad,** below the Hotel Cascade, lacks the pavement location but offers air-conditioning. Abderazak and Abdullah at **La Palma** provide freshly squeezed juices and milkshakes. All of the eateries around here open slowly during the morning but are lively by around 10am and continue through to at least 10pm daily.

Cafe Clock ✷✷✷ *Finds* INTERNATIONAL/CAFE   Mike Richardson, formerly of The Ivy and The Wolseley restaurants in London, has moved to Fes and recently opened up this vibrant, fresh alternative to the medina's traditional cafes. Set within a restored 250-year-old dar, Cafe Clock consists of a quaint, cool courtyard surrounded by two floors of rooms that include a relaxed juice bar, an open kitchen, nonsmoking lounge, and "red room" for parties and events. There's also a projector room for showing movies on select evenings, a book exchange, and information on Fes and Morocco, and the whole place is wired for Wi-Fi. The multilevel roof terrace is filled with plants and is a great place to view the sunset as the call to prayer carries out from the Bou Inania Medersa next door.

The menu is fresh and modern, with crunchy salads, grilled sandwiches, soups, great burgers (try the lamb with feta and mint), and daily Moroccan specials. The juice bar pumps out a welcome stream of smoothies, fresh juices, ice creams, home-made cakes and pastries, ice coffees, and a selection of teas. Mindful of Western tastes and concerns, Mike's breakfast choices include scrambled eggs and muesli, and the ice cubes are made with bottled water.

The atmosphere is very relaxed and friendly, and diners include both residents—it's "in" with the local creative crowd of writers, artists, and musicians—and travelers who enjoy its very convenient location only steps away from busy Tala'a Kebira.

7 Derb el Magana, off Tala'a Kebira, opposite Bou Inania Medersa. ✆ **061/183264**. www.cafeclock.com. Breakfast 20dh–50dh ($2.50–$6.25/£1.25–£3.15); lunch 25dh–80dh ($3.15–$10/£1.55–£5). No credit cards. Daily 9am–11pm.

Cremerie la Place ✪ JUICE BAR   This little hole-in-the-wall juice and tea stop— run by Hakim, Mustapha, and Rihab—is a godsend for travelers treading the alleys and lanes in the busy Kairouine/Seffarine area. Located right on place Seffarine next to the Kairouine Library, a few welcome tables are usually filled with thirsty folks recharging on Rihab's freshly squeezed apple, avocado, orange, and pineapple juices, or on a freshly brewed mint tea and pastry courtesy of waiter-extraordinaire Mustapha. Background music ranges from Moroccan folk to The Doors, and will have you up and marching in no time.

Place Seffarine. No phone. Juice 8dh ($1/50p); tea and pastry 15dh ($1.90/95p). No credit cards. Sat–Thurs 8am–9pm; Fri 3–9pm.

VILLE NOUVELLE
Moderate
Chez Vittorio ITALIAN/INTERNATIONAL   A dark-stained wood interior, checked tablecloths, and the smell of pizza greet diners as they enter this long-time favorite for Fassi families who live in the ville nouvelle. The menu includes classic pasta dishes such as *tagliatelle al forno* and a selection of pizzas; locals love the slightly charred, thin-crust *margarita*. Some ex-pats who have eaten here recommend skipping the Italian items and trying the international salads, onion soup, and beef brochettes. The atmosphere is usually lively, which is helped along by the reasonable wine list.

21 rue Brahim Roudani. ✆ **035/624730**. Pizzas 50dh–85dh ($6.25–$11/£3.15–£5.30); main courses 80dh–150dh ($10–$19/£5–£9.40). Alcohol served. MC, V. Daily noon–3pm and 7–11pm.

Restaurant Isla Blanca INTERNATIONAL   Since 2003, this has been a welcome alternative in Fes for those looking for something other than Moroccan cuisine. Although conveniently positioned on busy avenue Hassan II, double-glazed doors and air-conditioning keep the noise outside. The interior is modern and intimate in the nonsmoking front dining room, while a larger room in the rear can get quite smoky and is more of a meeting place for locals who wish to eat—and drink—away from prying eyes. The varied menu includes a good selection of cold and hot starters includ-ing Andalusian minestrone soup and a large cheese platter, while entrees range from pastas and thin-crust pizzas to grilled meats including brochettes *de dinde* (turkey pieces on skewers) and grilled Saint-Pierre (John Dory). There's also a three-course Moroccan set menu and a very good selection of local wines available. Friendly wait-ers—some English speaking—and monogrammed crockery add a touch of class. A separate entrance leads up to a very smoky local bar upstairs.

32 av. Hassan II. ✆ **035/930357**. Fax 035/942153. Starters 25dh–85dh ($3.15–$11/£1.55–£5.30); pizzas 55dh–80dh ($6.90–$10/£3.45–£5); main courses 40dh–115dh ($5–$14/£2.50–£7.20). Alcohol served. MC, V. Daily noon–3pm and 7pm–midnight.

Restaurant Marrakech 🍴🍴 MOROCCAN   Mustapha Aziz's little restaurant has been a travelers' favorite for more than 20 years. Renovated in 2005 in a Marrakchi-colored *tadelakt* with plush burgundy and gold furnishings, the atmosphere is intimate yet relaxed and friendly, with a mixed clientele of Moroccans and travelers. Six set menus offer various three-course combinations of salads, *harira* soup, tagines, brochettes, couscous, chicken *pastilla*, fruit, and mint tea. It's all well cooked and a very good value.

Corner of rue Omar el Mokhtar and bd. Mohammed V. ⓒ 035/930876 or 064/437862. Set menus 115dh–125dh ($14–$16/£7.20–£7.80). No credit cards. Daily noon–3pm and 6–10:30pm.

Inexpensive

Al Khozama 🍴 INTERNATIONAL   Run by a hard-working father-son team, this is my favorite place in the ville nouvelle for a cheap meal. The small kitchen offers an amazing—considering its size—range of dishes that lean toward the quick and tasty. Pizzas, pasta, grilled meats, salads, omelets, sandwiches, and savory crepes are all served with a smile and in good portions. There are tables inside, but the outside tables are the best spot for people-watching.

23 av. Mohammed es Slaoui. ⓒ 064/143424. Sandwiches 15dh–20dh ($1.90–$2.50/95p–£1.25); pizzas 35dh ($4.40/£2.20); main courses 25dh–70dh ($3.15–$8.75/£1.55–£4.40). No credit cards. Daily 8am–10pm.

Le Paris CAFE/BREAKFAST   Located a couple of doors down from Hotel de la Paix on busy avenue Hassan II, this is a perfect spot for breakfast. The on-site bakery ensures a steady supply of croissants, *petit pain,* and *pain au chocolat,* as well as Moroccan *msemmen* and *baghrir.* A set breakfast allows for a selection of these along with freshly squeezed orange juice and coffee or tea; ask for Lipton if you don't want mint tea. If you're here at any other time, the bakery also dabbles in a delicious range of gâteaux. A spacious interior and mezzanine level affords some privacy, while the outdoor tables are for those who like to watch and be watched.

40 av. Hassan II. No phone. Breakfast 15dh–20dh ($1.90–$2.50/95p–£1.25). No credit cards. Daily 7am–11pm.

Le Mamia 🔍 ITALIAN   This little pizzeria is great for a quick, cheap meal of wood-fired pizza, hamburgers, spaghetti bolognaise, or a fresh salad. A grilled steak with fries, rice, and vegetables is available for those looking for something more substantial. Alfresco tables look out over a busy city square, or there are more private tables upstairs—a warm option during the colder months. The service can be a bit up and down, but the food is dependable and does the trick.

Place Yacoub el Mansour (formerly place de Florence), av. Hassan II. ⓒ 035/623164. Pizzas 30dh–67dh ($3.75–$8.40/£1.90–£4.20); main courses 22dh–50dh ($2.75–$6.25/£1.40–£3.15). No credit cards. Daily noon–3pm and 6–10:30pm.

WHAT TO SEE & DO

There's no particular sight within Fes's aging walls that defines its attractions; it's what you experience—through sight, smell, sound, taste, and touch—that you remember most. Within the largely confining walls of Fes el Bali and Fes Jdid is the world's last great medieval city, and *this* is what you come here to see. When Fes was declared a UNESCO World Heritage site in 1980, the organization's director-general described the city as "a single example of what men, moved by the same faith and the same ideal, and coming together from different horizons . . . have been able to achieve."

Besides the very worthy attractions listed below, there are an infinite number of possible attractions just waiting to be discovered down every one of the medina's 9,500

Tips Watch Out!

As you are exploring the medina, listen out for cries of "Balak! Balak!" This is a warning that coming up in front or behind you is one of the medina's thousands of working donkeys and mules.

twisting alleys, blind corners, dark lanes, and frustrating dead ends. Heaving masses of impatient people, mules laden with anything from stinking animal hides to baskets of fresh flowers, giggling school girls skipping home from school, grizzly old men playing checkers in a cafe, an impromptu game of street football—open yourself up to these possibilities, and you'll begin to know the real Fes.

FES EL BALI (OLD FES)

Bab Bou Jeloud ★★★   Bab Bou Jeloud is a monumental gateway that spans one the medina's busiest thoroughfares and is a good starting point for your explorations inside the medina walls. This gate (*bab* in Arabic) was constructed by the French in 1913, but the 12th-century original—positioned with an indirect entrance to negate battering rams—can still be seen next to it. The gate's Mauresque-Andalusian style is replicated in the Morocco exhibit in Orlando's EPCOT center, and the horseshoe arches are decorated with Fassi blue tiles on the outside and green tiles on the inside, patterned in the form of stars and swirls. Standing outside looking in, you can see two minarets. The one on the right belongs to the crumbling 11th-century Sidi Lazzaz mosque and is usually topped with a stork's nest. The other minaret, topped by two golden orbs, is part of the 14th-century Bou Inania Medersa (see below).

For much of the day, the cobbled artery that slices through Bab Bou Jeloud is a constant movement of people, donkeys, mules, and mopeds, and once you've viewed its exterior beauty, this is the real attraction of Bab Bou Jeloud. There are a number of cafe-restaurants both just inside the gate (p. 224) and outside that afford some quality viewing of everyday life in this medieval city.

Note: Look for the huge bolt on the outside of the French-built gate. In a complete reversal of function, during the protectorate era, the medina was closed at night and locked from the outside.

Bou Inania Medersa ★★★   The most celebrated of the many *medersas* (theological colleges and dormitories) built by the Merenid dynasty, Bou Inania Medersa is a group of buildings built between 1350 and 1356 by Sultan Abou Inan. It simultaneously functioned as both an educational institute and as a congregational mosque, and accommodated shops and a large public latrine along the front facade. Not a particularly pious man, it is thought that Abou Inan built the *medersa*, with its accompanying mosque and minaret, as his personal rival to the powerful Kairouine complex to its east. Legend has it that upon being presented with the total cost of its construction, Abou Inan tore apart the accounts, threw them into the river, and responded dismissively, "Whatever is beautiful cannot be expensive at any price. What is enthralling is never too costly." *Zellij,* carved wood, and panels of stucco, originally a mix of plaster and egg whites, finely carved with Koranic verses decorate every available surface of the courtyard. Wood *mashrabiyya* screens separate the marble-paved courtyard from the arcaded corridors leading to the student rooms. The contrast between the excessive decoration in the courtyard and the spartan accommodations for the students, in use up to 1956, is quite alarming. The green-tile roof and tall minaret are noticeable from Bab Bou Jeloud (see above). As part of the ongoing Réhabilitation de la Médina de Fès project, the *medersa* is currently undergoing restoration and should reopen to visitors sometime in 2008.

Tala'a Kbira (main entrance), 150m (490 ft.) from Bab Bou Jeloud. Admission 10dh ($1.25/65p) adults and children 12 and older. Daily 8:30am–5:30pm.

Chouwara Tannery ☆☆☆   Northeast of the Kairouine Mosque and Seffarine Square is Fes's most visited—and aromatic—sight. A picture straight out of medieval times, the Chouwara tannery is the largest and busiest of the four traditional tanner-ies still operating in the medina. Sheep, goat, and cow skins are cured, stretched, scraped and dyed in numerous honeycombed earthen pits in a process that is still as manual as when it began in the 13th century upon the decline of Cordoba. The skins are cured by a concoction that includes cow urine and pigeon guano and are then laid atop the rooftops to dry. The final dying process involves the leather being mixed and soaked by hand in the vats before being trimmed for the medina's leatherworkers. The vegetable dyes—poppy (red), turmeric (yellow), mint (green), indigo (blue)—have been replaced by chemicals that, along with the odd rinsing machine, are the only modern concessions to have infiltrated the process. It's both a confronting and fasci-nating view at the same time, and strongly challenges your sense of voyeuristic tourism. Perhaps the knowledge that the tanneries are still one of the most important sources of income and trade for the city may temper any misgivings. The Chouwara tanneries are best viewed in the morning, from the roof-terrace leatherware shops along Derb Chouwara (p. 236), where a well-placed sprig of mint will help those who find the smell perhaps more confronting than the sight.

Derb Chouwara, Blida, Medina. Daily 9am–6pm.

Dar Batha Museum   This late-19th-century palace was built by Sultan Moulay al-Hassan I during the final years of decadence before Morocco's occupation by the French (this is where the French Protectorate Treaty was signed in 1912) and now houses excellent exhibits of Morocco's renowned craftsmanship. On display are fine examples of woodcarving, stucco, and *zellij*, much of it rescued from Fes's crumbling *medersas*, along with embroidery, Berber carpets, jewelry, musical instruments, textiles, and calligraphy. Also check out the small collection of ancient astronomical instru-ments. At the far end of the palace is its head-lining ceramic collection, with pieces dating back from the 14th century. Here you can easily distinguish the unique Fassi style. Specialists since the 10th century, they invented the famous "Fes blue" obtained by the use of cobalt. Always on a background of white enamel, the stylized floral motifs interweave in a manner that is sophisticated yet harmonious.

The displays are explained in Arabic and French only, but there is usually an Eng-lish-speaking guide at the entrance, which I recommend to get full value of the exhibits. The palace's interior Andalusian-style garden is surrounded by a covered walkway with finely crafted wood ceilings, and is a pleasant place to take a break.

Ahmed Mekouar Sq.; museum entrance is 60m (195 ft.) up the narrow road separating it from the Hotel Batha. Admission 10dh ($1.25/65p) adults and children 12 and older. No credit cards. Wed–Mon 8:30am–4:30pm.

Kairouine Mosque and University   The most important mosque in Morocco, and one of the oldest universities in the world, can only be seen from the outside for non-Muslims. It was built in 859 by Fatima el Fihria, the daughter of a wealthy immi-grant from Kairouan, Tunisia, and by the 10th century had become the congregational mosque of the Kairouine quarter of the medina. Surrounded by *medersas,* it became a major intellectual center in medieval Mediterranean; a popular tradition suggests Pope Sylvester II, who was instrumental in western Europe's adoption of Arabic numerals, was once a student here. This Mediterranean connection is evident in both the 12th-century Almoravid *minbar* (pulpit), made from precious wood and inlaid ivory and originally from the then-great Islamic center of Cordoba, and two flanking early-17th-century Saâdian pavilions modeled on those of the Lion Court in the Alhambra at Grenada. Two chandeliers inside the mosque were church bells of Andalusian origin.

Such is the mosque's concealment by the surrounding shops and businesses that it's hard to tell from the outside that more than 20,000 worshippers can attend prayers inside, under the vaults supported by 270 columns.

The best interior view non-Muslims can manage is from the main entrance opposite the Attarine and Mesbahiya *medersas,* from where it's possible to see the Saâdian pavilions to the far right (if you're standing on the far left side of the door). If you continue around the perimeter of the mosque to Seffarine Square, you'll come to the entrance to the Kairouine Library, unfortunately also off-limits to non-Muslims. This once held one of the greatest collections of Islamic literature in all of Arabia and was a place of pilgrimage for those seeking intellectual and spiritual knowledge. Much of the library's collection was lost in the 17th century, but some precious manuscripts and volumes have survived. The present reading room was built in 1940 by Mohammed V and has recently been restored and reopened to Muslim scholars.

Nejjarine Museum of Wooden Arts & Crafts ★★★ When the Nejjarine Foundouk, "Inn of the Carpenters," first opened its doors in the 12th century, it was one of the largest "hotels" in the world, comparable to palaces being built in Europe at the same time and capable of housing 100 or more merchants. The *foundouk* was designed to meet the needs of the thriving commercial center that Fes had become. The massive double door that can be seen today marked the *foundouk*'s entrance and was designed to admit a traveler on camel or horseback; it also includes two smaller panels that swing open to admit people on foot. The *foundouk*'s purpose eventually shifted toward accommodating traveling merchants who would stay upstairs and keep their animals and sell their wares downstairs. Reflecting the decline of the city in the 17th and 18th centuries, the *foundouk* was used solely to house pack animals, although in more recent times it was also used as lodging for students at the nearby Kairouine University.

Standing proudly in a corner of the small Nejjarine Square and the carpenter's souk from which it is named, the *foundouk* has been beautifully restored and now houses three levels of exhibits centered around a large, pleasant courtyard. Each floor has three or four rooms to a side, each opening onto an internal veranda that overlooks the central courtyard. The ground floor and the first floor are strengthened by heavy cedar beams; the top-floor veranda boasts geometric latticework railing. The *foundouk*'s former rooms now house displays of traditional woodworking tools, cooking implements, musical instruments, Islamic literature, and other artifacts. With explanations only in French and Arabic, the displays are really only interesting as a whole; it's the restored building itself that is the star attraction. In reference to the building's original function, hanging in the courtyard are two sets of scales big enough to weigh a small child. On the rooftop terrace is a pleasant cafe and a wood *minbar* of four small steps that offers a sweeping view of the northern medina. The entire square and souk were also restored, and in the alleys leading off there are the carpenters' workshops, surrounded by the sweet smell of cedar wood.

Place Nejjarine. Admission 20dh ($2.50/£1.25) adults and children 12 and older; free for children under 12. No credit cards. Daily 10am–5pm.

Seffarine Square   This is one of the busiest stops on the guided-tour circuit. One of the oldest trades practiced in Fes is that of the copperware craftsmen, and surrounding Seffarine Square—and the source of the noisy clanging and banging—are coppersmiths shaping and polishing all manner of pots, cauldrons, plates, and buckets. It's best viewed while sipping a mint tea at Cremerie la Place (p. 227) in the northeast corner of the small square.

Seffarine Sq., Kairouine, Medina. Daily; some workshops closed Fri and Sun.

FES JDID (NEW FES)

At the beginning of the 14th century, Fes's Jewish community was relocated to an area known as the Mellah in the Merenid-built Fes Jdid. This concentration of the community's skills—and wealth—led to a prosperous neighborhood of multistory houses with large interior patios and balconies hanging over the street, many of them decorated in the stucco and *zellij* designs from the Jew's Andalusian heritage. Take a walk along wide, straight rue de Merenides (also known as Derb el Mellah) to see the faded grandeur of these houses and balconies.

In the south of the Mellah abutting the medina walls is a blinding mass of more than 18,000 whitewashed tombs dating from the beginning of the Mellah itself to as recent as 2004. Row upon row of rounded rectangular tombs are lined up in sections for children, adults, priests, and distinguished persons. Two tombs rising above the others are those of Sol the Just and Yehuda ben Atar, both of whom are considered saints and are subject to ongoing annual pilgrimages. An elegant white tomb with green trim is that of Solica, a 14-year-old girl who, in 1834, was killed after rebuking an offer of marriage—along with the necessary conversion to Islam—by the Governor of Tangier. The elderly *gardien* is usually on hand at the main gate (ring the bell) to

---

Salt & the Jews

Mellah is the name given to all the Jewish neighborhoods in Morocco. The Mellah in Fes Jdid was the country's first, built in 1276 for the Jewish Syrian archers employed in the army of the ruling Merenid dynasty. Eventually all of the city's Jews were relocated to this district and fell under the direct protection of the sultan and his nearby palace. The Saâdian rulers took similar action in Marrakech in 1558. Both relocations may have occurred to install the Jewish population as a physical buffer zone between the ruling sultan and his subjects should there have been any unrest and violence. Another school of thought is that it simply made it easier for the sultan to collect taxes from the Jews. Even up until the early 20th century, Moroccan Jews were relatively wealthy compared to their Muslim and Berber countrymen, comprising a large majority of the country's bankers and jewelers. Historically, they also controlled Morocco's sugar and salt trade. It's this latter connection to salt, *maleh* in Arabic, and the Fes neighborhood's close proximity to the Oued el Maleh (Salty River) that the name Mellah was derived.

---

show you around. Enter via the door at the junction of Derb Temara and Derb Taourirt. A second entrance is located on the first street to the right after entering through Bab Lamar. The garden is open daily and is free, but a 10dh ($1.25/65p) gratuity is recommended.

OUTSIDE THE MEDINA
Medina Viewpoints

At some stage of your visit, try to head up to one of the convenient viewpoints looking over the medina. Borj Sud and Borj Nord were both lookout towers built in the late 16th century by the Saâdians to keep watch over any potential unrest within the medina. Nowadays they offer up the best views of the medina. Borj Nord is the most accessible of two from Bab Bou Jeloud. About 500m (⅓ mile) past Borj Nord are the Merenid Tombs, which also have a great view and usually play host to a sunrise concert during Fes's Festival of World Sacred Music. Any other time of the year, however, it's not safe to hang around at the ruins too long after dark. For all three lookout points, catch a *petit* taxi for 5dh to 10dh (65¢–$1.25/30p–65p) one-way. The Merenid Tombs are the closest to both the main road and the medina walls, should you wish to walk one or both ways.

ESPECIALLY FOR KIDS

The inherent joy and untainted affection that Fassis have for all children can open up doors to experiences that parents may not have otherwise been offered. On the other hand, however, exploring the medina can be a tiring experience with small children, largely due to the human traffic congestion that occurs along narrowing lanes and at various junctions. Keeping your children's attention level on high, however, shouldn't be difficult in the medina, thanks to a veritable circus of music shops with lots of drums; Berber pharmacies (called *herboristes*) with brightly colored concoctions; butcheries with the odd sheep's or camel's head prominently displayed; and tanneries of brightly colored leather and grown men jumping up and down in colored baths. Even having to dodge the regular trails of equine refuse can lead to squeals of laughter. Worth a visit, especially during summer, is **Baghdadi Square** between Bab Bou Jeloud and Bab Mahrouka. In the late afternoon you'll normally find a few musicians, storytellers, and potion salesman. Other than the offerings in the medina, Fes is sadly lacking in any other activities that can claim to be child friendly. Out in the ville nouvelle, at the junction of avenue Hassan II and avenue des F.A.R., a few *calèches* have begun to appear during the warmer months, offering rides for tired little legs. Come meal time, those who are missing their familiar burgers and fries can be accommodated at the McDonald's on place de la Résistance in the ville nouvelle.

SHOPPING

To shop, or even browse, in Fes requires large doses of patience, humor, or money—preferably all three. Fassi shopkeepers are the doyen of hagglers, and it takes a concerted effort to go head to head with one. Keeping this in mind, it must be said that Fes el Bali is Morocco's shopping center. Here you can find whole streets of artisans devoted to just one specific trade. Woodwork, *babouches,* jewelry, tailored clothing, leatherwork, pottery, mosaic tiling, brass and copperware, cotton and silk weaving, drums—all can be bought direct from the factory, so to speak. Approach each experience with a smile and positive thoughts, and your shopping in Fes can prove memorable.

Items that particularly require the three previously mentioned qualities are carpets, *kélims,* and rugs. It seems everywhere you turn in Fes el Bali, a *maison du tapis* is right there. Unfortunately, this seemingly excess supply doesn't equate to bargain prices. Carpets aren't cheap in Fes. If you're traveling into the Atlas mountains or beyond into central Morocco and the palmeraies, then frankly you are better off waiting until then. The carpet emporiums of Fes know this and can be annoyingly persistent for your business once you show even a flicker of interest. If you intend on shopping for carpets and rugs here, have a good idea of how much you are willing to pay before you begin any negotiations. It's your choice, and remember that you can always walk out of the shop. Once you've started, however, sit back and enjoy the banter, mint tea, and plethora of choice displayed before you.

Caution: When shopping in Fes's medina, don't rely on being able to use your credit card. For most of your purchases, cash—usually dirham but sometimes euros or dollars—will be the only form of payment accepted. Some carpet emporiums and antiques shops may accept credit cards, but be aware of the full amount being charged to your card prior to signing off the transaction. The purchase should be charged in dirham, so be aware of current exchange rates; if you're not sure, ask the proprietor to show you where the day's rate has been procured from and the calculation conducted to arrive at the price. On no occasion should you agree to pay for your purchase in monthly installments. There's every chance that the multiple slips that you signed will either be banked all together or, worse, that you discover the amounts were manipulated upon your arrival back home.

For everyday items, head to the **Central Marché** in the ville nouvelle on boulevard Mohammed V, 2 blocks north of place Mohammed V. Here you'll find fresh produce, dried fruits and nuts, and dairy products. There are also a couple of alcohol shops on either side of the entrance opposite the Hotel Olympic. For fresh produce, groceries, toiletries, and alcohol, there's an **Acima** supermarket in the ville nouvelle, on avenue Mahmoud al Aqqad, in the direction of the Fes-Meknes auto route (© 035/931374), which is open daily from 9am to 10pm. On the western edge of the ville nouvelle, on the old highway to Meknes, is the Western-style, air-conditioned **Marjane Hypermarket** (© 035/957814), open daily from 9am to 9pm and selling everything from groceries and general foodstuffs (including bacon) to cookware and computers. There's also an ATM, pharmacy, and well-stocked liquor store that stays open for tourists during Ramadan.

SHOPPING A TO Z
Antiques
On or around Derb Sidi Moussa, southeast of the Foundouk Nejjarine Museum, are a smattering of antiques shops, the best of which is Chakib Lahkim Bennani's **Les Mystères de Fes,** 53 Derb Bin Lemsarri, off rue Sidi Moussa, Guerniz (© 035/636148 or 061/483195). Chakib's family have been antiques dealers of note since 1922, and their three-story, 13th-century riad is all class. "I am obliged to find and sell the best of the best," Chakib says. You can spend a whole day here wandering around and marveling at the craftsmanship required to produce a 19th-century pure silver settee with blue-velvet cushions; twin 2m-high (6½-ft.) bronze urns; carpets interwoven with silk and silver; Berber turquoise pottery; antique Arab jewelry; and a calligraphy-engraved crystal *terriya,* or chandelier. Most of the pieces are of Moroccan origin, but there are also items from Syria, Turkey, and India. There are small pieces that make great souvenirs; large items can be bought, wrapped, and shipped in handmade wood chests to anywhere in the world. Open daily 9am to 7pm.

(Tips) Guided Shopping

Guides will invariably lead you to their shops of choice while showing you around the medina. As this is their livelihood, a guide will want you to purchase something so that he will earn a commission from the sale, sometimes up to 30%. This incentive for you to buy can work in your favor if you're a good haggler and stick to your guns. If you prefer to shop on your own, then strongly advise your guide of this before you begin. He may then request you to increase the rate for the tour by 100dh ($13/£6.25)—from 250dh to 350dh ($31–$44/£16–£22) for example—which is fair enough if it then affords you more time to visit the sights and profit from his knowledge rather than his shopping contacts.

Carpets & Rugs

"If a carpet talks to your heart, it will make you happy," says carpet salesman extraordinaire Hakim Hamid, *directeur* of **Aux Merveilles du Tapis,** 22 Derb Sbaâ Louyat, Seffarine, Medina (next door to Dar Seffarine; p. 219; ℂ **035/638735** or phone Hakim direct on 063/672068). Sit back and enjoy your mint tea while he explains the connection between Morocco's architecture (the shop itself is housed in a grand 14th-century palace) and its carpets; the difference between Berber rugs and Royal (Arabic) carpets; and the importance of knots, lambs' wool, and reversible carpets. His sales pitch is so corny it's funny, is not at all pushy, and makes for an enjoyable experience even if you don't buy. If you are buying, then you'll be spoilt for choice in design, color, and size. Hakim estimates there are 3,000 carpets, rugs, and *kélims* within this shop, and I don't doubt him. Prices vary greatly depending on the quality of craftsmanship and your negotiation skills, but small *kélims* can go for as little as 1,000dh ($125/£63); a medium-size (2m×2m/6½ ft.×6½ ft.) Berber rug for 5,000dh ($625/£313); and a 4m×4m (13 ft.×13 ft.) reversible carpet can sell for 32,000dh ($4,000/£2,000). Open daily 9am to 7pm.

For cotton and silk rugs, visit **Chez Alibaba,** 7 Derb el Mitter, Blida, Medina (between Pension Dalila and Restaurant Zohra; ℂ **035/636932**). Mustapha Jamila and his jovial staff will gladly show you the weaving process; cotton, wool, and Algarve silk are some of the threads being used on the traditional loom here. Rugs and throw blankets can be ordered in a rainbow of colors and made within a day, and there is also a wide choice of lamp shades, bed covers, curtains, and cushion covers. Open daily 9am to 7pm.

Embroidery

Rachid Alaoui's **Maison de Broderie,** Derb Blida (20m/66 ft. southwest from the junction with Derb Hassan; ℂ **035/636546** or 070/857675), is one of the premier embroidery shops in the medina. English-speaking Rachid is a wealth of knowledge on the craft and will gladly explain the work being produced on-site, except Fridays when the women have a day off. Crisp, white bedspreads, cushions, napkins, and tablecloths are all decorated with exquisitely embroidered Berber designs. Open daily 9am to 7pm (American Express, MasterCard, and Visa are accepted).

Fashion

Chez Alami's **Caftan Saâda,** on Tala'a Kbira just east of the Bouanania Medersa (℃ **067/188873** or 067/334000), is the place to go for *jellabahs* and caftans. Alami has been operating from this 1312 riad for 22 years, and the wall-to-wall choice of designs and colors is staggering. For high quality shawls and scarves, visit **Chez Alibaba** (above).

Leatherware

Terrasse de Tannerie, 10 Derb Chouwara at the Chouwara Tanneries (℃ **035/ 636625**), is a veritable rabbit's warren of all things leather. Camel, cow, and goat leather products—*babouches, poufes,* belts, jackets, wallets, and every size bag imaginable—are crammed within a series of rooms that eventually lead to a split-level covered terrace with the best view of the tanneries down below. It's a busy shop (guides bring their groups here throughout the day), but the staff are always keen to sell and are usually willing to give you time to absorb the atmosphere, view, and even smell before choosing something. Pay attention to the varying qualities of leather (camel leather is the most supple); bad-quality leather will crack over time. A well-placed basket of fresh mint leaves is at the top of the stairs as you enter. Open daily 9am to sunset.

Music

Lajaj Ali's **Fabrication de Percussions & de Poterie,** 23 Derb el Horra (20m/66 ft. from Tala'a Sghira; ℃ **035/635954** or 060/916750), is a rustic, ramshackle treasure trove of the many different styles of percussion instruments played in Morocco. Since the 1930s, Lajaj's father and now Lajaj himself have been producing quality drums—*darbuka, bandia, tabla, tahr,* and *djembe*—from the 200-year-old riad. Drum makers are often at work in the front rooms, while in the courtyard is a mass of drums stacked in amongst Fassi pottery, antique carpets, and what can quaintly be described as bric-a-brac. Lajaj is a very genuine man who loves nothing more than to explain the historical context behind each drum. An average-size *darbuka* sells for around 200dh ($25/£13) and a *tabla* for 250dh ($31/£16). Open Saturday to Thursday 9am to 6pm; sometimes open Friday morning.

Pottery & Ceramics

Direct from the potter, the pieces at master potter **Serghini Maître Potier,** 32 Aïn Nokbi (℃ **035/761629** or 035/649726), are the best in quality and consequently not the cheapest. Two floors house everything from ashtrays to fountains. Most of the common housewares—bowls, vases, cups—are decorated in the distinctive Fassi style and colors. If you have the time, take the free guided tour at the rear of the property to see the entire process from raw clay to the finished product; note that some workers are absent on Fridays. There's usually a steady stream of shoppers traipsing through, but there's always a staff member on hand to assist you—and haggle with. English-speaking Azzeddine Khaloui is one of the most respected sales assistants in the quarter, and can be contacted after hours at ℃ **072/723683** if required. Open daily 8:30am to sunset.

If you can't make it out to the quarter, Abdelfettah Dahhouki's **Le Bleu de Fes,** on the corner of Tala'a Kbira and Rhat Shems (℃ **067/254079**), has a nice selection of both pottery and *zellij.* Easily packed items include square-tile house numbers for your home (150dh/$19/£9.40) and small, *zellij*-topped mosaic tables weighing only 3kgs (6.5 lb.) and selling for around 275dh ($34/£17). Open daily 8am to 8pm; closed Friday during the colder months.

Spices & *Herboristes*

Recognizable by the cone-shape mounds of green (henna), red (paprika), and yellow (turmeric) on display at their entrances are the medina's spice shops. An essential item in everyday Moroccan cooking, spices can be bought readily and without any haggling. Prices should be fixed (around 20dh/$2.50/£1.25 per 100 grams/¼ lb. for any standard spice, perhaps a little more for saffron; see p. 387) and the transaction drama-free.

The medina's *herboristes,* on the other hand, provide much more entertainment for your money. Along with selling spices, including a mixture of 35 different varieties known as *ras el hanout* that is great for stews and casseroles, these Berber chemists show off their stock of herbal medicines, oils, and teas said to "cure" everything from bladder problems and constipation to depression and obesity; there's even a Viagra tea for impotence. Abdou Belkhaid, aka **Herboriste Abdou,** 148 rue Sidi Moussa, Guerniz (© **035/638127**), has more than 350 jars of goodies to show you, along with a huge line-up of perfumed oils—cedar wood, jasmine, orange, amber, rose—and natural cosmetics. He's open every day from 9am to 7pm. In a similar vein is Amina's and Sanae's **Aux Mille Epices,** 42 Derb Blida (20m/66 ft. southwest from the junction with Derb Hassan; © **035/741879** or 066/514825).

Tip: If you are anywhere near the Acima or Marjane supermarkets (p. 234), have a look at their spice section. Although obviously lacking the atmosphere of shopping in the medina, you are very likely to find the exact same spices at a cheaper price.

FES AFTER DARK

As befits this spiritual, conservative, and orthodox city, most nightlife in Fes revolves around family activities and nonalcoholic pursuits, namely enjoying an ice cream or drinking coffee or mint tea in one of the city's cafes. From late afternoon to late evening, you'll often find families and young Fassis hanging out on **Baghdadi Square,** between Bab Mahrouk and Bab Bou Jeloud. Quite often you'll find musicians, storytellers, and even some African *herboristes*—a la Jemaa el Fna in Marrakech—entertaining the crowds and adding a noisy, lively atmosphere to the evening stroll. The newly opened **Cafe Clock** (p. 226) is a great place to meet both locals and travelers. It hosts irregular literary and film events, including movie nights in the special projector room. If you're looking for a drink in the medina, the long-time watering hole of choice is still the **Hotel Batha** (p. 221). The hotel's colonialesque Churchill lounge is a popular haunt with both ex-pat residents and hotel guests, while the Le Consul bar at the rear can sometimes have quite a party happening and stays open until 2am. For a refined, though expensive, after-dark drink, head to the **Sofitel Palais Jamaï,** Bab Guissa (© **035/634331;** www.sofitel.com). This 1879 former palace has a piano bar—which actually has a piano—and also offers glorious sweeping views over the medina. Come here for sunset.

Out in the ville nouvelle, the cafes surrounding place Mohammed V are always a good spot to watch the evening throngs. There are also a few male-only bars around here. The only other options for a drink are in the enclosed bars of the Hotel Mounia (p. 223) and Hotel Splendid (p. 223).

For evening pursuits of the cultural kind, contact the **Arabic Language Institute in Fes (ALIF)** and the **American Language Center,** 2 rue Ahmed Hiba, Ville Nouvelle (© **035/624850;** fax 035/931608; www.alif-fes.com), to see if they have any upcoming events.

2 Meknes *

60km (37 miles) from Fes

Meknes is Morocco's third imperial city and perhaps its most overlooked. Most visitors to Meknes at best stay one night as part of an itinerary that includes visits to Volubilis and Moulay Idriss Zerhoun. Some see the city only as part of a day trip from Fes. Perennially compared to Fes, Meknes is certainly yet to embrace tourism with the same vigor. The city boasts no great hotel chains, very few decent restaurants, and less than a handful of restored *maisons d'hôte* in its medina. Meknassis, the residents of Meknes, themselves are different from their Fassi cousins; they are somewhat more dark skinned and diminutive in stature, speak with a distinct accent, and often have different political views. For the traveler, however, the differences are the very reason to visit Meknes. The city has its fair share of monuments within a medina that is still largely residential and hassle-free. Untainted by a desperate desire to cash in on the increase in tourism to Morocco, Meknes is a joy to discover.

Meknes joined the select group of imperial cities when Moulay Ismail became the second sultan of the Alaouite dynasty that still rules today. Ascending the throne after his brother's untimely death from a horse fall, Moulay Ismail promptly moved the seat of power from the desert-fringed Tafilalt to fertile and well-watered Meknes, less rebellious than Fes or Marrakech. The town itself had been settled in the 10th century by the Berber Meknassis tribe and had, over different periods, housed Almohad and Merenid sultans. Meknes's greatest—indeed, its only—golden age was solely due to the reign of Moulay Ismail. His 55-year rule was the longest in Moroccan history and is regarded as one of its greatest. Inheriting a country weakened by internal tribal wars and royal successions in 1672, the 26-year-old Ismail became, at least in European eyes, the most notorious of Morocco's rulers. The builder of an imperial city intended to equal Versailles (Louis XIV was building his palace at the same time and the two grew to become close allies), Moulay Ismail is the sire, according to legend, of more than a thousand children, yet also a monster of cruelty in his treatment of both his slaves and subjects. For those who crossed the sultan's path or were in the wrong place at the wrong time, death was their imminent fate. He constructed his Imperial Palace with captives from military campaigns in Algeria and Mauritania, along with Christian slaves captured by the notorious Sallee Rovers (p. 300) during their raids on western Europe. He would often use these Christians as bargaining tools with the European powers, receiving vast sums of money in exchange for their return.

The sultan was also an extremely able ruler who kept a tight hold on the country and based his power on a standing army of 150,000 West African slaves called the Black Guard. During his reign, Ismail expelled the British, Ottoman Turks, and Spanish from Morocco's shores, and was a prodigious builder of roads, bridges, kasbahs, and mosques. His vision for his beloved Meknes was grand, and before his death at the age of 80, he had endowed the city with more than 25km (16 miles) of protective walls, seven monumental *babs*, or gates, and a vast palace complex.

Moulay Ismail's death in 1727 also signaled the demise of Meknes's stature, and within 30 years his grandson, Mohammed III, had transferred the Alaouite capital to Marrakech. The city's fortunes were somewhat revived during the protectorate era as the French installed Meknes as their military headquarters. As elsewhere throughout Morocco, they constructed their ville nouvelle apart from the medina and encouraged French settlers to farm the land around the city. The majority of the country's vineyards are still to be found here.

ORIENTATION
ARRIVING

BY TRAIN Meknes has two train stations *(gare)*. Gare Meknes is inconveniently located on the eastern edge of the city, although it's closer to the CTM bus station. The one at which most travelers will disembark is the small **Gare el Amir Abdelkader** (© 035/522763), 2 blocks and a very short walk east of avenue Mohammed V in the ville nouvelle. Inside the station are a couple of cash machines, a cafe, and a small news agent. Both *petits* and *grands* taxis are usually waiting right outside the station. A *petit* taxi ride into the medina shouldn't cost more than 10dh to 15dh ($1.25–$1.90/65p–95p). *Note:* Insist the driver use his meter, as he is legally bound to.

Grands taxis can be chartered for the drive to Volubilis and/or Moulay Idriss Zerhoun (see "By *Grand* Taxi," below).

Trains depart daily for Meknes from most of the western half of Morocco (there are no trains in either the Atlas or Rif mountains or central Morocco and the oases). Some of the more popular routes are from Casablanca (3¼ hr.; 86dh–128dh/$11–$16/£5.40–£8); Fes (45 min.; 18dh–26dh/$2.25–$3.25/£1.15–£1.65); Marrakech (7 hr.; 162dh–247dh/$20–$31/£10–£15); Rabat (2¼ hr.; 59dh–86dh/$7.40–$11/£3.70–£5.40); and Tangier (4–5½ hr.; 80dh–121dh/$10–$15/£5–£7.55). From destinations such as Agadir, Essaouira, and Tetouan, you will be traveling all or part of your journey on the ONCF bus service called Supratours. Reservations are only accepted up to 1 month prior to departure and can be made either over the phone (© **090/203040** from within Morocco only), at ticket booths at each station, or through authorized agents. Payment at the station is by cash only, but some agents will accept credit cards.

BY BUS Buses to Meknes arrive daily from almost everywhere in Morocco, including Agadir (11 hr.; 200dh–230dh/$25–$29/£13–£14); Casablanca (5 hr.; 80dh–90dh/$10–$11/£5–£5.65); Chefchaouen (5½ hr; 60dh–80dh/$7.50–$10/£3.75–£5); Erfoud (10 hr.; 100dh–110dh/$13–$14/£6.25–£6.90); Fes (1 hr.; 20dh/$2.50/£1.25); Marrakech (9 hr.; 140dh–160dh/$18–$20/£8.75–£10); Rabat (3½ hr.; 50dh–60dh/$6.25–$7.50/£3.15–£3.75); and Tangier (6 hr.; 80dh–90dh/$10–$11/£5–£5.65). Besides CTM services, which operate from their office in the ville nouvelle (see below), all long-distance bus companies arrive at the *gare routière* just outside the medina gate of Bab el Khemis, which is a 10-minute walk west of place el Hedim. Open around the clock, it has the usual selection of restaurants, cafes, and ticket counters, and offers a handy luggage storage service (5dh/65¢/30p per bag) open 6am to midnight.

If you don't want to walk up to place el Hedim or are heading for the ville nouvelle, there are usually plenty of light-blue *petits* taxis waiting outside the station to transport you. It shouldn't cost more than 10dh to 15dh ($1.25–$1.90/65p–95p) to reach your destination.

For onward travel from Meknes, all companies except CTM depart from the bus station, where they each have their own ticket booths (you must pay in cash). For an early-morning departure or during high season to Chefchaouen, Marrakech, and Tangier, it's advisable to purchase your ticket the day before. **CTM** (© **022/438282** central reservations; www.ctm.ma) operates from their own station at the junction of avenue des F.A.R. and avenue Yacoub el Mansour (© **035/522585**) in the ville nouvelle. CTM's international services to Spain and France also operate from here. Inside the station, open 24 hours, is a luggage-storage counter (5dh/65¢/30p per bag), open 6am to midnight, and a small cafe. It's a 10-minute walk (about 500m/⅓ mile) along avenue des F.A.R. to the southern end of avenue Mohammed V, or *petits* taxis can be hailed from the street. There are also usually *grands* taxis across the street at the CMH petrol station.

BY *GRAND* TAXI   Most long-distance *grands* taxis operate throughout the day from a vacant lot adjoining the *gare routière,* including those for Fes (45 min.; 20dh/$1.75/90p); Ifrane (1 hr.; 25dh/3.15/£1.55); Ouezzane (for Chefchaouen; 3 hr.; 60dh/$7.50/£3.75); and Rabat (2 hr.; 45dh/$5.65/£2.80). Those plying the route to Moulay Idriss Zerhoun (35 min.; 15dh/$1.90/95p) are located opposite the Institute Français on avenue des Nations Unies (the road to Tangier/Chefchaouen), from where you can also charter a *grand* taxi for the round-trip to Moulay Idriss Zerhoun and Volubilis. This can also be arranged with *grands* taxis outside the CTM bus station, the train station, and at the junction of avenue des F.A.R. and avenue Allal ben Abdallah. Round-trips from Meknes to Volubilis are currently 300dh ($38/£19) per taxi, and an extra 100dh ($13/£6.25) for a stop in Moulay Idriss Zerhoun. A *grand* taxi can take four passengers comfortably, six at a squeeze. *Note:* Remember to pay at the end of the journey, not the beginning, and make sure that all costs and itinerary are agreed upon upfront.

BY CAR   Driving into Meknes is pretty straightforward. Entering the city from the Fes-Meknes toll road—take the Meknes-*est* (east) exit—will bring you to the large intersection between the ville nouvelle and the medina. Coming from Chefchaouen or the coast will bring you to the intersection with avenue Hassan II on the edge of the ville nouvelle. In the medina there is secure parking on place Lalla Aouda, entered through the arches just east of Bab Mansour. Street parking in the ville nouvelle is watched over by local *gardiens,* who appreciate 10dh ($1.25/65p) for each day and night that you are parked. *Note:* Red-and-white-stripe curbing means no parking.

VISITOR INFORMATION

There's a Délégation Régionale du Tourisme, or tourist office, opposite the Hôtel de Ville (Town Hall) on place d'Listiqlal in the ville nouvelle (© **035/524426; fax 035/ 516046**), open Monday to Thursday 8:30am to noon and 2:30 to 6:30pm, and Friday 8 to 11:30am and 3 to 6:30pm. However, the only information on hand is a list of accommodations posted up on their notice board. ONMT, the national tourism body, has opened a small booth on the southeast corner of place el Hedim. It's open from Monday to Friday 8:30am to noon and 2:30 to 6:30pm, and Saturday 9am to noon and 3 to 6pm.

CITY LAYOUT

Meknes's medina and ville nouvelle are clearly defined, thanks to the riverbed of the normally dry Oued Bou Fekrane. The medina is only one section of Moulay Ismail's huge walled city, but it is here and the adjacent neighborhood known as Dar el Kebira—the remnants of the sultan's palace residential quarter—that travelers will spend their time. Place el Hedim is the focal point of the medina and most exploration here will bring you back to the square or along rue Sekkakin, running northward from the northwest corner of the square. Dar el Kebira can be entered from either its northern face, place Lalla Aouda, or from Hay al Amal, the narrow road running along its southern end. Although its winding lanes and alleys can be confusing, you should eventually emerge somewhere near these two thoroughfares.

The French-designed ville nouvelle is easy to navigate thanks to the two double-lane streets of avenue Hassan II and avenue des F.A.R., which run parallel to each other from west to east. Most hotels, restaurants, and banks are located between these two streets.

GETTING AROUND

BY *CALECHE* A fun way to tour the medina is by horse-drawn carriage, or *calèche*. Seating up to five passengers, they are usually parked at the entrance to place el Hedim or beside place Lalla Aouda on the street leading to the Mausoleum of Moulay Ismail. You can hire a *calèche* for around 80dh ($10/£5) per hour.

BY FOOT It's easiest to get around the medina and most of the central ville nouvelle by foot. From place el Hedim you can easily reach the main sights, accommodations, and restaurants by foot. A *petit* taxi would only need to be considered if you are heading out to the CTM bus station. The walk between place el Hedim and the ville nouvelle will take about 30 minutes.

BY TAXI *Petits* taxis are the most convenient way to travel between the medina and ville nouvelle. You'll find the small, pale-blue, government-regulated vehicles everywhere. At your hotel, you can usually ask the reception staff to organize one for you, or you can simply stand on the side of the street and hail one. Drivers are only allowed to carry up to three passengers at a time, but be aware that if there is a vacant seat, you may pick up an additional passenger. At all times, request the driver to put on the meter, which he is supposed to do no matter the time of day or night. Most trips between the ville nouvelle and medina should cost no more than 10dh ($1.25/65p) during the day and a bit more after 8pm, when a 50% evening surcharge kicks in. *Petits* taxis operate solely within the city environs; for transport to Moulay Idriss Zerhoun and Volubilis, you will need to charter a *grand* taxi (see above).

FAST FACTS: Meknes

Banks & Currency Exchange There are a few banks and ATMs within the medina and considerably more dotted throughout the ville nouvelle. The most convenient in the medina is the **BMCI** branch on place el Hedim (② **035/583190**). The branch is open Monday to Friday 8:15am to 3:45pm, but there is also an exterior exchange booth that opens on weekends from 10:30am to 12:30pm and 4 to 6 pm. There is also an ATM. About 70m (230 ft.) west of place el Hedim, on rue Dar Smen, is a bureau de change and ATM of **Banque Populaire,** open the normal banking hours of Monday to Friday 8:15am to 3:45pm. In between the medina and ville nouvelle is the Dawliz Complexe, where there's another **Banque Populaire** bureau de change and ATM with the same hours as above. Next door, between McDonald's and the Ibis Mousaffir Meknes hotel, is a **BMCI** ATM. In the ville nouvelle proper, on or near place al Wahda al Ifriquia, you'll find branches, with ATMs and exchange facilities, of **SGMB, Banque Populaire,** and **BMCE,** all open Monday to Friday 8:15am to 3:45pm. Behind SGMB is a **WafaCash** exchange open Monday to Friday 8am to 7pm, and Saturday 8:30am to 1pm and 3 to 6pm. Along avenue Mohammed V are more banks, including a branch of **Banque Populaire** (② **035/540058**) conveniently next door to the Majestic Hotel (p. 246). An after-hours **BMCE** bureau de change, with ATM, is located next to their branch at 98 av. des F.A.R., open Monday to Saturday 10am to 1pm and 4 to 7pm. If all else fails, try one of the more expensive hotels.

Car Rentals Very few travelers commence their car rental in Meknes, hence the lack of any major international firms in the city. Try local operators **Bab Mansour Car,** 8 av. Idriss II, Ville Nouvelle (*(C)* **035/526631**); **Stop Car,** 3 rue Essaouira, Ville Nouvelle (*(C)* **035/525061**); or the travel agents **Drissi Voyages,** 18 rue Antisrabé, Ville Nouvelle (*(C)* **035/512831**), and **Zeit Wagen,** 4 rue Antsirabé, Ville Nouvelle (*(C)* **035/525918**).

Consulates See "Fast Facts: Morocco" in chapter 2.

Doctors **Dr. Mohammed Dbab** is a French-trained G.P., located at 4 rue Accra, in the ville nouvelle (*(C)*/fax **035/521087** or 061/159356 after hours). **Dr. Rahal Rahalli** practices from the Polyclinique Cornette on Esplanade du Dr. Giguet (*(C)* **035/520262** or 035/520263).

Drugstores Pharmacies are very prevalent throughout Meknes. In the medina, **Pharmacie el Fath** (*(C)* **035/846110**) is on the far northwest corner of place el Hedim. In the ville nouvelle, **Pharmacie Centrale** (*(C)* **035/843246**) is on the corner of avenue Mohammed V and rue de Tarfaya. Meknes pharmacies open Monday to Thursday 9am to 12:30pm and 3:30 to 8pm, Friday 9am to noon and 3:30 to 8pm, and Saturday 9am to 1pm. After hours, look for a list of open pharmacies on the front door of the above. **All-night pharmacies** (*(C)* **035/523375**) operate from the Hotel de Ville (Town Hall) on place de l'Istiqlal in the ville nouvelle and from behind the bus stands 60m (195 ft.) south of place el Hedim.

Hospitals There is a small cluster of private medical clinics on or close to avenue des Nations Unies (the Tangier/Volubilis road), including **Polyclinique el Menzah** (*(C)* **035/400330**). **Trauma-Med** has doctors on duty 24 hours, just south of avenue des F.A.R. on avenue Nehru in the ville nouvelle (*(C)* **035/528070** or 061/476306). The state-run **Hospital Moulay Ismail** (*(C)* **035/522805**) is to the south of the ville nouvelle on rue Kiffa, off avenue des F.A.R.

Internet Access Compared to other major cities, cybercafes are few and far between in Meknes, but there are still a few in handy locations for travelers. Usually they will permit cheap, overseas, Internet-based phone calls, and the rates are generally a very reasonable 8dh ($1/50p) per hour. In the medina, **Meet Net** is on the busy rue Rouamazine, close to Hotel de Paris, and is open Monday to Saturday 10am to 1pm and 3 to 9:30pm. Out in the ville nouvelle, **Club Cyber** is located next to the WafaCash just north of place al Wahda al Ifriquia; **Club Leisure Company** is on the pedestrian-only section of rue Dakhla (formerly rue de Paris); and **Cyber de Paris** is on rue Accra, two doors down from Hotel de Nice. All of these ville nouvelle cybercafes are open daily from 9am to midnight.

Laundry & Dry Cleaning There are no self-service laundries in Meknes, but *pressings* (dry cleaners) are widespread. A shirt or pair of pants costs around 15dh ($1.90/95p). **Pressing Marhaba** is on rue Rouamazine in the medina, at the corner of the steps with a sign leading up to Collier de la Colombe restaurant. **Pressing Atlas** is at 26 av. Allal ben Abdallah, just past rue Atlas. Both are open Monday to Saturday 8:30am to 12:15pm and 2:30 to 7:30pm.

Maps There are no Meknes city maps available in Morocco. Editions Laure Kane publishes a glossy, colorful Fes-Meknes map with easy-to-read symbols and names of the major streets in both cities' ville nouvelles and medinas. It's usually available from major online booksellers.

Newspapers Newspaper stands outside the Cinema Camera on place al Wahda al Ifriquia and opposite the Majestic Hotel on avenue Mohammed V sell the weekly international versions of *The Guardian* and *Herald Tribune.*

Photographic Needs **Nasr Colour,** at the beginning of avenue Mohammed V, off place al Wahda al Ifriquia, burns digital images to CD; sells memory cards, batteries, and film; and does processing. It's open Monday to Saturday 8:30am to noon and 3 to 8:30pm.

Police For **general emergencies** and the **police,** call © **19.** The main police station is at place Ferhat Hached, in the ville nouvelle.

Post Office & Mail Meknes's **main post office,** which receives all *poste restante* mail, is on place de l'Istiqlal, and is open Monday to Friday 8am to 4:15pm and Saturday 8 to 11:45am. There's a small branch in the medina on the corner of rue dar Smen and rue Rouamazine open the same hours.

Restrooms In the medina there is a clean WC on the north side of place el Hedim, costing 5dh (65¢/30p). In the ville nouvelle, your best bet is to politely ask for the *toilette* in any reasonable-looking restaurant. Sometimes there might be a small fee or, if there is an attendant keeping them clean, 2 to 3 dirham (40¢/20p) is expected.

Safety Meknes could be considered one of the safest cities in Morocco, and very rarely will you encounter anything more than the odd tout looking for business at the train and bus station or in the medina. Both the medina and ville nouvelle can become deserted by midnight, so at this time it's best to take normal precautions and not walk alone.

Telephone The **city code** for Meknes has recently changed from 055 to **035** (the same as Fes).

WHERE TO STAY

Meknes's medina is yet to attract any great immigration of Moroccan or European hoteliers renovating its riads and dars into chic guesthouses, or *maisons d'hôte.* This only adds to the attraction of staying in the few that are located within its walls, as you will be immediately ensconced into authentic, residential medina life and be very much a curiosity in the neighborhood.

The most recently built or renovated accommodations within the city have been in the ville nouvelle, where there is a good selection of reasonably priced hotels that are all within walking distance or a very short taxi ride from the train station.

Meknes lacks any great number of accommodations, and the better hotels can be full by early afternoon, so arriving in the morning or prebooking your accommodations is a wise move. ***Note:*** Read my "Tips on Accommodations" on p. 60.

DAR EL KEBIRA

Riad Meknes   Ismaïli Raouf's family are distant descendants of Meknes's founding father, Sultan Moulay Ismail, and this riad was once part of the sultan's vast Imperial Palace. Ismaïli is a collector of note, and the fruits of his efforts—especially antique radios—are dotted around this labyrinth property. The rooms vary in size and style ranging from rustic to opulent, some with private terraces. For those looking for something different, the Berber suite is decorated to emulate a burgundy, gold, and army-green Moroccan tent. The walled entrance passes by a very welcoming swimming pool, through to a central courtyard with an established garden, where the popular restaurant (p. 247) is located. The rooms are to be found either coming off this courtyard, and therefore lacking, at times, in privacy, or farther into the building. A large upstairs salon is sometimes for family celebrations. English-speaking Ismaïli is a relaxed host, and this carries through to his friendly, young staff. At press time, a couple of new rooms were being built.

79 Ksar Chaacha, Dar Lakbira Medina, Meknes. ⓒ 035/530542. Fax 035/531320. www.riadmeknes.com. 6 units. 600dh–900dh ($75–$113/£38–£56) double. Rates include breakfast. Accessible by foot only; follow the signs from place Lalla Aouda or Bab er Rih. MC, V. **Amenities:** Restaurant; pool. *In room:* A/C.

MEDINA

Ryad Bahia 🅐🅐 *Kids*   Abdellatif and Bouchra Jamaï have converted two houses, joined by a small bridge spanning the lane below, into easily the best *maison d'hôte* in the medina. Entering through a nondescript front door brings you into a ground-floor courtyard and a number of salons. Decorated in earthy reds, oranges, and yellows, it's a communal area for guests to chat and eat, although there are also quiet corners for reading and privacy. A first-floor sitting room has a small library, armchairs, and a fireplace. The rooms are spread out over the top floors of the main house, which was Abdellatif's childhood home, and across to the quieter little "old" house. Abdellatif and Bouchra, both tour guides, have traveled in India, and the decor and furnishings throughout the riad reflect that.

A good option for families is to rent out one floor, called the Masria suite, consisting of two bedrooms and a small living room. For couples, either of the rooftop doubles, though small, are private and romantic. The riad's restaurant offers cuisine that mirrors the two influences of India and Morocco and easily convinces most guests to dine in. Meals can be taken on the Marrakchi ochre–colored rooftop terrace; its shaded upper level is high enough to look down upon most of the medina.

13 rue Tiberbarine, Medina, Meknes. ⓒ **035/554541** or 061/815237. Fax 035/554468. www.ryad-bahia.com. 7 units. 660dh–990dh ($83–$124/£41–£62) double; Masria suite 1,650dh ($206/£103). Children under 5 stay free in parent's room. Low-season rates available. Rates include breakfast. Accessible by foot only; follow the signs from northeast corner of place el Hedim. MC, V. **Amenities:** Restaurant; babysitting; Internet; Wi-Fi. *In room:* A/C.

VILLE NOUVELLE
Expensive
Hotel Malta *Finds*   The newest hotel in Meknes, opened in 2006, is tucked in a quiet street close to the main roads and offers very reasonably priced rooms in almost palatial surroundings. The red carpet is still fairly new in this five-story hotel, and along with the marble columns, floor, and staircase, the hotel's efforts of grandeur look the part. The good-size rooms are a mix of tile flooring, wood paneling, and white walls with modern bathrooms and tub/shower combos. In-wall Internet modem connections are a modern touch. There are two suites that are only slightly larger than the rooms, though they do come with a private balcony. An in-house restaurant, two bars, and a ground-floor nightclub ensure that it's best to ask the English-speaking reception staff for a room on one of the top floors.

3 rue Charif el Idrissi, Ville Nouvelle, Meknes. ⓒ 035/515020 or 035/515021. Fax 035/515018. hotelmalta@ menara.ma. 58 units. 540dh ($68/£34) single; 730dh ($91/£46) double; 870dh ($109/£54) triple; 1,500dh ($188/£94)

Meknes Medina

M E D I N A

Bab el Jdid

Blvd. el Haboul

O. bou Fekrane

Rue Abderzak

to Meknes
Ville Nouvelle

Rue Rouamazine

Rue Souk es Sebaat **1**

Kissaria Lahrir

Bab Berrima

Ave. de Mellah

Rue Sekkakin

2

3

4

5

Rue Dar Smen

7

5

PLACE
EL HEDIM

PLACE
LALLA
AOUDA

Marché
Couvert

BERRIMA

Ave. Zine el Abidine

6

DAR EL
KEBIRA

8

Hay al Amal

9

10

Rue Palais

Bab er Rih

ACCOMMODATIONS ■
Riad Meknes **8**
Ryad Bahia **2**

DINING ◆
Le Collier de la Colombe **7**
Mille et Une Nuits **3**
Place el Hedim
    cafe-restaurants **5**
Restaurant Riad **8**
Restaurant Salma **9**

ATTRACTIONS ●
Bab Mansour **6**
Bou Inania Medersa **1**
Dar Jamaï Museum **4**
Mausoleum of
    Moulay Ismail **10**

0   1/8 mi
0   1/8 km

suite. Children 6–12 stay half price in parent's room; under 6 free. TPT not included. Breakfast 60dh ($7.50/£3.75). Secure street parking available. MC, V. **Amenities:** Restaurant; 2 bars; nightclub; ATM in lobby. *In room:* A/C, satellite TV, Internet, fridge.

Moderate

Hotel de Nice ✦   This 1920s hotel underwent a complete renovation in 2003 and is one of the better options in the ville nouvelle. Located on a busy corner close to everything you'll need, the good-size tiled rooms are light and clean with modern furnishings and new bathrooms. Good options for those traveling in a group are the triple rooms, which are large enough to comfortably fit three singles with a bit of space between each bed. The top-floor suites can also comfortably accommodate a third bed and come with a large private terrace. A first-floor restaurant serves up a decent breakfast, while a ground-floor bar and separate piano bar (more of a smoky den) looks after those wanting a drink.

Corner of rue d'Accra and rue Antsirabé, Ville Nouvelle, Meknes. ✆ **035/520318**. Fax 035/402104. www.hotel denice-meknes.com. 46 units. 343dh ($43/£21) single; 420dh ($53/£26) double; 462dh ($58/£29) triple; 600dh ($75/£38) suite. Children under 6 stay free in parent's room. Breakfast 42dh ($5.25/£2.60). Limited street parking. MC, V. **Amenities:** Restaurant; 2 bars. *In room:* A/C, satellite TV.

Ibis Moussafir Meknes *(Value (Kids)*   A step up from Ibis's usual standard in Europe, this Meknes offering is an extremely good value. Conveniently located between the medina and ville nouvelle, and very well signposted from the outskirts of Meknes, this chain hotel offers no surprises, but the rooms are spacious, modern, clean, and functional. Some rooms look out toward the medina—a view partly obscured by a popular McDonald's—while others face inward overlooking the large pool. Surrounded by a nice garden and a plentiful supply of sun lounges, the pool (a rarity at the accommodations in this city) is what lures many to stay here. Within the hotel is a restaurant that serves rather bland lunches and dinners, but offers a pretty good buffet breakfast until noon. Opening onto the pool is a cozy bar, where you can enjoy a quiet drink along with a burger or panini from the snack menu. *Note:* This has become a popular hotel for both Moroccans and travelers, so it's best to prebook if you can.

Av. des F.A.R., Ville Nouvelle, Meknes. © 035/404141. Fax 035/404242. www.ibishotel.com. 104 units. 490dh ($61/£31) double. Children under 11 stay free in parent's room. TPT not included. Buffet breakfast 47dh ($5.90/£2.95). Secure parking available. MC, V. **Amenities:** Restaurant; bar; pool. *In room:* A/C, satellite TV.

Inexpensive

Majestic Hotel   This 1930s hotel was once the toast of the ville nouvelle, and even though it is now definitely in the budget category, there is still some elegance left in the old girl. A wide, spiral marble staircase (be warned, there's no elevator) leads up to three floors of rooms, some recently renovated and with a private bathroom, others with just a basin and shared facilities in the hallways. As with all accommodations in this price range, there are some sacrifices to be made, and the major one here is the lack of any heating in winter that, combined with the dark-wood walls and tile flooring throughout, can make things a bit chilly. Inward-facing rooms look out over a pleasant courtyard, while a large Moroccan salon on the rooftop terrace can be converted to dorm-style beds if requested. On the ground floor is a small breakfast room with a TV that is also a good place to meet up with other travelers.

19 av. Mohammed V, Ville Nouvelle, Meknes. © 035/522035 or 035/520307. Fax 035/527427. 23 units. 136dh–214dh ($17–$27/£8.50–£13) single; 178dh–241dh ($22–$30/£11–£15) double. Children under 6 stay free in parent's room. No credit cards.

WHERE TO DINE

The dining scene in Meknes is certainly no gastronomic adventure. Options are largely restricted to restaurants offering Moroccan or French/Italian cuisine, with the widest choice of locations being in the ville nouvelle. As I find throughout most of Morocco, the highlight of eating out in Meknes, for me, is the postmeal mint tea or coffee. Great people-watching cafes are located in the medina on place el Hedim or on avenues Mohammed V and Hassan II in the ville nouvelle.

DAR EL KEBIRA
Moderate

Le Collier de la Colombe MOROCCAN   Come for the view and the *pastilla,* and you won't be disappointed. On the edge of the medina, this restaurant has two floors with glorious uninterrupted views across the Oued Bou Fekrane valley to the ville nouvelle. The grand dining room has large picture windows affording all diners—it can seat more than 100—a view. The rooftop terrace, however, is where you want to be, with tables shaded by umbrellas during the day; it's a simply stunning location to watch the sunset. The mainly Moroccan, very reasonably priced menu includes the regular line-up of grilled lamb and meat dishes, brochettes, and tagines, but it is the house specialty *pastilla*—for once not overdry or too sweet—that is highly recommended here.

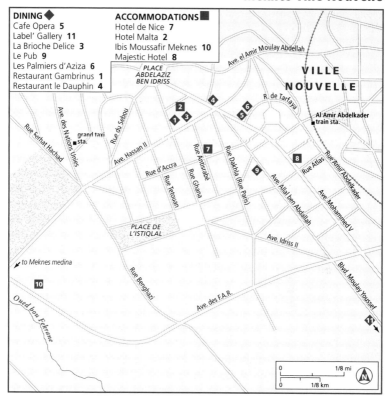

DINING ◆	ACCOMMODATIONS ■
Cafe Opera **5**	Hotel de Nice **7**
Label' Gallery **11**	Hotel Malta **2**
La Brioche Delice **3**	Ibis Moussafir Meknes **10**
Le Pub **9**	Majestic Hotel **8**
Les Palmiers d'Aziza **6**	
Restaurant Gambrinus **1**	
Restaurant le Dauphin **4**	

67 rue Driba (best reached from place Lalla Aouda), Medina, Meknes. ✆ **035/555041.** Fax 035/556599. Main courses 80dh–135dh ($10–$17/£5–£8.45). Alcohol served. MC, V. Daily 11am–4pm and 7–11pm. Accessible by foot only; parking at place Lalla Aouda.

Restaurant Riad MOROCCAN   Also known as Riad Meknes (p. 243), this is renowned for its fine Moroccan cuisine. Diners can choose from one of five set menus—the vegetable couscous is well prepared, as is the pigeon *pastilla*—or the very reasonably priced a la carte menu. Tagine *kadra* (beef) with prunes is a house specialty, as is the roasted lamb *mechoui,* which requires a few hours' notice. Choose to dine in the Moroccan salon or a separate, less authentic but air-conditioned dining room. Better still, dine outside on the wrought-iron *zellij*-topped tables in the courtyard amongst the garden.

79 Ksar Chaacha, Dar Lakbira Medina, Meknes. ✆ **035/530542.** Fax 035/531320. www.riadmeknes.com. Set menus 110dh–170dh ($14–$21/£6.90–£11); main courses 60dh–80dh ($7.50–$10/£3.75–£5). MC, V. Daily noon–3pm and 6:30–10pm. Accessible by foot only; follow the signs from place Lalla Aouda or Bab er Rih.

MEDINA
Moderate
Mille et Une Nuits MOROCCAN   Abdellah Garmat welcomes diners into his family home (they still live on the first floor) to experience true home-cooked Moroccan

cuisine. The ground-floor courtyard has been converted (though one gets the feeling it looks much the same) into a restaurant with cushioned lounges, *zellij* tables, colorful stucco, and Moroccan lanterns. This is merely the setting, though, to experience Lalla Garmat's exceptional cooking. A limited but varied menu of Moroccan classics is offered. Specialties include a sweet and savory *pastilla* with almonds and honey, *harira* soup, and Lalla's vegetable tagine. If you're around on Friday, join the family for their midday couscous.

Off place el Hedim; follow the signs from the northeast corner. © 035/559002. Main courses 85dh–90dh ($11/£5.30–£5.65); set menu 100dh ($13/£6.25). No credit cards. Daily 10am–11pm. Accessible by foot only.

Restaurant Salma *Kids* MOROCCAN/INTERNATIONAL   Around the corner from the Mausoleum of Moulay Ismail, a welcome rooftop terrace combines with a varied menu to make this a popular traveler's choice. Diners can choose between an a la carte or snack menu, the latter providing Western comfort foods such as hamburgers and sandwiches. The a la carte menu covers the Moroccan spectrum of tagines, couscous, and brochettes along with fresh seafood from Mohammedia, near Casablanca, and a few pasta choices. A reasonably priced three-course *menu du jour* offers salads and soups, fruit desserts, and a choice of a Moroccan entree. There's also a large air-conditioned salon on the first floor resplendent in *zellij* and stucco, furnished with traditional low-lying tables and lounges with oversize, plush cushions. On the large rooftop terrace—high enough to catch a breeze if it passes by—is a rustic setting of terra-cotta tiling, wrought-iron furniture, and grass umbrellas. Samir, the English-speaking manager, keeps things moving and the waiters on their toes.

2 Derb Hammam Moulay Ismail. ©/fax 035/556708 or 061/253502. www.restaurantsalma.com. Burgers 35dh–40dh ($4.40–$5/£2.20–£2.50); main courses 60dh–110dh ($7.50–$14/£3.75–£6.90); *menu du jour* 110dh–130dh ($14–$16/£6.90–£8.15). MC, V. Daily 9am–10:30pm. Secure parking available.

Inexpensive
Place el Hedim SNACK/CAFE   Alongside both the eastern and western fringe of this central square in the medina is a string of cafe-restaurants popular more for their location than their inspiring cuisine. Nonetheless, there are always plenty of tables to choose from, and they offer the best people-watching location in Meknes. Menus span a basic range of tagines, brochettes, *chawarma,* and sandwiches. For a familiar, quick bite, try the omelet with fries at Snack Ifoulki, on the western edge, which can also rustle up a cheap breakfast of eggs and bread.

Place el Hedim. Main courses 25dh–45dh ($3.15–$5.65/£1.55–£2.80); breakfast w/tea or coffee 20dh ($2.50/£1.25). No credit cards. Daily 8am–10pm.

VILLE NOUVELLE
Moderate
Le Pub ✾ INTERNATIONAL   Besides a popular watering hole, this is also a very nice restaurant with a menu that comes as a surprise considering Meknes's staid gastronomic scene. Diners can choose from no less than a dozen entrees including *escargot à la Provençale* (sautéed snails in a white wine–and–garlic butter sauce) and a beef carpaccio topped with shaved Parmesan. Main courses include seafood, pastas (try the crab ravioli or the lasagna *quattro formaggio*), pizzas, French grills such a beef filet in a Roquefort sauce, and *rognons de veau* (baby beef kidneys) in a ginger and mustard sauce. The dessert menu isn't to be ignored; the chocolate profiteroles are a personal favorite. The restaurant, separated from the bar and lounge by a carved cedar-wood room divider, is nicely furnished in a modern design. Reflective windows

ensure privacy from the outside, while low lighting and candle-lit tables make for a nice atmosphere in the evening. Arrive after 10pm, and the live Moroccan music coming from the club below may be an unpleasant distraction.

20 bd. Allal ben Abdallah. © 035/524247. Appetizers 50dh–70dh ($6.25–$8.75/£3.15–£4.40); main courses 55dh–110dh ($6.90–$14/£3.45–£6.90); desserts 35dh–55dh ($4.40–$6.90/£2.20–£3.45). Alcohol served. MC, V. Daily 11am–midnight. Street parking available.

Restaurant le Dauphin ⚑ INTERNATIONAL/MOROCCAN   One of Meknes's
best restaurants is hidden by a very unassuming exterior that thankfully opens onto a lovely shaded garden and elegant tiled interior. Manager Aziz Bennouna presides over a long-serving team of uniformed waiters that are typically unobtrusive and professional. The menu covers a wide range of French and Italian cuisine, with more than 30 cold and hot starters; my favorite is a deliciously simple onion soup. These are followed by a variety of grilled meats, pastas, and seafood, delivered fresh every morning. There are also Moroccan standards such as lamb and beef tagine, and a *couscous aux sept legumes* that will easily feed two happy vegetarians. A three-course *menu du jour* usually consists of a grilled meat entree with soup and dessert. Speaking of desserts, try the crêpes suzette or *flambée banane* for something different.

5 av. Mohammed V (entrance is on rue el Leanissa). ©/fax 035/523423 or 063/459549. Appetizers 40dh–80dh ($5–$10/£2.50–£5); main courses 80dh–100dh ($10–$13/£5–£6.25); desserts 25dh–40dh ($3.15–$5/£1.55–£2.50); *menu du jour* 130dh ($16/£8.15). Alcohol served. MC, V. Daily noon–3pm and 7:30–11pm.

Inexpensive
Cafe Opera & Les Palmiers d'Aziza CAFE/PATISSERIE   Two of the best cafes
in Meknes sit within 50m (165 ft.) of each other in the heart of the ville nouvelle. **Cafe Opera,** on busy avenue Mohammed V, is an old fashion-style cafe with uniformed waiters in bow ties and aprons. A very large air-conditioned interior allows for some privacy away from the hustle and bustle outside. A delectable selection of pastries and gâteaux is also on display. The outside seats—if you can grab one—are great for people-watching.

Around the corner on rue de Tarfaya is the shady, multilevel **Les Palmiers d'Aziza,** recognizable by the huge palm tree in its center. There are various areas both inside and outside for a quiet coffee or tea break, and they also offer a small selection of gâteaux and ice creams. Both of these cafes are female and traveler friendly while still retaining their local atmosphere.

7 av. Mohammed V and 9 rue de Tarfaya. No phone. Coffee or mint tea 5dh–10dh (65¢–$1.25/30p–65p); ice cream 5dh–15dh (75¢–$1.90/40p–95p); gateaux 10dh–15dh ($1.25–$1.90/65p–95p). No credit cards. Daily 7am–10pm.

Label' Gallery ASIAN/LEBANESE/TEX MEX   On the top of this three-level
shopping center is a clean and modern food hall. The three takeaway-style counters don't hold any surprises in comparison to similar eateries across the globe, but in Meknes they are worth a mention if only for those suffering from couscous and tagine overload. Bangkok serves up a very decent *salade vietnamienne* with chicken and *crevettes* (prawns or shrimps) along with the usual Asian stir fries and rice, noodle, and meat dishes. Petit Libanaise is a falafel haven for vegetarians, while Tacos Tex Mex is a little disappointing other than a decent fajita. There are plenty of tables, it's air-conditioned, and there are clean toilets.

Corner of av. Moulay Youssef and bd. Ibn Khaldoune. No phone. Main courses 25dh–55dh ($3.15–$6.90/£1.55–£3.45). No credit cards. Daily 10am–10pm.

La Brioche Delice CAFE/PATISSERIE   This classy and friendly little cafe is a great spot for a quiet rest without the smoky masculinity of the other cafes in this area. Right on busy avenue Hassan II, an effort has been made to create a female- and child-friendly environment, with a couple of outdoor tables with umbrellas. The small interior—all nonsmoking—has modern tables on the ground floor and a mezzanine level at the rear. A decadent selection of gâteaux is on display to accompany freshly squeezed juices, milkshakes, or the more traditional coffee and mint tea. A separate ice-cream stand provides a popular treat for families walking past on their evening stroll.

8 av. Hassan II. ⓒ 035/526780. Juices/milk shakes 8dh–15dh ($1–$1.90/50p–95p); ice cream 6dh (75¢/40p), gâteaux 10dh–15dh ($1.25–$1.90/65p–95p). No credit cards. Daily 8am–10pm.

Restaurant Gambrinus MOROCCAN   Good, cheap, wholesome Moroccan food is what you'll get here. Located opposite the busy Marché Centrale and enclosed by old lace curtains, the tired interior of the Gambrinus isn't exactly inspiring or modern. However, this doesn't seem to concern the steady stream of Meknassis. They come here for the good choice of Moroccan standards such as lamb, beef, chicken, or veggie couscous or tagine; chicken and beef brochettes; and grilled steaks. They have a bargain three-course set menu that includes a choice of entree, including soups and omelets, and a couple of fruit desserts. Alternatively, you can just order the same items a la carte.

Rue Omar Ibn Aïss. ⓒ 035/520258. Main courses 45dh–65dh ($5.65–$8.15/£2.80–£4.05); set menus 70dh ($8.75/£4.40). Taxes not included. No credit cards. Daily noon–3pm and 7–10pm.

WHAT TO SEE & DO

For a medina lacking any great number of sights, those that Meknes offers visitors are up there with the best in the country. Located relatively close to each other, they make for at least a pleasant morning's walk. In addition to these sights, however, it is very much the Meknassis themselves that make exploring their walled city so pleasurable. The hassle from guides and shopkeepers is minimal here, especially when compared to Fes. As in the rest of Morocco, take some time out to sit in a cafe and observe the relatively relaxed everyday life in Meknes, preferably over a mint tea, said to be the best in the country.

MEDINA

Bab Mansour   The gate for which Moulay Ismail created place el Hedim, this is one of the grandest of Moroccan gateways. Eventually completed by Moulay Ismail's son, Moulay Abdallah, in 1732, it is quite often overlooked by travelers who become ensconced in the activity and sights on the square opposite. The gate has had a recent clean-up, and along with a smaller gate beside it, Bab Jemaa en Nouar, stands watch over the busy pedestrian and vehicle traffic, resplendent in green and blue *zellij* and towering columns. The interior of the *bab* is sometimes used to house art exhibitions.

Rue Dar Smen, opposite place el Hedim.

Mausoleum of Moulay Ismail 🕊🕊🕊   This peaceful and spiritual resting place of Sultan Moulay Ismail is one the few sacred sites in Morocco open to non-Muslims. Constructed during his lifetime, Ismail chose this location as it had once housed Meknes's Palais de Justice (courthouse), and he hoped in death to be judged in his own court by his own people. A nondescript building from the outside, the serenity of the series of pale-yellow courtyards leading to the tomb is in contrast to the turbulent and cruel reign of Ismail while he was alive. In the far left corner of the last courtyard is a door that leads into the sanctuary—completely renovated in the 1950s by King Mohammed V—in which the sultan is buried. Respectfully remove your footwear before entering. The anteroom to the tomb has walls with a series of levels consisting of exquisite *zellij,* enamel-painted wood, elaborately carved plaster, graceful arches, and marble columns. This is a beautifully cool and tranquil room, and grass mats on the floor allow for rest and quiet contemplation. To the right of this is the tomb itself, of which non-Muslims cannot access, but it's visible from the anteroom through a Moorish doorway. Two antique clocks, one on each side of the doorway, were gifts from Louis XIV, which the king is said to have sent when he refused Ismail's request to add his daughter, Princess de Conti, to the sultan's harem.

Rue Palais, Dar el Kebira, Medina, Meknes. Free admission, though 10dh ($1.25/65p) donation appreciated. Sat–Thurs 8:30am–noon and 2–6pm.

MEDINA

Bou Inania Medersa ⭐⭐
This theological college was started by the Merenid sultan Abou el Hassan and completed by his son Abou Inan, after whom it is named and who also constructed the Bou Inania medersa in Fes in 1358. It is now open to visitors and ranks alongside the mausoleum of Moulay Ismail as a must-see monument in Meknes. The building is centered around a single courtyard decorated in stucco finely detailed with carved calligraphy, carved olive wood, and a *zellij* floor. The three crafts have achieved an amazing combination of intricacy and simplicity—no space has been left unworked, but it's not chaotic or overbearing at all. The courtyard is encircled by two levels of cell-like rooms that used to house up to 60 students. Head up to the rooftop terrace that affords a sweeping view of the medina, including the nearby green-tile roof and minaret of the off-limits Grand Mosque.

Souk es Sebaat. Admission 10dh ($1.25/60p) adults; 3dh (35¢/20p) children under 12. Daily 9am–noon and 3–6pm.

Dar Jamaï Museum
This is one of Morocco's finest and most underappreciated museums. Overlooking place el Hedim, this 1882 former palace was built by the influential Jamaï family *viziers,* or high government ministers, to Sultan Moulay Hassan I before they fell from grace upon the death of the sultan in 1894. The French converted it into a military hospital in 1912 before it became the Museum of Moroccan Art, better known as the Dar Jamaï Museum, in 1920. In contrast to most other museums in Morocco, the exhibits here look fresh and are well lit. However, there are no English-language descriptions. Exhibits cover a wide range of Moroccan decorative arts such as jewelry, ceramics, woodcarvings, and embroidered textiles. A selection of antique guns is also interesting. Dar Jamaï itself is also an exhibit; head upstairs to a reception salon with a stunning *koubba,* or domed sanctuary, and finish your visit with a few moments rest in the cool courtyard shaded by citrus trees.

Place el Hedim. Admission 10dh ($1.25/60p) adults; 3dh (35¢/20p) children under 12. Wed–Mon 9am–5pm.

Place el Hedim
The heart of Meknes's medina, place el Hedim was originally the western corner of the medina until Moulay Ismail demolished the houses to enable a royal approach to his palace. Besides public executions—of which Moulay Ismail was particularly fond—and royal announcements, the square was also used as a storage area for the masses of construction material he had pillaged from around Morocco to build his capital. Meknes authorities have recently cleaned up the square, and during the day it is the medina's premier spot to while away some quality people-watching time. Come here in the early evening, especially in the warmer months, to witness

musicians, storytellers, and African *herboristes* taking center stage in a smaller version of Marrakech's Jemaa el Fna spectacle.

SHOPPING

As far as sheer size and choice are concerned, the souks of Meknes's medina don't match up to others in Morocco. What they do offer, however, is a relatively hassle-free shopping experience. Browsing the area to the north of place el Hedim can be both enjoyable and rewarding. Carpets and *babouches* especially are of high quality and reasonable price here, and make sure to seek out the one true specialty of Meknes—souvenirs decorated with silver damascene. The souks are open daily from 9am to late, sometimes closing for midday prayers and lunch on Friday.

For fresh produce and flowers, go to the **Central Marché** on the north side of avenue Hassan II, between rue Tetouan and rue Omar Ibn Aiss, in the ville nouvelle. Fodassi Mini-Marché is opposite the market's entrance on rue Omar Ibn Aïs and sells everyday grocery items, toiletries, and alcohol. It's open Monday to Saturday 8am to 6pm and Sunday noon to 6pm. The modern **Label' Vie** supermarket is on a below-ground level of the Label' Gallery shopping center, corner of avenue Moulay Youssef and boulevard Ibn Khaldoune, in the ville nouvelle. It's open daily 9am to 9pm. Signposted on the road between the Meknes-Fes toll highway and the city is **Marjane Hypermarket** (© 035/520385), open daily from 9am to 9pm.

Covered Market 🏠🏠 Along the west side of place el Hedim is a covered market that is an attack of the senses. Under this one roof are olive stalls, *herboristes,* pet shops, spice sellers, butchers, live chickens, and confectionery stalls. The shops between the covered market and place el Hedim sell a good range of pottery, musical instruments, and souvenirs.

Silver Damascene Kissaria Lahrir is the traditional souk for silver damascene work. Thin silver threads are slowly tapped into designs on pieces of steel and then attached to all forms of pottery. It's a delicate art that is sadly beginning to die away as consumer tastes have turned away from this style of decoration. There are, however, a few shops in the Kissaria to the southeast of Bou Inania medersa that continue on with the craft. Abderrazak el Bettani's **L'Art des Villes Imperiales,** 2 Derb Hammam, between place Lalla Aouda and rue Palais (© 035/553740), is below Restaurant Salma (p. 248) and has a good selection of jewelry, souvenirs, and pottery decorated in silver damascene. Most of the figurines—elephants, antelope, peacocks, horses, lions, kangaroo—are painted black so that the silver damascene stands out.

Souk es Sebbat The area behind the Dar Jamaï Museum on place el Hedim is where you'll find the best *babouches* in Meknes. Each tall, narrow stall has row upon row of colored *babouches*—pointed and yellow for men and petite and multicolored for women. Expect to pay around 120dh ($15/£7.50) for a quality, handmade pair.

Souk Joutiya es Zerabi Just west of Souk es Sebbat is the carpet souk. Here you'll find carpets from Middle Atlas cooperatives. The quality is quite high—360,000 double knots per square meter (11 sq. ft.) and up to 8 months' work for one woman to produce a 1.8 by 2.8m (6 ft.×9-ft.) carpet.

MEKNES AFTER DARK

Meknes is sadly lacking when it comes to offering modern and friendly—especially for females—entertainment once the sun sets. In the medina there is the mini Jemaa el Fna spectacle on **place el Hedim** (p. 248). Apart from this, you can usually enjoy a wine (the waiters will sometimes ask you to order a salad or similar to accompany it) on the terrace of **Le Collier de la Colombe** (p. 246), with its sweeping view of the ville nouvelle at night. At the main roundabout connecting the medina and ville nouvelle is a newly terraced and **landscaped garden** that is floodlit at night and has quickly become the place for women and children to while away the early evening hours.

There are quite a few **bars** in the ville nouvelle, especially near place Ifriquia on avenue Hassan II, and along avenue Allal ben Abdallah, although they are all men-only and decidedly seedy. At the southern end of the pedestrian-only section of rue de Paris is **Novelty** (© 035/521885). Formerly a bit of a dive, Novelty has recently been renovated by an elderly Italian gent who has cleaned the place up and added some nice tables and draught beer. It's now very female friendly, offers free tapas, and is an enjoyable stop for a late-night drink. Novelty is open Monday to Saturday noon to 11pm.

Close by is **Le Pub,** which besides its fine restaurant (p. 248) is a very popular drinking hole. The ground-floor bar is well stocked, has satellite sports TV, and a few tables, bar stools, and a salon to choose from. Downstairs is a smoky—from both cigarettes and *shisha* pipes—bar and lounge that starts filling up late each night with Meknassi men and women coming for a bit of live Moroccan music. It's open daily noon to midnight.

Other choices are limited to hotel bars, of which the **Hotel Rif,** on the west end of rue Accra (© 035/522591), is usually liveliest with cheap beers, free snacks, and comfortable seats. During the warmer months, treat yourself to an expensive beer (50dh/$6.25/£3.15) in the garden of the otherwise overrated **Hotel Transatlantique,** rue el Merinyne (© 035/525050), in the ville nouvelle. The expansive, shaded grounds at the rear of the property give a sweeping view of the medina and are a pleasant place to spend a couple of hours. Kids will love the large, green lawns; take their swimsuits and ask the staff if the kids can have a swim in one of the hotel's two pools.

If your French is up to par, call the **Institut Français,** on the corner of avenue Moulay Ismail and rue Ferhat Hachad (© 035/515851; fax 035/510170; www.ambafrance-ma.org). They have a monthly calendar of cultural events such as movies, plays, concerts, lectures, and exhibitions.

SIDE TRIPS FROM MEKNES
MOULAY IDRISS ZERHOUN
4km (2½ miles) S of Volubilis; 29km (18 miles) N of Meknes; 74km (46 miles) W of Fes

Coming around the bend from Meknes, the town of Moulay Idriss Zerhoun is a dramatic sight, a jumble of houses and mosques almost hidden between the twin hillsides of Khiba and Tasga. Moulay Idriss Zerhoun is a pilgrimage center, home to the tomb of its namesake, Idriss Ben Abdallah Ben Hassan Ben Ali, great grandson of Ali and Fatima, the Prophet Mohammed's daughter. The descendants of Ali and Fatima, the Alids were persecuted by the ruling Abbaysid Arabs in Baghdad, and after being implicated in a rebellion against them, the Alid Idriss fled to the western extremity of the then-known Islamic world. By 788, the Muslim Auraba Berbers, who resided in the ruins of the Roman city of Volubilis and rebelled against Damascus' efforts to rule the entire Islamic empire, accepted Idriss as their spiritual leader, or *imam*. Endowed with a charismatic personality and venerable heritage, Idriss united the warring Berber tribes and thus founded what is regarded as the first Moroccan dynasty, the Idrissids. At this time he began the construction of his capital, Fes. Word of his growing influence reached Baghdad, however, and in 792 he was fatally poisoned by the jealous Caliph Harun al Rachid. The Berbers laid their leader to rest between two craggy hills on the western slopes of the Zerhoun Range, within sight of Volubilis. Today he is referred to as Idriss El Akbar (the Great). Idriss's son, Moulay Idriss II, proceeded to develop Fes into the first significant focal point of urban Arabic culture in Morocco.

The actual town of Moulay Idriss Zerhoun was mainly developed in the 18th century by Sultan Moulay Ismail, in part using materials pillaged from nearby Volubilis. Off limits to non-Muslims until 1912, it is still primarily a sacred village and best visited during the day as an excursion from Meknes.

The tomb and sanctuary, or *zaouia,* with its green-tile roofs, prayer halls, ablution areas, and tombs, is closed to non-Muslims—and coincidentally beasts of burden—courtesy of a low wood bar. For a much better view from above, take the stairs to your left and climb through the winding streets to the summit of the town. There is usually a local guide who will show you the way for 50dh ($6.25/£3.15). On the way up you will pass the Persian-inspired cylindrical minaret of the Sentissi Mosque, which was donated in 1939 by a pilgrim freshly returned from Mecca. It's a bit of a steep hike, but at the top there is a rewarding view over the sanctuary, showing the courtyards, roofs, and adjacent royal guesthouse (the royal family are regular pilgrims).

Once back in the town, the little street below the main square has a string of cafe-restaurants and is a good spot to absorb the festive pilgrimage atmosphere.

It goes without saying that this is a holy place and should be treated as such by visitors. Restraint in picture-taking and dressing respectfully (covering the knees and elbows) is recommended. That said, the townsfolk of Moulay Idriss Zerhoun are very welcoming and seem to be genuinely embracing a recent increase in non-Muslim visitors. Saturday is market day and, as a result, an especially lively day to visit.

GETTING THERE Buses for Moulay Idriss Zerhoun depart hourly between 8am and 6pm (10dh/$1.25/65p) from Meknes's *gare routière* outside Bab el Khemis. *Grands* taxis depart when full (15dh/$1.90/95p) throughout the day from opposite the Institute Français, on avenue des Nations Unies (the road to Tangier/Chefchaouen). See Meknes arrival information (p. 239) regarding chartering a *grand* taxi. If you're driving yourself, take avenue des Nations Unies, at the junction of avenue Hassan II and avenue Moulay Ismail. After 5km (3 miles), veer right onto the Chefchaouen road on which the turnoff to Moulay Idriss Zerhoun is signposted.

VOLUBILIS

4km (2½ miles) N of Moulay Idriss Zerhoun; 33km (20 miles) N of Meknes; 70km (44 miles) W of Fes

The Roman ruins of Volubilis (Latin for "morning glory") are the most impressive in Morocco. The existence of a Roman city in Morocco surprises some people, and while much has been pillaged over the centuries to adorn other cities (mainly Meknes) or taken to museums such as that in Rabat, the structure of the town is still clearly visible from the ruins. A visit to this UNESCO World Heritage site is highly recommended.

Although the Roman influence on Volubilis was the greatest, archaeological evidence points to the possibility of a Neolithic settlement, while recovered tablets show there was a 3rd-century B.C. Phoenician village here. However, it was under the Berber Mauritanian king Juba II, descendant of Hannibal and husband to the daughter of Cleopatra and Marc Antony, that Volubilis began to flourish, and from A.D. 45 to A.D. 285 it was the capital of the Roman province of Mauritania Tingitana. Under the Romans, this province—once in Horace's phrase "the arid nurse of lions"—became one of the granaries of the Empire, and Volubilis grew to a city of 20,000 inhabitants on the back of exporting vast quantities of olives and wheat to Rome. The number of

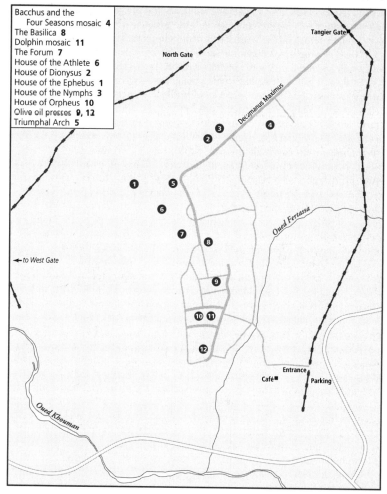

Bacchus and the
Four Seasons mosaic **4**
The Basilica **8**
Dolphin mosaic **11**
The Forum **7**
House of the Athlete **6**
House of Dionysus **2**
House of the Ephebus **1**
House of the Nymphs **3**
House of Orpheus **10**
Olive oil presses **9, 12**
Triumphal Arch **5**

Tangier Gate

North Gate

Decumanus Maximus

Oued Fertassa

← to West Gate

Entrance
Café ■
Parking

Oued Khouman

presses that have been found on the site reflect the importance of the olive to the city's fortunes. Volubilis was also a noted exporter of wild animals—in particular the Barbary lion—to figure in the legendary gladiator games in the Colosseum. The city was also the meeting point between Berbers and Romans, where the two cultures met to trade even though the indigenous nomads of Morocco were never subdued by the Roman legions. Volubilis's weakness was that it was on the fringes of the Empire, only connected to Rome through the Atlantic ports. Although numerous emperors had dreams of taming the Atlas and forging on into the Dark Continent, they never came to fruition. With the empire beginning to crumble in the late 3rd century, Emperor Diocletian withdrew his legions to the coastal areas, leaving Volubilis at the mercy of neighboring tribes.

With its established olive and farming industries, however, the city continued to function for centuries afterward. Latin was still the common language amongst the city's population of Jews, Greeks, Syrians, and Berbers until the Islamic Arabs arrived in the late 700s. The proclaimed sultan in Volubilis, Moulay Idriss, preferred his new city of Fes, however, and the demise of Volubilis is echoed by the rise of early Islam in Fes.

The city and its Christian and Jewish population survived with diminished importance, becoming the Christian enclave of Oualila during the 8th century, but by the 11th century Volubilis was virtually deserted. In the 18th century, Sultan Moulay Ismail raided the city's remains for building materials to construct his vast palace at nearby Meknes, while the devastating earthquake of 1755, which flattened Rabat and Lisbon, brought the city to the ground.

French excavations and reconstruction began in 1915, with more reconstruction in 1962. The site covers 40 hectares (99 acres)—about half has been excavated so far—and contains more than 30 mosaics and buildings with poetic names such as the House of the Athlete, the House of the Nymphs, and the House of Orpheus. The Decumanus Maximus is the main street, at the end of which is the Triumphal Arch, dedicated to Emperor Caracalla. On one side of the street is the Forum, with its restored Corinthian columns. The best preserved houses include the house of Dionysus near the Decumanus Maximus, the House of the Euphebus next to the triumphal arch, and the House of Orpheus to the south near the olive presses. Although fading in the open light, the floor mosaics are still fascinating to view. Featured are various mythological figures such as Bacchus, the un-Islamic god of wine Dionysus, Medusa, and Orpheus. Hunting, music making, and scenes from the natural world—such as the dolphin mosaic—can also to be seen.

With encouragement from UNESCO, the Moroccan government has begun a complete rebuilding of the site's entrance area, which will hopefully include a visitor information center. At the moment there are a couple of cafes in the parking lot, one of them a Berber tent, and a temporary ticket office. Visiting Volubilis requires a bit of effort and planning, and the site itself is quite large and can take a couple of hours at least to discover properly. Only a few of the sights are accompanied by information panels—and only some of them in English—and although roped off, the mosaics are easily visible. English-speaking guides are always hanging around at the entrance, and I recommend hiring one if your interest is anything more than fleeting. There is very little shade through the ruins and it can be oppressively hot in the middle of the day, so be sure to take a hat (an umbrella works superbly) and plenty of water. Conversely, during winter it can at times be cold and miserable out in the ruins, and warm, protective clothing is then recommended.

Large tour groups are usually traipsing through the ruins from 10am to noon and again from around 2 to 5pm. As a result, the best time to visit is first thing in the morning or as the sun is setting.

Volubilis is signposted from the main road. Admission is 20dh ($2.50/£1.25) adults and children over 12, and hours are daily 9am to sunset. Secure parking is available; gratuity of 10dh ($1.25/65p) to the *gardien* is expected.

The **Volubilis Inn** (© **035/544405** or 035/544281; fax 035/544280; www.ilove-morocco.com/hotelvolubilisinn; 826dh/$103/£52 double) opened in 2007 and is 1km (⅔ mile) from Volubilis, situated on the side of Jebel Zerhoun overlooking the ruins. Although leaning throughout to an obvious Romanesque theme, the 50-room hotel is nicely decorated and furnished. All the rooms are spacious and modern, most with a balcony and views of the ruins. The hotel is also a very pleasant lunchtime stop and offers three restaurants and two bars, open from noon to 11pm. In a large panoramic terrace, the summer sunset views, accompanied by a glass of "Roman red" and a plate of Volubilis olives, are stunning.

GETTING THERE   There are no buses to Volubilis. You can catch the bus to Moulay Idriss Zerhoun (see above) and then either walk about 45 minutes or charter a *grand* taxi for around 40dh ($6.25/£3.15) one-way. Arrange a time for the *grand* taxi to return to pick you up. *Note:* Only pay him once he picks you up, especially if you are visiting in the afternoon, or you may end up hitchhiking on the main road. The best option for two or more travelers is to charter a *grand* taxi from Meknes. See Meknes arrival information on p. 239.

3 Ifrane ⟨★⟩

63km (39 miles) S of Fes; 84km (52 miles) SE of Meknes; 143km (89 miles) N of Midelt

The mountain resort of Ifrane is like no other in Morocco. Built by the French in 1929 as a colonial retreat, the first impression upon entering the village is of a "little Switzerland"—hence the marketing slogan used by tourism bodies to promote it. Within the village are tall, triangular-roof Alpine chalets, neatly-trimmed gardens, a leafy park surrounding a mountain-fed lake, and a central square surrounded by stone-wall cafes and restaurants. What attracted the French—and now affluent Moroccans—is the heavenly cool climate during summer. As Fes and Meknes swelter, Ifrane is pleasant and refreshing. This climate is also an attraction in winter, when the surrounding mountainside can be blanketed in snow.

The addition in the 1990s of a royal palace and a private university, Al Akhawayn University, has added extra prestige to the village's status as a favored location. Some hard-core travelers scoff at the chance to stop and visit Ifrane, citing it's not the "real" Morocco. I personally enjoy wandering around the village. The beautifully fresh air is revitalizing to say the least, and I also like the happy and vibrant atmosphere that prevails here. Many Moroccans come here on day visits, no doubt wanting to see this "foreign" town and how the other half lives. While families play in the park and have their picture taken next to the village stone lion—carved by an Italian soldier during World War II—university students mingle in cafes and check out each other's new cars. Ifrane offers a different view of Morocco, and many travelers leave here refreshed and surprised that such a village can exist.

ESSENTIALS
GETTING THERE
BY BUS & *GRAND* TAXI   The bus and *grand* taxi stations sit side-by-side behind the municipal market off the Ifrane-Meknes road, about .5km (⅓ mile) from the village square. CTM and private buses from Casablanca (4½ hr.; 90dh/$11/£5.65) travel via Rabat (3½ hr.; 65dh/$8.15/£4.05) and Meknes (1 hr.; 25dh/3.15/£1.55). Those coming from Marrakech (8 hr.; 95dh–125dh/$12–$16/£5.95–£7.80) travel via Beni Mellal (4 hr.; 60dh/$7.50/£3.75). There are also both CTM and private buses from Fes (1 hr.; 20dh/$2.50/£1.25) and Midelt (3½ hr.; 40dh/$5/£2.50).

Grands taxis depart throughout the day from Fes (1 hr.; 23dh/$2.90/£1.45); Meknes (1 hr.; 30dh/$3.75/£1.90); and Midelt (3 hr.; 50dh/$6.25/£3.15).

Monkeys in Morocco

Known in Morocco as the Barbary ape, this medium-size primate is actually a macaque monkey, the mistake arising from their lack of a tail. Like all macaques, they have powerful jaws and long canine teeth. The Barbary macaque, which lives for up to 22 years, is the only macaque outside of Asia and is found in Morocco and North Algeria, along with a small population, under the protection of the British army, in Gibraltar.

Barbary macaques live in multimale, multifemale troops of 20 to 30, with females as the head of the troop. They differ from other macaques in that the males help to care for the young, often grooming and playing together for hours. This occurs because the females mate with all the male members of the troop, ensuring they are never sure of the offspring's paternity. This situation then forces the males to collectively look after all the offspring. The females give birth to a single offspring every one or two years.

Barbary macaques are equally at home on the ground as in the trees, and feed on a wide variety of leaves, roots, sprouts, fruit, and invertebrate. When food is scarce, however, they forage for bark, and this has put them at odds with the Moroccan forestry services who have considered culling the macaques in the past because of their bark stripping, even though the species is listed as vulnerable by the World Conservation Union. This bark stripping is due to the macaque's range being reduced by drought, logging, and overgrazing.

VILLAGE LAYOUT   The road from Meknes, boulevard Mohammed V, intersects with avenue des Tilluels, which eventually passes the north side of the village square. Two parallel roads head south for 50m (165 ft.) from the square—avenue de la Marché Verte and rue de la Cascade—before intersecting with avenue Hassan II, the main road north to Fes.

FAST FACTS   Within 100m (330 ft.) south of the open village square, you'll find branches of Banque Populaire, Credit du Maroc, and BMCE, all with ATMs and open Monday to Friday 8:15am to 3:45pm.

The post office is located on the square, and is open Monday to Friday 8am to 4:15pm and Saturday 8 to 11:45am. Just south of the square is Pharmacie Mischlif-fen, open Monday to Thursday 9am to 12:30pm and 3:30 to 8pm, Friday 9am to noon and 3:30 to 8pm, and Saturday 9am to 1pm.

The mini-supermarket Superette Al Akhawain faces the south side of the square, while Superette des Cigognes, which is also the local beer depot, is 50m (164 ft.) to the west. Both are open daily from 9am to 1:45pm and 3:30 to 8:30 pm (closed Tues afternoon).

There are a couple of souvenir and photo shops south of the square. On avenue de la Marché Verte is Caprice Shop, which sells postcards and the *Guardian Weekly,* and Labo Photo Ismailia, which both stocks and processes film. On rue de la Cascade is the Atlas Souvenir Corner with Moroccan trinkets, maps, and souvenir books. They are all open daily 9am to 7pm and closed between 12 and 2:30pm on Fridays.

GETTING AROUND   The bus and *grand* taxi stations are only a 10-minute walk from the square.

WHERE TO STAY

Hotel Chamonix   This well-priced hotel is in a good location just south of the square. The rooms are light, modern, and (importantly) come with heating and 24-hour hot water in the private bathrooms. The restaurant and bar downstairs are the most popular in town. In winter, a nice fireplace warms up the restaurant, and the hotel also rents out ski equipment, albeit dated. During the summer holiday season, a nightclub opens on weekends.

Av. de la Marché Verte, Ifrane. ℃ 035/566028. Fax 035/566826. 64 units. 440dh ($55/£28) single; 672dh ($84/£42) double; 968dh ($121/£61) triple. Rates include breakfast. No credit cards. **Amenities:** Restaurant; bar. *In room:* A/C, heating, satellite TV.

Hotel Mischliffen   At press time, a complete makeover of this five-star ski lodge was just about complete. Sitting atop a hill overlooking Ifrane, the huge complex is going to be a statement in luxury and is a vote of confidence in the future of the village. Rooms will be various sizes and offer either village or mountain views. A large restaurant will hang over the hillside and offer sweeping views toward the lake and royal palace.

Av. Hassan II (Ifrane-Fes road), .5km (⅓ mile) south of the village square. ℃ 035/566607. Fax 035/566622. 200 units. 900dh–1,300dh ($113–$163/£56–£81) double. MC, V. **Amenities:** Restaurant; bar; hammam; conference center. *In room:* A/C, heating, satellite TV.

WHERE TO DINE

Cookie Craque ✮✮ CAFE/INTERNATIONAL   Located on the north side of the village square is this popular cafe and restaurant. There's a pleasant outdoor veranda and both an informal dining area with a fireplace and more formal restaurant inside. Cookie Craque is good for both a light snack or something more substantial. An open kitchen under the veranda produces some tasty pizzas, savory crepes, and toasted sandwiches, while the kitchen inside prepares a selection of grilled meats, pastas, and tagines. In summer there's a good supply of Häagen-Dazs ice cream to accompany the sweet selection of pastries and gâteaux. A variety of teas is also available.

Av. des Tilleuls. ℃ 035/567171. Pizzas 40dh–60dh ($5–$7.50/£2.50–£3.75); main courses 25dh–90dh ($3.15–$11/£1.55–£5.65). No credit cards. Mon–Fri 7am–10pm; Sat–Sun 7am–11:30pm.

Hotel Chamonix MOROCCAN/INTERNATIONAL   The large restaurant of this hotel has tables both inside and outside and has the most varied menu in town. Diners can choose light meals of salads and omelets, pizzas, Atlas trout (a specialty), grilled meats, brochettes, and tagines. They open for breakfast, but I recommend Le Croustillant (below) around the corner.

Av. de la Marché Verte. ℃ 035/566028. Fax 035/566826. Light meals 20dh–35dh ($2.50–$4.40/£1.25–£2.20); pizzas 50dh–80dh ($6.25–$10/£3.15–£5); main courses 60dh–130dh ($7.50–$16/£3.75–£8.15). No credit cards. Daily 7am–10:30pm.

La Paix Cafe Restaurant MOROCCAN/INTERNATIONAL   This modern and simply furnished restaurant is popular with Moroccan families visiting Ifrane for the day. The spotless kitchen offers a reasonably varied menu of soups and salads, pizza, pastas, and tagines.

Av. de la Marché Verte. ℃ 035/566675. Main courses 40dh–60dh ($5–$7.50/£2.50–£3.75). No credit cards. Daily 10am–10pm.

Le Croustillant CAFE/PATISSERIE/BAKERY This is the best spot on the square to get fresh bread and pastries. The seating is all indoor, but large windows allow for a view of the goings-on outside. This is also a popular spot for a coffee or tea.

Rue de la Cascade. No phone. No credit cards accepted. Daily 7am–11pm.

WHAT TO SEE & DO

Ifrane is a pleasant place to walk around. The royal palace takes up the south side of the village lake, complete with white swans, and a public walkway runs parallel on the northern side, just 100m (330 ft.) from the village square. A couple hours' walk alongside the lake and around the village center is best topped off by a meal or drink in one of the cafes or hotels overlooking or surrounding the square.

For a full day's outing into the mountainside, a trip to the volcanic crater of Mischliffen and the Barbary apes south of Azrou is highly recommended. The Mischliffen is surrounded on all sides by Atlas cedar forests and is a pleasant place for a hike and picnic. An interesting sight here is the rustic clubhouse of the Ifrane Ski Club. Returning to Ifrane via Azrou, troops of Barbary apes can usually be seen on the side of the road, in far more natural surroundings than those encountered on Marrakech's Jemaa el Fna and elsewhere.

4 Midelt

206km (128 miles) S of Fes; 193km (120 miles) S of Meknes; 133km (83 miles) N of Er Rachidia

Quietly sitting on the high plains to the south of the Middle Atlas, Midelt is a convenient stopover between Fes and Meknes to the north and Er Rachidia and Erfoud to the south. The town itself lacks any great appeal, but the surrounding countryside offers some beautiful landscapes and pictures of rural Berber life. Midelt is a French creation—second in the country after Casablanca to receive electricity—built to coordinate the large-scale mining of lead and gypsum in the area. The region is now a major fruit-growing area; most of the country's apples, walnuts, apricots, and plums come from here. All of this is largely incidental to the traveler, however, who generally arrives late in the day, beds down for the night, and continues on the next day to destinations better known.

ESSENTIALS
GETTING THERE

BY BUS & *GRAND* TAXI The bus station sits in the center of town, with *grands* taxis parked 100m (330 ft.) to the south. CTM and private companies operate services from Casablanca (8 hr.; 100dh–120dh/$13–$15/£6.25–£7.50); Erfoud (4½ hr.; 55dh–75dh/$6.90–$9.40/£3.45–£4.70); Er Rachidia (3 hr.; 40dh–60dh/$5–$7.50/£2.50–£3.75); Fes (5 hr.; 70dh–90dh/$8.75–$11/£4.40–£5.65); Meknes (5 hr.; 60dh–80dh/$7.50–$10/£3.75–£5); and Rabat (7 hr.; 85dh–100dh/$11–$13/£5.30–£6.25).

Grands taxis depart throughout the day from Er Rachidia (2 hr.; 35dh/$4.40/£2.20); Fes (4 hr.; 55dh/$6.90/£3.45); and Meknes (4 hr.; 55dh/$6.90/£3.45).

TOWN LAYOUT Midelt is almost a one-road town. The main road from either the Middle Atlas (Fes, Meknes, Azrou) or the High Atlas (Er Rachidia) splits into avenue Mohammed V and avenue Moulay Abdallah between the bus station and the *grand* taxi station before rejoining again and heading out of town.

FAST FACTS A new branch of **Banque Populaire** can be found 50m (164 ft.) north of the bus station on the main road heading to the Middle Atlas. There is also a **BMCI** branch across from the *grand* taxi station. Both branches are open Monday to Friday 8:15am to 3:45pm.

The **post office** is located south of the *grand* taxi station, 1 block back from the main Midelt-Er Rachidia road. Across the road from the *grand* taxi station is **Pharmacie la Cascade,** open daily 8:30am to 8pm. **Cyber Cascade Internet** cafe is above the Cascade Cafe on the roundabout at the bus station.

WHAT TO SEE & DO

Atelier des Soeurs Franciscaines

Operated by Franciscan sisters since 1926, this weaving *atelier* (workshop) is an enlightening example of cooperation between the faiths. Franciscan sisters are inspired by the spirit of St. Francis of Assisi, who during the Fifth Crusade in 1219 met with the Muslim Sultan of Egypt in an unprecedented gesture of dialogue and peace. Although the nun's established a convent shortly after their arrival in Midelt, an implicit aspect of their presence has also been a profound respect for the Muslim faith and a desire to collaborate with their Muslim neighbors. In an effort to respond to the needs of the local people, the sisters have over the years opened an orphanage, embroidery and weaving workshops, and a dispensary, as well as a primary school. Along with earning additional income for their families through the sale of their embroidery and weaving, the workshops allow the local women to pass on their skills to the younger generation.

Currently, there are six sisters based in here who cover an impressive mix of nationalities (French, Irish, Polish, Korean, and Spanish). The sisters have moved from the convent to a smaller house within the compound, and the convent is now a monastery, Nôtre Dame de l'Atlas (www.notredameatlas.com), occupied by four Trappist monks. Visitors are welcome to visit the monastery, as well as attend the daily mass. Madame Nicole de Bono (embroidery section), Sister Monique (embroidery section), and Sister Teresa (weaving section) are usually on hand to show visitors through the workshop (an understanding of French is advantageous), though the local women have Fridays and Sundays off. The embroidery and weaving work is exceptional, and is available for sale in the form of blankets, tablecloths, and wool carpets.

Kasbah Myriem, Midelt-Tattiouine road (1km/⅔ mile from Midelt center). ☎ 035/361255, or after hours 035/582443 or 064/447375. debono@menara.ma or donlon_me@yahoo.fr. Workshop: daily 8:30am–12:30pm and 2:30–5:30pm. Monastery: daily; Mon–Sat Mass 7:15am, Sun Mass 11am.

WHERE TO STAY & DINE

Kasbah Asmaa

Part of the Asmaa chain, this kasbah-style hotel is the best in town, though that's not saying much. A lonely property on the road heading south, the hotel is protected by a large roadside wall. A front courtyard leads into a massive reception and dining area. The L-shape building looks inward to a pleasant garden and swimming pool. Two standards of rooms are available. Those in the older wing are perfectly adequate, if a little dusty and tired, while the newer rooms still have some shine to them and enjoy a view of the garden. Besides the Moroccan lounge-style restaurant, there's also a large restaurant–cum–dining hall under the new wing, facing onto the garden. This hotel is the main lunchtime stop for tour buses ploughing through from the south to Fes or vice versa. An a la carte menu and three set menus offer the usual Moroccan fare of tagines, brochettes, and couscous. They serve a nice *harira* soup as well.

Midelt–Er Rachidia road, 4km (2½ miles) from Midelt center. ☎ 035/580405. Fax 035/583945. 35 units. 350dh ($44/£22) double (old wing); 600dh ($75/£38) double (new wing). Restaurant: set menus 100dh–125dh ($13–$16/£6.25–£7.80); main courses 60dh–100dh ($7.50–$13/£3.75–£6.25). Alcohol served. Daily 7am–10:30pm. No credit cards. **Amenities:** 2 restaurants; pool. *In room:* A/C, heating, satellite TV.

9

Northwest Morocco

Unlike anywhere else in Morocco, the forgotten northwest corner of the country has suffered the most from a long history of selfishness and neglect by the very same powers that have fought so hard to possess it. Subtly different to the rest of the country, thanks to its relatively recent Spanish occupation, the northwest has historically welcomed far fewer tourists than the more popular regions of Morocco to its south. This was partly due to a well-earned reputation as the country's worst region for hustlers and conmen, but also as a result of a long period of disownment from a king who seemed to genuinely dislike the region—perhaps as a direct consequence of two failed attempts on his life that supposedly emanated from here.

Tangier, one of the oldest ports known to man, has been exploited almost since its beginning, when the Phoenicians settled here in 1500 B.C. at the western edge of the then-known world. Many nations have since passed through the port and proceeded to accept all the gifts provided by its strategic location without any real commitment toward bettering its residents or developing its infrastructure. This exploitation reached its peak during the first half of the last century when no less than 14 nations—begrudgingly including Morocco—were involved in the city's administration. This was the "InterZone" period of Tangier, a time of excess and vice that earned the city a reputation that still lingers today.

Chefchaouen sits hidden away in the Rif mountains, the wildest of the country's ranges. Isolation by xenophobia—rather than exploitation by outsiders—was the curse of this little village. For more than 400 years, the villagers (Andalusian refugees who came here to start a new life after expulsion from reconquered Christian Spain) determined never again to let the "Christian dogs" rule over them. They denied entry to all Westerners, even poisoning one who made it through the village's gates. The region was placed under Spanish "protection" from 1912 to 1956. However, rather than a time of prosperity under colonialist rule—as it could be argued occurred in the rest of the country under the French—the northwest was again subject to a reign of plunder and neglect, with little or no infrastructure, education, or health initiatives. This very isolation and lack of development, however, has over the past 10 years seen Chefchaouen deservedly becoming a must-see destination on both the backpacker and mainstream tourist route. Travelers now come here to see the medina's photogenic and once-off-limits blue-washed houses and kick back for a couple of days, enjoying the fresh air—both natural and narcotic—and small village friendliness.

The quaint fishing village of Asilah was also settled by the ancient Phoenicians before witnessing through the centuries a steady stream of invaders and conquerors. Also under the jurisdiction of the Spanish until Moroccan independence, the village was headed for obscurity up until the late 1970s, when a prominent ex-Asilan who grew up in its historic, and by then crumbling, medina launched a festival of arts that has turned the town's fortunes around. The festival, held every August, is so popular that the city's hotels are often booked out a year in advance and property prices within its once bargain-basement medina have risen to levels matched only by Marrakech.

Both Chefchaouen's and Asilah's current popularity is finally being duplicated in Tangier. For the past 5 years—thanks to a new king who makes no secret of his affection for the city—a frantic amount of restoration, landscaping, and foreign investment has resulted in the city being coined "Morocco's St-Tropez." Its once-seedy past is now looked upon with nostalgia by those Westerners old enough to remember the days of beat writers and Barbara Hutton, while hordes of Spanish visitors arrive every morning for a day's exploration of an Islamic kingdom only a 2- to 3-hour ferry ride away. Moroccans themselves also come to the city for a beach holiday and the city's cosmopolitan atmosphere.

While most independent Western travelers will still choose to take a taxi between Tangier's port and train station to head straight out of the northwest for more "glamorous" regions farther south, those who delay that journey for even just a few days will have the chance to experience a world-weary part of Morocco with a charm and style all its own.

1 Tangier

Tangier is one of the oldest cities in North Africa and has also been one of the most highly sought after. Founded by Phoenician traders sometime around 1500 B.C., it's since seen Carthaginians, Romans, Vandals, Byzantines, Arabs, and a succession of European powers come and go. Even when the Arabs arrived in A.D. 706 on a wave of Islamic fervor across North Africa toward the Iberian Peninsula, Tangier was subsequently fought over by a succession of Muslim factions. The Umayyads of Andalusia; the Idrissids, the Almohads and Almoravids of Morocco; and even the Fatamids of Egypt all captured and eventually lost the city over a period of 765 years. During this period of the Middle Ages, Tangier was already making a name for itself in Europe as a materially rich but immoral city.

The Portuguese, during their brief period of world maritime power, captured Tangier in 1471. Nearly 200 years later, in 1661, they handed the city—along with Bombay, India—to the British as part of Catherine of Braganza's dowry to Charles II. During their time, the Portuguese had built beautiful residences, chapels, monasteries, and a new cathedral, but a series of corrupt and inept British governors, along with their ill-disciplined troops, drove away both the Portuguese colonists and the sizable and economically important Jewish community.

Sultan Moulay Ismail of Meknes was determined to regain Tangier as part of his campaign to rule over all Morocco, and in 1678 he eventually surrounded the city and cut off supplies from the interior. In 1680, England's parliament refused any further funding to defend it, and by 1683 the British were ready to abandon Tangier.

Secretary of the Admiralty Samuel Pepys was sent to help oversee the withdrawal. What he found shocked him. "Never surely was any town governed in all matters both public and private as this place has been . . . an excrescence of the earth and nothing but vice in the whole place of all sorts, for swearing, cursing, drinking and whoring." The British blew up a lengthy seawall they had built to protect the harbor—the only public work they had undertaken in their 20 years—and left behind their one enduring character and now Morocco's national drink, tea.

Tangier fell back to Moroccan rule and was repopulated with Berbers and Arabs from the countryside. The British, who in 1704 captured Gibraltar, still kept an interest in the strategically important city, giving the citizens guns and ammunition in exchange for supplies, and in doing so denied other European powers, especially the French and Spanish, any great foothold. Over the next 200 years, Tangier gradually became an enclave where European diplomats and merchants could establish bases close to Europe and took on the character of an international city.

By the end of the 19th century, as Moroccan power waned, the contest for control of Tangier heated up. The French, Spanish, Italians, and Germans all tried to exert their power over the city.

In 1912, as the European "Scramble for Africa" was finally run and Morocco came under French and Spanish "protection," Tangier was accorded status as an International Zone whose system of government was to be decided later (not until 1925 due to World War I). It was in this year that the Statute of Tangier, a document drawn up by the major European powers, formalized the city's status as a permanently neutral, demilitarized International Zone. Officials from 12 European countries and the United States combined with native Tanjawis to make up a 26-member Legislative Assembly. Overseeing the activities of the assembly, and with veto power over their decisions, was a group of eight Western consuls known collectively as the Committee of Control. Of course, this entire bureaucratic structure was hopelessly unworkable, and thus Tangier began its 31-year run as a wild, lawless city of decadence and vice. The city expanded rapidly prior to World War II, and by 1934 there were an estimated 50,000 residents, a quarter of whom were European residents of various nationalities, called Tangerinos.

At the outbreak of World War II, Franco's fascist Spain marched into Tangier from the Spanish zone and took power. However, Franco curiously still allowed access to everyone. Americans, British, French (both Free and Vichy), Germans, and Italians—many still in uniform—moved freely about the city. Tangier became a hotbed of espionage. The Petit Socco and place de France would be rendezvous points for spies and their secret messages. Neutral nationalities, from Moroccan shoeshine boys to Portuguese aristocrats, were recruited to inform on the enemy, whoever they might be. Not surprisingly, then, Tangier was never attacked, never bombed, and continued with business as usual throughout the entire war. At war's end, the Spanish marched back to their protectorate zone and the Committee of Control resumed administration of the city, with the obvious absence of its former German member.

The dozen years immediately after the war were Tangier's greatest as a center of vice and freedom, a black cloud that is only just starting to clear 50 years later. There were no drug laws, no corporate or personal taxes, no currency or banking restrictions, no censorship laws, no import duties, and no morality or vice laws. By 1952, nearly 150,000 people lived in Tangier, almost a half of whom were foreign. The Tangerino community included many British and Americans escaping their socially restrictive, postwar countries. American writers Paul and Jane Bowles were some of the first to arrive, settling in Tangier permanently in 1947, followed by William Burroughs, Truman Capote, Allen Ginsberg, Tennessee Williams, and others.

In 1957, control of the city was returned to the newly self-governing Moroccans, and within a year the authorities began to clean up, instituting a municipal police force, raised import duties, and press censorship. By the late 1970s, those Europeans who weren't attracted by or stuck in the new Morocco left, and the city fell on hard times.

Mohammed VI's ascension to the throne in 1999 has heralded a new dawn for the city. Tangier's aging port will soon become a passenger-only marina for yachts, cruise ships, and ferries, as a new commercial harbor half way between Tangier and Ceuta—Tanger Mediterranée—is due to be fully operational sometime in 2008. A spate of renovation and building projects have been undertaken, including the beautification of many of the city's public spaces such as the Grand Socco, place el Oumame, and the beach promenade that now bears the king's name.

ORIENTATION
ARRIVING

BY PLANE All domestic and international flights land at **Tangier's Ibn Battouta airport** (© **039/934717** or 039/393720), 15km (9⅓ miles) southeast of the city on the road to Asilah. At press time, a new terminal was being constructed. Presently the small arrivals and departures hall houses two currency exchange booths open daily, but irregularly, from 8am to 8pm. They'll usually change your unused Moroccan dirham notes back to euros or British pounds if you're departing from here. There are also two ATMs, desks for most of the international car-rental companies, and a small cafe.

There are no buses or public shuttle services to or from the airport. Cream-color *grands* taxis are located directly outside of the terminal building. The fare into the city, including Tanger Ville train station, is currently fixed at 160dh ($20/£10) up to 8pm and 200dh ($25/£13) after. Taxis from the airport (but not those operating around town) generally accept euros and sometimes U.S. dollars or British pounds, but you will receive change only in dirham. The drive from the airport to the city takes around 15 minutes. Many hotels and *maisons d'hôte* are happy to arrange an airport pickup for you, usually with one of their preferred taxi drivers, for around 150dh ($19/£9.40). This is especially recommended if you are staying in the medina as not all taxi drivers will know the location—and best drop-off point—of your accommodations.

BY TRAIN Tangier has two *gare ferroviaire*, or train stations: Morora and Ville. Tanger Morora (the second-to-last stop) is 4km (2½ miles) from the city center on the Tetouan road and is really only useful for locals. The final stop on the line is Tanger Ville (© **039/952555**), at the far east end of boulevard Mohammed V, 3km (1¾ miles) from the port and 2km (1¼ miles) from the city center. Inside the modern station are an ATM, Budget car-rental desk, cafe, and small bookshop.

Petits taxis can be found directly outside the station and cost around 15dh ($1.90/95p) depending on your destination in the city; make sure the driver uses the meter. Trains depart daily for Tangier from Asilah (45 min.; 15dh–23dh/$1.90–$2.90/95p–£1.45); Casablanca (Voyageurs only; 6 hr.; 118dh–175dh/$15–$22/£7.40–£11); Fes (5–6 hr.; 97dh–145dh/$12–$18/£6.05–£9.05); Marrakech (9–10 hr.; 190dh–290dh/$24–$36/£12–£18); Meknes (4–5½ hr.; 80dh–121dh/$10–$15/£5–£7.55); and Rabat (5 hr.; 91dh–135dh/$11–$17/£5.70–£8.45).

From destinations such as Agadir and Essaouira, you'll first travel to Marrakech on the ONCF bus service called Supratours. Reservations are only accepted up to 1 month prior to departure and can be made either over the phone (© **090/203040** from within Morocco only), from ticket booths at each station, or through authorized agents. Payment at the station is by cash only, but some agents will accept credit cards.

There is also a popular overnight sleeper service from Marrakech that currently departs at 9pm and arrives in Tangier at 7:25am, the return journey departing Tangier at 9:05pm and arriving in Marrakech at 8:05am. If you want to sleep in a couchette, there is an additional 100dh ($13/£6.25) supplement to the above fare.

BY BUS   Buses to Tangier arrive daily from most destinations west of the Atlas, including Agadir (16 hr.; 250dh–280dh/$31–$35/£16–£18); Asilah (45 min.; 20dh/$2.50/£1.25); Casablanca (6 hr.; 110dh–130dh/$14–$16/£6.90–£8.15); Chefchaouen (4 hr.; 30dh–40dh/$3.75–$5/£1.90–£2.50); Fes (6 hr.; 70dh–80dh/$8.75–$10/£4.40–£5); Marrakech (11 hr.; 150dh–170dh/$19–$21/£9.40–£11); Meknes (6 hr.; 80dh–90dh/$10–$11/£5–£5.65); Rabat (4½ hr.; 80dh–110dh/$10–$14/£5–£6.90); and Tetouan (1 hr.; 20dh/$2.50/£1.25).

CTM (© **022/438282** central reservations; www.ctm.ma) buses operate from their office at the entrance to the port (© **039/324916**). All other bus companies use the *gare routière* on place Jamai el Arabia (© **039/946928** or 039/363290), 2km (1¼ miles) southwest of the city center. Open around the clock, it's a busy building with cafe-restaurants and ticket counters, and offers a handy luggage-storage service (5dh/65¢/30p per bag, open 6am to midnight). A *petit* taxi into the city center won't cost more than 10dh ($1.25/65p).

Tip: The CTM service direct to Chefchaouen currently departs Tangier daily at noon. If you miss this one, there are other departures to Tetouan from where you can catch a *grand* taxi. Or, there are other departures to Chefchaouen from Tangier's *gare routière.*

BY *GRAND* TAXI   Most long-distance *grands* taxis operate throughout the day from the bus station, including those for Asilah (15dh/$1.90/95p) and Tetouan (30dh/$3.75/£1.90).

BY CAR   Driving into Tangier can be traumatic, as the roads are always busy and the inner-city center is a frustrating maze of one-way streets. All roads into Tangier from either the Atlantic coast (Asilah, Rabat, Casablanca) or Tetouan/Chefchaouen meet at the busy place Jamai el Arabia; look for the large Syrian mosque Masjid Suri. From here it is best to take avenue Beethoven (the west side of the bus station) to the junction with boulevard Mohammed V. Here you can turn west (left) into the city center or continue straight to the beachside avenue Mohammed VI (formerly av. des F.A.R.), from where you can then access the port and the hotels on rue el Antaki.

There are guarded parking lots around the south end of boulevard Mohammed V, which are handy for long-term parking (25dh/$3.15/£1.55 for 24 hr.). Otherwise, most street parking will be attended by a *gardien* who expects a tip of around 20dh ($2.50/£1.25) per 24 hours. For the medina, there is a guarded parking lot on the corner of rue d'Amerique du Sud and rue d'Angleterre. *Note:* Red-and-white-stripe curbing means no parking.

Unless you are driving out of Tangier directly from the airport or port, car-rental pickup is best organized from your hotel. Conversely, if you are driving into Tangier from elsewhere and flying or sailing straight out, then dropping off your rental car at the airport or port, respectively, is a good idea, as both are easy to locate.

BY FERRY   Arriving by ferry or hydrofoil into Tangier is relatively straight forward once you know what to do. Immigration formalities, including your passport being stamped, always occur on board the ship. Announcements are made sometime during the journey as to where and when this is taking place. These announcements aren't always in English, but don't worry: simply look for the line-up of passport-clutching passengers that usually begins to occur shortly after the boat leaves the harbor. The immigration officials pack up long before the ship reaches Tangier, so get all of this done earlier rather than later.

Most arrivals berth at the main ferry terminal building where a customs and passport check occurs (this can still take a while if the boat is full and two have berthed at the same time). Some ferries may alternatively berth at one of the three outer terminals, especially during the hectic August holiday season, in which case you will be directed to a smaller customs building alongside the port wall. In the entrance parking lot is a cafe-restaurant, ticket offices for the various ferry companies, and a string of bureaux de change, most with an attached ATM. They are open daily but operate irregular hours depending on the season; usually at least one will be open between 8am and 10pm. Exchange rates are fixed in Morocco, so you'll find little variance between the bureaux, and very rarely will you be approached by a moneychanger.

In this parking lot you'll also find *petits* and *grands* taxis. The *petit* taxi drivers are notorious for refusing to charge by their meter, which they are legally bound to, and instead charge up to a ridiculous 50dh ($6.25/£3.15) for the short journey into the city center. *Grands* taxis don't operate with a meter, and are also well known for overcharging unsuspecting port arrivals. Currently the strongly negotiated rate for either taxi—*petits* take only three passengers, *grands* taxis up to a squashed six—is 30dh ($3.75/£1.90) into the city center and perhaps 10dh ($1.25/65p) more to be taken straight to Tanger Ville train station or the bus station. Frustratingly, when taking a taxi in the opposite direction, the rate can fall to as little as 10dh ($1.25/65p) on the meter.

Note: Avenue Mohammed VI begins just outside the port gates, which are 400m (¼ mile) from the ferry terminal building. The medina and the hotels on rue el Antaki are therefore only a 10-minute walk away from the entrance.

Just outside the port entrance—around the corner from the CTM office and about 20m (65 ft.) up rue du Portugal toward the medina steps—is a *consigne* (luggage storage). One bag costs 10dh ($1.25/65p) for 24 hours.

Although not as bad as years past, faux guides and hustlers still lurk around the port entrance. Quite simply, a guide is not needed in Tangier. The small medina is a joy to discover on your own, and the city's hotels are easily accessible. The train and bus stations are easily reached by *petit* taxi, and don't believe the age-old scam of "the trains/buses don't run on a Sunday."

Note: Try to avoid traveling from Spain to Tangier during the first week of August and in the opposite direction during the last week of August. The port can be exceptionally frantic—and ferries full—during these periods with the holiday rush of Moroccan workers traveling to/from Europe.

Current one-way fares from Tangier to Spain are between 390dh and 407dh ($49–$51/£24–£25), plus 20dh ($2.50/£1.25) departure tax; both can be paid in either dirham or euros. If you have a vehicle, expect to pay an additional 700dh ($88/£44).

VISITOR INFORMATION

The **ONMT Délégation Régionale du Tourisme,** 29 bd. Pasteur (© **039/948050;** fax 039/948661), is open Monday to Friday 8:30am to noon and 2:30 to 6:30pm. It carries the usual friendly yet ineffectual staff and stacks of uninformative glossy brochures.

There's an **American Language Center,** 1 rue Emsallah (© **039/933616;** fax 039/935566; www.aca.org.ma), which is mainly for Moroccans studying English, but can provide information to visitors regarding cultural events in the city.

If your French is up to scratch, you can call the **Insitut Français,** 41 rue Hassan ibn Ouazzane (© **039/942589;** www.ambafrance-ma.org). They have a monthly calendar of cultural events such as movies, plays, concerts, lectures, and exhibitions.

CITY LAYOUT Tangier's streets can be initially confusing, especially if this is your first Moroccan city. The city's medina and ville nouvelle aren't as clearly defined as others in the country. However, most major landmarks can be easily located thanks to the natural beach-facing axis of the city.

The small medina is tucked away in the north corner, directly above the port and looking out over the Straits of Gibraltar, while the ville nouvelle surrounds it to the south and east. The major junction between the two is a large square officially called place du 9 Avril 1947, better known by its old Spanish name of the Grand Socco (p. 280). From here the medina can be accessed by rue Semmarine and rue Siaghine, and the kasbah, in the medina's northwest corner, via rue d'Italie.

Running parallel to the long beach-side thoroughfare avenue Mohammed VI (formerly avs. d'Espagne and des F.A.R.) is boulevard Mohammed V, which becomes boulevard Pasteur at its north end. At the top of boulevard Pasteur is place de France, from which the Grand Socco is reached via rue de la Liberté (officially renamed rue el Houria).

GETTING AROUND

Generally, Tangier is a pleasant place to explore. In keeping with the general clean-up of the city in recent years, most of the notorious hustlers and faux guides have softened to a level of merely irritating. The city is always busy with Spanish day-trippers and holidaying Moroccan families, which adds a vibrant atmosphere, especially within the medina and along the beachfront.

BY FOOT Most travelers will be happy to get around Tangier by foot, although be aware that the incline between avenue Mohammed VI and boulevard Mohammed V or the Grand Socco is quite steep in parts. To walk from the east end of the beach promenade up to the Grand Socco can take up to 30 minutes whether via boulevard Mohammed V or the easier route along the flat avenue Mohammed VI and up the medina-hugging rue Salah Eddine al Ayoubi. The beach promenade is well lit and safe to walk along at nighttime. In August the city can get quite humid during the day until the afternoon sea breeze makes its way on shore.

BY TAXI Aqua-blue *petits* taxis are everywhere in the city and are handy if you don't feel like walking between the medina and the beach restaurants; simply stand on the side of the street to hail one. Drivers are only allowed to carry up to three passengers at a time, but be aware that if there is a vacant seat, you may pick up an additional passenger. At all times, request the driver to put on the meter, which he is supposed to do no matter the time of day or night. Most trips should cost no more than 10dh ($1.25/65p) during the day and a bit more after 8pm, when a 50% evening surcharge kicks in. *Petits* taxis operate solely within the city environs; for transport to the airport you can charter a *grands* taxi through your hotel or at the *gare routière*. These beige-color Mercedes sedans take a maximum of six passengers and cost around 160dh ($20/£10) for the one-way trip.

FAST FACTS: Tangier

Banks & Currency Exchange The closest banks to the medina are on the Grand Socco: **SGMB** (© 039/334783) and **BMCE** (© 039/933564). Both branches are open Monday to Friday 8:15am to 3:45pm, and SGMB also has a 24-hour exchange ATM. In the ville nouvelle, there is a string of banks on boulevard Mohammed V and boulevard Pasteur. **Banque Populaire,** on the corner of boulevard Mohammed V and rue Allal ben Abdellah (© 039/933651), exchanges traveler's checks and is open Monday to Friday 8:15am to 3:45pm; it also has a 24-hour exchange ATM. **WafaChange,** across from the Banque Populaire on boulevard Mohammed V, is open Monday to Friday 8am to 6pm and Saturday 9am to 1pm. **WafaCash,** corner of boulevard Pasteur and rue Ahmed Chaouki (© 039/932177), will process a cash advance on your credit card and is an agent for Western Union. It's open Monday to Friday 8am to 9pm, Saturday 9am to 2pm and 4 to 9pm, and Sunday 10am to 2pm and 4 to 9pm. The **SGMB** branch on the corner of avenue de Mexique and avenue Prince Héritier has a 24-hour exchange ATM. The state-run **Bank al Maghrib,** on boulevard Mohammed V (Mon–Fri 8am–3pm), will usually cash traveler's checks, damaged notes, pre-1999 U.S. notes, and the new British pound notes, all of which may be rejected at other banks.

Car Rentals The major international firms can be found in the ville nouvelle, including **Avis,** 54 bd. Pasteur (© 039/934646); **Europcar,** 97 bd. Mohammed V (corner of place el Oumame; © 039/941938); **Hertz,** 36 bd. Mohammed V (corner of rue Allal ben Abdellah; © 039/322165); and **National/Alamo,** corner of boulevard Mohammed V and rue Libanais (© 039/325159). **Budget** (© 039/301045) is based in the Tanger Ville train station, at the far southwestern end of boulevard Mohammed V. Those with desks at the airport include **Avis** (© 063/053432), **Hertz** (© 039/322210), and **National/Alamo** (© 063/053432). A reputable local company is **Doukka Car Hire,** 3 rue Allal ben Abdellah (© 039/940400).

Consulates See "Fast Facts: Morocco" in chapter 2.

Dentist & Doctors **Dr. Hassan Cherqui** and **Dr. Abdelmalek Takkal** are both based in the Clinique Assalam (see "Hospitals" below). For a pediatrician, English-speaking **Dr. Abdelouahid Torres** is at 62 rue Moussa ben Noussaire (© 039/934600). For dentistry, **Dr. Minhal Kodeih** is at 2 rue Kendy (© 039/320332).

Drugstores Pharmacies can be found easily throughout Tangier. In the medina, on rue Siaghine, is **Pharmacie Anegax** (© 039/378973). In the ville nouvelle, **Pharmacie du Paris** and **Grande Pharmacie Pasteur** are both located on place de France. Farther down boulevard Pasteur is **Pharmacie Centrale** (© 039/940982). Pharmacies in Tangier generally operate Monday to Friday 9am to 1pm, 4 to 8pm, and 9pm to 1am. All pharmacies will have a list of after-hours pharmacies listed on their front doors.

Ferry Tickets There are plenty of travel agencies lining avenue Mohammed VI (formerly av. d'Espagne) leading to the port, all of them selling ferry tickets. You can purchase tickets, however, direct from the ferry companies at their ticket offices just in front of the ferry terminal building inside the port; ignore touts' and hustlers' advice to the contrary. The ferry companies also have ticketing offices in the ville nouvelle: **Comanav,** 43 rue Abou Alaa al Maari (© 039/940488); **Comarit,** corner of avenue Mohammed VI (formerly av. des F.A.R.) and rue de Marseille (© 039/320032); **EuroFerrys,** 31 av. de la Résistance (© 039/322253); **FRS,** 18 rue Farabi (© 039/942612); **IMTC,** 2 bd. Pasteur (© 039/336002); and **Limadet,** 13 rue Prince Moulay Abdellah (© 039/933621). All of the above sail to Algeciras, Spain. FRS also operates a Tangier-Gibraltar and Tangier-Tarifa service, although Tarifa isn't an international port so therefore can only be used by E.U. passport holders. *Tip:* Make sure you're given an immigration departure card when purchasing your ticket to sail from Tangier. Immigration formalities take place in the ferry terminal building, not on the boat. Hustlers hang around in the building distributing cards and assisting passengers expecting a tip in return.

Hospitals For a **private ambulance service,** call © **039/954040** or 039/946976. The best private clinic in Tangier is **Clinique Assalam,** 10 av. de la Paix (© **039/322558**).

Internet Access Close to the medina on the Grand Socco is **Soconet,** open daily from 10am to 11pm. Back in the ville nouvelle is the **Maroc Telecom Téléboutique,** on the corner of boulevard Pasteur and rue Prince Moulay Abdellah, open daily 8am to midnight. **IB Nord Internet,** 3 rue Allal ben Abdellah, is open daily 9am to 11pm. Club Internet 3000, 27 rue el Antaki, sells computer accessories and is open daily 9am to midnight (closed Fri noon–3pm).

Laundry & Dry Cleaning **Laverie Ouazzani,** 50 rue Zariab (© **039/949883**), washes by the kilo and is open daily from 9am to 9pm. Pressing 7/7 dry cleaning is on rue el Antaki (between hotels Marco Polo and Bristol). A shirt or pair of pants costs around 15dh ($1.90/95p). It's open daily 9am to 9pm.

Maps & Books There aren't too many maps of Tangier to be found. On my last visit, **Librairie des Colonnes,** 54 bd. Pasteur (© **039/936995**), was selling a *Tanger Plan Ville* color map (20dh/$2.50/£1.25), which has good plans of both the medina and ville nouvelle, with a street directory for the ville nouvelle. You'll also find a small selection of English-language fiction and some French-language Morocco guide books and coffee table-style photographic books here.

Newspapers Along avenue Mohammed VI, boulevard Mohammed V, and boulevard Pasteur, you'll find various newsstands and minisupermarkets selling international weekly versions of the *Guardian* and *Herald Tribune,* including Superette Normandie, 82 bd. Mohammed V, open daily 9am to 9pm. *Les Nouvelles du Nord* is a weekly French-language publication dedicated to the news and gossip of Tangier and is available (4dh/50¢/25p) at the same locations.

Photographic Needs **Labo Photo Samar,** corner of boulevard Pasteur and rue Prince Moulay Abdallah (© **039/932187**), sells and processes a range of film and can transfer your digital images onto CD. It sells a few digital accessories and secondhand equipment, too, and is open Monday to Saturday 9am to 1pm and 3 to 9:30pm and Sunday 4 to 9:30pm. Since 1935, **Labo Studio el Minzah** (© **039/931399**) has been housed just down from the El Minzah Hotel at 79 rue de la Liberté. It sells used cameras, filters, and battery chargers, and will transfer digital images to CD. Daily hours are 8am to 1pm and 4 to 9pm.

Police For **general emergencies** and the **police**, call (C) **19**. Tangier's **Brigade Touristique** is located in the old Tangier Port train station at the entrance to the port ((C) **039/931129**).

Post Office & Mail Tangier's main **post office**, which receives all *poste restante* mail, is in the ville nouvelle at 33 bd. Mohammed V, open Monday to Friday 8am to 4:15pm and Saturday 8 to 11:45am. There is a section outside for sending parcels (that must be inspected first) and Western Union services. **DHL**, 98 rue Sidi Bouabid ((C) **022/972020** central reservations), is open Monday to Friday from 8:30am to 6:30pm, Saturday 8:30am to 12:30pm, and public holidays 9am to 1pm. **FedEx**, 4 rue Allal ben Abdellah ((C) **039/320074**), is open Monday to Friday 8am to 7:30pm and Saturday 8am to 12:15pm.

Restrooms There are no public restrooms in Tangier. If you're caught short in the medina, go to the refurbished **Cafe Centrale** on the Petit Socco. Just up from the Grand Socco, in the Complexe Dawliz on rue de Hollande, is a **McDonald's**, or try the nearby **Café de Paris** on place de France. There's also a **Pizza Hut** near the beach on the corner of avenue Youssef ibn Tachfine and rue Abou Alaa al Maari.

Safety Tangier has lost a good deal of its sleaze in the past few years, and most travelers will feel quite at ease safety-wise. Most annoyances nowadays come from pavement salesmen, especially in the medina, trying to sell their wares. Also, some travelers find themselves targeted by those selling *kif,* the Moroccan hashish, purely because they have long hair or look slightly alternative. Solo women travelers may also attract some lewd or suggestive comments and looks, but this isn't solely in Tangier.

Telephone Tangier's **city code** is **039**.

WHERE TO STAY

Tangier has always had a good selection of accommodations, and as some hotels get a bit outdated, others are built or refurbished. Most accommodations are outside the city's small, walled medina, as only recently has there been any interest in staying there. That said, there are three gems that I recommend below.

Heading up to the medina from the port entrance, there is a line of *pensions* along rue Salah Eddine al Ayoubi, but my preferences are mainly on rue El Antaki, only .5km (⅓ mile) farther along but an altogether more pleasant and quieter street.

Hotels can fill up quickly during the day in Tangier, as both travelers and Moroccans arrive in the city either on their way to or from Spain. If possible, reserve your accommodations before your arrival, especially during high season. Also, read my "Tips on Accommodations" (p. 60) in chapter 2.

MEDINA
Very Expensive

Riad Tanja (⋆)   Just inside the medina and practically next door to the American Legation Museum is one of Tangier's premier *maisons d'hôte*. Behind the thick, green door is a peaceful, covered courtyard with a rose petal–strewn fountain, *tadelakt* and *zellij* interior, and *bejmat* floor. Steps lead up to the restaurant (p. 276) and past a small patio to the rooms, all with the same *tadelakt, zellij,* and *bejmat* combination. Room Petit Socco lives up to its name by being a bit on the small side, while the large El Minzah suite can easily accommodate two adults and a child. Individually furnished, some rooms come with day beds, small libraries set in wall niches, and medina views. The views from the rooftop terrace are even better, looking across to the port and into the Bay of Tangier. This is a true medina *maison d'hôte* in both its levels of superior, personal service (provided by the mostly young and very personable staff), and the little quirks that come with its location. It's in a very old corner of the city, and some rooms look out onto the busy corner of rue Salah Eddine al Ayoubi and rue du Portugal, where taxis wait for business and fresh produce and seafood are sold in the covered *fondouk.*

Off rue d'Amerique, American Steps, rue du Portugal, Medina, Tangier. ℂ 039/333538. Fax 039/333054. www. riadtanja.com. 6 units. 800dh–1,500dh ($100–$188/£50–£94) double. Children under 2 stay free in parent's room. Rate includes breakfast. Parking at American Steps. Accessible by foot only (just inside the medina, signposted from the top of the steps). MC, V. **Amenities:** Restaurant; room service; laundry; Internet. *In room:* A/C, hair dryer.

Expensive

Dar Jameel *(Finds)*   The ancestry of the three young owners of Dar Jameel reads like a travelogue: Poland, Syria, India, and the Berber heartlands of Morocco. Between them, Stefan, Talib, and Driss have pumped new life into this 150-year-old house and now easily host Tangier's funkiest medina *maison d'hôte,* only a short walk from the port entrance. Dar Jameel comprises five levels surrounding a covered central courtyard. The lower floors have been kept in their original style with exquisitely carved stucco breaking up the pinks, blues, and greens of the walls and doors, Iraqi glass windows, and a black-and-white-tile floor. The bedrooms are in pastel colors and are simply furnished—some with a four-poster bed, others with a small, low-lying lounge; some also have a private bathroom. An iron staircase and railing winds its way up (there are lots of stairs here) to the newer section of the house, where you'll find plenty of communal chill-out space in keeping with the Moroccan-Indian influences. The bottom half of a split-level roof terrace offers more resting, reading, and sunbathing space, while the watchtower-like top level affords 360-degree views from its enclosed lounge and is *the* place to watch the sunset. Dinner can be arranged with the in-house kitchen for groups of six or more.

6 rue Mohammed Bergach, Medina, Tangier. ℂ 039/334680 or 061/092780. www.magicmaroc.com. 7 units. 825dh ($103/£52) double. Children under 14 100dh ($14/£6.25) in parent's room. Low-season discount applies. Closed Feb. Rates include breakfast. TPT not included. No credit cards. Accessible by foot only. Off rue Dar Baroud; follow the signs to the Hotel Continental parking lot, and turn left for 20m (66 ft.) **Amenities:** 2 lounges. *In room:* No phone.

Dar Nour *(★★★)*   Phillipe Guiguet Bologne opened the lime-green doors of his enchanting Dar Nour (House of Light) in 1999. Tucked away in the high northern reaches of the medina's 14th-century kasbah (the unmarked green door is impossible to find on your own) with sweeping views of both the old city and the Straits, Dar Nour is two adjoining houses offering individually furnished rooms and suites that just beg exploration. The blue-hued Hafa Suite has its own cozy Andalusian-style living room and a private terrace, while the smaller, split-level Itaf Room is adorned with Far Eastern tapestries on its ochre-color walls. An eight-seat dining table takes pride of place in the communal dining room where guests are encouraged to engage in lively conversation. The floppy couches in the adjoining living room provide a welcome retreat should the discussion become too much for you.

Tangier

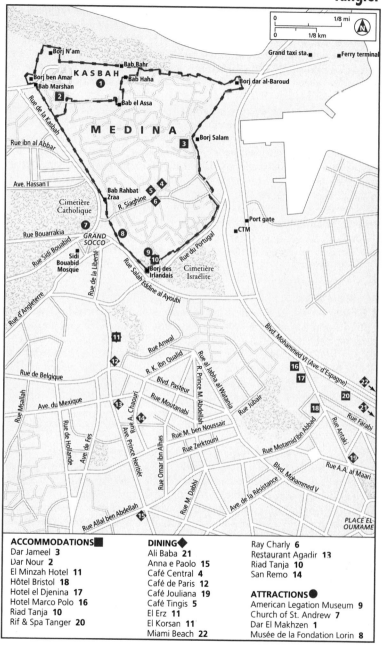

0   1/8 mi
0   1/8 km

Grand taxi sta. ■ Ferry terminal

Borj N'am

KASBAH   Bab Bahr

Borj ben Amar
Bab Marshan   Bab Haha   Borj dar al-Baroud

Rue de la Kasbah

Bab el Assa

M E D I N A   Borj Salam

Rue ibn al Abbar

Ave. Hassan I   Borj Salam

Bab Rahbat
Zraa
R. Siaghine   Café Central 4
Cimetière   5   6
Catholique   Port gate
CTM

Rue Bouarrakia
GRAND
SOCCO
Sidi
Bouabid
Mosque

Rue Sidi Bouabid

Rue de la liberté   Borj des
Irlandais   Cimetière
Israélite

Rue d'Angleterre   Rue Salah Eddine al Ayoubi

Rue du Portugal

Blvd. Mohammed VI (Ave. d'Espagne)

Rue Amwal   16
17
Rue de Belgique   R. K. ibn Oualid   20
21
Rue Msallah   Blvd. Pasteur   19
Ave. du Mexique   Rue Moutanabi   18
Rue de Hollande   Rue M. ben Noussair
Ave. de Fès   Rue A. Chaouri   Rue Zerktouni   Rue Motamid Ibn Abbad
Ave. Prince Héritier   Rue al Jabha al Watania   Rue A.A. al Maari
Rue Omar ibn Alhas   Rue Prince M. Abdellah   Rue Juabar
Rue M. Dabhi   Blvd. Mohammed V
Rue Allal ben Abdellah   Ave. de la Résistance

PLACE EL
OUMAME

ACCOMMODATIONS ■
Dar Jameel **3**
Dar Nour **2**
El Minzah Hotel **11**
Hôtel Bristol **18**
Hotel el Djenina **17**
Hotel Marco Polo **16**
Riad Tanja **10**
Rif & Spa Tanger **20**

DINING ◆
Ali Baba **21**
Anna e Paolo **15**
Café Central **4**
Café de Paris **12**
Café Jouliana **19**
Café Tingis **5**
El Erz **11**
El Korsan **11**
Miami Beach **22**

Ray Charly **6**
Restaurant Agadir **13**
Riad Tanja **10**
San Remo **14**

ATTRACTIONS ●
American Legation Museum **9**
Church of St. Andrew **7**
Dar El Makhzen **1**
Musée de la Fondation Lorin **8**

Throughout the interior of Dar Nour are various objets d'art from Phillipe's personal travels, along with an enticing and extensive library that guests are encouraged to browse. The whitewashed roof—with bright blue chimney stacks—is split into three terraces, all with their own sitting areas that are a godsend during the steamy summer months when the limp afternoon sea breeze finally makes its way to land. During the winter months when the nights can get quite chilly, each room is supplied with a portable heater.

Dar Nour exudes a coziness more attuned to a home-stay than a boutique hotel, due as much to the warm and rustic Arabic-Andalusian decor as the personal yet unobtrusive attention from the small staff. A sumptuous breakfast of pancakes, pastries, fruit, honey, yogurt, and fresh *khübz* (Moroccan flatbread) is included in the price. Dinner is on request and is usually traditional home-cooked Moroccan fare of *harira* soup and beef or lamb tagine with couscous and vegetables. Nadia, the house cook, can also cater the evening meal for any special dietary needs. Mint tea is, of course, available any time of the day or night. Dar Nour can be the perfect quiet romantic hideaway but is equally suitable for families or small groups.

20 rue Gourna, Kasbah, Medina. (C) 062/112724. www.darnour.com. 7 units. 600dh–1,100dh ($75–$138/£38–£69) double. Low-season discounts apply Nov–Dec. TPT not included. Rates include breakfast. MC, V. Accessible by foot only; directions given upon reservation. **Amenities:** Restaurant; library. *In room:* TV/DVD (in some), no phone.

VILLE NOUVELLE
Very Expensive
El Minzah Hotel   El Minzah is the one hotel to name-drop in Morocco. Built in 1930 by a British aristocrat heavily mired in the shady business of the InterZone, this grand old dame has entertained kings and queens, presidents and prime ministers, a string of red-carpet Hollywood stars, and a few dodgy spies. Today, stranded like a colonial island between her Moroccan-ized former cohorts the Grand Socco and place de France, the El Minzah is still worthy of at least four of her five stars. Carpeted corridors lead to large rooms, some with frescoed doors, archways of intricately carved stucco, and carved-wood armoires; others in a more rustic Moroccan style with earthy colors and Berber carpets. Most rooms have a view looking over the lush gardens to the Bay of Tangier and beyond into the Straits of Gibraltar.

Along with that view, it's the amenities that make this place something special. A large Andalusian courtyard leads off in all directions—a wine bar offering light meals; Moroccan and international restaurants (p. 277); a wellness center and spa; and Maclean's Bar that leads through to the large pool. The pool is set in a spacious, peaceful garden of green lawns; palm, citrus and umbrella trees; roses; hibiscus; and lilies. During summer, guests can enjoy a lovely buffet lunch while lounging in the sun. The large staff of uniformed *garçons* is presided over by 30-year veteran Monsieur Ahmed ben Nasar. To stay at the El Minzah is to overlook the gruff reception, sometimes wheezing air-conditioning, and the odd bit of flaking paint and soak up the atmosphere of a true colonial relic that still has the best view in town.

Tip: Booking through a travel agency often includes *demi-pension* (half board), but sometimes there is miscommunication between agencies and the hotel. Be fully aware when checking in as to what the hotel is including in your room rate.

85 rue de la Liberté, Tangier. (C) 039/935885 or 039/937844. Fax 039/934546. www.elminzah.com. 140 units. 1,600dh–2,400dh ($200–$300/£100–£150) double. Children 2–12 400dh/$50/£25 (bed only) in parent's room; under 2 free. Rates include breakfast. TPT not included. AE, MC, V. **Amenities:** 3 restaurants; 2 bars; pool; spa and wellness center. *In room:* A/C, satellite TV, fridge, hair dryer.

Expensive

Rif & Spa Tanger   The old Rif has had a makeover and is back to its worthy position as the best hotel on the beach strip. While it once welcomed the likes of Sir Winston Churchill and Elizabeth Taylor, it now panders to the tour group brigade and is also a good choice for independent travelers. Those looking for large, modern rooms in a prime location (away from the noise and grime of the city center or medina) will appreciate the Rif. A dusty blue-and-red color combination throughout the hotel works well, especially with the carpeted floors, lending a hint of luxury. In the rooms, marble floors with Berber carpets mix well with the accent wall and reproduced prints of 18th-century Tangier. A small recess with comfortable lounge chairs is well positioned under the window, and the mosaic and marble bathrooms have a welcoming step-in shower. There's a choice of higher-end rooms and suites as well.

The Rif's amenities are numerous. The first floor lends access to a choice of restaurants (Moroccan and international), bars, and a reasonable-size pool with a waterfall. The central hallway on this floor is a piece of art in itself, with original floorboards, carved-cedar wood ceiling, chandeliers, and original artworks depicting Atlas and Rif scenes. The Rif has always been a big hotel but is currently handling the new attention well, with enough staff to offer a good level of friendly service.

152 av. Mohammed VI (formerly av. des Espagne), Tangier. (C) 039/349300. Fax 039/321904. www.hotelsatlas.com. 127 units. 824dh–2,189dh ($103–$274/£52–£137). TPT not included. MC, V. **Amenities:** 3 restaurants; 2 bars; nightclub; pool; spa and wellness center; boutique; Wi-Fi. *In room:* A/C, satellite TV, fridge.

Moderate

Hotel el Djenina   This is the middle of three hotels on this street and a decent fallback to the other two (reviewed below). This is a child of the 1950s and was refurbished in late 1990s. The rooms, which are still a good value, are modern but beginning to show signs of age. The combination of compact rooms and heavy gold drapes serves to keep the rooms a bit warmer in winter than other hotels, with each room furnished with a small coffee table and two chairs. The bathrooms are adequate with walk-in showers. Request a rear-facing room, as those overlooking the road can get a bit noisy.

8 rue el Antaki, Tangier. (C) **039/942244.** Fax 039/942246. 30 units. 451dh ($56/£28) double. Interconnecting rooms available. TPT not included. No credit cards. *In room:* Satellite TV, no phone.

Hotel Marco Polo 🏆🏆   This old mainstay of the Tangier hotel scene underwent a full renovation in 2006 and now offers exceptionally good-value modern rooms in a prime location. Although the hotel sits on a very busy corner, the rooms are set quite a distance back from the road, some reached by a fair hike up a few sets of stairs. Pastel tones have been used throughout, and I'm very impressed with the restraint in garish furnishings that usually accompanies a hotel refurbishment in Morocco. Built-in cupboards and bathrooms with ventilator fans are also welcome touches. The rooms on the first floor are a bit larger than those on the ground floor and come with a small lounge and coffee table. Besides the well-known bar and shaded outdoor patio-restaurant, there's also a small hammam that can be heated up with a couple of hours' notice.

2 rue El Antaki (corner of av. Mohammed VI), Tangier. (C) **039/941124.** Fax 039/941508. 33 units. 460dh ($58/£29) double. Children under 10 stay free in parent's room. Low-season discounts apply. Breakfast 35dh ($4.40/£2.20). TPT not included. MC, V. **Amenities:** Restaurant; bar; hammam; laundry service. *In room:* A/C, satellite TV, fridge.

Inexpensive

Hôtel Bristol *Value*   Conveniently located on rue El Antaki and a 10-minute walk from the beach, medina, and city center, the 1950s Bristol still has some of the best-value rooms in Tangier. An old, creaking elevator ascends the three levels of large, simply furnished rooms, all with private bathrooms and big, breezy windows. The rooms can be a bit cold in winter, but it's to be expected at this level of accommodations. The English-speaking reception is staffed around the clock, so don't worry about a late-night ferry arrival. They have one studio with two rooms that is an exceptional value for two couples looking for an affordable stay. There's also a street-level bar (p. 284), so it's best to request a room in one of the upstairs floors in case the music pumps up during the night.

14 rue El Antaki, Tangier. (C) **039/942914** or 039/944347. Fax 039/343094. 38 units. 200dh ($25/£13) single; 250dh ($31/£16) double; 400dh ($50/£25) triple; 500dh ($63/£31) suite (4 people). Peak-season supplement applies July–Aug. No credit cards. **Amenities:** Restaurant; bar. *In room:* Satellite TV.

WHERE TO DINE

There's a fair choice of dining options in Tangier, as you'd expect from a bustling port city. Finding something different from the usual Moroccan/international combination, however, proves difficult. At the time of writing, there were rumors that a Thai and perhaps a Japanese restaurant were going to open, but for the time my recommendations revolve around the city's best offerings of traditional and *nouvelle marocain* cuisine, and those restaurants influenced by Morocco's neighbors across the Mediterranean.

At last count there were almost 15 beachfront restaurants below the street level of avenue Mohammed VI. And though most aren't particularly renowned for their food, a lot of them offer a lively atmosphere during the summer months. Once the holiday season tapers off, however, some of them close their doors. Besides a notable exception mentioned here, it's best to simply wander along the beach promenade and see what takes your fancy.

MEDINA

Very Expensive

Riad Tanja *✦✦✦* MOROCCAN   Moha Fedal, of Dar Moha fame in Marrakech, is behind this fantastic Moroccan salon-restaurant. The menu is described as *nouvelle marocain*, and is just as popular with Tanjawis as with visitors. A set five-course menu travels the length and breadth of Morocco. Starters are a mosaic of Mediterranean salads including a ratatouille *taktouka*, mashed sweet pumpkin, and a red-pepper paste with almonds. A *pastilla* of pigeon or monkfish or veggie-filled pastry triangles follows. Entrees are all Moha's takes on the standard tagine and can be accompanied by a spicy house couscous. I love the dessert selections, which include a Hispano-Moorish tart and a simply delectable *chakhchoukha* (almond and apple in a phyllo pastry) served with saffron-infused stewed apples. The twin salons are decked out with thick, red Berber carpets; dark-wood chairs with comfortable linen cushions; antique drawings, paintings, and maps adorning the shiny *tadelakt* walls; and soft lighting and candles. On pleasant evenings, ask for a table to be set on the balcony overlooking the edge of the medina and across to the Bay of Tangier.

Off rue d'Amerique, American Steps, rue du Portugal. (C) **039/333538**. Fax 039/333054. www.riadtanja.com. Reservations recommended. Set menu 300dh ($38/£19). Alcohol served. Parking at American Steps. Accessible by foot only (just inside the medina, signposted from the top of the steps). MC, V. Tues–Sun noon–3pm and 8–11pm.

Inexpensive

Café Central & Café Tingis CAFE   These legendary cafes still pull in the travelers and the odd dodgy local. Located on Petit Socco, the Central (the historical haunt of William Burroughs) was recently refurbished and now boasts trendy outdoor tables and a welcoming air-conditioned interior. Paul Bowles' Café Tingis is still in its "traditional" phase and has infinitely more character and the odd *kif*-smoking local.

Petit Socco, Medina. No phone. Coffee/mint tea 5dh–10dh (65¢–$1.25/30p–65p). No credit cards. Daily 8am–11pm.

Ray Charly FAST FOOD   If you're in the medina and looking for a quick bite, head for the Petit Socco and plonk yourself down on one of Ray Charly's stools. The lads at this hole-in-the-wall diner will fry you up a burger with egg or slice off a piece of rotisserie chicken, add a side of fries, and serve it to you on a piece of white paper. Add the great people-watching location, and you couldn't ask for more.

Petit Socco. No phone. Half rotisserie chicken 20dh ($2.50/£1.25); burger 15dh–30dh ($1.90–$3.75/95p–£1.90). No credit cards. Daily 10am–10pm.

VILLE NOUVELLE
Expensive

El Erz INTERNATIONAL   This is one of the restaurants inside the grand El Minzah Hotel (p. 274) and worthy of the accolades it receives from its regular Tanjawi clientele as well as hotel guests. Although it's a large restaurant with tables for more than 150 diners, the marble arches, wood beams, leather-studded chairs, and piano exude some romantic charm. The menu covers a range of international dishes to satisfy most tastes. An appetizer of spinach salad with line fish could easily be a main course; other entree offerings include sole filet with mustard sauce, traditional pepper steak, and a half baby chicken in a *diable* sauce. One of the house specialties is *magret de canard* (duck breast) in a honey sauce. During the summer months, prebook a table for dinner on the outside terrace and enjoy a balmy evening with a cooling sea breeze and views of Tangier Bay.

85 rue de la Liberté. ℂ 039/935885 or 039/937844. Fax 039/934546. www.elminzah.com. Starters 50dh–80dh ($6.25–$10/£3.15–£5); main courses 130dh–170dh ($16–$21/£8.15–£11). Reservations recommended. Alcohol served. AE, MC, V. Daily 1–3pm and 8–11pm.

El Korsan 👁👁 MOROCCAN   Another of the restaurants inside the El Minzah Hotel (p. 274), the "Corsair" serves up some of the best Moroccan cuisine in the country. Upon entering the split-level salon, diners know they're somewhere special by the uninterrupted view of the Straits through 3m-high (10-ft.) bay windows. The menu includes Moroccan staples with a twist; a *harira Marrakchi* soup with Tafilalt dates and a beef kebab tagine with eggs in a paprika sauce, for example. Those who can give 3 hours' notice can indulge in the house specialties of sea bream stuffed with seafood or *mechoui* (roast lamb) with prunes and almonds. The large salon has traditional low-lying tables and lounges, and at night diners are entertained by Andalusian musicians and traditional dance.

85 rue de la Liberté. ℂ 039/935885 or 039/937844. Fax 039/934546. www.elminzah.com. Starters 40dh–60dh ($5–$7.50/£2.50–£3.75); main courses 130dh–160dh ($16–$20/£8.15–£10); specialties (for 2 people) 320dh ($40/£20). Reservations recommended. Alcohol served. AE, MC, V. Daily 8–11pm.

Miami Beach SEAFOOD   Since 1999, Farah Ahmed and his son Hicham have been consistently serving some of Tangier's best seafood dishes. In a great beachside location, Miami Beach is popular with locals and visitors, and is often one of the livelier places along the beach strip. The French menu covers mainly fish dishes, including filets of

Saint-Pierre (John Dory), *espadon* (swordfish), or the daily line fish, all accompanied by sauces such as an apple Normand, Roquefort, pepper, mushroom, or white-wine *bonne femme*. The *carte du vin* has a reasonable selection of mainly local wines at very reasonable prices. I highly recommend the chocolate mousse with almonds for dessert. Windows all around the restaurant take advantage of its great location, and low lighting, atmospheric music, and comfortable woven chairs accompany the uniformed waiters to make this an all-round pleasant dining experience. *Note:* As with most restaurants in Morocco, smoking is allowed inside Miami Beach and can at times be particularly thick.

3 Plage de Tangier, av. Mohammed VI (formerly av. des F.A.R.). ℭ 039/322463. Main courses 100dh–130dh ($13–$16/£6.25–£8.15). Reservations recommended. Alcohol served. MC, V. Daily noon–4pm and 7:30–11:30pm.

Moderate

Anna e Paolo ℱ ITALIAN   This is Tangier's most authentic Italian restaurant. Dark and nondescript on the outside, the interior is classic Italian, from the flag over the entrance and the black-marble floor to the simple wood furniture and the pictures of old Italy adorning the walls. The menu follows the authentic line with starters such as Caprese salad or beef carpaccio and entrees including a Milanese-style scallopine and *Mellanzane alla Parmigiana* (eggplant). There's also some delicious seafood dishes, and a host of pasta and pizza choices that can be *plats à emporter* (takeaway). Leave room for the obligatory tiramisu dessert.

77 av. Prince Héritier (corner of rue Allal ben Abdellah). ℭ 039/944617. Fax 039/940408. Starters 30dh–60dh ($3.75–$7.50/£1.90–£3.75); main courses 45dh–115dh ($5.65–$14/£2.80–£7.20). Alcohol served. MC, V. Mon–Sat noon–3pm and 7:30–11pm.

San Remo INTERNATIONAL   Popular with locals, the family-run San Remo prides itself on a wide menu of international standards with a high level of attentive service. On a quiet corner not far from the bustling boulevard Pasteur, the restaurant's inward-facing focus allows for privacy, and the pale yellow and green walls, white linen–covered chairs, and fresh flowers on the tables add a fresh, modern feel. The menu reflects Italian/French influences with pasta dishes including a range of ravioli, cannelloni, tagliatelle, and *bavette* (thin, flattened strands of egg-free pasta) combinations, along with a good choice of pizzas that are also available from their small takeaway across the road. Other dishes include a filet of Saint-Pierre with roasted almond and a hearty beef stroganoff. Gourmet carnivores will no doubt lean toward trying San Remo's tournedos Rossini. Make sure to keep room for a divine *citron tart* (lemon cheesecake). A *plat des enfants*—hamburger with fries or spaghetti and a crème caramel dessert—is also available.

15 rue Ahmed Chaouki. ℭ 039/938451. Pizzas 40dh–60dh ($5–$7.50/£2.50–£3.75); main courses 50dh–150dh ($6.25–$19/£3.15–£9.40); tournedos Rossini 200dh ($25/£13). Alcohol served. MC, V. Daily noon–3pm and 7–11pm.

Inexpensive

Ali Baba LEBANESE   Despite the corny name, this family-run eatery across the road from the beach serves delicious, authentic, eastern Mediterranean cuisine. Vegetarians will delight in the choices of hummus, tabbouleh, and falafel that are offered with other standards such as kibbe and *chawarmas*. All dishes come with warm, thick pita bread. The open kitchen also rustles up a fairly good panino "Ali Baba" (with *kefta* mince, cheese, and egg), along with a few pizza and pasta dishes. The restaurant stays open almost 24 hours and is very handy for those who have been indulging in the bars and nightclubs across the road.

136 av. Mohammed VI (formerly avs. d'Espagne and des F.A.R.). ℭ 039/321294. Hummus 15dh–25dh ($1.90–$3.15/95p–£1.55); main courses 15dh–35dh ($1.90–$4.40/90p–£2.20). No credit cards. Daily 8am–4am.

Café de Paris 🎐 CAFE   It's said that many a spy during World War II came to his double-crossing grief after talking to the wrong person over a coffee at one of Café de Paris' studded-leather tables. The decor hasn't changed much since those dangerous times, but the clientele certainly has. The pavement tables are where you want to be nowadays, enjoying one of the best people-watching sites in the city overlooking place de France. The large interior has a few different areas; walk to the rear section for a nice quiet table and a view of the Bay of Tangier. The uniformed waiters are suitably rushed, efficient, and even bordering on friendly (when they let their guard down). Nice, big teacups and a fertile imagination of past days of espionage make this one of my favorite tea stops.

Place de France. 🕾 039/938444. Coffee/mint tea 5dh–10dh (65¢–$1.25/30p–65p). Daily 6am–midnight.

Café Jouliana 🎐🎐 *(Finds* BREAKFAST/CAFE   This unassuming stock-standard Moroccan cafe doesn't see many travelers but is regularly full, especially in the mornings when Tanjawis pop in for one of the cheapest and tastiest breakfasts in town. Choices include a Moroccan flat loaf with goat cheese, fresh cake, and *miel* (honey) or *khalii* (poached) egg on toast; a personal favorite is a fresh *baghrir* (a large pancake with lots of little open pockets) smothered in argan *amlou* paste and topped with crushed almonds. These can all be ordered as a *petit déjeuner* (breakfast plate), which includes fresh orange juice, tea, or coffee and a side of olives. Its location at the top of rue el Antaki is one of the first spots to catch the sea breeze; sit outside under the awnings or inside in one of the two air-conditioned levels. Although the cafe is local, it's also female friendly.

Corner rue El Antaki and rue Abou Alaa al Maari. 🕾 039/321144. Breakfast dishes 7dh–14dh (90¢–$1.75/ 45p–90p); *petit déjeuner* 16dh ($2/£1). No credit cards. Daily 6am–11pm.

Restaurant Agadir INTERNATIONAL/MOROCCAN   Behind lace curtains (it's often mistaken as closed) is this favorite restaurant of backpackers. Ex-Tafraouti Mohammed Akellal works wonders out of his little kitchen and then doubles as the waiter while still finding time to chat and offer you a beer. His menu is surprisingly diverse, offering both French and Moroccan menus. The former includes a grilled *espadon* (swordfish) filet or pepper steak, a seafood paella, and simple spaghetti bolognaise. The Moroccan dishes include a very tasty *harira* soup, a chicken tagine *aux citron,* and a simple beef couscous. There's also a very reasonably priced three-course set menu with a variety of choices for each course.

21 av. Prince Héritier. 🕾 068/827696. Main courses 35dh–75dh ($4.40–$9.40/£2.20–£4.70); set menu 58dh ($7.25/£3.65). Alcohol served. No credit cards. Daily noon–3pm and 7–11pm.

WHAT TO SEE & DO

Tangier's small medina is a delight to walk around, and in the past few years has shed its sleazy image and taken on the vibrant, tourist-friendly atmosphere of other, better-known medinas in the country. Rue Siaghine and rue de la Marine are now lined with souvenir shops, and the lanes up to the kasbah are becoming well trodden by wandering travelers. The few sights and noteworthy shops are easy to find, but if this is your first visit to Morocco and you're feeling a little overwhelmed at the thought of having to negotiate the medina's alleys and lanes, contact Saïd Nacir (🕾 071/045706; www.d-destination.com), a Tangier specialist. There's not much to see in the ville nouvelle, but as always there are a few good people-watching spots.

American Legation Museum This fascinating museum is a treasure trove of both Tangier and Moroccan history. In 1786, just 3 years after the United States gained its independence from the British, Thomas Jefferson and Sultan Mohammad III signed the Morocco–U.S. Treaty of Friendship. This was the first recognition of the United States by any nation and is the longest unbroken treaty in U.S. history. In 1821, Sultan Moulay Slimane presented the original two-story building as a gift to the United States, and it proceeded to house the U.S. Embassy until Moroccan independence in 1956, when all embassies moved to Rabat. The building then continued as the U.S. consulate for another 5 years, before a new one was built outside the medina. It was the first building outside the United States to be registered under the National Historic Landmarks program.

The property has been extended over the years and now sits astride rue d'Amerique, connected by a covered walkway; it still contains the original building. Various rooms house exhibits on the history of Tangier, much of it as seen through a Westerner's eyes. The museum's diverse collection of 17th- to 20th-century art includes works by Scottish engraver and painter James McBey and more recent works by resident American artists. A portrait of former American Ambassador to Morocco, Joseph Verner Reed, by renowned painter William F. Draper hangs in the atrium of the museum's extensive research library. "The Final Portrait of Paul Bowles," by James Krone, is one of the more recent additions and is located in a room dedicated to the late-resident American author. A small selection of literature and paraphernalia is for sale, including a copy of the first correspondence, in 1789, between George Washington and his "Great and Magnanimous Friend, the Emperor of Morocco," Sultan Moulay Ben Abdallah.

English-speaking guides are on hand to provide a free tour of the museum. The museum's entrance is always locked due to heightened security at U.S. landmarks worldwide; just ring the bell.

8 rue d'Amerique (via the American Steps, off rue d'Portugal), Medina. (C) **039/935317**. www.legation.org. Admission free; donations accepted. Mon–Thurs 10am–1pm and 3–5pm; Fri 10am–noon and 3–5pm.

Grand & Petit Soccos The Grand Socco (a French-Spanish hybrid for the Big Square) is the best point of departure for an exploration of the medina and souks. Thanks largely to personal interest from King Mohammed VI, this former market square underwent a makeover in 2005. A large marble fountain is now encircled by park benches and grass areas shaded by large palm trees; it's a popular spot to rest and watch the world go by. Place du 9 Avril 1947 (its little-used official name) refers to a visit to Tangier by the king's grandfather, Sultan Mohammed V, when he aligned himself with the Moroccan independence movement. Head into the medina via the main rue Siaghine (Silversmith's Street), and for a great introduction to Morocco's souks, detour immediately right into the covered market on rue Touahin. At stalls and cave-like shops, travelers can taste and smell fresh fruit and aromatic spices and see and feel bolts of cloth sparkling with sequins or metallic thread. As witness to Tangier's location as a crossroads between Morocco's Riffian north and its Arabic-Berber south, some women wear veils and leave only their henna-dyed hands exposed, while others walk about with their faces bare, showing off the cryptic blue tattoos on their chins, foreheads, and cheeks.

Rue Siaghine meanders downhill to the Petit Socco (Little Square). In the heart of the medina, this was the meeting place of choice for many of the writers, painters, and

A Grave Society

The whitewashed **Church of Saint Andrew,** dedicated to the patron Saint of Scotland but regularly flying the cross of Saint George, was built in 1894 and consecrated in 1905. The interior has a wonderful ceiling of carved cedar and an Arabic version of the Lord's Prayer around the chancel arch. A walk through the shaded gravestones bears witness to an isolated, aged community where burials were frequent and marriages were rare. After noting the sheer number of titled persons—sirs, ladies, envoys, vice consuls, knights, commanders, and the like—one can begin to understand the wealthy exclusive club that this particular ex-pat community cocooned themselves in as late as the 1980s.

Saint Andrews is at the bottom of rue d'Angleterre. The caretaker, Mustapha, lives on site and is usually around to open the church for visitors; otherwise Sunday service is at 11am. The grounds are always open. British aristocrat society aside, some of the more colorful characters laid to rest here include:

- **Caid Sir Harry Maclean** (1848–1920). Descended from an ancient and noble Scottish family, Maclean served in H.M. armed forces before resigning his commission in 1876 to enter the service of the then Sultan of Morocco, Moulay Hassan I.
- **Dean** (d. 1963), owner of Dean's Bar and buried with a simple gravestone saying "Missed by all and sundry," was a popular bartender in the El Minzah Hotel, and his clients moved with him when he opened his own bar around the corner. The bar (2 rue Amérique du Sud; daily 9am–11pm) is still open today, albeit lacking any of the character of its heyday.
- **Emily Keene** (1849–1944), also known by her official title as Her Highness the Sherifa of Wazan, was born in Britain and came to Tangier as governess for a local household, where she fell in love with and married His Highness Moulay Abdeslam ben Alarbi, the Grand Sherif of Wazane (the town, also spelled Ouezzane, is on the southern edge of the Rif mountains). A wise woman, she made the marriage conditional upon the sherif not taking any additional wives. When he did just that, she enforced the contract conditions and lived the rest of her days in relative luxury in Tangier. She founded the first school in North Africa for Muslim girls and introduced the smallpox vaccine to Morocco.
- **Jay Haselwood** (1914–66) hailed from Kentucky and served in France during World War II before making his way to Morocco and eventually to Tangier. A notorious gossip, Haselwood was known as Radio Tangier.
- **Paul Lund** (1915–66) was imprisoned in Italy for a time after a shootout with the Italian Coast Guard. Upon release he returned to Tangier and managed a bar on the Petit Socco. He was almost deported in the late 1950s along with the American writer William Burroughs after involvement in a drug scandal.
- **Walter Harris** (1866–33), a British author and longtime Morocco correspondent of *The Times,* wrote many articles on Morocco and several travel books.

other creative types who breezed through the city from the 1930s to 1950s. The coffee houses surrounding the square once served up much sleazier offerings but are today pleasant places to while away an hour and let your mind wander back to how it must have been. Thanks to the many touts and hawkers hanging around, you can even do some souvenir shopping from your seat.

Kasbah   Set atop the town's tallest coastal promontory, the kasbah has served as Tangier's military and political center since the Roman era. Within its walls, the former royal palace, or **Dar El Makhzen** (© **039/932097;** Sun–Mon and Wed–Thurs 9am–12:30pm and 3–5:30pm, Fri 9–11:30am; admission 10dh/$1.25/60p), houses a museum of mosaics from the Roman city of Volubilis (p. 254), as well as a fine selection of Moroccan crafts. A room dedicated to Fes includes some superbly bound manuscripts with exquisite calligraphy, as well as examples of the city's famous ceramics. Other regions and cities are also represented, while the building itself is a display of Morocco's renowned *zellij*, hand-carved stucco plaster work, and painted ceilings.

Just south of the kasbah, in the medina proper on rue Amrah, is Sidi Hosni, former home to "poor little rich girl" Barbara Hutton. Sidi Hosni is constructed from seven separate homes that had housed during their time both a Moroccan saint and the writer Walter Harris; Hutton, the Woolworths heiress, lived here from 1947 to 1975. The three-time princess by marriage (the only one of her seven husbands not to hold a title was Cary Grant) styled herself as the princess of Tangerine society. Her parties were legendary—she once had 30 camels transported from the desert to stand as a guard of honor—and typical of the ex-pat decadence seen in 1950s and 1960s Tangier. True to princess form, she even convinced the mayor of Tangier into widening the kasbah's gates so that her Rolls-Royce could pass through them.

There's a great view of the Bay of Tangier and the Straits of Gibraltar just outside the kasbah's Bab Bhar gate. If you have time, take a stroll to Cafe Hafa, off rue Assad ibn el Forrat, west of the kasbah. The aging, terraced cafe looks out across the Straits of Gibraltar and is a magical, tranquil place to enjoy the sea breeze and sip a mint tea or two. On a clear day, you can even make out the Rock of Gibraltar.

Musée de la Fondation Lorin   Simply signposted as LORIN FOUNDATION, this former synagogue houses an interesting collection of pictures and memorabilia of Tangier from the 1940s to 1960s. A look through the rows of black-and-white photographs affords a glimpse of the changing times experienced in Tangier—and Morocco—during this period. Subjects range from Mohammed V at a function with a very young Hassan II to visits by Sir Winston Churchill, along with portraits depicting the everyday life on Tangier's streets. The second floor houses an art gallery displaying work from local disadvantaged children, sponsored by the foundation, which was named after its founder and former long-time Tangier resident Marisha Lorin.

44 rue Touahine, Medina. © **039/930306.** Admission free; donations accepted. Sun–Fri 11am–1pm and 3:30–7:30pm.

Place el Oumame   Better known by its French name, place des Nations, this is the new square for Tangier and is often the setting during the summer holiday season for royal parades and celebrations. The north side of the square has recently been landscaped and closed to traffic, and is a great spot to watch Moroccan families enjoying the grassed area and young lads playing football on the square's paved center.

Place el Oumame, bd. Mohammed V.

SHOPPING

Tangier's shop owners—and their commission-only touts—were notorious for persistent, aggressive sales tactics in the very recent past. On my last visit, however, things seemed to have settled down a bit, especially for independent travelers. With the steady stream of Spanish day-trippers currently visiting the city, everyone seems to be getting their fill. Shopping in Tangier is really only for those that aren't traveling any farther into Morocco or need some last-minute souvenirs to take back home. Nothing is made in Tangier, so all the various arts and crafts for sale are transported from elsewhere in the country. Obviously the cost of this necessity is added on to the final product. With that in mind, the few shops mentioned below have something special about them and will hopefully satisfy those that need to shop here.

For a Western-style supermarket, there is an **Acima** in the ville nouvelle, on avenue Hariri, southwest of place El Oumame (formerly place des Nations). Farther out on the road to Asilah and Rabat is the **Marjane.** Both are open daily from 9am to 9pm and sell everything from alcohol and general foodstuffs (including bacon) to cookware and computers.

Caution: When shopping in Tangier, don't rely on being able to use your credit card. For most of your purchases, cash—usually dirham but sometimes euros or dollars—will be the only form of payment accepted.

Lawrence-Arnott Gallery This respected art gallery is the North African agent for Bonhams of London and represents some of Morocco's leading contemporary painters. Open Monday to Friday 10am to 12:30pm and 4 to 7pm, and Saturday 10am to 12:30pm. 68 rue Amr Ibn el Ass, Ville Nouvelle. Ⓒ **039/333482.** Fax 039/333486.

Marrakech la Rouge Opened in 1968, this is one of the most respected artisanal shops in Tangier and is very easy to locate. All of Morocco's crafts are for sale here—ceramics from Fes and Safi; leatherwork from Marrakech; carpets and rugs from the Atlas mountains; *thuya* woodwork from Essaouira and the Souss; and lamps and lanterns from all over. Open daily 9am to 7pm. 50 rue Siaghine, Medina. Ⓒ **039/931117.**

Parfumerie Madini For more than 500 years, the Madini family have been *parfumeurs d'Orientale* of note, and the tradition is continuing as strong as ever. Sidi Madini oversees two shops in Tangier that boast reproductions of more than 115 brands and styles including Allure, Coco Chanel, Jazz, and Opium. Bottles (50ml) sell for 50dh ($6.25/£3.15). Also available is a wide selection of essential oils (6ml for 40dh/$5/£2.50). Open Monday to Thursday and Saturday 10am to 1pm and 4 to 9pm; Friday and Saturday 4 to 9pm. 5 bd. Pasteur, Ville Nouvelle (Ⓒ **039/375038**) and 14 rue Sebou, Medina (Ⓒ **039/934388**).

Volubilis Art Gallery Karla and Mohamed Raïss el Fenni own and manage this small, multilevel gallery in a quiet corner of the kasbah. The works are all for sale and exclusively feature Moroccan artists. Open Tuesday to Sunday 10:30am to 1pm and 3:30 to 7pm. 6 rue Sidi Boukouja, Kasbah. Ⓒ **039/333875.**

Fun Fact **What's in a Name?**

The easy-to-peel tangerine fruit is a type of mandarin orange and was first shipped to Europe from Tangier in 1841, hence its name.

TANGIER AFTER DARK

Finding somewhere to drink isn't a problem in Tangier; it's finding somewhere decent that's the challenge. Most of the bars from Tangier's decadent past have closed down or are in an irretrievable state of unfriendly seediness. Apart from the riad restaurants, the medina is strictly nonalcoholic—a situation that hasn't changed for 50 years—and perhaps as a consequence, there's been no nightlife development here. The beach strip, on the other hand, sees new or refurbished bars open their doors every summer. After extensive research, the list compiled below is a good mix of local and friendly, colonial and modern.

Atlas Bar Ⓖ This friendly pub has cold beer, free tapas, and some stories to tell—it's been open since 1928. There's a central oblong-shape counter to drink from plus a few corner tables and satellite sports TV. Open Monday to Saturday 7pm to midnight. 30 rue Prince Héritier, Ville Nouvelle. ⒸⒻ **061/924052.**

Caid's Bar More than anywhere inside the El Minzah Hotel (p. 274), this is the place that has the most stories to tell. Named after Caid Sir Harry Maclean (p. 281), his life-size portrait still watches over a bar that was one of the drinking holes of choice during wartime Tangier and is said to be the inspiration for Rick's Cafe in *Casablanca*. Caid's is a true lounge bar with plush velvet seats, lingering cigar smoke, and live piano jazz most nights. Open daily 10am to midnight. 85 rue de la Liberté. ⒸⒻ **039/935885** or 039/937844. Fax 039/934546. www.elminzah.com.

Chellah Beach Club ⒼⒼ Despite old bar stools, hard chairs, and a very smoky interior, this continues to be the most popular bar on Tangier's beachfront. There's live music every night (usually kicked off by the owner stepping up and belting out everything from Elvis to Frank Sinatra) including flamenco, Gnaoua, jazz, and often a fusion of all three. The best place to tap your toes and show off your moves is around the bar, which serves pints of draught beer as well as pizzas, tapas, and tortillas. There's also a reasonable restaurant, El Carabo, if you want something more substantial. Daily noon to 3pm and 7pm to midnight. Av. Mohammed VI, opposite av. Beethoven, Ville Nouvelle. ⒸⒻ **039/325068** or 063/647066.

Churchill Lounge One of the in-house bars of the Rif & Spa Tanger (p. 275), this is *the* place for a cigar and cognac. This lounge bar has a nice mix of traditional (*zellij* flooring and stucco walls) and contemporary (plush chairs and sofas), all underneath a blood-red chandelier. The bar looks out over the Bay of Tangier, smooth jazz and blues play in the background, there's a fireplace for the colder months, and the beer's not too pricey. Open daily 6 to 11pm. 152 av. Mohammed VI (formerly av. des Espagne). ⒸⒻ **039/349300.** Fax 039/321904. www.hotelsatlas.com.

Hôtel Bristol The street-level bar of this hotel (p. 276) is a good place for a beer, pizza, and a game of pool. The music can be a bit on the loud side and a few "professional" ladies seem to work from here, but this is Tangier after all. Open daily noon to 11pm. 14 rue El Antaki. ⒸⒻ **039/942914** or 039/944347. Fax 039/343094.

Hotel Marco Polo At the front of the hotel (p. 275) is a small, smoky, and well-stocked bar that's full most nights with both Moroccan men and women. There's also a nice, shady outdoor terrace with tables. Open daily 11am to 11pm. 2 rue El Antaki (corner of av. Mohammed VI). ⒸⒻ **039/941124.**

2 Chefchaouen ★★★

113km (70 miles) SE of Tangier; 192km (119 miles) N of Fes

Secluded beneath the twin Rif peaks of Jebel ech Chaouen (the Horned Mountain), the Andalusian village of **Chefchaouen** (*shef*-sha-wen) is one of Morocco's prettiest. Its little medina is fascinating to explore—and photograph—with an uphill maze of quiet, cobbled alleys that twist through rows of blue-washed houses and a large open square where you sit down for breakfast and end up staying for lunch.

Chefchaouen today is a welcoming place, but it hasn't always been this way. Chaouen (as it's often called) was founded in 1471 by Moulay Ali Ben Rachid, follower of a nearby saint (one of many whose tombs were scattered in the mountains). Moulay Rachid used the village as a base for guerilla attacks on the Portuguese, who were expanding southward from their coastal garrison at Ceuta. This anti-European sentiment increased over subsequent decades with the arrival of Jewish and Muslim refugees fleeing the Christian reconquest of Spain. For centuries onward, Chefchaouen increasingly turned inward, welcoming only Muslim and Jewish pilgrims who had journeyed to pay homage to the surrounding saints and locking the gates of its protective walls each night.

By the time the Spanish made their way here in 1920, only three Westerners had braved entering Chefchaouen: Frenchman Charles de Foucauld spent an hour in the village—disguised as a rabbi—in 1883; Walter Harris, Morocco correspondent for the *London Times* in 1889; and American missionary William Summers, who was poisoned here in 1892. The Spanish were amazed to find the village Jews still speaking a language that hadn't been heard in Spain for 400 years.

Now well and truly discovered, Chefchaouen still retains its village atmosphere and strong Riffian culture. Here you will see the distinctive dress of the women of the Rif: a red-and-white-striped *fouta*, or overskirt, and large conical straw hat with wool bobbles. Combined with a lingering Spanish influence, Chefchaouen is like no other place in Morocco and is worth visiting for a day or two.

ORIENTATION
GETTING THERE

BY BUS   Chefchaouen is well serviced by buses originating in Fes (5 hr.; 50dh–60dh/$6.25–$7.50/£3.15–£3.75) and Tangier (3 hr.; 30dh–35dh/$3.75–$4.40/£1.90–£2.20). Buses from Tangier will often pass through Tetouan, where there are also buses traveling directly to Chefchaouen (1½ hr.; 15dh–25dh/$1.90–$3.15/95p–£1.55). There are also daily departures from Casablanca (6 hr.; 70dh–80dh/$8.75–$10/£4.40–£5) and Rabat (5 hr.; 55dh–65dh/$6.90–$8.15/£3.45–£4.05). All buses, CTM included (© **039/988769**), operate from the small *gare routière* 1.5km (1 mile) southwest of town at the very far end of avenue Mohammed V. It's a 20- to 30-minute hike uphill or 10dh ($1.25/65p) in one of the *petits* taxis that are usually parked at the station.

Tip: Very few bus services originate in Chefchaouen, and many of those passing through the village are full with passengers heading to through destinations. When departing Chefchaouen, try purchasing your ticket the day before or, at the very least, arrive at the station early.

BY *GRAND* TAXI   Beige-color Mercedes *grands* taxis depart throughout the day to Tetouan (from where others then depart for Tangier) from avenue Jamal Dine el Afghani, just west of place Mohammed V (1 hr.; 30dh/$3.75/£1.90). Some ply the

The Rif & Her *Kif*

In 2004, the United Nations Office on Drugs and Crime (UNODC) named Morocco as the single biggest supplier of hashish, or *kif* (Arabic for "bliss"), in the world. They reported that cannabis production was expanding so rapidly in the Rif that it was causing deforestation and soil erosion. The area under cultivation had increased from 5,000 hectares (12,350 acres) in 1950 to 200,000 hectares (494,000 acres) at present.

The Moroccan government now plans to completely eradicate the cannabis crops by 2008. However, the government is in a tough situation. It's estimated that up to two-thirds of the Rif's population depend on the crop for their income. True to the historical treatment of the Riffians, the vast majority of the 112 billion dirham ($14 billion/£7 billion) annual profits from the *kif* industry are taken by the British, Dutch, Spanish, and German drug lords ensconced in their hideaways on Spain's Costa del Sol. The average annual income from cannabis for a Rif farmer is just 20,480dh ($2,560/£1,280) compared to the industry's annual 112 billion dirham ($14 billion/£7 billion) profit.

It's said that there's so much cannabis being farmed that the Rif region cannot even feed itself and needs to import up to 80% of its food from elsewhere in the country. Alternative crops such as avocadoes and olives are being encouraged, but supply is always influenced by demand, and in Europe this is increasing every year: 22 million Europeans consumed cannabis in 2006.

For the traveler, the streets of Chefchaouen may appear a cannabis smoker's utopia, where many shops sell the local smoking pipe, a *sebsi,* and invite those who look even slightly alternative to share in a smoke. *Warning:* Smoking and possession of *kif* is illegal, and there have been highly publicized arrests of Westerners who violate this law.

route direct to Tangier (2 hr.; 60dh/$7.50/£3.75), but nowhere near as regularly. For Fes, you'll have to catch a *grand* taxi to Ouezzane from behind the Central Market at the junction of avenues Abdelkrim el Khattabi and Moulay Idriss (1½ hr.; 40dh/ $5/£2.50); from there it's onward to Fes (3 hr.; 70dh/$8.75/£4.40).

BY CAR   From either north or south, all roads into Chefchaouen end up on place Mohammed V or its offshoot, avenue Hassan II. The best long-term parking is at place el Makhzen, at the far east end of avenue Hassan II. Although it's in front of the Hotel Parador, nonguests are allowed to park here for around 20dh ($2.50/£1.25) per night. There's also another parking lot outside the Hotel Madrid, about 300m (990 ft.) south of place el Makhzen, still on avenue Hassan II.

TOWN LAYOUT   Travelers will spend most, if not all, of their time within Chefchaouen's medina, which occupies the eastern half of the ever-expanding town. The main entrances are Bab el Aïn and place el Makhzen. Coming from the town center and bus station, the main entrance into the medina is under the busy arches of Bab el Aïn, from where you can wander uphill all the way along rue Lalla el Hora to the medina's heart, place Outa el Hammam. A second, smaller square, place el

Chefchaouen

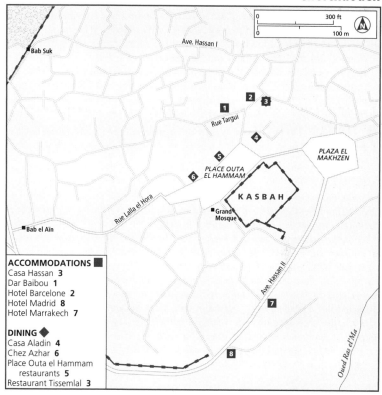

ACCOMMODATIONS ■
Casa Hassan **3**
Dar Baibou **1**
Hotel Barcelone **2**
Hotel Madrid **8**
Hotel Marrakech **7**

DINING ◆
Casa Aladin **4**
Chez Azhar **6**
Place Outa el Hammam
    restaurants **5**
Restaurant Tissemlal **3**

Makhzen—connected to place Outa el Hammam by a short pedestrian-only road—is the easiest entrance for self-drivers and those staying in accommodations on the west side of the medina on avenue Hassan II. The lanes and alleys north of the two medina squares can be confusing at times, though the general north-south descending slope and the medina's overall small size usually helps to regain one's bearings.

Avenue Hassan II curls around the southern wall of the medina and is the principle street of the Spanish-built new town, where you'll finds banks and the post office along a 300m (990-ft.) stretch heading west from Bab el Aïn to place Mohammed V.

FAST FACTS   In the medina there's a **Banque Populaire** bureau de change in the south corner of place Outa el Hammam, open daily (in theory) from 9:30am to 1pm and 3:30 to 9pm. Note that these hours are rarely adhered to. On avenue Hassan II, you'll find branches of **Wafa** (✆ 039/986783), **Banque Populaire** (✆ 039/986531), and **BMCE** (✆ 039/986094), all with ATMs and open Monday to Friday 8:15am to 3:45pm.

Chefchaouen's **post office** is on avenue Hassan II, open Monday to Friday 8am to 4:15pm and Saturday 8 to 11:45am.

Hospital Mohammed V (✆ 039/986228) is on avenue al Massira al Khadra, west of place Mohammed V.

Pharmacie Utaa Hammam (© 039/987132) can be found between the two medina squares, and **Pharmacie Chefchaouen** (© 039/984692) is at the north end of avenue Moulay Idriss, just below avenue Hassan II. Both are open Monday to Friday 8:30am to 1pm and 4pm to 1am, and Saturday 8:30am to 1pm.

Internet access can be found in the cybercafes **Outahammam.com,** between place el Makhzen and place Outa el Hammam; the air-conditioned **Elkhadarine,** up the steps on the north side of place el Makhzen; and at **Saadoune.net,** the north end of place Outa el Hammam. All are open daily from 9am to 10pm, often later in summer.

GETTING AROUND   This is a village to be explored by foot, and the need for one of the town's blue *petits* taxis should only occur when needing to get to/from the bus station.

WHERE TO STAY

Considering its size, Chefchaouen has a pretty good range of guesthouses, called *pensions,* and hotels. Located both inside and outside the medina, they generally cater to the middle and lower end of the tourism market.

No matter where you stay in Chefchaouen, the village's valley location ensures that noise travels far. Well into the night, the general noise of the village can often be heard from your hotel window. This also applies to early morning *muezzin* calls to prayer from the numerous mosques surrounding and within the village, as well as the typical rooster crowing. Hotels can be very cold in winter, but are usually well endowed with character and a very friendly, laid-back staff. High season in Chefchaouen can be exceptionally busy, so it's worth ringing ahead and making a reservation rather then traipsing around the medina looking for a room. Read my "Tips on Accommodations" (p. 60) before deciding where to stay within Chefchaouen's walls.

EXPENSIVE

Casa Hassan ✿✿   This has continually been one of the most popular dars in Chefchaouen, and subsequently there's always a happy, busy atmosphere. The rooms are spread out over the ground and first floor, and though most are fairly compact, they have been thoughtfully furnished and make the most of their space. Each has its own individual character—earthy *tadelakt* walls and Berber rugs; Chefchaoueni blue and hand-painted four-poster beds; split-level with beds on top and a lounge down below; and some with a fireplace and small lounge. The roof terrace has some covered seating but also plenty of warm, sunny spots with great views. There are lots of lanterns, and little moons and stars have been carved out of the walls to add a magical touch. The well-known restaurant (p. 290) occupies part of the ground floor.

22 rue Targui, off place Outa el Hammam, Medina, Chefchaouen. © 039/9866153. Fax 039/988196. www.casa hassan.com. 7 units. 600dh–800dh ($75–$100/£38–£50) double. Children under 7 75dh ($9.40/£4.70) in parent's room. Rates include breakfast. TPT not included. No credit cards. Accessible by foot only. **Amenities:** Restaurant. In room: A/C.

Dar Baibou ✿✿   This sister property to the nearby Casa Hassan (above) opened in 2004 after an unbelievable 5-year restoration. The two 100-year-old connecting houses offer some of the most atmospheric rooms in the medina. Facing inward to two courtyards, the rooms all come with *tadelakt*-rendered bathrooms, small lounges, and locally woven bed covers. There's plenty of comfortable seating spread out over the two elegant courtyards—covered in winter and with a fireplace—and the rooftop terrace offers a great view overlooking the kasbah. A recently opened in-house hammam is a godsend during the colder months. At the time of writing, work was still being carried out on a back garden that will make this open and uncluttered dar feel even more spacious.

8 rue Targui, off place Outa el Hammam, Medina, Chefchaouen. ℂ **039/9866153**. Fax 039/988196. www.casa hassan.com. 14 units. 600dh–800dh ($75–$100/£38–£50) double. Children under 7 75dh ($9.40/£4.70) in parent's room. Rates include breakfast. TPT not included. No credit cards. Accessible by foot only. **Amenities:** Hammam. *In room:* A/C (in some), fridge (in some), no phone.

MODERATE

Hotel Madrid   Sister hotel to the Moroccan House Hotel in Marrakech (p. 125), this Chefchaouen family member is just as quirky and entertaining. Hotel Madrid is a barrage of colors and styles, starting from the reception and lounge area, with heavy red-velvet drapes, multicolor cushions, traditional hand-painted ceiling and furniture, and a *zellij*-covered fountain. While some rooms are relatively plain, with only pink walls and floral bedding, other rooms are endowed with four-poster beds wrapped in sheets of lace and marble floors warmed by Arabic carpets. A complete range of toiletries is set up in the bathroom, everything from a toothbrush to a nail scrubber. Located about a 10-minute walk up avenue Hassan II to place el Makhzen, the neighborhood is relatively quiet, and parking is right outside.

Av. Hassan II, Chefchaouen. ℂ **039/987496**. Fax 039/987498. www.moroccanhousehotels.com. 26 units. 280dh ($35/£18) single; 364dh ($46/£23) double; 459dh ($57/£29) triple. Low-season discount available. TPT not included. Breakfast 38dh ($4.75/£2.40). MC, V. *In room:* Satellite TV, safe.

INEXPENSIVE

Hotel Barcelone   Owner Saïd Bennasser has given his popular *pension* a new lick of blue and yellow paint and refurbished a couple of the rooms. A range of room configurations are available, giving options for solo travelers and couples, as well as small groups of friends. The refurbished doubles now offer either air-conditioning *or* a TV, but what matters more is the new hot-water system; stay here in winter and this will mean more than any other luxury. Locally made bed coverings add a nice rustic touch to each room. Barcelone's rooftop terrace has a brilliant view of both the kasbah and the hills behind the village, and is the perfect spot to meet up with fellow travelers and enjoy a leisurely breakfast. *Note:* Nine rooms share only one bathroom.

14 rue Targui, off place Outa el Hammam, Medina, Chefchaouen. ℂ **039/988506**. 13 units, 4 with private shower. 80dh ($10/£5) single shared room; 250dh–350dh ($31–$44/£16–£22) double. Child under 3 stay free in parent's room. Rates include breakfast. TPT not included. No credit cards. Accessible by foot only. *In room:* A/C, satellite TV (in 2 rooms), no phone.

Hotel Marrakech   Despite the name, this budget hotel is all Chefchaouen, with a Chefchaouani blue exterior and small, airy rooms that are decked out with blue walls, blue curtains, and blue bed covers. The outward-facing windows allow for fresh air to filter through. Some rooms have private showers, while the shared bathrooms are small and kept reasonably clean. Breakfast can be served on either the covered rooftop terrace, which houses a well-used lounge area and is a popular spot for a summer's sunset, or in the large ground-floor salon with fireplace. This is a cheap, simple, and clean accommodations with street-side parking and is just a few minutes' walk to place el Makhzen.

41 av. Hassan II, Chefchaouen. ℂ **039/987774** or 067/543915. 15 units, 6 with private shower. 140dh–150dh ($18–$19/£8.75–£9.40) single; 200dh–250dh ($25–$31/£13–£16) double; 250dh–300dh ($31–$38/£16–£19) triple. Children under 2 stay free in parent's room. Rates include breakfast. MC, V. **Amenities:** Lounge. *In room:* No phone.

WHERE TO DINE

There aren't a lot of fine dining options in Chefchaouen, but there's normally a fair selection of standard dishes reflecting the village's combination of Moroccan, Spanish, and French influences.

Place Outa el Hammam is the heart and social hub of the medina, and at last count, this elongated square had 10 restaurants and cafes lining its edge with another couple on rue Targui sitting directly overhead. It's not so much the food that you'll come here for, which for the greater part is almost identical down to the last dessert, but the atmosphere. From very early in the morning to just before midnight, there's something, or someone, to see. Seeing that it's rude to just sit and stare, travelers find themselves choosing a particular eatery for no other reason than the tables are placed in the best people-watching position. No matter where you dine, make sure to stop off here for an after-dinner mint tea.

Casa Aladin (aka La Lampe Magique) MOROCCAN   Low lighting with lots of candles, plenty of cushions, and a world-music soundtrack make this one of the most atmospheric restaurants in Chefchaouen. Located on the hotel and restaurant strip just off place Outa el Hammam, the ground floor is very much the winter dining room, with wrought-iron tables and chairs seated next to a welcoming fireplace and under an oversize Moroccan lantern with colored Iraqi glass. The first floor has tables, lounges, and deep-red cushions and drapes—all under a high, hand-painted wood ceiling. There's also a private enclave at the back. The split-level rooftop terrace includes the open kitchen and offers both covered seating and a fantastic 360-degree view. The set menu is one of the most diverse in town, though it's still heavy on the Moroccan standards. Try the chocolate crepe for dessert. The service is at times a bit *too* cool and casual.

26 rue Targui, off place Outa el Hammam, Medina. ✆ 065/406464. Set menu 75dh ($9.40/£4.70). No credit cards. Daily noon–3pm and 7–11pm (Aug 11am–11pm). Accessible by foot only.

Chez Azhar ITALIAN   English-speaking Tarik's small eatery is tucked away in the southwest corner of place Outa el Hammam and offers something different from the other places on the square. His kitchen can rustle up a tasty breakfast of toast, jam, and egg, or later in the day you can choose from a select range of pastas and pizzas. There's a small outdoor dining area to people-watch while you eat, or a more private room and terrace upstairs.

Place Outa el Hammam. Main courses 25dh–60dh ($3.15–$7.50/£1.55–£3.75). No credit cards. Daily 7am–10pm.

Hotel Parador BAR   If you're looking for somewhere to have a drink, the best—and pretty much the only—bar in town is within the otherwise overrated Hotel Parador. The bar itself isn't that great, but the outdoor pool and covered terrace have a fantastic view of the hills and the Spanish Mosque. It's a pleasant spot to enjoy a cold beer or a coffee.

Place el Makhzen, Medina. ✆ 039/986136. Beer 15dh ($1.85/90p); coffee 5dh (60¢/30p). No credit cards. Daily 11am–11pm.

Restaurant Tissemlal MOROCCAN   The restaurant within the popular Casa Hassan (p. 288) is one of the better choices in the medina. Depending on the season, diners can sit in the downstairs restaurant—with various salons, tables, and lounges and a fireplace—or enjoy an open-air meal with views on the terrace. For the evening meal, there are lots of lanterns, candles, and low lighting to set the mood. The very reasonably priced set menu has a small selection of starters including a Greek salad, and entrees include Moroccan standards such as tagine, couscous, grilled meats, fish, and omelets.

22 rue Targui, off place Outa el Hammam, Medina. ✆ 039/9866153. Fax 039/988196. www.casahassan.com. Set menu 75dh ($9.40/£4.70). No credit cards. Daily noon–3pm and 7–10:30pm. Accessible by foot only.

WHAT TO SEE & DO

Medina ✶✶✶ As previously mentioned, Chefchaouen's medina is one of the most rewarding in Morocco to explore. It's sufficiently compact enough to not get lost, and is exceptionally pleasing to the eye. An exploration along any number of its winding, cobbled, sometimes sneaky and hidden streets will present marvelous examples of traditional Andalusian architecture, arches, arcades, and porches, not to mention the photogenic white- or blue-washed houses with ochre-tile roofs.

Place Outa el Hammam & Kasbah Outa el Hammam, the central square, is dominated by the 15th-century kasbah, now the Musée de Chefchaouen, and the town's Grand Mosque. The kasbah was constructed by Morocco's greatest builder, Sultan Moulay Ismail. As a prison it housed the leader of the 1920s Riffian revolt, Abd al-Karim. The museum has an exhibition of local dress, musical instruments, pottery, weapons, and a collection of photos depicting place Outa el Hammam and the kasbah in the 1920s. It's worth climbing to the top for a sweeping view of the town, as well as a look at the dungeons and prison cells below. There's also a quiet Andalusian garden in which to relax, and an art gallery often housing temporary art exhibitions.

Next door is the Grand Mosque—currently receiving a much-needed exterior makeover—with its unusual octagonal minaret.

Musée de Chefchaouen, Kasbah, place Outa el Hammam. Museum: ✆ 039/986343. Admission 10dh ($1.25/65p) adults; 3dh (40¢/20p) children 3–12. Wed–Mon 9am–1pm and 3–6:30pm.

Spanish Mosque This mosque sits alone and ruined on a hill overlooking Chefchaouen to the east and is a pleasant morning's hike from the medina. The trail begins from Bab al Ansar, the medina's eastern gate, and passes the Ras el'Ma river, where you'll often find the local Riffian women going about their daily laundry chores. The trail then meanders past fences of prickly pear and *agarve* cacti up to the ruin. This is one of the main paths coming into Chefchaouen from the villages higher up, and there's usually a nice trickle of locals and their livestock walking by. The mosque was built by the Spanish for the local population, but it never gained favor and was simply abandoned and fell into disrepair. It's still standing, however, and gives you some idea of the interior of a mosque. The hilltop view is essentially what you come up here for, and on a clear day the limestone peaks of the Rif range seem shiny white against the green fields and blue sky. It's a slow 45-minute walk one-way.

SHOPPING

Chefchaouen is known for its weaving, particularly the blue, white, and red–striped Riffi blankets, which are worn by most rural women in the Rif. Mohammed Hazim's 40-year-old **Bazar Hicham,** on place Outa el Hammam (✆ 064/826252), was the first *artisinat Marocain* (Moroccan handicrafts shop) in the village. Here visitors can see wool and silk blankets being handwoven on a traditional loom. The shop is open daily 9am to 9pm.

In the eastern corner of place el Makhzen is the town's **Ensemble Artisinal,** where Riffi blankets, along with other crafts, can be bought at fixed prices. Hours are Monday to Friday 9am to noon and 3 to 6pm. There's also a line of small shops on place el Makhzen selling jewelry, trinkets (including the *sebsi*, or *kif*-smoking pipe), and the usual selections of lanterns, lamps, and carpets.

On the corner of place Outa el Hammam and rue Targui is **Aladin the Herboriste.** This small two-story store is filled with spices, soaps, oils, crystals, and 101 natural concoctions to help every human condition known to science—and perhaps a few that aren't. It's open daily 9am to 9pm.

Around the village you'll see both locals and travelers wearing thick, woolly beanies and berets. These are made in Chefchaouen and are particularly popular during the cold months, when funky leg warmers are also a smart purchase. Farther up rue Targui, at its junction with rue Garnata, is the tiny shop of the well-known *kif*-smoking **Hatman.** Pop in for a chat and a look at his range of wildly colored woolly warmers.

3 Asilah

42km (26 miles) S of Tangier; 191km (118 miles) N of Rabat.

Asilah (also spelled Assilah) is an attractive fishing port and coastal town with a medina of white and blue houses surrounded by imposing ramparts and lying alongside a quaint harbor and an extensive beach. It's the northernmost of the former Portuguese outposts, and today has a strong Mediterranean feel, assisted by the hordes of Spanish weekenders who drive down here once disembarking from the ferries in Tangier.

History began here more than 3,500 years ago. Ancient Greek geographers Ptolemy and Strabo mentioned it, as did 10th-century Arab traveler and writer Ibn Hawqal. Over the centuries, the little village saw Phoenicians, Romans, Normans, and Arabs come through. In 1471, the Portuguese garrisoned themselves here, constructing the town's still-impressive fortifications. Their king, Dom Sebastian, landed here in 1578 on his way to defeat at what was to become known as the Battle of the Three Kings. This defeat led to the Spanish absorption of Portugal, and thus of Asilah. The notorious Alaouite sultan Moulay Ismail then recaptured the village in 1691. During the 19th century, Asilah was used as a base for piracy, which led to bombardments in 1826 by Austria and 1860 by the Spanish. In the late 19th and early 20th centuries, Moulay Ahmed er Raissouli, a bandit chief who terrorized much of northwestern Morocco, was based in the town and described by his one-time hostage and later friend, Walter Harris (p. 281), in the book "Morocco That Was." Er Raissouli built his palace in the medina, from where he reigned in terror over much of the northwest region, eventually fleeing to the Rif mountains once Spain took control of the town in 1911 as part of their protectorate.

Asilah can be a pleasant introduction or relaxing end to traveling in Morocco. Hassle is negligible, and even when the town is jam-packed with August holidaymakers, it becomes lively and not intolerable. In the 1970s, the town was just a backwater fishing village, its medina crumbling, filthy, and lacking electricity. In 1978, former resident Mohammed Benaïssa, now Morocco's foreign minister, and local artist Mohammed Melehi organized a cultural and arts festival as a vehicle for rejuvenating the medina and inspiring its residents. Thirty years later, Asilah's International Cultural Festival is one of the country's best and is truly an international event, with recent programs including artists, musicians, intellectuals, and lecturers from countries including Germany, Austria, Chile, Spain, Italy, Mexico, Portugal, Japan, Senegal, Syria, the Czech Republic, Tunisia, and Morocco. It runs for most of the month of August and is worth organizing your travels to coincide a visit during this time, although you'll need to pre-book your accommodations or visit as a day trip from Tangier.

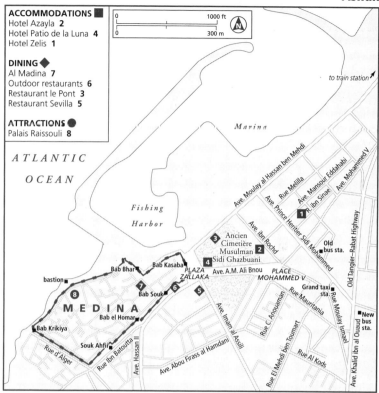

Asilah

ACCOMMODATIONS ■
Hotel Azayla **2**
Hotel Patio de la Luna **4**
Hotel Zelis **1**

DINING ◆
Al Madina **7**
Outdoor restaurants **6**
Restaurant le Pont **3**
Restaurant Sevilla **5**

ATTRACTIONS ●
Palais Raissouli **8**

ORIENTATION
GETTING THERE

BY TRAIN Asilah is easily reached by any train heading to Tangier. The *gare* (© 039/417327) is located about 2km (1¼ miles) north of the town on the old Tangier-Rabat highway and has recently been refurbished. There are usually *petits* taxis waiting to meet the trains; it shouldn't cost more than 10dh ($1.25/65p) for the voyage into town. Trains depart daily from Casablanca's Voyageurs station (5 hr.; 102dh–154dh/$13–$19/£6.40–£9.65); Fes (4–5 hr.; 82dh–121dh/$10–$15/£5.15–£7.55); Marrakech (9 hr.; 175dh–268dh/$22–$34/£11–£17); Meknes (4 hr.; 66dh–96dh/$8.26–$12/£4.14–£6); Rabat (4 hr.; 78dh–116dh/$9.75–$15/£4.90–£7.25); and Tangier (45 min.; 15dh–23dh/$1.90–$2.90/95p–£1.45).

The overnight sleeper between Marrakech and Tangier stops in Asilah; prebook your ticket (9¾ hr.; 340dh/$43/£21)

BY BUS Asilah is very well connected with the national bus network. Most southbound services originate in Tangier and can already be full, so try to prebook your seat if possible. Buses depart for Asilah daily from Agadir (13½ hr.; 275dh/$34/£17); Casablanca (4½ hr.; 60dh–70dh/$7.50–$8.75/£3.75–£4.40); Fes (5 hr.; 65dh/$8.15/£4.05); Marrakech (9 hr.; 205dh/$26/£13); Meknes (4 hr.; 55dh/$6.90/£3.45); Rabat (3½ hr.; 60dh/$7.50/£3.75); and Tangier (45 min.; 20dh/$2.50/£1.25).

At the time of writing, the *gare routière* was about to be relocated to a new site on the north side of the Tangier-Rabat road. From here it's only a 10-minute stroll down rue Moulay Ismail to the medina. Some operators may continue to use the old bus station for a while; it's located on avenue Prince Héritier Sidi Mohammed (formerly av. de la Liberté) opposite the central market, 1 block north of avenue Moulay Ismail. The CTM (℃ 039/418091) office is currently still at the old bus station.

BY GRAND TAXI *Grands* taxis operate from either the new bus station or on avenue Moulay Ismail. Departures from Tangier depart throughout the day (40 min.; 15dh/$1.90/95p).

Tip: Tangier's airport is roughly halfway between the city and Asilah, on the main highway between the two. Buses and the train will only take you into Tangier city center. Catch a *grands* taxi from Asilah and ask the driver if he'll drop you off at the airport on the way into Tangier.

BY CAR The exit off the national auto route (the toll road) is on the southern edge of town. If coming from Tangier on the old Tangier-Rabat highway, you'll enter the town from the north. The streets are pretty quiet, and there's usually parking available outside all the hotels and restaurants. There's also a guarded parking lot—used by overnight campers—at the Bab Bhar entrance to the medina; tip the *gardien* 10dh ($1.25/65p) for the day.

TOWN LAYOUT Asilah is a very compact town. The old road from Tangier or Rabat runs along the northern edge of town, almost bypassing it altogether. From here it's only 1km (⅔ mile) to the harbor, with the medina adjoining its south wall and the beach beginning off its north. Avenue Moulay al Hassan ben Mehdi—with its wide, paved promenade—runs parallel to the harbor and is the main thoroughfare connecting the beach with the medina. Avenue Hassan II and rue Ibn Batoutta run alongside the medina wall, and it's here that most people gravitate during the day and evening.

FAST FACTS On place Mohammed V you'll find branches of **Banque Populaire** (℃ 039/418895) and **BMCE** (℃ 039/417294), with bureaux de change and ATMs, open Monday to Friday 8:15am to 3:45pm.

The **post office** is between the Tangier-Rabat highway and avenue Mohammed, open Monday to Friday 8am to 4:15pm and Saturday 8 to 11:45am.

Hospital d'Asilah (℃ 039/417217) is located on avenue 2 Mars, behind the new bus station.

On place Mohammed V you'll find **Pharmacie L'Océan** (daily 8:30am–1pm, 3–7:30pm, and 8–11pm), a combined **Internet/*téléboutique*** (daily 10am–11pm), and **Labo Studio L'Océan,** which sells and processes film and stocks memory cards (daily 9am–1:30pm and 3:30–9pm).

WHERE TO STAY

The beauty of Asilah is that it has managed to retain a small fishing village atmosphere. As a consequence, however, good hotels are rather hard to find. If you're coming anytime from May to September (especially on a weekend), I recommend phoning ahead and making a reservation. There are no hotels—yet—within the medina, but the following are all only a short walk away, located between the medina and the beach.

Hotel Azayla *(Value) (Kids)* Opened in 2001, this hotel is on a quiet street and is the best value in town. Light and clean throughout, a white stairway—adorned with black-and-white photos of Asilah taken by Moroccan foreign minister Mohamed Benaïssa in the '70s—leads up to the very spacious rooms. The standard rooms continue the light and airy feel, and are comfortable but not luxurious. The pastel-color suites are even larger and come with U-shape lounges that can accommodate up to three small children; some have a small balcony. The bathrooms are small but clean, with walk-in showers and individual hot-water systems. At the rear of the reception is a large salon and breakfast room with a pleasant fireplace for the colder months.

20 rue ibn Rochd, Asilah. ℂ 039/416717. Fax 039/417600. 15 units. 296dh ($37/£19) single; 360dh ($45/£23) double; 420dh–456dh ($53–$57/£26–£29) suite. Children 10 and under stay free in parent's room. Rates include breakfast. MC, V. **Amenities:** Lounge w/fireplace. In room: A/C, satellite TV.

Hotel Patio de la Luna　This rustic Spanish guesthouse is a favorite on the backpacker circuit and fills up fast during summer. Just a stone's throw from the medina's ramparts, the welcoming reception area with fireplace leads to a small shaded patio and up to the terrace. The simply furnished rooms are tiled throughout and have small bathrooms with good showers and comfortable beds covered with local textiles. The rooms are cool in summer but can be quite cold in winter (extra blankets are provided). Blue-and-white, limestone-washed walls throughout add a Mediterranean seaside feel. It's very simple and friendly.

12 Plaza Zelaka, Asilah. ℂ 039/416074. www.patiodelaluna.com. 7 units. 350dh ($44/£22) single; 500dh ($63/£31) double; 600dh ($75/£38) triple. Children 10 and under stay free in parent's room. No credit cards. **Amenities:** Fireplace. In room: No phone.

Hotel Zelis　This large and friendly hotel is the one skyscraper in town, set back from the harbor promenade and a 10-minute stroll to either the medina or beach. Leading off from the marble-tile reception is a large cafe-restaurant and pleasant pool area. Unfortunately, depending on the season, the condition of the pool varies between crystal clear and decidedly neglected, so check before you dive in. The bright and breezy modern rooms are all spotlessly clean, tiled throughout, and have large bathrooms with bath/shower combos. Ask for an oceanview room on one of the top floors (there's an elevator). The first-floor restaurant serves up a small buffet breakfast but isn't recommended for other meals.

10 av. Mansour Eddahabi, Asilah. ℂ 039/417069. Fax 039/417098. 55 units. 604dh ($76/£38) double. Children 10 and under stay free in parent's room. MC, V. On-site parking. **Amenities:** 2 restaurants; pool; Internet. In room: A/C, satellite TV.

WHERE TO DINE

Thanks to the small fishing fleet that operates from the harbor, fresh seafood is a given in Asilah. Combine this with the town's Spanish influence, and you'll then know why every restaurant specializes in *pescado* and seafood paella. The best restaurants are along avenue Moulay al Hassan ben Mehdi and avenue Hassan II, and place Zallaka between them.

There's a string of outdoor restaurants lined up alongside the medina walls on avenue Hassan II. Under the shade of eucalyptus trees, these are the most popular—and best value—eateries in Asilah. There's not much difference between them—their kitchens are actually over the other side of the narrow road—but **Restaurant Rabie** is perhaps the pick of the bunch. Each restaurant's menu is much the same as the next, and includes a long list of daily seafood specials as well as standard Moroccan tagines and couscous. Main courses range from 30dh to 80dh ($3.75–$10/£1.90–£5). All the restaurants here operate seasonal hours and are open daily 10am to 11pm during the warmer months and noon to 9pm during winter.

Al Madina CAFE   The largest and best-positioned cafe in the medina, Al Madina has a nice outdoor area with tables right on the pavement. It's on one of the busiest corners of the medina, looking straight down rue al Kasaba to Bab Kasaba, and diagonal from the medina's two schools. The menu offers the usual Moroccan fare, and it's best for a spot of mint tea and prime people-watching.

Place Sidi Abdellah Guennoun, Medina, Main courses 30dh–45dh ($3.75–$5.65/£1.90–£2.80). Daily 7am–10pm.

Restaurant le Pont ⭐   For 17 years, Aziz Maazouzi has been serving fresh seafood from his simply furnished restaurant looking out over the harbor. There are newer and better dressed restaurants around, but Aziz's friendly, easy-going manner and his simple menu do the trick for me. The seafood is very reasonably priced and is, of course, fresh. His filets of *espadon* (swordfish) and *merlan* (hake) are grilled with just a touch of lemon and are exquisitely delicious. He can also rustle up a plate of grilled lobster or sautéed king prawns if you wish. He also offers a good Moroccan menu; a fish *pastilla* is an unusual combination worth trying if only because you won't find it elsewhere. In the warmer months, there's outdoor seating across the road on the promenade. There is no alcohol for sale, but you can bring your own.

24 av. Moulay al Hassan ben Mehdi. ℂ **039/417463** or 067/987116. Main courses 35dh–60dh ($4.40–$7.50/£2.20–£3.75); fish *pastilla* 150dh ($19/£9.40). No credit cards. Daily 11am–5pm and 7–11pm.

Restaurant Sevilla SEAFOOD/MOROCCAN   This little restaurant is only 50m (164 ft.) off place Zallaka and misses a lot of the tourist traffic, but is popular with the locals. The menu is classic Asilan, with a large choice of seafood dishes—their paella is one of the best in town—along with Moroccan standards. They've also got a good selection of salads and soups, and overall offer a nice dining experience for lunch or dinner. You can dine alfresco, or there's a small split-level dining area inside.

18 av. Imam al Assili. ℂ **039/418505.** Starters 10dh–35dh ($1.25–$4.40/£.65–£2.20); main courses 30dh–110dh ($3.75–$14/£1.90–£6.90). No credit cards. Daily 11am–10pm.

WHAT TO SEE & DO

Asilah's medina is a quaint, compact circuit of lanes and alleys of predominately white and blue buildings (reflecting the influence of past Iberian powers) and makes for a pleasant hour's exploration. It's largely a residential quarter and lacks the intensity or haggling that accompanies some other medinas in the country. Make sure you head down to Bab Krikiya, where there's a popular viewing platform affording sweeping views of the coast and is a great spot to watch the sun go down. From here you'll also see Palais Raissouli, built by Riffian rogue, thief, kidnapper, and all-round troublemaker Moulay Ahmed er Raissouli. Raissouli was known for kidnapping Westerners for large ransoms in the early 1900s. The palace is now a cultural center used during the culture festival, and it's said that captives who incurred Raissouli's wrath were literally made to walk the plank from the palace windows, falling to their death on the rocks below. As you're walking around, note the modern murals on some of the houses in the medina, painted—and repainted—over the years by artists during the festival. Just outside Bab Bhar, early-morning wanderers will see the town's fishermen repairing nets and scrubbing the decks.

SHOPPING

There are a few shops in the medina selling the usual assortment of crafts imported from elsewhere in Morocco. Jordi el Gaabouri's **Bazar Atlas,** at the east end of rue Tijara (© **039/417864**), has a quality range of ceramics, lamps, mirrors, and housewares coated in colorful, shiny *tadelakt*. It's open daily 10am to 9pm. Calligrapher **Sadik Haddari** (© **078/326084**) has works on sale at his small shop at 6 rue Borj Ghouja. For fresh produce and a look at local life, visit **Souk Ahfir** alongside the medina walls on rue Ibn Batoutta.

10

The Atlantic Coast

In ancient times, Morocco's Atlantic coastline was the farthest west known to man. These were shores rarely ventured to, and only after the great European maritime nations began their exploration of the world in the 15th and 16th centuries did the area receive regular visitors. Settlements along this seaboard have included Roman, Portuguese, French, and, of course, Berber and Arab, and their influences can still be seen today. A classic example is Rabat, the nation's relaxed capital, which boasts a history that reads like an adventure novel, including occupation by a notorious band of pirates, along with other tribes and nations. Its combination of an Andalusian-influenced kasbah, distinctly Moroccan residential medina, and French-designed centre ville—all lying within 12th-century Almohad walls—is perhaps the best introduction to Morocco for first-time visitors.

Rabat's big sister to the south, however, is another matter. Casablanca is Morocco's economic and industrial heartland, a new modern city that in 200 years has grown from an abandoned village to a heaving metropolis, and is still expanding thanks to a continuous wave of rural migrants hoping to make a better life in the "big smoke." Casa, as it's known, was the showpiece for colonialist France, and its town planners were at the forefront of nouvelle architecture. Some fine examples can still be seen in the city center today.

South of Casablanca is a seemingly uninterrupted stretch of beach that goes to Essaouira and beyond. This is the country's summer holiday coast, where Moroccans pitch tents for the whole month of August, playing beach football by day and loud music by night. For the traveler, this coast can be enjoyed at any time of the year, with the various seasons bringing opportunities for bird-watching, surfing, and relaxation.

Oualidia is one such place, which is heaving in August and deserted for the rest of the year. This small fishing village offers a natural, sheltered lagoon and a wild, deserted beach, along with a small selection of hotel-restaurants serving up the country's freshest and cheapest seafood. Perhaps the finest (and definitely most popular) of this region's settlements is the alluring port town of Essaouira. With a special combination of a quaint walled medina; quality *maison d'hôte* accommodations; a wide, crescent-shaped bay; and exceptionally relaxed and friendly townsfolk, the Essaouira of today is a result of both past and present influences. Here you can see craftsmen plying their traditional trades on streets that were designed as recently as the 18th century. This mix of ancient and modern can also be seen during the town's world-renowned Gnaoua & World Music Festival, when hundreds of thousands of visitors come to listen and dance to the trance music (fused with jazz and pop music) that was brought here by West African slaves.

At least a fifth of the country's population lives along this section of the Atlantic (from Essaouira to Rabat), which brings about the advantage of a good network of public transport, but also confronts the traveler with a perhaps more cosmopolitan Morocco than expected. With a little further exploration, however, I feel that of all of the regions covered in this book, it's the Atlantic coast that truly portrays the Morocco of today—sometimes conservative yet often liberal, and yearning to be modern while respecting tradition.

1 Rabat

250km (155 miles) S of Tangier; 91km (57 miles) N of Casablanca

Rabat is considered Morocco's most conservative city. The nation's capital displays a civilized orderliness more akin to Europe, with its citizens quietly going about their business, void of the frantic pace experienced in many other African and Arabic capitals. For some, this conservativeness lacks any attraction, and Rabat is often overlooked in many travelers' itineraries. However, upon investigation, this low-profile yet cosmopolitan city offers a well-proportioned package of sights, restaurants, and history within the walls of its easily negotiated and largely hassle-free centre ville, medina, and kasbah. Spend a day or two exploring Rabat's relatively clean but still mazelike medina, its adjoining cliff-top kasbah, and the tree-lined boulevards of the French-designed centre ville, and you'll discover the city's fascinating past.

Rabat has been the nation's capital since the beginning of the protectorate era in 1912, the French preferring its coastal, defendable location to the then-nationalistic capital of Fes. Prior to this, the city's fortunes ebbed and flowed with that of the Oued Bou Regreg ("Father of Reflection" river), which separates Rabat from its historical sister city and now southern suburb, Salé. Early history shows evidence of both Phoenician and Carthaginian settlements on the southern banks of the Bou Regreg. They were followed by the Romans, who established a trading post here around 150 B.C. as an integral access point to their westernmost colony. Known as Sala Colonia, the settlement was based in the citadel known today as the Chellah. The settlement withstood the eventual collapse of the Roman Empire, and by the 8th century had transformed into the capital of a self-governing Berber kingdom. Typical to the independent nature of Morocco's Muslim Berbers, the kingdom was governed under an amalgamation of Koran-based principles and Berber customs and needs. This didn't sit well with the orthodox Idrissid sultans of the interior, who were at the beginning of their rule as the country's first imperial dynasty.

As other coastal settlements became the Idrissids' favored ports of trade and commerce, Rabat's decline was hastened by the silting of the river's mouth. Around the 10th century, a local Berber tribe, the Beni Ifren, built a new settlement on the northern banks of the river called Salé. Continuously at war with a rival tribe to the south of the Bou Regreg, they constructed a fortress, or *ribat,* where Rabat's kasbah now stands. This *ribat* was extended in the 12th century by the Almohads, and the resulting kasbah served as a launching point for their eventually successful campaigns in returning Andalusia to Islamic rule. From 1170 until his death in 1199, the Almohad sultan, Yacoub el Mansour, transformed Rabat into a fine imperial capital. During this golden age, the city's imposing medina walls were constructed along with the kasbah's impressive entrance gate, Bab Oudaïas. El Mansour also began the construction of his empire's showpiece, the Hassan Mosque, intended at the time to be one of the largest in the Islamic world. El Mansour's death initiated the decline of the entire Almohad dynasty, which subsequently lost its control of Andalusia, as well as much of its

African territory. By the 13th century, Rabat's economic power had shifted to Fes, and the city entered into a long period of obscurity, recorded in the 16th century as having no more than 100 households huddled together within the kasbah.

The city's fortunes were revived in the 17th century, when an influx of Muslim refugees fleeing the Christian reconquest of Andalusia settled here, renaming it New Salé. Along with these immigrants came all manner of unsavory types, including a band of pirates that became known as the Sallee Rovers. Safely entrenched in the Almohad-era kasbah, this community, which included Christians and Moors, owed no allegiance to the Saâdians or their successors, the Alaouites, and for a time enjoyed virtual self-rule as the Republic of Bou Regreg, trading with some European nations and entertaining their consuls. The pirates specialized in looting merchant ships returning to Europe with stores of gold from the Americas and West Africa, and roved as far as the southern English coast, capturing Christian slaves for labor. Rabat finally came under Moroccan authority with the rise to power of the ruthless Meknes-based Alaouite sultan, Moulay Ismail. However, the pirates continued their plundering until the 19th century, when in 1829 they were finally curtailed by a concerted bombardment from the Austrian navy in revenge for the loss of one of that country's ships. Again, the city's fortunes declined until the French, fearful of the potential for revolution in Fes and Marrakech, established their seat of power in Rabat, the coastal city much more accessible by their navy should the need for defense arise. The French built an extensive ville nouvelle as well as a new centre ville within the old Almohad walls, both developing within an orderly grid of wide boulevards lined with trees, palms, and impressive colonial buildings. Rabat quickly established itself as the diplomatic center of the country, so much so that upon independence in 1956, it remained the seat of government and the home of the king, as it is today.

ORIENTATION
ARRIVING
BY PLANE   Seven kilometers (4⅓ miles) northeast of the city is the small Rabat-Salé airport (℡ **037/808090**). There's not much inside besides a lone currency exchange booth with erratic operating hours, a post office agency, and desks for the various international car-rental companies. The only public transport to/from the airport is by *grand* taxi, located directly outside the airport. The fare into Rabat—15 minutes' drive away—costs 150dh ($19/£9.40), and payment is usually only accepted in dirham, though some drivers may also accept euros.

To reach Rabat direct from Casablanca's Mohammed V airport, the easiest option is to catch a train to Casa-Voyageurs station (35 min.; 30dh/$3.75/£1.90; departs every hour, 6am–midnight), and then change for Rabat Ville station.

BY TRAIN   Rabat Ville station (℡ **037/736060**) is very conveniently located in the centre ville on avenue Mohammed V, close to many hotels and about a 10-minute walk from the edge of the medina. Inside the station are a cafe, Budget car-rental booth, ATM, and currency exchange booth (usually open Mon–Fri 8am–8pm). There's also luggage storage, where locked/padlocked items can be left for 10dh ($1.25/65p) per item per day, that's open 7am to 10:30pm. Outside on avenue Moulay Youssef is a stand for Rabat's blue *petits* taxis. Rabat also has a second station, Rabat Agdal, servicing the suburbs to the south and west of the city, though it's of little use to travelers.

Trains depart daily for Rabat Ville from Casablanca's Casa-Port (1 hr.; 30dh/$3.75/£1.90) and Casa-Voyageurs stations, as well as Fes (3 hr.; 76dh–115dh/$9.50–$14/£4.75–£7.20); Marrakech (4½ hr.; 112dh–170dh/$14–$21/£7–£11); Meknes (2¼ hr.;

59dh–86dh/$7.40–$11/£3.70–£5.40); and Tangier (5 hr.; 91dh–135dh/$11–$17/ £5.70–£8.45). From destinations such as Agadir, Essaouira, and Tetouan, you will be traveling all or part of your journey on the ONCF bus service Supratours. Reservations are only accepted up to 1 month prior to departure and can be made either over the phone (© **090/203040** from within Morocco only), at ticket booths at each station, or through authorized agents. Payment at the station is by cash only, but some agents will accept credit cards.

BY BUS   Buses to Rabat arrive daily from Agadir (11 hr.; 180dh–190dh/$23–$24/ £11–£12); Casablanca (1½ hr.; 20dh–25dh/$2.50–$3.15/£1.25–£1.55); Er Rachidia (10 hr.; 125dh/$16/£7.80); Essaouira (8½ hr.; 150dh/$19/£9.40); Fes (4½ hr.; 50dh– 60dh/$6.25–$7.50/£3.15–£3.75); Marrakech (5½ hr.; 80dh–105dh/$10–$13/ £5–£6.55); Meknes (3½ hr.; 50dh–60dh/$6.25–$7.50/£3.15–£3.75); Ouarzazate (14 hr.; 150dh/$19/£9.40); and Tangier (4½ hr.; 80dh–110dh/$10–$14/£5–£6.90).

Besides CTM services (see below), all long-distance bus companies arrive at the *gare routière,* or bus station (© **037/795816**), inconveniently located 5km (3 miles) southwest of the city on the road to Casablanca. Open around the clock, it's a busy building consisting of ticket counters and a luggage storage service (5dh/65¢/30p per bag; daily 6am–11pm). CTM (© **022/438282** central reservations; www.ctm.ma) operates from their own just as inconveniently located station (© **037/281488**) just south of the *gare routière.* Blue *petits* taxis are usually waiting outside either station, and it shouldn't cost more than 20dh ($2.50/£1.25) to get into town. *Tip:* If you're coming from Asilah or Tangier, it's quicker—though not necessarily cheaper—to disembark at Salé and catch a *grand* taxi (5dh–15dh/65¢–$1.90/30p–95p) into central Rabat.

BY *GRAND* TAXI   *Grands* taxis from Casablanca (1 hr.; 30dh/$3.75/£1.90) arrive throughout the day to a rank just outside the *gare routière* and less frequently to a rank outside Rabat Ville train station. If you're traveling between the two cities, I recommend taking the train, which is safer, more comfortable, and just about as quick. *Grands* taxis plying the route from Fes (2½ hr.; 55dh/$6.90/£3.45), Meknes (2 hr.; 45dh/$5.65/£2.80), and Salé (10 min.; 5dh/65¢/30p) arrive at a busy rank opposite the Hotel Bou Regreg, on the corner of boulevard Hassan II and rue Nador.

BY CAR   Rabat's roads are some of the least congested of the country's cities, although it's best to avoid arriving into the city after dark, as many road signs are not well lit. Entering the city during the day is pretty straightforward, with the centre ville well signposted from most access roads (from here you can then orientate yourself for entry by foot into the medina or kasbah). Within the centre ville, however, parking can sometimes be difficult to find from Monday to Saturday. Most parking is controlled by meters, costing 2dh (25¢/15p) for 48 minutes and up to 10dh ($1.25/65p) for every 4 hours. Guarded parking is offered in a parking lot on the medina side of the junction between avenue Hassan II and avenue Mohammed V, and in a small side street between the Jardins Triangle de Vue and the Royal Hotel.

VISITOR INFORMATION

The **Office National Marocain du Tourisme (ONMT)** office is on the corner of rue Oued el Makhazine and rue Zellaka, in the suburb of Agdal (© **037/673918;** fax 037/674015). To be honest, it's not worth the effort to get here, as all you can expect are a couple of free brochures (big on pictures and low on information) and friendly but overwhelmingly useless staff. It's open Monday to Friday 8:30am to 4:30pm.

The office for **Le Conseil Régional du Tourisme de Rabat,** 23 av. de la Victoire (© 037/776400), isn't open to the general public, but they have a handy website (www.visitrabat.com).

The French-language *Rabat de A à Z* is a 180-page, spiral-bound glossy handbook and city map. It's full of contact details for all manner of establishments—including most of the city's better hotels, restaurants, and shops—and sells for 55dh ($6.90/£3.45) from a few bookshops on or near avenue Mohammed V, including Librairie Populaire on 4 rue Ghazza (next door to the Hotel Splendid).

Although a little out of the way, the Rabat branch of the **British Council,** 36 rue Tanger, Ministères (off the southern end of av. Mohammed V; © 037/760836; www.britishcouncil.org.ma), has a large library of English-language books and current newspapers, and also offers limited assistance and information to travelers and a monthly program of exhibitions, lectures, and social functions. It's open Monday from 2 to 6pm, Tuesday to Friday 9:30am to 12:15pm and 2:30 to 6pm, and Saturday 9:30am to 1:45pm.

CITY LAYOUT

Rabat's centre ville and pedestrian-only medina are both within the 12th-century Almohad-built walls, bound to the north and west by the Oued Bou Regreg. Within the centre ville, and running parallel to the southern wall, is avenue Mohammed V, which connects Rabat Ville train station with the medina; many hotels and restaurants are also found close by. Also within the walls are the suburbs of Hassan and Ministères, where many embassies and government departments are located.

Avenue Hassan II neatly separates the medina from the centre ville and provides access to the medina extension of avenue Mohammed V, as well as rue Oukassa, which becomes rue des Consuls. Connecting avenue Mohammed V and rue Oukassa/rue des Consuls is rue Souika, which becomes Souk as Sabbat. At the northern end of the medina, separated by the busy avenue al Marsa, is the Kasbah des Oudaïas, a compact and likeable mini-medina overlooking the mouth of the Oued Bou Regreg.

Rabat's ville nouvelle sprawls southward of the Almohad walls and includes the university suburb of Agdal, along with the upmarket suburb of Souissi, where a few embassies have recently relocated.

GETTING AROUND

For most travelers, Rabat is easily navigated on foot. Most of Rabat's sights and points of interest are within walking distance from each other, though on warmer days you may wish to catch a *petit* taxi between those that are located farther apart, such as from the Kasbah des Oudaïas to the Chellah. Unless you are loaded down with luggage, accommodations in the centre ville can be reached by foot. The accommodations that I've recommended within the kasbah and medina are best reached by first taking a *petit* taxi to the appropriate entrance and then walking a short distance to your hotel.

BY FOOT Walking around the centre ville is easy enough, though at times the street grid between avenue Mohammed V and the river can be a little confusing. Heading west from avenue Hassan II, the lay of the land progressively rises, which is something to consider if you plan on walking all the way to Le Tour Hassan or the Chellah. Both the kasbah and medina are easily navigable under your own steam.

BY TAXI Rabat's blue *petits* taxis can be found everywhere other than the pedestrian-only medina. The main ranks are at the junction of avenues Mohammed V and

Hassan II, and outside Rabat Ville station on avenue Moulay Youssef. At your hotel, you can usually ask the reception staff to organize one for you, or otherwise you can simply stand on the side of the street and hail one. Drivers are only allowed to carry up to three passengers at a time, but be aware that if there is a vacant seat, you may pick up an additional passenger. At all times, request the driver to put on the meter, which he is supposed to do no matter the time of day or night. Most trips within the centre ville should cost no more than 10dh ($1.25/65p) during the day and a bit more after 8pm, when a 50% evening surcharge kicks in. *Petits* taxis operate solely within Rabat's environs and aren't supposed to travel across to Salé or beyond to the city's airport; for both of these destinations, take a *grand* taxi.

FAST FACTS: Rabat

Airport See "Arriving" in "Orientation," above.

Banks & Currency Exchange There are plenty of banks—with ATMs—in the centre ville, mainly along avenue Mohammed V and the parallel avenue Allal ben Abdellah. The **BMCE** branch, 260 av. Mohammed V (© 037/216167), also has a bureau de change, conveniently open daily from 8am to 8pm.

Car Rentals The major international firms can be found in the centre ville, including **Avis,** 7 rue Abou Faris Al Mairini (© 037/721818 or 037/769759); **Budget,** Rabat Ville train station (© 037/705789); **Europcar,** 25 bis rue Patrice Lumumba (© 037/724141); **Hertz,** 467 av. Mohammed V (© 037/707366 or 037/709227); and **National/Alamo,** corner of rue de Caire and rue Ghandi (© 037/722731).

Doctors **Dr. Mohammed el Kabbaj,** 8 rue Oued Zem (© 037/764311), and **Dr. Youssef Alaoui Belghiti,** 6 place des Alaouites (© 037/708029), both come recommended.

Drugstores There are plenty of pharmacies in Rabat. In the medina, at the kasbah end of rue des Consuls, is **Pharmacie Oudayas** (© 037/727770), which also usually has a doctor in résidence, while halfway along rue des Consuls is **Pharmacie Souk Tahti** (© 037/711290). In the centre ville, **Pharmacie du Maroc** (© 037/723981) and **Pharmacie Soha** (© 037/722145) are on avenue Mohammed V. All general pharmacies in Rabat open Monday to Friday 8am to 8pm (some closing for lunch from 12:30–2:30pm) and Saturday 8am to 2pm. They then work on a roster system after hours; the list of open pharmacies is on the front door. The **Pharmacie du Nuit,** on avenue Moulay Rachid, is open nightly from 8pm to 8am Monday to Friday, and 2pm Saturday to 8am Monday.

Embassies **Canada,** 13 bis, rue Jaâfar as Sadiq, Agdal (© 037/687400); **South Africa,** 34 rue des Saâdians, Hassan (© 037/706760); **U.K.,** 28 av. SAR Sidi Mohammed, Souissi (© 037/633333 or 061/134375 in an emergency); and **U.S.,** 2 av. Marrakech, Ministères (© 037/762265). **Australia** is represented by the Canadian embassy.

Emergency For **general emergencies** and the **police,** call © **19.** For a private ambulance service, phone **Service d'Assistance Médicale Urgente (SAMU;** © 037/737373). In a medical emergency, call **SOS Médicins** (© 037/202020). Also see "Doctors," above, and "Hospitals," below, for more options.

Hospitals **SOS Médicins** (© 037/202020) is a 24-hour emergency clinic, located at 6 rue Moulay Slimane. Up in the suburb of Hassan is **Polyclinique de Rabat,** 8 rue de Tunis (© 037/204914).

Internet Access There aren't as many cybercafes around the city center as you'd expect, with most being located in the university suburb of Agdal. On avenue Hassan II is **Phobos,** located next door to the Hotel Majestic, and **Student Cyber,** 83 av. Hassan II. Both are open daily from 9am to 10pm.

Laundry & Dry Cleaning There are no self-service laundries within the medina or centre ville. Dry cleaners in the centre ville include **Process Clean,** 186 av. Hassan II (© 037/205890), and **La Reine des Neiges,** 73 rue Patrice Lumumba (© 037/766472). Both are open Monday to Friday 8:30am to 12:30pm and 3 to 7pm.

Maps & Books **Le Conseil Régional du Tourisme de Rabat,** 23 av. de la Victoire (© 037/776400), annually produces the free *Carte Touristique* Rabat city map. It will help you to initially get your bearings, but unfortunately its scale is too large and therefore lacks a detailed look at the streets of the centre ville and the lanes and alleys of the medina. It's available from most hotels and some of the better restaurants. In a similar vein is the map accompanying the spiral *Rabat de A à Z* handbook (see "Visitor Information," above), which is available from the bookshop **Librairie Populaire,** 4 rue Ghazza, Centre Ville (© 037/388677). Here you'll also find a good range of Arabic-English and French-English dictionaries. **English Bookshop,** 7 rue al Yamama, off avenue Moulay Youssef (© 037/706593), sells both new and secondhand English-language fiction and nonfiction titles. The small **American Bookstore,** on the corner of rue Moulay Abdel al Hafid and rue Annaba (formerly rue Boujaad; © 037/761269), stocks a small selection of English-language books on Morocco, as well as secondhand English-language paperbacks.

Newspapers Try the newsstands along avenue Mohammed V, between Rabat Ville train station and the junction with avenue Hassan II, which occasionally stock the weekly international edition of the U.K.'s *Guardian.*

Photographic Needs There's a string of photo-processing shops along avenue Mohammed V, between Rabat Ville train station and the junction with avenue Hassan II. At the time of writing, none were able to download digital images to disk, however. **Phobos** (see "Internet Access," above) sells a few memory cards.

Police There's a **Préfécture de Police** on avenue Tripoli, south of avenue Moulay Hassan in the centre ville, and a police post on the medina side of the junction of avenue Mohammed V and avenue Hassan II.

Post Office & Mail Rabat's main **post office** is in the centre ville, on the corner of avenue Mohammed V and rue Soekamo. There's also a smaller post office at the northern edge of the medina, on rue Loubira off avenue Laâlouj. Both are open Monday to Friday 8am to 4:15pm and Saturday 8am to noon. **DHL** has an office located in the suburb of Agdal, 40 av. de France (© 037/779934), open Monday to Friday 8:30am to 6:30pm and Saturday 9am to 1pm. **FedEx,** 23 av. Tariq ibn Ziad, Hassan (© 037/661166), is open Monday to Friday 8am to 6:30pm and Saturday 8am to 12:15pm.

Restrooms There are no public restrooms within the medina or centre ville. Your best bet is to try one of the better dining establishments mentioned below.

Safety Rabat is considered one of the safest cities in Morocco, and travelers can expect minimal hassle from shopkeepers, touts, and faux guides. Most nights, however, the streets can become rather deserted after 10pm, and the usual precautions should be taken.

Taxis See "Getting Around," above.

Telephone Rabat's **city code** is **037,** but you need to drop the "0" if you are calling from outside the country.

WHERE TO STAY

For a capital city, Rabat offers a very limited range of quality accommodations. Most of the international chains are here, but they can be disappointing for the price they charge. At the other end of the scale, there is a plethora of budget-priced accommodations, which are frequented more by rural and up-country Moroccans than travelers. Here I've recommended those that offer at least some character, good value for money, or both. The compactness of Rabat's medina and adjacent centre ville lessens the importance of the location of your accommodations, with most sights and restaurants within walking distance. It's always worth trying to prebook your accommodations here, or at least arrive early in the day, as hotels begin to fill up during the afternoon with a steady stream of overnighters. Very few people—Moroccans or travelers—stay in Rabat for longer than 1 night.

KASBAH
Very Expensive
Dar Baraka ⋆⋆⋆ *Finds* *Kids*   This little gem enjoys a spectacular position overlooking the Oued Bou Regreg, and is the friendliest *maison d'hôte* in Rabat. Though it's located at the end of the main street in the kasbah (taxis can drop you right outside the front door), peace and seclusion await behind the nondescript blue door. Pauline de MaziÃres's Dar Baraka ("luck") has only two bedrooms; both are light and breezy, with original artwork and antique furnishings. The bathroom in the spacious double has kept its ivory tiling and original bath with 1950s fittings, while the compact twin combines white Italian marble with traditional *zellij*, and has a beautiful terrace opening to the split-level garden. An outside staircase leads to the garden, where there's also a large living room with fireplace, TV/DVD, and Internet/Wi-Fi.

Delicious lunches and dinners can be taken here or on one of the two terraces. An Andalusian terrace of citrus trees and bougainvillea looks out to the river and across to Salé. A second terrace is shaded by ancient fig trees and also has views. Underneath the house is a vaulted cellar, where cannonballs recall the city's pirate past. Pauline or one of her staff are on hand at any time of day or night, and will even assist with shopping excursions. The rooms can be booked separately, but together are a great option for families. A free basket of fruit and bottled water is offered upon arrival.

26 rue de la Mosquée (aka rue Jemaa), Kasbah des Oudaïas, Rabat. ✆/fax **037/730362** or 061/783361. www.dar-baraka-rabat.com. 2 units. 990dh ($124/£62) twin; 1,430dh ($179/£89) double; 2,310dh (289/£144) entire dar; 165dh ($21/£10) extra (sofa) bed. Peak-season supplement Jul–Aug and Dec 23–Jan 5. Rates include breakfast. No credit cards, but can prepay with PayPal. **Amenities:** Restaurant; 24-hr. room service; TV/DVD room; Internet/Wi-Fi. *In room:* No phone.

MEDINA
Expensive

Dar al Batoul   The Khribeche family have turned this former merchant's house into a peaceful dar with low-key service. The central courtyard (covered in winter) is a pleasant blend of simple comfort and traditional style, with tall columns, black-and-white tiling, hand-carved stucco, and potted plants. The Diwan room—a former ante chamber used to greet guests—is now a warm, split-level reading room with a small library and TV. Other communal rooms and the large, brightly colored Alia bedroom lead off from the courtyard. A first-floor terrace with original wood railings lends access to the other bedrooms. Compact and tastefully furnished, each room is individual and true to the style of medina *maisons d'hôte*—small windows and not a lot of privacy. The roof terrace affords a glorious sweeping view of the medina. The family is very unobtrusive and hands-off in their service (only French and Arabic are spoken), preferring to leave their guests to enjoy quality personal time. Lunches and dinners, often eaten with the family, can be arranged upon request. The dar is easy to locate, and guarded parking is close by.

7 rue el Jirari, Laalou, Medina, Rabat. © 037/727250. Fax 037/727316. www.riadbatoul.com. 9 units. 870dh ($109/£54) double; 1,400dh ($175/£88) suite. Children under 8 stay free in parent's room. No taxes included. MC, V. **Amenities:** Restaurant; library/TV salon. *In room:* No phone.

CENTRE VILLE
Moderate

Hotel Bou Regreg   Good, moderate-priced accommodations are hard to find in Rabat, and while this hotel isn't perfect, there are still a few good points to focus on. The hotel is in a great location for exploring the medina, and is within walking distance to the Hassan Tower and Mausoleum of Mohammed V. A secure parking lot at the rear is a bonus for self-drivers. Some of the rooms have recently been renovated and offer modern bathrooms and balconies, while others are a bit smaller with dated furnishings. However, the hotel is located on an extremely busy corner—it's one of the city's main *grand* taxi terminals—and the outside facing rooms are subject to incessant car and street noise. There's a ground-floor restaurant, which I don't recommended, and separate bar, both of which look onto a central, covered courtyard, where there's live Moroccan music most nights. *Tip:* Prebook your room—there's usually English-speaking reception staff on duty—and request a rear-facing room on one of the higher floors.

Corner of bd. Hassan II and rue Nador, Centre Ville, Rabat. © 037/724110. Fax 037/734002. 58 units. 540dh ($68/£34) double. Children under 10 stay free in parent's room. Rates include breakfast. TPT not included. MC, V. On-site parking. **Amenities:** Restaurant; bar; elevator; Internet. *In room:* A/C, satellite TV.

Royal Hotel 🏩🏩   Located conveniently between Rabat Ville station and the medina, the recently refurbished Royal is the best in this price range. All the rooms are bright and airy, with simple furnishings, white walls, tiled floors, and large windows overlooking either the shaded street or Triangle de Vue park. There's plenty of floor space for luggage, and the bathrooms are modern with walk-in showers. Red-carpeted steps lead to a small reception area, where English-speaking Jamal Bouhouch is usually on hand to welcome guests. The Mediterranean-style in-house restaurant is accessed from here, and is open for all meals, though I recommend it only for the included breakfast.

There's a very handy elevator, which works most of the time. *Tip:* Some of the rooms are yet to be furnished with new beds, so check out a few before deciding. Also, the single rooms can be quite small.

Rabat

KASBAH DES OUDAÏAS

Le Plateforme du Semaphore **1**

Cimetière Musulmane

Bab Oudaïas

Palace Museum

Ave. al Marsa

Oued Bou Regreg

SALÉ

Blvd. al Jaych al Malaki

Blvd. Fès

21

Blvd. al Alou **2**

Bab al Alou

MEDINA

Rue des Consuls

Bab el Bahr

Rue Sidi Fatah **3**

4

Ave. Mohammed V

Ave. Misr

Rue S. Sabbat

Rue Oukassa

MELLAH

Rue Souika

R. Bab Chellah

Bab el Mellah

Rue Abdelmoumen

HASSAN

Rue des Saadians

Central Marché

5

Bab al Bouab

Bab Chellah

Ave. Hassan II

Rue Melilya

9

PLACE MELILYA

Rue al Hoceima

Rue al Mouahidine

Rue Marininiye

Rue al Adarisa

Ave. Moulay Ismaïl

Ave. al Alaouyine

20

Blvd. Tour Hassan

Rue de Taza

Bab el Had

6 **7**

R. de Beyrouth

Ave. Abdallah

8

Jardin Triangle de Vue

R. al Monastir

R. al Mansour ad Dhabi

11 **10**

Rue Makka

Rue al Kahira

Rue Patrice Lumumba

Ave. Abderrahman Aneggay

Rue d'Oran

Rue Idriss al Akbar

Rue de Tunis

12

CENTRE VILLE

13
14

PLACE AL JOULANE

Blvd. Abi Regreg

PLACE A. LINCOLN

Ave. Mohammed V

Rue al Ouds

PLACE MOHAMMED V

Rue Abou Nan

R.A.F. al Marini

R. H. Dunant

R. d'Annaba

Rue al Jazair

R. de Dennate

Blvd. Tarik ibn Zijad

Rue d'Azrou

Ave. Ibn Toumert

Rue de Baghdad

15 **16**

Ave. Allal ben Adbellah

17

Rabat Ville train sta.

Ave. Moulay Hassan

R.M. Abdel al Hafid

Blvd. de Meknès

R. Sana'a

Ave. Moulay Youssef

Rue Fès

Rue d'Agadir

Bab er Rouah

R. Moulay abd el Aziz

Assounna Mosque

18

Rue de Safi

Ave. Yacoub el Mansour

Rue Patrice Lumumba

Rue Tanger

Rue de Ouarzazate

Ave. Marrakech

Ave. Ibn Batouta

Ave. Bab Soufara

MINISTÈRES

Ave. du Près. Roosevelt

19

Blvd. Moussa Ibn Noussaïr

ACCOMMODATIONS ■
Dar al Batoul **2**
Dar Baraka **1**
Hotel Bou Regreg **9**
Hotel Majestic **7**
Hotel Splendid **8**
Royal Hotel **10**

DINING ◆
Café Restaurant
   la Jeunesse **5**
Casa el Ouazzani **4**
Chahrazad **6**
La Bamba **14**

La Mamma **13**
La Pagode **15**
Le Grand Comptoir **12**
Restaurant Saidoune **17**
Riad Oudaya **3**
7éme Art Café & Snack **11**
Tajine Wa Tanjia **16**

ATTRACTIONS ●
Archaeological Museum **18**
Chellah **19**
Le Tour Hassan &
   Mausoleum of Mohammed V **20**
Salé **21**

Corner of av. Allal ben Abdellah and rue Amman, Centre Ville, Rabat. ⓒ **037/721171** or 037/721172. Fax 037/725491. www.royalhotelrabat.com. 67 units. 450dh ($56/£28) single; 600dh ($74/£38) double; 771dh ($96/£48) triple. Children under 10 stay free in parent's room. Rates include breakfast. TPT not included. No credit cards. Limited street parking available. **Amenities:** Restaurant; elevator. *In room:* A/C, satellite TV, fridge.

Inexpensive

Hotel Majestic   A popular budget option, the Majestic is well located, especially for self-drivers, opposite the medina on avenue Hassan II. There's a choice of rooms with a balcony and medina view (and subsequent street noise), or quieter rooms at the rear. All the rooms are spacious, simply furnished, and have compact, modern bathrooms, although on my last visit the hotel's broken hot-water system resulted in only a quick wash in the walk-in shower. I've always found the staff friendly, and its popularity ensures that you should prebook or arrive early.

121 av. Hassan II, Centre Ville, Rabat. ⓒ **037/722997.** Fax 037/708856. 21 units. 239dh ($30/£15) single; 279dh ($35/£17) double. TPT not included. No credit cards. Limited reserved parking. *In room:* TV.

Hotel Splendid   The best cheapie in the city, the Splendid was once a grand hotel that has aged gracefully. Surrounding a pleasant courtyard, the spacious, high-ceiling rooms are pretty simple but functional, with firm mattresses and big, old wardrobes. Some rooms come with large, private bathrooms, and those without have a basin with hot water. The plumbing can be a bit dodgy at times, but everything is kept sparkling clean. The reception staff is always friendly, though reservations are difficult to make if you don't speak French. It's about a 10-minute walk from Rabat Ville station.

8 rue Ghazza, Centre Ville, Rabat. ⓒ **037/723283.** 28 units. 104dh–128dh ($13–$16/£6.50–£8) single; 159dh–187dh ($20–$23/£9.95–£12) double. TPT not included. No credit cards. **Amenities:** Cafe. *In room:* No phone.

VILLE NOUVELLE
Very Expensive

Villa Mandarine ★★★ *(finds)*   This former mansion is now a family-run luxury *maison d'hôte,* and is quite possibly the finest accommodations in Rabat. Claudy Imbert, her daughters, and son-in-law have been welcoming guests into their 36-room "country house" in the city for 5 years, yet Villa Mandarine is still one of Rabat's, if not Morocco's, best-kept secrets. The rooms are set out on two levels surrounding a large central courtyard of palm trees, rose bushes, and a mosaic fountain. Tastefully furnished and personally decorated by Claudy herself, the well-appointed rooms are beautiful combinations of natural colors, Berber rugs, Moroccan lamps, and contemporary and traditional art works; all rooms have their own balcony. The public areas are numerous and include a rustic African bar, large lounge and library, billiards room and fireplace, and a private beauty salon with hammam, Jacuzzi, spa, and on-site masseuse. There's also an open and sunny restaurant serving fine international fare. The large grounds are dotted with citrus trees and have lots of private areas for reading and relaxing, along with a large swimming pool. Villa Mandarine is located in the southern suburbs, close to the Hilton, away from all the sights and restaurants, but the payoff is worth it for both travelers and businesspeople who are looking for class and character over convenience.

19 rue Ouled Bousbaa, Souissi, Rabat. ⓒ **037/752077.** Fax 037/632309. www.villamandarine.com. 36 units. 1,800dh–2,200dh ($225–$275/£113–£138) double; 2,500dh–3,800dh ($313–$475/£156–£238) suite. Breakfast 100dh ($13/£6.25). MC, V. **Amenities:** Restaurant; bar; pool; sauna; hammam; massage; library. *In room:* A/C, satellite TV, Internet, fridge, safe.

WHERE TO DINE

Rabat has a good selection of eateries ranging from fine dining establishments to local haunts. Those recommended here are all within the Almohad-walled medina and centre ville, and are therefore within strolling distance of most hotels and the train station.

MEDINA
Very Expensive

Riad Oudaya ✦✦✦ MOROCCAN   This riad restaurant serves up delicious home-cooked cuisine in a serene, romantic setting. Candle-lit, wrought-iron mosaic tables with comfortable high-back chairs are nicely spaced around an inner courtyard of clay *bejmat*, a gurgling *zellij* fountain, and Moroccan lanterns. In-house cook Aïcha prepares each dish with the freshest ingredients brought straight from the nearby vegetable souk. The meal commences with an alcohol-free aperitif, small *samosa*-like *briouattes* with an olive tapenade, and hors d'oeuvres of savory seasoned vegetables. The first of two main courses includes choices ranging from the very traditional *pastilla au pigeon* to *aumônière* crepes of Dorade filets. The second main course offers a tasty, fluffy vegetable couscous, tagines of beef or Dorade, or a *mechoui* of roasted mutton. There's plenty to follow, with two dessert courses offering a selection of homemade pastries, seasonal fruits, tarts (the apple and cinnamon is a personal favorite), crepes, or a sweet almond *pastilla*. There's also a lunch menu that is practically the same but reduces the main and dessert courses to one choice.

46 rue Sidi Fateh. © 037/702392. www.riadrabat.com. Reservations strongly recommended. 220dh ($28/£14) lunch; 330dh ($41/£21) dinner. Wine served. No credit cards. Daily noon–2:30pm and 7:30–10pm.

Inexpensive

Cafe Restaurant la Jeunesse MOROCCAN   Cheap and cheerful, this is where you'll find Moroccan city workers enjoying lunch or an early dinner. The menu is as standard as they come, with a range of tagines and couscous, along with brochettes, omelets, and the cheapest, tastiest bowl of *harira* (4dh/50¢/25p) you'll ever find. The downstairs section affords the best people-watching, while the larger upstairs dining hall—with plastic chairs, tables, and tablecloths—is more spacious. Don't expect five-star; here you'll find tasty, cheap Moroccan food.

305 av. Mohammed V. No phone. Main courses 10dh–23dh ($1.25–$2.90/65p–£1.45). Daily noon–10pm.

Casa el Ouazzani PIZZERIA/SNACKS   This little hole-in-the-wall eatery, opened by the Ouazzani family in 2006, is a good spot for a quick and cheap lunch or dinner, with some excellent people-watching, too. Located in the medina, on the pedestrian-only section of avenue Mohammed V, the space is limited to four mosaic tables with wrought-iron and woven-raffia chairs, shaded by a small awning. The menu, also limited, includes a selection of pizzas along with panini, toasted sandwiches, fries, and a *plat du jour* that is usually a couscous or tagine dish.

157 av. Mohammed V. © 037/713341 or 010/274865. Pizzas 25dh–35dh ($3.15–$4.40/£1.55–£2.20); panini and sandwiches 8dh–20dh ($1–$2.50/50p–£1.25). No credit cards. Daily noon–10pm.

CENTRE VILLE
Expensive

Le Grand Comptoir FRENCH   Casablanca-born brothers Louis-B and Yann Lechartier took 2 years to renovate this former derelict cafe before finally opening up their classy and refined bar/cafe/restaurant in 2004. It's the combination of the building's classic 1930s French brasserie design, a chic and trendy clientele, and fine French cuisine that makes this one of the "in" places to dine and drink in Rabat. Chef Frederic Biette specializes in prime cuts of meat, but also enjoys the city's plentiful supply of fresh seafood; serious diners are encouraged to peruse the day's catch and even suggest to Frederic how they would like it done. There are also a couple of Japanese-style sashimi dishes for those looking for something different. The menu also includes a selection of comfort foods such as hamburgers and a quiche Lorraine. There's valet parking and an upstairs bar with live jazz or African music.

270 av. Mohammed V. Ⓒ 037/201514. Fax 037/707322. www.legrandcomptoir.ma. Reservations recommended. Entrees 45dh–125dh ($5.65–$16/£2.80–£7.80); burgers and light meals 52dh–75dh ($6.50–$9.40/£3.25–£4.70); main courses 95dh–280dh ($12–$35/£5.95–£18). Alcohol served. MC, V. Daily 9am–1am.

Moderate

La Bamba MOROCCAN/INTERNATIONAL   Located on a quiet street just off avenue Mohammed V, this restaurant offers very affordable set menus for a pleasant sit-down lunch or dinner. The choices are varied for each menu; most have a choice of five appetizers and five main courses followed by two to three desserts. Salads of *zaalouk* (pulped eggplant) and *chakhchoukha* (finely chopped peppers, cucumber, and tomato) are offered, as are delightful seafood *briouattes*. Main courses range from seafood brochettes and *pastilla* of chicken and almonds to *méchoui* roasted lamb and beef, chicken, and lamb tagines. As always, room needs to be left for dessert, especially a divine chocolate mousse. While the restaurant can be very quiet for some meals, it can be lively and busy for others.

3 rue Tanta. Ⓒ 037/709839. Set menus 80dh–120dh ($10–$15/£5–£7.50). Tax not included. Alcohol served. MC, V. Daily noon–2:30pm and 7–10:30pm.

La Mamma ⊛ ITALIAN   Since 1967, this little piece of Italy has been the authentic restaurant of choice for locals and businesspeople. An interior of dark-wood beams greets diners as they walk through the nondescript doors, and an open kitchen separates the two dining areas. The wood-fired pizza oven and charcoal grill lend an aroma that makes you want to start eating right then and there. A fairly broad menu of Italian classics includes a recommended Sicilian tomato, basil, and mozzarella salad appetizer, followed by main dishes such as cannelloni *bolognaise* and tagliatelle carbonara. More than 20 pizza choices are offered—the recommended Mamma Speciale is topped with ham, anchovies, capers, mushrooms, oregano, and mozzarella. For those who like authentic *gelati*, more than 40 flavors are available courtesy of the family's ice-cream parlor, La Dolce Vita, located next door.

6 rue Tanta, Centre Ville. Ⓒ 037/707329 or 037/702300. Appetizers 30dh–55dh ($3.75–$6.90/£1.90–£3.45); pizza 45dh–60dh ($5.65–$7.50/£2.80–£3.75); main courses 50dh–95dh ($6.25–$12/£3.15–£5.95). Alcohol served. MC, V. Daily noon–3pm and 7–11pm.

La Pagode ASIAN   Reopened in 2007 after an extensive refurbishment, La Pagode offers mainly Chinese and Vietnamese dishes in a tranquil, authentic—and now air-conditioned—atmosphere. The French-only menu is very extensive, with pork, seafood, beef, chicken, and duck available in every form. There's also a good choice of soups and salads, which for vegetarians makes up for the lack of main-course choices. The restaurant is located alongside the train station, but a very heavy metal door ensures the noise stays outside. The red, white, and black interior is your typical

Asian-style decor, and the waitstaff—dressed in an appropriately kitsch uniform—are attentive and speedy. A *plats emporter* (take-out) service is also offered.

13 rue Baghdad. ⊘ 037/709381. Starters 56dh–88dh ($7–$11/£3.50–£5.50); main courses 65dh–98dh ($8.15–$12/£4.05–£6.15). Alcohol served. MC, V. Tues–Sun noon–3pm and 7–10:30pm.

Tajine Wa Tanjia ✦✦✦ *Kids* MOROCCAN   Since they opened their restaurant in 2004, the Jabbour family have managed to find that perfect combination of reasonably priced authentic cuisine, served in a warm, intimate atmosphere. The extensive menu reads like a Moroccan cookbook, and offers just about every national dish possible. The house specialties are their *tanjias* and tagines—try their succulent beef and camel *tanjia*, or *M'rouzia* (lamb with raisins and almonds in honey), *Mechmach* (beef with apricots), or *Mokj m'charmel* (shrimp in herbs) tagines. If you're around on Friday, definitely try their couscous with onions and raisins.

Vegetarians are well catered for, and there's a kids' menu including old-fashioned fish and chips. The list of traditional desserts includes a highly recommended saffron cheesecake. Rita, the delightful multilingual (she speaks six languages) owner/manager and her mother Valentina are on hand each night, while architect brother Karim (who designed the restaurant) manages the lunchtime session. I love the interior of this restaurant, with low lighting subtly highlighting the *tabout* walls, which are adorned with Moroccan lanterns and mirrors. The wrought-iron tables and comfortable chairs are well spaced for intimate dining, or can be brought together for larger groups; dinner is accompanied by a live *oud* (lute) player.

9 rue Baghdad. ⊘ 037/729797. Reservations recommended. Starters 28dh–54dh ($3.50–$6.75/£1.75–£3.40); main courses 64dh–82dh ($8–$10/£4–£5.15); desserts 18dh–45dh ($2.25–$5.65/£1.15–£2.80); kids' menu 54dh ($6.75/£3.40). Alcohol served. MC, V. Mon–Sat 11:30am–3pm and 7–11:30pm.

Inexpensive

Chahrazad CAFE/PATISSERIE   Uniformed waiters with bow ties and waistcoats shuffle around the two floors of tightly set tables inside this welcome alternative to the city's smoky and male-dominated cafes. Family friendly and with a large nonsmoking section, Chahrazad offers a large choice of brightly colored and deliciously creamy gâteaux and pastries, along with ice-cream sundaes, pizza slices, and a selection of different coffees and teas. The U-shaped, gold-and-rust-colored interior doesn't offer much people-watching, but does allow for some privacy and an escape from the hustle and bustle outside.

119 av. Hassan II. No phone. Gâteaux and pastries 8dh–15dh ($1–$1.90/50p–95p); ice cream 15dh–23dh ($1.90–$2.90/95p–£1.45). No credit cards. Daily 6am–9pm.

Restaurant Saidoune ✦ LEBANESE   In a handy location across from Rabat Ville station, this little restaurant is great for either a quick snack or a sit-down meal. Vegetarians will be happy with the choice of Lebanese standards such as falafel, hummus, and tabbouleh. Of course, there's also chicken or beef *chawarma,* offered with sides of hummus, *moutabbal* (spicy eggplant dip), fries, or rice. Diners can choose to sit outside in a small arcade or inside at the counters or tables.

467 av. Mohammed V. ⊘ 037/769226. Main courses 12dh–45dh ($1.50–$5.65/75p–£2.80). Alcohol served. No credit cards. Sat–Thurs noon–3pm and 7–11pm; Fri 7pm–midnight.

7ème Art Café & Snack *Kids* CAFE/LIGHT MEALS   Adjacent to the Cinéma du 7ème Art, this cafe's relaxed garden setting is a great spot to stop for a drink or bite to eat during your exploration of the city. The menu covers a wide range of snacks and light meals, including salads, omelets, hamburgers, and sandwiches. There's also a good selection of panini and pizzas, as well as a simple grilled chicken and fries. The choice of ice creams and milkshakes makes this a good stop for an afternoon sugar fix as well. Small tables sit under white umbrellas, frequented by businessmen at lunch as well as young students coming to the cinema.

Av. Allal ben Abdellah. ℂ 037/733887. Main courses 14dh–49dh ($1.75–$6.15/90p–£3.05); pizza 26dh–55dh ($3.25–$6.90/£1.65–£3.45); ice cream 22dh ($2.75/£1.40). No credit cards. Daily 7am–11pm.

WHAT TO SEE & DO

The nation's capital offers a choice selection of sights, most of them within walking distance of one another. Combined with some general meandering within its hassle-free medina, there's enough here for a relaxing day or two of sightseeing. Adding to the city's attractions will be the major redevelopment of both the Rabat and Salé river-banks, intended to be completed by the end of 2008. The result will see long prome-nades on both sides of the river, with grassed areas, restaurants, and berths.

Archaeological Museum   Tucked away in the top end of the centre ville, this under-visited and underfunded museum is nonetheless Morocco's most important. Two floors and a separate annex house exhibits displaying the full ancient history of Morocco, from prehistoric times to the stone age, and beyond to Phoenician, Carthaginian, and Roman times. The undoubted highlight is the Salle des Bronzes, housed in the separate annex. Here is a fascinating collection of Roman-era ceramics and artifacts—procured largely from excavations of the Volubilis ruins near Meknes (p. 254)—dating back to the first and second centuries A.D. The bronzes include evocatively named pieces such as "Drunken Donkey," "Volubilis Dog," "Young Man Crowned with Ivy," which is said to be that of Cato the Younger, and "Heads of Young Berbers," as well as a beautiful, real-istic bust reputed to be that of Juba II, the Romanized Berber Mauretanian king and son-in-law to Cleopatra and Marc Antony. The exhibits are explained only in Arabic and French, but a visit is still worthwhile purely on aesthetic grounds.

23 rue Ifni al Brihi. ℂ 037/701919. Admission 10dh ($1.25/65p) adults; 3dh (40¢/20p) children 5–12. Mon and Wed–Fri 8:45am–4:30pm.

Chellah   Sitting just outside Rabat's Almohad-era walls and standing sentry over the river that has served the city since ancient times, the Chellah is both a Roman ruin and Islamic burial place. As the Roman city of Sala Colonia, it was a bustling trading post of the empire's southernmost colony from A.D. 40 onward, and was one of the last to eventually sever links with the empire. Signposted as SITE ANTIQUE, the mainly scat-tered ruins include a main road, the Decumanus Maximus, that passes through a tri-umphal arch and past the Jupiter Temple (on the left), coming to an end at the forum. The city was finally abandoned in 1154 for the new settlement of Salé, across the river. Used as a royal burial ground by the Almohads, the site was extended into a holy necropolis, or *chellah,* by the Merenids, in the 14th century. Most visible today is a tall stone-and-*zellij* minaret and a small theological school, or *medersa.* Near the minaret is the tomb of one of the greatest Merenid rulers, Abou el Hassan, who was known as the Black Sultan. El Hassan's rule saw the entire Maghreb (Tunisia, Algeria, Morocco) under Merenid control. There's no one great sight within the ruins, but it remains a vis-ible reminder of the historical significance that the city of Rabat has held. It's a pleas-ant and tranquil place to wander around; the ruins are overgrown with aged fruit trees and are habituated by a colony of storks, which is considered a sign of good fortune.

Corner of av. Yacoub al Mansour and bd. Moussa ibn Nassair. Admission 10dh ($1.25/65p) adults; 3dh (40¢/20p) kids 5–12; under 5 free. Daily 9am–5:30pm.

Kasbah des Oudaïas ✹✹✹   Built by the Almohads in the 12th century on the site of the original 10th-century *ribat* fortress, Rabat's cliff-top kasbah is a delight to explore. Standing sentry over the mouth of the Oued Bou Regreg, the kasbah has been the one constant in the city's history, inhabited during both the good times and the bad. Today it's a quaint villagelike quarter, only 150m (500 ft.) from one end to the other, and crammed with rows of whitewashed houses with brightly colored doors. It still exudes a whiff of its Andalusian heritage, though little of its notorious pirate past. The main entrance gate is the ornately decorated Bab Oudaïas. Constructed during the late-12th-century building spree of the Almohad sultan Yacoub el Mansour, it houses a series of chambers that would have originally been the city's courthouse and staterooms, and are now used regularly to house art exhibitions. The kasbah's main thoroughfare, rue Jemaa, runs from here straight through the kasbah, passing a couple of art galleries and the 12th-century mosque from which the street gets its name. About halfway is the junction with rue Bazo, which winds down to the Andalusian Gardens (free admission; daily from sunrise to sunset), which is accessed via Café Maure, a popular stop for mint tea and biscuits with a great view of the river mouth, open daily from 9am to 5pm.

The gardens were actually constructed during the protectorate era and occupy the grounds of a former palace, built in the 17th century by the Meknes-based Sultan Moulay Ismail. Ismail was the first sultan to have any control over the Sallee Rovers, a feat accomplished largely due to his garrison of Saharan tribesmen, called the Oudaïas, which were housed here. The palace is now a museum (10dh/$1.25/65p adults, 3dh/40¢/20p kids 5–12; Oct–Apr daily 9am–noon and 3–5pm, closes at 6pm May–Sept), with various exhibitions of jewelry, clothing, ceramics, and traditional musical instruments now housed in its former reception rooms. It can also be accessed via a small outside entrance halfway between Bab Oudaïas and the southwestern corner of the kasbah. At the end of rue Jemaa is a wide-open area called Le Plateforme du Semaphore. This former signal station was built during the times of the Salle Rovers, affording them a sweeping view of any seafaring enemy, and would have been lined with cannon. Today it's a social gathering point for locals, and one of the best places to head should the summer humidity become unbearable; it also affords a great sunset view. The city's beaches are also accessible from here down a series of steps.

Tip: As you make your way up to Bab Oudaïas, you may be accosted by young women armed with syringes. These are the city's henna ladies, and their syringes are filled with harmless green henna. They have a very irritating sales pitch, initiated by surreptitiously squirting henna on your hand without your consent. If you'd like a temporary Berber-designed tattoo, then by all means enjoy the experience. If you don't, then be aware that the henna can stain your clothes, so be wary when they approach you.

Le Tour Hassan ✹ **& Mausoleum of Mohammed V** ✹✹   Rabat's two major attractions stand opposite each other looking out over the Oued Bou Regreg. Le Tour Hassan (the Hassan Tower) was the towering minaret of the Hassan Mosque, which began construction in 1195 under the Almohad Yacoub el Mansour. Intended to be 60m high (200 ft.)—and subsequently one of the tallest in the world—the tower stands today at 44m (145 ft.), having been abandoned upon the death of the sultan in 1199. It's still a formidable structure and looms over the remains of its ruined mosque, flattened by an earthquake in 1755. The mosque was designed to hold 20,000 worshippers, and even though all that is left today are rows of reconstructed columns, the scale of its grandness is still visible.

Facing the tower is one of the country's most important shrines, the Mausoleum of Mohammed V, which is open to non-Muslims. Here lie the tombs of the nation's—and the current king's—grandfather, King Mohammed V, and his two sons King Hassan II and Prince Moulay Abdellah. Designed by a Vietnamese architect and inaugurated 6 years after Mohammed V's death in 1961, the building's surprisingly plain exterior white walls and green-tile roof betray an interior of exquisite traditional Moroccan craftsmanship. Mosaics of *zellij* rise from the marble floor to a ceiling of gold leaf and hand-carved cedar wood, while the three ground-floor tombs are carved from white onyx. The tomb of Mohammed V is flanked by those of his two sons, all of which are visible from an interior balcony and guarded by elaborately dressed royal guards and fez-topped security agents.

Next door is the Mohammed V Mosque, constructed at the same time and used mainly for Friday midday prayers and on important holy days. The whole complex, which encompasses Le Tour Hassan and the Mohammed V Mosque, is open daily and guarded by royal guards, who are mounted on steeds and are usually open to being photographed. It's a pleasant, though gradually uphill, 30-minute walk from most accommodations, though on humid summer days you might want to catch a *petit* taxi and then stroll back. Visitors should dress respectfully—covering the shoulders and the knees—and avoid coming between noon and 2pm, when the mausoleum closes for midday prayers in the adjoining mosque.

Medina 🖈   Rabat's medina lacks the chaotic hustle and bustle of its imperial sister cities. Its typical maze of narrow streets is largely residential, and its whitewashed houses reflect the city's Andalusian heritage, resulting in one of the country's more photogenic and authentic-feeling walled cities. It's a great place to stroll around, taking in the everyday lives of its residents, which include businessmen walking to their offices in the centre ville, children rushing to and from a dwindling number of medina schools, dust-filled workshops staffed by artisans and tradesmen, and, of course, shopkeepers selling everything from fresh produce to wedding gowns. Depending on the time of day, it can take from 30 minutes to 1 hour to wander through the medina from avenue Mohammed V, along rue Souika and Souk as Sabbat, and up the wide rue des Consuls, a quarter reserved for diplomats from the 18th century until the French construction of the centre ville and ville nouvelle. The late-afternoon congestion on rue Souika, as both hawkers and buyers cram the narrow street, can make progress slow, though it's a fantastic time to absorb the medina atmosphere.

Salé   The walled city of Salé lies on the northern banks of the Oued Bou Regreg. Although nowadays it's effectively a suburb of Rabat, in the past Salé has at times been the more favored of the two. The settlement was first established in the 10th century as an alternative to the aging Sala Colonia across the river. In the 13th century, the ruling Merenid dynasty built the city's walls, which can still be seen today, in response to raids by Spanish looters. The Merenids also constructed a canal that passed through the main entrance gate, Bab Mrisa. The canal, no longer visible, offered secure access for merchant ships to sail right into the city, and as a result, Salé grew in stature to become one of the most important ports on Morocco's Atlantic coastline. Its stature grew even more during the 17th and 18th centuries, along with that of its twin sister across the river, when the two cities benefited from an influx of Muslim refugees from southern Spain, and the ensuing activities of the infamous Sallee Rovers. The Bab Mrisa canal was especially useful to the shallow-keeled vessels used by the pirates.

Once the renegade cities returned to central rule and European interest became focused on Rabat, Salé quickly fell from favor. The 1957 construction of the bridge, Pont Moulay Hassan, connecting the two only hastened Salé's decline as many of its citizens, called Slawis, shifted to the newer suburbs on the Rabat side of the river. Those that have stayed have kept their independent streak and "tribal" sense of belonging, however, and Slawis are considered amongst the more pious and conservative in the country. Some of the first independence demonstrations took place here, and Slawis are well represented in the upper echelons of government and the palace. Wandering around Salé's compact medina is a great half-day's excursion from Rabat, including the boat ride across the river that the city historically relied upon for its existence.

In the far western reach of Salé's maze of streets and lanes is the Almohad-era **Grand Mosque.** Constructed between 1163 and 1184, and one of the oldest in the country, the mosque sits in the top end of town, surrounded by a concentration of mansions and other religious monuments. Although non-Muslims can only see the mosque's stepped, main entrance and tall minaret; entrance into its adjacent theological college, or *medersa,* is open to all (rue Ras ash-Shajara, aka rue de la Grand Mosque; 10dh/ $1.25/65p adults, 3dh/40¢/20p kids 5–12; daily 9am–noon and 2:30–6:30pm). The *medersa* is a Merenid construction, built by Sultan Abou el Hassan in the 14th century and recently meticulously restored by the current government. Similar to sister *medersas* in Fes and Meknes, the *medersa* follows a basic plan of a central courtyard opening onto a prayer hall, with upper floors of cell-like rooms for the students. The interior craftsmanship is superb, with *zellij,* stucco, and cedar woodwork covering the ground-floor walls. From the flat rooftop there's a great view looking over Salé toward Le Tour Hassan and the Kasbah des Oudaïas. The annual Moussem of Sidi Abdallah ibn Hassoun is one of the more important in the country, and sees pilgrims paying homage to the patron saint of Salé (p. 20).

Your best options for getting across the river from Rabat to Salé are by boat or *grand* taxi. At the time of writing, boat taxis had ceased operating between the two river banks due to a major redevelopment of the riverside promenades on both sides. However, this popular and cheap (only 1dh/15¢/6p per person) public transport should be running again by early 2008; the boats leave when full from an area opposite the medina's Bab el Bahr in Rabat. *Grands* taxis for Salé depart from the rank next to Hotel Bou Regreg, arriving at another rank opposite Salé's Bab Mrisa—an unusually high entrance due to its original accommodations of merchant vessels.

ESPECIALLY FOR KIDS

Rabat offers very few attractions specifically for children. As always, however, a stroll through the city's medina will produce a visual feast of shops with large mounds of brightly colored spices, musical instruments, and gory splendors such as hanging goat and camel heads. Catching a boat taxi between the two riverbanks could also be fun. On the Salé side of the Oued Bou Regreg is the city's fun fair, **Magic Park,** on avenue du Bou Regreg. There are plenty of rides, including bumper cars and carousels, as well as a great view overlooking the river. It's open daily from May to September, and Wednesday, Saturday, and Sunday from October to April, operating from 11am to 9pm. Special hours during Ramadan are Monday to Friday 8pm to 1am and weekends 1pm to 1am. Admission costs 5dh (65¢/30p) for children up to 12, 10dh ($1.25/65p) for accompanying adults, and 25dh ($3.15/£1.55) for adults with no children. A 40dh ($5/£2.50) ticket per child or adult gives access to all rides.

If you're in Rabat for a number of days, then consider contacting French potter Marilyn Bottero (© **061/224268** or 037/674798), who offers a range of art workshops for kids including fabric painting, pottery, and papier-mâché.

SHOPPING

Rabat's medina and kasbah offer limited but rewarding shopping opportunities. Mingling in with those selling everyday wares such as olives, cooking utensils, plasticware, and clothing are shops stocked with all the same fine handicrafts as those in the more well-known shopping souks of Marrakech and Fes. The difference in Rabat is the relative lack of hard sell, with most shopkeepers either selling at a fixed price or only bartering out of some sort of respect for this ingrained local custom.

For fresh produce, visit the Central Marché, located on the medina side of avenue Hassan II between Bab el Had and Bab al Bouab, open daily from 8am to 8pm. There's a Label 'Vie supermarket, 4 av. al Maghreb al Arabi, 100m (330 ft.) west of Bab al Had, which also sells fresh produce along with standard supermarket groceries. It's open daily 8:30am to 9pm.

MEDINA

As the day draws to a close, hawkers converge on **rue Souika** to spread out their wares and seemingly compete with each other over who has the loudest and catchiest sales pitch. Although the goods are largely domestic products and housewares and of little interest to travelers, wandering along the crowded street at this time is one of my favorite pastimes, as the street comes alive, and the true sense of being in a residential medina can be experienced.

Rue Souk as Sabbat is a covered extension of rue Souika, and houses many small shops selling jewelry, *jellabahs, babouches,* musical instruments, and modern clothing and footwear. At the southwestern entrance to Souk as Sabbat, on the corner with rue Bab Chellah, is the small, dusty treasure trove of **Ben Hamou Metloub** ✦. The septuagenarian has been here for "only 15 years," and his shop is packed to the rafters with trinkets and curios. Inside you'll find, amongst other things, ancient trade beads, *darbuka* drums, fossils, gemstones, *kif* pipes, tambourines, leather wallets, and walking sticks. He's open daily, usually from 9am to 9pm.

At its northeastern end, rue Souk as Sabbat meets the junction of rue Oukassa and rue des Consuls. **Rue des Consuls** is Rabat's main shopping street. Here you'll find many shops selling handicrafts from other parts of Morocco, such as Marrakchi leatherwear and Fassi pottery, along with locally made colored-hide lamps, *babouches, jellabahs,* and carpets. Rabat carpets can have as many as 150,000 stitches per square meter (13,935 stitches per sq. ft.), and were traditionally made in workshops within the medina and kasbah. There's still a carpet auction held here every Monday and Thursday morning.

On the corner of rue des Consuls and rue el Harrarine (aka rue el Kheddarin) is the small Rabat boutique for French potter **Marilyn Bottero** ✦✦ (© **061/224268** or 037/674798). Her fun, brightly colored creations come in all manner of forms, from cloth bags and lamp shades to tagines and teacups. Marilyn also conducts creative workshops for both adults and kids. Two doors up is **Pop Art–L'Art Moderne** ✦ (© **079/781526**), the tiny workshop-cum-outlet for metalworking brothers Mohammed and Mohssin. The brothers fashion both traditional and contemporary lamp shades from various metal sources, including old olive oil tins and other canned goods. The shades are fashioned with designs from hundreds of tiny holes punched into the metal, casting fantastic shadows on the nearest wall. Both shops are open daily from roughly 9am to 6pm, usually with a break for lunch between noon and 2pm.

KASBAH DES OUDAÏAS

Toward the end of the kasbah's main street, rue Jemaa, is a wonderful art gallery, **Nouiga Galérie d'Art** (✆ 037/711646). Inside you'll regularly find original works from local artists, especially photographers, as well as a large range of different size prints taken from watercolors depicting everyday life within Morocco. There's also a selection of quality coffee table–style souvenir books, and information regarding upcoming cultural events. At the end of rue Jemaa is a **carpet co-operative,** where you can watch local women toiling away on the traditional looms, though they expect a gratuity (5dh/65¢/30p) for the privilege.

RABAT AFTER DARK

True to Rabat's standing as the country's diplomatic center, nightlife in the city tends to lean toward the cultural spectrum. **Théâtre Mohammed V,** on rue Moulay Rachid (✆ 037/707300), is the country's preeminent theater, hosting a wide variety of productions ranging from Moroccan comedy to European classical dance. **Cinéma du 7ème Art,** on avenue Allal ben Abdellah (✆ 037/733887), is popular with the student crowd, showing mostly Arabic and European art-house movies nightly. There's also the local cultural centers attached to some of the foreign embassies. The **British Council,** at 36 rue Tanger, Ministères (off the southern end of av. Mohammed V; ✆ 037/760836; www.britishcouncil.org.ma), offers a monthly program of functions, as does the **Institut Français,** 2 rue al Yanboua (✆ 037/701122; www.ambafrance.ma), and the German-aligned **Goethe Institut,** 7 rue Sana'a (✆ 037/732650; www.goethe.de), in the centre ville.

I find most clubs in Rabat highly overrated, both staffed and frequented by persons full of self-importance and costing an arm and a leg (by Moroccan standards) just to get in, let alone to have a drink. The most consistently popular in downtown Rabat is **Amnesia,** 18 rue de Monastir, centre ville (✆ 037/701860). American-themed right down to the diner-style backroom, the music is a mix of European and American chart pop, and the clientele largely well-to-do Rabat 20-somethings. It's open nightly 7:30pm to 2am; admission for men is 80dh ($10/£5) Monday to Friday and 100dh ($13/£6.25) Saturday and Sunday; women are always free. For a more relaxed drink, head to **Le Grand Comptoir,** 270 bd. Mohammed V, centre ville (✆ 037/201514; fax 037/707322; www.legrandcomptoir.ma). A brasserie in its truest French form, the upstairs bar offers somewhere to enjoy a reasonably priced drink without any stuffiness. Weekend nights can get quite busy and provide a fun night out, especially when accompanied by some live jazz or African music. It's open daily 9am to 1am.

2 Casablanca

91km (57 miles) S of Rabat; 238km (148 miles) SW of Marrakech; 289km (180 miles) W of Fes

Modern-day Casablanca is Morocco's capital in all ways except ceremonial. The teeming city is the country's largest, with a population going on four million, the majority of whom are only first- or second-generation inhabitants. Casa, as the city is popularly called, is a new city, having grown from a small village of less than a few thousand only 150 years ago. The settlers are coming even today, drawn by the mostly false hope of finding a job, housing, and a better life than what rural Morocco can offer. Some do make their fortune here, and the display of wealth on Casa's streets and in its trendy bars and restaurants gives the impression of a city in southern Europe.

For travelers, modern and cosmopolitan Casa never fails to surprise. The veil is rarely seen here, and the mixing of men and women is the most open of anywhere in Morocco. With its small medina lacking any of the exotic atmosphere of the country's better-known ancient cities and a dearth of sights bar the grand Hassan II Mosque, many travelers pass through Casa with only a fleeting glimpse—or bypass the city altogether. Those who stay, however, find the city grows on them, offering a good choice of fine restaurants, a few places to let the hair down and enjoy a drink, and a buzz of a city striding forward.

The city's origins trace back to the medieval town of Anfa. Set on a plateau overlooking the coastline and a small port, Anfa (nowadays one of Casa's more affluent suburbs) became the capital of an independent Berber state in the aftermath of the Islamic Arab invasions of the 7th and 8th centuries. The state was known as Berghouata, after the tribe that lived here. The pious Almoravids considered the Berghouata heretics, and commenced a holy war against them in the 11th century. The battle was continued, and finally won, by the Almohads in the late 12th century, with the Merenids taking control of the state during the 13th century. The Merenid dynasty began to falter by the early 15th century, and the local Berbers again rose up to take control. Anfa quickly became a port centered around piracy activity, and continuously incurred the wrath of the Portuguese navy. After two failed attempts to subdue the rebellious seamen, the Portuguese finally landed in 1575, erecting whitewashed fortifications and renaming the settlement Casa Branca (White House). Although under almost constant attack by the surrounding tribes, the Portuguese stayed here until 1755, when they abandoned the city after it was severely damaged by a devastating earthquake that also flattened their capital, Lisbon. The town was rebuilt shortly after by the revered Saâdian ruler, Sultan Sidi Mohammed ben Abdallah, who bestowed upon it the Arabic translation of Casa Branca: Dar al Baïda. The area struggled to regain its former importance, however, and by 1830, Dar al Baïda housed no more than 600 inhabitants.

The city we see today only really began to take shape in the mid–19th century. Europe was flourishing, and nations such as Britain, France, and Spain looked toward Morocco's fertile plains to help feed and clothe their people. The Dar el Baïda region became a major supplier of both wheat and wool, and European merchants converged on the city they called Casablanca—after the Spanish translation—to secure trade agreements. At the beginning of the 20th century, the French were granted permission to construct a bigger, artificial port to keep up with the growing demand, and regular maritime services soon commenced to the port of Marseille. European influence grew quickly, and although the city as a whole prospered from the increased economic activity, tolerance between the Europeans and Moroccans wore thin, eventually erupting into violence when in 1907, nine European workmen were killed after they commenced construction of a railway that crossed a Muslim cemetery. Pro-colonialist France had been looking to increase its presence in Morocco, and in response to the ensuing riots, promptly bombarded the town and sent in its navy. After fierce battles with both locals and Berber tribes from the inland, the militarily superior French troops gained the upper hand and occupied the city, setting in motion a process of colonization that culminated with Morocco being declared a French protectorate in 1912.

Under Resident-General Louis Lyautey, Casablanca became the blueprint for France's plans throughout the country. With Tangier declared an International Zone, Lyautey completed the construction of Casablanca's harbor, confirming its status as the country's new economic center. True to his respect for Morocco's ancient medinas, he proceeded to build a ville nouvelle outside the walls of the original Dar el Baïda. Casablanca became colonial Morocco's showpiece, sporting a unique architectural style, called Mauresque, which combined French colonial with Moroccan traditional.

French Morocco was supposedly an ally of Vichy France and Hitler's Germany during World War II. However, in 1942, U.S. General Eisenhower landed more than 25,000 troops here—presuming correctly that the Vichy soldiers were reluctant to shoot at U.S. soldiers—and declared the city as his air force base for the Allied North African campaign. A year later, the leaders of the Allieds, including Prime Minister Churchill and President Roosevelt, met in Casablanca to discuss the progress of the war. At the same time, Bogey and Bergman's classic *Casablanca,* loosely based on current events but shot entirely in Hollywood, was released. While Casa was gaining international recognition, it was also fast outgrowing its initially well-planned suburbs. Moroccans flocked to this new "capital," looking to make a quick fortune before returning home. Although some prospered, most didn't, spawning vast slum areas of shantytowns, or *bidonvilles.* By war's end, the city was fast approaching a population of one million, where only a century before there was less than 1,000.

Official recognition of the *bidonvilles* only commenced toward the end of Hassan II's reign, with his government preferring to ignore the problem, mirrored by many Moroccans who saw the rural immigrants as lower-class citizens. The early 2000s saw many *bidonville* families forcibly moved into high-rise apartment blocks, merely paying attention to their accommodations and not their socioeconomic problems. Casa's concentrated urban poor has developed into the country's most serious domestic situation. In 2003, the city experienced a coordinated attack from suicide bombers, attributed to an Islamist extremist group based in the largest of Casa's slums, Sidi Moumen. This directed attention onto the plight of the city's slums, said to house up to a third of its population. Some voluntary organizations moved in, teaching skills such as basic literacy and IT. The progress has been slow, however, with most slum dwellers still facing a desperate future void of any meaningful employment and social acceptance. More suicide bombings in 2007 only served to reiterate the problem.

The casual traveler, usually confined to the city center, won't be exposed to much of this internal discord. Indeed, the city center is experiencing a miniboom, with new hotels going up, old ones being refurbished, and an ever-expanding restaurant scene. There's no doubt that Casablanca lacks the allure of some other cities and regions, but taken for what it is, this modern city could be considered a true reflection of today's Morocco.

ORIENTATION
ARRIVING

BY PLANE   Casablanca's **Mohammed V airport** (© **022/539040**) is the country's hub, accepting most international flight arrivals along with the majority of domestic flights. Located 25km (16 miles) southeast of the city center, international flights originating from North America, Germany, Italy, and the Netherlands arrive at Terminal 3, a short, free shuttle ride from Terminals 1 and 2, where all domestic flights are operated from and where the main arrivals and departures building is located. Inside this building there are numerous ATMs and bureaux de change; it's worth exchanging some money into Moroccan dirham here, a necessity if you are using public transport to get into the city center. Most major airlines flying into Morocco have offices located here, as do the international car-rental firms. There's also a small pharmacy and post office located between the arrival and departure halls. If departing, there are a few duty-free shops after immigration, but they only accept major currencies and credit cards—and not Moroccan dirham.

Organizing an airport pickup with your hotel is a good idea for arrival into Casablanca, and usually costs around 300dh ($38/£19). This saves having to negotiate the sometimes busy, and late, public trains or a *grand* taxi driver intent on taking you to a hotel from which he will receive a commission. Whether by private transfer or *grand* taxi, the drive into Casa's city center can take up to 45 minutes depending on the traffic. *Grands* taxis are located directly outside the arrivals building, and are supposed to charge a set fee of 250dh ($31/£16) for up to six passengers. In reality, this can increase for night-time arrivals and if the driver is aware that his passengers are not traveling together. Taxis from the airport (but not those operating around town) generally accept euros and sometimes U.S. dollars or British pounds, but you will receive change only in dirham.

The airport is served by the national rail network, with an hourly train service connecting it with Casa-Voyageurs station between 6:50am and 9:50pm, with one final service at 11:50pm. The ride takes around 35 minutes and costs 30dh ($3.75/£1.90) for a second-class seat. Casa-Voyageurs is a short *petit* taxi ride from Casa-Port train station and the city center.

BY TRAIN There are five train stations in Casablanca, of which two are of most use to travelers. **Casa-Port station** (© 022/223011) is the more conveniently located of the two, located at the entrance to the port and at the northern end of boulevard Houphouet Boigny, only a 10-minute walk or a 3dh (40¢/20p) taxi ride from place des Nations Unies. Unfortunately, only trains from Rabat, Kenitra, El Jadida, and Mohammedia arrive here. All long-distance trains, and those originating from Mohammed V airport, arrive at **Casa-Voyageurs station** (© 022/243818), located at the far eastern end of boulevard Mohammed V, 2km (1¼ miles) east of the city center. *Petits* taxis are usually waiting outside the station, and it shouldn't cost more than 10dh ($1.25/65p) to get into town. *Note:* Insist your *petit* taxi driver use his meter, as he is legally bound to.

The service from Rabat to Casa-Port runs throughout the day, taking 1 hour and costing 30dh ($3.75/£1.90). Trains depart daily for Casa-Voyageurs from most stations in Morocco. Some of the more popular routes include Fes (4 hr.; 103dh–155dh/ $13–$19/£6.45–£9.70); Marrakech (3½ hr.; 84dh–125dh/$11–$16/£5.25–£8); Meknes (3¼ hr.; 86dh–128dh/$11–$16/£5.40–£8); and Tangier (6 hr.; 118dh–175dh/ $15–$22/£7.40–£11). From destinations such as Agadir, Essaouira, and Tetouan, you will be traveling all or part of your journey on the ONCF bus service called Supratours. Reservations are only accepted up to 1 month prior to departure and can be made either over the phone (© 090/203040 from within Morocco only) or from ticket booths at each station, as well as through authorized agents. Payment at the station is by cash only, but some agents will accept credit cards.

BY BUS Buses to Casablanca arrive daily from literally all over Morocco, including Agadir (9 hr.; 130dh–160dh/$16–$20/£8.15–£10); Chefchaouen (6 hr.; 70dh–80dh/ $8.75–$10/£4.40–£5); Er Rachidia (11 hr.; 170dh/$21/£11); Essaouira (7 hr.;

120dh/$15/£7.50); Fes (5 hr.; 80dh–90dh/$10–$11/£5–£5.65); Marrakech (4 hr.; 50dh–80dh/$6.25–$10/£3.15–£5); Meknes (5 hr.; 80dh–90dh/$10–$11/£5–£5.65); Ouarzazate (9 hr.; 130dh–140dh/$16–$18/£8.15–£8.75); Rabat (1½ hr.; 20dh–25dh/ $2.50–$3.15/£1.25–£1.55); Tangier (6 hr.; 110dh–130dh/$14–$16/£6.90–£8.15); and Taroudannt (10 hr.; 130dh–150dh/$16–$19/£8.15–£9.40). All of the above services bar Chefchaouen are best traveled on **CTM** (✆ **022/438282** central reservations; www.ctm.ma), which operates from their very conveniently located *gare routière* (bus station) in the city center, on rue Léon l'Africain (✆ **022/541010**). CTM's international services to Spain and France also operate from here. It's a clean, efficiently run setup, with a small cafe and a luggage storage *(consigne)* open between 6am and 11:30pm, charging 5dh (65¢/30p) per bag. From here, it's a short walk to most of the city's accommodations and many of its restaurants.

All non-CTM services—including all those from Chefchaouen—operate from the Ouled Ziane *gare routière* (✆ **022/444470**), 4km (2½ miles) southeast of and a 20dh ($2.50/£1.25) *petit* taxi ride from the city center. The modern building also houses a *consigne,* open around the clock and charging 5dh (65¢/30p) per bag.

BY *GRAND* TAXI   Most long-distance *grands* taxis operate throughout the day from a rank in front of Ouled Ziane *gare routière,* except those plying the route from Rabat (1 hr.; 30dh/$3.75/£1.90), which usually deposit passengers on boulevard Hassan Seghir, near the CTM *gare routière.* Travelers may be better advised, however, catching the train to Rabat, which departs from Casa-Port station (see above), as it's safer, more comfortable, and almost as quick.

BY CAR   For first-time self-drivers, driving into Casablanca is not recommended. The complicated grid of streets (some one-way) within the city center is extremely difficult to negotiate for the nonlocal, and that's not taking into consideration the busy traffic that manages to congest many of the thoroughfares during the week. Added to this is the lack of parking, making it almost impossible to find a parking spot during working hours. For a visit of only a day or two, perhaps consider leaving your car in Rabat and catching the train into the city. If hiring a car from here, wait until your day of departure to collect your vehicle, and have the company deliver it to your hotel.

VISITOR INFORMATION

Casablanca's **Syndicat d'Initiative,** or tourist information bureau, is conveniently located at 98 bd. Mohammed V (✆ **022/221524**). It's open Monday to Friday 8:30am to 4:30pm, and has the usual friendly but largely ineffectual staff. The **Casablanca Conseil Regional du Tourisme** (www.visitcasablanca.ma) has a website (in French) with some handy practical information and phone numbers.

The **Dar America Information Resource Center (IRC),** 10 place Belair (✆ **022/221460;** www.usembassy.ma/usmission/pas/irc/daramerica.htm), is the Public Affairs Office of the U.S. Consulate, and has an extensive research and library center available to library members. The IRC staff provides researchers and professionals with in-depth information and documentation on a wide variety of political, economic, social, and cultural issues. Members (Moroccan and non-Moroccan) also have access to Internet, films, round-table discussions, and other programs. Membership is open to Moroccan-based business professionals, journalists, professors, and university students, and costs 60dh ($7.50/£3.75) per year. You'll need to present two passportsize photos and a photocopy of your passport. The IRC is open Monday to Friday 10am to 6pm.

CITY LAYOUT

Casablanca is a sprawling metropolis, with a city center that can be overwhelming upon arrival. For most travelers, however, once ensconced in the city center, getting your bearings becomes a little easier. The busiest street junction is that at place des Nations Unies. Most of the city's major streets branch out from here, including the east-west running avenue des Forces Armées Royales (av. des F.A.R.); boulevard Houphouet Boigny, which connects the port area, including Casa-Port train station, with the city center; the easterly boulevard Mohammed V; avenue Moulay Hassan I, which heads southwest; and avenue Hassan II, which runs directly south via the large public square called place Mohammed V. Directly north of place des Nations Unies is the city's old medina. Typically mazelike though relatively compact, it's hard to imagine nowadays that only 100 years ago this was all there was of Casablanca. The grand Hassan II Mosque is 1km (⅔ mile) to the northwest of here, and 3km (1¾ miles) farther west lies the beach suburb of Aïn Diab.

GETTING AROUND

Casablanca is Morocco's largest city, and traffic congestion can be horrendous during most days and early evenings. The city center is relatively compact, however, and fairly easy for travelers to negotiate when accompanied by a good map. The city's small medina is pedestrian only, and is the usual labyrinth of small streets and lanes. The restaurants located along its northern port-facing wall, along with the Hassan II Mosque and the beaches of Aïn Diab, are really only reached from the city center by *petit* taxi.

BY FOOT   As mentioned, the city center is best navigated with a map and your feet, and its complex grid of one-way streets can often result in this being the quickest way to get around. Just be careful when walking around certain areas come nightfall (see "Safety" in "Fast Facts," below). The compact medina can be surprisingly challenging to negotiate, with very few tall landmarks to assist in navigation. Most travelers stick to wandering the busy souk area in the southeastern corner, invariably exiting the walls through one of the gates along avenue des F.A.R. The long beachfront promenade at Aïn Diab is a pleasure to stroll along, as witnessed every evening when locals converge here in numbers.

BY TAXI   Casa's *petits* taxis are the most convenient way to travel between the city center and any other part of the city. You'll find the small, red, government-regulated vehicles everywhere. At your hotel, you can usually ask the reception staff to organize one for you, or otherwise you can simply stand on the side of the street and hail one. Drivers are only allowed to carry up to three passengers at a time, but be aware that if there is a vacant seat, you may pick up an additional passenger. At all times, request the driver to put on the meter, which he is supposed to do no matter the time of day or night. Daytime trips within the city center should cost no more than 8dh ($1/50p), while a fare out to Aïn Diab will cost around 20dh ($2.50/£1.25). Remember that after 8pm, a 50% evening surcharge kicks in.

FAST FACTS: Casablanca

Airport See "Arriving" in "Orientation," above.

Banks & Currency Exchange There are banks dotted throughout the city center, most with ATMs and exchange facilities. On place du 16 Novembre, you'll find branches of **Banque Populaire** (🕿 **022/202540**) and **BMCI** (🕿 **022/224198**). There's an **SGMB** branch (🕿 **022/438888**) with 24-hour exchange ATM on the corner of rue Mohammed el Quorri and boulevard Mohammed V. If you've got traveler's checks, try the branch of **Crédit du Maroc** (🕿 **022/477000**) at 48 bd. Mohammed V. There's a **BMCE** bureau de change within the Hyatt Regency hotel on place des Nations Unies, which is open daily 9am to 9pm.

Car Rentals All the major international firms are located in the city center, including **Avis**, 19 av. des F.A.R. (🕿 **022/312424**); **Budget**, Tour des Habbous, avenue des F.A.R., near the Sheraton Hotel (🕿 **022/313124**); **Europcar**, Tour des Habbous, avenue des F.A.R., near the Sheraton Hotel (🕿 **022/313737**); **Hertz**, 25 rue Araibi Jilali (🕿 **022/484710**); and **National/Alamo**, 12 rue Araibi Jilali, 1st floor (🕿 **022/277141**). They also all have desks at the airport: **Avis** (🕿 **022/539072**), **Budget** (🕿 **022/539157**), **Europcar** (🕿 **022/539161**), **Hertz** (🕿 **022/539181**), and **National/Alamo** (🕿 **022/539716**); all are usually open 8am to 10pm.

Consulates The **U.S.** maintains a consulate in Casablanca, 8 bd. Moulay Youssef (🕿 **022/264550**; http://casablanca.usconsulate.gov), as does the **U.K.**, 36 rue de la Loire, Polo (🕿 **022/857400**).

Doctors Recommended English-speaking doctors include **Dr. Alain Guidon**, 6 rue Jean Jaurès (🕿 **022/267153**); **Dr. Mohammed Bennani**, 45 rue Atlas Maarif (🕿 **022/982323** or **022/391413**); **Dr. Solange Lahlou-Bouflet**, 14 rue Saad ben Abi Oakkas, off boulevard Hassan II (🕿 **022/200249**); and pediatrician **Dr. Dalila Ghazali**, Residence Mawlid, rue ibn Katir, Maarif (🕿 **022/983390** or **061/133298**).

Drugstores There are pharmacies all over the city center, including **Pharmacie du Progress** (🕿 **022/270489**) on place du 16 Novembre. All general pharmacies in Casablanca operate Monday to Friday 8:30am to 12:30pm and 3:30 to 8pm, and Saturday 8:30am to 1pm. They then work on a roster system after hours; the list is on the front door. The **Pharmacie du Nuit** (🕿 **022/269491**) is located within the Préfecture building, on place Mohammed V, open nightly from 9pm to 8am. There's a **24-hour pharmacy** on the corner of place Oued al Makhazine and boulevard d'Anfa.

Emergency For **general emergencies** and the **police**, call 🕿 **19**. For a **public ambulance**, call 🕿 **15**. **SOS Médicins Maroc** (🕿 **022/252525**) is a private ambulance service offering home visits by doctors (350dh/$44/£22 per visit) and emergency evacuation. See "Doctors," above, and "Hospitals," below, for more options.

Hospitals Private clinics with 24-hour admittance include **Clinique Badr**, 35 rue el Allouissi Bourgogne (🕿 **022/492800** or **022/492380**), and **Clinique Yasmine**, boulevard Sidi Abderrahman Hay el Hana (🕿 **022/396960**).

Internet Access **LGNet**, 81 bd. Mohammed V, 1st floor, is open Monday to Saturday 9am to midnight and Sunday 10am to midnight. **Gig@NET**, 140 bd. Mohammed Zerktouni, is open daily from 9am until past midnight, and **CyberNet**, 38 rue Mouftaker Abdelkader, is open daily from 8:30am to 11pm.

Laundry & Dry Cleaning There are no self-service laundromats in Casa's city center. City dry cleaners include **Lavomatic International** (no phone), 24 rue Salah ben Bouchaib, and **Elegance Pressing** (🕿 **022/295674**), on the corner of rue Charif Amiane and rue Prince Moulay Abdellah. Both are open Monday to

Saturday 8:30am to 12:30pm and 2:30 to 8pm. A shirt or pair of pants costs around 15dh ($1.90/95p). Otherwise, you can ask at your hotel reception, though this can prove expensive as they usually charge per item. Often your hotel's cleaning staff will do your laundry privately to earn some money on the side; a practice usually accepted by the management. A plastic shopping bag of laundry shouldn't cost you more than 30dh ($3.75/£1.90) this way, although perhaps don't trust them with your favorite white shirt or dress.

Maps & Books The series of maps produced by **Plan Guides du Maroc** (© 022/310281) includes a 2005 edition of Casablanca. Like others in the series, it's a full-blown map of the entire city, and would serve travelers' interests better if it were more concentrated on the city center. Nonetheless, it's helpful for self-drivers trying to navigate their way into the city, and gives a good overall view of the city's size. Have a look in your arrival airport's news agencies to see if the map is available. On the same scale, but even less effective due to the omission of many street names, is a city map produced by the **Casablanca Conseil Regional du Tourisme** (www.visitcasablanca.ma). Both maps are infrequently available. **Librairie de France,** 15 bd. Mohammed V, just off place des Nations Unies, sometimes stocks city maps of Agadir, Fes, Marrakech, and Rabat, along with a selection of mostly French-language Moroccan guidebooks and coffee table–style books. There's also a very small selection of English-language fiction. Hours are Monday to Friday 9am to noon and 2 to 7pm, and Saturday 9am to noon. **Mohammed Lamkhantar** operates a newsstand on the corner of boulevard Mohammed V and place des Nations Unies, and often has English-language Morocco guidebooks and maps. He's open Monday to Saturday 7am to 9pm.

Newspapers Dotted around place des Nations Unies are newsstands selling weekly international versions of the U.K.'s *Guardian* and the U.S.'s *Herald Tribune* newspapers, along with the odd English-language copy of *Time,* *Newsweek,* and *The Economist.*

Photographic Needs There are quite a few photo-processing studios located on or near the pedestrian-only section of rue Prince Moulay Abdallah. There's also **Studio Restinga,** 27 rue Tahar Sebti (© 022/275388), where you can get your digital images copied to CD. It's open Monday to Friday 9am to 7pm, Saturday 9am to 1pm.

Police There's a **Commissariat de Police** (© 022/989865) on boulevard Brahim Roudani. For **emergencies,** dial © **19.**

Post Office & Mail Casablanca's main **post office,** which receives all *poste restante* mail, is on place Mohammed V, at the junction of avenue Hassan II and boulevard de Paris, open Monday to Friday 8am to 4:15pm, Saturday 8 to 11:45am. There is a section inside for sending parcels (that must be inspected first) and Western Union services. There's a handy branch on the corner of boulevard Mohammed V and rue Chaouia (aka rue Colbert), which is open the same hours. **DHL** has an office located at 52 bd. Abdelmoumen (© 022/548904), open Monday to Friday 8am to 7pm and Saturday 9am to 1pm. **FedEx** has its Moroccan headquarters in the Globex building, 313 bd. Mohammed V (© 022/541212), open Monday to Friday 8am to 7:30pm, and Saturday 8am to

12:15pm. There's another office at 262 bd. Zerktouni (© **022/264470**), open Monday to Friday 8am to 6:30pm, and Saturday 8am to 12:15pm.

Restrooms There are no public restrooms within Casablanca's city center. Your best option is to duck into one of the larger hotels, such as the **Hyatt Regency** on place des Nations Unies, or the Sheraton, halfway along avenue des F.A.R. There's also a **McDonald's** on rue Allal ben Abdellah, not far from the junction with place des Nations Unies, and another one along the boulevard de la Corniche, out in the beachside suburb of Aïn Diab.

Safety For such a frenetic city by day, much of Casablanca's city center closes down by 10pm. Up to this time, most streets are safe to walk around, though the area around the Marché Centrale can always feel a little rough. Late at night, travelers should be aware of their surroundings if walking back to accommodations, especially from the restaurant-bar strip along rue Allal ben Abdallah, the seedy bar area along rue Mohammed el Quorri, and within the medina. My general advice for late night is that it's best to catch a taxi unless your accommodations are close by.

Taxis See "Getting Around," above.

Telephone Casablanca's **city code** is **022**.

WHERE TO STAY

Because Casa is Morocco's economic hub, as well as a forced stopover for some travelers flying in and out of the country, many of the city's hotels operate close to full capacity for most of the year. No matter where you intend to stay in Casa, book ahead or arrive early. Summer in the city center can be quite oppressive, with little of the Atlantic's sea breeze making its way into the concrete jungle. Rooms with air-conditioning are considered a necessity for most travelers during this time. During the winter months, however, Casa can get extremely cold, and a room heater can be the difference between a good night's sleep and a bad one. During these off-season months, it's also worth asking for a discount.

All hotels in the medina, and many of the budget establishments located close to the CTM bus station, have not been recommended, as I consider them overpriced and underequipped. Some national and international hotel chains are represented in Casa, and are mostly characterless, concrete blocks located along avenue des F.A.R. The following are all located in the city center and have something special to offer—be it location, value for money, personal service, or a combination of all three.

VERY EXPENSIVE

Oum Palace Hotel 👁👁   Opened in early 2007, this is one of the newest high-end hotels in the city and is a local alternative to the better-known international chain hotels nearby. Set out over 10 floors, the rooms are well designed and feature contemporary furnishings in colors of ochre or pastel green. Large enough to also include a coffee table and chairs, rooms come with all the modern conveniences including PC modem access points and Wi-Fi. Five suites are slightly larger than the rooms, and come with a private balcony and Jacuzzi. The contemporary design filters down into the two restaurants—one serving Moroccan fare and the other international—and reception area, while an in-house beauty center includes a hammam, sauna, and masseuse. Located near most of the city's expensive hotels, Oum Palace is also very close to most of its quality restaurants.

12 rue Mohamed Kamal (formerly rue Léon l'Africain), Casablanca. © 022/201500. Fax 022/204090. www.oumpalace.com. 106 units. 1,230dh ($154/£77) double; 3,000dh ($375/£188) suite. Kids under 12 stay free in parent's room. Rates include breakfast. MC, V. **Amenities:** 2 restaurants; conference room; beauty center; elevator; disabled rooms. In room: A/C, satellite TV, PC wall connection, Wi-Fi, fridge, safe.

MODERATE

Hotel Guynemer ★★★   This Art Deco, family-run hotel is a traveler's favorite and beats all others hands-down for friendly and helpful staff. Most of the rooms have been recently refurbished—now with brightly colored walls and newly tiled and fitted bathrooms. Ask to see a few rooms when checking in. Special touches such as free Internet and Wi-Fi and staff that is happy to assist with any query or difficulty are what make Guynemer different. Their licensed Moroccan restaurant (now air-conditioned) can get lively with tour groups, and has live *oud* music nightly; otherwise you're only a short walk to the city's better restaurants. You'll need to book your stay ahead of time, and you can also request an airport or railway station pickup.

2 rue Brahim Belloul (formerly rue Pegoud), Casablanca. © 022/277619 or 022/275764. Fax 022/473999. www.geocities.com/hotelguynemer. 29 units. 372dh ($47/£23) single; 538dh ($67/£34) double. Rates include breakfast. TPT not included. MC, V. Street parking. Airport pickup 200dh–250dh ($25–$31/£13–£16). **Amenities:** Restaurant; Internet; Wi-Fi. In room: Satellite TV.

Hotel Maâmoura ★★ (Value (Kids   After 6 long years of restoration, this once-derelict 90-year-old building is now one of Casa's best-value hotels. Father and son team Mohammed and Mbark Boudad are personally on hand each day to welcome guests and oversee the running of their hotel. The rooms are very spacious and not overdone with ornate decoration or garish color schemes, but rather neutral walls and tiled floors, heavy dark-brown bed coverings, built-in cupboards, and modern bathrooms. For those with children, there are eight interconnecting rooms. There are a few suites the size of a small apartment, which have a large, L-shape lounge, fridge, and balcony. A first-floor conference room is watched over by portraits of the Alaouite dynasty's present and past kings and sultans; the room is multipurpose and was being used for meditation and yoga on my last visit. A sparkling marble-floor reception area (check out the exquisite stucco plasterwork and *zellij* fountain) leads to an in-house cafe on one side and a large restaurant on the other. The restaurant should be fully operational by mid-2008. There are quite a few traders on the street, and while it's often littered with rubbish later in the day, it's cleaned up by morning. Most of the staff speaks at least some English, and the hotel is within walking distance to most restaurants.

59 rue Ibn Batouta, Casablanca. © 022/452967 or 022/452968. Fax 022/452969. www.hotelmaamoura.com. 60 units. 380dh ($48/£24) single; 468dh ($59/£29) double; 750dh ($94/£47) suite. Children under 13 stay free in parent's room. TPT not included. Breakfast 40dh ($5/£2.50). MC, V, Limited street parking. **Amenities:** Restaurant; cafe; elevator; Wi-Fi. In room: A/C, satellite TV.

Hotel Volubilis   Built in 1919 by renowned French architect Marius Boyer, this hotel sat derelict through the 1990s until it reopened in 2005, offering modern albeit small rooms for a very reasonable price. The owners kept the original floors in the rooms, but have refurbished the bathrooms with blue and white tiling and new bath/shower combos. Most rooms face onto the street—usually quiet at nighttime—but some rooms at the rear are even quieter. Thick red carpets line the hallways and

Casablanca

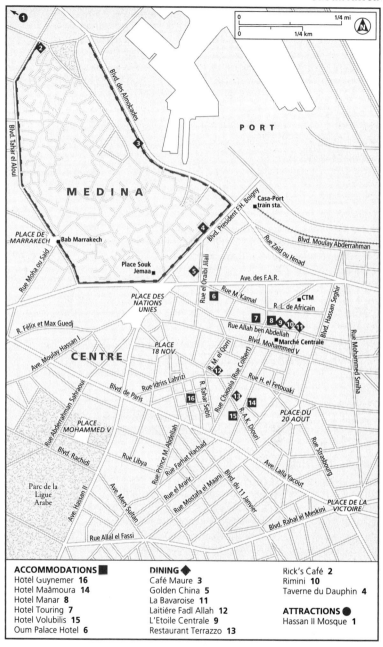

P O R T

Casa-Port
train sta.

M E D I N A

PLACE DE
MARRAKECH

Bab Marrakech

Place Souk
Jemaa

PLACE DES
NATIONS
UNIES

CTM

R. L. de Africain

Marché Centrale

CENTRE

PLACE
18 NOV.

PLACE
MOHAMMED V

Parc de la
Ligue
Arabe

PLACE DU
20 AOUT

PLACE DE LA
VICTOIRE

ACCOMMODATIONS ■
Hotel Guynemer **16**
Hotel Maâmoura **14**
Hotel Manar **8**
Hotel Touring **7**
Hotel Volubilis **15**
Oum Palace Hotel **6**

DINING ◆
Café Maure **3**
Golden China **5**
La Bavaroise **11**
Laitiére Fadl Allah **12**
L'Etoile Centrale **9**
Restaurant Terrazzo **13**

Rick's Café **2**
Rimini **10**
Taverne du Dauphin **4**

ATTRACTIONS ●
Hassan II Mosque **1**

help to warm up the hotel during the colder months. The reception area received a full makeover and is now resplendent in rough sandstone and Roman statuettes (in keeping with the hotel's namesake near Meknes). A small restaurant opening onto the street serves light meals and a pastry and tea/coffee breakfast. The Volubilis is only a short walk from the restaurant strip along rue Allal ben Abdellah, and there's usually parking right outside. *Note:* The single rooms here are very small; you'll get better value for your money at the nearby Hotel Maâmoura (above).

20–22 rue Abdelkrim Diouri, Casablanca. ✆ 022/272772 or 022/272771. Fax 022/294792. 45 units. 350dh ($44/£22) single; 450dh ($56/£28) double. Rates include breakfast. TPT not included. MC, V. **Amenities:** Restaurant. *In room:* Central A/C, satellite TV, fridge.

INEXPENSIVE

Hotel Manar *(Value*   This is perhaps the newest hotel in Casablanca (it opened in mid-2007), and is easily the best budget option. While it lacks any real character, the simply furnished rooms are all still sparkling with their new tiling and built-in cupboards, while the modern bathrooms are a decent size, with bath/shower combos. Heavy wood doors keep any hallway noise to a minimum; the inward facing rooms will be quieter than those with windows over the road. The reception area is suitably grand with a large chandelier and wall mural depicting charging horsemen. An in-house cafe occupies the split-level area at the reception's rear. The hotel is very centrally located, just around the corner from both the restaurant strip and CTM bus station.

3 rue Chaouia (formerly rue Colbert), Casablanca. ✆ 022/452751 or 022/452752. 50 units. 315dh ($39/£20) single; 358dh ($45/£22) double. Children under 10 stay free in parent's room. TPT not included. No credit cards. **Amenities:** Cafe; elevator. *In room:* Central heating, satellite TV.

Hotel Touring   This friendly old girl has had a fresh lick of paint and is the best of a number of budget hotels along this street. Popular with backpackers simply looking for a cheap bed for the night, the large rooms are clean and simply furnished. Some have a private bathroom, otherwise there are showers and toilets out in the hallways. It's only a 5-minute walk from the CTM bus station and restaurants.

87 rue Allal ben Abdellah, Casablanca. ✆ 022/310216. 20 units. 90dh–125dh ($11–$16/£5.65–£7.80) single; 130dh–165dh ($16–$21/£8.15–£10) double; 170dh–225dh ($21–$28/£11–£14) triple. TPT not included. No credit cards. *In room:* No phone.

WHERE TO DINE

Casablanca's selection of restaurants is amongst the best in Morocco, with many specializing in seafood. All those recommended here are fairly easy to find, with a section of rue Allal ben Abdallah, opposite the Marché Centrale, recently becoming a lively restaurant-bar strip within walking distance of many city center hotels. Besides the eating establishments listed here, there are plenty of *snak* restaurants to be found, serving up cheap rotisserie chicken, fried seafood, *chawarmas,* and sandwiches.

EXPENSIVE

La Bavaroise *(★★★* INTERNATIONAL   This former 1940s German beer house is now one of the finest dining experiences in Casa. Maitre'd Mehdi Touhami—a young wine specialist who's done stints in France and with The Dorset in England—and classically trained chef Bernard Bremond from Marseille are proving a hit combination with both locals and visitors. Located across from the busy local central market along a string of restaurants and bars, La Bavaroise has a wonderful atmosphere. The original floorboards, rough whitewashed walls, jazz music, and intimate setting make you feel like staying here for a long meal, fine wine, and good conversation. The menu is extensive and seasonal, though Bernard recommends the seafood, as he personally places the order at midnight and has it collected at 5am when the boats arrive back into port. Current entrees range from a grilled vegetable and smoked Herring salad to roasted shrimp and tomatoes in an artichoke sauce. Beef, duck, lamb, and ostrich are charcoal-grilled and served on a wood slab, while the catch of the day is roasted or grilled with olive oil, Atlas herbs, and pink garlic. There's a small brasserie at the entrance, where diners can select from Mehdi's extensive wine collection.

135 rue Allal ben Abdallah. ⓒ 022/311760. Fax 022/541843. www.bavaroise.ma. Appetizers 60dh–125dh ($7.50–$16/£3.75–£7.80); main courses 120dh–195dh ($15–$24/£7.50–£12). Reservations recommended. Alcohol served. MC, V. Mon–Sat noon–2:30pm and 7:30–11pm; Sun noon–2:30pm.

Rick's Café 𝕲𝕲 INTERNATIONAL   Bogey and Bergman may have never set foot in Casablanca, but the spirit of the movie is alive and well in downtown Casa. Rick's Café is the fruition of a 2-year tourism project by Kathy Kriger, or Madam Rick, an American woman who has lived in Morocco since 1998. Kathy opened the doors of Rick's in 2004, and has been greeting every customer since. The interior of the multi-level former medina residence has been restored to resemble the era depicted in the movie, and is dominated by the central courtyard with its authentic 1930s Pleyel piano, where local pianist Issam Chabaa recreates the '40s and '50s Tuesday to Sunday night; the Sunday night jam session regularly hosts international jazz musicians. If you've never seen the movie, it's screened nightly in an upstairs dining room that's decked out in movie memorabilia.

The menu has Moroccan standards such as a lamb tagine, but also offers such diverse dishes as giant shrimp with papaya and avocado, a good old-fashioned hamburger, and even fish and chips. The American breakfast (on the lunch menu) is a respectable splurge at 80dh ($10/£5). Saturday night is oyster night, which sees the oyster supplier's son, resplendent in nautical attire, shucking out the fleshy meat for each guest. The bar is easy-going and satisfies every thirst, from the local Casablanca beer to French champagne. There's also a recently opened Bar'n'Barbeque on the roof terrace.

248 bd. Sour Jdid (corner of bd. des Almohades and bd. Ziraoui), Medina. ⓒ 022/274207 or 022/274208. Fax 022/487884. www.rickscafe.ma. Reservations recommended. Appetizers 40dh–110dh ($5–$14/£2.50–£6.90); main courses 70dh–150dh ($8.75–$19/£4.40–£9.40); light meals 50dh–95dh ($6.25–$12/£3.15–£5.95). MC, V. Daily noon–3pm and 6:30pm–midnight.

MODERATE

Café Maure 𝕲𝕲 INTERNATIONAL/MOROCCAN   Away from the hustle and bustle yet only a 10-minute walk from Casa-Port train station, this very pleasant indoor-outdoor restaurant is a great place to eat and drink at any time of day or night. It's set within the walls of an 18th-century fortification, or *sqala,* and is part of a small complex that includes a boutique—a satellite shop to Stéphanie Bénetère's Kif Kif in Marrakech (p. 149)—and a gallery housing temporary art exhibitions and fashion shows. The outdoor section is where you want to be—mosaic tables, wrought-iron chairs, large linen umbrellas, and plenty of shade under a large trellis covered with bougainvillea. The menu is extensive and begins with a choice of breakfasts that are large enough to fill you for the whole day; the *F'tor Sqala* includes traditional breads, poached eggs, jams and *amlou* (argan spread), and freshly squeezed orange juice and tea or coffee. Dishes from midday onward include a delicious *Kémia Mauresque* salad of *zaalouk* (pulped aubergine/eggplant), *choukchouka* (finely chopped peppers, cucumber, tomato), artichoke, olives, *haricot* beans, and tomato. More substantial dishes include a *lotte et gambas* (burbot and shrimp) tagine cooked in saffron. There's also a range of desserts and gâteaux, which can be enjoyed with a coffee, tea, or delicious fruit cocktail. The waitstaff are young and friendly, and the clientele range from businesspeople to travelers to city 20-somethings.

Bd. des Almohades, Medina Wall. ℂ **022/260960.** Fax 022/262035. Breakfast 35dh–70dh ($4.40–$8.75/£2.20–£4.40); appetizers 45dh–70dh ($5.65–$8.75/£2.80–£4.40); main courses 55dh–160dh ($6.90–$20/£3.45–£10); coffee and cake 45dh ($5.65/£2.80). MC, V. Tues–Sun 8:30am–midnight. Wi-Fi connected.

Golden China CHINESE   Casablanca's best Chinese restaurant opened in 1993, and is a traveler-friendly establishment with English-language menus and a large choice of dishes to accommodate all tastes. There are standards such as Mongolian sizzling beef and sweet-and-sour pork, as well as a few different choices such as the Triple Delight fish, prawn, and calamari soup, or sliced duck in mustard sauce. Vegetarians will be pleased with options that include a delicious Szechwan tofu and eggplant sautéed in garlic and soy. The decor is as you'd expect—a laughing Buddha at the entrance, Asian-style lamps—with Chinese background music and air-conditioning adding a sense of tranquillity. They're licensed to sell alcohol and open during Ramadan.

12 rue el Oraibi Jilali. ℂ **022/273526.** Fax 022/273521. Appetizers 35dh–45dh ($4.40–$5.65/£2.20–£2.80); main courses 60dh–103dh ($7.50–$13/£3.75–£6.45). Alcohol served. Mon–Fri noon–2:30pm and 7:30–11pm; Sat 7:30–11pm.

Restaurant Terrazzo ITALIAN   From the outside, Terrazzo appears no more than an Italian take-away, but inside you'll find a modern, classy restaurant serving very good authentic cuisine. There's a good choice of salads—I like the simple tomato and mozzarella in basil and olive oil—and wood-fired pizzas topped with true mozzarella. Pasta dishes include your choice of sauce with fettuccine, spaghetti, penne, or lasagna, and there are also a few meat dishes such as *scaloppine al limone* and beef stroganoff. Perhaps the most difficult choice is deciding between the chocolate profiteroles or an Irish coffee for dessert. It's a popular venue for business lunches, as well as travelers staying in the numerous hotels close by.

Corner of rue Abdelkrim Diouri and rue Chaouia (formerly rue Colbert). ℂ **022/279650** or 022/271946. Fax 022/204771. Pizza 50dh–80dh ($6.25–$10/£3.15–£5); main courses 50dh–95dh ($6.25–$12/£3.15–£5.95); dessert 25dh–70dh ($3.15–$8.75/£1.55–£4.40). Alcohol served. MC, V. Daily 10am–3pm and 7–11pm.

Taverne du Dauphin 🐟 SEAFOOD   Since it opened in 1958 to feed Casablanca's hard-working, hard-living French sailors, the "Dolphin Tavern" has been the city's seafood restaurant of choice. Madame Besniard has since passed on, but her two grandsons, Jean-Claude and Marcel, are still on hand every night, ready for a chat and to recommend the day's freshest catch. Popular dishes include a filet of John Dory grilled in a lemon-and-butter *meunière* and served with sautéed mushrooms, and a half-dozen 000-class (the highest quality possible) Oualidia oysters. Diners can choose to eat alfresco (enclosed and heated during winter) or in the more refined air-conditioned restaurant in the back with a separate entrance. In between the two is a lively bar that serves up a nice cold beer with free seafood tapas. A selective wine menu includes a good choice of both local and imported reds and whites. *Note:* The back section can get a little smoky at times.

115 bd. President Félix Houphouet Boigny. ℂ **022/221200** or 022/277979. Fax 022/221551. www.taverne-du-dauphin.ma. Main courses 32dh–115dh ($4–$14/£2–£7.20). Alcohol served. MC, V. Mon–Sat noon–11pm.

INEXPENSIVE

Laitière Fadl Allah JUICE BAR/BREAKFAST   This is my favorite spot in Casa for a quick and easy breakfast or afternoon tea. The narrow interior is pleasantly non-smoking, and a croissant or *pain au chocolat* can be accompanied by any number of combinations of freshly made juices including apple, avocado, banana, orange, papaya, and pineapple. I recommend the date and almond milkshake, but coffee and tea are also available.

Rue Mohammed el Qorri (near the junction with av. Houmane el Fetouaki). No phone. Juice and croissant 15dh ($1.90/95p). No credit cards. Daily 7am–11pm.

L'Etoile Centrale MOROCCAN   For 40 years, this restaurant has been serving authentic Moroccan cuisine at a very reasonable cost. Popular with travelers, the restaurant's two salons (blue or red) are outfitted with traditional low lounges and walls of faux *zellij* and hand-carved stucco. The menu includes more than 15 choices of tagine, but owner Ahmed Mribed also recommends his Couscous Royale with either lamb, chicken, skewered beef, or vegetables. A chicken-and-almond *pastilla* is also a tasty offering. The restaurant is rarely busy—though it deserves to be—and is conveniently located on the restaurant strip and close to most hotels.

107 rue Allal ben Abdellah. (© **022/018625** or 061/637524. Main courses 60dh–100dh ($7.50–$13/£3.75–£6.25). No credit cards. Daily 11:30am–3:30pm and 6–11pm.

Rimini FAST FOOD   What makes Rimini different from all the other pizzerias in town is its wood-fired oven. There's a choice of 18 pizzas, all reasonably priced and delicious. The menu also includes other comfort food such as pastas—including a tasty seafood tagliatelle—panini, hamburgers, sandwiches, and a few grilled meat dishes. The split-level interior of yellow and red walls, mosaic tables, and wrought-iron chairs is bright and breezy, and is popular with young locals and late-night revelers leaving the nearby bars.

127 rue Allal ben Abdellah. (© **022/451042.** Pizza 24dh–40dh ($3–$5/£1.50–£2.50); other dishes 22dh–38dh ($2.75–$4.75/£1.40–£2.40). No credit cards. Mon–Sat noon–midnight.

WHAT TO SEE & DO

Casablanca's attraction is its cosmopolitan modernity (what sets it apart from any other Moroccan city), and is perhaps best appreciated at the end of your Moroccan travels. This is a city where people come to work and make money, and it's this big-city atmosphere that is best absorbed through a stroll around the city center or along boulevard de la Corniche in the beachside suburb of Aïn Diab. Complimenting these nontraditional sightseeing options is the impressive Hassan II Mosque, which also breaks with Moroccan tradition by allowing entrance to non-Muslims, and Casablanca's Museum of Moroccan Judaism, the only one of its kind in the entire Islamic world.

Aïn Diab *(Kids*   Casa's seaside suburb runs along the Atlantic coastline west of the city center, with a long beachside promenade called the Corniche flanked by bars, clubs, restaurants, and hotels. The beach itself isn't so fantastic, especially if you've already been farther south, but a walk along the 3km (1¾-mile) beachfront boulevard de la Corniche is highly recommended. Here you'll see Casablanca in all its contrasting beauty, where locals dressed in the latest European fashions walk past others dressed in traditional *jellabah* and *babouches*. It's an understandably popular stretch for families, who bring their children here to escape the confines of the heaving city's inner suburbs. Dotted along the beach are the city's beach clubs; they all usually offer a swimming pool or two, private sunbathing areas, and perhaps a basketball, tennis, or volleyball court. Sometimes you can feel on show, as the masses on the Corniche above look down upon you. Entrance can be as much as 100dh ($13/£6.25) adults and 35dh ($4.40/£2.20) kids up to 12, but it's worth checking a few clubs out before choosing. The largest is **Miami Plage** (© **022/797133**), while **Tahiti Beach** (© **022/783472**) is also popular. They usually open daily from 9am to 7:30pm, but often operate shorter hours or close up altogether from November to March. There are plenty of cafes along the strip, as well as *gelateries* selling ice cream in large waffle cones. For those missing Western comfort food, there's also a very popular McDonald's on the beach side of the road.

Art Deco Architecture   General Lyautey's nouvelle Casablanca brought about an architectural style known as Mauresque, which blended traditional Moroccan designs with the more liberal influences of early-20th-century Europe. By the 1930s, Mauresque architecture began to reflect the Parisian Art Deco style, characterized by ornate wrought-iron balconies, staircases, and windows; carved facades and friezes; and rounded, rather then straight, exterior corners. Some of these buildings have been restored or kept in good condition, and are a visual reminder of Casa's early protectorate history. Many of the city's best examples are in an area roughly bordered by boulevard Mohammed V to the north, avenue Lalla Yacout to the south, rue du Prince Moulay Abdellah to the west, and rue Ibn Batouta to the east. Buildings to look out for include: **Cinema Rialto,** on the corner of rue Mohammed el Quori and rue Salah ben Bouchaib; **Hotel Guynemer,** 2 rue Brahim Belloul (formerly rue Pegoud); **Hotel Lincoln,** opposite the Marché Central, on the corner of boulevard Mohammed V and rue Ibn Batouta; **Hotel Transatlantique,** 79 rue Chaouia (aka rue Colbert); and **Hotel Volubilis,** 20–22 rue Abdelkrim Diouri, where you should ask the staff to point out the World War II bullet holes on the front facade.

Walking along boulevard Mohammed V, the pedestrian-only section of rue du Prince Moulay Abdellah, and around place du 16 Novembre will afford more fine examples. Over on **place Mohammed V** are a cluster of classic Mauresque public buildings, including the 1930 former **Préfécture,** or police headquarters, the 1925 **Palais de Justice,** and the 1918 **General Post Office.** *Tip:* Make sure to look up while you're wandering around. Most of the city's Mauresque and Art Deco buildings now house shops or offices on their ground floors, which have long since been modified.

Hassan II Mosque ⟨⟨⟨   Acknowledging Casablanca's lack of historical monuments, King Hassan II stated (on his birthday in 1980) his desire for the city to "be endowed with a large, fine building of which it can be proud until the end of time." Thirteen years later, he inaugurated the Hassan II Mosque. Built on a rocky outcrop of reclaimed land—in response to Hassan II's translation of the Koranic verse that proclaims God's throne was built upon water—the mosque is a truly marvelous piece of architecture. Designed by French architect Michel Pinseau, it can accommodate 25,000 worshippers inside and 80,000 more outside. At the time it cost more than $750 million, all of it paid by public money. It took 6 years and more than 6,000 craftsmen to build. They used marble from Agadir, cedar wood from the Middle Atlas, and granite from Tafraoute; Venetian glass was the only imported material. The mosque's most exquisite examples of Moroccan craftsmanship are the blankets of *zellij,* some designs more than 10m (33 ft.) high. The mosque is not only one of the world's largest, it's also one of the world's most high-tech, with heated flooring, a retractable roof, a section of clear-glass flooring—for worshippers to see God's water below—and even a laser light atop its 210m-high (690-ft.) minaret, pointing the way to Mecca each night. There's also an ablutions hall with more than 40 fountains and two public hammams.

To see the mosque's interior, you have to take a guided 1-hour tour, which I highly recommend. It's only from within the vast prayer hall that you can appreciate the enormity and grandness of its scale. Visitors must be dressed respectfully (shoulders covered and preferably long trousers or skirt), and shoes are removed once you step inside. The mosque is located about a 10-minute *petit* taxi ride (around 15dh/$1.90/95p) from the city center.

Bd. Sidi Mohamed ben Abdallah. Guided tour in English, French, German, and Spanish 120dh ($15/£7.50) adults; 60dh ($7.50/£3.75) students with ID; 30dh ($3.75/£1.90) children under 12. Sept–June Sat–Thurs 9am, 10am, 11am, and 2pm; July–Aug 2:30pm.

Museum of Moroccan Judaism   Better known as simply the Jewish Museum, this is the only of its kind to be found in the Islamic world, and is often highlighted as an example of Morocco's historic tolerance between the two faiths. Opened in 1997 and set in a modern villa out in the suburb of Oasis, 5km (3 miles) south of the city center, the museum's exhibits follow the 2,000-year-old history of Morocco's Jews. A number of rooms display various aspects of their traditions and daily life such as torahs, Chanukah lamps, *ketubofs* (marriage contracts), and traditional clothing. There are also life-size replicas of the interior of a synagogue and a jeweler's workshop, referring to the Jews' historical dealings in silver. A photo library displays many of Morocco's ancient synagogues, cemeteries, holy sites, and various Mellahs and other Jewish landmarks within Morocco. Although you don't really require one, English-speaking guides can sometimes be arranged with prior notice. The museum is best reached by *petit* taxi, about 15 minutes and 25dh ($3.15/£1.55) from the city center.

81 rue Chasseur Jules Gros, Oasis. (C) 022/994940. Fax 022/994941. www.casajewishmuseum.com (in French). Admission 20dh ($2.50/£1.25) adults; free for children under 12. Mon–Fri 10am–6pm.

CASABLANCA FOR KIDS

Morocco's biggest city is not particularly child friendly, with plenty of traffic, noise, hustle, and bustle. To the southwest of the city center, about a 10-minute walk from place des Nations Unies, is the **Parc de la Ligue Arabe.** Casa's "Central Park" has plenty of grassed and shaded areas for little ones to run around and play. There's also a string of cafes and **Parc des Jeux Yasmina,** a small amusement park with fairground rides. The grounds are always open, while Yasmina is open daily from 11am to 7pm, with a nominal charge of 2dh (25¢/15p) per child. Another good option for the day is to head out to the beach suburb of **Aïn Diab** (p. 331), where there's a choice of beach clubs with various sporting facilities and swimming pools. Along the beachside promenade, there are plenty of places to eat lunch or grab an ice cream, including a McDonald's.

SHOPPING

Modern Casablanca lacks souks or quarters where artisans practice their traditional crafts, thus all souvenirs are imported from elsewhere in the country. The quality can therefore be low and the prices high, making shopping for souvenirs in Casa really only an option if you're about to leave the country. There's a string of **craft shops** on both sides of boulevard Felix Houphouet Boigny, opposite the medina walls. No one shop is recommendable over the other—they are all selling the same stuff, and are all extremely keen to secure your business at the highest negotiable price—but perhaps begin at no. 37, where owner Mohammed al Bouchaib (© 061/589347) makes a lovely pot of mint tea before the haggling begins. Also offering the same overpriced souvenirs, but without the hassle, is the **Exposition Nationale d'Artisanat**, at the junction of avenue Hassan II and rue Maarakat Ohoud (© 022/267064). This three-story building is stuffed with every imaginable craft product from around Morocco, and offers fixed-price, hassle-free shopping. It's open daily from 9am to 12:30pm and 2:30 to 8pm.

For everyday grocery items, fresh produce, and fresh flowers, head to the **Marché Centrale (Central Market).** Worth a visit even if you're not shopping, this large undercover market is a hive of activity each day from early morning through evening, and takes up a whole block in the city center, bordered by boulevard Mohammed V, rue Allal ben Abdellah, rue Abdallah Almedouini, and rue Chaouia (aka rue Colbert). A couple of blocks farther east is an **Acima** supermarket, on the corner of boulevard Mohammed V and rue Mohammed Smiha (© 022/297864). Here you'll find all the usual supermarket items such as groceries, toiletries, fresh produce, dairy products, and so on. It's open daily 9am to 9pm.

CASABLANCA AFTER DARK

Within Morocco, Casa runs second only to Marrakech in nightlife options. Having said that, the offerings are still relatively limited, with the two most popular options being the beachside strip in Aïn Diab and a cluster of restaurant-bars in the city center, on rue Allal ben Abdellah. *Warning:* Solo females may find themselves under a constant barrage of male admirers in Casa's clubs.

Along the beachfront boulevard de la Corniche in Aïn Diab are the nightclubs **Pulp Club,** no. 3 (© 022/759088); **Le Village,** no. 11 (© 022/723541); **Mystic Garden,** no. 33 (© 022/798877); and **Candy Bar,** no. 55 (© 022/710934). Pulp Club and Candy Bar are the least pretentious, while Le Village is gay friendly and Mystic Garden attracts Casa's ultrahip. Weekend nights are the most popular, as well as any night during the summer holidays, and some clubs may close on some weeknights during the winter. Admission is usually controlled by self-important doormen and fashionable, disinterested cashiers. Some clubs will deny entrance on the basis of wearing jeans, though this policy seems to change nightly and on the whim of the aforementioned doormen. Expect to pay around 100dh ($13/£6.25) to get in, and at least half this again for your drinks. If you're looking for something a little lighter and less formal, the street-level cafe of the beach club **Tahiti Beach** serves a great selection of ice creams, sundaes, and gâteaux, along with coffee and tea. Glass wind breakers keep the night chill at bay, and there's usually a happy, friendly atmosphere.

Back in town is **La Bodega** ⊛⊛⊛, 127 rue Allal ben Abdellah (© 022/541842; www.restopro.ma/bodega), which has serious doormen but no admission charge. The atmosphere inside this Spanish *taverna* is refreshingly vibrant and fun. The ground floor section is both a tapas bar and a restaurant serving light meals. Downstairs is a cavernous nightclub with a dance floor and lounge section. It's the one place in Casa where the alcohol flows freely—there's beer on tap—and female travelers can enjoy a hassle-free time, particularly on ground floor. It's open Monday to Saturday 7pm to 1am.

A few doors down from La Bodega are a couple of traditional all-male drinking dens, where the beer also flows freely, as does the cigarette smoke. For a quiet drink in classy surroundings, try **Rick's Café** ⊛⊛ (p. 329) or the **Casablanca Bar** in the Hyatt Regency Hotel, on place des Nations Unies; both are themed on the classic movie.

There's also a bar inside the restaurant **Taverne du Dauphin** (p. 330), which is popular with businessmen, or try a fruit cocktail at **Café Maure** (p. 329).

Finally, there's the Art Deco **Cinema Rialto,** on the corner of rue Mohammed el Quori and rue Salah ben Bouchaib (© **022/487040**), where the latest Hollywood releases (usually dubbed in French) are screened nightly for 25dh ($3.15/£1.55) Monday to Friday, and 30dh ($3.75/£1.90) Saturday and Sunday. Around the Rialto are a few bars, but they're pretty seedy and not recommended for female travelers.

3 Oualidia ★ ★

170km (105 miles) SW of Casablanca; 193km (120 miles) NW of Marrakech; 195km (121 miles) NE of Essaouira

Midway between the port cities of El Jadida and Safi, Oualidia (pronounced "wa-lid-ee-ah" is a small fishing and holiday resort overlooking one the finest natural lagoons of the North African coastline. It's a perfect spot to break a journey between the bustling northern centers of Tangier, Rabat, and Casablanca, and the southern tourist hot spots of Marrakech, Essaouira, and Agadir. Named after the Saâdian Sultan el Oulalid—whose 17th-century kasbah sits in ruins on a wooded hillside overlooking the lagoon—this former sleepy village is famous for its seafood, caught nightly by a small fleet of local fishermen, and its oysters, farmed along the lagoon's shores since the late 1950s. More than 200 tons of oysters are produced annually, most for local consumption, and a small selection of lagoon-side hotel-restaurants specialize in serving the succulent flesh for the cheapest prices in Morocco. Oualidia is a popular summer holiday destination; from late June to early September, both Moroccans and Europeans flock to the lagoon and its sheltered shore, as well as the adjacent beach facing the open sea. Besides the seafood and oysters, they come to enjoy a variety of watersports such as surfing, sailing, and fishing; the festive atmosphere; night-long music and dance; and endless cups of mint tea, all of which make up for the lack of secluded sunbathing. The beaches can get very crowded during these months, but come at any other time of the year, and you'll have the beautiful surroundings to yourself.

ESSENTIALS
GETTING THERE
BY BUS & _GRAND_ TAXI   Buses and _grands_ taxis operate from a small parking lot in the middle of the village, on the main El Jadida–Safi road. CTM buses operate from their own office, just 80m (260 ft.) farther south. Both CTM and other bus companies, as well as _grands_ taxis, depart throughout the day for Oualidia from Safi (1–1½ hr.; 20dh–30dh/$2.50–$3.75/£1.25–£1.90), and there are at least three departures per day from El Jadida (1¼–1¾ hr.; 25dh–30dh/$3.15–$3.75/£1.55–£1.90).

VILLAGE LAYOUT
The "commercial" center of the village straddles either side of the El Jadida–Safi road, sitting above the lagoon and beach down below. Along this 200m (655-ft.) stretch are the bank, Internet cafes, pharmacies, a covered market, and the stop for both buses and _grands_ taxis. Opposite the covered market—the busiest section of the road—is the road winding down 1km (⅔ mile) to the lagoon and beach; down here is where the village's best hotel-restaurants are located.

FAST FACTS
All the following are located on the El Jadida–Safi road running through the village. **Banque Populaire,** with a bureau de change and an ATM, is opposite the _grand_ taxi

park. It's open Monday to Friday 8:15am to 3:45pm. There are three pharmacies: **Pharmacie La Mosque** (② 023/356477), **Pharmacie Oualidia** (② 023/366494), and **Pharmacie La Lagune** (② 024/366255), all open Monday to Friday 8:30am to 12:30pm, 2:30 to 7:30pm, and 8 to 11pm. They then operate on a roster system after hours and on weekends. For Internet access, try **Cyber Club Oualidia,** at the southern end of the road, and **Cyber La Lagune,** at the northern end near the covered market; both are open daily from 9am to midnight.

WHERE TO STAY & DINE

All accommodations in Oualidia also double as restaurants. For the traveler, this has resulted in a limited range of pretty good sleeping and dining establishments.

VERY EXPENSIVE

La Sultana Oualidia ★★   Opened in 2007, this luxury resort is in a class of its own in Oualidia, and is the place to stay for a couple of days of indulgence and relaxation. Designed to showcase the skills of local craftsmen using natural materials (such as local limestone), this sister property to the well-established La Sultana Marrakech presents the best of contemporary Moroccan style. An entrance garden of green grass, palm trees, and mini-wetlands leads to a low-set reception, with the accommodations set at the rear of the property for maximum privacy. It has the feel of a villa apartment complex rather than a hotel, with carved steps leading to private entrances. The very spacious rooms are all individually styled, with painted-wood furniture, marble floors, oleander ceilings, and *tadelakt* walls. Most rooms include luxury touches such as a fireplace and outdoor Jacuzzi; some have a retractable dome roof over the sitting room. Uninterrupted lagoon views can be enjoyed from each private balcony.

The crowning glory of La Sultana Oualidia is its two freshwater swimming pools. One is heated and sits amidst Romanesque limestone columns, with a Jacuzzi on one side and salon-bar with fireplace on the other. Here you'll also find a hammam and sauna. Coming off the entrance gardens is an elevated outdoor pool that looks directly onto the lagoon. Set above the little private beach below, it's surrounded by wood decking and sun loungers, plus individual Jacuzzis that can be filled with seawater and operated by the guest. Nonguests can use this pool for 400dh ($50/£25), including nonalcoholic drinks from the bar. Below is the house restaurant, also open to the public. Chef Simou Mohamid has come from La Sultana Marrakech to lend his expertise to the new kitchen. Oualidia oysters take pride of place, with a dozen 000-rated oysters costing a very reasonable 160dh ($20/£10). There's also a fully stocked bar and an extensive list of Moroccan and French wines, plus a set kids' menu of a cheeseburger or roast chicken with fries and ice cream.

The hotel is accessed from a signposted dirt track at the northeastern entrance to Oualidia, which could be considered the hotel's one drawback. This end of the lagoon is very tidal—even at high tide the water is too muddy to swim in—and the beach is no more than a thin strip of hardened sand. A jetty has been built for fishing boats–cum–water taxis to ferry guests to the nicer parts of the lagoon.

Parc à huîtres, no. 3. ② 024/388008. Fax 024/389809. www.lasultanahotels.com. 2,888dh–5,177dh ($361–$647/£181–£324) double. Children 2–18 414dh ($52/£26) in parent's room; under 2 free. Low-season discount applies. Rates include breakfast and nonalcoholic in-room drinks. TPT not included. AE, MC, V. Guarded parking at entrance. Closed Jan 10–Feb 1. **Amenities:** Restaurant; bar; 2 pools; gym; hammam; sauna; salon. *In room:* Satellite TV, fridge, hair dryer, safe, towel warmer. Restaurant: ② 023/366595. Fax 023/366594. www.lasultana oualidia.com. Main courses 110dh–250dh ($14–$31/£6.90–£16); kids' menu 95dh ($12/£5.95). Alcohol served. AE, MC, V. Daily noon–3pm and 7:30–9:30pm.

MODERATE

Issa-Blanca ⚘ Newly opened in 2007, Issa-Blanca has six rooms—three of which have sea views—all tiled and tastefully decorated with modern furnishings and Asian antiques. The stylish ground-floor restaurant (air-conditioned in summer) offers a varied menu of seafood and Italian and Moroccan dishes. The large, spotless kitchen specializes in Oualidia's *fruits de mer*—a dozen local oysters for 70dh ($8.75/£4.40) or a seafood paella for 75dh ($9.40/£4.70)—and also serves home-style breakfasts. Attentive owner/manager Nadia el Khadri's friendly hotel-restaurant is at the far southern edge of Oualidia and just a walk over the dunes to the beach.

Beach Rd. Turn-off opposite tennis courts, 800m (½ mile) on left-hand side. ✆ 023/366148 or 070/751861. issa-blanca@hotmail.com. 6 units. 600dh ($75/£38) double. Children 3–15 50% discount in parent's room; under 3 free. TPT not included. Rates include breakfast. MC, V. **Amenities:** Restaurant; Internet. *In room:* Heater, satellite TV. Restaurant: Main courses 70dh–145dh ($8.75–$18/£4.35–£9.05). Alcohol served. MC, V. Daily 7am–10pm.

L'Initiale Hôtel Steps away from both the lagoon and the Atlantic beach, this established hotel-restaurant has new owners and is basking in a new lease of life. The rooms have been totally refurbished and now offer new and modern (if slightly small) bathrooms and bedrooms in warm shades of apricot and ruby red. Some offer sea views and balconies. The ground-floor restaurant has tables both inside and out, with a shaded verandah surrounded by a garden of bougainvillea and palms. The menu offers a wide selection of seafood, including a dozen local oysters for 70dh ($8.75/£4.40), calamari *a la provençale,* and a house paella. There are also a few pizzas and grilled meat dishes, plus a good wine and alcohol list. L'Initiale is a great spot for a meal (long Sunday lunches are popular) or to just enjoy a drink between sunbathing sessions.

Oualidia Beach, opposite tennis courts. ✆/fax 023/366246. laurenhuillet@menara.ma. 6 units. 350dh ($44/£22) single; 400dh ($50/£25) double. Rate includes breakfast. MC, V. **Amenities:** Restaurant. *In room:* Satellite TV (in some), balcony. Restaurant: Appetizers 35dh–90dh ($4.40–$11/£2.20–£5.65); main courses 70dh–100dh ($8.75–$13/£4.40–£6.25); pizza 45dh–60dh ($5.65–$7.50/£2.80–£3.75). Alcohol served. MC, V. Daily 8am–10pm.

INEXPENSIVE

A l'Araignée Gourmande This is the oldest hotel-restaurant in Oualidia (opened in 1983), and although the rooms are looking a bit tired, the restaurant still serves some of the best seafood in town. A lush garden—and owner Ahmed Adhaem—welcomes guests into the large building, where dark stained-wood paneling and fish nets adorn the interior. The rooms are located on an upper floor, and although there hasn't been much refurbishment undertaken over the years, most offer fantastic lagoon views and they're the cheapest in town. The large ground-floor dining hall is located on the lagoon's edge, and is usually packed on the weekends with Moroccans from Casablanca and Marrakech. The set menus are popular (entrees of a half-dozen oysters with salad, followed by two courses of seafood and dessert), or you can choose from a menu packed with very reasonably priced fresh seafood.

Oualidia Lagoon, opposite campsite. ✆ 023/366447. Fax 023/366144. 15 units. 206dh ($26/£13) single; 300dh ($38/£19) double. TPT not included. Breakfast 23dh ($2.90/£1.45). MC, V. **Amenities:** Restaurant. *In room:* No phone. Restaurant: Main courses 70dh–150dh ($8.75–$19/£4.40–£9.40); set menus 125dh–280dh ($16–$35/£7.80–£18). Alcohol served. MC, V. Daily 7am–11pm.

WHAT TO SEE & DO

There's only one reason to come to Oualidia, and that's to enjoy the sun and sand from the sheltered lagoon, or the long, open beach a short walk away. As mentioned, they can both get busy during the holidays, but walk a little past the open beach, and you'll find endless stretches of unoccupied sand; just be wary of the strong undercurrent if you go swimming. **Surfland** (© 023/366110) operates a surf school from their base, located halfway between the village and the lagoon, with weeklong camps for kids and beginners of all ages. **Oualidia Maroc Aventure** (© 061/157743; www.oualidia-maroc-aventure.com) is at the southern entrance to the village, on the main El Jadida–Safi road. They hire out mountain bikes (100dh/$13/£6.25 per half-day) and watersports equipment such as kayaks and canoes. During the holiday season, a few temporary operators set themselves up between the lagoon and the Atlantic beach, hiring out quad bikes and jet skis. The **Oualidia Tennis Club** (© 023/366262) has two well-kept clay courts, available for hire to nonmembers via a temporary social membership, which costs 100dh ($13/£6.25). If you're feeling a little sore and tired after a day of fun in, and on, the water, **La Sultana Oualidia** (see above) offers a vast choice of massage and beauty treatments from their in-house hammam and spa.

4 Essaouira ★★★

351km (218 miles) S of Casablanca; 174km (108 miles) W of Marrakech; 173km (107 miles) N of Agadir

Essaouira is one the most enchanting spots in Morocco. Both a laid-back port town and a chic seaside resort, it has quietly become one of the must-sees for backpackers, surfers (wind, kite, and stand-up), art enthusiasts, and crafts shoppers. Essaouira's appeal is its charming blend of 18th-century medina, temperate climate, slightly alternative atmosphere, photogenic port, and wide sandy bay. Add to this the renowned warmth and easy-going nature of the local inhabitants, called Souiris, and it becomes clearer as to why Essaouira (pronounced "essa-*wee*-ra") is currently riding the crest of a small tourism wave, becoming more than just a day trip from Marrakech.

Although the town we see today largely dates from the 18th century onward, the port has featured in Morocco's history since it was discovered by the Phoenicians in the 7th century B.C., who named it Migdol after their word for "watchtower." By 450 B.C., their maritime successors, the Carthaginians, established a colony of around 30,000 people. Excavations on the islands in the bay have confirmed this settlement, where locals extracted purple dye from the island's *murex* mollusks (hence its alternative name as the Iles Purpuraires [Purple Isles]). In the 15th century, another great maritime nation, the Portuguese, established a commercial and military base here, which they named Mogador, from the original Phoenician name. But by the mid–16th century, they had lost most of their Atlantic strongholds to the Moroccan Saâdian dynasty, and Mogador fell into decline as Agadir became the preferred trading port. However, as political power shifted to the nation's current ruling dynasty, the Alaouites, the citizens of Agadir, called Gadiris, declined to support the new power. Agadir's port was promptly closed, and all trade was diverted back again to Mogador. It was the Saâdian ruler, Sidi Mohammed ben Abdallah, who is responsible for the medina of Essaouira that is standing today. The forward-thinking ruler wanted the port redesigned as both a strong military base and as a free-trade port (the only one south of Tangier). In 1765, he entrusted French architect, Théodore Cornut, to design a walled city different to the country's other haphazard Arabic medinas, and more along the French gridlike street system. Liking what he saw, the sultan renamed the city Essaouira, meaning "well designed," and it prospered from both it's free-port status and a subsequent wave of immigrants that included wealthy Jewish traders, influential European merchants, thousands of local Arabs and Berbers, and a small community of African ex-slaves. This was Essaouira's golden age, from which much of the town's enduring architectural grace hails from.

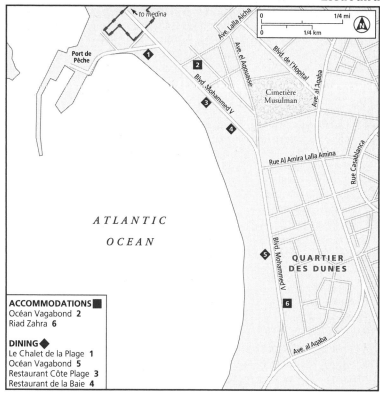

ATLANTIC
OCEAN

ACCOMMODATIONS ■
Océan Vagabond **2**
Riad Zahra **6**

DINING ◆
Le Chalet de la Plage **1**
Océan Vagabond **5**
Restaurant Côte Plage **3**
Restaurant de la Baie **4**

Upon the establishment of the French protectorate in 1912, the town fell into decline due to the favored port of Casablanca. Upon independence in 1956, this decline intensified with the exodus of the Jewish community to Israel. Although the town enjoyed irregular bursts of international attention over the ensuing decades—Orson Welles shot his 1950s *Othello* here, and visits by Cat Stevens and Jimi Hendrix led to a brief hippie fling in the late '60s and early '70s—it has only been in the past decade that the sleepy backwater has come back into its own. The city received a boost in 2001, when the medina was awarded UNESCO World Heritage status in recognition of its unique mix of European and North African architecture. Essaouira continues to welcome all manner of creative types—artists, photographers, movie stars, musicians—but now also hosts those more interested in wind, surf, and relaxation.

ORIENTATION
ARRIVING
BY PLANE   Essaouira's small international airport, 15km (9 miles) south of the town, welcomes a few flights from Paris and Casablanca each week. *Grands* taxis are usually waiting outside the terminal for each incoming flight, and will charge around 80dh ($10/£5) for up to six passengers (so long as they think you are traveling together) for the drive into town.

BY BUS   Buses to Essaouira arrive daily from Agadir (4 hr.; 40dh–60dh/ $5–$7.50/£2.50–£3.75); Casablanca (7 hr.; 120dh/$15/£7.50); Marrakech (3½ hr.; 35dh–60dh/$4.40–$7.50/£2.20–£3.75); Rabat (8½ hr.; 150dh/$19/£9.40); and Safi (2½ hr.; 50dh/$6.25/£3.13). **CTM** services (✆ **024/784764,** or 022/438282 central reservations; www.ctm.ma) and all other long-distance bus companies (except Supratours) arrive at the *gare routière* (✆ **024/784764**), located 500m (1,640 ft.) northeast of Bab Doukala. Open around the clock, it's a fairly straightforward building with ticket counters for the various routes and companies and a 24-hour luggage storage service (5dh/65¢/30p per bag). If you've got a bit of luggage, or if it's after dark, take a *petit* taxi to your preferred medina entrance (around 8dh/$1/50p). **Supratours (✆ 024/ 475317)** runs daily services from Essaouira to Agadir (3 hr.; 60dh/$7.50/£3.75), departing at 4pm; Marrakech (2½ hr.; 65dh/$8.15/£4.05), departing at 6:10am, noon, and 3:30 and 6:45pm; and Safi (2 hr.; 40dh/$5/£2.50), departing at 11am. They have a small office from where their buses depart, located just off avenue Lalla Aïcha, between Bab Marrakech and Bab Sbâa.

BY *GRAND* TAXI   *Grands* taxis to Agadir (1½ hr.; 40dh/$5/£2.50) and Marrakech (3 hr.; 100dh/$13/£6.25) operate throughout the day from outside the *gare routière*. When arriving into Essaouira, ask your driver to drop you off outside Bab Marrakech on the way to the *gare routière*.

BY CAR   Arriving into Essaouira is as easy as driving along boulevard Mohammed V. There are parking lots outside Bab Sbâa and Bab Marrakech, guarded around the clock and costing 25dh ($3.15/£1.55) per day, payable in advance; there's also some street parking (same cost) around place Orson Welles.

VISITOR INFORMATION

The **Office National Marocain du Tourisme (ONMT;** signposted SYNDICAT D'INITIATIVE) is within the medina at 10 rue de Claire, just inside from Bab Sbâa (✆ **024/783532**). The recently renovated office gives out more helpful information than usual, including the latest cultural events taking place. It's open Monday to Friday 9am to noon and 3 to 6:30pm.

CITY LAYOUT

Essaouira is delightfully compact and very easy to navigate. Everything you'll need is within the medina or along the beachfront down to the Quartier des Dunes. The one entrance into town comes in from the southeast, along the beachfront boulevard Mohammed V. This road terminates at the port, from where the medina can be accessed via place Moulay Hassan, Bab el Menzeh, or Bab Sbâa. The other main medina entrances—Bab Marrakech and Bab Doukala—are accessed by turning off boulevard Mohammed V onto avenue Lalla Aïcha, which leads onto avenue Moulay Youssef.

The medina itself is dissected by avenue Zerktouni, rue Souk Jdid, avenue l'Istiqlal, and avenue Oqba ibn Nafiaa, one continuous street running northeast to southwest, joining Bab Doukala and Bab el Menzeh. The other major streets include avenue Mohamed el Qouri, accessed by Bab Marrakech, and the busy tourist street of rue Lattarine. At the far southwest corner of the medina is the large square, place Moulay Hassan. Between Bab el Menzeh and the beach is place Orson Welles, dedicated to the great filmmaker who shot his famous *Othello* here in the 1950s.

GETTING AROUND

For travelers, Essaouira is a place to explore on foot. There are a few *petits* taxis usually hanging outside the medina (remember the medina is pedestrian only), but travelers will only need their services if they don't want to walk to the bus station.

FAST FACTS: Essaouira

Airport See "Arriving" in "Orientation," above.

Banks & Currency Exchange There's an **SGMB** branch with 24-hour exchange ATM in the medina at 10 rue Youssef el Fassi (℃ **024/475201**); the ATM accepts all cards and also changes foreign currency. **Banque Populaire** (℃ **024/476902**) and **Wafa** (℃ **024/486903**) are both located on place Moulay Hassan, and **BMCE** (℃ **024/489456**) is just around the corner; both have bureaux de change.

Car Rentals Of the major international firms, only **Avis** is here, with offices in town, 28 bis av. Oued el Makhazine (℃ **024/475270**), and at the airport (℃ **024/474926**). The two reputable companies located along boulevard Mohammed V are Dzira Location, 50 bd. Mohammed V (℃ **024/473716**), and Isfaoun Rent-a-Car, 62 bd. Mohammed V (℃ **024/474906**; www.essaouiracar.com).

Doctors & Dentists **Dr. Said el Haddad** (℃ **024/478675**) is located on avenue l'Istiqlal, opposite the mosque. Outside the medina, **Dr. Omar Farkhssi** (℃ **024/477621**) is located on place Dar Talib, on the corner of avenue Al Aqaba and avenue Fes, along with a number of dentists and Pharmacie Najib.

Drugstores There are plenty of pharmacies around Essaouira. In the medina are **Pharmacie Haddada,** on avenue l'Istiqlal (℃ **024/473714**), and **Pharmacie La Kasbah,** 12 av. Allal ben Abdellah (℃ **024/475151**). All general pharmacies in Rabat open Monday to Friday from 9am to 12:30pm, 3 to 7:30pm, and 9pm to 1am. They then work on a roster system after hours and on the weekend.

Emergency For **general emergencies** and the **police,** call ℃ **19.** The main police station, **Gendarmerie Royale,** is located outside the medina on avenue El Aqouasse. For a private ambulance, call **Ambulance Tassorte** (℃ **073/209562** or **061/064839**) or **Mogador Assistance** (℃ **061/247624**). Also see "Doctors & Dentists," above, and "Hospitals," below, for more options.

Hospitals The **public hospital** (℃ **024/475716**) is located just outside the medina from Bab Marrakech, on boulevard de l'Hôpital.

Internet Access **Cyber les Ramparts,** 12 rue du Rif, behind the restaurant Les Trois Portes (℃ **024/474728**), has more than 20 computer stations and is open daily from 9am to 2am.

Language Schools **Alliance Franco-Marocaine de Essaouira,** in the medina at 9 rue Mohamed Diouri (℃ **024/472593**; www.ambafrance-ma.org/institut/afm-essaouira), is the Essaouira branch of the nationwide Instituts Français. They offer semester-long French classes (44 hr.; 900dh/$113/£56) and various Arabic courses in both Moroccan Arabic and Modern Standard Arabic (MSA).

Maps & Books Plan d'Essaouira is a map of both the medina and the greater Essaouira town, and is very well formatted and easy to read. Most of the town's accommodations are marked. It costs 15dh ($1.90/95p) and can be bought from many hotels and *maisons d'hôte,* as well as numerous shops within the medina. On place Moulay Hassan are two bookshops, **Jack's Kiosk** (ⓒ **024/475538**) and **Librairie La Fibule** (ⓒ **024/476790**). They both sell a fair selection of English-language guidebooks, nonfiction books, postcards, and the above-mentioned *Plan d'Essaouira.* They're both open daily from 10am to 10pm, closing earlier in winter and later in July and August.

Newspapers **Jack's Kiosk** and **Librairie La Fibule** (see above) both sell various week-old U.K. and U.S. dailies and weekly international versions of the *Guardian* and *Herald Tribune.* **L'horloge Bureau,** located at the base of the clock tower on avenue Oqba ibn Nafiaa, sells 1- and 2-day-old U.K. dailies such as *The Daily Telegraph, The Independent,* and *The Sun.*

Photographic Needs The best photo shop in town is **Labo Photo Flash,** next to Patisserie Chez Boujmaa on avenue Allal ben Abdellah (ⓒ **024/475657**). It sells and processes a good selection of film, transfer digital images to CD, and sell memory cards. The shop is open daily from 9am to 9pm, often closing later during July and August.

Police The main police station, **Gendarmerie Royale,** is located outside the medina on avenue El Aqouasse. Dial ⓒ **19.**

Post Office & Mail Essaouira's main **post office** is outside the medina on the corner of avenue Lalla Aïcha and rue Al Mokaoama (between Bab Marrakech and bd. Mohammed V) and is open Monday to Friday 8am to 4:15 pm. There's a newly renovated branch office on rue Laâlouj, open similar hours.

Restrooms There are no public restrooms within the medina or centre ville. There are some ablution shower/toilet blocks (signposted wc) south of the outdoor seafood grills on place Moulay Hassan, but they're mainly used by the local fishermen. Your best bet is to try one the better dining establishments mentioned below.

Safety Essaouira is very safe to walk around during the day, but certain areas can feel a bit threatening come nightfall. The Mellah neighborhood within the medina, located north of avenue Zerktouni, is best avoided after dark, especially around the derelict areas along rue Mellah and rue Kowait. I've seen drug dealers doing business here even in broad daylight. During the Gnaoua & World Music Festival in June, take care of your belongings as you're squeezing through the jam-packed crowds.

Taxis See "Getting Around," above.

Telephone Essaouira's **city code** is **024,** but you need to drop the "0" if you are calling from outside the country.

WHERE TO STAY

Essaouira's selection of *maisons d'hôte*—all located with the walled medina—is amongst the best in the country. If you're on a budget or have preferred to stay out in the ville nouvelle of other cities for various reasons, I highly recommend considering a few "splurge" nights here in Essaouira's old town. Its easily navigable, pedestrian-only, and largely hassle-free streets are still only a short walk from the town's other

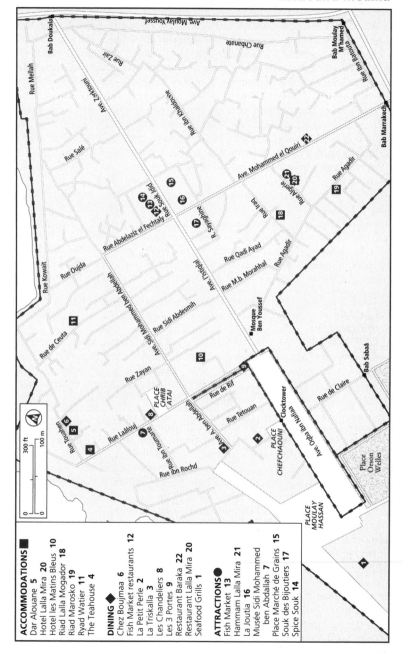

Essaouira Medina

ACCOMMODATIONS ■
Dar Alouane **5**
Hotel Lalla Mira **20**
Hotel les Matins Bleus **10**
Riad Lalla Mogador **18**
Riad Marosko **19**
Ryad Watier **11**
The Teahouse **4**

DINING ◆
Chez Boujmaa **6**
Fish Market restaurants **12**
La Petit Perle **2**
La Triskalla **3**
Les Chandeliers **8**
Les 3 Portes **9**
Restaurant Baraka **22**
Restaurant Lalla Mira **20**
Seafood Grills **1**

ATTRACTIONS ●
Fish Market **13**
Hammam Lalla Mira **21**
La Joutia **16**
Musée Sidi Mohammed
  ben Abdallah **7**
Place Marché de Grains **15**
Souk des Bijoutiers **17**
Spice Souk **14**

main attraction—the beach—most of the town's restaurants are within its walls, and the standard of accommodations offered is pretty good and reasonably priced. Other than the medina, Essaouira's other accommodations area is at the entrance into town, where a group of hotels are bunched together in what is called the Quartier des Dunes, or "Dunes Quarter." Families might prefer staying here, as some hotels have pools, and the beach is only minutes away by foot. The downside is that you're about a 15-minute walk (though it's a pleasant one along the beach promenade) from the medina.

Tip: Waiting at each entrance to the medina, especially Bab Marrakech and Bab Sbâa, are Essaouira's "trolley boys." For 10dh to 20dh ($1.25–$2.50/65p–£1.25), depending on the load, they will transport your luggage to your accommodations within the medina. Don't be shy to use them; it doesn't cost much and will let you take in the atmosphere. It's especially worthwhile if you're going to look at a few establishments before deciding.

Essaouira's peak tourist season is during the summer holiday months of July and August, though June is also quite busy largely due to the Gnaoua & World Music Festival (p. 21), along with the Christmas/New Year period. During these months, it's best to prebook. The winter months from November to February can be exceptionally cold, and most residences within Essaouira's medina, *maisons d'hôte* included, suffer badly from dampness. During this time, enquire about the availability of heating before deciding on where to stay. For more information, read my "Tips on Accommodations" (p. 60).

MEDINA
Very Expensive

Ryad Watier *(Kids)* Built in 1913 as Essaouira's first Islamic school, this derelict building was discovered in 2003 by journeyman Jean-Gabriel Nucci, who restored it to what it is today: an elegant *maison d'hôte*. The riad is located in one of the less touristed areas of the medina, yet it's only a short walk away from most restaurants and shops. Frenchman Jean-Gabriel's diverse background is seen around the riad (he was born in Algeria and used to run an art gallery in Australia's outback) in Aboriginal artwork and traditional French landscape paintings. Although larger than most riads—the 10 rooms are set out over four levels—Ryad Watier still exudes a homely atmosphere with no television or phones. There's a well-stocked library, a cozy dining/sitting room with open fireplace, plenty of potted plants and Berber carpets, Moroccan lanterns hanging from hand-carved stucco ceilings, and a small hammam.

Surrounding the covered, central courtyard are a range of different-size rooms, architect designed and named after historical Moroccan figures, with lots of wood furniture, Berber carpets, and *tadelakt*-rendered bathrooms with separate toilets. Some come with two bedrooms, a lounge, and a fireplace, and are an exceptional value for a family of four. Twin rooftop terraces host either sunbathers (bring your own towels, though) or diners (breakfast served, dinner on request). The riad kitchen also opens at midday for those who purchase food from the local market and want to make their own lunch. *Tip:* First-timers may find Ryad Watier a bit hard to locate, so ask for an escort to meet you upon your arrival outside the medina walls.

16 rue de Ceuta, Medina, Essaouira. ⓒ/fax **024/476204** or 061/346818. www.ryadwatier.com. 10 units. 935dh–1,320dh ($117–$165/£58–£83) double; 1,485dh–1,650dh ($186–$206/£93–£103) 2-room suite. Children 2–12 165dh ($21/£10) in parent's room; under 2 free. Rates include breakfast. No credit cards. **Amenities:** In-house restaurant; hammam; kitchen for lunch; library. *In room:* No phone.

Expensive

Hotel Lalla Mira ★★★ Felicitas de Christ's hotel is Morocco's foremost environmentally responsible establishment, and is also one of Essaouira's friendliest and most comfortable. Felicitas built the hotel above the town's oldest hammam (p. 352), and the freedom of not having to renovate an existing building allowed her, along with her German designer and Moroccan architect, to construct Hotel Lalla Mira as true to her environmental beliefs as possible. Open since 2004, this hotel boasts a sophisticated solar-powered underfloor heating system, which subsequently nullifies the humidity (and moldy smell) that many of Essaouira's other hotels constantly suffer from. This system also heats the renovated hammam, whose water is then pumped into the hotel's toilet cisterns. The walls were constructed from handmade clay bricks, and the bathrooms are rendered in different colors of hand-polished *tadelakt*. The rooms are of varying sizes and configurations, and boast allergy-friendly furnishings such as pure wool curtains, organic cotton linens, and firm mattresses filled with a locally made, nonabsorbent, mite-free natural fiber called *kapok*. Some of the smaller rooms are for single travelers only, while the suites offer separate lounges or a private terrace. A small split-level rooftop terrace allows for some quality sunbathing, while the restaurant (p. 349) sources as much local, organic produce as possible, some of it from the hotel's own plot in the countryside. Led by manager Khalid Saadi, the very friendly and attentive English-speaking staff includes a private wheelbarrow porter who will meet guests at a pre-organized time and place outside the small medina to transport luggage to the hotel.

14 rue d'Algérie, Medina, Essaouira. ℂ 024/475046. Fax 024/475850. www.lallamira.net. 13 units. 436dh ($55/£27) single; 692dh ($87/£43) double; 772dh–920dh ($97–$115/£48–£58) suite. Children under 4 70dh ($8.75/£4.40) in parent's room. Rates include breakfast and hammam entry. TPT not included. MC, V. **Amenities:** Restaurant; hammam; Internet. *In room:* Satellite TV.

Riad Lalla Mogador *Finds* This recently renovated 1930s dar offers a variety of good-value rooms in a homely environment, where guests are handed a key to the front door and management is discreet and unobtrusive. Located in a small alcove just a short walk from the Bab Marrakech medina entrance, guests step through a low, heavy door into a tranquil ground-floor courtyard, where the four original columns are accompanied by a gurgling fountain. The rooms—located on the three upper floors off verandahs of blue railings and accessed by a steep, narrow staircase—are all individually furnished with cotton and wool bed linens; carpets; and curtains in colors of ocean blue, deep burgundy, and gold. Some rooms offer a private balcony, others a fireplace or small lounge; there are both split-level and single-floor configurations that can accommodate up to five people. Most have *tadelakt*-rendered bathrooms with welcoming exterior windows. Breakfast can be taken privately in the courtyard or on the communal rooftop terrace with great beach and medina views. Guests are welcome to venture out to the Quartier des Dunes to use the pool at sister property Riad Zahra (below).

12 rue Iraq, Medina, Essaouira. ℂ 024/476744. Fax 024/473404. www.riadlallamogador.com. 7 units. 400dh–1,000dh ($50–$125/£25–£63) double. Children 4–12 65dh ($8.15/£4.05) in parent's room; under 4 free. Rates include breakfast. MC, V. **Amenities:** Laundry service; Internet. *In room:* Satellite TV, Ethernet connection, no phone.

The Teahouse ★★★ *Value Kids* This 200-year-old classic Souiri residence was formerly owned by a wealthy trader dealing in exotic fabrics and spices. Thanks to Anglo-Moroccan couple Alison and Jandal, it's now a captivating combination of a traditional Moroccan dar and an English country cottage. The Teahouse's two floors of apartments are outfitted in soft hues of sage, turmeric, rose, and mauve, and filled (by Alison) with a quirky assortment of Moroccan antique furnishings. Each floor, or apartment, has two en suite bedrooms, a kitchen, and sitting room complete with fireplace, which is much needed in the winter. Each apartment can sleep four, and will accommodate an additional small child if need be. Solo travelers and couples are given the same exclusivity of each apartment, and are only charged per person. The whole house can also be rented. Alison's personal touches include lavender-scented linens, a personal orientation tour, and a candle-lit roof terrace for romantic sunsets. She's also very knowledgeable about Morocco's traditional artisan history, and is one half of the highly recommended Craft Treasures of Morocco tour (www.styles-morocco.com) mentioned in chapter 2. Guests can choose to be totally self-sufficient (breakfast is included in the cost and delivered fresh each morning), or can join Alison's housekeeper for a visit to the fresh produce souks and enjoy an impromptu cooking lesson. The Teahouse isn't for everyone, but it's definitely peaceful, homely, and attracts a slightly alternative, artsy guest.

74 bis rue Laâlouj, in a short alley off the street, Medina, Essaouira. ☎ 024/783543. www.theteahouse.net. 2 units. 448dh ($56/£28) per person. Children under 12 80dh ($10/£5) in parent's room. Rates include breakfast. Optional 3-course dinner 100dh ($13/£6.25) per person. Credit card details required to secure bookings of up to 7 days. For stays of 8 days and longer, U.K. bank deposit of 50% required. Credit cards not accepted for payment; payment in cash upon arrival. **Amenities:** Kitchen; babysitting; small library; rooftop terrace; Internet. *In room:* Jellabahs.

Moderate

Dar Alouane This small dar lives up to its alternative name, La Maison des Couleurs, with shades of green, yellow, orange, and pink throughout—and an owner/manager who is just as bright. It took 4 years of renovation before German native Petra Köppe—formerly a teacher of English and Japanese—opened this decidedly un-Moroccan *maison d'hôte* in 2004. Guests are greeted by a courtyard with a small garden, Roman columns, and large black-and-white floor tiles. One interior wall, which is shared with the dar's neighbors, is where two bathrooms sit almost suspended in air in a very creative feat of construction. The compact, colorful rooms are simply furnished; some come with a window that adds light and air to the whole house. A small kitchen is available for use by guests, and the bright-green, split-level rooftop terrace offers up superb 360-degree views. It's very reasonably priced, and is close to most of the medina's restaurants and shops.

66 rue Touahen, Medina, Essaouira. ☎/fax 024/476172. www.geocities.com/hausderfarben. 7 units. 350dh–450dh ($44–$56/£22–£28) double with shared bathroom; 600dh ($75/£38) double with private bathroom. Low-season discounts available. No credit cards. **Amenities:** Kitchen. *In room:* No phone.

Hotel les Matins Bleus *(Value (Kids* In the heart of the medina, this 18th-century former school and *caid*'s (judge) residence has been in the Maboul family since 1920. English-speaking brothers Abdel and Samir, and their cousin Youssef, have converted the family home into one of the most welcoming *maisons d'hôte* in Essaouira. There's a range of different size and furnished rooms: The original bedrooms have had bathrooms added and are more traditional in design, while there are newer rooms on the rooftop terrace that are relatively smaller and more simply furnished. Families are welcome and encouraged to stay in one or both of the two large suites. The covered central courtyard leads to a communal dining room. Other rooms on the ground floor include a lounge with a TV and stereo, and the house kitchen, where resident cook Myriam offers home-cooked meals, afternoon tea with pastries, kid's meals, special high-carb dishes for surfers, and cooking lessons. She will even create a special dinner menu for guests and their invited friends. This accommodating attitude stems from that of the three young lads, who are part of the surf culture in Essaouira and have a management style that is very professional and courteous, but also unobtrusive and easy-going. *Tip:* Room no. 5 is classified as a single because of its solitary double bed and private outside shower. However, it can also accommodate a couple, and is a bargain at 300dh ($38/£19).

22 rue de Draa (off rue L'Attarine), Medina, Essaouira. ℂ/fax 024/785363. www.les-matins-bleus.com. 10 units. 275dh–420dh ($34–$53/£17–£26) single; 300dh–460dh ($38–$58/£19–£29) double; 840dh–920dh ($105–$115/£53–£58) suite. Children under 11 90dh ($11/£5.65) in parent's room. Rates include breakfast. TPT not included. MC, V plus 5% admin fee. Closed last 2 weeks of Nov. **Amenities:** Restaurant; laundry service; solar hot water. *In room:* No phone.

Riad Marosko *(Kids)*   Located at the end of a small lane close to the medina's Bab Marrakech, this quiet and intimate riad is the creation of multilingual French couple Rosko and Mari Becquet, who fell under Essaouira's spell during the Gnaoua Music Festival in 2000. The house's original Portuguese columns stand in a yellow and white courtyard with a central fountain. The narrow yet spacious rooms are located on multiple levels and are mainly split level, with a ground-floor lounge and separate bathroom, and two open bedrooms located on steep mezzanines, accommodating up to five people (better for families with teenagers rather than tots). There are, however, two single-level rooms on the ground floor that also offer wheelchair access. A delightfully cozy salon is furnished with numerous Gnaoua musical instruments and a small library, while throughout the house are paintings, objets d'art, and souvenirs from Rosko's and Mari's North African travels. Breakfast is served from the small kitchen on the rooftop terrace, where guests are encouraged to relax, sunbathe, and enjoy the ocean views.

66 Impasse, rue d'Agadir, Medina, Essaouira. ℂ 024/475409. www.riad-marosko.com. 7 units. 550dh–650dh ($69–$81/£34–£41) double. Children under 12 stay free in parent's room. TPT not included. Rates include breakfast. No credit cards. **Amenities:** Library; wheelchair accessible rooms. *In room:* No phone.

OUTSIDE THE MEDINA
Very Expensive
Océan Vagabond   This chic hotel, opened in 2006 by French couple Sebastien and Marie Deflandre and managed by daughter Juliette, is only 1 block from the beach and a short walk from Essaouira's medina. The multilevel white building features plenty of natural sandstone and dark wood throughout, with wavelike curves and Islamic arches. The spacious rooms are all individually furnished, with themes such as India, Bali, Borneo, Berber, Samurai, and Masai giving some indication of each room's style. Families are accommodated with interconnecting rooms. Rooms have either a medina or sea view; however, those with a medina view are very close to the street and tend to be noisy, so I recommend those with a sea view, which also look out over the pleasant back yard with its grassed lawn and heated pool. A health center on the far side of the garden offers a hammam and beauty and massage treatments. The hotel's ground floor centers around a large salon with fireplace, leather lounges, and plenty of oversize floor cushions, and the hotel bar and restaurant serves a delicious buffet breakfast daily. The restaurant also offers a dinner menu of mainly French and Asian cuisine, though meals inconveniently must be ordered in the morning.

4 av. Lalla Aïcha, Essaouira. ℂ 024/479222 or 010/079227. Fax 024/474285. www.oceanvagabond.com. 14 units. 1,320dh–2,310dh ($165–$289/£83–£144) double. Children 2–12 165dh ($21/£10) in parent's room; under 2 free. Rates include breakfast and entry to hammam. MC, V. Guarded parking. **Amenities:** Restaurant; pool; hammam; beauty and massage center; babysitting; laundry service; safe; salon w/TV/DVD; library; Internet. *In room:* Satellite TV, hair dryer.

Expensive

Riad Zahra *(Kids)* In 2006, Xavier and Edith Panades bought this established hotel in Essaouira's Quartier des Dunes and set about adding to its already wide range of rooms and amenities. Zahra is a large hotel constructed in a traditional design, with most rooms surrounding a two-level, columned central courtyard while offering full or partial sea views. The spacious and airy rooms feature brightly colored local fabrics and large bathrooms with ochre or pale yellow *tadelakt*-rendered walls. There are four newer rooms on the rooftop terrace that are Moroccan in design, with carved-cedar wood and Berber carpets. These rooms in particular are family friendly, as they are separated from the other rooms and share a common entrance, although some of the large suites—with two beds and a seaview balcony—are also options for those with children. A large pool is protected from the strong sea breeze and is surrounded by plenty of sun lounges, with a shady Berber tent located in the corner. The in-house restaurant features low-lying tables with cloth lounges of bright oranges and reds, and offers an all-day snack menu of hamburgers, chicken dishes, and pastas, along with an evening *menu du jour* (120dh/$15/£7.50). A second, more intimate bar-restaurant will soon be constructed on the rooftop terrace to take advantage of the fantastic sea views.

90 Quartier des Dunes, Essaouira. © 024/474822. Fax 024/474312. www.riadzahra.com. 23 units 450dh–750dh ($56–$94/£28–£47) single; 550dh–850dh ($69–$106/£34–£53) double; 500dh–650dh ($63–$81/£31–£41) suite. Children 4–12 65dh ($8.15/£4.05) in parent's room; under 4 free. Rates include breakfast. MC, V. Secure parking. Follow signs from the junction of the Marrakech-Agadir roads. **Amenities:** Restaurant; pool. *In room:* Satellite TV, Ethernet connection.

WHERE TO DINE

Essaouira's culinary scene is one of the most relaxed and varied within Morocco, with styles ranging from beachside cafes and outdoor fish grills to trendy establishments and some of the finest seafood restaurants in the country. Unlike the country's other medinas, here many places serve alcohol, though most will still close for lunch on Friday. As with the accommodations within the medina, it's best to prebook your dinner reservation during the peak holiday months of July and August, and definitely during the Gnaoua & World Music Festival in June.

MEDINA
Moderate

Les Chandeliers INTERNATIONAL/MOROCCAN This relaxed, casual restaurant offers an intimate atmosphere and a varied menu that covers most tastes. Seafood dishes include *briouates de l'océan* and a couscous *aux poissons*. Meat eaters are offered dishes such as lamb tagine with apricots and prunes, and a succulent beef tagine with figs and nuts. There are four three-course set menus (including a vegetarian), as well as a selection of pizzas. Those with a sweet tooth will have to decide between chocolate *crepeiteroles* or chocolate *profiteroles* for dessert. The ground floor is a more formal setting with candle-lit tables and wrought-iron chairs, while a small mezzanine level with salon-style lounges and mosaic tables is the preferred spot for a drink with tapas, accompanied by background world music.

14 rue Laâlouj. © 024/475827. Main courses 60dh–115dh ($7.50–$14/£3.75–£7.20); pizza 55dh–85dh ($6.90–$11/£3.45–£5.30); set menus 75dh–95dh ($9.40–$12/£4.70–£5.95); tapas 35dh ($4.40/£2.20); desserts 35dh–50dh ($4.40–$6.25/£2.20–£3.15). Alcohol served. No credit cards. Daily 6:30–11pm.

Restaurant Baraka MOROCCAN This former Jewish school may not be inviting at first sight, but by the end of your meal, you'll be ordering another juice cocktail and enjoying the eclectic mix of patrons that this restaurant seems to draw. Tasty appetizers include fried phyllo cigars of cheese and a range of salads including tabbouleh. The menu is mainly local with various couscous dishes, tagines, grilled meats, and fresh seafood, often charcoal grilled in front of you. Desserts are suitably decadent, although unfortunately the tantalizing chocolate and Bailey's Irish Cream crêpe is usually not available. The dining rooms surround a wild, central garden, and are a strange combination of silver, gold, and mustard yellow, while the background sounds can range from Andalous and opera to swing and rock.

113 av. Mohammed el Qouiri. ℂ 024/473561. Fax 024/473899. Appetizers 30dh–50dh ($3.75–6.25/£1.90–£3.15); main courses 40dh–85dh ($5–$11/£2.50–£5.30); desserts 30dh–55dh ($3.75–$6.90/£1.90–£3.45). Alcohol served. No credit cards. Daily noon–2:30pm and 6:30–10:30pm.

Restaurant Lalla Mira 🌟🌟🌟 MOROCCAN/SEAFOOD/VEGETARIAN   This split-level restaurant is on the ground floor of the hotel of the same name (p. 345), and continues with its owner's high standards of organic, natural, and environmentally friendly beliefs. The menu offers simple and healthy olive oil–based cuisine, with as much locally sourced and organic produce as possible. Vegetarians will delight in diverse dishes such as falafel with tahini and julienned vegetables, and corn polenta with niçoise ratatouille. Fresh seafood is offered daily, including a fish tagine cooked in sesame oil, and a filet of Dorade in a basil-and-tomato sauce accompanied by fresh seasonal vegetables. Traditional dishes include lamb *tanjia* for four and chicken-and-almond *pastilla*. Come time for dessert, bypass the delicious lemon cheesecake for a selection of locally made cheeses. Rounding off the menu nicely are a range of fresh juices, salads, omelets, soups, and a choice of four filling breakfasts or the breakfast buffet.

14 rue d'Algérie. ℂ 024/475046. Fax 024/475850. www.lallamira.net. Breakfast buffet 60dh ($7.50/£3.75); breakfast a la carte 20dh–40dh ($2.50–$5/£1.25–£2.50); appetizers 25dh–50dh ($3.15–$6.25/£1.55–£3.15); main courses 40dh–95dh ($5–$12/£2.50–£5.95); *tanjia* 150dh ($19/£9.40). Alcohol served. MC, V. Daily 7:30–11am, noon–2:30pm, and 7–10:30pm.

Inexpensive

Essaouira's **fish market,** located next to the spice souk off rue Souk Jdid, is where the town's two daily catches are bought and sold, and is also where you can indulge in the freshest seafood meal you'll ever have. The first catch usually comes in around 9 or 9:30am, and the second between 5:30 and 6:30pm. If you can stomach the smell, there are two simple restaurants tucked away in one of the corners, where you can take your purchase to be grilled or fried, served with olives, bread, and salad.

In between place Moulay Hassan and the port are Essaouira's well-known outdoor **seafood grills** 🌟🌟🌟. A selection of the day's catch is on display at each stall, and diners simply choose their meal and have it grilled on the spot. There are wood benches in front of each stall, or you can sit nearby on the medina's ramparts, overlooking the ocean below. The grills are open daily from mid-morning to late, depending on the season and daily catch.

Chez Boujmaa PATISSERIE   Open all day, every day, this small shop is the best spot to grab some delicious Moroccan pastries and biscuits. There's usually a choice of around 20 different delicacies, all sold by weight, as well as a range of dairy products for those who are self-catering. It's very conveniently located around the corner from the cafes off place Moulay Hassan.

Corner of av. Allal ben Abdellah and rue el Hajjali. No phone. 10dh ($1.25/65p) per 100 grams. Daily 6:30am–11pm (later in summer).

La Petite Perle ℛ MOROCCAN   For 25 years, this travelers' favorite has been serving simple and tasty local cuisine at very reasonable prices and with efficient, friendly service. The menu includes all the Moroccan standards—their *harira* soup is one of the best in town—plus a few pasta dishes. Vegetarians are relatively well catered for with tagine, couscous, spaghetti, and omelet options, and the five set menus are an excellent value for those looking for a three-course meal. The simple interior of traditional low-lying tables, walls and floor adorned with carpets, and plenty of cushions and candles makes for a relaxed and cheap meal.

2 rue el Hajjali. ℂ 024/475050. *Harira* soup 8dh (50¢/25p); main courses 40dh–60dh ($5–$7.50/£2.50–£3.75); set menus 55dh–95dh ($6.90–$12/£3.45–£5.95). No credit cards. Daily noon–3:30pm and 7–10:30pm.

La Triskalla ℛℛ VEGETARIAN/CAFE   This cavernous cafe is in a quiet section of the medina and attracts a young crowd of both locals and travelers who enjoy the mainly veggie dishes and chilled-out ambience. The largely un-Moroccan menu is a breath of fresh air, and mirrors the young and modern English-speaking staff, ably led by manager Saïd Enmili. Miso or *bissara* (fava bean) soups, fresh and crunchy salads, omelets, and specialties such as vegetarian lasagna are joined by delicious delights such as buckwheat pancakes—try the carrot and pumpkin. For something sweet, try the daily fruit tart, perhaps accompanied by a freshly squeezed juice (try the carrot, lemon, and garlic if you're feeling a bit run down) or one of a large selection of herbal and *chai* teas. The stone and *tadelakt* interior consists of a ground floor and mezzanine level, with low-lying candle-lit tables and artwork from up-and-coming local artists. It's Wi-Fi connected, and on selected nights Saïd sets up the DVD player and screens various environmental, wildlife, and cultural movies.

58 rue Touahen. ℂ 024/476371 or 066/252065. Soups and salads 10dh–30dh ($1.25–$3.75/65p–£1.90); pancakes 15dh–25dh ($1.90–$3.15/95p–£1.55); main courses 26dh–40dh ($3.25–$5/£1.65–£2.50); juices and teas 10dh–18dh ($1.25–$2.25/65p–£1.15). No credit cards. Daily noon–4pm and 6–10:30pm (longer hours June–Sept).

Les 3 Portes ITALIAN   This hip and intimate pizzeria—located underneath a section of the medina's ramparts—is owned and managed by a group of young and vibrant sisters and cousins hailing from Casablanca, who after initial local resistance are now operating one of Essaouira's most popular restaurants. A welcome variant for those suffering from tagine and couscous fatigue, the menu offers a fairly simple yet delicious range of Italian standards. Eleven choices of toppings from their wood-fired pizza oven include a Mogador with tuna, prawns, and calamari, and an Indian with chicken and onions. There's also a selection of pastas and risotto; the saffron and seafood is a personal favorite. There are veggie options as well, and a take-away service is handy for those wishing to eat on the beach. Alcohol is not available for purchase, but you can bring your own.

34 rue L'Attarine. ℂ 075/548792 or 012/014117. Pizzas 45dh–60dh ($5.65–$7.50/£2.80–£3.75); main courses 45dh–55dh ($5.65–$6.90/£2.80–£3.45). No credit cards. Tues–Sun 10:30am–3pm and 7–10:30pm.

BEACHFRONT
Expensive
Le Chalet de la Plage SEAFOOD   This beachfront institution has some of the best seafood in town. Built entirely of wood in 1893, the restaurant is in its fourth family of proprietors, the Jeannots, and the dark, maritime-theme interior is adorned with pictures and mementos of a past guest list that includes a French president and Hollywood movie stars. The favored tables (and they squeeze a fair few in) are under a weathered blue-and-beige pergola that looks directly onto the beach and around to

the port. While smooth jazz and swing plays in the background, diners feast on items from a French-language menu that offers Oualidia oysters, shrimp, calamari, lobster, and a wide selection of line fish. There's also a small choice of other meats, soups and salads, three-course set menus, and Chez Jeannot's *suggestions du jour*. A well-stocked bar is complimented by a select wine list, chosen by local vintner Charles Melia. It's not cheap (there's a minimum charge of 100dh/$13/£6.25 per person) and can at times be frightfully chi-chi, but the cuisine and views are worth the indulgence.

Bd. Mohammed V. (€) 024/475972. Fax 024/476419. Appetizers 45dh–75dh ($5.65–$9.40/£2.80–£4.70); main courses 70dh–180dh ($8.75–$23/£4.40–£11); set menus 150dh ($19/£9.40) and 180dh ($23/£11). Alcohol served. MC, V. Tues–Sat noon–3pm and 7–10pm; Sun noon–3pm; Mon 7–10pm.

Restaurant Côte Plage INTERNATIONAL   This restaurant's stylish maritime-theme interior, beachfront location, and exquisite menu is a winning combination that deserves more clients than it usually entertains. Formerly also a tapas bar, the restaurant now solely focuses on its fine cuisine. Chef Menad Berkani's delicious dishes include goat-cheese *croustillant* with walnuts and crystallized vegetables, sword-fish carpaccio marinated in aged Parmesan and lime juice, and wolfish cooked in aniseed butter with a fine ratatouille. Vegetarians unfortunately have to make do with a basil, tomato, and Parmesan penne pasta, or a platter of cheeses, salad, and argan oil. There's a three-course *menu du jour*, as well as a kids' menu with a hamburger or fried fish, french fries or rice, and ice cream. Diners can choose from the air-conditioned interior with contemporary European tables or an outside area with large blue umbrel-las, wood furniture with white-vinyl cushions, and glass wind breakers.

Bd. Mohammed V (opposite the Sofitel Hotel). (€) 024/479000. Appetizers 95dh–120dh ($12–$15/£5.95–£7.50); main courses 70dh–160dh ($8.75–$20/£4.40–£10); menu du jour 300dh ($38/£19); kids' menu 95dh ($12/£5.95). Alcohol served. AE, MC, V. Daily noon–3pm and 7–10:30pm.

Inexpensive

Océan Vagabond INTERNATIONAL/CAFE   This is a great place for a late breakfast or long lunch, and is the only beachfront establishment directly on the sand. The blue-and-white "beach shack" is set around two shady acacia trees, with lots of low-level tables, lounges and deck chairs, and umbrellas of woven grass. Funky Latino and world music plays in the background, as diners choose from the varied menu or simply relax with a beer or juice. There's a good selection of breakfasts, homemade cakes and tarts, as well as fresh juices and ice creams. Most main dishes are light meals, including some great salads—try Le Chèvre with goat cheese, lettuce, tomato, onion, and dried fruits—along with baguettes, panini, hamburgers, pizza, and grilled chicken and fries. There's also a *menu du jour* that is usually a tagine, couscous, or pasta dish. In keeping with the relaxed atmosphere here, the young waitstaff is easygoing—if at times a bit too casual—and friendly.

Bd. Mohammed V (next to Club Mistral). Breakfast 35dh–50dh ($4.40–$6.25/£2.20–£3.15); light meals 30dh–70dh ($3.75–$8.75/£1.90–£4.40); menu du jour 80dh–100dh ($10–$13/£5–£6.25). Alcohol served. No credit cards. Daily 9:30am–6pm.

Restaurant de la Baie INTERNATIONAL/CAFE   Another beachfront establish-ment, the de la Baie is less formal than those to its north, and is a good spot for lunch or a drink, accompanied by some great people-watching. The interior is split into two sections—a simply furnished restaurant and separate glassed cafe—but it's outside where you want to be, with tables set on the pedestrian promenade and overlooking the wide beach. The menu offers a good variety of light meals, including grilled calamari, savory crepes, panini, and pizzas. More substantial dishes are available, such as grilled chicken, beef brochettes, bolognaise or seafood spaghetti, chile shrimp, or a choice of beef or chicken tagine. For those just wanting a drink, the beer and wine selection is very reasonably priced, or you can order from the cafe for a coffee and tea.

Bd. Mohammed V. © 024/474076. All dishes 30dh–60dh ($3.75–$7.50/£1.90–£3.75). Alcohol served. MC, V. Wed–Mon noon–9pm.

WHAT TO SEE & DO

Essaouira is both a seaside port and beach resort, and although it lacks any great official sights, when combined with its artisan's markets, relaxed cafe-restaurant scene, and photogenic ramparts, it's a great place to while away a few days. The secret to enjoying Essaouira is to not be in a rush. Try to budget in a few days here, and you'll leave feeling refreshed, relaxed, and may very well plan to come back for an even longer stay.

MEDINA

Hammam Lalla Mira 𝒦𝒦   This is the oldest traditional public bath in Essaouira, traditionally used by Gnaoua slaves who gave it the name of their yellow spirit, "Lalla Mira." Since its renovation during the building of the hotel now located above it (p. 345), it has become the country's first hammam to be heated with solar thermal equipment, in keeping with owner Felicitas de Christ's strong environmental ethics. It's also a very beautiful, yet small, hammam, resplendent in natural *tadelakt* walls and green polished-clay tiling. The hammam's main clients are women—locals and travelers—who come for a traditional wash with black soap, a body scrubbing, or *grommage,* which uses a scrubbing mitten, a finely ground pumice stone, and argan oil all for 180dh ($23/£11). Separate *grommage* or massages cost 75dh ($9.40/£4.70) each.

14 rue d'Algérie. Daily 9:30am–7pm (for women) and 7–10pm (for men, by reservation only).

Musée Sidi Mohammed ben Abdallah   If you're wandering along rue Laâlouj, pop your head into the Musée Sidi Mohammed ben Abdallah, located next to the post office. Named after the town's founding father, this recently renovated, two-story, 19th-century mansion hosts an interesting collection of old coins, antique carpets, weapons, and examples of traditional Moroccan dress, along with a small gallery of pictures of late-19th-century Essaouira.

Rue Laâlouj. © 024/475300. Admission 10dh ($1.25/65p) adults, 3dh (40¢/20p) children 5–12. Wed–Mon 8:30am–noon and 2:30–6:30pm.

Place Moulay Hassan   The medina's focal point, this pedestrian-only square is lined with cafes and shops, and is perfect for a lazy morning or afternoon of people-watching. During the Gnaoua & World Music Festival (p. 21), a large portion of the square becomes one of the festival's main stages. The cafes are lined up side by side in the narrow, northeastern section of the square, and all operate roughly from 8am to 11pm. One of the old-timers is **Café du France,** which serves an older, local clientele. Close by is **Chez ben Mostafa,** one of the newer, alfresco-style establishments. Their woven-cane chairs and large umbrellas are popular with travelers looking for surroundings a little more stylish. Around the corner from these cafes, facing the square's large open area, is **Gelateria Dolce Freddo** 𝒦𝒦𝒦. This local institution serves homemade Italian ice cream by the scoop, and is open daily until late.

Skala de la Kasbah   Surrounding Essaouira's UNESCO World Heritage medina are its 18th-century walls, or ramparts. On the northern and western flanks, these ramparts protect the medina from the crashing Atlantic waves, and are accessible from rue Skala. This section of the ramparts is called Skala de la Kasbah, and a climb up the steps to the top platform—with a line of Portuguese brass cannons still pointing out to sea—and its northern bastion, Bab Ljhad, offers a fantastic view of both the medina and the ocean, and is a popular meeting point for the town's youngsters. Built into the Skala de la Kasbah are a number of wood workshops (see "Shopping" below). The platform is always accessible, but Bab Ljhad closes at sunset.

Rue Skala. No admission fee. Year-round 24 hr., except Bab Ljhad, which closes at sunset.

Souks   Essaouira has a few small souks that are definitely worth exploring. **Souk des Bijoutiers,** the jeweler's souk, used to be a flea market, but today it's a small collection of jewelry shops, similar to the one in Tiznit, south of Agadir. Located between avenue l'Istiqlal and rue Sayaghine, many of the shops house generations of jewelers, their forefathers originally exposed to the trade by the town's 19th-century Jewish population. Although traditionally trained, some of the work presently produced by these jewelers is delightfully contemporary.

Coming off rue Sayaghine is rue el Khabbazine, where a collection of Berber cafes is a perfect place to join in with the locals for a mint tea or coffee and perhaps a game of checkers. Opposite rue Sayaghine are two squares, **Le Joutia** and **place Marché de Grains.** They are connected by a small laneway occupied by the town's tailors, where handmade suits can be fashioned, sewn, and ready in a day or so. La Joutia, the smaller of the two, is the town's flea market. An amazing assortment of trash and treasure is on display here, much of it put up for auction every morning. Place Marché de Grains is better known as the Corn Market, which harks back to the square's original purpose as the weekly souk for the surrounding farmers to sell their corn and grains. Sadly, all that remains of this today are one or two lonely vendors selling their bags of corn kernels the old-fashion way, courtesy of a massive set of antique scales.

In one corner of the square is Toulaoui Café, a small family-run eatery serving sweet, piping-hot cups of mint tea; it's a great spot for rest and people-watching. They also cook a delicious couscous for lunch, every Tuesday and Friday. Most of the shops in the Corn Market are now spice stores, spilling over from Marché d'Epices (Spice Souk) across the road. The **Spice Souk** is still called Souk el Ghezel by some old Souiris, referring to its original function as the wool souk throughout much of the 19th and 20th centuries. Like the Corn Market, nowadays there is only one wool vendor selling his wares, as he has done every day since 1954. From 7 to 10am every Monday and Wednesday, his raw wool is washed and put up for auction. Outside the shop are traditional spinning spindles for sale, as well as an oversize set of antique scales. The remainder of the shops in the square are now Souiri versions of Morocco's famous *herboristes,* selling brightly colored spices, herbs, and concoctions. Adjacent to the Spice Souk is the **Fish Market** (see "Seafood Grills" under "Where to Dine," earlier).

OUTSIDE THE MEDINA

The Beach   Essaouira's wide, crescent-shaped bay is one long stretch of golden sand, and while perfect for a stroll, is often too windy for sunbathing. When the tide is out, the area closest to the medina becomes one large temporary football (soccer) pitch, and if you feel so inclined, is best viewed with a bottle of wine from the outdoor patio of the restaurant Le Chalet de la Plage (p. 350). South of the football pitches is the main entry point for kitesurfing and windsurfing (see "Active Vacation Planner"), but is also where most beach-goers congregate. From May to September, a large children's

The Good Oil

"Imma yargan igh ibbi neff mat ittarin" (Even when it is fallen, the argan tree will leave heirs). The evergreen, leathery leafed and spiny argan tree, also called Moroccan ironwood, is endemic to the Souss Valley and the lower slopes of the Atlas Mountains of southwest Morocco. Currently covering an area of approximately 8,000 sq. km (3,100 sq. miles) and numbering some 20 million, the trees bear fruit after 5 years, but only reach maturity at 60, with an average lifespan of 150 to 200 years, some living for up to 400 years. The olivelike drupes, or fruits, of the argan tree mature between May and July. The fruit is collectively gathered by hand in July and August, but this is only allowed after agreement within local councils; public criers relay the decision shouting from village to village "The argan is authorized!" Women gather the drupes (*afiash* in Berber) and dry them in the sun. They separate the nut from an outer white flesh, then crack open the nut to recover the kernels—usually one but sometimes up to three—within, which can contain up to 50 percent oil. These they roast and then grind to extract the oil. It takes 15 to 20 hours—depending on skill—to crack the 2 kilograms (4⅓ lb.) of nuts required to produce 1 liter of oil.

The argan woodland is a major contributor to the economic livelihoods of some two million Amazigh, the indigenous Berbers of the region. The trees are of such value to the Amazigh that they are often specifically included in legal lists of the assets of an estate. They also provide important forage for camels and goats, which have learned to climb up to the leaves and drupes. On top of this economic value, the deep-rooted, heat-resistant trees provide an important ecological anchor against erosion of soil and the encroaching Saharan sands.

However, drought, overgrazing, and firewood collecting are endangering the trees to the point that researchers estimate the argan population has decreased by at least 40% over the last 100 years. This motivated Dr.

playground is set up on the beach here, in front of the Restaurant de la Baie. Farther south are some camels and horses offered for (photogenic) rides along the beach by their overly competitive owners.

The Port ⚘   Essaouira's compact fishing port is the country's third largest (after Agadir and Safi) and is a very photogenic, atmospheric, and aromatic place to wander around. Most of the day, you'll find fishermen tending to their nets, wood fishing vessels being repaired or constructed, and the daily catches, usually around 9am and 5:30pm, being brought in. Also here is another of the town's bastions, Skala du Port, which can be climbed for a view of both the ocean and the medina. From the port you can also catch a boat ride around the uninhabited islands, Iles Purpuraires (Purple Isles), out in the bay of Essaouira. The largest island, Ile de Mogador, has some rusting, crumbling reminders of its history as both a bastion protecting the port and a 19th-century prison. Today the islands are a nature reserve, primarily to protect the endangered Eleanora's falcons, a migrant breeder that resides here from late April to

Zoubida Charrouf, a chemist and researcher at Rabat's Mohamed V University, to take a look into the active ingredients of argan oil. She found it to be rich in vitamins A and E, anti-oxidants, and unsaturated fatty acids, including omega 6. Dr. Charrouf joined with local officials to persuade the government to declare 2% of the argan forest off limits to grazing. In 1998, UNESCO took up the cause and declared part of the argan forest—including the 504-sq.-km (208-sq.-mile) Souss-Massa National Park—an international biosphere reserve.

Since women are the keepers of tradition, Dr. Charrouf turned to them and formed the Amal Women's Cooperative in the village of Tamanar, 70km (44 miles) south of Essaouira. There are now more than 30 argan oil women's cooperatives and a government body, the Mohammed V Foundation for Research and Argan Tree Preservation, that reports back to the king himself. There are two cooperatives south of Essaouira that are used to showing visitors around. Very few of the women speak English, but if you understand a little French, you'll be fine. **Co-opérative Amal** (© 024/788141) is in Tamanar, on the main Essaouira-Agadir road (68km/42 miles south of Essaouira), and **Co-opérative Tamounte** ✸✸✸ (© 024/476591 or 024/476092), opened by King Mohammed VI in 2007 and managed by the vivacious and vibrant Madame Taarabt, is in Tnine-Imi-n-Tlit (17km/11 miles east of Smimou, 39km/24 miles south of Essaouira).

Throughout most of southern Morocco, travelers can purchase a range of argan-based products including argan oil for cooking—its light, hazelnut-like flavor is perfect sprinkled on salads, couscous, and even popcorn—and massage; jars of an aromatic and delicious spread of ground almonds, honey, and argan oil called *amlou;* and soaps, lotions, and skin creams. Some roadside stalls are not selling the real deal, and may mix argan oil with cheaper olive oil.

the end of October. During this time you won't be allowed near the island, but at other times it's a pleasant outing if the weather is nice. Boats leave daily at 10:30 and 11:30am, and 3, 4, and 5:30pm, depending on the weather. Cost is 80dh ($10/£5) adults, 40dh ($5/£2.50) kids 5 to 12.

Skala du Port, Port du Pêche. Admission 10dh ($1.25/65p) adults; 3dh (40¢/20p) children 5–12. Daily 8:30am–noon and 2:30–6:30pm.

SHOPPING

Although lacking the vast array of medina shops or *foundouks* found in Marrakech and Fes, Essaouira's medina offers a terrific, small range of shopping experiences. Given the ease of navigation through the compact medina and a general lack of hassle from shopkeepers, some travelers prefer shopping here than in the bigger centers.

For those looking for groceries and alcohol, there are a few fresh produce stalls along avenue Zerktouni and a couple of small grocery shops at the southern end of avenue l'Istiqlal. There's a small supermarket outside the medina, Superette la Plage, off boulevard Mohammed V, on rue al Amira Lalla Amina, open daily from 9am to 9pm. Just outside Bab Doukala, on avenue Moulay Youssef, are a couple of shops selling alcohol, open Saturday to Thursday from 9am to 9pm.

ART

A number of art galleries displaying local and internationally recognized artists can be found close together within the medina. The most well-known is **Galeries Damgaard,** on avenue Oqba ibn Nafiaa (© **024/784446**). Danish art dealer Frederic Damgaard first visited Essaouira as an art student in 1969, returning frequently to collect works by local artists and eventually opening the gallery on the ground floor of a stone mansion in 1988. It's open daily from 10am to 1pm and 3 to 7pm. Nearby is the recently renovated **Espace Othello,** 9 rue Mohammed Layachi (© **024/475095**), owned by Belgian Mochel de Saint-Maux. **La Petite Galerie** ★★, under the archway at the beginning of rue ibn Rochd coming off place Moulay Hassan (© **065/660630;** fax 024/476431; www.artmajeur.com/soulaiman), is the showroom of local artist Slimane Drissi. His style of abstract humanism is both compelling and uplifting. Framed prints are on sale for 500dh to 3,000dh ($63–$375/£31–£188). Drissi's gallery is open daily from 9am to 9pm.

BEAUTY & FASHION

Argan oil and its associated beauty products (see "The Good Oil," above) are sold from shops throughout the medina. Products made specifically from Co-opérative Tamounte, under the product name Arganad, are for sale at **Chez Boujmah,** on the corner of avenue Allal ben Abdellah and rue el Hajjali. It's open daily from 6:30am to 11pm (later in summer). **Arga d'Or,** 5 rue ibn Rochd (© **061/601471** or 061/ 109287), is a dedicated argan shop with assistants on hand to display the various creams, soaps, and other beauty products, as well as selling cooking oil, argan honey, and the sweet *amlou* paste. It's open daily from 9am to 12:30pm and 2:30 to 8pm.

Raffia Craft, 82 rue d'Agadir (© **024/783632;** fax 024/474892), is the small outlet shop for local raffia fashion designer Miro. Most of his woven shoes and sandals are sold directly to European outlets, but there's still a quality selection of both men's and women's footwear to be found in this compact shop, open Monday to Saturday from 10am to 1pm and 3 to 7pm, and Sunday from 10am to 1pm. French fashion designer Litza Chemla's popular range of funky handbags and fashion accessories, **Poupa Litza,** is now available from her cavernous boutique at 135 bis av. Mohamed el Qouri (© **024/783565;** www.poupalitza.com), open Monday to Saturday from 9am to 12:30pm and 2:30 to 7pm.

CARPETS

In the far left corner of the small Le Joutia souk (see above) is shop no. 160, the only carpet shop within this souk and owned by **Abdellatif al Koujdaih** ★★ and his father for the past 40 years. In what must be the smallest shop in Morocco, Abdellatif has carpets stacked up to the walls. Most of the carpets are antique, or "preloved" as Abdellatif puts it, and are of Berber design. He also has a small selection of traditional marriage belts and other antiques, such as wood boxes specifically designed for holding mint tea glasses. He's open daily from 10am to 1pm and 3pm to "sundown."

FABRIC

For the past 30 years, Mohammed Oulad el Hajja has been selling the finest handwoven fabrics from his small shop, **Tissage Artisinal,** 15 rue Oudja (© **065/209297**).

Throw-overs, scarves, tablecloths, curtains, and yards of cloth—in wool, chenille cotton, and vegetable silk—come in all the colors of the rainbow. During weekdays, there are usually some local women at work on the loom within his shop. Credit cards are accepted. Hours are Monday to Saturday 9am to 9pm.

JEWELRY

Within the Souk des Bijoutiers (see above), shop no. 2 is owned by **Hamid El Asri** ✮✮✮ (© **068/515217**) and his two sons, Abdallah and Saïd, who produce some beautiful and original silver jewelry. Having learned the trade from their father, the two brothers are now letting their creativity flow, creating necklaces and pendants in designs influenced by such things as the stars and planets, combined with symbols of Arabic and Berber origin. Their prices are very reasonable, and have the customer, rather than the guides' commission, in mind. The shop is open daily from 10am to 10pm.

LEATHER

Along **rue Lattarine** you'll find a string of shops selling leather goods, such as bags, briefcases, *poufes*, and sandals. About halfway along this street, next to Hotel Souiri, is **Mohammed Schumacher,** who, as his name suggests, is a shoemaker. Mohammed's little shop is where he makes a range of footwear, mostly sandals, by hand; if there's none that fit, give him a day or so, and he'll make a pair to order. He's open daily from 9am to 7pm, but closes for Friday midday prayers.

MUSIC

The home of the Gnaoua & World Music Festival has surprisingly few music shops. One of the best is **Azza Lafnak d'Essaouira** ✮✮, Youssef Boumald's little musical treasure house at the base of the clock tower, on avenue Oqba ibn Nafiaa. He sells a wide range of Arabic, jazz, and world music, as well as CDs of past festivals. Daily hours are from 9:30am to 9:30pm. Mustapha Lacheb operates a similar shop, on avenue l'Istiqlal, close to the Wafa bank. Local Rasta-man Zak Zakaria's **Happy Shop** ✮✮, on the corner of rue ibn Rochd and rue Mohammed Diouri (© **077/325755**), is full of percussion instruments from all over the world, including West African *djembe* drums, Australian didgeridoos, and Arabic *darbuka* drums. He'll also provide lessons. Happy Shop is open daily from 9am to 5pm. Directly across from Happy Shop, on rue ibn Rochd, is the small workshop of local **drum maker Tigui Abdellah.** He styles West African *djembe* drums from the dried shells of the local agave cacti. His workshop is open daily from 9am to 5pm.

WOODWORK

Built into the ramparts of **Skala de la Kasbah** are a number of woodwork shops. These skilled craftsmen are working largely with both the trunk and the roots of the aromatic *thuya*, a short, scrublike conifer found only in northwest Africa, with small and endangered populations in Malta and southern Spain. The *thuya* tree produces a golden brown-red hard wood that is highly figured with small clusters of tight burls and can be polished to a fine luster. The craftsmen turn the wood into all manner of pieces, the more popular of which are chess boards, jewelry boxes, letter holders, book ends, and salad bowls. Some pieces also combine fine examples of marquetry. Shops selling *thuya* products are found all over Morocco, but these workshops are the real deal, and offer the chance to purchase a souvenir straight from the craftsmen's hands. Having said that, the tree is under pressure in Morocco from illegal logging, purely for the making of the products mentioned above. While it's easy to propose to travelers a boycott of these products, the livelihoods of the craftsmen also have to be taken into consideration. They work varying hours, but are generally open from Saturday to Thursday, 9am to 12:30pm and 3 to 8pm.

ESSAOUIRA AFTER DARK

There's no raging nightlife scene in Essaouira, but there are a few select places (most doubling as restaurants) where you can enjoy a drink. For a sunset drink with a view, try the beachfront **Le Chalet de la Plage** (p. 350), which has a pretty good wine list that includes a selection from a nearby winery. They usually prefer clients to eat, which can be solved by ordering an appetizer or two. Farther south along the beach is **Restaurant de la Baie** (p. 351). One of the more popular watering holes, especially around Gnaoua & World Music Festival time, is within the medina at the rooftop **Taros,** 2 rue Skala (© **024/476407**). Overlooking place Moulay Hassan, there are a couple of levels of lounges and tables, and an L-shape bar with overhead gas heaters during the colder months and live music over summer. It can be a bit windswept at times, but there are plenty of protected corners to enjoy your drink. It's also the "in" place for local ex-pats, and has a pretty good vibe on Friday and Saturday nights. Taros is open Monday to Saturday 8am to 11pm. Some of the restaurants in the medina that are also good for a drink: **Les Chandeliers** (p. 348), a cozy spot, especially upstairs on their mezzanine-level tapas lounge; **La Triskalla** (p. 350), where a younger, slightly alternative crowd comes to chill out; and **Restaurant Baraka** (p. 348), which often hosts live music on the weekends to accompany its menu of cocktails.

11

Southern Morocco:
The Souss & Anti-Atlas

Southern Morocco is vastly underappreciated compared to the more popular destinations over the High Atlas mountains to its north or the palm-fringed desert oases to its east. Most travelers stay in Agadir, Morocco's premier beach resort, and unfortunately bypass the rest of the region, preferring to fly in/fly out and sit on the beach. A city rebuilt from the ground up—after a devastating earthquake shortly after Morocco broke free from its colonial shackles—Agadir offers miles of golden beach and more than 300 days of sunshine. An obvious attraction for those wishing to soak up the rays and have some fun in the water—the country's best surf breaks are to the north—the city also provides a hassle-free break from the intensity that can be encountered farther north. Unfortunately, this is as far as many travelers go. The few who do venture away from the coast discover a Morocco of saffron-laced tea, pink-hued boulders, and rustic silver jewelry. The area is inhabited by indigenous Berbers who are fiercely proud of their heritage and overwhelmingly enthusiastic to show it to visitors.

The Oued Souss meanders its way between the High Atlas and Anti-Atlas mountains to its mouth just south of Agadir, along the way watering a wide and fertile valley and affording prosperity to its largest town, Taroudannt. This walled town is essentially still a market village and its inhabitants are largely ambivalent toward its billing as one of the country's most authentic and photogenic traveling experiences. East of the Oued Souss and in the foothills of the Anti-Atlas is one of the world's premier saffron-producing regions, where the price of the precious spice is a fraction of that to be found on grocer's shelves in the Western world.

Intrepid travelers exploring farther into the Anti-Atlas will be rewarded with the strikingly picturesque, boulder-strewn mountains protecting the idyllic Ameln Valley. The town of Tafraoute is a quiet gem here waiting to be discovered.

Tiznit is a mere hour's drive south from the bright lights of Agadir. The town has a history of jewelry making that began in the 19th century with Morocco's now-departed Jewish population and continues today with the town's Berber silversmiths, witnessed by the exquisite jewelry on display in this small town's *bijouterie* souk.

1 Agadir

Lying on the Atlantic coast at the mouth of the fertile Souss Valley and almost in the shadow of the Anti-Atlas mountains in the distance, Agadir is popular for one thing—its beach. Crescent-shaped Agadir Bay and its 9km (5½-mile) stretch of golden sand attracts large numbers of all-inclusive holidaymakers nearly year-round. Currently experiencing an increase in popularity as an alternative for those looking for a resort holiday with a twist, the city is largely hassle-free and has a pleasant, relaxed air about it, with the local Gadiris enjoying the current rise in prosperity.

Agadir's history is dotted with 16th-century Portuguese and 20th-century French interference, as well as a brief moment of German interest in the heady "Scramble for Africa" days pre-World War I. This is interspersed with Saâdian and Alaouite rule, but the greatest influence on today's Agadir occurred just 4 years after independence at 11:47pm on February 29, 1960. In 15 seconds, a violent earthquake shook the old city and buried 15,000 Gadiris alive under fallen rubble, leaving the remaining 50,000 inhabitants homeless. It was a particularly traumatic event for young Morocco, and King Mohammed V reacted quickly by declaring to his people, "If destiny decided to destroy Agadir, then its reconstruction depends on our faith and our will." The reconstruction was seen as a chance to build a modern city that would be a showcase of the "new" Morocco. The result is a well-designed (and earthquake-proof) city, unlike any other in Morocco, that's similar to a European beach resort but lacks any of the flamboyance or decadence. Travelers who have experienced other areas of Morocco (such as Essaouira, just 200km/124 miles up the coast) regularly bemoan a lack of any real atmosphere or personality, while some new arrivals to Morocco compare the city to more established resorts on the Mediterranean. To me, both points of view could be considered harsh. To stay in Agadir is to enjoy a city that is still developing its character and substance, influenced by the very people who have come to holiday here. It is only just starting to realize its potential as both a base to explore southern Morocco (convenient direct flights from Europe arrive at Agadir's al Massira airport daily) and a destination in its own right.

ORIENTATION
ARRIVING

BY PLANE   Due to Agadir's fly-in/fly-out beach resort status, the city's al-Massira airport ((**C** **028/839102**), located 25km (16 miles) east of the city center, is a large, modern building offering most of the services one would expect. There is only one terminal for both arrivals and departures, where you'll find desks for rental-car services, a ONMT tourist office (though it only hands out glossy brochures) open between 6am and midnight, a *téléboutique,* a couple of small souvenir shops, and a cafe/news agency that sells the odd English-language magazine and Agadir city maps.

There are also an ATM and three currency exchange booths that operate between 8am to 7pm but can sometimes be closed for no apparent reason or open outside of these hours. Though you will generally find a bank or bureau de change near your hotel or can usually exchange cash (they may not accept traveler's checks) at your hotel, it's best to pick up some Moroccan dirham at the airport just in case.

Many hotels are happy to arrange an airport pickup for you, and if you're on a package holiday, this should be included. *Grands* taxis are located straight outside the terminal and charge a set rate of 200dh ($25/£13; ignore the outdated sign stating a daily fee of 150dh) for the drive into town. Apart from dirham, they will normally accept euros and sometimes U.S. dollars and British pounds, but you will receive change only in dirham. *Tip:* Although they can take up to six passengers, these airport taxis will usually refuse to take multiple passengers who have only just met at the airport. This is to ensure that business is spread out. If you can, try to group up with any fellow independent travelers while still in the terminal.

Agadir

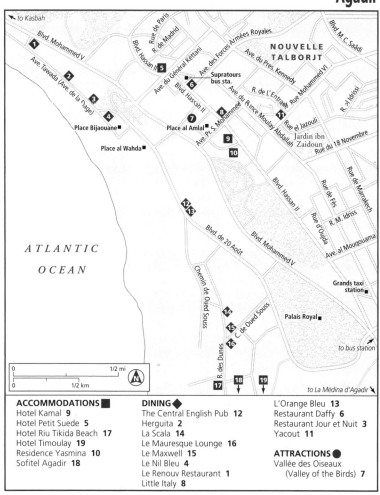

ACCOMMODATIONS ■
Hotel Kamal **9**
Hotel Petit Suede **5**
Hotel Riu Tikida Beach **17**
Hotel Timoulay **19**
Residence Yasmina **10**
Sofitel Agadir **18**

DINING ◆
The Central English Pub **12**
Herguita **2**
La Scala **14**
Le Mauresque Lounge **16**
Le Maxwell **15**
Le Nil Bleu **4**
Le Renouv Restaurant **1**
Little Italy **8**

L'Orange Bleu **13**
Restaurant Daffy **6**
Restaurant Jour et Nuit **3**
Yacout **11**

ATTRACTIONS ●
Vallée des Oiseaux
  (Valley of the Birds) **7**

A modern airport shuttle-bus departs for the city nine times a day between 8:30am and 12:30am. Tickets are bought at a counter in the arrivals area, and cost 60dh ($7.50/£3.75) per adult and 30dh ($3.75/£1.90) for children up to 12.

BY BUS   Buses to Agadir arrive daily from numerous cities in Morocco, including Marrakech (4 hr.; 70dh–90dh/$8.75–$11/£4–£5.65); Casablanca (9 hr.; 130dh–160dh/$16–$20/£8.15–£10); El Jadida (9 hr.; 110dh–130dh/$14–$16/£6.90–£8.15); Essaouira (4 hr.; 40dh–60dh/$5–$7.50/£2.50–£3.75); Fes (12 hr.; 230dh–250dh/$29–$31/£14–£16); Meknes (11 hr.; 200dh–230dh/$25–$29/£13–£14); Ouarzazate (8 hr.; 90dh–110dh/$11–$14/£5.65–£6.90); Rabat (11 hr.; 180dh–190dh/$23–$24/£11–£12); Tangier (16hr.; 250dh–280dh/$31–$35/£16–£18); Tafraoute (5 hr.; 60dh/$7.50/£3.75); Taroudannt (2½ hr.; 30dh/$3.75/£1.90); and Tiznit (2 hr.; 20dh/$2.50/£1.25).

Besides the ONCF-aligned Supratours, all long-distance bus companies arrive at the recently built *gare routière* on the outskirts of the city on rue Chair Alhamra Mohammed ben Brahim. From here it's at least a 20-minute trudge northwest into the city center. Alternatively, there are usually plenty of orange-color *petits* taxis around that will take you this short distance for around 10dh to 15dh ($1.25–$1.90/65p–95p). For onward travel from Agadir, all companies except Supratours depart from the bus station, where they each have their own ticket booths (you must pay in cash). For an early-morning departure, it's advisable to purchase your ticket the day prior to both ensure your seat and allow you time to ignore the touts and peruse the options available. Supratours and CTM buses to Marrakech are regularly full, so it's best to prebook your seat as early as possible. Supratours (© 028/841207), 10 rue des Orangiers, at the northern end of boulevard Hassan II, is open daily 9am to 7:30pm for ticket sales (cash only). The CTM ticket office (© 028/822077 or 022/438282 central reservations; www.ctm.ma) is still located across from the old, now demolished bus station on rue Yacoub el Mansour, is open 24 hours, and usually accepts credit cards (MasterCard or Visa) for payment.

Note: Just to confuse the issue, some long-distance buses to Agadir only travel as far as Inezgane, a bustling city some 13km (8 miles) southeast of Agadir and more conveniently located to the major access highways. If this is the case, there are plenty of *grands* taxis at the bus station plying the route between the two cities (7dh/90¢/45p). Ask upon purchasing your ticket so you may avoid this inconvenience or at least be preadvised.

BY *GRAND* TAXI   Long-distance *grands* taxis are located on the southern edge of the city on the corner of rue de Fes and rue d'Essaouira. The most regular routes include Essaouira (1½ hr.; 40dh/$5/£2.50); Marrakech (3½ hr.; 90dh/$13/£6.25); Taroudannt (1½hr.; 40dh/$5/£2.50); and Tiznit (1½ hr.; 40dh/$5/£2.50).

BY CAR   Driving into Agadir is pretty straightforward thanks to the modern, well-designed network of roads leading into and within the city. The coastal road from Essaouira enters the city at the northern end of boulevard Mohammed V, while the major highways from Tiznit, Taroudannt, and Marrakech converge at the hub city of Inezgane. From here a two-lane highway heads into Agadir's city center, where three of the four major parallel streets of boulevard Hassan II, boulevard Mohammed V, and boulevard du 20 Août make navigation relatively easy. Parking within the city usually isn't a problem, and the aggressive driving in other parts of the country is not a problem here.

A two-lane highway connecting the airport and the city center is one of the most hassle-free and navigable in all Morocco, and if you're picking up or dropping off a rental car here, there's a 24-hour petrol station, selling both leaded and unleaded, at the airport's entrance.

VISITOR INFORMATION

The **ONMT (Office National Marocain de Tourisme)** regional tourist office, on the upper level of Building Iguenouane, opposite the post office on the corner of avenue du Prince Moulay Abadallah and avenue Prince Sidi Mohammed (© **028/846377**), is open Monday to Thursday 8:30am to noon and 2:30 to 6:30pm, and on Friday from 8:30 to 11:30am and 2:30 to 6:30pm. This is the main tourist office of the region and has some useful lists of recommended accommodations and restaurants. There is also a local **Syndicat d'Initiative,** or tourist information bureau, on avenue

Mohammed V opposite avenue du Général Kéttani ((C) **028/840307**), which is open daily 9am to noon and 3 to 6pm. It carries a few pamphlets on local restaurants and attractions, as well as lists of emergency medical centers.

CITY LAYOUT

Agadir is very easy to navigate, and most travelers spend their time between the beach and the four parallel main roads heading away from the beach: boulevard du 20 Août, boulevard Mohammed V, boulevard Hassan II, and avenue du Prince Moulay Abdallah. Here you will find the city's restaurants, banks, and many of its moderate hotels and self-catering apartment blocks, along with a large number of fixed-price souvenir shops. A couple of blocks north of avenue du Prince Moulay Abdallah is an area known as *Nouvelle Talborjt*, where a number of basic hotels have replaced the old bus station. The northern end of Agadir Bay rises up past a new marina complex to the large industrial port and beyond to the beaches around Taghazout (p. 378). Boulevard du 20 Août provides access to the beach and its long promenade, where more restaurants and nightlife are to be found. At press time, this promenade was being extended farther south to eventually connect with the first of the beachfront resorts. Branching off south from boulevard du 20 Août are Chemin de Oued Souss and rue des Dunes, where an ever-increasing number of resorts are lined up side by side along the southern bay.

GETTING AROUND

Getting around Agadir is very easy. The beach-facing city center affords a degree of direction to even the most geographically challenged, and because there's no medina, streets are wide, straight, and well signposted.

BY FOOT This is how most people discover Agadir. Those based in the city center will find themselves walking everywhere, as most travelers' needs are met within a relatively small area. For those staying in one of the southern beachfront resorts, the 20-minute walk into the city center or beach promenade usually depends on the heat and the desire to leave the confines of the resort.

BY SCOOTER More for heading to the beaches north of Agadir rather than to get around the city itself, hiring a scooter or motorcycle is an option for a fun day out. Plan on paying around 250dh ($31/£16) per day for a scooter; 300dh ($38/£19) per day for a 125cc motorcycle. There's a string of pavement operations located along the shaded, southern stretch of boulevard du 20 Août, but I would steer clear of them. These boys are unlicensed, uninsured, and uninterested in anything other than your money. It's better to hire from a reputable agency such as **Transrent** ((C) **028/843378** or 061/385000), on the corner of boulevard du 20 Août and rue de la Jeunesse, open Monday to Saturday 9am to 7pm.

BY TAXI *Petits* taxis are really only needed to get around town if you are staying in a beachside resort, and this is where you'll find many of the orange-color vehicles waiting for business. Travelers heading to/from the bus station should also consider using one. At all times, request the driver to put on the meter. Most trips within the main tourist areas of Agadir should cost no more than 10dh ($1.25/65p) during the day and a bit more after 8pm, when a 50% evening surcharge kicks in. For transport to the bus station, the metered fare should only rise 5dh (65¢/30p) at the most. *Petits* taxis are only licensed to operate within the city environs. If you wish to head to Taghazout and the beaches north of the city (p. 378), charter a *grand* taxi. These Mercedes sedans take a maximum of six passengers—though four is comfortable—and cost around

250dh ($31/£16) for the day. You can find them on the southern edge of the city on the corner of rue de Fes and rue d'Essaouira.

BY CAR   As with scooter hire, renting a car for the day is only an option if you want to explore the coastline north of Agadir, which is easy to navigate and makes for a fun day. The high number of car-rental firms based in Agadir can equate to some very good deals amongst the local companies; however, make sure they have acceptable logistical and mechanical assistance to match the major international companies, who also offer one-way rentals. Rates vary greatly between seasons, and sometimes discounts of 10% to 40% can be negotiated, especially with the local companies. For a general idea, plan on 350dh to 500dh ($44–$63/£22–£31) per day for a small, four-door sedan with unlimited mileage and insurance.

The major international firms can be found on or near the northern ends of boulevard Hassan II and boulevard Mohammed V and include **Budget,** Residence Marhaba, boulevard Mohammed V (✆ **028/848222**); **Europcar,** corner of boulevard Mohammed V and rue Hubert Giraud (✆ **028/840203**); **Hertz,** Residence Marhaba, boulevard Mohammed V (✆ **024/449984**); and **National/Alamo,** Immeuble Sud Bahia, boulevard Hassan II, opposite rue des Orangiers (✆ **028/840026**).

Companies with desks at the airport include **Avis** ✆ 028/839244 or 061/530618); **Budget** (✆ 028/839101 or 075/386175); **Europcar** (✆ 028/840337); **Hertz** (✆ 028/839071 or 067/619069); **National/Alamo** (✆ 028/839121 or 067/199979); and **SixT** (✆ 068/190570); all are usually open from 8am to 10pm.

Reputable local companies include **Abid Rent A Car,** Complexe Tivoli, at the junction of Chemin de Oued Souss and rue des Dunes (✆ **028/827777** or 061/5742660), which offers one-way rentals to Marrakech; **Transrent** (✆ **028/843378** or 061/385000), on the corner of boulevard du 20 Août and rue de la Jeunesse; and **Always Rent-A-Car,** Agadir Toyota, southern end of boulevard Hassan II (✆ **028/842543** or 066/019385), which also has a desk at the airport (✆ **028/846061**).

BY TRAIN   It's not really a train, but it sure looks like one. **Petit Train d'Agadir** (✆ **061/164384**) is a battery-operated tourist train that takes visitors on a 40-minute circuit of the city, encompassing the southern beach resorts all the way to the northern edge of the beach promenade and up to avenue Hassan II and avenue du Prince Moulay Abdallah. The main pickup/drop-off is on boulevard du 20 Août, at the bottom entrance to the Vallée des Oiseaux (p. 374). The circuits commence at 9:15am and continue on the hour to 6pm, costing 18dh ($2.25/£1.15) per adult and 12dh ($1.50/75p) children 5 to 12.

FAST FACTS: Agadir

Banks & Currency Exchange Banque Populaire (✆ **028/837265**) and **Wafa** (✆ **028/817692**) have branches with ATMs on avenue du Général Kéttani, open Monday to Friday 8:15am to 3:45pm. Places with ATMs and exchange services include **BMCI,** on the corner of avenue du Prince Moulay Abdallah and avenue Prince Sidi Mohammed (formerly rue du Prince Héritier) (✆ **028/840710**); and **Banque Populaire,** boulevard du 20 Août (opposite English Pub; ✆ **028/886785**). Banque Populaire and Wafa both operate bureaux de change underneath the Hotel Kamal, corner of boulevard Hassan II and avenue Prince Sidi

Mohammed, as well as farther south on the corner of boulevard Hassan II and Passage Aït Souss. Banque Populaire, corner of rue des Dunes and rue Oued Souss, operates a bureau de change, ATM, and credit card-advance service. If all else fails, try one of the more expensive hotels.

Doctors Most of the beach resorts will have contact details for English-speaking doctors. The **Syndicat d'Initiative**, or tourist information bureau, on avenue Mohammed V opposite avenue du Général Kéttani (© **028/840307**), has a list of medical contacts on their front window. **Dr. Lazarak** (© **061/162567**) speaks good English and comes highly recommended.

Drugstores Pharmacies are very prevalent in the city. There are several along boulevard Hassan II and avenue Prince Moulay Abdallah. **La Grande Pharmacie d'Agadir** (© **028/842989**) is next to Centrale Post Office. Close to the beachfront resorts is **Pharmacie Valtur,** at the junction of Chemin du Oued Souss and rue des Dunes (© **028/822132**). Most pharmacies are open 9 to 11:30am, 3:30 to 8pm, and 9pm to 12:30am Monday to Saturday, with after-hours pharmacies listed on the front door as well as at the **Syndicat d'Initiative** on avenue Mohammed V opposite avenue du Général Kéttani (© **028/840307**). An all-night pharmacy **(Pharmacie du Nuit)** operates from the hôtel de ville (town hall), behind the main post office, on avenue Prince Sidi Mohammed.

Emergency For **general emergencies** and the **police,** call © **19.**

Hospitals There is a cluster of private medical clinics on or close to boulevard Hassan II between rue de la Foire and avenue al Mouqaouama. **Clinique Argana,** corner of boulevard Hassan II and rue d'Oujda (© **028/846000** or 028/846100), has a 24-hour emergency ward, as does **Clinique al-Massira,** corner of avenue du Prince Moulay Abdallah and boulevard Mohammed VI (formerly rue du 29 Février; © **028/843238**).

Internet Access **Cyber Cafe Indrif,** 60 av. du Prince Moulay Abdallah (© **028/ 824326**), also sends faxes and sells postage stamps. **Skoutti** is located at the entrance of Les Almohades Hotel on boulevard du 20 Août (© **028/846722**).

Laundry & Dry Cleaning There are no self-service laundromats in Agadir, but *pressings* (dry cleaners) are widespread. A shirt or pair of pants costs around 15dh ($1.90/95p). **Pressing les 4 Saisons,** 20 rue des Orangiers (© **028/840242**), and **Pressing Blanc Bleu,** on avenue du Prince Moulay Abdallah (© **028/ 848373**), wash and dry and charge per kilo. Both are open 8:30am to 12:15pm and 2:30 to 7:30pm Monday to Saturday.

Maps & Books Maps of Agadir are available at most newsstands and souvenir shops around the city. The *Plan Agadir Principale* map is the most tourist friendly and normally sells for 10dh ($1.25/65p). There's also a larger map, *Agadir Souss & Regions,* which has a more detailed city map as well as a regional map. It can usually be found at the airport, as well as various shops in the city, and sells for 45dh ($5.65/£2.80). **Librairie Papetrie la Lecture Pour Tous,** 11 Passage Aït Souss (© **028/843427**), is a new bookshop selling maps of both Agadir city and country maps, as well as a surprisingly good selection of English-language guide books and mainly French-language coffee table–style books on Morocco. It's open 9am to 12:30pm and 3 to 8pm Monday to Saturday.

Newspapers **Kiosque de Club Med,** outside the entrance to Club Med at the northern end of Chemin de Oued Souss, sells day-old copies of various U.K. and U.S. newspapers, as well as a small selection of English-language paperbacks. Hours are 9am to 7pm daily. Various shops around the city center also sell the weekly international versions of *The Guardian* and *Herald Tribune*.

Police A 24-hour tourist-friendly **police post** is located at the southern end of the beach promenade between place Bijaouane and place al Wahda, where regular patrols of the main beach are undertaken on quad bikes. Farther south at the junction of Chemin de Oued Souss and rue des Dunes is another similar post. The main **Brigade Touristique** station is opposite the Centrale Post Office on avenue du Prince Moulay Abdallah.

Post Office & Mail Agadir's **main post office,** which receives all *poste restante* mail, is on avenue Prince Sidi Mohammed and is open Monday to Friday 8am to 4:15pm and Saturday 8 to 11:45am. The Centrale branch is located on avenue du Prince Moulay Abdallah and is open the same hours. There's a small branch on boulevard du 20 Août, opposite the junction with Chemin de Oued Souss, open Monday to Friday 8:30am to 12:20pm and 2:30 to 6:30pm. You'll also find many souvenir shops within the city center, as well as most expensive hotels, that sell postcard stamps. A **FedEx** office, 9 rue Changuit, New Talborjt (© **028/844406**), is open Monday to Friday 8am to 6:30pm and Saturdays 8am to 12:15pm.

Restrooms There are no public toilets in the city. Your best bet is to politely ask for the *toilette* in any reasonable-looking restaurant. Sometimes there might be a small fee or, if there is an attendant keeping them clean, 2 to 3 dirham (40¢/20p) is expected.

Safety Generally, your personal safety never feels threatened in Agadir, and although some hawkers selling souvenirs or young Moroccans wanting to practice their English may approach you on the beach, it's normally pretty low key. During the warmer months, quad-bike police regularly patrol the main beach in front of the promenade. Sunbathing female travelers may feel more comfortable, however, at one of the roped-off private areas here or a similar area at their beachfront resort. As a precaution, I wouldn't recommend walking at night between the city center/beach promenade and the beachfront resorts on rue des Dunes; catch a *petit* taxi instead.

Telephone Agadir's **city code** has recently changed from 048 to **028**.

WHERE TO STAY

Although Agadir has plenty of accommodations, the choice becomes very limited when looking for that often rare combination of good value, good service, and good rooms. The location of accommodations in the city is influenced by the standard. Most inexpensive hotels are located a 20-minute walk from the beach in the area known as Nouvelle Talborjt; these are of a very low standard. My one inexpensive recommendation, below, bucks the trend with a very convenient location to both the beach and city center, and is of a good standard. Many independent travelers struggle to find midrange accommodations that aren't 30 years old and living off past glory.

Staying in a tourist apartment, or *résidence,* can be a good option. There are quite a few located in the city center and can be a good value, although the majority are getting a bit faded around the edges. Agadir's top-end beachfront resorts have designed themselves around individual, all-inclusive packages marketed toward particular nationalities. The two that I have recommended are known for their experience with English-speaking holidaymakers.

Out of peak season (Christmas/New Year, Easter, and July–Aug), accommodations in Agadir are rarely full and often offer up to a 40% discount.

VERY EXPENSIVE

Hotel Riu Tikida Beach *Kids*   Opened in 1995 and renovated in 2004, this four-story beachfront complex has more than 200 rooms and suites and is a popular all-inclusive choice for English-speaking travelers. Package tours aside, this is a pleasant place to spend a holiday and offers a plethora of amenities that includes restaurants, bars (including a pool bar in summer), a recently renovated nightclub, a massive heated pool, and a thalassotherapy center (p. 373). They also have their own private beach with a watersports center and 27-hole golf course 7km (4⅓ miles) away. Parents will love the kids' Mini-Club; it's open daily from 9am to noon and 3 to 5pm, for kids ages 4 to 12, and offers activities such as table tennis, basketball, *boules,* swimming, and sailing. The large, modern rooms are accessed by several interior courtyards and come with a choice of views. And, unusual for this standard, a single rate is offered for solo travelers. A range of payment options allows you to go from room-only to all-inclusive. The 1.2-hectare (3-acre) property is a 30-minute walk from the city center, and *petits* taxis are always waiting outside.

Rue des Dunes, Baie des Palmiers, Bensergao, Agadir. ✆ **028/845400.** Fax 028/845488. www.agadirtikida.com. 233 units. 1,158dh ($145/£72) single garden view, 1,244dh ($156/£78) single pool view; 1,258dh–1,776dh ($157–$222/£79–£111) double garden view, 1,492dh–1,949dh ($187–$244/£93–£122) double pool view. MC, V. **Amenities:** 4 restaurants; 4 bars; nightclub; pool; private beach; tennis courts; thalassotherapy center; watersports; salon; children's club; free golf shuttle. *In room:* A/C, satellite TV, minibar, hair dryer, safe.

Sofitel Agadir   This sleek and chic resort is a good mix of traditional architecture with some classy touches. The low-rise kasbah has a grand entrance—10m-high (33-ft.) wood doors and oversize, rooftop Moroccan lanterns—and it doesn't disappoint once inside, either. A courtyard of sandstone, marble, *zellij,* and *tabout*-rendered (rammed earth) walls houses a lounge of plush velvet chairs. Though the hotel has more than 270 rooms and suites, one doesn't feel cramped when staying here except within the rooms themselves, which for the most part are on the small side. It's worth paying more for the rooms with a balcony for the extra space.

The resort has four restaurants, six bars—including a cigar and cognac lounge—and a beautifully designed and landscaped pool. King-size, four-poster sun beds and oversize hammocks add a luxuriant touch. A wood path through palms and succulents leads to the private beach where you'll find more sun beds, a watersports center, and a small, well-kept horse stable (2-hr. rides cost 350dh/$44/£22).

Rue des Dunes, Baie des Palmiers, Bensergao, Agadir. ✆ **028/820088.** Fax 028/820033. www.sofitelagadir.com. 273 units. 1,760dh–3,300dh ($220–$413/£110–£206) double; 6,050dh ($756–£378) poolside junior suite. Children under 12 stay free in parent's room. Rates include breakfast (except for children under 12). MC, V. **Amenities:** 4 restaurants; 6 bars; heated pool; private beach; tennis courts; hammam and salon; watersports; concierge; 24-hr. room service. *In room:* A/C, satellite TV, Wi-Fi, minibar, hair dryer.

EXPENSIVE

Hotel Timoulay   This relatively small hotel has all the touches of a luxury property yet is very reasonably priced. The sandstone-brick building is an agreeable blend of traditional Moroccan/Berber decor with modern and Art Deco finishes. The rooms are large and bright and some have balconies with wood sun chairs. Most of the 58 rooms look inward to a central garden and pool area with timber decking and thick-cushioned sun lounges and beds. There are three deluxe rooms, which are slightly larger than the standard rooms, while a few suites look out over the beach resorts to the ocean; and that's the catch—the hotel is located about .5km (⅓ mile) from the nearest accessible beach and 1km (⅔ mile) from the nearest shops and restaurants. Timoulay tries to make up for this by offering a pretty good restaurant serving both Moroccan and international cuisine, served in a classy dining room of polished wood flooring or on a terrace overlooking the pool.

Cité Founty F6, Baie des Palmiers, Agadir. ⓒ 028/234220. Fax 028/230461. www.timoulayhotel.com. 58 units. 902dh ($113/£56) single; 1,210dh ($151/£76) double; 1,001dh ($125/£63) single deluxe; 1,298dh ($162/£81) double deluxe; 1,518dh ($190/£95) suite. TPT not included. Rates include breakfast. MC, V. **Amenities:** Restaurant; bar; pool; hammam; Internet; Wi-Fi. *In room:* A/C, satellite TV, Internet modem connection, minibar, hair dryer, safe.

MODERATE

Hotel Kamal   If hotels were rated solely on friendliness and service, this aging gent would be a five-star. Guests repeatedly comment on the genuinely good service they receive at Hotel Kamal. The building reflects the block-standard design of 1980s Agadir, and the rooms are definitely starting to age, although they still offer comfortable beds and private bathrooms. Ask for a pool-view room rather than one looking out onto busy boulevard Hassan II. The good-size swimming pool is kept spotlessly clean and is frequently in use—as is the attached pool bar—although the hotel is only a 10-minute stroll to the beach. It's also very close to the city's restaurants, and I recommend utilizing them rather than the in-house restaurant, which can be a bit up and down and charges extra for many breakfast items. This is a good-value hotel that is past its due date but is still a deservedly popular choice with English-speaking travelers.

Bd. Hassan II, Agadir. ⓒ 028/842817. Fax 028/843940. www.hotelkamal.ma. 400dh ($50/£25) single; 457dh ($57/£29) double. MC, V. **Amenities:** Restaurant; snack bar; pool. *In room:* Satellite TV (extra charge), no phone.

Residence Yasmina (Value (Kids   This is one the best-value apartment-hotels in the city center and is only a 10-minute walk from the beach. The main building houses 68 aging but spotlessly clean rooms that have separate bathroom, bedroom, kitchen, and lounge areas; most also have a balcony. The full kitchen has a large fridge, microwave, electric hot plates, cupboards full of crockery and cutlery, and a small table that looks onto a lounge room with satellite TV and twin sofas; these become extra beds if needed. The small bedroom is functional but a little stuffy when you close the door. The bathrooms are hospital-like but are large and airy, with a tub/shower combo. There are two suites on each of the four floors; the largest can squeeze up to eight people. A new, separate block will be completed by the beginning of 2008, with 30 rooms of a similar configuration to those in the old block.

Split-level swimming pools sit side-by-side, including a shallow pool for the kids. There is also a ground-floor cafe that offers an in-room drinks service (nonalcoholic) from 7am to 9pm. Yasmina is located next door to Agadir's Royal Tennis Club, and the pool-facing rooms include a great view of the action on the courts. A rarely used rooftop terrace has a few sun lounges, but it's a long way down to the pool. The well-stocked Anaprix supermarket (p. 376) is only 50m (165 ft.) away, and many of the city's restaurants are close by.

Rue de la Jeunesse, Agadir. ℂ **028/842620,** 028/842565, or 028/842430. Fax 028/845657. www.residence-yasmina. com. 76 units. 477dh–949dh ($60–$119/£30–£59) room 1–5 people; 551dh–1,171dh ($68–$146/£34–£73) suite 1–6 people, 643dh–1,524dh ($80–$191/£40–£95) suite 1–8 people. Children under 4 stay free in parent's room. 25% discount Dec 18–Apr 15 and Jul 16–Sept 9; 40% discount Apr 16–May 15 and Sept 10–Dec 17. MC, V. **Amenities:** Cafe; pool. *In room:* Central heating, satellite TV, safe.

INEXPENSIVE

Hotel Petit Suede   This small hotel at the northern end of the city center is only a 5-minute walk to the beach, albeit across the busy boulevard Mohammed V, and is both a good value and extremely friendly. It offers simply furnished but clean rooms, most of which come with their own shower and basin; common toilets are located in the hallway. A few rooms also have their own balcony, but the trade-off for this is the street noise, so ask for one overlooking the inner courtyard. Breakfast is served on the roof terrace and is a good place to meet other travelers. The hotel offers cheap car rental and has promised a 10% discount on accommodations for Frommer's readers.

Corner bd. Hassan II and av. Général Kettani, Agadir. ℂ **028/840779.** Fax 028/840057. lapetitsuede@hotmail.com. 20 units. 168dh ($21/£11) single; 250dh ($31/£16) double; 350dh ($44/£22) triple; 450dh ($56/£28) quad. Rates include breakfast. MC, V. **Amenities:** Rooftop breakfast room. *In room:* No phone.

WHERE TO DINE

Agadir's restaurant scene is alive and well despite the influx and attraction of all-inclusive resorts. The three areas for dining, as with most things in Agadir, are the city center, the beach promenade, and south of the city near the beachfront resorts. Although there are plenty of restaurants to choose from, the range of cuisine is limited to European—with one very notable British exception—and Moroccan, reflecting the nationalities of the majority of visitors to Agadir. Dining in Agadir generally lacks the Asian ambience prevalent in Marrakech or the strong traditional atmosphere of many restaurants in Fes, but this young city has never been a follower and can be looked upon as refreshing rather than lacking.

All of the recommended restaurants listed below are easy to locate and will perhaps require transport if you are staying at one of the beachfront resorts.

No matter where you dine, finish off your evening with a stroll along the beach promenade, perhaps partaking in an ice cream or mint tea at one of the many restaurants and cafes running along its length.

VERY EXPENSIVE

La Scala 🌟🌟🌟 SEAFOOD/INTERNATIONAL   Consistently one of the best in Agadir, this restaurant is one of the few places that doesn't require any touting to bring in the diners. Although not in the most convenient of locations, between the beach promenade and the beachfront resorts, the restaurant's menu reflects the establishment's elegant atmosphere. A wide selection (40 in total) of seafood dishes includes Oualidia oysters, filet of dorade grilled with saffron, and the La Scala Special (550dh/ $69/£34) seafood platter of shrimp and prawn offerings (scampi, king prawns, gambas) and monkfish on skewers. Other carnivorous dishes include a succulent beef filet in Roquefort, and duck in ginger and honey. Make sure to leave room for the Norwegian crepe flambéed in Grand Marnier (60dh/$7.50/£3.75). Outdoor and indoor seating is available, and the service is what you'd expect from a place of this price point.

Chemin de Oued Souss, behind Complexe Touristique de Tamlalt. ℂ **028/846773.** Fax 028/827502. Reservations recommended. Main courses 110dh–150dh ($14–$19/£6.90–£9.40). Alcohol served. MC, V. Daily noon–3pm and 5pm–midnight.

Le Mauresque Lounge MOROCCAN/INTERNATIONAL   One of the newer restaurants in Agadir, Le Mauresque is a feast for both the eyes and the palate. Craftsmen from La Médina d'Agadir (p. 374) were involved in the construction and decoration of this Moorish villa–cum–rustic lounge, and the result is as visually varied as the menu, which covers traditional Moroccan (try the lamb tagine with figs), seafood (oven-baked stuffed sea bream), Mediterranean, set menus, and European specialties from owner/chef Stéphane. The kitchen will also prepare simple grilled chicken, beef kebabs, or spaghetti for the kids.

Diners can choose from alfresco tables under grass umbrellas; a table on the villa's wide, raised veranda; the formal dining room with Victorian-style furniture and fireplace; or the small lounge area with its low-lying, chunky wood seating. The restaurant is conveniently located near the beachfront resorts but is also worth a taxi if those in the city center feel like a bit of a splurge.

Complexe Valtur, corner of Chemin de Oued Souss and rue des Dunes. ℂ 028/820444. Fax 028/820415. Alcohol served. Main courses 105dh–285dh ($13–$36/£6.55–£18); 2-course set menu 75dh–95dh ($9.40–$12/£4.70–£5.95). V. Daily 11am–midnight.

EXPENSIVE

Le Maxwell (Kids MOROCCAN/MEDITERRANEAN   This relaxed restaurant/ bar is close to the beachfront resorts and is a good choice for either lunch or dinner. Plenty of outdoor tables allow for enjoyable, lingering meals, and strategically placed glass wind breakers are a thoughtful touch. The compact interior is tastefully decorated with *tabout* walls and includes a small bar with satellite TV, regularly tuned to the sports channel. The menu spans the Mediterranean Sea by offering Moroccan standards such as beef tagine with prunes and chicken or fish *pastilla,* as well as a range of pizzas and pastas; try the tagliatelle with mixed fish for only 55dh ($6.90/£3.45). The added offerings of hamburgers, omelets, soups, and salads make Le Maxwell a good choice for families or groups. They also have an extensive Moroccan wine list.

Complexe Touristique de Tamlalt, corner of Chemin de Oued Souss and rue des Dunes. ℂ 028/840580. Alcohol served. Main courses 45dh–150dh ($5.65–$19/£2.80–£9.40). MC, V. Daily 10am–11pm.

L'Orange Bleu (Kids MOROCCAN/INTERNATIONAL   The "Blue Orange" has a wide menu of local fare and pays homage to the saffron-growing region inland from Agadir with one of the *plats du maison,* an exquisite saffron-infused chicken and lemon tagine. Other tagines (lamb with prunes, vegetarian) are offered along with seafood paella for two and a good selection of beef dishes including a carpaccio. For the little ones, a *menu les enfants* includes orange juice, soup, spaghetti, and a crepe for 65dh ($8.15/£4.05). Alfresco dining is available and leads into a very pleasant interior of *tabout* walls, an open kitchen, comfortable high-back wrought-iron chairs, and good music.

Bd. du 20 Août (at the junction with Chemin de Oued Souss). ℂ 028/846930. Alcohol served. Main courses 60dh–110dh ($7.50–$14/£3.75–£6.90); set menus 85dh–210dh ($11–$26/£5.30–£13). MC, V. Daily 9am–midnight.

MODERATE

The Central English Pub ENGLISH   Those looking for something other than the standard Moroccan fare should head to Peter Hanger's British-theme pub, which opened in January 2007. The large outdoor and indoor areas are filled with a young, friendly, and fun staff and a clientele ranging from homesick Brits to Moroccan businessmen. The all-day breakfast options range from a plate of sausage, egg, chips (fries for Americans), and baked beans (55dh/$6.90/£3.45) to a major fry-up of eggs, bacon, mushrooms, sausage, baked beans, tomatoes, and toast for 60dh ($7.50/£3.75). The menu also includes other British standards such as shepherd's pie, fish and chips in beer batter, and a steak and kidney pie with chips and peas. Pasta dishes, pizzas, and toasted panini are the sum of the international fare. There are no gastronomic surprises here: The food is well prepared and hearty in taste, and the servings are very generous.

Bd. du 20 Août (at the junction with Chemin de Oued Souss). ℂ 028/847390. Fax 028/847610. Alcohol served. Main courses 55dh–85dh ($6.90–$11/£3.45–£5.30). MC, V. Daily 9am–midnight.

Le Nil Bleu MOROCCAN/PIZZA/SEAFOOD   One of a line of beachfront restaurants on the promenade, Le Nil Bleu may not look like the classiest or trendiest, but it's the only one where you'll find a magical mix of generous servings of good food, genuinely friendly waitstaff, a million-dollar view, and nightly entertainment that ranges from an Egyptian plate dancer to Moroccan versions of "Love Me Tender." Hugely popular despite—or because of—the entertainment, Le Nil Bleu opens early and closes late and offers diners a full range of seafood, steaks, pizzas, pastas, and Moroccan standards such as couscous, various tagines, and *pastilla*. A few hundred diners can easily fit under the awning. Candle-lit tables for dinner, clear wind barriers, and gas heaters during the cooler months are all nice touches.

Av. Tawada (formerly rue de la Plage). ℂ **028/841617**. Alcohol served. Main courses 35dh–130dh ($4.40–$16/£2.20–£8.15). MC, V. Daily 8am–1am.

Le Renouv Restaurant *(Finds* FRENCH   Visitors often walk right past this little corner restaurant, but it's only 20m (66 ft.) from the beachfront promenade on avenue Tawada (formerly rue de la Plage) and well worth seeking out. Owner Cathy opened this place in 2006 and offers French classics such as chicken fricassee in fine herbs; seafood cassoulet; and both savory and sweet quiches and tarts (I recommend her fish and leek pie). Le Renouv is a popular choice with both foreign residents and Moroccan businessmen, and is simply furnished with both inside and alfresco tables. The ambience can be a bit lacking on a quiet night, but that's only because this is still the best-kept secret in town.

4 av. Tawada (formerly rue de la Plage). ℂ **064/914335** or 079/067288. Alcohol served. Main courses 45dh–80dh ($5.65–$10/£2.80–£5); 3-course set menu 95dh ($12/£5.95). MC, V. Daily 11:30am–3pm and 6–11pm.

Little Italy *(Finds* ITALIAN   Linda Rapisarda opened her piece of Italy in 2005, and though the name is a little ambitious, the ambience and cuisine here is as authentic as they come. Filled with both Gadiris and foreign residents, the restaurant consists of a small alfresco area on the front pavement and two floors of closely placed seating inside. The interior is decorated with scenic Italian pictures and Linda's personal mementos, and any spare space seems to be filled with bottles of wine. Efficient waiters offer a menu with a large selection of pastas—the house gnocchi is superb—and pizzas, along with various meat dishes that include a *saltimbocca alla romana* (beef escalope with a ham-and–white wine tagliatelle) and a filet of St. Pierre (John Dory) in a shrimp-and-mushroom-cream sauce. Traditional thin-crust pizzas are made in a wood-burning clay oven, and a take-away service is available. As with most restaurants in Morocco, smoking is tolerated inside, and the lack of any air-conditioning can sometimes leave the air a little stuffy inside.

Bd. Hassan II (opposite place al Amal). ℂ **028/820039**. Reservations recommended from 9pm. Alcohol served. Main courses 65dh–125dh ($8.15–$16/£4.05–£7.80). MC, V. Daily 10am–midnight.

Restaurant Jour et Nuit INTERNATIONAL/CAFE   Although the original "Day and Night" restaurant is still open, it's this newer, sleeker version across the road that is the "in" place in Agadir to enjoy a morning coffee or midafternoon drink. The contemporary sandstone and white design is enclosed by glass wind barriers and operates (like the original) 24 hours a day. It offers both indoor and outdoor tables, with a menu that allows for a simple coffee-breakfast served until 11am to main dishes such as an avocado and prawn salad, a bacon (yes, bacon) and tomato club sandwich, a meaty mixed grill, or a chicken breast roasted with cumin. The location can't be beat; it's slightly raised from street level and affords a great people-watching view of the promenade and beach. Upstairs is a fine-dining restaurant with a menu of expensive French classics, and although the setting is very nice, the food doesn't quite justify the price and the waiters tend to be on the gruff side.

Av. Tawada (formerly rue de la Plage). ⓒ 028/822347. Alcohol served. Main courses 40dh–110dh ($5–$14/ £2.50–£6.90); salads and sandwiches 25dh–55dh ($3.15–$6.90/£1.55–£3.45). MC, V. Daily 24 hr. (skeleton staff 3–5am).

INEXPENSIVE

Herguita BREAKFAST/JUICE BAR   This healthy juice bar is located on the beachfront promenade and pumps out a steady stream of the freshest juices and milk shakes. At last count, there were 37 different juices on offer, some of them only seasonal, as every ingredient is fresh. For something different, try a date milkshake, coconut juice, or the Herguita Speciale of mango, pineapple, papaya (paw paw), kiwi, nuts, date, and grape, all for just 15dh ($1.90/95p). They also whip up a tasty Moroccan breakfast of fresh *msemmen* or *harcha* flatbreads or a *baghrir* crepe with delicious *amlou* argan-oil spread, fried eggs, and coffee or tea. The alfresco tables are a great, umbrella-shaded spot to stop at any time of the day or night.

Av. Tawada (formerly rue de la Plage). No phone. Juices 7dh–15dh (90¢–$1.90/45p–95p); breakfast 18dh ($2.25/ £1.15). No credit cards. Daily 7am–midnight.

Restaurant Daffy MOROCCAN   Head waiter Omar has been welcoming travelers into this little restaurant for years. Located toward the northern end of the city and just around the corner from the Supratours bus stop, Restaurant Daffy attracts independent travelers and a regular stream of Gadiris rather than resort guests. There are alfresco tables outside, and the interior feels like a small Moroccan tent, draped with burgundy and deep-green material and filled with low-lying leather couches. The menu offers Moroccan standards including *harira* soup (10dh/$1.25/65p), tagines, brochettes, and a "king" couscous for a not-so-grand 48dh ($6/£3). A couple of seafood dishes are also available, and set menus offer a range of three-course meals. The restaurant opens early for a croissant-and-coffee breakfast and also offers sandwiches for the lunchtime crowd. Omar's service is always friendly and efficient, and the food is always good.

Rue des Orangiers. ⓒ 028/820068. Main courses 30dh–58dh ($3.75–$7.25/£1.90–£3.65); set menu 55dh–60dh ($6.90–$7.50/£3.45–£3.75). No credit cards. Daily 8am–10pm.

Yacout BREAKFAST/CAFE   This is one of the most popular cafe-restaurants in the city center and is especially well known for its cheap breakfast. Every morning, Gadiri businessmen, Moroccan visitors, and the odd traveler come to Yacout to enjoy both the pleasant garden setting and the house breakfast: a basket of pastries, muffins, croissants, and baguettes; saucers of jam, honey, oil, and olives; a bowl of *harira semoule* (semolina porridge); freshly squeezed orange juice; and tea or coffee. Under the garden pergola is a central fountain around which the tables are squeezed, and although it's more spacious inside, the pergola is where everyone sits and a good deal of people-watching takes place. If you come here at other times of the day, there are set menus of Moroccan fare available, plus a limited choice of pizzas and sandwiches.

Corner of rue de L'Entraide and bd. Mohammed VI (formerly rue du 29 Février). 𝒞 028/846588. Breakfast 16dh ($2/£1); 3-course set menu 65dh ($8.15/£4.05). No credit cards. Daily 6am–10pm.

WHAT TO SEE & DO

Agadir lacks any great attractions other than the one thing that brings everyone here—the beach. Everything else in this city only dates back to the reconstruction phase that began in the 1970s. There are a couple of sights that are worth a look between morning and afternoon sunning sessions, and day outings to the beach village of Taghazout or the jewelry souk in Tiznit are particularly recommended (p. 377).

The thalassotherapy center in Hotel Riu Tikida Beach (𝒞 **028/842120;** www.agadirtikida.com) offers a large range of massages, body wraps, and beauty treatments. One-time entry to the hammam is 70dh ($8.75/£4.40); a body scrub or henna body wrap is 120dh ($15/£7.50); and the Oriental Break, which includes a body scrub, 50-minute massage with argan oil, and a hydromassage in essential oils is 800dh ($100/£50). Reservations required. It's open daily 9am to 1pm and 2:30 to 7pm (restricted hours during Ramadan).

Agadir Bay   The crescent-shape bay in which Agadir rests is one of Morocco's best. Fine, golden sand stretches for about 9km (5½ miles), and the Atlantic Ocean is usually calm enough for swimming, though be wary of a strong undertow. No matter where in Agadir you are staying, you won't be too far from the beach; it's mere steps away for those staying in the resorts lining the shore south of the city center. Avenue Tawada (formerly rue de la Plage) is the official name for the promenade that looks over the main beach (or *plage*), and here you'll find roped off areas with umbrellas, sun lounges, and waiters serving drinks.

During the warmer months there are usually motorized watersports such as jet-skiing (400dh/$50/£25 for 30 min.) and surfboard and windsurfing equipment available for rent. **MTS Travel,** in Complex Manader on boulevard du 20 Août (𝒞 **028/827429** or 069/837345), organizes 2-hour camel rides along the beach for 200dh ($25/£13) adults and 100dh ($13/£6.25) children 12 and under; the cost includes tea and pastries. They also offer a yacht cruise, including lunch and nonalcoholic drinks, from 9:30am to 4:30pm for 450dh ($56/£28) adults, 225dh ($28/£14) children 12 and under.

Kasbah   The remains of the ancient kasbah are worth a look if only to grasp the complete destruction that befell the city in 1960. Located on a hill to the north of the bay and visible from anywhere along the sandy beach, the kasbah was largely destroyed by the quake, but the outline of eroding walls and an entrance arch are still visible today. It was built in 1540 by the Marrakech-based Saâdians to launch an attack on the Portuguese below, and was still inhabited before 1960. There are great views of Agadir Bay. Down below the kasbah is Ancient Talborjt, where Agadir's medina used to stand and where many of the 15,000 quake victims were buried alive and still rest today. This area has been made into a memorial park—look for the inscription engraved in one of the walls from King Mohammed V: "If destiny desired the destruction of Agadir, its reconstruction depends on our faith and our determination." This,

Agadir's New Medina

On the Inezgane road heading south of Agadir is builder-designer Coco Polizzi's **La Médina d'Agadir** ⨌. Polizzi, born in Rabat into an Italian family of architects, was involved in much of the construction that took place in Agadir through the 1980s and 1990s. In 1983, he built his own workshop in the city, partly to supply his booming building business but also to take the first step toward realizing a dream of building a new medina to replace the earthquake-devastated original. After receiving local government approval in 1992, a 4½-hectare (11-acre) site was leased, and over the next 4 years, using his own capital, Polizzi's new medina took shape. The medina is built entirely of bricks, hewn stone, and wood, and the only concessions to modernity are the plumbing and some electricity; there are no reinforcing bars or metal beams.

A continuing work in progress—there are plans for a museum, art gallery, hammam, artist studios, and a small lake with landscaped gardens—the site workshops produce nearly everything, from the mosaics that decorate the floors and walls of the buildings to the intricately carved doors and *roshans* (latticed windows). Much of the interior work inside many of the Agadir's resorts and restaurants (Sofitel, Riu Tikida Dunas, Le Mauresque Cafe) was produced in these workshops. Artisans work with only natural local products—terra cotta from Marrakech, marble from Casablanca, slate from Tafraoute, and limestone, *thuya,* and eucalyptus from the surrounding area. Basically a craft and culture village, the medina is a maze of arches and alleyways, each housing a small workshop with a local craftsperson making and selling his or her wares. Most traditional Moroccan art and crafts are represented: textiles, jewelry, lantern making, weaving, woodwork, henna art, *herboristes,* and glassware. Crafts that produce larger items or ones that are integral to building the medina are located in the rambling workshops to the rear of the property.

An agreement with the government results in every craftsperson in the medina training at least two others, which is integral to Polizzi's ethos of

combined with a visit to the kasbah, affords the visitor at least some chance to visualize old Agadir. If you feel like walking, it's best to take a taxi (15dh/$1.90/95p) from the city center/beach to the kasbah and walk back.

4km (2½ miles) northwest of the city center. Memorial park open 24 hrs.

Vallée des Oiseaux (Valley of the Birds) *(Kids* Located in the city along a former dry riverbed, this isn't a zoo by definition, but it's a nice distraction for those with children. It's a pleasant, shaded, narrow walkway of about 800m (½ mile) that runs between boulevard Hassan II and boulevard du 20 Août (and under bd. Mohammed V) with a range of animals including South American llamas, Australian wallabies, Moroccan moufflon (also known as Barbary sheep), and Dorcas gazelles. There are, as the name suggests, heaps of birds, including a large walk-through aviary. For the little ones, there's perpetuating Morocco's artisan heritage. Each craftsperson (there are currently 64) is interviewed by Polizzi or his daughter Claudia, who lives within the medina, and must offer something innovative or unique from that already being produced. For me, this is what makes the visit worthwhile. Although lacking the atmosphere of Morocco's ancient medinas, the craftsmanship and subsequent items on display and for sale are of an exceptional quality and some are really quite unique and perhaps more in tune with modern-day tastes. The prices are fixed, and each shopkeeper/craftsperson is most willing to show you how each product is made (a good time to ask that *herboriste* what is in the Viagra tea) without the pressure to buy that you find in the other city's medinas. The larger workshops are only available for viewing with a guide (English speaking and included in the cost of admission), which I encourage you to use. This is a great opportunity to see these skilled artisans at work in a nonintimidating environment. True to medina working hours, most of the shops close for lunch between noon and 2pm. There is a small restaurant, Cafe Mauré, on-site serving traditional Moroccan cuisine; main dishes of tagine or couscous are 40dh to 60dh ($5–$7.50/£2.50–£3.75). It's open 24 hours.

The medina is located at Ben Sergao, 4km (2½ miles) south of Agadir on the Inezgane road (© 028/280253; www.medinapolizzi.com; 40dh/$5/£2.50 adults, 20dh/$2.50/£1.25 children 2–12, free for kids under 2). Hours are Tuesday to Sunday 8:30am to 6:30pm. A shuttle-bus service from Agadir operates daily from 9am to 6pm and charges 60dh ($7.50/£3.75) adults, 30dh ($3.75/£1.90) children 2 to 12, free for kids under 2; ticket includes admission. The best pickup/drop-off point in the city center is La Medina's own kiosk at the junction of boulevard du 20 Août and Chemin de Oued Souss. Other stops include the beachfront resorts of Riu Tikida Beach and Sofitel.

a sand-floor playground. It's also a popular spot for young male and female Gadiris to meet and chat. This is also a start/finish point for Petit Train d'Agadir (p. 364).

Entrances on both bd. Hassan II and bd. du 20 Août, 50m (164 ft.) north of av. Prince Sidi Mohammed. Admission 5dh (65¢/30p) adults; 3dh (40¢/20p) children 2–10; free under 2. Daily 9:30am–12:30pm and 2:30–6:30pm.

SHOPPING

Agadir is no shopper's paradise, and apart from La Médina d'Agadir (p. 374), all shops import their souvenirs from other parts of Morocco. Most of these advertise their goods at fixed prices, though some of them will be up for a haggle should you feel the urge.

The **Municipal Market** (Marché) is a two-story complex of shops selling all manner of Moroccan-made souvenirs such as leatherwork from Marrakech, ceramics from Fes, and fossils from Erfoud at fixed, though inflated, prices. Round-nosed yellow *babouches* are a specialty of the Souss region and have a thicker sole than normal. Look at paying 250dh ($31/£16) for a pair. The concrete building is between avenue des F.A.R. and avenue Prince Sidi Mohammed and is open daily 9am to 7pm.

Close by is the **Uniprix** supermarket, which sells a large range of fixed-price souvenirs including T-shirts, beachwear and accessories, toiletries, general grocery items, and alcohol. It's on the corner of boulevard Hassan II and avenue Prince Sidi Mohammed and is open daily 9am to 1:30pm and 2:30 to 9pm. Similar supermarkets to Uniprix, only smaller, include **Anaprix,** on boulevard Hassan II at the junction with rue de la Jeunesse, open 9am to 1:30pm and 2:30 to 9pm daily; **Quick Service,** in the Tafoukt Complex between boulevard du 20 Août and place al Wahda, open 8am to 8pm daily; and **SM Supermarket,** Complexe Touristique de Tamlalt, corner of rue des Dunes and Chemin de Oued Souss, open Monday to Thursday and Saturday 9am to 1pm and 4 to 9pm and Friday 9am to noon and 4 to 9pm.

In 2001, Farah Habibi and her aunt Rachida Bouzendaga joined forces with a women's cooperative from the Berber Aït Baâmran tribe to offer a wide range of products derived from the indigenous argan tree (p. 354) found in the Souss region. Their *très chic* first-floor shop, **Argan House** , is located in a back street not far from the tourist area and is decorated with an African-Asian flavor combined with the sultry smells from their selection of essential oils and potpourri. Over a mint tea, Farah, who speaks the best English of these two dynamic ladies and is a combination *herboriste* and naturopath, will run through the array of different argan products, which include oil for both cooking and massage, bath soaps, creams, and cosmetics. There are also nice-size gift packs and other natural beauty products for sale. On the second floor is a massage room where Rachida specializes in a 2-hour traditional body massage (200dh/$25/£13). The Argan House, at 30 rue Moulay Idriss Boutchakat (corner of rue de Fes; ⓒ **028/842613** or 077/812157), is open Monday to Saturday 8:30am to 7pm; hotel visits are by appointment.

On the outskirts of the city on the southern edge of boulevard du 20 Août is the Western-styled, air-conditioned **Marjane Hypermarket,** open daily from 9am to 9pm. It sells everything from groceries and general foodstuffs (including bacon) to cookware and computers. There's also a well-stocked liquor store here that stays open during Ramadan.

AGADIR AFTER DARK
BARS & DANCE CLUBS

Some ill-informed travelers come here expecting something bordering on Ibiza and find themselves disillusioned at the complete absence of anything like it. When compared to the rest of Morocco, Agadir offers a fun albeit small mix of drinking establishments.

For a quiet alcoholic drink and some people-watching, the restaurants **Jour et Nuit** (p. 372) and **Le Nil Bleu** (p. 371) usually allow you to just have a drink or, at the most, ask you to order a small salad. There are a number of other restaurants along this busy promenade that should allow you to do the same. At the other end of the beach is **Le Mauresque Lounge** (p. 370), which has a great inside lounge/bar area where you can enjoy a drink and order some tapas. You can also drink outside under the woven-grass umbrellas and watch the beach resort pedestrian traffic shuffle by; happy hour specials are offered between 4 and 7pm.

At the busy junction of boulevard du 20 Août and rue du Oued Souss is the trio of **The Central English Pub, Jockey Bar,** and **L'Orange Bleu.** You can drink at the Pub (p. 370), either alfresco or inside, which consists of a sunken floor with heaps of cushioned seating as well as traditional bar stools and wine cask tables. Two separate sections play host to pool tables and a darts/sports bar. If there's a special sporting event that you want to watch, then this is the place. Low lighting and low ceilings allow for enough space and the right atmosphere for both Moroccans and tourists to enjoy somewhere to drink that's fun, lively, has good music, and isn't seedy or overly smoky. L'Orange Bleu (p. 370) has a popular bar at the rear with a long, thick wood counter and good music. Jockey Bar, located in the middle of the Pub and L'Orange Bleu, gets a mainly young crowd attracted to the 5 to 8pm happy hour and the resident DJs. Monday is reggae night, Tuesday Arabic, Wednesday house and retro, Thursday serves up tapas, and weekends are Jack Daniels nights with special drink offers throughout the night. It's open daily from noon to midnight.

Papa Gayo, at the Hotel Riu Tikida Beach (p. 367), has recently been refurbished and recommenced its tenure as the city's most popular nightclub. During the summer months, this is still the place to go after midnight, and although it's pricey and the crowd can sometimes be pretentious, a fun night can still be had as the resident DJ pumps out a popular mix of the latest Arabic and Western dance numbers.

SIDE TRIPS FROM AGADIR
TIZNIT ★★
98km (61 miles) S of Agadir

Between the Atlantic coast and the southern fingers of the Anti-Atlas mountains, this young city has an easily navigable medina, is historically renowned for its silver jewelry, and is a world away from the bright lights of Agadir.

Tiznit's pink-walled medina was built by Sultan Moulay Hassan (Hassan I) in 1882 to establish a base from which he could stabilize the unruly south. Eight kilometers (5 miles) of thick walls were constructed around 12 existing kasbahs, Jewish silversmiths were relocated into this "new" medina, and the town quickly established itself as one of the major trading centers of Morocco's south. Thirty years later, and in response to the beginning of French occupation, El Hiba the Blue Sultan—named after his flowing blue robes that are still worn today by men of the south—declared himself sultan of Morocco in Tiznit, and proceeded to fight the French until his death in 1919 in nearby Taroudannt.

Tiznit today is a peaceful, easy-going town, and the medina, if perhaps a little too open and lacking the bustle of other medinas, is a delight to walk around. Despite the immigration of the town's Jews to Israel, its reputation for producing quality silver jewelry lives on, and a browse through the Souk des Bijoutiers, or jeweler's souk, is highly recommended. Enter the medina through the main gate, Bab Jdid (you'll see the cluster of banks opposite), and the souk is 50m (165 ft.) to the left. In keeping with this young medina, the souk's shops are all modern and well lit, so don't expect a maze of little stores down twisting alleyways. There are more than 100 shops here, and the majority of customers are locals. There's a fair bit of tacky gold on show, but there are also plenty of shops selling authentic antique Berber jewelry, as well as more recent creations of bracelets, belts, brooches, earrings, ceremonial daggers, and necklaces. Bijouterie Aziz has two locations, at shop nos. 5 and 22, and offers fine examples of all. A farther 100m (330 ft.) or so into the heart of the medina is Tiznit's Grande Mosque. Its minaret is more typical of the Saharan style in Islamic West Africa, with wood perches sticking out of the sides to assist the recently departed on their climb to paradise.

GETTING THERE   Buses for Tiznit (2 hr.; 20dh/$2.50/£1.25) operate throughout the day from the recently built *gare routière* on the edge of Agadir on rue Chair Alhamra Mohammed ben Brahim. The *gare routière* in Tiznit is on the Tafraoute road, about a 15-minute walk along avenue Hassan II from Bab Jdid (sometimes called Bab Mechouar). Long-distance *grands* taxis in Agadir are located on the southern edge of the city on the corner of rue de Fes and rue d'Essaouira, and arrive in Tiznit (1½ hr.; 40dh/$5/£2.50) at a parking lot at the junction of avenue Mohammed V and avenue du 20 Août, 100m (330 ft.) from Bab Jdid. Chartering a *grand* taxi from Agadir for the day might be an option if there are a few of you, perhaps adding in a visit to La Médina d'Agadir along the way; plan on paying at least 500dh ($63/£31).

If you're driving yourself, the road to Tiznit is well signposted heading south out of Agadir. Once you enter Tiznit, head straight through the roundabout (keeping the medina's walls on your right) until you come to the busy junction of avenue Hassan II and avenue du 20 Août, which continues on through Bab Jdid. Major Travel Services (MTS) in the Complex Manader, boulevard du 20 Août (© **028/827429** or 069/837345), offer a half-day tour to Tiznit for 250dh ($31/£16) adults, 125dh ($16/£7.80) 12 and under. They also offer a full-day tour to Tiznit and Tafraoute (p. 388) for 980dh ($123/£61) adults and 490dh ($61/£31) under 12; the cost includes lunch.

TAGHAZOUT (TARHAZOUTE) ★★
21km (13 miles) N of Agadir

Each day, just after dawn, a fleet of bright blue-and-white boats splutters back into Taghazout's bay, and villagers greet them on the shoreline to inspect the morning's catch. Everyone helps to haul the boats onto the beach, and for the rest of the day, not much else happens except for a bit of net-mending and beach football. This is the Taghazout of old that can still be seen today—but you'd better visit soon. The village and its surrounding beaches, discovered long ago by surfers who reveled in the choice and variety of the surrounding breaks and European camper-vacationers seeking some winter sun, are attracting the attention of tourism developers drawn to such a pristine coastline so close to Agadir. The Agadir-Essaouira road now cuts through the village, and a large tourism complex is up for tender just to the south.

GETTING THERE   Bus no. 14 departs irregularly throughout the day to Taghazout (5dh/65¢/30p) from the main local bus station, located next to Agadir's long-distance *grand* taxi rank, on the southern edge of the city on the corner of rue de Fes and rue d'Essaouira. *Grands* taxis (20dh/$2.50/£1.25) departing for Essaouira will stop at Taghazout, or you could charter one for the day (400dh/$50/£25). The cluster of houses and apartments on the beach side of the road makes for a pleasant stroll, finished by a cheap meal of fresh seafood at one of the local restaurants located on a beachside promenade that runs the length of the small bay.

WHERE TO STAY & EAT   **Auberge Amouage** (© **028/200272** or 070/809785) is toward the southern end of the promenade and fries up an excellent plate of calamari or fish for only 40dh ($5/£2.50). If you feel like staying, they also have a range of simple, clean rooms for 100dh to 200dh ($13–$25/£6.25–£13) double. Serving similar fare at the northern end is the more rustic **Café Resto Come Back** (© **028/200260**). Fifty meters (165 ft.) back on the busy road are some more restaurants, surf-rental shops, and the bus/*grand* taxi stop. If you have your own transport, the drive north from here up to Cap Rhir (60km/37 miles north of Agadir) passes a few small villages along an almost constant stretch of beach and surf. For more surfing information, see p. 98.

2 Taroudannt ⋆⋆

223km (138 miles) SW of Marrakech; 79km (49 miles) E of Agadir

Enclosed by an almost complete circuit of high, rammed-earth walls and lacking any sprawling ville nouvelle outside, Taroudannt could very well be that quintessential untouched, ancient Moroccan city that you've been looking for. Its location, at the heart of the fertile Souss Valley, has always ensured a steady stream of powers keen to have the town under their wing before moving on to grander conquests. This was certainly the case with the Saädians, who made Taroudannt their capital in the 16th century, when they constructed most of the walls while plotting their eventual victory over Wattasid-held Marrakech and eventually ruling over all Morocco. The town has had its share of tragedy, however. In 1687, it was left virtually uninhabited when the feared, some would say barbaric, Alaouite sultan Moulay Ismail massacred most of the town's inhabitants in response to their opposition to his Meknes-based rule. In 1919, El Hiba the Blue Sultan was killed here while leading a fierce resistance to the French occupation.

Berber down to its core, this is essentially still a market town that doesn't rely on tourism or even seem that interested in it. The town lacks any great monuments or sights other than itself, which is exactly what draws some travelers here. It's a pleasant place to visit most times of the year, with warm winters and summers that, apart from the months of July and August, are cooled by the prevailing winds coming off the Atlantic Ocean.

For much of the year, the snowcapped Western High Atlas make a perfect backdrop to the ochre walls that seem to change color during the day. Taroudannt is exceptionally friendly and relaxed and the sort of place that you intend to stay the night and end up staying a week.

ORIENTATION
ARRIVING

BY BUS   Buses to Taroudannt arrive daily from Agadir (2½ hr.; 30dh/$3.75/£1.90); Casablanca (10 hr.; 130dh–150dh/$16–$19/£8.15–£9.40); Marrakech (6½ hr.; 80dh–90dh/$10–$11/£5–£5.65); and Ouarzazate via Taliouine (5 hr.; 65dh–75dh/$8.15–$9.40/£4.10–£4.70). All long-distance bus companies arrive at a large vacant expanse outside the medina walls at Bab Zorgane. From here it's a 10-minute walk into place al Nasr within the medina or an easy 15-minute stroll around the outside of the medina to Bab el Kasbah. If you don't feel like walking, there are usually a few *petits* taxis hanging around that will take you for around 5dh (65¢/30p). For onward travel from Taroudannt, all companies depart from Bab Zorgane. Some companies will simply issue a ticket once you are on the bus, or there are a couple of companies with ticket offices just inside Bab Zorgane. Although their buses operate from the same place as the private companies, the CTM ticket office is on place al Alaouyine (place Assarag) and is open daily from 9am to 8pm (no credit cards).

BY *GRAND* TAXI   Long-distance *grands* taxis to and from Taroudannt operate from the same place as the long-distance buses. The most regular routes for foreign travelers are Agadir (1½ hr.; 40dh/$5/£2.50); the transport hub of Inezgane (1¼ hr.; 40dh/$5/£2.50); and Taliouine (45 min.; 25dh/$3.15/£1.55), with irregular services to Marrakech (4½ hr.; 80dh/$13/£6.25). Chartering a private *grand* taxi to travel between Marrakech and Taroudannt will cost around 1,000dh ($125/£63).

Taroudannt

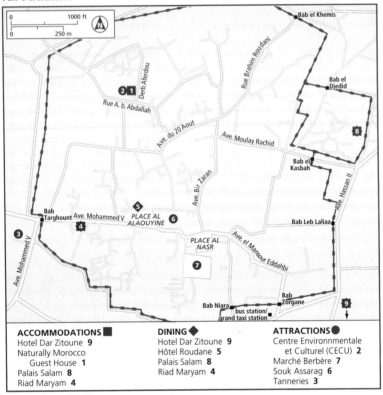

ACCOMMODATIONS ■
Hotel Dar Zitoune **9**
Naturally Morocco
Guest House **1**
Palais Salam **8**
Riad Maryam **4**

DINING ◆
Hotel Dar Zitoune **9**
Hôtel Roudane **5**
Palais Salam **8**
Riad Maryam **4**

ATTRACTIONS ●
Centre Environnmentale
et Culturel (CECU) **2**
Marché Berbère **7**
Souk Assarag **6**
Tanneries **3**

BY CAR   Driving into Taroudannt can be confusing depending on where you're coming from. The entrance to the city from the Tizi n'Test pass and Ouarzazate is along the main avenue Hassan II, which skirts the eastern wall of the medina past Hotel Palais Salam (p. 383) and continues on out of the city, past Dar Zitoune (p. 382) heading toward Agadir. Arriving from the Tizi Maachou pass will bring you into the southwest corner of the medina, where you can drive directly into place al Alaouyine, past Riad Maryam (p. 384). There are guarded parking lots at the Hotel Palais Salam and place al Nasr, but the streets are usually pretty quiet traffic-wise, and you can often park on the side of the street.

CITY LAYOUT
Taroudannt was left largely unaffected by the French occupation, and hence there are no separate medina and ville nouvelle sections. Travelers will spend most, if not all, of their time within the medina, which can initially be a little disorienting, although it lacks the overall intensity of Marrakech. Most travelers will spend their time between the twin squares of place al Alaouyine (formerly place Assarag) and place al Nasr (formerly place Talmoklate), or in the labyrinth Souk Assarag (also called the Arab Souk) that sits between the two.

GETTING AROUND

The best ways to discover this market town's compact medina are all environmentally friendly. Getting around on foot is easy, as there's not a lot of traffic and you'll never be too far away from the sights or your hotel; it's a 20- to 30-minute stroll from one wall to the other. A pleasant way to explore the medina further is by *caléche*. These horse-drawn carriages are an attraction themselves and are an especially good way to view the medina's walls, or ramparts. Their "taxi ranks" are either opposite the kasbah, at the junction of avenue Hassan II and avenue Moulay Rachid, or on place Assarag. A tour of the ramparts costs 30dh ($3.75/£1.90) and is especially pleasant at sunset. For the more intrepid, exploring the back streets of the medina by bike can be fun. These can be hired from the **Centre Environnmentale et Culturel** (CECU; p. 385) for 15dh ($1.90/95p) an hour. *Petits* taxis are always zipping around town and shouldn't cost you more than 5dh (65¢/30p) to anywhere in the medina; make sure they are using their meter before you commence the journey.

FAST FACTS: Taroudannt

Banks & Currency Exchange There's a cluster of banks with ATMs and/or bureaux de change on or around place al Alaouyine. They all operate the regular banking hours of Monday to Friday 8:15am to 3:45pm. There's also a **BMCI** branch on nearby place al Nasr with the same business hours. On avenue Hassan II—the main road coming from Ouarzazate or the Tizi n'Tichka pass—are branches of **WAFA, Credit Agricole,** and **Banque Populaire,** all with ATMs. WAFA also claims to cash American Express traveler's checks.

Drugstores There are a number of pharmacies dotted around town. **Pharmacie Taroudannt** (© 028/851392) is on place al Alaouyine, while along avenue Moulay Rachid are **Pharmacie Ibn Sïna** (© 028/850700) and **Pharmacie al Kasbaa** (© 028/850222). At the junction of avenue Moulay Rachid and avenue Hassan II is **Pharmacie el Baladia** (© 028/850700). They all operate daily between 9am to 1pm and 3 to 8pm, with a list of after-hours pharmacies posted on their front windows. An all-night pharmacy, **Pharmacie du Nuit,** is on avenue Prince Héritier Sidi Mohammed, .5km (⅓ mile) east of place al Nasr.

Emergency For **general emergencies** and the **police,** call © **19.**

Hospitals The public hospital, **Hôpital Mokhtar Souissi,** is located on avenue Moulay Rachid. **Clinique Taroudannt** (© 028/854100) is a private clinic located on avenue Hassan II.

Internet Access **Club Roudani** is on avenue Bir Zaran, just north of place al Nasr, and **Internet-Cyber** is located at the far west end of avenue Moulay Rachid. Outside the medina, **Cyber el Ayadi** is close to Hotel Palais Salam, behind the police station and Banque Populaire, on avenue Hassan II.

Photographic Needs **Labo Photo Ennakhil,** on place al Alaouyine, and **Labo Photo Bourar,** on place al Nasr, both offer digital downloading onto CD as well as the usual supply and processing of film. **Labo Photo Bourar** also has a small supply of memory cards, card readers, and USB hubs. All three are open daily from 9am to 12:30pm and 2 to 9pm.

Police The main police station **(La Commissariat)** is located just off avenue Hassan II, behind Banque Populaire and across from M'Haita mosque. There is also a police station on place al Alaouyine.

Post Office & Mail Taroudannt's main **post office**, which receives all *poste restante* mail, is across from M'Haita mosque and the police station, just off avenue Hassan II. Within the medina, there's a small post office on rue du 20 Août off avenue Mohammed V. Post offices operate Monday to Friday 8am to 4:15pm and Saturday 8 to 11:45am.

Restrooms There are no public toilets in Taroudannt. Within the medina, your best bet is to politely ask for the *toilette* in one of the budget hotels around place al Alaouyine. If you're anywhere near the kasbah, duck into the Hotel Palais Salam.

Safety Personal safety generally isn't an issue in Taroudannt. Some of the streets and vacant lots surrounding the medina walls aren't well lit at night, including the bus/*grand* taxi station, but even then only normal precautions need to be considered.

Telephone Taroudannt's **city code** has recently changed from 048 to **028**.

WHERE TO STAY

Taroudannt may be described as "a little Marrakech," but when it comes to accommodations, Taroudannt can't compare. Decent accommodations, for any budget, are hard to come by, and the following recommendations are pretty much it. Taroudannt's sublime climate—warm in winter, not oppressively hot in summer—largely negates the need for rooms with air-conditioning and heating other than in the oppressively hot months of July and August and perhaps on a few chilly nights in December or January.

EXPENSIVE

Dar Zitoune 🖝 Opened in 2005, this luxurious villa-style property on the edge of Taroudannt is a peaceful place to both explore the surrounding sights and unwind for a couple of days. Upon first glance of the large front wall and its heavy wood doors, you may wonder what could override such a nonluxurious location. However, this plain, heavy-set frontage only serves to keep the dust and noise outside and the peace and quiet inside. The whole property is low-rise and low key, built from natural materials and in earthy colors. It's set in 1.2 hectares (3 acres) of grounds with citrus, papaya (paw paw), and olive (*zitoun* in Arabic) trees and gardens of roses, geranium, and rosemary, all manicured by no less than four gardeners. A large, dome lobby made from local clay bricks leads onto a popular restaurant to one side and an even more popular bar and lounge on the other. All three rooms lead to a patio with mosaic and wrought-iron tables with oversize linen umbrellas, where a delicious breakfast of fruit, yogurt, eggs, cereal, and *msemmen* (crepes) is served each morning. There's also a squeaky clean, keyhole-shape 25m (82-ft.) pool surrounded by sun lounges and umbrellas.

The well-appointed bungalows and suites are scattered around the rear of the property and are rustic in feel but luxurious in fittings, with clay-tile *bejmat* floors; large *tadelakt*-rendered bathrooms with fluffy, white bath linens and domed walk-in showers; satellite TV; and a small sitting area. The larger suites can accommodate up to two adults and two children. Also at the rear is a small beauty center with hammam.

Despite its roadside-motel location—it's about 3km (1¾ miles) from the southern walls of the medina—Dar Zitoune is all class and worth the splurge if you feel like staying for a couple of nights.

Boutarialt el Barrania, Taroudannt-Agadir Road, Taroudannt. ℂ 028/551141 or 024/551142. Fax 028/551143. www. darzitoune.com. 22 units. 900dh ($113/£56) double; 1,220dh–2,720dh ($153–$340/£76–£170) suite. Rates include breakfast. AE, MC, V. **Amenities:** Restaurant; bar; pool; hammam; free Internet. *In room:* A/C, satellite TV, Internet modem connection, hair dryer, safe.

Hotel Palais Salam   Anchored into the wall of the kasbah, this former pasha's palace is definitely aging but still manages to hold on to some of its decadent past. The best feature of this hotel is its public spaces, beginning with a grand reception area that leads to a large garden of banana palms, jacaranda trees, bougainvillea, and tall date palms, dotted with small aviaries housing musical finches and love birds. A large pool has its own bar—ironically designed like a Muslim shrine—and is best for sitting around rather than swimming in. The constant noise of water from a small pond, complete with resident tortoises, adds to the peaceful ambience. Two large Moroccan lounges separate the gardens from the majority of the rooms, which are located in two-story blocks around a central courtyard garden, while the lobby leads to another garden courtyard surrounded by more rooms.

The rooms vary in size and standard. The old rooms are the ones in the courtyards and are definitely starting to feel, and look, their age. The separate wing has new rooms that are both large and airy, if a trifle bland, and also houses a second swimming pool; I recommend this pool for a dip, as it's infinitely more private than the garden pool and is regularly empty because many guests don't know it's here. You should also consider climbing one of the hotel's two towers toward the rear of the old wing. This is the only building that has a view of the kasbah and medina, so don't miss it. The hotel's two restaurants are its crowning glory (p. 385).

Bd. Moulay Ismail, Kasbah, Taroudannt. ℂ 028/852312 or 028/852501. Fax 028/852654. palsalam@menara.ma. 142 units. Old wing 550dh–600dh ($68–$75/£34–£38) single, 650dh–750dh ($81–$94/£41–£47) double; new wing 1,000dh–1,400dh ($125–$175/£63–£88) single, 1,400dh–1,600dh ($175–$200/£88–£100) double; 2,400dh ($300/£150) apt up to 4. Children 3–12 50% in parent's room; under 3 free. Taxes not included. MC, V. **Amenities:** 2 restaurants; bar; 2 lounges; 2 pools; gym; shop. *In room:* A/C, satellite TV, fridge, safe.

MODERATE

Naturally Morocco Guest House ★★★ *Value* *Kids*   The Taroudannt base for U.K. responsible-travel company Naturally Morocco used to be a family home and still feels like one; such is the happy and busy atmosphere that prevails throughout. The three-story building has up to 11 rooms depending on bedding configurations, plus a large communal dining room. Tiled throughout, the rooms are all furnished simply yet elegantly, some with a private bathroom. The ground floor can be rented as a two-bedroom, two-bathroom apartment, complete with its own kitchen, and is perfect for groups or large families. Twin, rooftop terraces are good spots to enjoy your meals. While only clients of Naturally Morocco can stay here, everyone is welcome to come for dinner (if reserved in the morning), where manager Latifa and the forever smiling Fatima serve up superb home-cooked Moroccan meals that some diners rate as the best in Taroudannt. The guesthouse is tucked away in a small *derb* (lane) but is well signposted from avenue du 20 Août; if you get lost, ask anyone for La Maison Anglaise.

La Maison Anglaise, 422 Derb Aferdou, Taroudannt. ℂ 028/551628, or 0845/345-7195 within U.K. www.naturally morocco.co.uk. 11 units. Rates are based on a 7-night stay program and include most meals and 5 days of tours/activities; 4,000dh ($500/£250) double. Shorter stays sometimes available upon request. Dinner 150dh ($19/£9.40). MC,

V accepted for prebooked reservations. **Amenities:** Restaurant; kitchen; library; communal room and activities center; interconnecting rooms. *In room:* Fans, electric heaters, no phone.

Riad Maryam ★★ *Finds* *Kids*   This is a riad in every sense of the word, with overwhelming hospitality, home-cooked food, and a lived-in feel that isn't luxurious—but doesn't pretend to be, either. Habib and Latifa Moultazim don't speak a word of English, but that hasn't stopped them from greeting a steady stream of guests from around the globe into their family riad since 2002. Their five-bedroom house surrounds a large central courtyard with twin, bird-friendly gardens with umbrellas, orange trees, banana palms, and bougainvillea, separated by a dining area with a long, communal table. The rooms are more quirky than quaint, and haphazardly furnished but perfectly adequate. Three rooms can take at least one extra bed, which is a plus for families. Not all rooms have a private bathroom, but the common bathrooms are spotlessly clean. Latifa's kitchen (see below) produces some of the best Moroccan food I've tasted and negates the need to deal with the lack of quality restaurants in Taroudannt. Habib can organize any day trip or activities, including a day drive/trek into the Anti-Atlas for 300dh ($38/£19). Or, if you just want to stay in, the courtyard is entirely bordered with cushions and lounges, plus there is a satellite TV and a CD player.

140 Derb Maalen Mohammed (signposted from av. Mohammed V), Bab Targhount, Taroudannt. © 065/485453 or 066/127285. www.riadmaryam.fr.fm. 600dh ($75/£38) double; 700dh–900dh ($88–$113/£44–£56) 1-to 4-person rooms. Children 5–12 200dh ($25/£13) in parent's room; under 5 free. Rates include breakfast. No credit cards. **Amenities:** Restaurant; laundry service; Internet; Agadir transfers available. *In room:* A/C, no phone.

WHERE TO DINE

Taroudannt has very few restaurants outside of the city's accommodations and none to recommend from those that are available. All is not lost, however, as those restaurants within accommodations are of a very high standard and come thoroughly recommended because of their cuisine and not the lack of competition. Besides those mentioned below, you can also try Naturally Morocco Guest House (p. 383).

EXPENSIVE

Dar Zitoune MOROCCAN/FRENCH   This is Taroudannt's only fine-dining choice and is known as much for the setting as the food. The large restaurant within this villa-hotel opens onto an open-air patio that affords a pleasant, umbrella-shaded lunch or a romantic dinner under the stars. During the colder months, request a table inside next to the clay-brick fireplace. The menu is limited but offers a choice of Moroccan dishes such as chicken tagine with preserved lemon and green olives, pastas, and *menus du jour* for lunch and dinner that usually include an international dish such as a filet of Saint-Pierre (John Dory) in a rosemary-and-cream sauce or a smoked salmon tagliatelle. If there are no tour groups staying here, and there rarely are, the restaurant is quiet, and you may end up with your own personal waiter.

Boutarialt el Barrania, Agadir Highway. © **028/551141** or 024/551142. Fax 028/551143. www.darzitoune.com. Alcohol served. Main courses 90dh–130dh ($11–$16/£5.65–£8.15); set menu 150dh–200dh ($19–$25/£9.40–£13) lunch, 250dh ($31/£16) dinner. AE, MC, V. Daily noon–3pm and 7:30–10:30pm.

Riad Maryam ★★★ MOROCCAN   The food that comes out of Latifa Moultazim's kitchen is worthy of a grander stage, but until (it's inevitable) this happens, diners are part of a secret club that have tasted some of the best Moroccan cuisine in the country. Both guests and the public are welcome into Habib and Latifa's riad (see above) for lunch and dinner. A long, communal dining table surrounded by birdsong from the overhanging trees is the perfect setting for an informal dining experience that always includes more food than you can eat and wine, sometimes even champagne, specially delivered to the riad. A meze of hot and cold starters is usually enough to fill your stomach, let alone the proceeding courses that could include beef brochettes topped with fresh coriander and a lamb tagine stewed with whole baby onions and sesame seed–covered prunes. Forget the Moroccan pastries offered with the mint tea—you won't have any space left.

140 Derb Maalen Mohammed (signposted from av. Mohammed V), Bab Targhount. © 065/485453 or 066/127285. www.riadmaryam.fr.fm. Reservations required. Set menu 200dh ($25/£13) lunch and dinner. No credit cards. Daily 1–3:30pm and 8–10:30pm.

MODERATE

Roudhane MOROCCAN/INTERNATIONAL   Whether you come to this former pasha's palace for a meal under the shade of large palm and jacaranda trees or for a Moroccan fine-dining experience inside the gold-cushioned Moroccan salon, you'll walk away happy. Although the Hotel Palais Salam is regularly overrun with tour groups, there seems to be enough space for everyone when it comes meal time. Maître d' Sarami Mohammed has been personally setting the standard for excellent service here for the past 15 years, and it's refreshing in a country where other restaurants are less enthusiastic about their service. Choose from either an extensive international menu—with dishes ranging from a *risotto Neapolitan* to a beef filet in pepper sauce—or from the Roudhane restaurant's four-course Moroccan *menu du jour* with standards such as *harira* soup and couscous *aux sept légumes* offered alongside specialties such as *tomate monégasque* (baked tomato stuffed with rice).

Bd. Moulay Ismail, Kasbah. © 028/852312 or 028/852501. Fax 028/852654. Alcohol served. Main courses 50dh–150dh ($6.25–$19/£3.15–£9.40); set menu 150dh ($6.25/£3.15). Nonguests cash only. Daily noon–3pm and 7–11pm.

INEXPENSIVE

Hôtel Roudane CAFE   Musa Roudhani runs this very friendly cafe/restaurant on place al Alaouyine, and although it's not the most modernly furnished of establishments and the food offered is pretty basic, it's a great spot for people-watching accompanied by a simple mint tea or coffee.

Place al Alaouyine. No phone. Tea/coffee 8dh ($1/50p). No credit cards. Daily 8am–10pm.

WHAT TO SEE & DO

Taroudannt is essentially still a market town, and the attraction for most travelers is the actual *lack* of attractions. Life here is not put on for show and continues on as it always has, give or take a few modern concessions. The sights listed below are only sights in the eyes of a visitor; for the resident of Taroudannt they are part of everyday life, which is the beauty of the place.

Centre Environnmentale et Culturel (CECU) ⭐⭐⭐   This is the home for the U.K.-based sustainable tourism company Naturally Morocco. The company offers a wide range of cultural experiences within Taroudannt. Their Moroccan staff accompanies clients on outings as diverse as a visit to the local hammam followed by an argan-oil massage; a henna hair coloring or tattooing; Arabic language or Moroccan cooking lessons; and a live folk music performance from a local, all-female Berber band. Those who are not clients of Naturally Morocco are welcome to join the day's planned outings so long as there is space. Activities are 100dh ($13/£6.25) each.

La Maison Anglaise, 422 Derb Aferdou (off av. du 20 Août). © 028/551628 or 067/620608. ecotours@menara.ma. Sat–Thurs 8:30am–noon and 3–7:30pm.

Place al Alaouyine ✫ This large, central square is the heart of the medina and plays host to a mini Jemaa el Fna most evenings. Storytellers, musicians, and potion salesmen can be seen on the square, surrounded by crowds of mostly locals. Snake charmers are also sometimes present, offering the princely sum of 25dh ($3.15/£1.55) to anybody brave enough to touch the often sedated or ill reptile.

Ramparts Taroudannt medina is encircled by 5km (3 miles) of walls that are considered the best preserved in the country. Dating back to both the 16th and 18th centuries, these walls have seen their share of bloodshed—all of the city's inhabitants were massacred in 1687 after opposing the rule of Moulay Ismail (p. 238)—but today are popular with camera-wielding travelers who marvel at its different hues of red, pink, and gold depending on the time of day. To walk around the walls takes a pleasant 2 hours, or you can also enjoy it via *caléche* or bicycle (see "Getting Around," earlier).

Souks Between place al Alaouyine and place al Nasr are Taroudannt's two souks: Souk Assarag (sometimes called the Arab Souk) and Marché Berbère (the Berber or Municipal Market). Souk Assarag is home to Taroudannt's leatherworkers—still going strong thanks to the tanneries (see below)—and dotted within the souk are a number of small shops where you can see handbags and footwear being designed, cut, and stitched. There's a lane of leatherworkers running alongside the souk's northern wall, about 30m (100 ft.) from place al Alaouyine.

The Souss region is known for its distinctive silver jewelry, and there's a cluster of *bijoutiers* (jewelers) in the souk's center. Spread throughout the souk are other skilled workers such as tailors, embroiderers, and blacksmiths. **La Maison Berbere,** at the souk's west entrance, is a treasure trove of ceramics, rugs, lanterns, and teapots and is open every day from 9am to 7pm. **Marché Berbère,** off place al Nasr, is more for everyday items and foodstuffs, but there are also a few pottery shops and *herboristes* selling such sweet-smelling luxuries as musk, amber, and jasmine (2dh/25¢/15p per gram) as well as saffron (15dh/$1.90/95p per gram). This is also the place to stock up on dried fruits and nuts.

Enter Souk Assarag from either its eastern side, at the BMCI bank on av. Bir Anzarane, or western side, off place al Alaouyine. Marché Berbère is directly to the south of place al Nasr. Daily 8am–8pm.

Tanneries ✫ *(Kids)* Cleaned up by the local authorities in 2001 to attract more visitors, Taroudannt's small tannery quarter is a sight to behold, especially if you haven't visited the larger operations in Fes or Marrakech. Different to the latter two in both size and location, these tanneries are a small, but busy, operation, and are located outside the medina albeit close to one of the major gates, Bab Targhount. What I like about these tanneries is that they offer a real up-close-and-personal experience where visitors can easily walk up to the pits and watch the dyer in action. The leather is still cured in pigeon droppings and cattle urine, dyed in henna (green), indigo (blue), paprika (red), and turmeric (yellow), and immersed in clay vats and soaked (by hand and foot) until ready.

Shops selling all manner of leather and animal products surround the tanneries, and some bargains, especially compared to those found at the Fes tannery, are to be had. Youss Allal and Youss Brahim, at nos. 25 and 26, respectively, sell some lovely pure lambs-wool hides (50dh–150dh/$6.25–$19/£3.15–£9.40), funky lambs-wool/cowhide handbags (120dh–150dh/$15–$19/£7.50–£9.40), leather jackets (500dh/$63/£31), and a wide range of leather *poufes* (foot cushions; 300dh–800dh/$38–$100/£19–£50).

Note: Unfortunately, some shops still offer products made from such things as snake skin and fox hide. It goes without saying that, for both legal and moral reasons, these products are best left on the shelf.

Av. Mohammed V, 70m (230 ft.) south from Bab Targhount. Daily. Hours vary (usually 9am–6pm).

Spice Town

From the Sirwa mountains around Taliouine comes a small but significant portion of the world's most expensive spice, **saffron**—known to sell in New York for up to $8,000 (£4,000) a kilo (just over 2 lb.). The dry climate around Taliouine is ideal for the violet-blue flower from which the valuable saffron stylus is picked.

The saffron plant, *crocus sativus,* is a cultivar and thus instead of a seed, it produces an underground corm, similar to a bulb. *Crocus sativas* needs 2 years to produce three to four corms big enough to be separated, replanted, and harvested. Up to eight flowers blossom during the plant's lifespan (Morocco's saffron fields are renewed every 7 years), each flower with six beautiful blue-violet petals and a long yellow style out of which comes three precious red-orange stigmas.

The plant needs to be evenly watered, and in dry Taliouine, the saffron fields are irrigated 15 times per year to the equivalent of .6 to .7m (24–28 in.) of rainfall. Harvest takes 4 to 6 weeks, peaking at the end of October when 60% of the flowers bloom over a 2-week period. Though it requires little physical energy the rest of the year, harvesting saffron is back-breaking work. The flowers are hand-picked for 2 to 3 hours every morning at dawn, before the sun opens up the flower and the style is damaged. This work is done mostly by women. Once identified, the flower is picked, opened, and its precious style pinched and removed. It takes 140 flowers to make a single gram of dried saffron. The saffron harvest is very demanding, and whole families will work up to 20 hours a day in the field and in drying rooms. Saffron stigmas are dried in dark rooms or over a low fire. Air-drying results in a spicier saffron, whereas heat-drying produces a stronger fragrance.

Used as a pigment, saffron's deep yellow color can be seen on painted cedar ceilings within the kasbahs of southern Morocco, where it is also known for its healing effects on muscle spasms, toothache, and menstrual pain. Moroccan Berber women use the saffron in a paste that enhances their facial features and enriches the hair.

Saffron is one of the most counterfeited foodstuffs in the world, so it's preferable to buy it in its stigma form. Stigmas must be thin, long, and a deep red color. When put into water, a stigma of saffron will immediately release a dark orange color. In Morocco's souks, and sometimes the streets of Taliouine, you may be offered dried saffron. In Taliouine, some families keep a part of their harvest to sell themselves, so it's highly likely that what's on offer is genuine. If it's being offered much cheaper than the going rate of 15dh ($1.90/95p) per gram, however, then there's every possibility that you're not buying the real deal.

SIDE TRIPS FROM TAROUDANNT
TALIOUINE
114km (71 miles) E of Taroudannt; 170km (106 miles) SW of Ouarzazate

Nestled in a pass of the Sirwa mountains, halfway between Taroudannt and Ouarzazate, is the sleepy town of Taliouine. At its eastern edge is a once-grand kasbah that belonged to the Lords of the Atlas, the Glaoui (p. 168). Although it is rapidly crumbling into an uninhabitable ruin, presently there are still a few families—descendants of the Glaoui's servants—living in it who are usually keen to show you around for 20dh ($2.50/£1.25) or so. Morocco's saffron (see "Spice Town" below) is grown in the hills around Taliouine, which are becoming popular for intrepid hikers.

The **Coopérative Souktana du Safran,** Taliouine-Ouarzazate Road (© **028/ 534151,** 068/395215, or 066/979002), represents more than 350 local saffron growers and enriches the lives of around 1,200 people. Tasked with all post-production, marketing, and distribution of its members' saffron, the cooperative also acts as a quality controller, especially with respect to the nonuse of artificial fertilizers and pesticides. By using only cow and sheep manure and regularly plowing the fields rather than spraying for weeds, Souktana saffron is certified organic, adding value to an already valuable crop. The cooperative is managed by locals Driss and Salah who welcome visitors to their small center on the main highway at the eastern (Ouarzazate) end of Taliouine. An explanation of the production process and the many benefits of saffron is offered along with a cup of saffron tea, and, of course, the precious spice can be bought here as well. It's open daily 8am to 8pm.

Taliouine is a 2- to 3-hour bus ride from Taroudannt (40dh/$5/£2.50) or Ouarzazate (55dh/$6.90/£3.45). The town has one bank, Crédit Agricole, on the Taroudannt-Ouarzazate road, open Monday to Thursday 8:30 to 11:30am and 2:30 to 5pm, and Friday 8:30 to 11am and 3 to 5pm. Ahmed and Michelle Jadid, along with their son Hassan, run trekking tours from their very popular **Auberge Souktana** (© **028/ 534074;** souktana@menara.ma), located at the edge of town on the Ouarzazate road. Their small guesthouse offers a range of rooms, bungalows, and tents, some with a private bathroom, from 135dh to 165dh ($17–$21/£8.45–£10) double, including dinner and breakfast. Closer to the town, and still on the main road, is **Auberge le Safran** (© **028/534046;** www.auberge-safran.fr.fm; 120dh/$15/£7.50 double).

3 Tafraoute ★★★
143km (89 miles) SE of Agadir; 102km (63 miles) E of Tiznit

Nestled amongst the palmeraie and boulder-strewn mountains of the Anti-Atlas's remote Ameln Valley is Tafraoute. Roughly translated from Berber as "a trough" or "depression," Tafraoute was originally the name given to the whole Ameln Valley but was gradually used solely for the village where the main, weekly souk took place and still does every Tuesday. A relaxed, unassuming town at first glance, an exploration on foot to its outskirts reveals a smattering of mini-mansions amongst the boulders—testimony to the many Tafraoutis who work elsewhere in Morocco and in Europe, only returning for holidays each year. Coupled with the their conservative nature (women are generally heavily covered out in public), this hidden wealth has left Tafraoute refreshingly free of the intense hassle that can be experienced elsewhere, and one of the first senses that you experience here is how quiet it is. Boulders surround the village and extend through the entire Ameln Valley, changing from pink to gray to gold, depending on the time of day. Sculpted over millions of years from wind and water, the granite boulders appear as they have been randomly thrown over the landscape. Almond trees are also prevalent in the Ameln Valley and are harvested in late February or early March, sparking off all-night festivals amongst the villages. Sleepy Tafraoute is slowly beginning to cash in on its harsh beauty, and with the recent construction of two new hotels, the village now offers good accommodations and is a delightful place to stop for a night or two.

ESSENTIALS
GETTING THERE
BY BUS & GRAND TAXI Private bus companies from both Casablanca (14 hr.; 140dh/$18/£9) and Marrakech (7 hr.; 100dh/$13/£6.25) make the trip to Tafraoute daily. Trans Balady (© 028/843212) travels from Agadir (5 hr.; 60dh/$7.50/£3.75) via Tiznit (3½ hr.; 20dh/$2.50/£1.25) twice a day. *Grands* taxis from Tiznit (2½ hr.; 30dh/$3.75/£1.90) depart daily.

VISITOR INFORMATION Ahmed Ouardarass' **Tafraout Aventure** is the unofficial tourism office in town, located on place al Massira in the town center (© 028/801368; www.tafraout-aventure.com). It's open daily from 8am to 8pm. They have information, a map on Tafraoute and the Ameln Valley, hire out mountain bikes, and offer guided 4WD tours.

FAST FACTS BMCE (© 028/801582), on avenue Mokhtar Souissi, just west of place al Massira, has a bureau de change and ATM. It's open Monday to Friday 8:15am to 3:45pm. **Pharmacie al Massira,** on place al Massira (© 028/800160), is open daily from 8am to 9pm. Internet can be accessed at **Tafraout Club des Internantes,** opposite the BMCE bank, open daily from 10am to 10pm. Tafraoute's **post office** is on place al Massira and is open Monday to Friday 8:15am to 4:30pm.

GETTING AROUND
The best way to experience the natural and rugged beauty around Tafraoute is by foot or bicycle. For further exploration of the Ameln Valley, a 4WD is required.

BY BIKE Mountain bikes can be rented from Tafraoute Aventure for 70dh ($8.75/£4.40) per day without shock absorbers, 100dh ($13/£6.50) with shock absorbers.

BY ORGANIZED TOUR Tafraoute Aventure offers a range of tours, such as a day's guided walk farther along the Ameln Valley, including lunch in a Berber house (400dh/$50/£25) and a full-day 4WD and walking tour of the surrounding gorges, engravings, and rock formations (1,200dh/$150/£75 per vehicle). They also do a 3-day tour to Ouarzazate via Tata and the Dra Valley (p. 189) for 2,200dh to 2,500dh per person ($275–$313/£138–£156). In Agadir, Major Travel Services (MTS) in the Complex Manader, boulevard du 20 Août (© 028/827429 or 069/837345), offers a full-day tour to Tiznit and Tafraoute for 980dh ($123/£61) adults, 490dh ($61/£31) children under 12, including lunch.

WHAT TO SEE & DO
There are 26 villages in the Ameln Valley, and most of them are in dramatic, beautiful locations between the boulder-strewn cliffs and the lush palmeraie on the valley's floor. Easy walks from Tafraoute include a 2km (1¼-mile) stroll southwest to the village of Tazka, where there's a prehistoric graving of a gazelle plus a few more recent ones. Three kilometers (2 miles) south of Tafraoute is a rock formation known as Napoleon's Hat in the village of Agard Oudad.

Berber carpets made in the Anti-Atlas can be cheaper here than anywhere else in the country, depending on your bargaining skills. Carpets featuring the deep yellow saffron pigment, grown in the hills around Taliouine on the northern side of the Anti-Atlas (p. 388), are an especially good value. La Maison Touareg (© 028/800210), just off place al Massira on the road up to Hôtel les Amandiers, has a huge selection of carpets, rugs, and *kélims*, all made by the Touareg nomads of Morocco's deep south. Hours are daily 9am to 7pm.

WHERE TO STAY

Hôtel Saint Antoine (Value Opened in 2006, this hotel offers the best value rooms in Tafraoute. The grand, three-story building tends to stick out a bit in this decidedly low-rise town, but within it are a ground-floor cafe/reception and Internet area, a first-floor restaurant, and well-appointed bedrooms with rust and white tiling and large modern bathrooms. Some rooms also have a two-seater lounge, and six rooms open onto their own private balcony with sweeping views over the palmeraie. The ground floor leads out to a heavenly 25m (82-ft.) pool surrounded by a well-kept lawn and garden, and on the rooftop is a large terrace with 360-degree views. Especially convenient for families, some rooms are large enough to accommodate up to four beds.

Av. Mokhtar Souissi, Tafraoute. © 028/801497. Fax 028/800003. www.hotelsaintantoine-tafraout.com. 24 units. 390dh ($49/£24) single; 450dh ($56/£28) double; 50dh ($6.25/£3.15) each additional bed. Reservations recommended Feb 20–Mar 10 and Aug. Rates include breakfast. No credit cards accepted. Guarded parking. **Amenities:** Restaurant; cafe; pool; room service; Internet. *In room:* A/C, satellite TV.

Riad Tafraout It's hard to miss this modern kasbah on the edge of town, with banners and flapping flags adorning its front. Hassan Bonami, from the nearby village of Agard Oudad, opened up his faux riad in 2007 after an extensive building project that can be described as rustic, if not a little too authentic. In any case, this is as chic as you'll get in this part of Morocco. The large ground-floor cafe-cum-reception mixes traditional Moroccan furniture and brightly colored Iraqi glass windows with quaint wrought-iron tables and a shiny, apricot *tadelakt* wall. First-floor rooms have dark *tabout* walls and an assortment of decorations and antiques ranging from Moroccan lanterns to antlers. A two-sided terrace is accessed from this floor. The second floor is a lot brighter, and the rooms are more traditional in design. All the rooms are reasonably sized with modern bathrooms and nice touches such as fluffy white towels and bags of potpourri, not to mention an Internet modem connection. Up on the small rooftop is an enclosed Jacuzzi. It could all border on a bit too much were it not for the pleasurable service.

Route de l'hôtel Les Amandiers, Tafraoute. © 028/800031. Fax 028/280032. www.riad-tafraout.com. 8 units. 400dh ($50/£25) single; 600dh ($75/£38) double. Reservations recommended Feb 20–Mar 10 and Aug. Rates include breakfast. No credit cards accepted. **Amenities:** Cafe; Jacuzzi. *In room:* A/C, satellite TV, Internet modem connection.

WHERE TO DINE

Hôtel les Amandiers BAR Although its accommodations and restaurant are living on past glories and are not worth your money, this hotel is a fantastic spot for a late-afternoon drink, when you can watch the sunset over Taroudannt and the surrounding mountains. Sitting atop the closest hill overlooking Tafraoute, Hôtel les Amandiers' white exterior can't be missed and is a pleasant walk up from the rest of the town. At the very front of the hulking mass is an outdoor area with a few tables and chairs from where you can be served a nice chilled wine or cold beer.

Route de l'hôtel Les Amandiers. © 028/800088. Bar service available daily noon–10pm.

Hôtel Saint Antoine MOROCCAN   The restaurant of this recommended hotel (above) offers a very good menu of Moroccan standards. Both lunch and dinner can be taken either within the large restaurant, a nondescript room with faux antique furniture that's gloriously warm on chilly winter nights, or on a terrace at the rear that overlooks the pleasant garden and pool. Salads, omelets, tagines, and brochettes are the order of the day, with a wide range of choices of each. A beef tagine (150dh/$19/£9) serves four and is a fine feast that's a "hands-on" affair. They'll also whip up spaghetti or couscous if desired.

Av. Mokhtar Souissi. 🕿 028/801497. Fax 028/800003. www.hotelsaintantoine-tafraout.com. Main courses 40dh–50dh ($5–$6.25/£2.50–£3.15). No credit cards accepted. Daily noon–10pm.

Restaurant Etoile du Sud MOROCCAN   Ali Boukhsay has been welcoming travelers—a lot of them in big tour buses—into his restaurant for the past 45 years. A large, compoundlike area consisting of two separate but adjoining salons and a large outdoor Bedouin tent, the "Star of the South" pumps out very Moroccan dishes from noon until late every day. Diners have a range of choices from a set menu that includes the specialties of beef tagine with prunes and local almonds and a very tasty *harira* soup. If you come in the morning, you can order a chicken *pastilla* (150dh/$19/£9) for the evening meal. The decor and furniture have definitely seen better days, but the crowds keep coming hungry and leaving satisfied. Alcohol is served, but you can also bring your own.

Place al Massira. 🕿 028/800038. Set menu 90dh ($11/£5.65) lunch and dinner. Alcohol served. No credit cards accepted. Daily noon–10pm.

SIDE TRIP FROM TAFRAOUTE
COL DU KERDOUS
49km (30 miles) W of Tafraoute; 54km (33 miles) E of Tiznit; 153km (95 miles) SE of Agadir

The journey to Col de Kerdous is just as rewarding as the destination itself. The views from this mountain pass, 1,100m (3,609 ft.) above sea level, are simply spectacular, especially during the late afternoon when the pink Anti-Atlas starts to take on all manner of shades. The winding drive from Tafraoute passes numerous Berber villages, their earthen adobe houses and cultivated terraces sometimes clinging to the mountainsides. Heading toward Tiznit, the col, or mountain pass, signals the rapid descent to the coastal plain.

The **Kerdous Hotel** (🕿 028/862063; fax 028/600315; 665dh/$83/£42 double, including breakfast) is located right on the pass and is a very comfortable place to stop for a drink or even stay the night. Built from the remains of a former kasbah, it offers 38 rooms, all with private bathrooms, air-conditioning, and heating. The restaurant's large kitchen offers a surprisingly varied menu of mostly international dishes for both lunch and dinner. A bar/salon opens up to a cliffside outdoor patio, where you can enjoy your meal along with sweeping views toward the west. A small bar-cafe at the hotel's entrance offers drinks (alcoholic and nonalcoholic) and coffee for those stopping just for a look and a photo.

Appendix A:
Morocco in Depth

Independent for just more than 50 years, Morocco has, over time, been trod by many different feet. From the New Stone Age to the 21st century, Morocco's mountains, coast, plains, and desert have hosted settlers and nomads, invaders and conquerors. Today this is visible in the country's religion (indoctrinated by marauding Muslims in the 7th c.), artisans and musicians (an oral and visual mix of Berber, Andalusian, Jewish, and Arabic), and, of course, its cuisine. Acceding to the throne upon his father's death in 1999, 44-year-old King Mohammed VI is repositioning Morocco as one of the major gateways between East and West—a position it has held intermittently over the centuries. A young country in more ways than one—more than half the population is under 40—Morocco is one of the world's current hot spots for investment, particularly tourism. This all-embracing focus on modernization has the potential to both uplift and alienate Moroccans. King Mohammed VI consistently walks a tightrope between his dual roles as the country's spiritual leader—his dynasty, the Alaouites, claim to be direct descendents of the Prophet Mohammed—and ruler of a nation that labors under an illiteracy rate of just more than 50% with a fifth of its inhabitants still living below the poverty line.

1 A Look at the Past

It can be argued that Morocco has the purest human bloodline of any region in Africa. The natives, who inhabited the area more than 3,000 years ago, have been subjected to waves of foreign interference by everyone from the Phoenicians and Romans to colonial French and Spanish settlers. These immigrants never came in overwhelming numbers—even the Bedouin Arabs of the 7th and 8th centuries who exerted such a profound influence on the region's culture—and so the greater part of Morocco's present population can be regarded as descendants of the original inhabitants that occupied el Maghreb a millennia ago.

The migration of prehistoric peoples that led to the emergence of the current population of Morocco likely took place well before 5,000 to 40,000 B.C., as writings from Greek scholars of the time refer to a substantial and formidable tribe

(termed Libyans in reference to the tribe's name, Lebou) inhabiting the far western fringe of Egypt to the west of the Nile delta.

During the course of the 1st millennium B.C., the Punic-speaking Phoenicians and their predecessors, the Carthaginians from modern-day Tunisia, constructed a series of trading stations and other posts—most notably in Morocco near the modern-day cities of Tangier, Larache, and Essaouira—to jointly meet the needs of their seamen and to protect their monopoly of the coastal trade. The Carthaginians waged wars against the Greek city-states of Sicily and with Rome. They expanded their empire farther west along the coasts of both northwest Africa and southern Spain before they eventually capitulated to Rome. The far western outposts of Carthage initially remained largely unaffected from the change in power and even prospered for about another 100 years from waves of relocating Punic refugees. The Libyans of Morocco were treated harshly under Carthaginian rule, and many took refuge in the Rif, Atlas mountains, and beyond into the pre-Sahara where they began a seminomadic existence. From these inaccessible, harsh regions grew a largely ungovernable people who would ferociously guard their independence for centuries to come.

Rome's African colony—called Ifrikiya in medieval Arabic times and from which the continent now takes its name—was established in the Carthaginian homeland in northern Tunisia, and over the next 150 years, Roman influence spread over all the coastal districts of northwest Africa. The Romans termed all the native inhabitants that were not under their direct rule as *barbari*—"barbarians," a term that passed into modern usage as "Berber"—and by the time the Romans made their way to Morocco, a number of kingdoms had been created among the inland, independent Berbers of North Africa. In northern Morocco and western Algeria, these Berbers were known by the Romans as the Maures, and their kingdom became known as Mauretania. Rome initially tolerated the kingdom, which prospered first under the rule of Juba II, an Algerian Berber who was educated in Rome and married the daughter of Antony and Cleopatra, and then his son Ptolemy. By around A.D. 40, however, Rome eventually imposed a more centralized control and split its colony into Mauretania Caesarensis (Algeria) and Mauretania Tingitana (Morocco), with Tingis (Tangier) the latter's easily accessible capital. Mauretania Tingitana was to be the empire's westernmost province, but the empire was to crumble before any such feat could be considered.

Though it was considered a far-flung outpost by the cultured set in Rome, Roman urbanization flourished in Mauretania Tingitana, with estimates of more than 30 established cities scattered along the northern coast and adjoining plains. Volubilis, located squarely within the fertile farmlands, became a major seat of power and commerce as the province supplied the empire with more than half its requirement of agricultural produce such as olives and grain, as well as many of the African animals used in the barbaric gladiator games. It is estimated that within the 200-odd years of direct Roman rule in northwest Africa, the populations of Atlas bears, elephants, and lions were as good as wiped out.

The rule by the Romans was plagued by constant raids from the Berbers living beyond the Roman frontier boundary.

Dateline

- 10,000–5000 B.C. Neolithic cultures spread out across North Africa.
- 1100–150 B.C. The sea-faring Phoenicians, followed by the Carthaginians, settle along the North African coast.
- 146 B.C. After the fall of Carthage, Roman influence makes its way to North Africa.
- 27 B.C. Direct Roman rule extends to Morocco as far as Volubilis (near Meknes).
- A.D. 253 Roman Empire begins to crumble and withdraws from Morocco.
- 429–535 Vandals, followed by Byzantines, briefly occupy Morocco.
- 622 The spread of Islam begins from Medina.
- 700s Arab invasion installs Islam across North Africa.
- 788–923 The Idrissid dynasty is the first Moroccan Arab dynasty, established by Moulay Idriss I and his son, Idriss II, in Fes.
- 1062–1145 The Berber Almoravid dynasty is established in Marrakech. Eventual rule extends to Spain.
- 1147–1248 The orthodox Almohad dynasty comes down from the High Atlas to depose Almohads and extends its rule farther into Spain and across to Tripoli.

continues

With their empire starting to crumble, the Romans started retreating from Mauretania Tingitana around A.D. 250, and subsequent rule over the region (first by the Vandals and then the Byzantines) was largely restricted to the ports of Tingis (Tangier) and Ceuta. Consequently, tribal law reigned over most of Morocco over the ensuing centuries, and it was this isolated, largely clan-bound land that confronted the marauding Arabs from the east in the 7th century.

Between A.D. 639 and 700, Muslim Arab invaders, influenced by the new religion preached by the Prophet Mohammed, invaded Egypt and most of the Maghreb. Though they had conquered the richer lands of the Middle East in less than a decade with relative ease, Morocco was only occupied after 70 years of fighting against the Berbers. Although the reason for such determined fighting by the invading Muslims would have been their mission to convert and rule the local Berbers, this may have been secondary to their determination to invade the Iberian Peninsula with an eye on eventual western European domination. In 711, they achieved both missions when an army composed largely of Muslim Berber troops set out from Tangier and successfully invaded the Spanish port of Tarifa, from where they proceeded over the next decade to push the Christians almost into France. Although this signified acquiescence to Islam by some Berbers, it did not constitute an acceptance of the presence of the Arabs.

The Arab invasions attracted Muslims from all over western Asia to settle in North Africa, and their presence greatly stimulated the commercial economy of the region. By the late 700s, regular trade was established across the Sahara between Morocco and the great gold, ivory, and slave kingdoms of West Africa. This wave of Islam had a far more profound impact on the Berber population than Rome and Christianity ever had; it transformed the cultural orientation of the Maghreb by turning its face from the Latin West to the Arab East.

Such was the quick expansion of the Islamic empire that it rapidly became too expansive to rule from the centralized seat of power in Damascus; the religion now reached from Persia across to the western Maghreb and from Ghana up to Spain. As Arab rule was transferred from Damascus to local leaders, the age of the Moroccan dynasties began.

Moulay Idriss arrived at Volubilis in 787. An Arab refugee of distinguished ancestry, he was immediately welcomed into the city and very quickly took on the role of both spiritual and political leader.

- **1248–1465** Merenid dynasty builds extensively within Morocco. Portuguese invade Moroccan coast.
- **1465–1554** Wattasid dynasty takes hold. Andalusia falls, and there's a rise in Jewish and Muslim immigration to Morocco.
- **1554–1669** Marrakech-based Saâdian dynasty ejects the Portuguese and extends rule south to Timbuktu.

- **1669–present** The Berber Alaouite from the Tafilalt is established and is still in power today with the 15th sultan, King Mohammed VI. Morocco, through Sultan Mohammed III in 1786, is the first nation to formally recognize a newly independent United States.
- **Late 1800s** European interest in Morocco grows as the "Scramble for Africa" begins in earnest.

- **1906** Algeciras Conference in Spain; France and Spain designated by European powers to control Moroccan ports and collect customs dues.
- **1912** Morocco divided into French and Spanish protectorates, administered by resident-generals. The sultan's influence subsides to a largely figurehead role.
- **1943** Istiqlal, the Party of Independence, is founded

Leaving Volubilis as the thriving commercial (and perhaps decadent) hub that it was, Idriss immediately set about transforming the nearby village of Fes into the principal city of western Morocco and a model for all the Moroccan dynasties to follow. A devout Shia Muslim, Idriss was proclaimed the Commander of the Faithful, a title that has continued throughout the ages and is still the spiritual crown worn by the current king, Mohammed VI. Astonishingly, Idriss accomplished all this in only 4 years before the Baghdadi Shia powers had him poisoned. Moulay Idriss II was born after his father's death, and over his 20-year reign, he elevated the Idrissid state into Morocco's first true dynasty, establishing a certain measure of government and law. Fes developed into one of the major intellectual centers in the Islamic world and was a vital link in the trade routes between Andalusia and the Middle East as well as Morocco and the Sahara. The Idrissid's power began to wane by the 10th century, but Fes retained its level of importance up to the 20th century.

As the Idrissid state reverted back to a more localized rule, a group of nomadic Berber tribesmen, the Sanhaja, established a massive empire in the south. This movement originated from the preaching of Ibn Yasin, who settled in the camps of the Sanhaja to preach the Islamic gospel. But upon finding their faith and diligence lacking, he withdrew to the western Saharan coast (modern-day Mauritania), where he established a *ribat*, a fortified monastery of sorts. As the number of his devotees increased, he was able to launch his strictly disciplined el-Murabitoun, or Almoravids, in a *jihad*, or holy war. He took revenge on those Sanhaja that had rebuked his teachings and extended his power southward to the ancient kingdom of Ghana and northward to Morocco.

Within 30 years (1050–80), the Almoravids overran all of the by-now fractured states of the western Maghreb (Morocco and western Algeria) and by 1107 were also rulers of southern Spain. For the first time in Maghrebi history, the Berber tribes had been forced to obey a single ruler, and within this relatively short space of time, the concept of Moroccan unity was born. The very name Morocco was derived from the Almoravids' new capital, Marrakech.

The Almoravid empire, however, collapsed as rapidly as it had grown, and in 1147 they were eventually overthrown by a movement not altogether dissimilar from their own. Ibn Toumert, an Atlas Berber who preached a very strict, deeply spiritual form of Islam, saw the Almoravids as blasphemous and

---

with support from Sultan Mohammed V.
- **1956** End of protectorate era after unrest and strong nationalist sentiment. Spain keeps its two coastal enclaves of Ceuta and Mellila. Sultan Mohammed V becomes king in 1957.
- **1961** Death of King Mohammed V; son Hassan II accedes to the throne.
- **1963** Morocco holds first general election as the country moves from a tradi-

tional sultanate to a constitutional monarchy.
- **1973** Polisario movement formed—with Algerian support—to establish an independent state in Spanish Sahara.
- **1975** The Green March. King Hassan sends 300,000 civilian volunteers into Spanish Sahara. Spain hands over Spanish Sahara to joint Moroccan-Mauritanian control. Algeria objects.

- **1976** Moroccan and Algerian troops clash. Saharawi Arab Democratic Republic (SADR) formed with Algerian assistance as a government-in-exile. Morocco and Mauritania divide Western Sahara.
- **1976–91** Continuous fighting between Moroccan military and Polisario guerillas.
- **1984** Organization of African Unity (OAU) admits SADR;

continues

immoral. Provoking the Almoravid court in Marrakech until he was eventually banished to the mountains, Ibn Toumert gathered a small band of disciples around him, known as Almohads, and succeeded, before his death in 1130, in creating a political structure strong enough to hold together many of the mountain tribes who harbored a natural animosity to the desert-originating Almoravids. A disciplined military force was established and swept down onto the fertile plains to conquer the Almoravids, firstly in Fes and then Marrakech; this only 25 years after their banishment from the city. Over the next century, the Almohads extended their power northward into Andalusia and eastward over present-day Morocco, Algeria, and Tunisia. The latter half of the 12th century was possibly the Maghreb's finest hour, and Andalusian culture reached its peak under their reign. The Almohad leaders were behind the building of the new capital in Rabat as well as Marrakech's Koutoubia Mosque and Seville's Giralda tower.

Barely 100 years after sweeping to power, the Almohad empire collapsed under the weight of internal divisions, and within Morocco many Berber tribes reverted back to local rule.

The Merenids, a Sahara Berber tribe that had fought alongside the Almohads in Spain, turned on their former masters, and by 1250 regarded themselves as rulers of Morocco, although they lacked any great military base. It was during these turbulent times that Morocco came to acquire certain contradicting, localized religious characteristics. Most of the country's urban Arabized centers began to practice a strict observance of the orthodox Islamic faith. Meanwhile, a vigorous brotherhood of Muslim saints, or *marabouts,* developed in the countryside where their strong mystical appeal attracted the illiterate, rural Berbers.

Also witnessed during the Merenid reign was a strengthening of the Bedouin Arab influence on the Moroccan northern plains. During this time, the Merenids embarked on a considerable construction spree, largely financed by the Makhzen system. The Makhzen was Morocco's first real centralized government system of administration and taxation, but was only enforceable in the urban centers under Merenid control and only then by an army of Arab and Christian mercenaries. The Merenids ruled from Fes el Jdid, an extension of the original city, Fes el Bali, and to perhaps appease the popular orthodox faith of the time, constructed many of the mosques and *medersas,* or Islamic colleges, that still dominate the Fes medina today.

Morocco resigns membership in protest.

- **1991** U.N.-monitored cease-fire begins in Western Sahara. Proposed referendum on the territory's future fails to be agreed upon.
- **1998** Morocco's first opposition-led government comes to power.
- **1999** King Hassan II dies and is succeeded by his son, Mohammed VI.

- **2003** More than 40 people are killed when suicide bombers attack several sites in Casablanca, including a Jewish community center and Spanish restaurant.
- **2004** Devastating earthquake hits the north; more than 500 people dead.
- **2004** Free trade agreement begins with the U.S. following Washington's designation of Morocco as a major non-NATO ally.

- **2005** Truth commission set up by King Mohammed VI to investigate human rights abuses during the rule of his father, King Hassan II. Commission says 592 people were killed from 1956 to 1999.
- **2007** Suicide bombings in Casablanca. Morocco and the Polisario Front hold U.N.-sponsored talks in New York but fail to come to any agreement.

However, the Merenids and their successors, the Wattasids, were quite unable to deal with their external problems. Their Spanish territories, including the last great Moorish city of Granada, were lost during their reign, and in 1415, the Portuguese occupied the port of Ceuta on the Moroccan side of the Straits of Gibraltar. This marked not only an important shift of power between Muslims and Christians in the western Mediterranean, but also the beginning of Western European expansion into the wider world.

Between 1460 and 1520, the Portuguese occupied the greater part of the Moroccan coast, including modern-day Tangier, Asilah, Essaouira, and Agadir. The Portuguese set up trading posts along a great deal of Africa's northern Atlantic coastline, and this greatly affected Morocco's Saharan trade routes. Although the caravans from West Africa through the central and eastern Maghreb to the Middle East continued to flourish, Morocco's position as the middle man between Africa's west and Europe became increasingly redundant.

The Saâdians used the widespread revolt against the Merenids and Wattasids to make their move. They were the first Arabic dynasty to rule over Morocco since the Idrissids back in the 8th century, although they suffered the same dramatic rise and fall from power as the previous Berber dynasties. The Saâdians lacked any tribal allegiances from the Moroccan Berbers and gained a lot of their power from their claim of being direct descendents of the Prophet Mohammed and their leading role in driving the Portuguese from most of their strongholds. They built themselves a capital in Taroudannt before claiming Marrakech in 1520. At this stage, the Wattasids were still governing some parts of northern Morocco from their stronghold in Fes, but there was widespread revolt in protest to the addition of Ottoman Turks to their Arab and Christian tax-collecting armies. Unpopular and bankrupt, they eventually succumbed to the rising Saâdian power from the south.

Ahmed el Mansour (the Victorious) was the greatest of the Saâdian sultans and reigned for 25 years. The sultan had eyes for a larger stage than most previous rulers, and established close commercial and diplomatic ties with Elizabeth of England, who realized his value as an ally against Spain. He also sent an army across the desert and overpowered the mighty West African empire of Songhai, founding a Moroccan protectorate on the banks of the Niger River in the process that sent back so much gold that "the Victorious" was bestowed another title, el Dhabi, "the Golden," by his thankful subjects.

Upon el Mansour's death in 1603, none of his three sons could deliver the same leadership as their father, and Morocco plunged into familiar chaos and anarchy. The Saâdians retreated to their strongholds of Marrakech and the Souss, where they continued to reign over the south for another 60 years. The Saâdian Tombs in Marrakech lay witness to the obvious wealth that the dynasty still enjoyed after the death of el Mansour. At the same time, Catholic Spain was pursuing a vigorous purge of all non-Catholics, and waves of Jewish and Muslim refugees arrived on Morocco's shores, only adding to the general lawlessness sweeping the country. One group of refugees was a band of pirates called the Sallee Rovers, who lay claim to their own Republic of the Bou Regreg at the mouth of the Bou Regreg River in the twin cities of Rabat and Salé. Their pirate state added a distinct Andalusian touch to the medina and kasbah of Rabat that is still evident today.

Law and order was restored to Morocco in the 1660s by the Alaouites, who came from the Tafilalt town of Rissani, near the Saharan dunes of Merzouga. It was their second sultan, Moulay Ismail, who was to become Morocco's longest-serving ruler—and one of its most notorious. Sultan from 1672 to 1727, Moulay Ismail was a ruthless leader who demanded loyalty and service from his subjects and kept a tight hold on the country via a standing army of some 140,000 black troops, many of whom were enslaved from military expeditions that took the Moroccans as far south as Senegal. He is remembered today as one of the country's pre-eminent leaders whose imperial city of Meknes was intended to be the equal of Versailles. His reign also saw the construction of roads and schools, and such was his reputation in Europe that even though the country spiraled into anarchy after his death, it wasn't until 150 years later that the European colonial powers considered invading Morocco again.

Up until 1850, Morocco had been relatively successful in keeping the West at bay. At the time, there were fewer than 500 Europeans in Morocco compared with 12,000 in Tunis and more than 100,000 in Algeria. Moulay Slimane, Alaouite sultan of Morocco from 1792 to 1822, was a devout orthodox Muslim and extolled a particularly xenophobic style of rule that forbade his subjects from leaving the country, confined all Europeans to Tangier and Mogador (Essaouira), and generally imposed stringent restrictions on all commercial relations with the Western (Christian) world. All of this only served to leave Morocco ill-placed to deal with a European presence that was starting to be felt throughout Africa. European, particularly British, French, and Spanish, businessmen were beginning to show an interest in the potential Moroccan market, and the Moroccans themselves were acquiring a taste for foreign products—imports of tea, for example, rose by 20% between 1830 and 1840. At the same time, the French invasion of Algeria in 1830 handed Morocco

a powerful and dangerous neighbor, and in 1845 the Moroccans found themselves fighting the French in a brief war. In 1859, the Spanish army invaded Morocco in response to constant raids on its garrison ports of Ceuta and Melilla and inflicted a series of defeats over Moroccan forces before the Alaouite sultan, Abd er Rahman, signed the Treaty of Tetouan. Under the treaty, Morocco promised to pay Spain a huge indemnity for the raids. To pay this, the sultan had to raise a loan in London on the security of the Moroccan customs revenue and hand over control of this to foreign commissioners. Consequently, from the 1860s there was a rapid expansion of European influence in Morocco.

Moulay al Hassan was the last great Moroccan sultan (1873–94) before the French occupation. His reign was virtually a continual campaign to satisfy those in the *bled el makhzen* and extend his power into the *bled el siba*, "the unfriendly country." It also witnessed more European, especially French, involvement in the country's civil administration and commercial dealings. Al Hassan's determination to govern the *bled el siba*—something that had not been achieved since the 17th century—arose from trying to make certain that no ungoverned groups existed that could cause frontier incidents such as the previous disastrous confrontations with the French and Spanish. The fact that Morocco was able to keep its independence until 1912—considering France had occupied Algeria since 1830 and declared Tunisia a French protectorate in 1882—is a tribute to his enterprise and skill.

By 1906, with the vast majority of Africa under European rule, the still technically independent nation of Morocco was the subject of intense negotiations amongst a number of European players. In the Conference of Algeciras and with Morocco on the verge of bankruptcy,

France and Spain became the designated European interests in the country.

In 1911, with his capital Fes surrounded by rebellious tribes and his country bankrupt, Sultan Moulay Hafidh (great uncle of the present king) requested French military intervention and ceded control of Morocco. This agreement was ratified the following year on March 30, 1912, with the Treaty of Fes, which formally proclaimed the Sultanate of Morocco as a French protectorate, with its new capital in Rabat. A separate agreement between France and Spain then divided the country into a vast central French zone with Spanish zones to both its north and south.

Morocco by this time was exceptionally poor, having suffered from perennial droughts, outdated agricultural methods, and, above all, difficulties of communication and transport caused by the mountainous interior. Over the next 40 years, the French zone witnessed more than 43,000km (26,660 miles) of road construction compared to just 500km (310 miles) in the Spanish zone. The French also successfully promoted the new colony to potential settlers, whereas the immigration of Spanish settlers was decidedly less. The relative success in the French zone was largely due to the character of its first resident-general, Louis Lyautey, who held office for 13 years until 1925. Lyautey had already served in Indochina and Madagascar as well as Algeria, and he was determined to preserve the traditional institutions of Maghrebi Islam. At the same time he had a sure grasp of economic affairs, and the rapid modernization of the Moroccan economy was largely his work. In particular, he set to task on the pacification of the tribes of the *bled el siba,* and perhaps his greatest achievement was bringing law and order to areas that had never been controlled by a central government. Today his legacy is most visible in the retention of the medinas around the country. In Algeria he had witnessed the random destruction of medinas in the name of progress, so in Morocco he, along with urban planner Léon-Henri Prost, designed elegant, gridlike new cities, or ville nouvelle, which were carefully separated from the ancient cities.

Around this time, Lyautey's pacification was rudely interrupted by the Rif War. The Berbers of the Rif mountains in the northern zone of Morocco had risen as one against the Spanish military government. They defeated a Spanish force in 1921 and proclaimed a Republic of the Rif. The uprising in the Rif was the eventual downfall of Lyautey, who was seen as too pro-Moroccan.

In 1927, after the death of the old sultan Moulay Hafidh, the French arranged for a young prince, Sidi Mohammed V, to accede to the throne. The French imagined that they could educate the young sultan to rule entirely according to their wishes, but during World War II, Mohammed V became the leader of the Moroccan nationalist movement, even welcoming Churchill and Roosevelt to Casablanca for the Allies Conference in 1943. Toward the end of the war, after many years of secret meetings and political organization and with the support of both the sultan and the majority of the Moroccan people, the major resistance movements in Morocco combined to publicly form the Istiqal, the "Party of Independence." The sultan made himself the central figure of the nationalist movement. He refused to give his consent to French laws to ban the Istiqal and other nationalist parties. In a desperate effort to overcome the resistance to their rule in Morocco, the French sided with the nomadic groups in the Atlas mountains, who were traditionally hostile to the sultan. However, this attempt to "divide and rule" by playing off the Berbers against the Arabs only resulted in uniting them in opposition to

French rule. In 1953 the French deposed Mohammed V, and exiled him first to Corsica and then to Madagascar. In his place, the southern tribal *caid* Thami el-Glaoui, who had enjoyed virtual rule of southern Morocco under the French, was made sultan. Unrest broke out with the formation of an Army of Liberation by the nationalist groups, and eventually the French were forced to acknowledge defeat and agree to the principle of independence. In November 1955, Mohammed V returned to his country and was reinstated as sultan; Morocco became independent in March 1956. Upon independence, the government instigated a sweeping range of reforms, built more schools and universities, and dealt with the excesses of colonial rule, most notably by cleaning up the seedy port city of Tangier. The sultan changed his title to king while retaining his spiritual position as Commander of the Faithful.

Mohammed V died somewhat unexpectedly in 1961, and power moved smoothly to his son, Hassan II. Although initially intent on introducing a new constitution—as promised by his father even before independence—Hassan II, faced with ever present social and political unrest, delayed its introduction and proceeded to dismantle the opposition. The king reverted back to rule similar to the patrimonial mode of the precolonial sultans.

The 1970s and 1980s saw Hassan II play a leading neutralist role in the affairs of both the Middle East and North Africa, and over time this served to instill within Moroccans a sense of national pride. The last few years of his 38-year reign saw some democratization within the government plus some changes to the country's constitution. Hassan II died in 1999 after a relatively short struggle with cancer, and his 36-year old son, Mohammed Ben al Hassan, was immediately enthroned as Mohammed VI, the 18th Alaouite king of the Alaouite dynasty.

The king's former reputation as a "playboy prince" who preferred jet skis to *jellabahs* preceded him, and almost immediately the young monarch set about distancing himself from his father's past and modernizing his reign. He pledged to tackle poverty and corruption, stimulate the economy, and improve Morocco's human rights record.

Early in his reign, Mohammed VI, along with his sisters, princesses Lalla Meryem, Lalla Asma, and Lalla Hasna, strongly advocated women's rights and a key reform has been the creation of a new family code, or Mudawana, which raised the minimum age of marriage for women to the same as that for men (18 years), discourages polygamy, and allows for freedom of choice in both marriage and, perhaps more importantly, divorce—a freedom Princess Lalla Meryem exercised in 1999.

2 Morocco Today

Some Moroccans feel the level of personal freedom has actually eroded since Mohammed VI's ascension to the throne. New anti-terrorism laws and a campaign against Islamic extremists in the wake of the 2003 and 2007 bombings in Casablanca have been seen by some as an infringement of human rights. Media freedom is regularly questioned, and journalists are censored, even jailed, over the taboo subjects of the monarchy, Islam, political corruption, and the Western Sahara. International NGOs such as Amnesty International have recently publicized cases of excessive human rights abuses, in some cases resulting in deaths, against an increasing number of mainly sub-Saharan Africans—but also Moroccans—caught attempting to illegally cross the border between Morocco and the

Spanish enclaves of Mellila and Ceuta. For those Moroccans wishing to enter Europe legally, the depressingly long lines at the French and Spanish consulates constitute an infringement on their freedom of travel.

Although the economy has and still is undergoing an impressive liberalization that is attracting foreign investment—especially in the previously neglected Rif Mediterranean region—poverty, unemployment, and an illiteracy rate of more than 50% is the daily curse of many Moroccans who still see the majority of the political and military elite as untouchable and corrupt.

Some Moroccans also see a sense of hypocrisy in a king who espouses political and civil freedom while still enjoying almost absolute power over his subjects as both monarch and Commander of the Faithful. Although Mohammed VI seems to be slowly moving toward a constitutional monarchy, the albeit democratically elected parliament is effectively run by the king and his royal advisors, and the country's prime minister and his key ministers are still directly appointed by the king. Although there is speculation that the Moroccan monarchy will evolve like the Spanish one, Mohammed VI himself replies that there should be a Moroccan model specific to Morocco and that applying a Western democratic system would be a mistake.

In 2002, Mohammed VI married computer engineer Salma Bennani, and while his father's spouse (some say spouses) was never seen in public, Mohammed VI's marriage has been a very public affair. His wife was granted the title of princess while assuming a prominent role in women's rights. The births of a son in 2003 and daughter in 2007 provoked genuine celebration throughout the country.

Mohammed VI's popularity is hard to measure, as any negativity toward his rule is kept largely behind closed doors. The Islamist extremist threat is, at this stage, still largely confined to the country's major slum area in Casablanca, and it is from here that opposition to his policies and power are most visible.

TERRORISM IN MOROCCO In recent years, a spate of bombings and foiled suicide attempts has raised fears of a surge of radical Islamist violence previously unwitnessed in Morocco, with one Spanish anti-terror judge labeling the country as "the worst terrorist threat for Europe."

In 2003, Morocco sentenced three Saudi men to 10-year jail terms for attempting to form a Moroccan branch of Al Qaeda and plotting to attack NATO ships in the Straits of Gibraltar. That same year simultaneous suicide bomb attacks targeting Jewish, Spanish, and Belgian buildings in Casablanca killed more than 40 people, the first such coordinated terrorism attack in Morocco. In the 2004 terrorist bombings in Madrid, the majority of those accused are Moroccan nationals. In 2007, Casablanca was again struck with three separate suicide bombings within 2 months.

The 2003 attacks were attributed to the Moroccan Islamic Combatant Group (GICM), a hard-line Islamist group based in an impoverished slum in Casablanca called Sidi Moumen that advocates violence against Jewish and U.S. interests within Morocco. The Moroccan authorities' response to the Casablanca bombings was swift and predictably harsh, with 87 defendants facing trial that same year and receiving sentences ranging from 10 months imprisonment to the death penalty.

Two of the 2007 attacks took place within another poor district of Casablanca, El Fida. These bombings ran parallel to worse conditions in neighboring Algeria, and Moroccan authorities and civilians fear that the suicide bombings are the work of the Algerian-based Salafist Group for Preaching and Combat (GSPC), recently renamed Al Qaeda Organization in the Islamic Maghreb. Members allegedly receive training in Iraq, Afghanistan, and Algeria, where they have claimed responsibility for a number of bombings in the capital Algiers, and some are said to have infiltrated the relatively porous border between Algeria and Morocco. The group's main focus has historically been to establish strict Islamic rule in Algeria, but it is now thought to harbor regional, even global, ambitions since becoming a franchisee of Al Qaeda. Immediately prior to the 2007 incidents, Moroccan authorities arrested eight Algerians in Casablanca who were accused of being members of an armed group that was preparing an attack.

Morocco has been vocal about its alliance with the U.S. and its fight on terror, and it is said that there has been an increase of CIA presence in the country. King Mohammed VI has come under international scrutiny after it was known that some of those arrested or killed in the 2007 attacks had been jailed in connection with the 2003 Casablanca bombings but had subsequently received a pardon by the king in 2005. Mohammed VI constantly finds himself treading a fine line between his responsibilities as the country's reigning monarch and supreme Islamic leader.

Overall, Morocco appears to be at least on level terms with the extremists. The 2007 bombings could all be considered "foiled attacks," and subsequent sweeping arrests—assisted by anti-terrorism laws some human rights organizations describe as excessive—netted many of the alleged ringleaders, which was largely possible because of the isolation of the extremists within Morocco, and more specifically Casablanca. It is solely within the slums of Casablanca that the terror cells are gaining

a foothold. It's estimated that a third of the city's population resides there, most of them rural workers who journeyed to the "big smoke" in search of their fortune only to find themselves with no regular work, no family or institutional support, and socially alienated. Some slums are severely lacking in, if not totally devoid of, basic infrastructure, and to some, the Islamic fundamentalists offer a way out of the black hole.

While some Moroccans may sympathize with the extremists' views of a "Western war on Islam," the majority of the population deplore any violent action, as illustrated in the "No to Terrorism" march in 2003, when tens of thousands took to the streets in Casablanca just days after the bombings. Indeed, throughout my travels in the Islamic world it was a Moroccan who informed me that the true meaning of *jihad* simply means "striving," and that its generally accepted interpretation explicitly forbids killing an individual purely because of their religious preference.

The government's current strategy plays on this nonviolent emotion by encouraging Moroccans to inform them of anyone or anything suspicious, and security agents are beginning to watch new arrivals in the suburbs, account for casual workers on construction sites, and even mix in with the crowds waiting in front of certain consulates. For the first time the government has also begun to publicly advertise the names of those who are under suspicion.

The visible police presence throughout Morocco can be a bit disconcerting for the visitor upon arrival, but it actually lends itself to a more secure environment throughout the country. The police can be overly officious and, at times, blatantly open to corruption, but this is not the case when it concerns terrorism. Wherever you travel in Morocco, locals will be at pains to assure you of your safety and that they welcome your presence.

THE WESTERN SAHARA Morocco's deep south is a largely barren, desolate, good-for-nothing expanse that just happens to be the stage for Africa's longest territorial conflict and one of the United Nations' most protracted and expensive peace missions. Depending on which map you look at, this region is called the Western Sahara, the Disputed Territory of the Western Sahara, or even the Saharawi Arab Democratic Republic. The dispute over this sovereignty between Morocco and the indigenous Saharawis has been going on since 1975, when more than 300,000 unarmed Moroccans converged on the city of Tarfaya in what was dubbed the Green March. This peaceful "invasion" was orchestrated by King Hassan II in response to the rejection of Moroccan and Mauritanian territorial claims to the region by the International Court of Justice, which recognized the Saharawis' right to self-determination pending the imminent withdrawal of Spain after nearly 100 years of colonial rule.

Prior to the court ruling, tens of thousands of Moroccans had already crossed the border into Spanish Sahara to back their government's contention that the northern part of the territory was historically Morocco's. Following the ruling, King Hassan II sent his army to attack positions held by the Saharawi guerilla army (the Algerian-backed Polisario Front founded in 1973 to contest Spanish rule), followed by the Green March a week later. This forced Spain to ignore the court ruling and negotiate the Madrid Agreement, which partitioned two-thirds of the territory to Morocco and the remaining third to Mauritania. Polisario consequently launched an armed struggle that succeeded, 3 years later, in Mauritania withdrawing its territorial claims, but Morocco simply overran the remainder and has stood firm to the present day.

Between 1981 and 1987, Moroccan forces constructed a 2,700km (1,674 mile) wall to separate the Polisario-controlled areas from the rest of Moroccan Western Sahara. The United Nations brokered a ceasefire in 1991 and established a mission to both enforce the ceasefire and implement a peace plan that would eventually allow Western Saharans to choose independence or integration with Morocco. Although both parties initially agreed to the plan, the referendum has never eventuated largely due to disagreement over voter "identification"—the Saharawis wanted it based on a census carried out by Spain in 1973, thereby ruling out those Moroccans who settled in Western Sahara after the Green March. Morocco, perhaps eyeing the vast phosphate and fishing resources within the territory, proceeded over the next decade to consistently delay talks at resolving the issue. From 1997 to 2001, the U.N.'s special envoy, former U.S. Secretary of State James Baker, mediated talks between Polisario and Morocco and eventually came up with a new Framework Agreement. This agreement offered the Saharawi autonomy under Moroccan sovereignty—including Moroccan control of internal security and the judicial system—over a 4-year transition period, followed by a referendum in which Moroccan settlers residing in the territory for longer than a year were allowed to vote. Giving little way to their independence aspirations, the Saharawis rejected the plan and threatened to return to guerilla war.

In 2001 and 2002, Mohammed VI visited his southern provinces and reaffirmed his late father's position of Moroccan historical rights to the territory, proclaiming that Morocco "will not renounce an inch." Tensions between Morocco and Spain escalated at this time, apparently due to the latter's refusal to back a behind-the-scenes French initiative that would have strengthened Morocco's case at the U.N. It was at this time that former U.N. Secretary-General Kofi Annan proposed partitioning the contested territory between Morocco and the Saharawis, which was predictably and forcefully rejected by both parties.

The political tide started to turn in favor of the Saharawis when South Africa, followed by a number of other high-profile African countries, urged support for self-determination and opened diplomatic ties with the Saharawi Arab Democratic Republic, an act the Moroccan government called "disappointing." In recent years, the Saharawis have become more politically savvy. In 2005, the Polisario Front released Moroccan servicemen they had detained in southern Algeria for almost 20 years. The 404 men, considered the world's longest-serving prisoners of war, were released in a gesture that the Polisario Front hoped would pave the way to peace with Morocco.

Money is a silent, but inextricably strong, factor in the struggle for this piece of Saharan-battered land. In addition to the Western Sahara's phosphate deposits and fish reserves, oil has been discovered fairly recently. The 2000 U.S. Geological Survey of World Energy estimated substantial oil and gas resources off the Western Saharan shore, an appealing factor for Morocco, which produces less than 1,000 barrels of oil a day and heavily imports its energy needs. Western Saharan reserves will provide a direct route to the refineries of Europe and the eastern seaboard of the U.S., and with both regions publicly stating they are looking for alternative sources to the Middle East, the stakes are high.

Recently, a new struggle between Morocco and the Saharawis has developed over who has the authority to sign over the exploratory rights, with both countries granting licenses to separate gas and oil exploration companies. In a major blow to Morocco, the U.N. undersecretary for legal affairs ruled that Morocco had no right to award contracts since the "exploitation of natural resources in a non-autonomous territory" is only allowed "if it benefits local populations, is carried out in their name, or in consultation with them." In somewhat of a coup for the Saharwis, the 2004 U.S.–Morocco Free Trade Agreement specifically ruled out trade within Western Sahara, and a 2006 E.U.–Morocco Fisheries Partnership Agreement, which opens the Western Saharan coastline to European fishing fleets, has been opposed by some E.U. member countries.

In 2007, Morocco's Western Sahara policy shifted toward regional autonomy—but with no referendum on independence—while the Saharawi demand for outright self-determination has grown more vocal and public. Both parties have been treading the diplomatic streets, with the U.S. and France publicly backing their long-time ally Morocco, while various European nations, such as Belgium and Germany, hosted Saharawi independence activists and government members. Current U.N. Secretary-General Ban Ki-moon has reiterated the body's intention to stay in the Western Sahara until an agreement between the two countries is realized.

3 Religion

Muslims account for about 99% of Morocco's population, so it's no surprise that its practices and philosophy dictate most aspects of daily life.

The Arabic word "Islam" literally means "submission to God," and the core of the faith is the belief that there is only one God (Allah) who should be worshipped. And, in a line of prophets who included Adam, Abraham, Noah, Moses, John the Baptist, David, and Jesus, Mohammed was the last and most definitive. Muslims believe that Christianity, Judaism, and Islam are all essentially the same, but that the messages from the earlier prophets have been distorted and that Mohammed was chosen by God to revive, refine, and purify His message.

The main sources of Islam are the **Koran** (or Qur'an)—the revelations Mohammed received during his lifetime and Mohammed's own actions, the **Hadith.**

Mohammed was born in Mecca (in present-day Saudi Arabia) in 570 and began to receive revelations from God, via the angel Gabriel, around 610. These continued until his death in nearby Medina in 632. The illiterate Mohammed would pass on each revelation to his scribes, who would then input them as a particular verse in the Koran. The Arabic word *qur'aan* means "recitation," and Muslims regard the holy book's contents as the word of God. The Koran's 114 chapters were not revealed in the order presented, and in fact many were patched together from passages received by Mohammed at different times in his life. The year before he died, however, Mohammed finally recited in its entirety the order in which these original verses were to stay.

The Koran provided a basic framework for Islam, but it didn't go into specific detail: Of 6,616 verses, only 80 concerned issues of conduct. For more practical guidance, Muslims referred to Mohammed's actions and words while he was alive, even though he never claimed any infallibility beyond his intermediary status. The Prophet's actions and words were remembered by those who knew him and passed down through Muslim communities.

The **five pillars of Islam** are drawn from the Koran and the Hadith, and are the basic religious duties and cornerstones of the faith.

- **Statement of Faith** *(shahadah)* "I testify that there is no god but God, and Mohammed is the Messenger of God." If you say this with absolute sincerity, then you have become, or are, a Muslim.

- **Prayer** *(salat)* Prayer must be performed five times a day, preferably within a mosque, though in the modern world many Muslims make this effort only for the midday prayer. Since the Islamic calendar is a lunar one, the day, and the first prayer, begins at sunset. Prayers follow in evening, dawn, midday, and afternoon. The exact times for these are set in advance by the religious authorities and published in local newspapers. In the past, *muezzins* would climb to the top of the mosque's minaret and call the faithful to prayer, but today it is mostly prerecorded and played over electronic speakers. Prayer involves specific rituals, the most important being the act of purification. This is achieved by rinsing out the mouth, sniffing water into the nostrils, and washing the face, head, ears, neck, feet, and (lastly) hands and forearms. Even if there is no water available, one must go through the actions.

- **Alms** *(zakat)* It is believed that alms-giving purifies the heart of greed, while receiving charity purifies it of envy. The Islamic tolerance toward begging is drawn from this.

- **Fasting** *(sawm)* Fasting takes place during Ramadan, the ninth month of the lunar cycle.

- **Pilgrimage** *(hajj)* Every Muslim who has the means is bound by duty to make the pilgrimage to Mecca at least once in his/her lifetime. This usually takes place in the 12th month.

Although Islam permeates most aspects of their everyday lives, Moroccans practice their religion relatively conservatively. Besides being denied entry into the country's mosques—apart from the tourist-friendly Hassan II Mosque in Casablanca (p. 332)—and perhaps being woken in the pre-dawn by the *muezzin's* call to prayer, non-Muslims will find their daily travel largely unhindered by any Islamic codes of conduct. That said, it is considered respectful to dress conservatively when in public areas. For female travelers, this generally means dress that covers the knees and shoulders, while male travelers should be aware that sports shorts and sleeveless shirts are considered inappropriate dress unless on the sports field or beach. *Tip:* Female travelers will find it helpful to always have a sarong or large shawl on hand, as it can substitute as a long skirt or extra shoulder covering when the need arises.

RAMADAN Ramadan—the ninth month of the Islamic lunar calendar—is when Mohammed received the first of his revelations from God. Muslims observe a strict fast during the entire month—originally modeled after similar Jewish and Christian practices—and use the time for worship and contemplation. During the day, all forms of consumption are forbidden including eating, smoking, drinking, and any form of sexual contact. However, this is only the outward show of what is intended as a deeper, spiritual cleansing and strengthening of faith. One Hadith says, "There are many who fast all day and pray all night, but they gain nothing but hunger and sleeplessness."

All Muslims who have reached puberty are expected to observe the fast. It is generally accepted that the elderly and the chronically ill are exempt, as are those who are sick or traveling, mothers who are nursing, and menstruating or pregnant women, all of whom are encouraged, for every day of fasting missed, to provide a meal for one poor person who is breaking their fast. Children are not required to fast, though some families encourage them to do so for part of a day or for a few days during the month.

At the end of the day the fast is broken with a light meal followed by the sunset prayer, which is then followed by an evening meal called the *iftar.* Muslims are encouraged to share *iftar* with family, friends, and neighbors as well as the poor and non-Muslims. The fast is resumed the next morning, traditionally when "you can plainly distinguish a white thread from a black thread by the daylight."

The last 10 days of Ramadan are considered especially important, and many Muslims retreat to their mosque or other community centers for prayer and recitations of the Koran. Laylat al-Qadr (the Night of Power) is a special night of prayer commemorating Mohammed's first revelation. It is believed that this is when heaven is open to the faithful and God determines the course of the world for the following year.

When the crescent of the new moon of the 10th month rises, Ramadan ends with Eid al-Fitr (Feast of Fast Breaking). The feast lasts for 3 days and is a time of both religious significance and social festivities. Villages and towns may also hold festivals or events to celebrate this time.

Non-Muslims should be aware of the fast taking place and attempt not to eat, drink, or smoke with blatant disregard to those who are fasting. Some restaurants, cafes, and stores may be closed all, or part, of the day, and those that are open may be staffed by tired, irritated personnel. It may be just me, but it seems the country's taxi drivers become particularly argumentative during Ramadan. Morocco is a relatively modern country, and Moroccans understand that business must go on and that the non-Muslim world is still working and traveling.

Ramadan in Morocco doesn't mean going on your own fast, but in some rural areas it may be difficult to get freshly cooked food and drinks during the day. However, a little discreet enquiring should find you an open shop where you can stock up on dry foods and bottled drinks. Many accommodations throughout Morocco will also offer in-house daytime meals to accommodate their non-Muslim guests.

The half-hour before sunset is the busiest time during Ramadan for locals, who will be seen rushing to finish work, pack up shop, and head home for the breaking of the fast. Expect to find a ghost town if you arrive at this time of the day, even in Morocco's bigger cities. Many riads and dars, some hotels even, also close their doors for an hour. While irregular hours, abrupt service, and noise generated by locals enjoying the nightly freedom from the fast (which can last until dawn) are par for the course during Ramadan, travelers can still enjoy their experience by showing a little respect and restraint.

4 Moroccan Food & Drink

Displaying influences from Africa, Arabia, and the Mediterranean, the Moroccan cuisine of today is a reflection of the country's colorful past, blended with the culinary traditions of both its Arab and Berber inhabitants. Over time, these influences have been refined into a distinctly Moroccan flavor—thanks largely to centuries of imperial dynasties, where expectations and demands weighed heavily on the chefs of the royal courts, and thus inspired both experimentation and extravagance.

Moroccan cooking is strongly characterized by the subtle blending of spices, and Moroccans expertly use them to enhance, rather than mask, the flavor and fragrance of their dishes. Spices such as cayenne, saffron, chilies, cinnamon, turmeric, ginger, cumin, paprika, and black pepper are all commonplace in Morocco, as is a special blend of spices called *ras el hanout*, translated as "head of the shop," which is usually a mixture of between 10 to 30 different spices. Traditionally the proprietor of each spice shop sold his own unique—and secret—*ras el hanout* recipe. Fresh herbs are also present in Moroccan dishes, particularly garlic, coriander, parsley, and mint, as are fragrant additions such as orange or rose water, olives, and olive oil. *Harissa,* a fiery paste of garlic, chilies, olive oil, and salt, is often used as a condiment. Above all else, perhaps the defining characteristic of Moroccan cuisine is the blending of savory with sweet, most commonly witnessed by the addition of fruit to meat tagines.

Moroccan food is mostly homegrown, producing a wide range of fruits, vegetables, nuts, and grains, along with large quantities of sheep, cattle, poultry, and seafood. This range of seasonal and mostly organic produce is largely grown and cultivated by small-scale farmers and delivered daily to markets and souks around the country.

Eating in Morocco is a social ritual, and sharing meals at home is fundamental to most Moroccans' way of life. Families take great pride in all aspects of a meal, from purchasing the freshest produce to the preparation, cooking, and display of each dish. Such is the importance of mealtime that many urban families even employ a live-in cook—sometimes a poorer family relative—to boost their social standing. Most of the country's *maisons d'hôte* also employ full-time chefs to entice both residents and nonresidents to their doors. This has resulted in an impressively high number of quality eateries located throughout the country, as well as a new wave of international-Moroccan fusion cuisine.

FOOD

To get you started, here's a list of common Moroccan food items you'll certainly come across during your travels:

- *amlou:* sweet spread made from almond paste, honey, and argan oil
- *baghrir:* spongelike pancake with little open-air pockets on the top, similar to a large crumpet
- brochette: skewered meat grilled over a charcoal fire
- couscous: hand-rolled semolina grain steamed until plump and fluffy
- *harira:* soup usually made from vegetable or chicken stock with added chickpea and tomato
- *kefta:* minced lamb or beef generously spiced and either rolled into the shape of a sausage brochette or shaped into meatballs and cooked in a tagine
- *khalli:* poached egg, sometimes cooked and served in a tagine
- *khübz:* circular, flat loaf of bread
- *mechoui:* whole roasted lamb or beef
- *msemmen:* thin, oily, flat bread
- *pastilla:* flaky, phyllo pastry pie with a savory filling of chicken, pigeon, or sometimes seafood, topped with cinnamon or sugar icing
- tagine: meat, seafood, and/or vegetable casserole or stew, slowly cooked in a two-piece earthenware cooking vessel with cone-shaped lid
- *tanjia:* earthenware urn stuffed with seasoned meat and slowly cooked in the embers of the local hammam
- *zaalouk:* spiced eggplant dip

BREAKFAST & BREADS Morocco's culinary delights begin in the morning. Even the most basic of cafes will usually have an offering of fresh pastries or breads to accompany your coffee, tea, or a freshly squeezed orange juice. Baguettes, croissants, and *pain au chocolat* are the mainstays of most breakfasts, but you may also encounter Moroccan breads—best eaten fresh—such as *khübz, msemmen,* and *baghrir.* A personal favorite is a warm *baghrir* smothered in *amlou.* If you're staying in one of the country's *maisons d'hôte,* your breakfast will likely also include a selection of jams, or *confitures,* yogurt, and fresh fruits, as well as boiled eggs and omelets.

SANDWICHES & SNACKS *Snak* restaurants can be found all over Morocco, ranging from hole-in-the-wall pavement specials to larger, sit-down establishments. Dishes on offer will range from sandwiches, pizza, and *frites* (french fries) to *chawarma* (roasted meat in pita bread) and more substantial dishes such as brochettes. The Moroccan version of a sandwich comes in either a baguette or *khübz,* and usually involves choosing from a displayed selection of meats, salads, and sauces; ask for *plats emporter* if you want it as a takeaway. Boiled snails—not the large French variety but small brown-and-cream banded snails known as *babouche*—are commonly sold from street food stalls, and a bowl of snail soup is considered a great restorative. *Harira* is another soup, and can be eaten on its own or as part of a larger meal. During Ramadan, *harira* is often drunk at dusk to break the fast. There are many recipes for *harira,* with the basic stock including chickpea and tomato, bean, and pasta; or chicken and pepper. I recommend a squeeze of lemon to add a little sharpness to the taste.

SALADS The abundance of fresh fruits and vegetables throughout Morocco—even out to the edge of the Saharan dunes—lends itself to a delicious variety of salads. Almost everywhere you will be offered a *salade Marocain* (finely chopped tomatoes, cucumber, and sometimes green pepper) or at the very least a *salade vert* of lettuce and tomatoes. Vegetarians will prefer the salad course offered by many fine restaurants called *meze.* This mélange of small dishes can include spiced eggplant dip called *zaalouk,* herbed baby potatoes, honeyed carrots, puréed pumpkin with cinnamon, and roasted tomato relish.

SEAFOOD Morocco's Atlantic coastline, including the disputed Western Sahara, is a much sought-after fishing ground, and for good reason. The cold, nutrient-rich waters have always provided the country's markets and restaurants with a wide range of fresh seafood year-round. Lately, however, there has been a decline in the daily catch, widely attributed to overfishing. Still, on any given day along the coast, and in the major inland cities thanks to refrigerated transport, you're still likely to be spoilt for choice, with fresh catches of Saint-Pierre (John Dory), *dorade* (sea bream), *merlan* (whiting), and sardines. Oualidia's oyster farms ensure a steady domestic supply of the popular mollusk, while *crevettes* (prawns/shrimps) and *homard* (lobster) are also regularly featured in menus.

MEAT Moroccans love their meat, and the concept of vegetarianism causes some looks of confusion among locals, who presume that seafood will still be eaten; hence a vegetarian salad usually comes with tuna. Lamb is favored and enjoyed with couscous, in tagines, skewered over charcoal, braised, boiled, or slow roasted until delectably tender for *mechoui*. Beef and chicken are more affordable and are also served in a variety of ways, including flame-grilled *rotisserie* chicken, a popular *snak* meal.

COUSCOUS Originating in either Algeria or Morocco in the 13th century, couscous—Morocco's national dish—is a fine, semolina grain that is traditionally hand-rolled before being steamed over a simmering stew. Ready when plump and fluffy, the grains are then piled into a large platter or tagine dish, with the stew then heaped on top. It's traditionally served after a tagine or *mechoui*, and is the crowning dish from which most Moroccans will judge a meal. If you're invited to a Moroccan's home for the traditional Friday midday couscous, be aware that every Moroccan man's wife or mother cooks the best couscous in Morocco, and to state otherwise is comparable to treason.

PASTILLA Sometimes called *bisteeya*, this is a sweet and savory pastry consisting of shredded chicken or pigeon mixed with egg and crushed almonds. The mixture is enclosed in a phyllolike pastry called *warka*, which is topped with cinnamon and sugar icing. *Pastilla* is considered a delicacy, so some restaurants may not always have it available.

TAGINE Tagine is a casserole or stew traditionally cooked over a smoldering charcoal fire in a two-piece, cone-shape, earthenware vessel, which is also called a tagine and from where the dish gets its name. Tagines come in many delectable combinations such as beef with prunes, chicken with preserved lemon, and lamb with dates, but can also consist of *kefta* topped with egg, seafood, or purely vegetables.

TANJIA Like tagine, *tanjia* owes its name to the earthenware vessel in which it is cooked. A classic Marrakchi dish, large cuts of seasoned, spiced beef or lamb are stuffed into the *tanjia*, which is then tied with paper and string and taken to the local hammam. The hammam's *farnatchi*—the man responsible for stoking the furnace—buries the *tanjia* vessel in the embers and leaves it to slowly cook for a few hours, after which the meat is tender and ready to eat. This is traditionally a dish made by men for men and is prepared for a bachelor party or all-male gathering.

DESSERTS & SWEETS Besides mint tea (see below), dessert will usually consist of sweet Moroccan pastries dripping in sweet honey or dusted in cinnamon and sugar icing. Some top restaurants offer *pastilla au lait*—layers of crispy, flaky pastry smothered in sweetened milk and *amlou* and topped with crushed nuts. *Sfenj* is a deep-fried Moroccan doughnut, and can be seen threaded six at a time on a piece of bamboo reed or palm frond. Patisseries are everywhere in Morocco—a legacy left behind by the French—and the quality of pastries and gâteaux (cakes) is excellent. For something truly Moroccan, try the gazelle horns, which are small, crescent-shaped pastries stuffed with marzipan.

DRINK

BEVERAGES Night and day, Moroccans are rehydrated by two popular drinks—freshly squeezed orange juice and mint tea, the national drink. Both can be found in cafes and *snak* restaurants countrywide, and are an excellent pick-me-up for the overheated traveler. For more on mint tea, see p. 143.

Moroccan males are especially keen on their coffee; another legacy of the French occupation. No self-respecting Moroccan cafe would dare serve instant coffee, and coffee lovers can find fresh cappuccino, espresso, or coffee with milk just about anywhere at any time.

WATER Many Western travelers—especially those from colder climes—suffer from dehydration during their Moroccan travels. This needn't happen, as cheap bottled water is available everywhere. The best still-water brands are Sidi Ali and Ciel, while Oulmes is the most commonly available sparkling water. Most tap water in Morocco is also drinkable, but it's safer to stick to bottled water. For more information on water-related issues in Morocco, see p. 35.

BEER, WINE & LIQUOR Morocco is by no means a dry country, but drinking in public is still frowned upon and is extremely ignorant if practiced near a mosque. Besides a few select establishments—mainly in Marrakech—Moroccan bars, called brasseries, are all-male, smoky, drinking dens that are only for the desperately thirsty and are unpleasant for females. Most upscale restaurants, however, will have a liquor license, and should be able to offer beer, if not also wine and spirits. Many tourist hotels will also have an attached bar, although some of them are also the domain of chain-smoking businessmen and prostitutes.

Morocco has three local brands of beer—Casablanca, Stork, and Flag—of which the latter is my personal recommendation, while Heineken is the most readily available imported beer. There are also a few surprisingly palatable Moroccan wines available, including an elegant Gris de Guerrouane rosé along with many French brands.

The supermarket chains Acima and Marjane are found in various cities throughout Morocco and have well-stocked liquor stores, and have even been known to stay open for non-Muslims during Ramadan. Other liquor stores can be hard to locate, but you can ask at your hotel. Within most of the country's medinas, the only alcohol to be found will be in select tourist hotels and restaurants.

5 Moroccan Crafts

by Jennifer M. Scarce

Morocco's craft culture fuses indigenous Berber traditions with Arab, Jewish, Andalusian, and other European influences (particularly France), and marries local resources—stone, wood, metal, mineral and clay deposits, and supplies of leather and wool—with imports such as marble and silk.

Technique, passed on through specialist guilds where a master *maalem* instructs apprentices and examines their skills, is at the core of Moroccan crafts. An extensive repertoire of designs combines Arabic calligraphy, graceful foliage, and abstract geometry typical of urban design with the sharply stylized birds, animals, zigzags, triangles, and squares of Berber origin. Crafts were officially encouraged during the French protectorate (1912–56) through the research of scholars and teachers and during the reign of King Hassan II (1961–99), who sponsored government handicraft centers and training schemes and employed craftsmen on major projects such as the great mosque in Casablanca.

Foreign investment and the development of tourism are powerful incentives for the survival of these traditional crafts. Owners of hotels, guesthouses, and private homes employ builders, decorators, tile makers, wood and stucco carvers, metalworkers, weavers, and embroiderers to create beautiful and comfortably furnished environments. Meanwhile, souks are full of goods—ceramics, jewelry, clothes, leather bags, slippers—to attract tourists, and contemporary Moroccan fashion designers make brilliant use of traditional fabrics and decorative techniques in their collections.

ARCHITECTURE Within the imperial cities of Fes, Marrakech, Meknes, and Rabat, traditional life was based on the medina where houses, souks, and craftsmen's workshops clustered around public buildings such as the mosque, *medersa* (teaching institution), *fondouk* (travelers inn), communal fountain, and hammam (bathhouse). The ruler's palace was usually located in a defined space outside the medina.

Buildings conform to a basic square or rectangle with an open court concealed from the outside world by high walls. Columned arcades surround the courts of mosques and *medersas,* one or two stories of rooms enclose the small courtyard of a dar, and walls frame the garden of a riad.

Beyond the cities, the spectacular kasbahs—residences of local rulers—and the *ksar*—fortified villages—also have walls enclosing living and storage areas. Before the advent of concrete, bricks made of clay, gravel, and lime were the main building material, reserving local stone for specific features. Gray stone quarried near the port of Essaouira, for example, was used to build the columns and arcades of warehouses and the frames of doors and windows, carved in intricate designs of foliage, stars, and rosettes. Local marble is used in floors, columns, and fountains in wealthy homes. Brick walls are frequently decorated in the technique of *tadelakt,* which also gives walls a durable, waterproof, and attractive polished surface. This craft involves several stages, including the application of a plaster of powdered limestone mixed with pigments—usually yellow, rust, brown, or green—which are burnished when dry and polished with oily black soap.

Three major crafts decorate and furnish Moroccan buildings: **woodwork, carved plaster** known locally as *geps* but also called stucco, and ceramic mosaic tilework called **zellij.** They are seen at their best in the decoration of the *medersas* (built in the 14th–16th c.) of Fes, Meknes, and Marrakech, and in the surviving palaces and great houses of the 19th and early 20th centuries.

Moroccan interiors are remarkably uncluttered by fittings and furniture. Apart from the arched *mihrab* niche indicating the direction of prayer toward Mecca, mosques have a *minbar,* or pulpit, for the preaching of the Friday sermon and a few stands for copies of the Koran, while the *medersa* only adds a few mats, books, and personal possessions to the students' rooms. Households have little movable furniture except cushions, floor coverings, small tables, and stands, and rooms are multifunctional and easily converted into spaces for dining, sleeping, or entertaining.

Cedar wood from the forests of the Middle Atlas and Rif mountain ranges is used in various woodworking techniques. One of the most beautiful is *mashrabiyya,* an openwork lattice of small turned pieces of wood joined in patterns of squares, octagons, and stars to form the partitions in the court and rooms of a *medersa* and in private houses to control the flow of air, filter light, and separate private and public space. In Morocco's *medersas,* wood was traditionally carved in relief, with bands of religious inscriptions in Arabic, calligraphy in angular Kufic or a flowing cursive script, and panels of spiraling and interlaced foliage mingled with geometric motifs. Wood serves many uses in a household, including kitchen utensils and finely carved tables, shelves, storage chests, jewelry caskets, and containers for ink and cosmetics.

Among the regional variations is the prized marquetry of Essaouira, worked in the root of the *thuya* tree that grows near town. In specialized workshops, the wood is carved into a range of tables, stands, frames, boxes, and containers that are decorated with marquetry in citron wood, walnut, and ebony, often enriched with inlays of mother-of-pearl and copper and silver wire. Painted wood has mainly survived in the palaces and large private houses, seen in their domed and vaulted ceilings, doors, and shutters.

The technique of carved plaster—called *geps* or stucco—is one of the most difficult to master. The craftsman has to work fast, first spreading a thick layer of wet plaster and then shaping and incising many levels of relief in stages before it dries. The spectacular results can be seen throughout Morocco covering panels, friezes, arches, and vaults.

Deep friezes of brilliantly colored *zellij* line the lower walls of buildings and column bases with an explosion of radial and interlaced patterns. The craft flourished in Fes using the technology of ceramic glazing.

CERAMICS   Workshops in Fes and the port city of Safi have traditionally produced distinctive ranges of decorative wares using fine red clay. The kilns and workshops of Safi, the most extensive pottery center in Morocco, are outside town. Here the industry was revived in the late 19th century by potters from Fes who were attracted by the quality of the local clay. They also introduced the technique of polychrome decoration, which has simple borders and medallions of geometric motifs painted in blue, green, and yellow on bowls, plates, and vases. Berber pottery, in contrast, uses brown and red clay to make unglazed items that are painted with simple designs in vegetable-based colors of red and yellow.

CLOTHING   Moroccan dress requires the crafts of textiles, jewelry, and leather. While European dress is increasingly worn in the cities, it is still possible to see contemporary versions of traditional clothing worn by men and women, purchased ready-made in the local souk or commissioned from a tailor. The basic garment is the *jellabah,* an ankle-length, loose robe with long straight sleeves and a pointed hood. These are made in fabrics ranging from fine wool (usually worn in the city) to rough, homespun yarn of the rural Berbers, who also wear a large cloak, or *burnous.* Headdresses range from an embroidered or crocheted skull cap to a red felt fez for formal occasions.

Women's *jellabahs* are made in a greater range of fabrics, including light-weight cotton, silk, and blends of synthetic fibers. The clothing of Berber women consists of lengths of cloth fastened with silver pins and brooches, cloaks woven with geometric motifs, and elaborately folded headdresses.

Traditional dress is important in marriage rituals, especially in Fes where the bride is robed in layers of garments and wraps of brocaded silk and gold-embroidered velvet. They are then adorned with a gold crown hung with strings of pearls.

JEWELRY   The craft of jewelry is deep-rooted in Moroccan tradition. The skills of Andalusian and Jewish immigrants historically monopolized the workshops of Fes, Marrakech, Essaouira, and Tiznit up until as recently as the middle of the 20th century. Jewelry uses many techniques of casting, engraving, filigree, chasing, and enameling to communicate messages of wealth, status, and identity. City jewelry is usually gold crafted in intricate filigree and often set with pearls, garnets, emeralds, and rubies. Flamboyant Berber jewelry is made of silver and often embellished with coral and amber beads.

LEATHERWORK   Tanneries in Fes, Marrakech, and Taroudannt continue the traditional processes of transforming animal skins into soft leather suitable for shoes, bags, cushions, book covers, and more. The main style of shoe for both men and women are flat-soled, heelless slippers called *babouches.* These are usually made of white, beige, yellow, or red leather and can be decorated with embossed and embroidered patterns. The footwear of Berbers consists of closed leather shoes and boots suitable for rough country terrain.

METALWORK   The importance of metalwork is best seen in Moroccan architecture and furnishings. Doors studded with iron nails turn on iron hinges and are fitted with iron and bronze knockers. Openwork grills of wrought iron decorate windows and balustrades. The workshops in the souks of Fes, Marrakech, and Taroudannt equip homes with a wealth of objects in copper and brass and teapots of silver and pewter.

TEXTILES   Morocco has had a well-deserved reputation for textiles since Roman times, especially for the woven and embroidered fabrics of the Berbers. Today, Berber women continue to weave wool blankets, rugs, cloaks, storage bags, and pillow and cushion covers using natural black, brown, and white yarn (which can also be dyed). By the 16th century, Fes became Morocco's principal center for the weaving of fine wool and silk for both domestic and export markets. Since these times, the city's professional craftsmen have embroidered silk velvet with gold and silver thread using a flat couched stitch to work elaborate flower and foliage designs for luxurious house furnishings, wedding garments, and horse trappings. Many of the embroidered textiles required for a household—curtains, pillow cases, mattress and bed covers, runners—have been traditionally made by women. Apart from Fes, Meknes and Rabat are also known for their embroidery work.

6 Moroccan Music & Dance

by Rachel Blech

Just as Morocco's history can be revealed through its architecture, the country's intricate musical textures also have stories to tell. There are more than 700 dance and music festivals every year, and each region has its own particular flavor.

Tumbling quarter-tones and intoxicating rhythms beckon from every corner, be it Arabic pop or *chaabi* blaring from a taxi's radio, a snake-charmers' rasping oboelike *raita,* or simply the soulful call of the *muezzin* from the mosque summoning the faithful to prayer.

Morocco's indigenous people, the Berbers, provide the cultural firmament that gives the music a unique rustic flavor. For thousands of years, the Berbers have populated the coastal plains, desert, and mountains, and have incorporated the rich variety of musical influences brought from the Middle East.

Folk music performs ritualistic, celebratory, and social duties as well as providing a vehicle for broadcasting the news to generations of rural dwellers who might never have learned to read or write.

In many regions, traveling poets, or *rwais,* bring news of current affairs to the weekly souks. In small ensembles, they sing with accompaniment on hand-crafted instruments including double-sided *duff* tambourines and the one-stringed fiddle or *rabab.* The context is usually celebratory and as such there is a rich stream of folkloric dance styles accompanying the music. In the High Atlas, villagers in local costume will gather around an open fire for a dance called the *ahouach;* in the Middle Atlas it's the *ahidous,* where women will dance shoulder to shoulder in a large circle around the seated male musicians who play hand-held frame-drums called *bendir* and *ney* flutes.

If Berber village music represents a pastoral heritage, then the vestiges of Morocco's foreign military history can be found in its classical music, known as *andalous.* It stems from the Arabic invasion and subsequent Islamic domination of Spain's Iberian Peninsula from the early 8th century. For 500 years, the Moors ruled the region known as Andalusia—a melting pot of Spanish, Berber, Arabic, and Jewish influences. The complex structure of *andalous* music is largely attributed to a composer named Ziryab, who traveled to Cordoba from Baghdad in the 9th century and created a highly stylized system of suites called *nuba,* each *nuba* corresponding to a time of day. The music was traditionally performed in court settings on state occasions and, though it is still viewed as Morocco's high art, it remains very popular among the general public with concerts being broadcast every evening on TV during Ramadan. The typical *andalous* orchestra uses *rabab, oud* (lute), *kamenjah* (European-style violin played vertically), *kanuun* (zither), *darbouka* (goblet-shaped drum), and *taarija* (tambourine). When the Arabs were driven out of Spain during the Inquisitions of

the 15th century, the music was dispersed across Morocco, and today the most famous orchestras can be found in Fes, Tetouan, Tangier, and Rabat.

Morocco's position at the northern edge of Africa and at the western extreme of the Arab world gave it a key role in trade with Europe and beyond. From this emerged *gnaoua.* The Gnaoua people are descendants of slaves originally captured by the Arabs during the 17th century in Guinea, Mali, and Sudan and brought across the Sahara for onward trading and to serve the sultans in Morocco. *Gnaoua* music can be recognized by its call-and-response, blues-like style and its instruments: the bass lute or *gimbri,* the persistent rhythms of metal castanets or *qraqeb,* and the acrobatic leaps of the vividly robed dancer-musicians who form the troupe. The effect is intentionally hypnotic; tassels swirling from the dancers' skullcaps and the cyclic groove are all designed to induce a trancelike state in the audience. *Gnaoua* music is not just entertainment but has a deeply rooted spiritual and healing purpose derived from the Sufi tradition of Islam and ancient Sub-Saharan African rituals. The healing ceremonies, or *lilas,* take place from dusk till dawn and are conducted by a priestess who invokes ancient African spirits, or *djinn,* and Islamic saints. For many years, respectable Moroccans shunned the music, but now it is openly performed and has pride of place at the annual Gnaoua & World Music Festival in Essaouira, which attracts crowds of 400,000 people.

Heading south toward the Sahara desert, the insistent rhythms of the city slow to a more reflective pace in the valleys of Ziz, Dra, and Souss and beyond to the Western Sahara. Like the mountains, the desert also yields a wealth of folkloric music. The Souss valley is the home of the *guedra* dance of the Saharan nomads, or "Blue Men." The word *guedra* means cooking pot, and it is that pot, covered with an animal hide, which forms the drum. To a hypnotic heartbeat rhythm, a kneeling female dancer carves mesmerizing movements with her arms and fingers. It's said that the ritual can attract a mate from miles away.

From south of Agadir comes the *tissint,* or "dagger dance," which forms a central part of marriage ceremonies amongst desert nomads. To a crescendo of drums, the couple performs a passionate duet in which the groom holds a dagger and circles around the girl. He then raises the dagger and puts it around the neck of the young girl before collapsing to his knees. Farther north, where the rivers of Ziz and Rheris meet in the Tafilalt, *al baldi* draws upon Berber, Arab, African, and Andalusian influences in songs about religious and social issues.

Political and social themes find expression in many modern Moroccan music forms, and toward the fringes of the long-disputed territory of Western Sahara, one is far more likely to hear the yearning voice of Saharwi refugees living in exile in Mauritania than the classical strains of *andalous.* The music is sparse, poetic, and dominated by female singers who play a small stringed harp-lute called an *ardin;* they are often accompanied by a solo electric guitar. *Rai* music, originating from western Algeria and once rooted in Bedouin music, is also popular. The word *rai* means "opinion," and Moroccans have produced their own homegrown variety that reflects contemporary and controversial views on social issues.

Appendix B:
Useful Terms & Phrases

Although most Westerners presume Moroccans simply speak Arabic, the situation on the ground is definitely more complicated. Morocco's indigenous Berbers had already been speaking their native tongue—nowadays collectively called Amazight—for thousands of years before the Islamic-fuelled Arab invaders of the 8th century imposed the language of their holy Koran on the region. Over time this became known as **Classical Arabic.** Its relation to the spoken varieties of today can be compared with that of Latin to the modern Romance languages. It is still taught in most Arabic schools and has changed little since the days of Mohammed. Classical Arabic, however, is not used in the everyday lives of Arabic speakers. **Modern Standard Arabic,** or MSA, evolved from Classical Arabic into the *lingua franca* of the Arabic world, and is the official language of many nations, including Morocco. There are no native speakers of MSA, and it is rarely the mother tongue of most Arabic-speaking people. The vast majority of educated Arabs learn it in school, while others without formal schooling in MSA can understand it with varying degrees of proficiency. In Morocco, MSA is mainly used in formal situations (religious sermons, news broadcasts, government literature, and speeches) but rarely in conversation.

Moroccans, Arab and Berber, generally converse in what is called **Moroccan Arabic,** sometimes referred to as *Darija.* Moroccan Arabic contains fewer vowel sounds, sounds more guttural, appears to be spoken twice as quickly as MSA, and is at times very similar in pronunciation to Amazight. Influences from Morocco's most recent occupiers, the **French** and **Spanish,** are audible in many words, resulting in a distinctly local dialect that (other than for some Algerians and Tunisians) is difficult to understand for other Arabic-speaking people.

For the non-Moroccan, both French and Moroccan Arabic will be useful when traveling in the country. While Moroccan Arabic is the language of everyday conversation between Moroccans, most Moroccans instantly revert to French—or a confusing combination of both—when conversing with a Westerner. In the more heavily touristed areas (and in most regions covered in this book), English has become more prevalent, and I am constantly amazed at the ease with which many Moroccans have picked up English. My advice is to at least learn a few Moroccan Arabic words and phrases such as "thank you." As surprising as it may sound, very few travelers attempt this, even though the respect and extra assistance that this will garner may very well be the difference between getting a bargain or being ripped off, and being shown the way out of a medina or being ignored.

Most of the sounds in Moroccan Arabic are similar to English and correspond to the Roman letters used to represent them here. Notable exceptions are:

- "Ai" is pronounced as "eye."
- "Ei" is pronounced as the "ai" in "bait."
- "Gh" is a sound made in the back of the throat, similar to the rolling "r" sound in French and Spanish.

- "Kh" comes from even deeper in the throat and is a similar sound to the "ch" in the Scottish "loch."
- "Ou" is pronounced as "w."
- "Ow" is pronounced as the "ow" in "cow."
- "R" is pronounced with a rolling tongue.
- "S" should always be pronounced as in "say" and not as the middle "s" in season.
- "Zh" is pronounced as the "s" in "pleasure."

Other peculiarities for non Arabic speaking people are:

- The glottal stop ('); a sound like that made when pronouncing "uh-oh."
- The letters ä, ï, ö, ü are stressed vowels and should be spoken as a longer sound than is normal in English. For example, ä is pronounced as the "a" in "father," ï as the "ee" in "bee," ö as the "oa" in "coat," and ü as the "oo" in "boot."
- With double consonants, the stressed consonant should also be emphasized, as in the "z" in "bezzef."

1 Basic Vocabulary

ENGLISH-FRENCH-MOROCCAN ARABIC PHRASES

English	French	Moroccan Arabic
Yes/No	oui/non	ïyeh/la
Okay	d'accord	wakha
Please	s'il vous plaît	'afak
Thank you	merci	shukran
Thank you very much	merci beaucoup	shukran bezzef
You're welcome	de rien	bla zhmïl
Hello (during daylight)	bonjour	salamü 'lekum
Good evening	bonsoir	msel khïr
Goodbye	au revoir	beslama
What's your name?	Comment vous appellez-vous?	Ashnü smïtek?
My name is	Je m'appelle	Smïtï
How are you?	Comment allez-vous?	Kï deir? *or* Labas?
So-so	Comme ci, comme ça	Bekhïr lhamdü lläh
I'm sorry/excuse me	Pardon	Smeh lïya
Do you speak English?	Parlez-vous Anglais?	Wäsh kat'ref neglïzïya?
I don't speak French	Je ne parle pas Français	Matan'refsh lfaransïya
I don't speak Arabic	Je ne parle pas Arabe	Matan'refsh larabïya
I don't understand	Je ne comprends pas	Mafhemtsh
Could you speak more loudly/more slowly?	Pouvez-vous parler plus fort/plus lentement?	'Afak tkellem bezzäf/ beshwïya

GETTING AROUND

English	French	Moroccan Arabic
What is it?	Qu'est-ce que c'est?	Ashnü hada?
What time is it?	Qu'elle heure est-il?	Sh hal fessa'a?

English	French	Moroccan Arabic
What?	Quoi?	Kïfash? or Ashnü?
How? or What did you say?	Comment?	Ashnü gulti?
When?	Quand?	Ïmta?
Where is?	Où est?	F ïn?
Who?	Qui?	Shkün ?
Why?	Pourquoi?	'Läsh?
here/there	ici/là	hna/lhih
left/right	à gauche/à droite	lïser/lïmen
straight ahead	tout droit	sïr nïshan
I'm lost	Je suis perdu(e)	Tweddert
Fill the tank (of a car) please	Le plein, s'il vous plaît	'Afak dïr lïya lplan, lttumubïl
I want to get off at	Je voudrais descendre à	'Afak bghït nzel 'end
airport	aéroport	lmatär
bank	banque	lbänka
bridge	pont	lqentra
bus station	routière	lmehetta
bus stop	l'arrêt de bus	blasa dyal ttöbïs
By means of a car	en voiture	fttumubïl
Cashier	caisse	mzher dyal lflüs
Driver's license	permis de conduire	lpermï
Elevator	ascenseur	ssansür
Entrance (to a building or a city)	porte	dekhla
Exit	sortie	lkhrouzh
Gasoline	du pétrol/de l'essence	lpetrol/lgäz
Hospital	hôpital	sbïtär
Luggage storage	consigne	lkonsin dyal lehwayezh
Museum	musée	methef
No smoking	défense de fumer	mamnü' tedkhïn
One-way ticket	aller simple	werqa dyal lali
Police	police	lbülis
Round-trip ticket	aller-retour	werqa dyal lali wö rrutür
Second floor	premier étage	tebqa ttanya
Slow down	ralentir	beshwïya
Store	magasin	magaza
Street	rue	zenqa

English	French	Moroccan Arabic
Telephone	**téléphone**	telefün
Ticket	**billet**	werqa
Toilets	**toilettes/WC**	bït lma

ACCOMMODATIONS

English	French	Moroccan Arabic
I'd like	**Je voudrais**	'Afak bghït
a room	**une chambre**	wahed lbït
the key	**la clé (la clef)**	ssarüt
How much does it cost?	**C'est combien?/ Ça coûte combien?**	Shhal ttaman?
That's expensive	**C'est cher/chère**	Ghalï bezzef
Are taxes included?	**Est-ce que les taxes sont comprises?**	Wäsh ddärïba däkhla felhsäb?
Is breakfast included?	**Petit déjeuner inclus?**	Wäsh lftür däkhel felhsäb?
Do you take credit cards?	**Est-ce que vous acceptez les cartes de credit?**	Wäsh katqbel lakart krïdï?
balcony	**balcon**	lbälkon
bathtub	**bain**	lhemmäm
bed	**lit**	nnamüsïya
big	**grand/gross**	kbïr
hot and cold water	**l'eau chaude et froide**	lma skhün wö bäred
room	**chambre**	lbït
shower	**douche**	ddüsh
sink	**lavabo**	lavabo
small	**petite**	sghïr
suite	**une suite**	swït
We're staying for . . . days	**On reste pour . . . jours**	bghïna ngelsü shï . . . yüm

NUMBERS

0	**zéro**	ssifr
1	**un**	wahed
2	**deux**	zhüzh
3	**trois**	tlata
4	**quatre**	reb'a
5	**cinq**	khamsa
6	**six**	setta
7	**sept**	seb'a
8	**huit**	tmenya
9	**neuf**	tes'üd
10	**dix**	'ashra

20	vingt	'ashrïn
30	trente	tlatïn
40	quarante	reb'in
50	cinquante	khamsïn
60	soixante	settïn
70	soixante-dix	seb"in
80	quatre-vingt	tmanïn
90	quatre-vingt-dix	tes'in
100	cent	mya
1,000	mille	alf

DAYS OF THE WEEK

Monday	Lundi	nhar Letnïn
Tuesday	Mardi	nhar Ttlat
Wednesday	Mercredi	nhar Larb'
Thursday	Jeudi	nhar Lekhmïs
Friday	Vendredi	nhar Zhzhem'a
Saturday	Samedi	nhar Ssebt
Sunday	Dimanche	nhar Lhedd

NECESSITIES

English	French	Moroccan Arabic
I'd like to buy	Je voudrais acheter	bghït nshrï
gift	cadeau	hdïya
map of the city	plan de ville	kharïta dyal lmdïna
newspaper	journal	zharïda
phone card	carte téléphonique	lakärt dyal ttïlïfön
postcard	carte postale	kart pustal
road map	carte routière	kharïta dyal trïq
stamp	timbre	tanber

EMERGENCIES

English	French	Moroccan Arabic
I'm sick	Je suis malade	Ana mrïd
It hurts here	J'ai une douleur ici	Keidernï henna
I am allergic to	Je suis allergique	'Andi lhasasïya dyal
bees	abeilles	nhel
dairy products	produits laitiers	lmakla lli fiha lhlib
penicillin	pénicilline	lpiniselïn
wheat	blé	dgïg
aspirin	des aspirines/des aspros	aspirin
condom	préservatif	lkaput
diarrhea	diarrhée	kersh zhärya or s häl
doctor	docteur/médicin	tbïb

English	French	Moroccan Arabic
headache	mal de tête	keidernï räsi
medicine	médicament	dwa
tampons	tampons	zzif dyal ddem
Help me please!	Au secours, s'il vous plaît!	'Afak'awennï! or 'Afak 'ateqnï!
Call a doctor!	Appel un docteur!	'Ayyet 'la shï tbïb!
Call the police!	Appel l'police!	'Ayyet 'la lbülïs!
Thief!	Au voleur!	Sheffär!
I've been robbed	On m'a vole	Tsreqt
Go away!	Allez-vous-en!	Sïr fhälek!
Accident	accident	ksïda

2 Menu Terms

English	French	Moroccan Arabic
I would like	Je voudrais	'Afak bghït
to eat	manger	nnäkel
Please give me	Donnez-moi, s'il vous plaît	'Afak 'tïni
a bottle of	une bouteille de	wähed lqer'a dyal
a cup/glass of	une tasse/un verre de	wähed lkäs dyal
a plate of breakfast	une assiette de le petit-déjeuner	wähed ttebsïl dyal lftür
the check/bill	l'addition/la note	lehsäb
lunch	le déjeuner	leghda
dinner	le dîner	le' sha
a knife	un couteau	lmüs
a napkin	une serviettesserbïta or lfüta	
a spoon	une cuillèrelm'elqa	
a fork	une cuillère	lfurshïta
vegetarian	végétarien	makayakulsh lhem
fixed-price menu	un menu prix-fixe	lmeni dyal
Is the tip/service included?	Est-ce que le service est compris?	Wäsh sserbïs däkhel felhsäb?
Waiter!/Waitress!	Monsieur!/Mademoiselle!	Garson!
Appetizer	entrée	lontri
main course	plat principal	lpla
tip included	service compris	sserbïs däkhel felhsäb

MEAT

beef	boeuf	lbegrï
chicken	poulet	dzhäzh
lamb	l'agneau	lghenmï
meat	viande	lhem
meat on skewers	brochette	qetbän dyal lhem
minced meat	viande hachée	lkefta
veal	veau	du veau
fish (saltwater)	poisson de mer	lhöt
John Dory	Saint-Pierre	Ssanpyïr
sea bream	dorade	ddoräd
lobster	homard	llomär
oysters	huîtres	bozrüg
shrimp/prawn	crevettes	lkrüvït
smoked salmon	saumon fumé	saumon fumé
tuna	thon	ttön

FRUITS & VEGETABLES

almond	amande	llüz
avocado	avocat	lavoka
banana	banane	lbänän
carrot	carotte	khïzzü
corn	mais	lgemh
date	datte	tmer
eggplant	aubergine	denzhäl
french fries	pommes frites	lfrït
green beans	haricots verts	lübïya
lemon/lime	citron/citron vert	lhamed
lettuce	laitue	lkhess
peas	petit pois	zhelbana
pineapple	ananas	ananäs
potato	pomme de terre	batätä
prune	pruneau	lberqüq
raisin/sultana	raisin sec	zbïb
rice	riz	rrüz
spinach	épinards	lizippinar
strawberries	fraises	ttüt
tomato	tomate	mateisha
vegetable	legumes	lkhedra
zucchini	courgette	lger 'a

CONDIMENTS

bread	pain	khobz
butter	beurre	zebda
cake	gâteau	lhelwa
cheese	fromage	lfermäzh
egg	ouef	lbeid
honey	miel	l'scl
olive	olive	zzïtün
olive oil	huile d'olive	zït l'üd

DRINKS

beer	bière	lbïrra
milk	lait	lhlïb
orange juice	jus d'orange	'asir lïmün
water	l'eau	lma
red wine	vin rouge	lvan rrüzh
white wine	vin blanc	lvan blanc
coffee (black)	café noir	qehwa kehla
coffee (with cream)	café crème	qehwa belhlïb
coffee (with milk)	café au lait	caffee krïm
coffee (espresso)	café espresso (un express)	qehwa espresso
tea	thé	atei
with mint	thé la menthe	atei benna'nä'
without milk	sans lait	bla hlib
without sugar	sans sucré	bla sukkar

Index

See also Accommodations and Restaurant indexes, below.

ACCOMMODATIONS

RESTAURANTS

Frommer's® Complete Travel Guides

Frommer's® Day by Day Guides

Pauline Frommer's Guides: See More. Spend Less.

FROMMER'S® PORTABLE GUIDES

Acapulco, Ixtapa & Zihuatanejo
Amsterdam
Aruba, Bonaire & Curacao
Australia's Great Barrier Reef
Bahamas
Big Island of Hawaii
Boston
California Wine Country
Cancún
Cayman Islands
Charleston
Chicago
Dominican Republic

Florence
Las Vegas
Las Vegas for Non-Gamblers
London
Maui
Nantucket & Martha's Vineyard
New Orleans
New York City
Paris
Portland
Puerto Rico
Puerto Vallarta, Manzanillo &
Guadalajara

Rio de Janeiro
San Diego
San Francisco
Savannah
St. Martin, Sint Maarten, Anguila &
St. Bart's
Turks & Caicos
Vancouver
Venice
Virgin Islands
Washington, D.C.
Whistler

FROMMER'S® CRUISE GUIDES

Alaska Cruises & Ports of Call

Cruises & Ports of Call

European Cruises & Ports of Call

FROMMER'S® NATIONAL PARK GUIDES

Algonquin Provincial Park
Banff & Jasper
Grand Canyon

National Parks of the American West
Rocky Mountain
Yellowstone & Grand Teton

Yosemite and Sequoia & Kings
Canyon
Zion & Bryce Canyon

FROMMER'S® WITH KIDS GUIDES

Chicago
Hawaii
Las Vegas
London

National Parks
New York City
San Francisco

Toronto
Walt Disney World® & Orlando
Washington, D.C.

FROMMER'S® PHRASEFINDER DICTIONARY GUIDES

Chinese
French

German
Italian

Japanese
Spanish

SUZY GERSHMAN'S BORN TO SHOP GUIDES

France
Hong Kong, Shanghai & Beijing
Italy

London
New York
Paris

San Francisco
Where to Buy the Best of Everything.

FROMMER'S® BEST-LOVED DRIVING TOURS

Britain
California
France
Germany

Ireland
Italy
New England
Northern Italy

Scotland
Spain
Tuscany & Umbria

THE UNOFFICIAL GUIDES®

Adventure Travel in Alaska
Beyond Disney
California with Kids
Central Italy
Chicago
Cruises
Disneyland®
England
Hawaii

Ireland
Las Vegas
London
Maui
Mexico's Best Beach Resorts
Mini Mickey
New Orleans
New York City
Paris

San Francisco
South Florida including Miami &
the Keys
Walt Disney World®
Walt Disney World® for
Grown-ups
Walt Disney World® with Kids
Washington, D.C.

SPECIAL-INTEREST TITLES

Athens Past & Present
Best Places to Raise Your Family
·es Ranked & Rated
    ·ces to Take Your Kids Before They Grow Up
    's Best Day Trips from London
        Best RV & Tent Campgrounds in the U.S.A.

Frommer's Exploring America by RV
Frommer's NYC Free & Dirt Cheap
Frommer's Road Atlas Europe
Frommer's Road Atlas Ireland
Retirement Places Rated